Leoš Janáček   A Biography

LEOŠ JANÁČEK

A Biography
by Jaroslav Vogel

Revised and edited
by Karel Janovický

W • W • NORTON & COMPANY
NEW YORK • LONDON

Contents

PART THREE (1918-1928)

APPENDIX

Foreword

It is now 18 years since Jaroslav Vogel's famous book on Janáček first appeared. I believe it was first produced in German and English translation in 1962, and it was in a sense a work of pioneering. Up until then Janáček was not considered a world composer, but a strange, rather acquired musical taste, only for those who particularly loved Central European art, who were fascinated by that strange juxtaposition of cultures which made up the Austro-Hungarian Empire, and which in Janáček's lifetime fell apart into their various cultural ingredients, Viennese, German, Czech, Moravian, Hungarian, Polish, Serbian, Croatian, to name but a few.

Vogel had known and worked with Janáček, and was a fine conductor of his works, a man of wide culture both musical and otherwise, and so the shade of Janáček must have rejoiced somewhere in his Slavonic Elysium that it was Vogel who was chosen to write his first biography and the first really exhaustive study of his works.

Before Vogel's biography, there had been various books of reminiscences of people who had known Janáček, all of them interesting in their way, but none of them really fully presenting Janáček the man and the artist, especially to readers having no particular knowledge of Czech (or, more accurately, Moravian) culture at the turn of the century. In fact, Vogel himself had written a very interesting small 'paperback' on Janáček's operas *(Leoš Janáček dramatik)*, in which he referred for the first time in print to certain problems of orchestration and interpretation, which are further developed at the end of the present work (pages 385—395), and which I, as a student just getting to know Janáček, had always found tantalizingly incomplete.

A comprehensive biography by the great Czech musicologist Dr Vladimír Helfert was planned, but unfortunately he died with very little of it completed. So it was Vogel who had the honour of being the first in the field, and it is a marvellous (and indeed necessary) thing that this book, which is still the most comprehensive work on Janáček that exists, should now reappear in a revised edition.

In the last few years Janáček's reputation in the musical world has grown tremendously, his operas are performed everywhere from Stockholm to Sydney, and his concert works are equally popular. This popularity has brought about a spate of literature about the composer, mainly in Czech, written by experts to be read by other experts, but also quite a few books in English aimed at the general reader. Excellent as many of these are, not one of them comes anywhere near Vogel's work for sheer completeness in the field of Janáček research. Everything is contained in this one book. It is an exhaustive biography, showing Janáček's entire background and development and above all, it shows *why* he became the musician he did.

It is also the most complete musical analysis of Janáček's entire *œuvre* ever written, not just the famous operas, his Sinfonietta and the quartets, but *everything* down to the tiniest folk song arrangements and unfinished works. The music is described very penetratingly, not only in relation to Janáček's background, and the milieu of Central European musical life just before and after the creation of the Czechoslovak Republic, but also as comparison with other contemporary composers, especially those with similar nationalistic tendencies, such as Bartók. I feel when I read Vogel's descriptions of some work of Janáček that I do not happen to know, that I can imagine just what it is like.

Vogel has also been able to draw on his long experience as a conductor of Janáček's operas to describe how the many problems of interpretation can be overcome. I myself learned a great deal about conducting Janáček from reading this and his earlier above-mentioned work on Janáček interpretation. Vogel also has some wise things to say about the production side of the operas, and one feels his sympathy and lifelong experience with the music on every page of the book. In addition to all this, the plots of the operas are all given in a most detailed manner with an analysis of their literary backgrounds.

In fact, this book can be read through as a fascinating biography and account of one of the greatest composers of the twentieth century, or it can be used as the most valuable work of reference on Janáček in existence. For many years it has been my sole Janáček bible, and I predict that its usefulness will be permanent. One cannot imagine such a work becoming obsolete, however many more Janáček biographies may be produced by an ever-increasing number of Janáček enthusiasts for a continually-growing Janáček public.

SIR CHARLES MACKERRAS

Introduction

It has been said that when one of Mozart's admirers asked him to explain his works, he replied with innocent surprise, ('Ja—und woher soll ich die wissen?'). Needless to say, the most authentic explanation of a composer's work should nevertheless come from the composer himself. Janáček was of this opinion as he himself stated, in his preface to the extensive collection of Moravian folk songs which he edited in collaboration with Bartoš, warning the reader against accepting alien conjectures. 'Explanations of this kind (and in this case he was referring only to folk songs) should only be printed if their authenticity could be guaranteed by the composer himself. To invent an explanation, however interesting it may seem, is out of place, and explains neither the secrets of the song nor of the composer's mind, but only the vague, poetic thoughts of the writer.'

When it comes to analyzing Janáček's work, the question arises: how many and how reliable explanations has he himself left us? In his articles, autobiographical fragments, letters and press interviews, he dropped some interesting hints although in most cases they are more obscure than explanatory. The works themselves contain many half-revealed and half-solved problems. In addition, compositions hitherto unknown even by name keep coming to light. Janáček, who kept almost all his composition exercises, did not consider many of these works, especially his early ones, worth preserving. Even his PIANO TRIO based on Tolstoy's *Kreutzer Sonata* and the original score of JENŮFA are lost.*) On the other hand, a variety of letters and other documents are still being discovered which often serve to change, with a single sentence, many of the existing carefully worked out assumptions.

There is also the paradox which is Janáček himself. On the one hand a barbaric, independent rebel, and on the other an eccentric dogmatist: the contrast between the master in full control of his powers, and the slave of fixed ideas (how else can one explain the difference between his penetrating arrangement of the libretto for JENŮFA and the problematic quality of his own text for DESTINY, written so soon afterwards?); between the uniquely sensitive interpreter of human speech, and its most ruthless violator. Such are the paradoxes which rule out straightforward deductions.

These paradoxes and mysteries may account for the fact that although so much has been written about Janáček, no complete biography has, as yet, appeared. Max Brod's book is more a sensitive essay than a biography, as is

---

*) The story that he had burned it in a fit of depression (a vain effort since the theatre had a copy) was based on information by Mrs Marie Stejskalová, Janáček's housekeeper for many years, who declared that in 1910, before moving to his new house, he ordered her to burn, under his personal supervision, a whole pile of manuscripts, including the manuscript score of Jenůfa.

the lesser known book by the French expert on Stendhal, Daniel Muller,*) who translated JENŮFA into French. The books by Adolf Vašek, *Po stopách L. Janáčka* (In the steps of Leoš Janáček), Robert Smetana, *Vyprávění o Janáčkovi* (Stories about Janáček), Bohumír Štědroň, *Leoš Janáček: Letters and Reminiscences* and the memoirs of Mrs Janáček (written to her dictation and not published) only concern certain phases of Janáček's life. Dr Vladimír Helfert's untimely death unfortunately prevented him from completing more than a quarter of his very thoroughly planned biography, but it provides the basis for any study of Janáček's early life, as in the present instance.

I would have hesitated to write this book had not the late Dr Pavel Eisner, who subsequently translated it into German, encouraged me to add further material to my former book, *Leoš Janáček dramatik* (Leoš Janáček the Dramatist). It may be less the fault of the author than the extent of the material itself that this 'brief completion' has led to such a voluminous book. But the way it came into being from the study of Janáček's dramatic work (which is included more or less complete in this book) is not quite accidental.

Janáček is not only a dramatist in his operas but in all his work—in his choral works, his symphonic poems, even in his chamber music (as can be seen, for example, in his FIRST STRING QUARTET and THE DIARY OF THE YOUNG MAN WHO DISAPPEARED).

Few composers, in fact, have had a greater tendency to approach every subject from its dramatic point of view than Janáček. This was due to his extraordinary imagination, the vital need to place his works in a localized scenic context linked organically with the inner theme. Works such as THE OVERGROWN PATH, ČARTÁK ON SOLÁŇ, IN THE MISTS, SONGS OF HRADČANY are all good examples. In MARYČKA MAGDÓNOVA and in THE CZECH LEGION the locality is repeatedly emphasized. And it is certainly not by chance that many of his works, for instance OUR FATHER, ADVENTURES OF THE VIXEN SHARP EARS**) and NURSERY RHYMES were inspired by paintings. This is all the more conclusive in view of the fact that Janáček had no particular love of painting. Even works intended for the concert platform often led to experiments in scenic and choreographic representation.

There was also a strong element of self-dramatization in Janáček's personality. His own highly-strung temperament, passing from one crisis to another, was a living replica of drama. Few artists indeed could so whole-heartedly embrace Terence's '*Homo sum, nil humani a me alienum puto*' (I am a man, nothing human is strange to me).

Then there is the strong Slav streak which manifests itself when his characters, such as, for instance, Laca in JENŮFA, resort to violence, repenting their actions a moment later: or when they combine defiance with the deepest humility, or paganism with Christianity. There is the teasing sensuality of his Zefka in THE DIARY and Emilia Marty in THE MAKROPOULOS CASE, contrasting

---

*) *Maîtres de la Musique ancienne et moderne*, Rieder, Paris.
**) This work is also known as THE CUNNING LITTLE VIXEN which is a translation of the title which Max Brod gave it in German. The title ADVENTURES OF THE VIXEN SHARP EARS will be used throughout this book since it is a faithful rendering of the Czech title and of the vixen's name.

with the inexorable moral code expressed in the fate of Katya or in THE DIARY OF THE YOUNG MAN WHO DISAPPEARED. All this reveals how deeply the composer felt passion in both senses of the word: the fateful passion of the flesh and the inescapable passion of suffering which redeems and purifies.

It was precisely because Janáček experienced all and saw all that he was able to penetrate the souls of others and was unable to remain indifferent. His passionate sense of engagement is expressed in his choral works where all the anguish and hope of mankind hammers at the gates of heaven, for instance in the outcries 'May we live?' of the 70,000. Throughout his work one feels the searing need to express his attitude to all experiences, events and ideas, to participate in every struggle—whether a struggle against odds, the striving of outcasts for their place in the sun, or the struggle of the sinner for purification and atonement. This need of his is often so strong that one complete work is not enough to express it, and it overflows into works of a different nature, forming a complement or contrast to the first. For instance, during the First World War Janáček ridiculed, in his MR BROUČEK, mediocrity and cowardice, and then created, in TARAS BULBA, a monument of Slavonic might, an astounding contrast to the caricature and derision shown in MR BROUČEK. After KATYA KABANOVA, a passionate defence of an innocent sinner, he wrote a chamber work of similar content—his QUARTET based on Tolstoy's *Kreutzer Sonata*. Even after having written ADVENTURES OF THE VIXEN SHARP EARS he occupied himself with youth and the animal world in his WIND SEXTET, in his CONCERTINO and in his NURSERY RHYMES, while Elina Makropoulos in his MAKROPOULOS CASE extends her hand to the prisoners in THE HOUSE OF THE DEAD. 'You know, the terror, the inner feeling of a human being who will never cease to breathe, complete despair which wants nothing and expects nothing,' he says of his heroine, 'will have its continuation in THE HOUSE OF THE DEAD.'

Despite the chronological 'tangles' (to use one of Janáček's favourite expressions) which are created by complex associations in his work, three distinct periods may be distinguished, excluding his preparatory, traditional phase.

His first period, which may be called ethnographic, begins with his first choral songs and culminates in JENŮFA. He was born the son of a village schoolmaster in a corner of Moravia where folklore was unusually well preserved and whose music he was destined to discover, thus completing the role played earlier by Bedřich Smetana in Bohemia. At the same time he became increasingly Slav-conscious, as is seen by the development from his FAIRY-TALE to his TARAS BULBA and his GLAGOLITIC MASS.

His second period, which may be called revolutionary (revolutionary in three senses—social, national and ethical) did not express itself in revolutionary slogans but no less dynamically as the composer's '*J'accuse*': he lifted an accusing voice on the death of a workman demonstrating for national culture, and stepped forward in defence of victims of social and national oppression in the Těšín district. He also condemned the despotism of the family which drove Katya Kabanova to her doom, and at the end of his life accused those who leave 'God's spark' to languish in the bosoms of the prisoners in THE HOUSE OF THE DEAD. His most fiery accusations are naturally his choral works based on words by the 'Silesian bard', Petr Bezruč. But since he always concerned himself with the better arrangement of the things of this world, such works as THE ETERNAL GOSPEL and THE BALLAD OF BLANÍK also belong to this period.

His third period was intimately autobiographical, though already hinted at in a number of works in which he explored folklore—these include JENŮFA—and in early compositions like AMARUS, THE OVERGROWN PATH, and others.*)

But the subsequent brightening of his style which was brought about by the eagerly awaited independence of the Czech state, the recognition of his works and a great love affair, changed his bitter and tragic intimate compositions into joyful or at least reconciled works (as can be seen in THE MAKROPOULOS CASE) and this third, quite different, period of his work can be clearly distinguished, especially when considering works like ADVENTURES OF THE VIXEN SHARP EARS, YOUTH, CONCERTINO, SINFONIETTA, GLAGOLITIC MASS, CAPRICCIO, NURSERY RHYMES and the SECOND STRING QUARTET. Janáček had spoken out freely on the national and social struggle, and having lived to see the satisfaction of his fundamental demands, now sang his panegyric to life.

It is natural that these three periods, just as the three basic themes of Janáček's work, not only overlap and support each other, but also change as such: the Slav element, for example, finds its initial outlet in enchantment with folklore; then—during the first world war—in a defiant outburst against 'superior races' and finally, in the GLAGOLITIC MASS, in a religious subject.

Yet all these three periods have one common trait, their realism and their basic methods of expression. How could it be otherwise with a composer who so many times expressed his creed in the following words: 'I maintain that a pure musical note means nothing unless it is pinned down in life, blood, locale. Otherwise it is a worthless toy,'**) or 'The chord is for me a live being... my heart swells when I write it, it sighs, wails, crushes, dissolves in mist or hardens into stone. What do I care about the borrowed attribute, beautiful or unbeautiful!

'Its being coincides with my being in a flash of life.'***) Yet the sources of his inspiration were usually very simple: most frequently it was nature, often the simple nature, of his native Hukvaldy.

The realism of Janáček's work is naturally most strongly expressed in works portraying human life, namely, in his operas. If we accept the division of all dramatic music into two archetypes, the Western classical synthetic type where the idea of the work as a whole is uppermost while its individual characters and situations take second place, and the Eastern analytical type concerned primarily with the humanity of the individual figures and situations often only loosely attached to the principal theme, then there is no doubt that Smetana belongs to the first type and Janáček to the second. Like Mussorgsky, Janáček presents us with unique and original human beings. But Janáček was not at his best in constructing plots where even the most insignificant details have their unalterable place and form a complete whole. When he set novels

---

*) Among these 'intimate' works, in a broader sense, should be included the opera DESTINY.
**) Janáček to Max Brod, 2 Aug. 1926.
***) Janáček: 'Scestí' (Crossroads). *Listy Hudební matice*, Vol. IV (1924), p. 2.

as operas he did not even choose those which would offer him a simple and easily isolated plot but used THE EXCURSIONS OF MR BROUČEK, ADVENTURES OF THE VIXEN SHARP EARS, or THE HOUSE OF THE DEAD which, in their original forms, are mere sequences of episodes without any definite conclusion. No wonder then, that the action of some of his libretti is almost incoherent, with characters seemingly suspended in mid-air. (Even the original titles, the EXCURSIONS OF MR BROUČEK, the ADVENTURES OF THE VIXEN SHARP EARS or FROM THE HOUSE OF THE DEAD, betray their episodic character.) Janáček takes us to the primeval forests, to the realm of Czech legend, to the Moravian countryside, to worldly spas, to a composer's workshop, on to the moon, among the dour Hussites and the merchants of the Volga, the animal vermin of the forest or the human vermin of a lawyer's office, into the back-stage of a theatre and the back-stage of life in a prison camp in Siberia. He projects dream into reality, the present into the past, the world of humans into the world of animals, searching everywhere for the melody of the soul: and (though he most violently objected to this as a musician) he fashioned dramatic works out of these innumerable melodies of life, almost as if he were writing a mere diary, raising both figures and actions to some higher unity by symbolic parallels but relying mainly on the life inherent in them, on their human truth and persuasiveness. And thanks to this inherent truthfulness and their striking destinies, and naturally thanks to his musical genius, all fundamental objections are silenced. One can even say that there are few artists who have, in each one of their works, concentrated such a wealth of ideas and ethics. And, what is most rare—they are devoid of all rhetoric, slogans and preaching whether moral, national, social or of any other kind. Just as Smetana's *The Bartered Bride* is the most national Czech opera without ever using the words 'Czech' or 'nation', Janáček never uses the word 'people' although his work speaks no other language than the language of the people themselves.

It is self-evident that the realistic and genre style of the drama is also his style of composition. This will be seen most clearly if one considers the two contradictory traditions which were extant at the time of his arrival: the German symphonic abstract style (Wagner) with a tendency towards monumental subjects, and the more sensuous, melodious, Latin style, with a growing tendency towards subjects from everyday life, though not disdaining anything which could make 'the everyday' less common. And in between these two extremes, there was the Smetana—Dvořák tradition of Bohemia which, especially in the case of Smetana, could best be called 'idealizing realism', sometimes falling, however, by this idealization into romanticism. Janáček's intervention thus had the effect of putting this realism firmly on its own feet without any idealization and also without romanticism. The result is the loosening of all bonds of stylization and, in the words, a transition from verse to prose; later (in BROUČEK, THE VIXEN and THE HOUSE OF THE DEAD) there is a shift towards the style of a dramatic suite. Musically it means a reduction of the Latin cantilena in favour of the so-called speech-melodies, of the German symphonic style likewise in favour of the suite, and the restriction (but not abolition) of the part played by the Leitmotiv.

Once the border-line between self-contained numbers and recitatives disappeared, opera libretti in prose became commoner. The first to risk such

13

prosaic opera (1868) was Mussorgsky in his *Marriage* based on Gogol's play, solving this problem in a purely recitative style. (This was done shortly before him by Dargomyzhsky in his *Stone Guest* but with words in verse.) Mussorgsky was probably not satisfied with his experiment since he did not continue beyond Act I, but he repeated the experiment with greater success in *Boris Godunov* (1874) in which the tavern scene is based entirely on a prose text. By the turn of the century a number of composers were writing operas to prose words without knowing of one another: after the unsuccessful operas by Alfred Bruneau on realistic subjects by Zola came Charpentier (1900) with *Louise* to his own libretto in prose, Debussy (1902) with *Pelléas* on Maeterlinck's prose, Strauss (1905) with *Salome* based on Wilde and, in the meantime, Janáček (1904) with JENŮFA to prose by Gabriela Preissová.

As can be seen from these dates, Janáček could not have been influenced by any of these foreign examples (only after writing JENŮFA did he become acquainted with Mussorgsky) and, as in many other cases, he came to the new shores by his own route. At the beginning of the 1890s he started systematically taking down the melodic and rhythmic qualities of the spoken word—even sounds of animals and objects—and found that with the help of these 'speech melodies' he could 'form the motif of any given word, the most common or the most uplifted', and that he could thus 'encompass the whole of everyday life or the greatest tragedy—more than enough for the prose of JENŮFA'. And thus he 'composed to prose'.*)

Realistic speech melody, in Janáček's sense, does not attempt to record the standard, more or less idealized intonation of the word, but the living speech with all its individual and regional peculiarities, with all the uniqueness of a certain feeling, a certain moment in life, a certain milieu. That is also why Janáček had no use in his operas for princes or gods, but only for people more or less of his time and of his kind. That is why he transposes animals (Bystrouška the Vixen) and fantastic creatures (in MR BROUČEK'S EXCURSION TO THE MOON) into the world of humans, and historical figures (in MR BROUČEK'S EXCURSION TO THE FIFTEENTH CENTURY) into the present. That is also why he did not have to use folk songs in order to express the atmosphere of a milieu: the speech melodies, with their regional characteristics, sufficed.

Obviously even Janáček's speech melodies have their predecessors especially in works which set out to copy speech by the sole use of instruments. And there are examples of sung speech melodies before him. Janáček himself found a number of speech melodies in Mussorgsky, objecting only that he 'did not see their beauty or otherwise he would have followed them up'; and in Charpentier's *Louise*, who 'nevertheless' (according to Janáček) used in his opera the ready-made calls of the Paris hawkers. But Janáček made the speech melodies into the main principle of his realistic style and attributed to them such importance that he even wanted speech melodies to appear in the curriculum of the *conservatoires* and even advised actors to study them.

The speech melodies which Janáček collected throughout his life were not to be employed mechanically. They were to him what sketches are to a painter—a key to the inner life of people, animals and things. They became

---

*) Janáček in *Hudební revue*, Vol. IX (1916), p. 245.

the basis of his thematic work. The most striking ideas would be repeated either literally or in a free variation (usually in the form of a concluding phrase) in the voice itself or in the orchestra (here usually with some adaptations). It is interesting that already in JENŮFA, besides those places where the orchestra takes over logically the speech melody from the singer, there are many instances of the speech melody appearing in the orchestra first. The most drastic example of this is when Mr Brouček, in his excursion to the moon, resolutely replies:

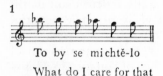

To by se mi chtě-lo
What do I care for that

to Blankytný's 'On your knees' (vocal score, page 63). This theme appears in the orchestra completely on its own as early as page 55! From such examples one may deduce (and Janáček's glosses in the libretti bear it out) that Janáček, while composing, used to have the speech melodies prepared at certain places in the text as dramatic reminders; such a method would also help to give the appearance of the vocal and orchestral parts deriving from a single emotional source.

Needless to say, not all Janáček's motifs and themes are derived from speech melodies but are also of instrumental origin. Neither have they always the same part assigned to them. As has been pointed out, the true bearers of the musical current are the brief motifs carried usually by one or two alternating harmonies and repeated in the form of an ostinato so that the style of 'dramatic suite' (continuity) mentioned earlier is here reflected in miniature. On the basis of this 'bedding', as Janáček used to call it, or by themselves, appear the more musically important motifs, but their role is usually complete as soon as the dramatic situation has changed. They may therefore best be called 'situation motifs'. Finally there are the themes spanning the whole opera or at least several of its sections, the principal or Leitmotivs. Some of these are occasionally put to all three uses either at one and the same time or subsequently, usually with the help of more or less idiosyncratic variation.*)

This variation represents, as is the case with more recent composers, the main means of Janáček's thematic work and is musically and descriptively

---

*) It may be surprising that I use the term Leitmotiv in respect to Janáček. The analysis of his works will demonstrate clearly that Janáček used Leitmotivs not only in all his operas but also in his symphonic poems and that like Wagner he used to give them, at least in his mind, definite names. It is, for instance, evident from a letter he wrote to Otakar Ostrčil, 6 Nov. 1917, concerning THE FIDDLER'S CHILD, where he expressly mentions the 'falling asleep' motif (see p. 192) and from Vilém Petrželka's reminiscences of the composing of the unfinished mass in Janáček's composition class (see p. 154), where he expressly mentions the motif of guilt in the *Kyrie*. The difference between Janáček and Wagner is that the number of Leitmotivs in Janáček's operas is much smaller—there is often only one—and a greater part is played by the situation motifs. Janáček (see his article, 'Some remarks on "Jenůfa" ', *Hudební revue*, Vol. IX, (1916), p. 245) was mainly concerned with the most faithful rendering of a definite moment, which again was the result of his above-mentioned attitude to drama in general.

15

a necessary complement to frequent ostinatos, while sequences (in the academic sense of the word) are relatively scarce.*)

Sometimes, when a variant serves as a preparation for the appearance of the theme proper, the incipient and end stages of it are so far apart that one cannot see with any certainty which is the correct version, whether it is the same motif or a new one, and whether they are not simply related by the use of the same elements. In such a case the surest guide is the thematic correlation and the musical development. One of the most sophisticated forms of transition consists of a gradual convergence of two quite independent motifs by the use of related elements so that in the end it is often doubtful whether a mere variation or a complete change of motif has occurred.

Of course, Janáček's monothematic variants never give the impression of being laboured or contrived but are an elemental flow of fantasy.**) This—besides the unity of tempi (much greater than might at first be assumed)—is the main secret of the surprising unity of form of most of Janáček's compositions despite the apparent maximum of freedom of form. (Janáček indulged in this freedom only in his operas; elsewhere he uses, in nearly every case, various types of rondo form, especially the so-called 'small rondo' on the well-known *ABA* pattern.)

Integral combinations of two equal themes, on the other hand, are very rarely found in Janáček's work—even though this was the pride of all composers since Berlioz and including even Verdi. Janáček's polyphony is limited to two voices, and his imitations are confined (as was the case with Debussy) to canon of the simplest character—namely, at the octave. 'Of all the musical tricks the contrapuntal ones are particularly pitiful,' he once declared.***)

Janáček's melodic invention has two specific characteristics: the melodies are usually short (as is to be expected in consideration of his system of speech melodies) but give the impression of a continuous flow, having, so to speak, neither beginning nor end (not unlike the melodies and motifs of Debussy); a sort of 'endless melody' of a different kind. Yet the more compressed the arches of his melodies are, the higher and bolder they become and their terseness of expression is heightened even harmonically by their over-reaching of the top note of the harmony so that the result is all manner of suspended sixths, sevenths, and especially ninths, usually unresolved. For instance, Ex. 191 from THE ETERNAL GOSPEL, or Ex. 277 (the lure of the Volga) from KATYA

---

*) Janáček's motivic variants are mainly diminutions which he uses either as figurative accompaniment or for his typical interjections. Augmentations are much rarer. And just as the time intervals diminish or augment, so the melodic intervals are diminished or augmented (especially when, at a moment of crisis, the theme 'bends' under the pressure of dissonant harmony) and individual notes are added or taken away from the theme. There are frequent cases of one theme being penetrated by echoes from another theme.

**) This is indirectly borne out by Janáček's letter of 7 March 1920, in which he thanks Otakar Šourek for his exact quoting of motifs in the analysis of the EXCURSIONS OF MR BROUČEK but at the same time he expresses surprise: 'What a number! I would never have known that there are so many! I know that my melodic ideas change according to how they are pressed by circumstances. You have perceived well the resulting relationships of all the motifs. They have to grow out of themselves, one cannot carve them out beforehand.'

***) In his article THE FIDDLER'S CHILD which appeared in the *Hudební revue*, Vol. VII (1914), p. 205.

KABANOVA or the related main theme of the FIRST QUARTET (Ex. 321).

In his lyrical motifs Janáček—like Weber and Chopin—preferred a decorative, or rather, a melodically enhanced repetition, as in Ex. 340 from the sextet YOUTH, or one which expressed overflowing emotion as for instance in KATYA KABANOVA (Ex. 273) or in the main theme of the original last movement of the VIOLIN SONATA (Ex. 213).

Otherwise Janáček's ornamentation is closely connected with the melodies and traditional system of ornamentation of the peasant fiddlers, used characteristically in the recruits' song in Act I of JENŮFA. But more of that in the chapter on Janáček's folklore period. For the moment I would like to mention his use of the trill. In his evocations of the buoyant folk gatherings he was able to conjure up, by garlands of trills, the whole frenzy of folk temperament. ('The trill is like a flaming hoop which we bowl along,' he once said.) How well he suggests the sparkling beauty of folk costumes in the last movement of his SUITE, opus 3, or in the dance *Odzemek* from Act I of JENŮFA. In Act II of JENŮFA, in the eerie monologue of Kostelnička, he conjures up—not unlike Mussorgsky in the scene of Boris's madness—by the same 'flaming hoop', a vision of terror, while at the end of KATYA KABANOVA he gives the trills a sweet soothing quality.

Harmonically, Janáček leans very much towards the Slavonic East and South by frequent use of old Greek or Church modes, especially in JENŮFA. But like Smetana, he gives a new charm even to the most ordinary tonic-dominant or subdominant-tonic progressions, as is also the case with his use of parallel thirds and sixths which, especially in his mournful melodies, are powerful and telling in effect—examples of this are: Jenůfa's mourning over her dead baby, Emilia's reflections on death in THE MAKROPOULOS CASE (Ex. 377 and Ex. 385), or the melody at Filka's death in Act III of THE HOUSE OF THE DEAD.

Janáček made many discoveries of the kind which, elsewhere, lead to the founding of whole new schools of composition. For instance, in JENŮFA (therefore independently of Debussy) he stumbled on the whole-tone scale which he later used, especially in the EXCURSION TO THE MOON and in the ADVENTURES OF THE VIXEN SHARP EARS, to 'enigmatic' effect. Similarly in DESTINY (therefore this time independently of Schoenberg) he enriched his harmonic palette by chords built up from fourths, although many such harmonies could be defined as second inversions of subdominant or dominant triads over dominant or tonic pedals. (More about Janáček's own controversial definition of them in 'Teacher and Theoretician' later.)

Considering the exciting effect of Janáček's music, it is surprising to note how inert his harmonies sometimes are even in the most dramatic moments, for instance the passage in Act III of JENŮFA where she is attacked by the chorus and where the harmony (the dominant of E flat) as well as the motif are repeated note for note. The secret of the effect of this procses used, for instance, by Beethoven (first movement of the Pastoral Symphony) and on the other hand by Smetana when he wants to convey the sense of peace, grandeur or well-being, is the addition of other means of expression; in this case, the attacking ostinato motif, the suspensive harmony and the mounting of the dynamics almost to a paroxysm, which give these repetitions an opposite effect.

Moreover, Janáček knew particularly well how to use, in such cases, one of his rhythmic peculiarities, the suspension of the accented beat—a peculiarity which gives his lyrical passages their brooding, sobbing quality.*) Other characteristics of Janáček's rhythm and metre are his frequent use of shortened or extended five-beat or seven-beat metres as they appear especially in Russian folk music and the music of the East in general. But while in these cases this type of metre usually runs throughout the whole composition or movement, in Janáček it only appears on the whole in single bars.**)

In common with the folk music of Slovakia Janáček made frequent use of the pert, defiant rhythm ♪ ♪. and of such mirror inversions of rhythmic figures as ♩. ♪₁ ♪♩.. (see Ex. 137), or ♩ ♩ ₁♩ ♩ (Laca's spiteful attacks on the old woman at the beginning of JENŮFA) or ♫♩ ₁♩ ♫ (see Ex. 399) and many others.

After JENŮFA, Janáček's style and technique remained basically unchanged. But there was, nevertheless, a marked development in some important details. This was mainly brought about by a new element which gradually became more marked in Janáček's work: symbolism and riddles. Janáček the realist was, at the same time, too much of a musician and poet not to love the atmosphere of mystery and enigma. He even intended to preface his down-to-earth JENŮFA with a symbolical symphonic parallel to a folk ballad. But withouth considering this, it is my opinion that even the seemingly common objects in JENŮFA influence the subconscious mind of the listener as unwitting symbols: for instance, in Act I, the contrast of the prosperous mill (the world of the rich Števa) with the modest shed (the world of the ignored Laca) or even the wooden foot-bridge over the mill-race which Števa crosses, leading the recruits like a conqueror entering a bastion; more so the menacingly turning mill-wheel (a symbol of fate), the clapping of the mill in the xylophone and the mill-race, forerunner of the fatal Volga in KATYA KABANOVA. It does not matter if such inobtrusive symbols are not fully understood by the audience—they always have their realistic function on the stage. On the other hand the absent, almost imaginary Terynka in the ADVENTURES OF THE VIXEN SHARP EARS is a deliberate erotic symbol, while 'the eagle, Czar of the forests' in THE HOUSE OF THE DEAD is a symbol of freedom. And in JENŮFA, DESTINY, KATYA KABANOVA and THE HOUSE OF THE DEAD there is the ever present, purely Slav, almost Dostoyevskian mysticism of inexorable fate.

With each successive opera, Janáček's thematic technique developed new characteristics. After the intrusions of abbreviated figures (interjections) into the fading out of a melodic phrase (for instance at the beginning of JENŮFA)

---

*) Vladimír Úlehla, in his book Živá píseň (The Living Song), page 310 ff., even goes so far as to maintain that most Moravian songs should begin not on the accented beat but after it as, he says, is evident from the beat which the folk singers consciously or unconsciously give by walking or rocking the body while singing (a peasant rider or soldier does it even on horse-back).
**) Sometimes Janáček complicates the rhythm unnecessarily as in the choral song REST IN PEACE (see Ex. 16) where every listener will certainly hear it as a regular four-beat bar, or he even indicates it wrongly as in the ballad In the Hills, In the Valleys ('Na horách, na dolách', No 7 of PÍSNĚ DETVANSKÉ; see p. 404, DVACET ŠEST BALAD LIDOVÝCH) which should be written in three-beat bars.

he develops, in the EXCURSIONS OF MR BROUČEK, a manner of regularly alternating whole sections of movement and rest, of agitation and peace, suspense and relief, again mostly by a simple variation of the same motif as, for instance, in the introduction to Act II of the EXCURSION TO THE MOON where he twice alternates the peaceful motif of the earth:

with its more lively variant:

Further typical examples of this can be found in THE HOUSE OF THE DEAD— the beginning of Act I or in Act III at Shishkov's story—and, the most typical example, the alternating of the same unchanged melody (of the comic hymn 'Blessed Thy Lips') once in quavers, once in crotchets—that is to say twice as slow—before Mr Brouček's flight from the moon.*)

In the ADVENTURES OF THE VIXEN SHARP EARS this system (for example in the great intermezzo in A flat minor after the first scene) is further ornamented by rhythmical shifts (see Ex. 297,) as is the case in the prelude to THE HOUSE OF THE DEAD:

In KATYA KABANOVA his use of verse-like repetitions of the text, so typical of JENŮFA, became less frequent. Another thing which disappeared later was the 'ensemble' in traditional operatic style found in Act I of JENŮFA.

What is more, the libretti of the operas which followed the EXCURSIONS OF MR BROUČEK gave this eminently choral composer very little scope for making use of the chorus. But the increased symbolism of some of his later subjects brought about the use of the chorus with a non-realistic function. For instance, at the end of KATYA KABANOVA, the chorus represents the voice of the Volga; in the ADVENTURES OF THE VIXEN SHARP EARS, it represents the voices of the forest in the wedding scene, the voice of humanity at the conclusion of THE MAKROPOULUS CASE and the 'heavy breathing' of the prisoners in THE HOUSE OF THE DEAD. The same atmosphere of unreality against a realistic background leads to the highly characteristic stylization of laughter in MR

---

*) Basically, this is the same alternation of two variants of the same motif—of the motif at rest and the motif in crisis—which marked the LACHIAN DANCES where, however, it was done only by alternating a consonant and dissonant harmonic basis.

Brouček, in the Adventures of the Vixen Sharp Ears (the poacher Ha-rašta), in The Makropoulus Case (Hauk), and in the play-within-the-play scene in The House of the Dead. In the operas that followed Jenůfa, Ja-náček makes up for the more limited possibilities of elementary contrast and melodic expansion by his masterly building up of not only the preludes (Katya Kabanova, The Makropoulos Case, The House of the Dead) but also the interludes, and sometimes in his almost over-exuberant conclusions of acts (where it is a case of contention whether to fill in the time with some additional action or drop the curtain as is prescribed). Janáček also likes to insert folk or quasi folk songs and sayings into the action (a practice which again brings him close to the Russians, especially Mussorgsky, but which is not only Russian: in Moravia, especially in the wine-growing districts, the people always have a serious or whimsical song ready for every situation and for every mood, bursting into song at the slightest provocation).

As to which other composers most influenced his ripest period (after all three whole generations passed during his life-time) one would have to say, almost no one. Despite all the changes and all the alluring contentions of the powerful musical schools of the day, the lonely and still unrecognized composer of Jenůfa saw no reason to falter—perhaps because he was so firmly attached to his native soil. Yet he never isolated himself from the work of other composers, whether local or from abroad, classical or modern, analyzing their work with enthusiasm, with the result which may well be described by the words: he recognized no one and learned from everyone.*) Yet he never copied any one. One of the so-called classical composers he admired, besides J. S. Bach, was Mozart. When he was 20 he compared Beethoven to Michelangelo and wrote from Leipzig to his fiancée after hearing Beethoven's Quartet in C sharp minor: 'It was a concert which penetrated deep into my soul. In this quartet Beethoven stops caring whether he will appeal to the public or not and gives expression to his innermost life. I think that Beethoven would have to rise again to be able to tell us how much he actually created and how much still remains to be done in continuation in this direction. Oh, if only there could be a part of this great spirit within myself.'

Besides Beethoven (from whom he later became estranged)**) the young Janáček admired and performed Mendelssohn, Rubinstein and Saint-Saëns.***) He admitted the virtues of Verdi, Boito (the music of his *Mefistofele* he described as 'beautiful, even excellent'), and Meyerbeer. (In his copy of the libretto of *Le Prophète* he wrote: 'The music is dramatic, full of effective passages in the orchestra and fascinating islands, which are like glowing light.') He dismissed

---

*) It is typical that, like Richard Strauss, he never lost an opportunity of hearing every promising novelty as soon as possible, especially in the field of opera. In 1906, for instance, he travelled to Prague to hear Strauss' *Salomé* at the Prague German Theatre. On 16 February 1908 he went to hear Puccini's *Madame Butterfly* performed for the first time at the Prague Vinohrady Theatre. In 1910 he went to hear Strauss' *Elektra* in Prague and Nouguès' *Quo vadis* (which he liked), and in 1914 he was one of the first 'heretics' to attend the first perform-ance of *Parsifal* at the Prague National Theatre.

**) See p. 351 of this book.

***) As will be seen, he even intended to go and study with the last two, and as late as the spring of 1911 he was preparing a special concert dedicated to Saint-Saëns.

Richard Wagner almost summarily, even accusing him, from the purely musical point of view, of rhythmic poverty, and (speaking of the overture to *Tristan!*) of a lack of melodic invention. And whenever he admitted—as in his book on harmony—that Wagner had contributed in no small way to the development of music, he seemed to be making (like Hanslick who influenced him considerably in his youth) a slip of the tongue. Besides Chopin, he admired Brahms, but as a full-blooded country man he was irritated by the 'city music' of Johann Strauss.

Of the Russian composers, it was not Mussorgsky who was nearest to his heart, although they had so much in common, but (at least in the 1890s) Tchaikovsky. Although in 1891 he criticized *Onegin*, saying of it that all the characters 'sing in the same pretty way', after the Brno première of the *Queen of Spades* he wrote of Tchaikovsky, in the paper *Lidové noviny* on 21 January 1896: 'A genius of originality, distinction and sincerity', and continued with enthusiasm 'on the music of horror', as he called the introduction to Act II built up mainly on the eerie pedal of C sharp. (Was not this introduction to a certain extent the pattern for Janáček's own introduction to Act II of JENŮFA—a composition one might equally call 'music of horror' and which is also built up on the pedal of C sharp?)

Of the Czech composers he admired Dvořák almost without reservation, suggesting, for instance, that a dictionary of Dvořák's motifs should be published. For many years he was almost an enemy of Smetana's work as can be seen from his cruelly unjust declaration, 'Dvořák is the only Czech national composer.' Besides evident personal reasons, as, for instance, his friendship with Dvořák and the hostile attitude of the Czech supporters of Smetana to his own works, his attitude was, in fact, dictated by Dvořák's—and his own—generally Slavonic sympathies. Smetana's orientation was specifically Czech and thus appeared to Janáček to be endangering his Moravian regionalism and his Pan-Slav ideals.*) Altogether his antagonism to composers such as Smetana and Wagner (who by his 'courage for breadth' was the antipode of Janáček with his 'courage for conciseness'), may perhaps be best explained as his instinctive self-defence against influences which appeared to him to be the greatest danger to his originality or, at least—as in the case of Mussorgsky—for the just appraisal of his personality. However, upon examining Janáček's early works, the main influences—apart from those of Dvořák—are none other than Wagner and, in particular, Smetana: in the latter case, we sometimes find whole quotations (SUITE FOR STRINGS, the chorus AUTUMN SONG, MUSIC FOR INDIAN CLUB SWINGING and in OUR SONG).

But even when Janáček's musical language had reached the stage of complete independence and when there can be no question of direct influence, Smetana's structural influence may still be found.**)

---

*) Janáček dreamed — at least in his younger days — that there would be no specially Czech, Russian, Polish music, but only one style of music common to all the Slavs. Naturally the old Moravian folk music was closest to this ideal.

**) Influences are usually picked out too one-sidedly by chance or by superficial and visual similarities. And yet it is far more interesting for anyone who does not want to be a mere 'hunter of reminiscences' to discover tectonic or at least technical analogies which may be found even in the works of the greatest composers. (For instance, the conclusion of Act I

In this respect it is possible that the long crescendo on the broken C major chord by which Smetana, in Act II of his opera *The Kiss*, accompanied the sunrise, led Janáček to a similar long drawn out crescendo of a C major chord before the end of JENŮFA. (Here also, at least figuratively, the sun is rising!) And a no lesser structural and expressive analogy is presented by the preparation of the moment when, at the end of Smetana's *The Kiss*, Lukáš and Vendulka fall reconciled into each other's arms, with the moment when, at the end of JENŮFA, Laca and Jenůfa take each other's hands in eternal union. But also in the realm of ideas—besides their reformatory influence from the point of view of composing, conducting and teaching—both masters are much nearer to one another than Janáček would probably have cared to concede: they both have the same, almost philosophical basis for their work, the same deep sympathy for the ordinary man, for their native soil and historical tradition, as well as the combination of manly strength with almost child-like tenderness of expression. Naturally there are differences, one of the main ones being the fact that Smetana was the poet of national freedom while Janáček was the poet of personal freedom. And Smetana was mainly a consonant while Janáček was a dissonant spirit. But in fairness to Janáček, it should be stressed that, besides some prejudiced and even trivial criticisms of Smetana, he wrote some truly revealing passages about him. And if he prepared for the Smetana Centenary in 1924 — the year of his own seventieth birthday— a speech which was, on account of its utter lack of piety, suppressed, he made up for this very largely in his essay 'The Creative Mind'.*) He had besides paid tribute to the composer of the fanfares for *Libuše*, when he wrote the fanfares of his SINFONIETTA.

In his compositions, Janáček shared with Debussy a preference for modulations formed by the use of a note common to both chords, an aversion to the 'embrace of the Old Lady', as Debussy used to call the perfect cadence, and the dislike of 'administrative' musical forms. On the other hand, the sophisticated sensitivity and wistful resignation of the composer of *Pelléas* must have been as alien to Janáček's full-blooded fighting spirit as the worldly sophistication and the emphatic subjectivism of Richard Strauss was to his peasant simplicity and humanitarian feeling. And the careful study he made of Puccini was mainly dictated by his wish to master the weapons of the opposite camp.**)

---

of *Die Meistersinger* is tectonically—the key of F included—almost a literal analogy to the finale of the first movement of Beethoven's Pastoral Symphony. And the dark bass motif of *Parsifal* in Act III, where the hero is about to faint, bears a striking resemblance to the way in which Mozart accompanies a similar moment when Donna Anna recognizes the murderer of her father, in *Don Giovanni*.
*) *Lidové noviny*, 2 March 1924, the day of Smetana's Centenary.
**) For instance, Janáček was evidently struck by the ostinato B flat, G, A flat, F in Act I of *Tosca* inspired by the ostinato of the bells in Wagner's *Parsifal*—judging, at least, from the fact that he jotted down this motif on the pro gramme of the performance. Yet the means by which such an ostinato gains its main attraction—the constantly changing harmonic pattern of the unchanged motif (a system used most successfully, for instance, by Richard Strauss in *Till Eulenspiegel* in the augmentation of the hero's motif and by which also the Russian composers liked to liven up their ostinato repetitions of folk dance motifs) is, in Janáček's ostinatos, very rare. His motifs usually 'bend' together with the harmonic basis.

The advent of the third generation of his time also left him untouched. This is the more remarkable in view of the fact that it was this generation which brought about the revival of absolute music, its forms and its pre-classical stylization aspiring to the ideal of '*musica pura*'. This he did not accept even though he himself was performed at International Festivals of Contemporary Music as one of the leaders of the avant-garde. In fact, for this peculiarly programmatic musician of ideas all superiority of form was alien, just as stylization was alien to his realism or the cold '*Neue Sachlichkeit*' to his elemental flame and passion. When he says in reference to this, 'If the mind was not aflame within the chord, I might compare harmony to the flowers which the frost conjures up on our windows,' he is hinting that he does not deny this type of music its peculiar 'cold beauty' but at the same time that he himself feels quite differently. And he underlines this by confessing, 'The tame look of a duckling, or the scanning glance of a hawk, an ardent kiss or the grasp of a cooling hand, the misty blue of the forget-me-not or the burning fire of the poppy, all these create in me a chord.'

There was, however, one thing which Janáček had in common with these trends: in the same way in which he had—though by other means—estranged himself from romanticism, he had also come nearer to that more sober generation by his growing sense of the slender charm of two voices singing together or even a solo voice, thus fulfilling what he attributed to Dvořák when he wrote:*) 'I believe that *Armida* would have been the last of his operas in which a dense impenetrable mist of full chords would have been rolling throughout—his last opera in the old style. He was searching for a libretto which would break up the customary tectonic structure.'

In any case the trend of modern music towards a chamber style influenced greatly the creation of Janáček's later works for chamber ensembles, as in the CONCERTINO, the CAPRICCIO and the NURSERY RHYMES.

And here it will not be out of place to say a few words about Janáček's orchestra.

It is necessary at the outset to point out that Janáček's development towards chamber ensembles was the logical result of the whole of his orchestral style. Even his setting of the old Czech chorale LORD HAVE MERCY UPON US is scored for a limited though in its way massive ensemble consisting of two choirs, a quartet of soloists, brass octet, harp and organ. And even when he was writing for the full orchestra he hardly ever made use of all the instruments. For instance, in the final tutti of the SINFONIETTA the bassoons are silent, although a specially enlarged brass ensemble is playing. Writing, as he was, at the time of mammoth orchestras, his scores and also his piano style are predominantly modest, making full use of clean, clear colour. It is noteworthy, for instance, to observe his sparing use of all uncommon, conspicuous instruments and superficial sound effects, and the perfect sense of balance and purpose which is revealed in his saving such instruments for exceptional moments. He uses them with all the more decisive and singular effect, with the exception, perhaps, of the unfortunate viola d'amore (in the SECOND STRING QUARTET)

---

*) *Hudební revue*, Vol. IV (1911), p. 433.

which evidently bewitched him more by the sound of its name than by the sound of the instrument itself. Take, for instance, the xylophone in Act I of JENŮFA or the use of the bass clarinet in the same work for expressing the anguish of guilt, the use of the high E flat clarinet for Ostap's torture in the second movement of TARAS BULBA, or the celesta's lilting accompaniment to the motif of the sensual Varvara in KATYA KABANOVA. Janáček made frequent use of the harp, even as early as the LACHIAN DANCES, and with great effect, probably under the influence of Berlioz. The same may be said of the *Glockenspiel* or its miniature military equivalent, the lyra, which he used especially in his earlier compositions, being at that time dependent on military bands. Of the percussion instruments, Janáček is most sparing in his use of the gong: in AMARUS, one single soft stroke marks the death of Amarus, in the Hussite part of the EXCURSIONS OF MR BROUČEK it is used to suggest the din of battle in the introduction, and in THE HOUSE OF THE DEAD, where it introduces, with a fortissimo stroke, the play acted by the prisoners. It is significant that the naturalist Janáček usually preferred the 'common' timpani, the least naturalistic and most stylized of all the percussion instruments, as Jarmil Burghauser has pointed out.*) To illustrate this let me quote a few examples: the conclusion of Act I and especially Act II of JENŮFA, the mighty crescendo of the choir *a cappella* in the ETERNAL GOSPEL, the virtuoso solo figuration accompanying the appearance of the devils at the beginning of the comic play acted in THE HOUSE OF THE DEAD, the characteristic tremolo glissandos in the BALLAD OF BLANÍK; the chiming timpani motif accompanying the fanfares in the SINFONIETTA. No doubt, there are in Janáček's scoring a number of realistic elements (though basically he uses the romantic orchestra of Wagner's *Lohengrin* augmented perhaps only by the celesta, a fourth flute or a number of piccolos as a result of his predilection for the extremes of pitch); and since Janáček drew much of his inspiration from folk songs, he found inspiration in the folk instruments themselves, using them either directly (the bagpipe in Act I of DESTINY or at the solemn entry of the Hussite leader Žižka into Prague in the EXCURSIONS OF MR BROUČEK**), or the child's trumpet and the village band in Act I of JENŮFA) or indirectly (the imitation of the cymbalom in the piano accompaniment at the beginning of the VIOLIN SONATA) and especially in many folk songs and, in a very stylized way, in the 9/8 G flat major section at the end of the wistful scene before the last part of the ADVENTURES OF THE VIXEN SHARP EARS—where I would like to point out the rubato alternation of long notes with fast figurations, so typical of nostalgic songs of Southern Moravia and further East.

His sparing use of some instruments is connected with a further peculiarity of his orchestral style. Even here symbolism is added to purely realistic elements. Entirely symbolical, for instance, is his habit (especially at the time when he was writing THE FIDDLER'S CHILD, the FAIRY-TALE for cello and the VIOLIN SONATA, but which may also be seen in the CAPRICCIO) of attributing to every musical idea and every poetic image what might be called its 'personal'

---

*) *Musikologie III*, p. 304.
**) He allowed however — partly for reasons of modulation — the replacement of bagpipes by oboes.

instrument, for instance, the viola d'amore to the mysterious heroine of THE MAKROPOULOS CASE or a whole group of instruments, for instance, in THE FIDDLER'S CHILD, a quartet of violas characterizing poverty. All this—together with Janáček's liking for chord notes at the extreme ends of the compass while leaving out the centre—gives his orchestration its highly individual character.

What then was Janáček's contribution as a whole? It neither begins nor ends with the speech melodies. They existed before him, as did the Wagnerian Leitmotiv before Wagner in Weber's *Freischütz* or Berlioz's *Symphonie Fantastique*. Neither does it begin or end with his use of the church modes, for these were resuscitated before him, in particular by the Russian composers. Even the use of his favourite D flat major for hymnic passages was known by Beethoven (second movement of the *Appassionata*), Richard Wagner (motif of Valhalla), Bruckner, Dvořák (*Dimitri*, the finale of *Rusalka*, the slow movement of the 'New World' Symphony), the assignment of a 'personal' instrument or group of instruments was used by Bach in *St Matthew's Passion* (strings accompanying only the Lord), Mozart in *Don Giovanni* (trombones for the slain Commendatore), by Berlioz in *Harold in Italy* (solo viola) and by Richard Strauss in *Don Quixote* (solo cello and solo viola) and in the *Sinfonia Domestica* (oboe d'amore). The milieu of the present-day town on the operatic stage had not only appeared in Verdi's *Traviata* but in comic opera right from its birth. I think, however, that Janáček was the first composer to write a whole opera in folk dialect (or two, if we count ADVENTURES OF THE VIXEN SHARP EARS), but even Bach allowed himself to write, in dialect, a sort of cantata—or almost a small opera buffa ('*Mer hahn en neue Oberkeet*'). Bach even knew the exciting effect of fragmentary interjections, as can be seen from the beginning of the C major Toccata which was well known to the young Janáček. In the sung declamation, similar rhythms blurted out to the last fragment of the bar are also often used by Richard Strauss. In the creating of an eerie effect by playing the lowest and highest chord notes while leaving out the firm middle, he was preceded by Beethoven in his later piano works. And from Beethoven Janáček probably got his habit of not writing long notes directly but joining smaller note values. There are countless other examples. Wherever he ventured someone had been there before him.

But he knew he was going 'his own way', and this not only in the prose which he was the first to use, at least in his country, for opera, unaware what experiments others were making at the same time. And thus he is, after all, different even where his steps meet those of other people—and perhaps that is where he is most different. 'My dear teachers—but each time I found myself on the opposite bank.'

Yet there were two teachers to whom he remained faithful throughout his life: nature and the simple human being who was, for him, what the mythical man was to Wagner. And thanks to these two teachers he made his greatest contribution: truthfulness, even to the point of ruthlessness, if necessary. And although from time to time his eye turned broodingly, sometimes defiantly to the 'other' bank, he always remained on this earthly side fighting, as perhaps no other musician since Beethoven, for a just and better life in this world.

Janáček reveals himself as a down-to-earth realist in his approach to work. In fact he composed permanently—in the streets, at the market, during his morning walks to the nearby Brno parks of Lužánky and Špilberk or to the more distant Imperial (later Wilson) Forest, and everywhere he listened and took down the speech of the ordinary people, often developing their melodies in his mind.*) He even composed during his classes at the Organ School, which became evident when he suddenly stopped in the middle of an explanation and went to the window, absorbed in an idea which had just entered his mind.

His creative work passed, usually, through three stages. The slow germination of the basic idea sometimes went together with a few motifs (in the vocal works these were, primarily, the speech melodies of the most prominent passages in the words) unless the work was actually inspired by a spontaneously appearing musical motif. If the subject came from a definite milieu, he set himself to study its 'cradle', striving to get as much as possible into the mood of the subject. For instance, before his prepared (yet abortive) rewriting of MARYČKA MAGDÓNOVA for choir and orchestra, he went, at the beginning of October 1908, to the Ostrava industrial basin to study there the 'tone chaos', another time he went to study the *genius loci* before his intended composition of the operas ANGELIC SONATA, THE FARMER'S WOMAN and JOHNNY THE HERO. While working on the ADVENTURES OF THE VIXEN SHARP EARS he used to go out with the gamekeepers at night to watch the foxes and at an interview which he gave to the press before the première of the EXCURSIONS OF MR BROUČEK he declared: 'Because of Brouček, in order to get soaked with the proper atmosphere, I spent many hours of the night on top of the tower of St Vitus's cathedral, as I wanted to have a fresh and deep impression of Prague sinking into night.'**) Otherwise he spent much time in 'long thinking' (as he called it in the case of the CONCERTINO), thinking still harder in the case of an opera where it also meant moulding the libretto. 'It is cetrain that each of my operas grew a good year or two in my mind without my stopping this growth by a single note. For every work I worried my head off.'***) This lingering sometimes had its deeper reason. 'It is not good to write straightaway after gaining some strong impression. When these impressions have been covered by another layer, the idea then works its way through with more strength and richness, like an Artesian well,' he wrote to Max Brod on 31 October 1924.

Although the passage of this first stage began comparatively calmly, the ripening of the thematic material gradually passed into a stormy phase. Janáček was too much of a full-blooded musician to be able to do without the inspiration of live sound. This is described most vividly by the Brno musicologist Dr Ludvík Kundera. At the time when he was secretary of the Brno *conservatoire*, the window of his office was opposite Janáček's study in the villa which he occupied in the garden of the Organ School. 'The whole morning I could hear his piano. But in a most unusual way. Janáček, with the pedal

---

*) See, for instance, his article, 'The Mouths', *Lidové noviny*, 5 July 1925.
**) *Janáček—Librettists*, p. 8.
***) *Veselý—Janáček*, p. 96.

firmly up, kept banging out as loud as possible a few notes of a motif of the kind one knows so well from his compositions. He repeated it many times unchanged or else with only a slight alteration. The verve of his playing made one realize how much he was carried away by the emotional contents of the motif... This, naturally, was not composing—by repeating one and the same motif he wanted to get into a certain mood in order to throw the composition, built up mostly from this motif, feverishly on paper without the piano.' After this preparatory stage, the second stage, the writing of the work proper, usually made very rapid headway as can be seen from the almost incredible dates on the manuscripts of both QUARTETS or on the GLAGOLITIC MASS.*)

The third stage was again a longer one and consisted mainly of the polishing up of the roughly finished composition. ('I write quickly but I polish for a long time', he told Max Brod in 1928 and ten years before that he said to the writer F. S. Procházka: 'I usually let a finished work lie until it gets over-run by another emotional deluge. After a time one gets different eyes. The work must not submerge one completely.')

It is typical that this process of selection and cleaning up consisted mainly of elimination and abbreviation. This can be most strikingly seen from the gradual condensing of his originally long-winded and romantic first opera, ŠÁRKA, or in the final version of the EXCURSIONS OF MR BROUČEK, on which he comments in a letter to the singer Gabriela Horvátová written on 18 January 1918. 'What a pleasure it is sometimes to throw away finished work. All the scenes of Brouček in his home which I wrote last year, I have now thrown away.'

A further phase of the polishing process was the testing of the sound and passages which seemed unsuitable from the point of view of performance. This was done at rehearsals. Here he used to drive the performers to despair, changing, up till the very last minute, not only the instrumentation and dynamics, but even the tempi. Even years after finishing and after the first performance of a work, he would return to it and make many alterations: he rewrote, for instance, his choruses to words by Petr Bezruč, the CELLO SONATA, and especially the VIOLIN SONATA, THE FIDDLER'S CHILD, THE ETERNAL GOSPEL, NURSERY RHYMES, not to mention ŠÁRKA and the PIANO TRIO based on Tolstoy's *Kreutzer Sonata*, which he changed into his FIRST STRING QUARTET.

For Janáček creation was life, and to live was to create. He could not bear to rest even after writing THE MAKROPOULOS CASE or the GLAGOLITIC MASS and, as he used to say, 'The end of one work is the beginning of the next one.'

Fate took away from him his baby son and later his daughter. Thus he became all the more attached to his music.

'By now my family consists of nothing but notes. They have got heads and

---

*) Janáček usually sketched his orchestral works directly in full score (putting only a few bars on each page so that he might easily eliminate what he wanted to leave out). And he used to rule his own staves because, as he maintained, empty lines would seduce him to write unnecessary notes. His wife, according to Adolf Veselý, writing in the Brno *Hudební rozhledy* of November 1928, explained this in another way: in order to be sure that Janáček took proper rest during the holidays she did not allow him to take any manuscript paper away with him and he was thus forced to rule the lines himself.

feet. They can run, play, bring forth tears or happiness. They are difficult to catch, and to understand them—that took a long time. And what a number of them in one line! At least they won't forget me; they won't deny me—we are Janáček's. Is that not happiness enough?'*)

Janáček's portrait would not be complete without mentioning briefly his activities as a writer. He has left us literary work which, if only by its volume and pioneering ideas, is by no means inferior to his musical legacy. It is actually quite natural that a musician of such original opinions and gifts of observation, a musician so inquisitive and temperamental as Janáček (see his sarcastic footnotes, question marks and exclamation marks with which he used to fill the books he read or his programmes of concerts of plays) often felt the need to resort to the pen in order to state his views on some burning subject or to express a strong emotion or to convey an important discovery.

Janáček's literary activities can be divided into three groups:

1. Musicology (studies, essays on folk songs, on composing; criticism and theoretical work, especially the comprehensive book on harmony).

2. Autobiographical sketches (in the form of articles for the newspaper *Lidové noviny* and other periodicals) in which the composer is most concerned with his favourite theme, the speech melodies. But since Janáček always looked for the human being as a whole when considering a speech melody, these sketches are often complete psychological studies, glimpses of the whole of life through the prism of a moment, miniature idylls or tragedies. For instance, the short story, *Alžběta* (Elizabeth), from his birthplace, Hukvaldy, unwittingly portrays the two sides of the life of the simple folk. Janáček by means of speech melodies describes the seemingly identical childhood of Lidka and Vinca—children of his friend the gamekeeper Sládek—and of the seven-year old Alžběta, the child of poor peasants, ending with the brief but all the more shattering remark that one day the unfortunate Alžběta was beaten to death by her own drunken father.

3. Janáček's arrangements of the poems and dramatic subjects which he set to music. Janáček, in such cases, added very little of his own text, even less, perhaps, than was necessary for the proper welding of the action, quite unlike Mussorgsky who did not hesitate to rewrite the whole Forest of Kromy scene in *Boris Godunov* quite independently. Perhaps Janáček was worried about the disunity of diction, which was certainly unnecessary since he became so deeply involved in every subject on which he worked. But the less Janáček added of his own words the more he cut out of the original. Janáček the writer was as fond of conciseness as Janáček the composer; with the same horror of banalities in both fields.

And he eventually became, although later than in his music, a true poet of the word. This can already be seen from his letters. Reading his exchange of correspondence with people who were often professional writers, one can distinguish his unconventional, sometimes terse, sometimes warm and human style from the writing of his correspondents (besides some grammatical peculiarities of his native dialect, like placing the attribute after the noun).

---

*) Janáček to Mrs Gabriela Horvátová, 7 January 1918.

His speeches and lectures are of particular interest. Their originality begins with their graphic arrangement: each sentence is a separate paragraph. As if Janáček wanted to give time to the reader to think of what he had just said. And this is often necessary, since the shorter the time needed for reading one of his sentences, the longer it takes to understand.

Sometimes one is almost flabbergasted by his trick of expressing, in so few words, something so highly puzzling… Fortunately, Janáček's riddles are usually well worth the trouble spent in solving them and when this has been done, one has a feeling that the idea could not have been expressed in a more attractive or even straightforward way.

Thus this self-taught and lonely man from Brno—or perhaps one of the great outsiders—the prisoner of narrow, one-sided and queer theories, is, in fact, one of the most prolific and original figures of modern music—and, perhaps, not only of music.

But now it is time to try and describe how—through his origin, life and art—Janáček came to be such a figure.

J. V.

PART ONE (1854·1903)

(I) Family Background

The little village of Hukvaldy, overlooked by the ruins of a once-mighty Moravian castle, lies among the Beskydy hills. Its name—*Ukvaly* in the local Lachian dialect and *Hochwald* in German—is derived from that of the castle's first known inhabitant, Count Arnold de Huckeswage (Huckswag, Hohenswag), whose name appears in ancient documents as early as 1234. His son, Frank de Huckeswage, sold the whole estate to Bruno of Schaumburg, Bishop of Olomouc and chief adviser to the unfortunate king Přemysl Otakar II. However, de Huckeswage continued to live in the castle as the bishop's vassal, entrusted with the task of colonizing the uninhabited surrounding land.

After 1311, Hukvaldy knew many owners, among them Sigmund of Hungary, and two Hussite captains, the second of whom, Jan Talafús of Ostrov, styled himself Lord of Hukvaldy. In 1581, Bishop Stanislav Pavlovský bought back the whole estate for the chapter of Olomouc, under whose administration it remained until recently. Glass-making and the exploitation of iron ore flourished on the estate, and in 1576 veins of silver and even gold were discovered.

During the seventeenth century, Hukvaldy was besieged in rapid succession by Mansfeld, the Turks, the Swedes and the Hungarians. The castle withstood all these attacks, but the unfortunate peasants suffered both at the hands of the besiegers who revenged themselves for their failure to conquer the castle by pillaging the surrounding countryside, and also of the lords of the castle who suppressed and exploited them when their enemies withdrew.

Finally, in 1695—the year of the Chod uprising in south-western Bohemia—disturbances broke out among the peasants on the Hukvaldy estate in protest against the exorbitant taxation and demands made on the serfs. Fifteen hundred men from thirty villages gathered at Kopřivnice, but the captain of Hukvaldy, Maximilian of Harasov, suppressed the uprising and threw the leaders into prison. The disturbances ceased but the conditions remained unchanged.

On 5 October 1762, a large part of the castle, then serving as a prison for delinquent priests, was burnt down and the archives, with their unique historic documents, were destroyed. Another fire broke out in 1820, after which no attempts were made at restoration. Only the splendid game reserve has been maintained, the haunt of herds of fallow deer. The castle on the hill, half hidden among huge beeches and limes, retains little of its former grandeur.

The buildings of interest in Hukvaldy village are all to be found on the slope under the castle, close to the entrance to the game reserve. They include a country house built in the year of Janáček's birth for the Archbishop of Olomouc, Friedrich von Fürstenberg, the little church of St Maximilian (built in 1759) and the village school.

In this very school, 'in a room where one window looked out on the church

33

and the other on the brewery'—as he himself said— Leoš Janáček was born on 3 July 1854. He was christened Leo Eugen on the following day, and this date is sometimes erroneously given as the day of his birth. He was the ninth child of a poor village schoolmaster and choirmaster whose ancestors had been weavers in the district of Těšín and again later, after the end of the seventeenth century, in Frýdek.

The first musician and founder of the musical tradition in the Janáček family was Leo's grandfather, Jiří (George). His mother's husband, Jan Janáček (born 20 February 1742, died 6 June 1774), died before Jiří's birth (17 April 1778), and his mother, Dorota, in the autumn of 1784 accepted the post of housekeeper to Father Antonín Herman, chaplain of Velký (Great) Petřvald. 'The reason why Father Herman chose this young woman from Frýdek was probably a personal and perhaps even intimate one' (Helfert, p. 17). We may guess it by comparing the dates of Jiří's birth and Jan Janáček's death. In any case this was the first providential occurrence in the family.

Father Herman was no ordinary country chaplain. He was the son of the burgrave at Count Vilček's castle of Klímkovice where he had been born on 10 November 1753. He became a priest and in 1778, the year of Jiří's birth, entered the Augustinian monastery of Fulnek, where he held the comparatively important position of administrator and preacher on festive occasions. His cell was equipped with all the comforts necessary to an educated and enlightened man of the world, from a well-stocked library to a complete riding outfit. This privileged life was brought to an end in 1784 when the Emperor Joseph II closed Fulnek, among other monasteries. Nothing remained for the members of the order but to become secular priests at the disposal of the Archiepiscopal Consistory in Olomouc. A sudden flood of surplus priests probably explains why Father Herman, accustomed to more magnificent surroundings, had to content himself with the post of chaplain of 'Great' Petřvald ('Great' as distinct from the even smaller neighbouring village of Little Petřvald) where at that time there was neither school nor vicarage, only a small wooden sixteenth-century church. Count Karl Vetter of Lilie, a friend of Father Herman, tried to get him appointed castle chaplain at his nearby residence, but the Emperor frustrated this plan with the remark, 'I have priests for poor villages but not for cavaliers.' Although his 'retreat from glory' embittered the priest and drove him to console himself by consuming a rather too liberal quantity of spirits, the circumstance proved a blessing to the six-year-old Jiří Janáček, whose rudimentary education was now taken in hand. Father Herman taught the young pupil such everyday crafts as bookbinding and gardening, but it was he who encouraged Jiří to set his sights higher and to become a teacher. After Father Herman's own experience as a priest and in view of the increasing state provision for schools this seemed a safe bet.

However, the beginning of Jiří's career was not particularly brilliant. In October 1797, at the age of 19, he was appointed assistant to the 'widely renowned' teacher (according to Jiří's biography written by his son Vincenc) and able musician, Karel Němec, in the town of Polish (later Silesian) Ostrava. His multiple duties included looking after the head-teacher's children, running errands, playing the organ in church and acting as bell-ringer and sacristan. He was always in imminent danger of being conscripted into the army, which at that time meant eight to fourteen years of service. This did not suit his plans, however, and when, one day, the commission arrived to find him seated at lunch with the priest's family, he seized the table, hurled it at the commissioners, plunged through a window (like Pushkin's Grishka in *Boris Godunov*) and escaped across the river Ostravice to Great Petřvald, where his mother hid him. The local educational authorities, moved by his mother's pleading, subsequently intervened on his behalf and had him officially registered as a future teacher, which exempted him permanently from military service.

He was appointed teacher at Albrechtice, a village only a few miles from Great Petřvald, where he found favour with Count Vetter of Lilie, patron of the local school and church, and one of Father Herman's former benefactors. He was entrusted with the private tuition of the Count's two sons, who repaid him by playing practical jokes on him. Once, on a cold autumn day, they forced him to bathe in the river Odra, causing him to contract rheumatism which was to trouble him for the rest of his life.

Nevertheless, Jiří proved himself worthy of his patron's interest, though inclined to display in his undertakings the same rather rash determination which he had shown in the recruiting episode. For instance, having demanded a new building for his school to replace the ramshackle cottage which lacked even the most elementary equipment, and realizing that his demands were fruitless, he arranged an apparently accidental collapse of the ceiling—considerately, out of school hours.

Yet, in spite of his explosive temper, he was a conscientious and respected teacher. He soon saw to it that in the hitherto almost entirely illiterate village—in the winter months the girls used to go to a herdsman who taught them reading; boys 'didn't need it'—there were no children who did not attend school regularly, nor any parents who objected to paying school fees. With equal zeal, he ran a course of Sunday classes for the older boys whose work prevented them from attending school on weekdays.

He put his knowledge of tree-grafting and gardening to good use, teaching his pupils to do the same, and he turned a stony slope next to the school into a flower garden and an orchard.

He also cultivated his other hobbies of bookbinding, wood-carving and paint-making. When the little village church burned down, he decorated the new one with commendable taste and skill.

His love of music led him to try his hand in yet another direction—organ building. With the help of the village tailor, Jan Huvar, he managed to build an organ for the new church which remained in use until 1891: he himself was not only a proficient organ player, but also possessed some knowledge of the technique of composition. When playing in church he would often improvise fugues, and, as recounted in the biography, enjoyed singing in a 'strong, pleasant voice' to his own accompaniment, with sufficient clarity for the congregation to understand every new hymn, 'both young and old joining in with joyful and enthusiastic singing'. He often was also an inspiring speaker, the fire and emotion of his words often reducing not only his listeners but himself to tears. But at other times he had his audience laughing till again the tears ran down their cheeks.

Owing to his social and artistic gifts and his manual skill, he enjoyed not only great popularity ('he was invited to every feast and entertainment') but also a fairly good income. His new wife, Anna Šajtarová (or Scheutterová) was equally hardworking. She was also a thrifty woman, and the marriage was happy and successful. They had seven children, six of whom lived to grow up. Of his four sons, the two eldest, Josef and Jan, were chosen for the priesthood; Jiří (born 4 October 1815, the father of Leoš) and Vincenc were to carry on the new family tradition of teaching and music.

The unbounded energy of Grandfather Janáček occasionally led to outbursts of violence, especially when he had been indulging his craving for liquor, a habit acquired in his youth from the disillusioned step-father who gave him drinks as a reward for smuggling spirits to him. On these occasions he flew into such a rage that this otherwise model father became an object of fear to his wife and children. On such days 'our sun shone no more', writes Vincenc in his biography, with only the vaguest hint at one particularly regrettable scene. His wife saved him from the consequence of that incident by 'a cloak of silence', although she herself had probably been the main sufferer. Vincenc refers to her as 'the golden pillar of the household who carried the burden of the family on her shoulders. Her quiet and placid nature and her kindness soothed our father's temper and guarded him against his own reckless actions... She left herself exposed to his outbursts, suffering all for the sake of her children.'

In later life the old man developed a heart disease and, at the age of 64, was obliged to give up teaching and live in retirement. His heart grew steadily worse, he became very deaf and, once so sociable and entertaining, he began avoiding people and sat listlessly at home. 'Then came the year 1848 when the sun of freedom shone brightly for the nations of Austria. His energy revived and he followed the development of events with avid interest. However, his strength was failing and we saw that his days were numbered. He died of pneumonia on 15 October 1848, at the age of 70. His patient wife outlived him by 21 years, reaching the venerable age of 86.'

A comparatively large amount of space has been devoted to Janáček's grandfather because—as Vladimír Helfert says (*Leoš Janáček*, p. 29) — his life, and more especially his character, resembled those of Leoš Janáček in so striking a manner. 'The tenacious energy and enterprising spirit which enabled him to raise himself from extreme poverty to a reasonably comfortable level of life, his keen intelligence and perception, his wide interests and his indefatigable work promoting culture through his own creativeness in an environment which was backward and primitive—these gifts and qualities recurred, in intensified form, in the person of his grandson, Leoš. Combine this explosive temperament with the ability to express it imaginatively in music, translating these emotions into creative terms—and we have a true picture of the future composer.'

The son who inherited both his profession and his name, Jiří, was taught the rudiments of piano and organ playing as well as singing by his father; but after a while young Jiří was sent to study at Velký Petřvald under Josef Richter, a severe and demanding teacher.

In August 1831, after a three-month preparatory course at the Piarist school in Příbor, Jiří, although still only 16, was appointed assistant teacher at the North Moravian town of Neplachovice. There, according to Vincenc's biography—and here we have another providential coincidence—'the little orphan Pavel Křížkovský attached himself to the new teacher. The child's mother begged young Jiří to give the boy music and singing lessons. Jiří undertook the task and later secured a scholarship for the child at the choir school of the church of the Holy Ghost in Opava and by so doing laid the foundations of his career as a composer of choral music, a service which was later repaid in Brno to Jiří's son, Leoš.' Křížkovský, the future founder of the Moravian choral style, was the illegitimate child of a village girl, and suffered not only from poverty but also from malicious prejudice. It was not surprising that he clung gratefully to his benefactor, scarcely six years his senior.

Jiří Janáček left Neplachovice after one and a half years to take up an assistant's post in Kateřinky near Opava where he increased his musical skills by playing the organ and singing in churches and elsewhere. After two years he went, in February 1835, to Příbor where he also became second and eventually first town *cantor*—teacher and music-master. Considering himself to be sufficiently well provided for he married, on 24 July 1838, the 19-year-old Amalie Grulichová, a daughter of one of the old burgher families of Příbor. However, he remained a mere 'assistant' for the next ten years, and it is hardly surprising that when in 1848, shortly before his father's death, the post of full teacher became vacant in the nearby village of Hukvaldy, he exchanged the town for the picturesque village (unless he was compelled to do so because of some rash act).

The significance of his move to Hukvaldy for the future of his family could not have been foreseen. When he arrived, the inhabitants of Hukvaldy numbered only 573. Most of them made a meagre living by weaving and keeping sheep. The teacher had no fixed salary, his income depending on the number of fee-paying children attending school. Attendance was, in fact, very poor and the villagers impoverished by bad harvests and by a compulsory levy of over 300,000 guilders imposed by their former overlords after the abolition of serfdom in 1848. Poverty reached its height when the state ran into bankruptcy after the disastrous Lombardian war of 1859.

These events had both a direct and indirect influence on the home of the new teacher, which was already far from comfortable. The living space was insufficient for the size of his family, quite apart from the fact that he was also obliged to provide his assistant with board and lodging. Leoš Janáček recollects: 'Hukvaldy school: one large room, raw wooden benches. On the left, the little ones—on the right, the older children. Two blackboards, father and the assistant teaching simultaneously. How did they manage? A huge stove in one corner, beside it a bed for the assistant. I too lay in it after I had once scalded myself.' Worse than the lack of space was the fact that the school building—once a manorial ice-store—was damp and badly in need of repairs for which Jiří Janáček waited desperately for ten years, long enough for him to develop severe rheumatism resulting in turn in hereditary heart disease. This illness, aggravated by his innate irritability, caused his premature death.

In these difficult conditions one child after another was born to the Janáčeks. They had left Příbor with five children, three daughters, Viktorie (b. 1838), Eleonora (b. 1840), Josefa Adolfina (b. 1842), and two sons, Karel (b. 1844) and Bedřich (b. 1846). The first children born in Hukvaldy were twins (b. 1849) one of whom was born dead, the other, František, dying soon after. There followed Rosalie (b. 1850), Jiří (b. 1852) who died in infancy, Leo Eugen (b. 1854), František (b. 1856), Josef (b. 1858), Adolf (b. 1861) and Marie (b. 1863); the two youngest lived only a few months. It is perhaps significant that of the five children born in Příbor all lived to grow up, while of the nine born in Hukvaldy, only four survived.

Jiří Janáček has been described as 'robust, tall and dark-haired'; his wife was small and fair. Leo Eugen, our Leoš, was a *mixtum compositum* of both: dark like his father (there is no picture extant of Janáček's father or grandfather, only of Janáček's mother) and short like his mother. Their life in Hukvaldy was far from easy and as Leoš recollected, 'music and bee-keeping were my father's only amusements.' Although overburdened with domestic worries, Jiří Janáček by no means neglected his teaching, on the contrary, he extended the school syllabus to include drawing, singing and geography and was, like his father, an active patriot, in itself risky for an employee of the Austrian establishment. Only a year before his death, he founded a reading and singing club whose aim was not merely educational, but which also sought to revive a feeling of national consciousness in its members. He himself was the club's first choir-master.

He inherited from his father a love of music and skill in bee-keeping and gardening. He unfortunately also inherited something of his father's rashness and bad temper, which seems to have been mainly directed against his unfortunate wife, who, he complained, was too extravagant. Luckily he did not make matters worse by excessive drinking as grandfather Janáček had done.

Jiří Janáček was unable to act as a real choir-master in Hukvaldy church where there was insufficient space for performing any but the simplest masses. However, he compensated himself by frequently visiting the neighbouring village of Rychaltice where he and his colleague, who was choir-master there, shared a mutual love of bee-keeping. The two teachers spent much of their spare time making music and they were not always the only performers. Jiří would sometimes add to their pleasure by bringing with him a daughter (Eleonora?) who played the viola and one of his sons, then about seven years old, who had a pleasant soprano voice. This small singer was none other than Leoš Janáček.

From the day of his birth, 3 July 1854, little Leoš lived in close contact with music, nature and poverty. On the other hand the household was supplied with fruit and vegetables from the school garden, it kept some domestic animals, the father kept his bees and was entitled to free beer, and as a fiddler he occasionally earned extra money by playing at dances.

Leoš Janáček retained few recollections of his childhood in Hukvaldy. He left the village when he was 11, not even completing his schooling; his marks placed him only seventh among his eight brothers and sisters. Looking back on his childhood, when in his seventies, he recollected the small yard with ducks, a cow in the stable, his sister Viki's loom; going to early Advent mass through the snow, carrying a candle; a pilgrimage to St Andrew's shrine at the castle; sliding down—'tobogganing'—on a sun-baked tin roof followed by an inspection of the seat of his trousers 'in their still warm condition'; the biting ants in the forest, and noisy, unpleasant strangers who nosed around the hunting-lodge.

His childhood memories of music consisted mainly of the festival masses at Rychaltice, and the equally festive lunches afterwards at the vicarage. (He still dreamed of them when he was a student in Leipzig.) 'There they had double music-stands, a gilded organ with plenty of stops on both sides of the manual, and at the back, near the window, two kettledrums, each as big as a kneading-trough.' Unfortunately, the two teachers had a quarrel one sunny afternoon in the Janáček garden, the very afternoon of the 'tobogganing' episode, which probably accounts for the severity of its consequences. The friendship, and the excursions to Rychaltice choir, came to an end.

The parting of the two teachers had still one more consequence. In order to provide drums for the special Easter mass, several youngsters from Hukvaldy, Leoš among them (without his father's knowledge), set out to 'borrow', under cover of darkness, the kettledrums from Rychaltice. The drums were dragged in triumph up the hill to Hukvaldy but—such is the lack of understanding on the part of fathers—the drum-sticks danced not on the timpani but, rather, on Leoš's back. However, his love of the timpani was not diminished by this event and he later remarked: 'Whenever they occur in my work I give them a special solo.'

The 'robbing' expedition and a fire in the neighbourhood were the most romantic occurrences in an otherwise uneventful childhood. For although the castle ruins and the countryside around Hukvaldy were steeped in romantic and historic associations, they must have conjured up memories of cruelty and oppression rather than of former glory.

(2) The Choirboy

In the summer of 1865, when Janáček was 11 years old, his pleasant singing voice led to the first change in his life; a change of considerable importance. His father decided to place him as a chorister either at the Archbishop's school in Kroměříž or at the school of the Augustinian monks at the so-called Queen's Monastery in Old Brno. According to Vladimír Helfert, Janáček's father took this step, apart from the boy's musical talent and good voice, in order to ease his ever increasing family expenses in the face of his deteriorating health. However, according to Janáček himself, the decision was taken in spite of these worries, purely as a result of his eagerness for independence and knowledge.

'I suddenly realized how I grew up,' said Janáček in 1926, at the unveiling ceremony of a commemorative plaque on the house of his birth in Hukvaldy. 'This Hukvaldy child didn't want to stay at home. Like a baby bird with only a few feathers, it wanted to get out of the nest, into the world and to learn from the world. I remember going from house to house collecting my father's fees. In spite of all, he let me go. I remember him with gratitude.'

A point in his favour at Kroměříž was that his father had been choirmaster under the patronage of the Archbishop. In Brno, his chances were equally good, as the choir-master of the Monastery school since 1848 was the very Pavel Křížkovský whom Jiří Janáček had cared for in such a paternal manner at Neplachovice, and who would now certainly do the same for young Leoš, quite apart from his undoubted excellence as a music-master. Křížkovský was by that time a well-known composer of choral music, his male voice chorus *Utonulá* (The Drowned Girl) having been received with enthusiasm at its Prague performance in 1862. In 1863, he achieved a further success in Brno during the Millennium to celebrate the bringing of Christianity from Byzantium to Moravia by the Saints Cyril and Methodius, when his cantata in praise of them was performed to an audience which included leaders of the Czech national movement (Palacký, Rieger, Purkyně and others). As Křížkovský was then taking a cure at Škrochovice spa near Opava, the Janáčeks did not have far to go for the audition. The journey resulted in Leoš's entering the Queen's Monastery school in September 1865 as a chorister, after another equally successful though somewhat superfluous audition at Kroměříž.

Even now he was not wedded to the idea of a musical career; in fact, the object was to train him in his father's teaching profession.*) However, his

---

*) Or perhaps make him a monk, as we can guess from his cryptic remark made at the unveiling of his memorial plaque in 1926: 'They wanted to make of me a monastery priest, later a teacher, but what man has in himself deeply rooted, that will never give way.' (*Vašek*, p. 106.)

admission as a chorister automatically developed his growing prepossession for music, and admirably prepared him for the time when he was to devote himself to it entirely. Křížkovský, in returning the former generosity of the father by taking special pains with the son, was making compensation in greater measure than he realized.

Despite this, young Leoš by no means found himself in paradise. He said of his arrival:

'Stricken with anxiety, mother and I spent the night in a tiny room on the Capuchin Square. I with wide open eyes. At crack of dawn, out, to be out.

'In the court-yard of the monastery mother walked slowly away. I in tears, she too.

'Alone. Strange people, uncongenial; strange school, hard bed, harder bread. No tenderness.

'My own world, exclusively mine, was beginning.'

Small consolation to be dressed in the light blue, white-bordered uniform of the choirboys which caused the citizens of Brno to nickname them 'blue-boys'. On festive occasions they wore long red coats with gold-edged collars. The school itself had been founded in 1648 and endowed by Countess Sibylla Polyxena of Montani, *née* Thurn-Wallesessin, to support a limited number of poor children to be instructed in the 'musical virtues' and the 'development of science' (on the model of, perhaps, the Italian *conservatorios* which originally were orphanages). 'We were told to remember with thanks our lady founders,' (Janáček thought Sibylla and Polyxena were two sisters!) 'when singing the *Salve* and the *Litaniæ Lauretanæ*.' The boys' conduct had to be irreproachable. Six to thirteen of them received free board, light, lodging and medical treatment. A further number were admitted for the sum of 100 florins a year. Documents from the 1820s give the following particulars:

Blue-boys were known throughout Brno. Their 'harmony' welcomed government ministers (Count Kolowrat) and other dignitaries (Count Žerotín). High state officials invited them to give 'Nocturnes' and 'Academies'. They helped out in the theatre—in the orchestra, on the conductor's rostrum and on the stage. They accompanied burials of persons of rank with funeral marches. No church-choir could do without their services. A high standard was required for admission. For instance, Hoffmann from Zlín could play the trumpet, flute, violin, viola and organ at the time of his admission, while Matouš David from Skalice near Červený Kostelec could play the horn, trumpet, viola, flute, organ and double-bassoon.

Boys were admitted between the ages of nine and twelve. (There were exceptions to this rule: Křížkovský, for instance, was admitted as a novice in 1843— he was 23 and had long before completed his eight years of secondary schooling.) The boys formed a band consisting of two oboes, two clarinets, two horns, two clarini (trumpets), two bassoons and a double-bassoon. There was no shortage of flutes, trombones and timpani. There were six violins. At a celebration in honour of the second founder, the abbot Cyrill František Napp, Beethoven's Symphony in C major was performed by an orchestra 70 strong. The most frequenty played composers were Mozart, Cherubini, Rossini and Haydn. And you may wonder at the efficiency of the blue-boys: according to one document, the argest-scale Mass in existence, Cherubini's Coronation Mass, was learnt in the short period between 19 and 24 September 1827. Beethoven's Mass, 'Eroica' Symphony and 'Coriolan' Overture were performed in 1828. The overture to Weber's *Oberon* and Mozart's Quintet were played from sight. Mozart's *Don Giovanni*, Auber's *La Muette de Portici* and *Frà Diavolo* and Méhul's opera *Joseph* were all produced in 1830. One of the Ladies-in-Waiting in Mozart's *Magic Flute* was sung by a blue-boy. How much musical education was necessary to accomplish all this! Every day the pupils practised singing and playing the piano as well as their own instrument. There was training in quartet playing as well as other ensemble classes. Special teachers taught figured bass, counterpoint, violin, horn and piano. The charge was 30 kreutzers per hour. Tricks and dodges in handling wind instruments were passed on from one boy to another. There is a long tradition of wind instrument playing in Bohemia and Moravia.

The blue-boys played at the more distinguished balls, and daily 'played in the roast' at the refectory lunch; every day at table and every Sunday in praise of God, in addition to all their other music-making. One's astonishment grows when one considers that every blue-boy was either studying philosophy and logic, classics, grammar or a normal school course and that here also he was obliged to show satisfactory progress.

As Janáček observed, the establishment was a *conservatoire* in the true sense of the word. He adds that when in 1919 the Brno *conservatoire* grew out of the organ school, which had itself originated in 1881 as a branch of the Thurn-Wallesessinian foundation, it was merely the culmination of an uninterrupted line of development. The 11-year-old Janáček could scarcely have entered a milieu more beneficial to his development as a musician. The abbot himself was a great lover of music and he and Křížkovský used to participate in quartet playing at the house of Count Michal Bukuvka. Opportunities were not wanting for Janáček to gain musical experience. 'I saw clearly copied scores of Haydn's Symphonies, sang a solo with Miss Hřímalá in Beethoven's second Mass, accompanied Miss Ehrenberger*) at a concert given in the Lužánky hall and I was only 11. We boys sang on the stage of the Brno Theatre in Meyerbeer's opera *Le Prophète*.'**)

These many advantages were dearly bought, however, considering the rigours of the choristers' time-table: At five o'clock in the morning, reveille. From then till a quarter to seven, prayers and study. At seven, Mass was sung, then breakfast and off to school. (During his first year, Janáček completed his preliminary schooling and in the three years which followed, attended lower secondary school.) At twelve, lunch. In the afternoon, a walk and further study. From six to seven, singing practice (on Sundays from eleven to twelve). At seven, supper. A short free period, then prayers before going to bed. The monastery provided the boys with board and lodging, but school fees, textbooks and

---

*) Eleonora of Ehrenberg, evidently the first Mařenka in Smetana's *Bartered Bride*. Janáček's memory for names, even from his own operas, was faulty: in one of his Prague lectures he consistently spoke of 'Schönberger' instead of 'Schönberg'.

**) Helfert (p. 54) assumes that Janáček, in his recollections, confused Meyerbeer's *Le Prophète* with *L'Africaine* as *Le Prophète* was first performed in Brno as early as 1851. *L'Africaine* however contains no children's chorus. *Le Prophète* makes use of one in the coronation scene.

42

the more expensive extras had to be paid for out of their own pockets.

On 8 March 1866, during Leoš's first year at Brno, his father died. ('Inconceivably cruel blow.') Leoš's mother, herself a talented musician and organist, took her husband's place in the village church. But this was only a temporary arrangement and she found herself with nine children to bring up on a pension of 200 guilders a year.

Leoš was taken in charge by his uncle Jan Janáček, at that time the village priest of Blažice, near Bystřice pod Hostýnem, and later of Znorovy (now Vnorovy). He was comparatively well off and sent his nephew money, shoes and other clothing (from which it appears that the choristers wore their uniforms only when on duty). These gifts were sent to the school and passed on by Křížkovský so that Leoš would not know the donor.

Křížkovský himself took a fatherly interest in the boy, at one time paying his school fees with the help of the headmaster of the secondary school, Matzenauer, on another occasion using his influence to save Leoš from failing an exam. Yet he fathered him in the truly old-fashioned sense of the word. Janáček, in an article entitled 'For a few apples', describes an expedition which he and some other boys undertook, rather like the one he had made to the neighbouring village church for the timpani, this time to raid the convent garden for the forbidden fruit. On their return, Křížkovský was waiting for them with a lighted candle, and greeted each one with slaps 'in the minor scale and in all octaves (I got it on my cheek in the highest octave)'. On another occasion, when relatives came to ask how little Leoš was doing, Křížkovský opened the door of a room to reveal the boy doing handstands and performing other irreverent antics, and remarked dryly, 'You can see for yourselves how he is doing!' There were also more serious incidents and Křížkovský was several times obliged to seek the aid of Leoš's guardian in order to master the boy's stubbornness, and even save him from expulsion.

Another crisis soon followed. 'The war of 1866 broke out and the blue-boys dispersed. The Queen's Monastery was crowded with 'our men' (meaning the Austrian troops billeted in the building). The square was more threateningly crowded soon afterwards, bristling with the bayonets of the Prussians. I was the only choirboy who remained.'

Fortunately all was soon over. The Prussians who had marched into Brno on 12 July (the Prussian king and Bismarck arrived the following day to remain there until 1 August) marched out again on 13 September at the beginning of the school year.

Although Janáček was able to resume his studies with the same teachers, things were no longer quite as they had been. The political change coincided by chance with a change, amounting almost to a revolution, in the style of church music. For some time it had been felt that church music was being written in a secular style incompatible with liturgy (Haydn and Mozart not excluded). In Moravia this tendency was voiced by the priest, František Sušil, known for his work as a collector of folk music, who said of Beethoven's *Missa Solemnis:* 'A magnificent creation, but alas, little can be heard of humble supplication. A Titan rises to conquer the heavens.'

Křížkovský, in 1854, showed himself to be in support of this view by performing a mass by Orlando Lasso. Similarly, Josef Foerster, father of the dis-

43

tinguished composer, J. B. Foerster, systematically revived the work of the pre-classical masters of *a cappella* music at the Prague church of St Vojtěch (St Adalbert) where he was choir-master.

Similar tendencies throughout Central and Western Europe reached a climax (presumably exceeding the intentions of many pioneers of the movement) when, in the years 1866—1867, Franz Xaver Witt, in his *Fliegende Blätter für katholische Kirchenmusik* laid the foundations for the so-called Caecilian Movement, demanding the abolition of large-scale High Masses with orchestra and the return of church music to the sixteenth-century style—to Palestrina and his contemporaries. (According to these extreme reformers, not even Bach was considered sufficiently pious; yet Palestrina himself had been obliged to defend his style at the Council of Trent against the accusation that it was insufficiently simple. Oddly enough, this reform, perhaps unintentionally, followed the Russian orthodox liturgy which even avoided the organ, not to mention the orchestra.) The influence of the Caecilian reform made itself felt in the Old Brno choir, especially after the death, in 1867, of the enlightened, liberally minded abbot Napp. Loud intradas were abolished, the orchestra restricted, and the repertoire suitably revised in accordance with the principles of the new reform movement. The teaching of wind instruments stopped entirely—the choristers, in fact, becoming a purely vocal ensemble.

In spite of this, Janáček still had plenty of opportunity to increase his musical knowledge. Křížkovský as a conductor, as Janáček stated at the age of 70, 'was unmethodical. He plunged forward, getting a general effect—our bearings were lost.' By 'unmethodical' Janáček was probably referring to Křížkovský's conviction that the singers would better understand the harmonic progressions and correct interpretation if they heard the entire work and rehearsed it together, rather than rehearsing each vocal part separately. However, 'no one probed more deeply into the spirit of a work, nor reached the soul of a composer with such boldness and certainty,' wrote Janáček of Křížkovský in 1902. The danger in this method of rehearsing, the uncertainty in controlling the individual voices, was warded off by Křížkovský's exceptionally sharp sense of hearing and his flair for holding the boys' attention not so much by severity as by his own enthusiasm. Janáček may be believed (at least the Janáček of 1875) when he wrote in the magazine *Cecilie:* 'Although I have heard many choirs, the only truly fine singing was under Křížkovský.'

Apart from his musical influence on Janáček, he also awakened his Slavonic sympathies. Křížkovský, like František Sušil and other priests in Moravia, as much from patriotic as from ecclesiastical motives, was an enthusiastic champion of the 'Cyrilo-Methodius' movement.*)

---

*) So called after the Slavonic missionaries SS. Cyril (Kyrillos) and Methodius, brothers who came from Salonica. They translated the Bible into the Old Slav language, which was gradually established as the ecclesiastical language of the Western Slavs. In 862 A.D., the Moravian Prince Rastislav asked the Byzantine Emperor Michael III for emissaries to be sent to Moravia to counteract the political influence being exercised from the Salzburg Archbishopric. The Byzantine Court sent the two brothers known for their diplomatic skill, their experience of church and legal matters, and their knowledge of the Slav language gained through the work they had done among the Slavs in the area of present-day Macedonia and

In Moravia, where the cult of St Wenceslas had never been as developed as in Bohemia, the two missionaries were equated with all forms of religious, cultural and patriotic endeavour.

Janáček was carried away by this movement, although it is probable that his main impulse was patriotic rather than religious. His enthusiasm reached its height when, in 1869, the final year of his scholarship, the millennium of St Cyril's death was celebrated at Velehrad. Křížkovský, who was entrusted with the musical part of the festivities, decided that the blue-boys should take part. 'You cannot imagine,' wrote Janáček to his uncle at Znorovy, 'how I long to see the sacred ground where once lived the great Svatopluk**) and the Slav missionaries Cyril and Methodius. I am unworthy of treading it.' He begs his uncle to send him a Slav costume (as worn by the members of the Sokol gymnastic association). Janáček's life at the Old Brno monastery not only instilled in him a respect for iron discipline—which lasted all his life—and laid the foundations of his musical studies, but also developed a trait which he owed to his Moravian origin, namely a tendency to identify himself with the Slavonic East. Although works like AMARUS give expression to the frustration and nostalgia which he felt in the monastery, his experiences there, especially his participation at the age of 15 in the Velehrad festivities, lead eventually to his GLAGOLITIC MASS. Daniel Muller is probably correct when he says: 'The imprint of the monastery (besides the imprint of Moravia and the imprint of life) had yet another influence on Janáček's work. At the monastery the young Janáček learned the simplicity of life. In its atmosphere he became aware of the idea of sin which plays such a vital part in his work. No composer before him ever stressed the despair of a young man losing his innocence as Janáček did in the DIARY OF THE YOUNG MAN WHO DISAPPEARED; although, how few young people become aware of such things in circumstances so poetic.'

Bulgaria. But friction arose between them and the German divines who tried to discredit them in the eyes of the Pope. Kyrillos died in 869 in Rome. Methodius became Bishop of Pannonia and Moravia, was deposed by the Synod of Regensburg, spent two years in custody, and was afterwards reinstated by the Pope, only to be charged once more. Thus the struggle over the ecclesiastical language in Bohemia and Moravia, simultaneously a struggle for decisive cultural and political influence between East and West, was carried on until the death of Methodius, ending with the victory of the German faction. Nevertheless, the activities of the two saints deeply influenced the cultural as well as the religious life of the whole region.

**) During the reign of Svatopluk in the ninth century, the Great Moravian Empire reached the peak of its prosperity, comprising Bohemia, Moravia, Slovakia and parts of present-day Hungary. Weakened by the dynastic feuds of Svatopluk's sons, it was overrun at the beginning of the tenth century by the Hungarian hordes and divided.

(3) First Choral Works

In September 1869, after completing his schooling, Janáček left the monastery and in accordance with his late father's wishes, entered the Brno Imperial and Royal Teachers' Training Institute, at that time housed in the Minorite Monastery. He studied there for three years with the aid of a state scholarship of 100 guilders a year and in July 1872 passed the final examinations, doing especially well (apart from singing and organ playing) in history and geography. His eagerness to apply himself to subjects other than music, in particular psychology, was already very marked. Psychology played a vital part in his works and figures significantly in his treatise on harmony.

He served the compulsory two-year period of unpaid teaching at the school run by the Institute, and at the same time was given an opportunity of starting what might be called a 'training school' for organ playing and conducting with the Old Brno Queen's Monastery choir. Křížkovský was entrusted with the task of carrying out Witt's reform at the Archbishop's cathedral in Olomouc and, in the autumn of 1872, appointed the 18-year-old Janáček as his deputy choir-master in Old Brno.

Although Janáček's deputizing as choir-master was more or less permanent, it was unpaid, since it was one of Křížkovský's monastic duties. On the other hand he partook of the lunches and suppers from the renowned monastery kitchen and received occasional gifts of money. His principal duty was to rehearse the choristers for an hour every afternoon for the Sunday mass. At mass Janáček would display his considerable repertoire—always within the limits of Witt's reforms—performing Palestrina, Orlando Lasso, Lodovico da Vittoria, Jacob Handl, F. X. Brixi, Joseph and Michael Haydn, as well as new ecclesiastical works by German composers and, among the Czechs, Křížkovský, Josef Foerster and Skuherský. The choir of Old Brno was one of the few where works were thoroughly and painstakingly rehearsed, and thanks, too, to Janáček's skill in organ playing and his daring improvisations*) it was not surprising that the church of St Martin gradually became the focal point of Brno's musical life.

From here it was but a small step for Janáček to participate in the concert life of Brno. On 13 February 1873, he was elected choir-master of the craftsmen's choral society, Svatopluk, founded in 1868. The members were mostly weavers, and Janáček's spirit of dedication was evident from the outset when

---

*) A vivid description of these improvisations has been given by one of the former blue-boys: 'When the prelate served mass the discipline relaxed. He would proceed down the central aisle to the altar and leave again in the same manner. After mass, we crowded the steps of the organ loft and listened enthralled to the magic his fingers performed.' (Štědroň, *op. cit.* p. 63.) Less delight in these 'acrobatics' by his unmanageable assistant was shown by Křížkovský.

he refused to accept an annual fee of 108 guilders which had been paid to his predecessors, so that he might command greater authority and avoid being indebted to anyone. He was determined to renounce the rather complacent and superficial methods by which the Svatopluk (as well as most other Czech choral societies) managed its affairs, and did his utmost from the very beginning to lift the repertoire out of the field of light, though patriotically angled, entertainment.

(The society's motto was 'United and loyal to the homeland'; and the band which accompanied the society's outings played its own small part in arousing local nationalistic fervour.) He also strove to raise the standard of the choral singing, insisting on full attendance at rehearsals, longer periods for studying the programmes and, for the more difficult works, a smaller choir of picked singers. For performances of mixed-voice choruses he would make use of the boy sopranos and altos from the monastery. He insisted that the dance with which the Society invariably ended its evenings should take place separately, and that the concerts be given not at the White Cross Inn in Pekařská Street, but in the concert hall of the newly built Beseda—the cultural and social centre of the Czech minority in Brno, thereby gaining for them significance and prestige. Leading soloists were engaged (the well-known Prague baritone Josef Lev participated in one of the programmes), and as a result of Janáček's efforts, the concerts of the Svatopluk choral society began to attract audiences who had previously scarcely known of its existence, even members of the German-speaking nobility.

Above all, the choir itself proved most worthy of his efforts, as Janáček wrote in the magazine *Moravská orlice* in 1875: 'Raining, snowing, freezing, all one to the worker stumbling out of the factory, tired out from his day in the dust. He remembers something still to be done, his singing rehearsal. Probably hungry and thirsty. His wife perhaps waiting at home, and his children. What keeps him from going home, why does he hurry to the rehearsal room? I cannot answer this question—but nowhere have I found such devotion, diligence, love and assiduousness among singers.'

Janáček's work with the Svatopluk choral society gave him a valuable opportunity to extend his own knowledge of choral music and also to try out his own first male-voice choruses. At the very first concert which he conducted, on 27 April 1873, his ORÁNÍ (Ploughing) and ŽENICH VNUCENÝ (The Imposed Bridegroom) were performed, and his festival chorus VÁLEČNÁ (War Song) on 5 July 1873, NESTÁLOST LÁSKY (The Fickleness of Love) on 9 November 1873, OSAMĚLÁ BEZ ÚTĚCHY (Alone Without Comfort) on 14 March 1874, were so successful that they were either immediately repeated or performed a second time soon afterwards.

The influence of Křížkovský can be felt in these and other of Janáček's youthful choral works in his choice, as a nationalistic activist, of folk-song material and in his musical treatment of it.

PLOUGHING, the earliest known composition by Janáček, is a simple choral setting of the folk song *Šohajko švarný, čemu neořeš?* (Bonny lad, why aren't you ploughing?) which had been noted down by Sušil, although to a different tune. It is not certain whether Janáček knew, as Helfert assumed, a different version of the song or whether he set it to a tune of his own in folk-song style.

47

A contemporary critic remarked, in the magazine *Moravská orlice,* on Janáček's colourful tunes to folk words.

Little can be ascertained about the second work, THE IMPOSED BRIDE-GROOM, as there is no known copy in existence and a criticism of it which appeared in the magazine *Dalibor* mentions only 'a very attractive arrangement of a Serbian folk song.'

The male-voice chorus WAR SONG was specially composed for the unfurling ceremony of the Svatopluk choral society's banner and its fifth anniversary. It was completed on 26 June 1873, and exists in two versions: one purely choral, the other with an accompaniment for piano, trumpets and three trombones and (very rare for Janáček) a well-developed fugato in the middle section. In this song Křížkovský's influence is less evident, but the rather pompous unison opening is reminiscent of Tovačovský who had also composed a war song.

THE FICKLENESS OF LOVE (dating from not later than October 1873) is again a folk song, *Šohajko švarný na vraném koni* (Bonny lad on a black horse) in the Křížkovský manner, except that in this song the melody is more varied and Janáček has taken some liberties with it by making use in the second verse of a phrase of another folk song, *Ej lásko, lásko, ty nejsi stálá* (O love, love, you are not constant). He had fallen in love with this song once when staying in the village of Znorovy and made, as will be seen later, a separate arrangement of it.

The chorus ALONE WITHOUT COMFORT is the most mature of the group. It dates from the beginning of 1874 and is reminiscent of the folk song *Ani tak nesvítá, jako svítávalo* (Dawn no longer breaks as it used to). The beautiful folk-like melody is interspersed with daring enharmonic modulations so typical of Janáček's maturity though it must be remembered that he revised this song as late as 1925.

On 18 November 1874, (having passed his examination), Janáček received his teacher's diploma. Shortly before, on 6 July, he had been very successfully examined in Czech and Czech literature by Professor Antonín Matzenauer whose lectures Janáček had been attending at the Moravian Academy in Brno*) and from whom he imbibed the elements of what later became his so very characteristic literary style.

He was now qualified to teach Czech, geography and history in schools where the children were taught in Czech. But there were now other things for which Janáček felt himself to be 'well-fitted'. He was now absolutely convinced that his real calling was music, and that if he had to be a teacher, it would be of music. This would involve passing a state examination and therefore a further period of preparatory training; Janáček's early successes, flattering as they were, did not blind him to the fact that he still had a great deal to learn.

Already in January 1874, before completing his period of unpaid teaching, he had decided to go to Prague in the following autumn to study with František Skuherský at the organ school. Thanks to the intercession of Křížkovský and

---

*) It is significant that Janáček chose philological and historical subjects for his final examination, doing particularly well in history, while his practical teaching was 'fair to medium'.

the understanding of the new director of the Teachers' Training Institute, Emilian Schulz, Janáček was granted the necessary one year's leave. It is understandable that, as the admirer and assistant of Křížkovský, Janáček should select the institution which specialized in training organists, choirmasters and composers of ecclesiastical music in the spirit of the Caecilian reform.

At the end of the summer holidays, Janáček set out for Prague.

(4) At the Prague Organ School

The Organ School in the Old Town quarter of Prague was founded in 1830 by the Society of Friends of Ecclesiastical Music in Bohemia. Its curriculum consisted of a three years' course. The first year was taken by Professor František Blažek, at one time Dvořák's teacher, who taught theory of music, harmony and figured bass (on which subject he wrote a valuable textbook). The second year was taken by the director of the school, Skuherský, who taught modulation, counterpoint and polyphonic forms. The third year was also taken by Skuherský and included orchestration and free form, as well as organ playing which formed the main part of the whole course. The first year also included liturgical chant and the second, history of music.

A three-year course, and only one year of leave, not to mention an almost total lack of funds. This meant cramming at least two years into one in order to pass the examination. Janáček got off to a bad start at his entrance exam with Professor Blažek.

'How would you resolve the chord of the dominant seventh?'

Silence.

'The seventh falls by step, the third rises, the fifth rises, the root falls. He does not know.'

'In my head I heard:

5

'The seventh did not move by step, the fifth did not rise and the root did not fall.'*)

Fortunately, thanks to the intervention of Křížkovský (who was satisfied that Janáček knew how to resolve a dominant seventh chord, and much else), Skuherský gave permission for the young man from Brno to study the first two years simultaneously.

In Prague, Janáček existed almost entirely on enthusiasm**) like Smetana when he had been studying with Proksch in Prague. He had not enough money to hire a piano and was obliged to use an imaginary one, 'the keyboard chalked on the table. My fingers learning Bach's preludes and fugues. It was maddening. I was longing for the living sounds!

---

*) D. Muller (*Leoš Janáček*, p. 23) quotes this example as a proof that already at that time Janáček was attracted by the key of C sharp, or D flat major.

**) According to the magazine *Dalibor*, he received a small subsidy from the Moravian 'Land' Council, and Janáček himself stated that a certain Neumann sent him fees for piano lessons which he was giving in Janáček's absence.

'One day, out of the blue, a piano appeared in my little room in Štěpánská Street. I told the story to Father Ferdinand Lehner, editor of the *Cyril*.*)

'A secret smile appeared on his kind face.

'At the end of the school year the piano vanished from my room in the same mysterious manner.

'Many were the suppers to which he invited my hungry self!'**)

Cold added to the discomfort of hunger and the frustration caused by the lack of a piano; in the winter months Janáček shivered in his unheated room. Then he 'stole warmth' by leaving ajar the door leading to the next room occupied by the concierge. To Janáček's great disappointment, this fortunate owner of the warmth was always slamming the door shut.

Happily, these material privations did little to dampen his ardour. He seemed to realize the importance of utilizing every available moment, and this resulted in his early maturity, a fact which his French biographer, Daniel Muller, deduced from a photograph taken at that time (a photograph so unlike his later ones as to cast doubt on its authenticity, had not Janáček himself confirmed it). 'He was then a young man, clean-shaven and emaciated by the austerity of his life. Slight short-sightedness caused him to wear pince-nez which he later abandoned. Tightened lips and eyes very alive behind the pince-nez, an expression of profound seriousness; everything in the photograph of 1874 indicates a character already formed, a strong will and unusually intense inner life. Nothing in the face is superficial, everything is concentrated inwards just as was later to be the case with his music.'

The pace imposed upon students of the Organ School was strenuous enough without the additional strain of compressing two years' work into one. Skuherský's methods, which combined strictness with liberality, are reflected in the four volumes of his *Treatise on Composition*. He would give only the briefest of explanations, or more frequently none at all, 'whereas he worked through each section of the *Treatise* giving practical exercises for as long as was necessary for even the least talented student to understand them thoroughly.'***) In the harmony class, Janáček made a particularly keen study of church modes which later played such an important part in his work. His diligence in studying counterpoint and fugue also won him approval, although he was unable then to master fully these techniques in the short time allotted to him. This is apparent not only from the selection of his exercises in modulation, counterpoint and fugue, published by Helfert, which teem with consecutive fifths and other faults, but also from works written after he had finished his studies in Prague.

But even at that early stage, some of his characteristics began to appear, like his habit of drawing his own staves and replacing foreign technical terms by Czech expressions.

His belligerent frankness almost put an end to his studies with Skuherský:

---

*) The magazine, *Cyril*, was at that time still called *Cecilie*.
**) Apart from the tactful anonymity of this procedure, Father Lehner was prompted by a certain *sacro egoismo*, seeing in Janáček a promising advocate of the Caecilian movement; this, however, in no way detracts from his generosity.
***) Ladislav Dolanský, *Memoirs*, p. 18—19.

he wrote in Lehner's magazine *Cecilie* (5 March 1875) an adverse, though probably well-founded criticism of Skuherský's performance of a Gregorian mass, which had taken place in the Piarist church on 24 January. In it he criticized his professor not only for the ragged ensemble of the choir, particularly noticeable in the unison Gregorian chant, and his improper interpolation of Palestrina and other polyphonic composers' motets with a Gregorian mass, but also for incorrect tempi, incorrect Latin accentuation, lack of rhythm and wrong breathing; not content with this, he went on to point out, using musical examples, how it should have been done. This 'reformatory' article resulted in his having to leave the school on 9 March before the term ended. He noted in his diary: 'A memorable day. I was persecuted for telling the truth.'

Fortunately—owing partly to the intervention of a former scholar at the Queen's Monastery in Old Brno, the tenor J. L. Lukes, and in particular to Father Lehner—Janáček was readmitted, presumably against the wishes of Skuherský, who immediately went on leave. However, he was probably aware of Janáček's exceptional gifts and would have regretted losing such a pupil. The only consequence, therefore, of the episode for Janáček was a prolonged Easter holiday in Brno. Janáček often acknowledged that it did not in the least shake the faith of the student in his professor; they intended, in fact, to collaborate on a treatise on composition which did not materialize (Skuherský wrote it alone) simply because they lived too far apart.

The reading in musical aesthetics with which Janáček strove to augment his studies at the organ school, and his choice of authors representing a formalistic tendency, (Durdík*) and Zimmermann**)) show plainly that he shared Skuherský's views. Skuherský in his preface to his *Treatise on Harmony,* published in 1886, upholds the theory of absolute music as expounded by Eduard Hanslick (*Vom Musikalisch-Schönen,* 1854). Skuherský's formalism differed from formalism as understood today, although Hanslick's definition of music as '*tönend bewegte Formen*' holds good even for programme music. Skuherský, unlike most musical theorists of his time, not only demonstrated the technicalities of music but explained their purpose—what they expressed and how.***) This animated type of exposition was subsequently adopted by Janáček in his own treatise on harmony. Janáček's interest in the Cæcilian movement induced him to pay frequent visits to St Vojtěch's church, where the choirmaster was Josef Foerster and where he made the acquaintance of Foerster's organist—Antonín Dvořák.

At that time he only got as far as seeing Bedřich Smetana, already deaf, at a concert given in his benefit at the Žofín Island Hall on 4 April 1875, where

---

*) *General Aesthetics,* at that time newly published, which was recommended to him by Emilian Schulz.

**) *Allgemeine Aesthetik der Formwissenschaft* (1865) which served as a model for Durdík's book. Janáček even began translating this work into Czech.

***) He writes in his *Treatise on Musical Composition,* Vol. I. (Cadences and Modulation), p. 95: 'A modulation which does not exceed the most closely related keys can only be used in works of quiet character and orderly structure. The case of works of a stormy, passionate nature, of dramatic works, is different. Here such simple means no longer suffice: it is necessary to modulate to remoter keys, using harsh, even abrupt transitions.'

the symphonic poems *Vyšehrad* and *Vltava* were being performed (*Vltava* for the first time). This was one of the rare occasions when Janáček went to a concert, for he could seldom afford to attend the musical events of Prague.

At this time—besides learning French—he began to show an interest in the Russian language. He mastered the Russian alphabet and, in order to guard against the curiosity of his fellow-students, used it for writing amorous out-pourings in his note-books to the girl he had left behind in Brno. She was his 16-year-old piano pupil and the pretty daughter of a local factory owner, Ludmila Rudišová.

During his year of study at the Prague Organ School, Janáček wrote a number of compositions in addition to the above-mentioned exercises,which, with the exception of the EXAUDI DEUS, were either entirely unknown or presumed to be lost; for example, his CHORAL FANTASY FOR ORGAN. In 1958, however, one of his notebooks from 1874—1875 was discovered in which the following compositions were found (unusually neatly copied out).

Gradual, SPECIOSUS FORMA, composed on 29 December 1874, a melody in the style of a Gregorian chant, of which the first part is arranged for four-part men's choir and the second for four-part women's choir with organ.

Introit, IN NOMINE JESU, which closely follows an original Gregorian chant and is arranged for mixed choir with organ, as is also the BENEDICTUS, composed 17 February 1875, and the original version of EXAUDI DEUS, composed 3 February 1875, the second version of which, composed exactly one week later, is for unaccompanied mixed choir.

SOUNDS IN MEMORY OF FÖRCHTGOTT—TOVAČOVSKÝ (second part) for three violins, viola, cello and double-bass. This begins with a Grave in the style of a canzone followed by a folk-like Andante:

and a modified reprise.

Communion FIDELIS SERVUS, composed 20 June 1875, for unaccompanied mixed choir. The melody is again almost identical with the Gregorian chant *Graduale Romanum*:

INTRADA in G minor, composed 25 November 1875, for four violins, the theme of which (the first nine bars of the work):

he used three years later in the Scherzo of his IDYLL for strings. Another

INTRADA for four violins was composed two days earlier, on 23 November 1875, in Brno and begins with a passage reminiscent of *Lohengrin*:

9

OVERTURE FOR ORGAN, composed 19 June 1875, (in G minor) and VARYTO (a harp-like instrument, possibly apocryphal, used in Czech legends by bards) FOR ORGAN (24 June 1875). The introductory recitative:

10

is developed into the theme:

11

which is used contrapuntally in different parts.

CHORAL FANTASIA for organ, composed 7 July 1875. This may be said to have been written in homage to Křížkovský since it contains a contrapuntal working out in notes of equal length, of the closing chorale from his cantata, *SS Cyril and Methodius*:

12

O - ro-duj - te   u   Bo - ha,   aťˇ   se vzdá - lí   má - to - ha
Pray,___ pray to the Lord_____   Let the phan - tom be   gone

This work, together with Bach's Toccata in C major, was played by Janáček at his exams with which, on 22 and 23 July 1875, he ended his studies at the organ school. On 24 July of the same year, he received his report in which all subjects were 'very good' with the exception of playing from a figured bass, which was 'good'. With this certificate he was considered 'excellently qualified' to fill the office of organist.

Immediately after this important first year of musical study followed the first free summer holiday spent in wandering through Moravia—more signific-ant than it may appear.

'Břeclav castle; on the ground floor of one of the wings lives the doctor. Across the river Morava to Strážnice.*) Through the pine woods of Písek,

---

*) Strážnice in the south-eastern district of Moravské Slovácko (Moravian Slovakia) is rich in folklore.

once more across the Morava and towards the small church of Znorovy. Sticking to the hill-side, the little town of Velká. In Břeclav Castle, the doctor's daughter. Strážnice waking up to an organized cultural and social life. Girls at the far side of Znorovy bridge: among them Běta Gazarková. On this side of the bridge, young men in a fight. Fiery coloured costumes, passionate songs! In Velká, the old bearded Martin Zeman, *slivovice,* and the fiddler Trn, bagpipes, fiddle and cymbalom—here was the paradise of my student days. This must have been where the first seeds of JENŮFA were sown.'*)

Běta Gazarková, who, apart from the doctor's daughter in Břeclav castle, put Ludmila from Brno out of his thoughts (at least temporarily), was referred to by Janáček in 1927 in an article which he called 'My Girl from the Tatras'. Why the Tatras? Because he identified her with the heroine of a novel of that name by Vítězslav Hálek (written in 1871) which he sent her as a token of love before he left Znorovy.

*) *Veselý — Janáček,* p. 37.

(5) Back in Brno

After the summer holidays Janáček once more returned to the severities of life. The first thing which faced him was the state music examination. He took it in mid-October 1875, both Skuherský and Foerster being among the examiners. He passed only in singing, organ and piano (all with honours) and on 30 August 1876, became a teacher, but in an as yet unconfirmed position. After passing an additional examination in violin playing (7 October 1878, with the same examiners) he was confirmed on 14 May 1880 as a teacher of music at the Teachers' Training School in Brno.

He also resumed his conducting of the Old Brno Choir, all the more readily since the monastery, at Křížkovský's instigation, had ordered a magnificent new organ to be built by the famous F. G. Steinmayer of Oettingen in Bavaria. On the first occasion it was played in public (30 August 1876), Janáček performed Bach's Toccata and Fugue in C major with which he had finished his studies at the Prague Organ School the year before. On this occasion he met Steinmayer who invited him to visit his workshops at Oettingen.

Janáček actually went there two years later, in the summer holidays of 1878. He remembered with amusement*) the small town 'where no one was supposed to patronise any one inn but in fairness to make the round of them all. I knew every one.' In nearby Munich he found other things of interest. 'The castle square enthralled me. I was dazzled by the marvels in marble of the Glyptothek and the marvels in paint of the Pinakothek.' He visited the Harz mountains where he met his brother (Bedřich?) and noted some Slavonic legends and place names. From there he went on to Berlin. 'I wanted to see Hamburg, but I had barely enough money for getting back via Prague to Brno.' In Oettingen, on 4 August, he composed an unnamed and uncompleted piece for organ (in the style of a ricercare). He probably did well to deface it. His motets, written at about the same time, are more mature. His abovementioned offertory, Exaudi Deus, the first of Janáček's works to be published (in the music supplement of the magazine *Cecilie*, 1877), his responsory, Regnum Mundi, first performed on 21 September 1878, his gradual, Suscepimus (final version, 28 January 1887) and his Exsurge Domine are all for mixed-voice choir and organ. His offertory Constitues is composed for male voices and organ. With the exception of the last, they are almost entirely homophonic works and according to the ideals of Witt's reform, reminiscent of the sixteenth century ecclesiastical style and Gregorian chant. Each one begins with a quotation of a Gregorian chant in one of the parts, apart from the two bars of organ introduction in the offertory Constitues.

---

*) *Veselý — Janáček*, p. 40.

This introduction is derived from the thematic material of the fourth bar of the chorus:

Only the antiphon Veni Sancte Spiritus for male voice choir, disregards, as its beginning shows:

the narrow limits of archaic style and of the church modes which will, however, continue to play an important part in Janáček's works, including the secular ones.

In the sphere of secular music, Janáček's driving energy could assert itself more fully. Here his 'overflowing desire to deliver Brno from the bonds of amateurishness and small-minded provincialism led him to interfere whenever given the slightest opportunity. One choral society was no longer sufficient for him. The fact that the first thing he undertook after his return to Brno was an attempt to organize a concert of massed choirs in which all the male voice choirs of Brno would take part, may be called symbolical.'*) He first achieved this project as early as 22 August when a benefit concert was given in aid of the Radhošť Society, and again on the following All Souls Day at an *in memoriam* concert for the renowned founder of Slavonic philology, Josef Dobrovský.

The Svatopluk choral society had been conducted in the meantime by two successive choir masters: František Musil, organist of St Peter's Cathedral in Brno, and František Budík, both of whom had been failures, due to their lack of interest. It followed quite naturally that Janáček, who had acted as a substitute for Budík on more than one occasion towards the end of the summer holidays, should return on 21 October to direct the Society.

Once more his work with the choir incited him to write choral works, and at their second concert, on 23 January 1876, the first performance of two new choruses, Když mne nechceš, což je víc (If you don't want me, what is left?) and Láska opravdivá (True love) took place. The programme also included the earlier choral piece, Ploughing, and the three works appeared under one title: Tři popěvky (Three Songs). Other choral songs from the same period are Divím se milému (I wonder at my Beloved), Vínek stonulý (The drowned wreath)**) and the funeral song Odpočiň si (Rest in peace).

---

*) *Helfert*, p. 203.
**) The last two together with True Love appeared in print thanks to the care of V. Steinman under the title Ohlas národních písní (Echoes of Folk Songs).

It is not known whether the first of these works was performed by the choir or as a tenor solo with piano accompaniment. A copy of the solo version is the only one that has survived.

Of the next three male choruses, I WONDER AT MY BELOVED is probably the earliest and is a choral arrangement of a folk song of unknown origin. As both the music and the words of the song are simple almost to the point of insipidity, it is difficult to see its attraction for Janáček. He harmonized it in an equally primitive style, note against note, only enlivening it with occasional passing thirds or sixths.

TRUE LOVE consists of two identical verses and is worked out in a similar fashion, although the melody is more attractive and the harmonization, thanks to aptly placed suspensions, is more interesting in spite of the original G major being strictly maintained. From the rhythmic point of view, it is worth noticing that Janáček, as once before in THE FICKLENESS OF LOVE, gives no time signature, but leaves the song in its uneven declamatory style such as the peasants would use. This, combined with effective dynamic contrasts and an intuitive sense for male-voice choral writing, lend interest to this work by the 21-year-old Janáček. The words tell of a girl comforting her lover who is anxious for a more passionate declaration of her love by assuring him that true love dwells in a silent heart, not in loud words.

The third work, THE DROWNED WREATH, an arrangement of the beautiful folk song from the district of Příbor, *A před vraty kámen zlatý, bílá leluja* (At the front gate, a girl like a rock of gold, white as a lily...), returns to normal 3/4 time, as František Sušil had noted it down:

15

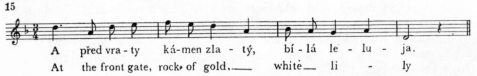

Janáček, however, enriches it by treating the first half of the second and fourth verses independently, in each case turning them into a continuation of the foregoing verse, and by charmingly expressive figurations that are more than mere word-painting and that pay little heed to contrapuntal rules.

The chorus REST IN PEACE, a setting of words by František Sušil, was composed about 1875, and was evidently intended to be sung at funerals. However, the harmonic, or rather enharmonic difficulties which occur especially in the middle section, make it unsuitable for ordinary use. The archaic style of the word accentuation gives it, in Czech, an unintentional, almost comic effect as, for instance, in the second statement of the main theme:

16

1. Rest in peace in silent shade

2. Now you may forever rest

58

from which develops the animated theme of the middle section:

revealing, in the sudden acceleration of the words as against the slowly descending inner parts, the germ of what later became the typical Janáček interjections. The hand of the master is evident also in other ways, as for instance in the impressive B flat minor gradation later on in the piece. It is probable, as was the case with the SUITE FOR STRINGS, that Janáček revised this work towards the end of his life, after it had been rediscovered by Hynek Bím. This is borne out by a letter to Mrs Kamila Stösslová (29 March 1926) in which among other things just 'being finished' Janáček mentions the SUITE FOR STRINGS and REST IN PEACE, a funeral chorus 'for those poor souls who must leave this beautiful world unwillingly'.

After the January concert, however, Janáček's zeal for Svatopluk began to wane. The reason for this apparently incredible change was that on 3 February 1876, the choir-master of the Beseda choral society—The Brno Beseda—Jan Nesvadba, resigned his post and on the same day Janáček was elected his successor. He gladly accepted, for although the Beseda was at that time artistically at a very low ebb, being a burghers' society, it had more funds at its disposal and its artistic prospects were therefore better than those of the workmen's and artisans' Svatopluk.

For the next half-year Janáček directed both societies simultaneously, but soon found himself forced to neglect his duty either to one or the other (in June the members of the Svatopluk complained that their choir-master did not attend rehearsals regularly) and in October he resigned the directorship of the Svatopluk society.

Janáček began rehearsing with the Beseda on the third day after his appointment and the society at once felt that they had entered a new era. There was an immediate increase in attendance at rehearsals and the members began to entertain hopes of performing, as did the Prague Hlahol choral society and the Brno Musikverein, some of the great oratorios and cantatas. This meant extending the choir to include sopranos and contraltos. (On one or two occasions Janáček invited the Vesna Women's Choral Society to collaborate with the Beseda, but when Vesna demanded to be consulted about the programmes, Janáček, typically enough, put an end to the co-operation.) On 27 April the Beseda became a mixed-voice choir, and whenever the need arose Janáček supplemented it again with choristers from the Queen's Monastery and pupils from the Teachers' Training Institute, sometimes raising the number of singers to as many as 250.

Janáček now proposed founding an orchestra, for there was as yet no Czech theatre in Brno. He did not want to depend (even if he were able to) on the German one, and the military band, which could only be conducted by army officers, had not enough strings anyhow. At the beginning of 1877, therefore, he proposed founding not only a singing school for boys in order to train fresh blood for his choir, but also a violin school. And to improve the situation in the meantime, he requested that ten permanent players be engaged at once.

Under Janáček's direction, the Beseda programmes which, until then, had consisted of an incongruous mixture of all kinds of music (operatic arias alternating with zither duets, recitations, and so on), took on a very different character. Throughout the many years of his activities with the Beseda, Janáček made great choral works, especially the classical ones, a staple of its repertoire, and a start was made on 14 December 1876 when Mendelssohn's *Psalm 95* was performed. Mozart's *Requiem* followed on 14 April 1877, and on 2 April 1879 (Palm Sunday) a peak in the society's achievements was reached, when they performed Beethoven's *Missa Solemnis* with leading Prague soloists (Eleonora Ehrenberg, Betty Fibichová, Antonín Vávra and Karel Čech), a choir numbering 100, and an orchestra of 30 violins, 13 violas, 7 cellos and 7 double-basses, 'such as was never heard in Brno before'.*)

Beside these large-scale works, Janáček's patiently built programmes included many fine vocal compositions as well as symphonic ones. He also showed his skill as a pianist in Rubinstein's Fantasia for Two Pianos, which he performed with Amalia Wickenhauser-Neruda, and in Mendelssohn's Capriccio for Piano and Orchestra, and Mendelssohn's and Saint-Saëns' Piano Concertos—all conducted by Amalia Wickenhauser's husband Ernst, conductor of the German Theatre in Brno. Neither did Janáček forget his teachers, and he performed Křížkovský's *Utonulá* (The Drowned Girl) and Skuherský's symphonic poem *Máj* (May).

His favourite Czech composer, however, was Dvořák, whose works he began to perform regularly. The first of Dvořák's compositions to be played in Brno was the Serenade for Strings. The *Moravian Duets* followed and on 15 December 1878, the choral songs *Grief, The Maiden in the Forest* and *The Magic Well* were performed with the composer himself at the piano. Then came four of the newly orchestrated first series of *Slavonic Dances*. Friendship sprang up between the two men and during the summer of 1877 they set off on a tour of Bohemia, visiting Říp hill, then south to Strakonice, Orlík castle, Husinec and Prachatice. 'We left Prague by train, but only a bit of the way. A bit of the way back, too, the rest was on foot. Our conversation during the three days could have been tied into a very small bag.'**) There was mutual understanding between them. 'You know how it is when someone takes the words out of your mouth? For me it was always like that in the company of Dvořák.'***) Why then do any talking? It was entirely Janáček's doing that Dvořák had been invited to take part in the above-mentioned concert, at which he had been ceremoniously received and shortly afterwards made an honorary member of the Beseda.

The means at Janáček's disposal stirred his imagination and extended his creative activities from the choral to the orchestral sphere. Thus ZPĚVNÁ DUMA (Choral Elegy) was written before 23 February 1876; SLAVNOSTNÍ SBOR (Festive Chorus) in 1877; OSUDU NEUJDEŠ (No Escape from Fate)

---

*) *Dalibor*, 10 April 1879.
**) *Veselý — Janáček*, p. 38.
***) Janáček: 'Reminiscences of Antonín Dvořák' (*Hudební revue*, October 1911).

before 29 October 1876; the orchestral melodrama (recitation with musical accompaniment) Smrt (Death) to words by Lermontov, before 27 March 1876; and two works for string orchestra, Suite (1877) and Idyll (31 July to 29 August 1878).

Of these works, the vocal one that taxed Janáček's creative energy to the utmost was undoubtedly the Choral Elegy. It is a setting of four lines from František Ladislav Čelakovský's *Ohlas písní českých* (Echoes of Czech Folk Songs) which tells the story of a forsaken girl whose grief deprives her of her senses and her beauty. The desolate character of the poem is expressed in slow 'tempo rubato' and long sustained or decorated notes, melismas, frequent repetitions. In spite of the shortness of the text, the work grew into one of Janáček's longest choruses. The use of the Dorian and Aeolian modes in addition to the figurations make this work consciously, though somewhat incongruously—in view of its simple, folk-like words—reminiscent of old church music, even organ music. It contrasts strikingly with Janáček's simple setting of similar words in the chorus Alone Without Comfort.

There is more of Wagner *(Lohengrin)* than of Janáček, perhaps owing to the festive occasion for which it was written, in Festive Chorus. It has been called a triple chorus but is really a mixed-voice chorus with male-voice quartet and piano accompaniment, set to rather pompous words by Karel Kučera and especially composed for the laying of the foundation stone of the Teachers' Training Institute in Brno, at which ceremony it was first performed, on 15 July 1877.

No Escape from Fate is a setting of a Serbian folk poem for male-voice choir. It tells how the frivolous girl, Toda, tries in vain to avert her marriage to an old man, which she brought upon herself by declaring that she would throw an apple and marry the man on whom it fell. Janáček was probably inspired by the metre of the folk poem to make use of an unusual, although typically Slav, alternation of $3/8 + 2/8 + 3/8$, $3/8 + 2/8 + 3/8$ and so on, with evident assurance. As in The Fickleness of Love and True Love he omitted the time signature and also the key signature, although the piece is clearly in G major.

No copy has as yet been found of the melodrama Death, a setting of Lermontov's poem commemorating Pushkin's death, *Death of a Poet*.*) Janáček probably set only the first section, which he performed at a Beseda concert on 13 November 1876. Helfert may have been right when he pointed out that the 'gloomy, disconsolate mood and preoccupation with death is closely connected with the Choral Elegy, both works belonging to the same period and both being an expression of the gloom and depression which was later to reveal itself in Leipzig'.

After this attempt at a melodrama Janáček turned against it and on principle never wrote another one.

Suite for String Orchestra is the first of Janáček's extant instrumental compositions. It is in six movements, the original titles of which were taken

---

*) Lermontov himself was later killed in a duel, when scarcely 27 years old.

either from old dance suites or from sonata movements. In both cases the titles were, for the most part, so inappropriate that Janáček certainly did wisely when he decided to abandon them.

The first movement (originally entitled Prélude) is enclosed, concerto grosso fashion, by a robust motif in octaves, their crushed notes reminiscent of Liszt:

The thickly-coloured motif with which the theme continues—still in octaves—in the violins and violas is then augmented to form the 'Brucknerian' middle section:

It should be noted, though, that the first of Bruckner's own truly 'Brucknerian' symphonies, No 3, had its premiere two weeks after the composition of Janáček's SUITE, and in Vienna at that. On the other hand, Helfert rightly traces a Wagnerian influence in this and the following Adagio (originally Allemande), especially *Lohengrin*, excerpts from which were often performed in Brno at that time. This is particularly noticeable in the chromaticism permeating even the middle and lower parts and in the high *divisi* violins. The simple third movement was originally called Saraband, although it is in common time and is more like a gavotte in character. It evokes a pleasant, old-fashioned Victorian atmosphere, with its capriciously forte up-beat followed by a sudden, well-mannered piano.

The fourth movement, with the original title of Scherzo, is not in D minor but in G minor, despite the concluding chord of D major, and modulates to C minor without any compensatory digression to brighter keys. But the trio with its charmingly asymmetrical melody is in G major:

Relatively most characteristic is the fifth movement, again an Adagio, originally called, appropriately enough, Air. It is a somewhat pensive dialogue between a recitative-like theme in the bass and a mellow theme in the low register of both first and second violins.

Unfortunately the last movement is the least effective, being utterly unlike a finale in character (once more an Andante). And by being written in B minor (it even modulates to B major) it wanders dangerously far from the main key of the work (G minor) which it is supposed to round off. It is also the least satisfying structurally owing to the somewhat hasty conclusion; the main theme is strongly reminiscent of the aria 'Ah, what sorrow' from Smetana's opera *The Brandenburgers in Bohemia*, while the second subject suggests the *Vyšehrad* theme by the same composer.

Considering the amount of unintentional consecutive fifths, close, constrained part-writing and other infelicities in this as well as the foregoing movements, we can hardly agree with Helfert when he says that 'the modulations and part-writing clearly show that Janáček had by now gained considerable mastery over the technique of composition.' It cannot be denied, however, that the SUITE is both emotionally and artistically sincere. This, together with its variety of mood and moments of interesting instrumental colour, probably account for its extraordinary success with both critics and public, when it was first performed in Brno on 2 December 1877, with Janáček conducting; a criticism which appeared in the paper *Moravská orlice*, written, judging by its elaborate style, by Janáček's admirer Berthold Žalud, reflects the good reception of the work.

Today the work is significant in as much as it shows the various elements most strongly influencing Janáček at a time when he was still struggling to master the technique of composition of 'absolute music'. A struggle which was not so much the result as the instinctive cause of the tendency in his earliest works—to be conservative.

The seven-movement IDYLL (also for string orchestra) composed a year later marks a definite step forward. Even here, however, Janáček has not quite succeeded in freeing himself from a certain *naiveté* fashionable in the musical atmosphere of Brno at that time (for example the second repetition of the second movement or the main section of the sixth movement). The IDYLL presents an even greater mixture of styles than the SUITE, reaching as far back as Handel, as in the last movement, and showing a very strong Dvořák influence both in the general structure of the work—for instance the typical Dvořákian *dumka* of the fifth movement—and in the use of certain melodic, harmonic and rhythmic patterns. Altogether there is greater coherence in structure, clearer part-writing and a surer sense of key (with the exception of the main section of the fifth movement which closes in the subdominant and the main section of the fourth movement (Scherzo) which closes in the dominant, whereas both should close in the tonic) than in his previous works. Of special interest are certain unusual rhythms typical of the later Janáček—for example the 5/4 bars in the third movement (a kind of barcarolle, slightly reminiscent of Mendelssohn, said to have been inspired by the Stahrenberg lake where Janáček stayed on his way back from Oettingen) and the slow quaver quintuplets at the beginning of the fifth movement.

Of even greater interest is the playful use of unusual accentuation in the Trio section of the fifth movement, and especially in the episode of the last movement (a rondo):

Janáček achieves variety of colour, as he did in the Suite, by a liberal amount of rests, especially in the lower parts, by the use of mutes (throughout the entire fifth movement), by borrowing Dvořák's graceful manner of using pizzicato (for example in the middle section of the third movement where cellos and violas imitate each other with quaver arpeggios, pizzicato and arco alternately), by short phrases tossed from one group of instruments to another and by other devices. He failed, however, to grasp Dvořák's use of high cellos and, in the last movement, took them so high, not in a slowly rising melody but in complicated figurations, that he was obliged after the first performance to double them with the violins, rendering the efforts of the cellists unnecessary.

Dvořák could be called the godfather of this work not only because so many of the ideas owe their origin to his influence but also because he happened to attend the first performance, conducted by Janáček, on 15 December 1878, while he was staying in Brno. He also accompanied some of his choral works on the piano and attended a performance of his *Slavonic Dances*.

Janáček's interests now began to extend beyond orchestral music to chamber music. In the paper *Moravská orlice* of 23 December 1876, he had recommended the establishment of a local chamber music society. At the beginning of the new year he began arranging chamber concerts to take place twice yearly at the Beseda Reading Society, at which he himself alternated at the piano with Amalie Wickenhauser-Neruda. Her sister, the well-known violinist Mrs Norman-Neruda (she was engaged by Queen Victoria) and other Brno instrumentalists played the string instruments. In this field also, as will be seen, Janáček tried his hand as a composer.

His efforts to reform the Beseda, however, met with opposition. There, the narrow-minded had raised their 'warning' voices even before the performance of the first large-scale work, Mozart's *Requiem*, and Janáček and his friend Mrs Wickenhauser had provided 15 guilders each to meet the necessary expenses. Owing to the tremendous success of the *Requiem*, no objections were raised to the subsequent performance of Beethoven's Mass; in fact, on that occasion Janáček was presented with a baton inlaid with silver and a velvet music-case. The respect he already commanded as a composer may be seen from the fact that on 10 December 1877, the committee officially thanked him for having allowed the first performance of his Suite for Strings to be given at a Beseda concert. On the other hand, a continuous campaign was being waged, both secretly and in the open, against serious programmes and constant demands made for a return to social events with light music. The conflict never came to a head, however, for the simple reason that in the summer of 1879 Janáček decided to interrupt his many activities in Brno and go abroad to complete his studies.

In the meantime, he had tried to make up for missing the third year at the Prague Organ School by a special study of musical form (in Prague between 20 June and 13 July 1877, probably with Skuherský), and by supplementing his study of Wilhelm Wundt, the German psychologist, in 1876—1877 with Helmholtz's *Lehre von den Tonempfindungen*. Towards the end of 1876, he began to improve his piano playing with the aid of Amalie Wickenhauser; but he remained dissatisfied. In the summer of 1878, he decided to study with Anton Rubinstein, hoping to benefit both as pianist and composer. Despite Kříž-kovský's objections, Janáček wrote to the famous pianist, but 'the registered letter chased him heaven knows where, to Paris, to St Petersburg... and after a year, came back into my hands unopened.'*) In the spring of 1879, Janáček's choice alighted therefore on the Leipzig *conservatoire*, which came closest to his own classicist ideas at the time.

Before his departure at the end of the summer holidays he was invited to play at the unveiling ceremony of a statue of František Palacký on 8 September at Rožnov. Janáček accepted and played, among other pieces, his DUMKY for piano, no known copy of which exists. It was his first and last 'concert tour' and provided him with an opportunity to revisit, after many years, the neighbourhood of his birthplace. It made a powerful impression on the 25-year-old Janáček, to see this stone carving of one of the leaders of the national movement, surrounded by the picturesque costumes of Valachian girls, and Radhošť hill towering in the background.

This was not the only strong feeling he carried away with him. He had just entered on his first serious love affair. He had had many passing infatuations which he commented on in his memoirs under the heading 'Flirting—Catching'. 'M.U., the Rychaltice landowner's daughter, M.V., the daughter of the manager of a princely estate. They held me, a boy of nine, spellbound. The most tantalizing was A.M. She laughed at my cap with its flat top. F.S., K.H., J.M. and K.R.; they were enchanting. She of the year 1881 bewitched me.'**)

The last bewitcher was Zdeňka Schulzová, daughter of the same Emilian Schulz who was Janáček's superior at the Teachers' Training Institute.

She was born on 30 July 1865 in Olomouc, where her father was a high school professor. In 1871 he was transferred to the German high school in Kro-měříž, and, one year later, appointed director of the Royal Imperial Institute for the Education of Teachers, as the Teachers' Training Institute in Brno was then called. Zdeňka was an only child. The family lived first at 37 Pekař-ská Street, later moving into the Institute, where they led a happy family life in spite of the fact that her father was Czech—the son of a doctor from Obří-ství near Mělník—and her mother German. (Her maternal grandfather, Gustav Kaluschka, who was of Polish origin, had been secretary to the Archbishop of Breslau.) Professor Schulz was, according to his daughter, 'extremely good and cheerful. In the early mornings he used to hum or whistle Czech folk songs to himself. His little pipe, visits to the coffee-housses and an occasional hunt sufficed to keep him content. He was much liked by his

---

*) *Veselý—Janáček*, p. 41.
**) *Veselý—Janáček*, p. 43.

pupils.' Mrs Schulzová was less lenient. 'I knew she loved me, but she was severe with me. Beautiful, slender, elegant, with austere moral principles, she lived solely for her household which she managed simply and economically. She brought me up in like manner.' Naturally enough 'Mama brought me up to speak German—her Czech was, for that matter, atrocious—and Papa yielded to her in everything.'

Zdeňka did not go to school, and it now sems odd that the director of an institute for training of Czech teachers should have given his own daughter education in German, helped by his Czech colleagues. One of the teachers at the Institute, professor Vorel, gave her piano lessons and by the time she was 12 years old she had made such good progress that Vorel suggested entrusting her further musical education to Janáček, then 23.

'I was in great fear of my teacher. I had heard from his pupils that he was very strict. There was something forbiddingly sombre to me in his appearance. He was slim and rather small in stature, his pale countenance strongly contrasting with his crisp curly beard, thick black curly hair and expressive brown eyes. Even then I loved his small, full, white hands which became animated whenever they touched the keyboard. My fear was unnecessary, Janáček never spoiled me, he never spoke except to the point, he expected me, as a matter of course, to have done my homework to perfection, but I cannot say that he was particularly strict, and never harsh as had been frequently said of him.'*)

One day, when she had grown up into a lovely young girl with long fair plaits, she looked up and saw her teacher, reflected in the mirror, gazing at her in a markedly non-academic fashion. She noticed the same look when he offered to give her—apart from her normal three lessons a week—lessons in duet playing, gratis, on Sunday mornings; and again, on Easter Wednesday, 1879, after the performance of Beethoven's *Missa Solemnis* when he almost missed the service at the Queen's Monastery because of her. Janáček was well aware of Zdeňka's reciprocal feeling for him, and when one day during the following August, he surprised her crying from the loneliness of being without him, he decided to ask her to marry him.

He had no difficulty in obtaining her mother's approval. Her father was not exactly enthusiastic about the course the lessons had taken but, in the end, gave his consent. He may have hoped that Janáček's departure for Leipzig would 'break the slender, newly-formed threads of this relationship'. In any event, the announcement of the engagement was delayed.

In the meantime, Janáček had been making arrangements for his departure. On Schulz's advice, he had sent in a request for a paid holiday in order to be able to support himself while abroad. His school colleagues very generously took over his teaching without demanding extra payment, each giving one of his lessons every week, so that the school would incur no extra expenses and the state be more inclined to grant his request. And after Janáček had been to Vienna to plead his case personally at the ministry, his leave was granted and nothing now prevented him from studying in Leipzig, at that time the most renowned musical centre of Germany.

---

*) *Zdeňka Janáčková*, p. 10.

(6) Studies in Leipzig and Vienna

Janáček arrived in Leipzig on the morning of 1 October 1879, and found lodgings in the centre of the city at 1/III Plauensche Strasse. On the same afternoon he presented himself to the director of the *conservatoire* and hired a piano. On the following day he easily passed his entrance examination and on 9 October began classes. The subjects for which he registered, with their teachers, were as follows:

Harmony and counterpoint	Dr Oskar Paul
Musical form	Leo Grill
Piano technique	Ernst Wenzel, Karl Reinecke
Piano performing	Dr Oskar Paul
Organ	Wilhelm Rust
Violin and chamber music playing	F. Hermann, C. Schröder*)
	H. Schradieck
Choral singing	K. Reinecke, H. Klesse
Score reading and conducting	H. Schradieck

In addition, he attended Paul's lectures on history of music at Leipzig University.

Janáček threw himself into his studies even more vigorously than in Prague five years earlier. Whereas he had then crammed the three years' course into two he now set out to work through three years in one. He spent 4—5 hours daily practising the piano, did some composing (mainly fugues), went to concerts, read a good deal, including Zimmermann's *Geschichte der Aesthetik*—the chapters on Plato and Aristotle, and wrote long letters to Zdeňka. He allowed himself neither leisure nor social distractions, not even on Sundays, and soon began to feel 'like Robinson Crusoe on a desert island', as well as to show signs of over-work.

He therefore decided to drop some of the subjects, a decision more easily arrived at considering the unbelievably primitive equipment of the *conservatoire***) which was at that time housed in a gloomy two-storied building in the courtyard of the Gewandhaus.

'A shed with a wooden partition. Very dark. At one end an old piano fitted with a pedal keyboard—this is where organ practice is done. All desire to go there soon vanishes.'***)

*) Later, author of a book on conducting.
**) A new building was allotted to the *conservatoire* only in 1887. The Gewandhaus concerts, so called after the drapers' hall where they originally took place, were given a new building three years earlier, in 1884.
***) *Veselý—Janáček*, p. 41.

Not even Professor Rust, the 57-year-old organist of St Thomas's, and member of the Bach Society, could sustain Janáček's enthusiasm: and though he had planned to spend the year 1880 touring as on organist, he now gave up the idea of specializing in that instrument.

He had also begun to lose interest in his choral singing classes although professor Klesse pronounced his voice capable of development—'*eine bildungs-fähige Stimme*'—and in spite of the fact that the classes were often taken by the famous 55-year-old composer, musicologist and pianist Karl Reinecke, who conducted the Gewandhaus concerts from 1860 to 1895.

'Rehearsal of Beethoven's *Missa Solemnis*. I was put among the first basses. Sluggish tempi: everything complacent. It drove me to distraction; after all, haven't I conducted this work?'

It was not long before he became rebellious over the remaining principal subjects—piano and composition. The 71-year-old Professor Wenzel, a contemporary of Mendelssohn, who had—in the *Neue Zeitschrift für Musik*—collaborated with Schumann, was too old. 'He often nods dozing over my left hand at my piano lessons.' Grill, the composer of several chamber-music works, although only 33, disconcerted Janáček at his first lesson by refusing even to look at the SONATA IN E FLAT which Janáček had brought. Grill expounded phrase construction with such relentlessness, and insisted upon such rigid adherence to the rules, that Janáček in desperation wrote to Zdeňka: 'If I were to work as Grill wants, I should need to forget what imagination is.' He refused to wear 'the iron cloak of rules' even though it meant Grill's doubting his sense of rhythm.

These were the reasons why Janáček took a liking to the 'free thinker' *(Freigeist)* Paul (born 1832) who, formerly a theologian, had become a historian, theorist and essayist on music. When Paul's lectures at the university began clashing with Grill's lessons, Janáček seized the opportunity to rid himself of the 'iron cloak'. Yet a few simple and frank words from Grill were sufficient to change his mind and he decided to remain in Grill's class while disengaging himself from Paul's lectures. From then on his confidence in Grill grew while the haphazard way in which Paul disregarded his own and his colleagues' timetable, coupled with his general inconsistency, gradually made Janáček lose confidence in him altogether. (Similarly the young Wagner had turned from the romantic *Freigeist* Dorn to the strict contrapuntalist Weinlig.)

Paul's authority as a teacher was throughly shaken for the first time when he set Janáček to write a symphony before teaching him anything about either symphonic form or orchestration.*) Later, Janáček discovered that Paul did not know the meaning of the terms *quinta* and *sexta vox*, when used in the old motets, and when he failed to notice a mistake which Janáček had deliberately made in a fugue, the last vestige of confidence was lost. He was not entirely glad when, on 25 January, he received news of the extension of his leave; he was anxious to continue studying, but not in Leipzig.

---

*) Janáček had read Berlioz's *Treatise on Orchestration* in his spare time and had attempted to acquaint himself with the *timbre* of the various instruments by frequent attendance at orchestral rehearsals.

As early as 24 November, shortly after his reconciliation with Grill, he had confided in Zdeňka his intention of going for the second part of the year to Paris—to Saint-Saëns. This decision was the result of the impression which a concert given by Rubinstein two days earlier had made on him. Suddenly he felt the need of being taught by a greater man than Grill. Janáček was overwhelmed with admiration for Rubinstein both as pianist and composer and was seized with the desire to develop along the same lines, even to become his heir *(einstens sein Erbe sein)*. He was painfully aware of the clumsy nature *(das Machwerk)* of his own compositions.

The Schulzes, however, gave him to understand, through Zdeňka, that they did not approve of his Paris plans, and this caused a temporary disagreement between the lovers. Therefore, on 26 January 1880, Janáček decided to enter the Vienna *conservatoire*. By the end of the month he had finished Paul's course in fugue-writing. He then took private lessons with Grill in order to complete some of the rest of Grill's course. The concert season had almost ended and Janáček, exactly one month after making up his mind, left Leipzig, not even waiting to make use of an opportunity to perform in public on 29 February his newly finished TEMA CON VARIAZIONI for piano.

Janáček's behaviour in this matter was apparently rash and inconsistent. Here was a village schoolmaster's son from remote Hukvaldy condemning, out of hand, the world's most renowned *conservatoires* (the affair was destined to be repeated even more drastically in Vienna). There is something almost tragic in his departure with so unfavourable an opinion of Paul, who had a sincere liking for Janáček to the end, and whom Janáček acknowledged to be an excellent piano teacher.

Janáček's actions, however, were far from being prompted by vanity; on the contrary, he complained bitterly of Paul's flattery. He hated making any kind of pretence and judged himself even more severely than he did other people. He was simply living through a *Sturm und Drang* period in the development of his creative talent, during which he strove desperately to find a musical idiom which he could genuinely call his own. This crisis was heightened by his awareness of his comparatively advanced age and of it being his last chance.

Apart from the crisis in his studies he was mentally crushed by the weight of his loneliness. 'There is not one among my fellow students for whom I feel the slightest attachment nor do they attempt to approach me,' he wrote to Zdeňka on 30 October. He was by nature, as he himself admitted, buried in himself, and was all the more in need of sympathetic help in mastering his inordinate, almost demoniacal state of mind. 'When I am happy, I am the most exuberant of men, but the next moment I may feel so crushed by despair that I cannot pull myself together without help, which I find only in thoughts of you, dear Zdenči.' He continues: 'I take so long before I become *wohltemperiert* once more.' In this state of unhappiness he turned for comfort to the 14-year-old girl of his choice. From Leipzig he had been able to visit her only once—at Christmas: and then only because his future father-in-law had paid for the journey and had invited Janáček to stay as his guest. From Vienna the journey would be easier.

Although Janáček left Leipzig with feelings little less than hostile, his time there was far from wasted. He himself admits: 'Here I have become acquainted with life in one of the most musical cities in the world. I have been to a great many concerts*) and, I hope, learned musical form thoroughly.'

His Leipzig compositions are numerous and, apart from the fugues written for Paul and the exercises written for Grill, consist of the following works, most of which are unfortunately lost:

PIANO SONATA IN E FLAT MAJOR. Begun in Brno and finished in Leipzig on 6 October — less than a week after his arrival. He showed it to Grill who, as previously mentioned, thought little of it. Lost.

TWO SONGS: DIE ABENDSCHOPPEN and A SONG written for Grill. Lost.

FOUR ROMANCES FOR VIOLIN AND PIANO. On 17 October Paul told Janáček to write three romances for violin and piano without giving him any indication of how such a work should be composed; Janáček simply let himself be guided by instinct. The three romances were completed—after several rewritings—on 9 November, but, still not satisfied, he wrote a fourth in E major (the only one to have been preserved) in 'song' form with a short, slow introduction reintroduced at the end of the composition. The work is permeated with a Mendelssohn-like lyricism. In a letter to his fiancée, Janáček said: 'Here, at last, I have expressed my joy, my Zdenči, my happiness.' The character of a romance which, in the first three, he had difficulty in suggesting, is here well maintained. From the technical point of view the only weakness is perhaps a little too much doubling of the violin in the piano part.

SANCTUS. This was an exercise in vocal fugue, which Janáček wrote for Paul in November. Lost.

MINUET FOR PIANO. The so-called 'Zdeňka's minuet' written specially for her, although set as an exercise by Grill, probably written during the Christmas holidays spent in Brno. Lost.

VIOLIN SONATA. Composed in January 1880. Probably only the first two movements were completed, of which Janáček himself wrote that they were 'not very original'. Lost.

SCHERZO. Written for the symphony which Paul told him to write on 6 November, setting him Easter as the time limit. Janáček failed to get beyond this one movement, which he completed only 'with the greatest difficulty', on 25 January 1880. Lost.

His last Leipzig composition, written for Grill between 29 January and 22 February 1880, was the one in which he took most pride at the time: his TEMA CON VARIAZIONI in B flat major, published, like the fourth ROMANCE, only after his death. It bears the sub-title 'Zdeňka's Variations' in fulfilment of a promise he had once made her. The theme (which contains a long passage in another key and seems therefore to require a slightly longer end in order to establish the main key) occurred to him, he said, in the early morning of 29 January 1880. It took such a strong hold of his imagination that by 2 February he was able to show it to his professor together with the first four variations (there were eventually seven). The fact that this fresh and

---

*) Among others, the Gewandhaus concerts, which took place every Wednesday (often attending the rehearsal as well), the Saturday concerts of church music given in St Thomas's church, and numerous chamber music concerts and recitals. He did not go to the opera and in conservative Leipzig heard nothing of the work of Berlioz, Liszt or Wagner.

sincere little work was not completed until 22 February may prove, as was the case with the ROMANCE, that Grill was largely responsible for the facile part-writing and other sure strokes in construction not evident in Janáček's completely independent compositions (SUITE FOR STRINGS) until some time later. Janáček at 25 was still very largely influenced by various Romantic composers, in particular Schumann, as is evident in the buoyant rhythm of the third variation:

and in the leaps of the seventh variation:

while the sixth variation, with its low octaves in the bass, suggests the sombre mood of Beethoven or Brahms. Following the example of these composers he enlarges some of the variations; the third by a repetition of its first bars and the seventh by a brilliant bridge passage in a style rather more reminiscent of Smetana:

which leads to the final statement of the theme.

A flash of the future Janáček is clearly discernible, however, in the first two bars of the concluding section of the theme:

with its polka-like circulation of the subdominant minor round the dominant, so typical of the future LACHIAN DANCES.

It seems that one more composition was written in Leipzig (according to Janáček's letter to Max Brod, certainly in 1880) — DUMKA for violin and piano, not performed until 1885. Helfert thinks it might be one of the lost ROMANCES. Compared, however, with the surviving ROMANCE, this DUMKA, which is in the key of C minor, is much more passionate. It also lacks the lighter contrasting touches characteristic of Dvořák's *dumkas*. Its consistent sadness makes it one of the works in which the painful loneliness of Janáček's early years comes through most strongly.

Having spent the Easter holidays in Brno, Janáček arrived in Vienna on 1 April 1880, on which day he was admitted to the *Conservatorium für Musik und darstellende Kunst der Gesellschaft der Musikfreunde in Wien* as a second-year student. The Vienna *conservatoire* was closely connected with the *Gesellschaft der Musikfreunde* concerts and from the time of its foundation in 1817 had been widely renowned as one of the best institutions of its kind. The director was at that time Josef Hellmesberger and the main composition professors, Anton Bruckner and the 64-year-old Franz Krenn. Janáček's classical leanings at that time probably account for his choice of Krenn rather than Bruckner.

The most celebrated of the piano professors was Julius Epstein, Gustav Mahler's piano teacher. Janáček joined the piano class of Josef Dachs with whom he remained only a short while, for Dachs demanded far more than Janáček's unpianistic small, round hands could cope with, and insisted on his changing the method of piano playing which he had just learned from Wenzel. Janáček gives yet another, perfectly simple reason for his latest desertion: 'No room for a piano in this tiny room overlooking the courtyard. Useless to learn.' However, in a letter to Zdeňka, dated 1 April 1880, he mentions having hired an upright piano immediately after his arrival. Whatever the reason, his piano classes ceased at the end of April much in the same way as the organ classes in Leipzig. There now remained no alternative to becoming a composer!

When Janáček entered Krenn's class he intended to complete his studies in musical form, having reached the so-called 'third rondo' involving two dissimilar episodes (*ABACA*); and his studies with Krenn began precisely where he had left off.

From the very first lesson, however, Janáček felt Krenn (who nevertheless had produced a composer of such early maturity as Gustav Mahler only two years before) to be lacking in Grill's thoroughness and strict discipline. The divided attitude towards the neo-classic and late romantic styles which the *conservatoire* adopted in the city of both Brahms and Bruckner was certainly reflected in Krenn's method of teaching, while most of the students were drawn more towards the new Romanticism.

In Vienna, the indefatigable Janáček lost none of his zeal, though disturbed at his lodgings by a nearby piano school and strolling musicians who played and sang in the courtyard. He brought new exercises in composition to every class, which he attended three times a week, whereas the other students brought theirs only once a fortnight. Determined to make up for Krenn's lack of strictness by being particularly strict with himself, he set out to write a movement in rondo form of the 'fourth' type followed methodically by a movement in sonata form. Between 16 April and 12 May he completed a violin sonata*) having rewritten the last movement, the first version of which he thought 'bombastic and meaningless'. At the same time, between 22 April and 7 May, he composed a song cycle, FRÜHLINGSLIEDER (Spring Songs) to words by Vinzenz Zusner. Krenn encouraged him to write the SONGS in order to enter them for a prize offered by Zusner for the setting to music of his worthless poems. Janáček next began a systematic study of some of

---

*) This was his SECOND VIOLIN SONATA but like the first, written in Leipzig, it is not extant.

Beethoven's string quartets and soon began writing his own QUARTET, of which at least three movements are known to have been completed.

He hoped that, in spite of adhering to a more classical style, his works would at least stand up to comparison with the 'Wagnerian bombast' of his fellow students. He was, however, to be bitterly disappointed.

On 25 June, the public competition for the *conservatoire's* Medal of Honour (a modest form of the Paris *conservatoire's Prix de Rome*) took place. On 28 May, the most advanced students, including Janáček, had to pass a preliminary qualifying examination at which Janáček wanted to enter his QUARTET, but as he could not finish it in time, Krenn decided that he should present his VIOLIN SONATA. The adjudicators, Hellmesberger, Epstein and a member of the board, heard only the slow movement (the other candidates had presented only one movement each), which, in Janáček's opinion, was very indifferently played by Julius Herzfeld, who was also competing as a composer.

Janáček's work was pronounced too academic and was not passed for entry in the competition, whereas Herzfeld's own work was not only passed but was then awarded first prize in the competition.

Janáček's indignation was roused and on 29 May he wrote an emphatic protest, pointing out that the selection of his Adagio put him at a disadvantage and demanding a further hearing, even going so far as to threaten exposure of the whole affair in a music magazine. He resolved to send the sonata to Hanslick for his opinion, and made up his mind to leave the *conservatoire*. He postponed this decision until 12 June by which time he would know the result of the Zusner competition although he now allowed himself no illusions; and indeed, he was again unsuccessful, in spite of Krenn being one of the judges.

At this point Janáček's unbounded selfconfidence began to give way to doubt. He suddenly found himself to be 'as stupid as blackest night,' and decided to go and finish his studies with Dvořák. However, owing to Zdeňka's or rather her family's objections, he abandoned the idea. Yet he felt he had succeeded with the Scherzo of his QUARTET: 'Without talent I could scarcely have done something like this.'

That he had talent was not denied at the Vienna *conservatoire*, as may be seen from Krenn's remark—presumably citing Hellmesberger—after he had unsuccessfully intervened on Janáček's behalf over the affair of the competition and been told it was a matter of principle. Janáček informed Zdeňka: 'I would need to forget all I learned in Prague and in Leipzig. The two schools have their good points, but they have stayed behind, I am told.' Janáček did not agree. 'This affair cannot divert me from my course for which I am indebted to Leipzig's Grill. I will never dedicate myself to musical stylelessness (he probably meant formlessness), empty effects and gradations of pompous chord progressions; the time for this is now past.'*)

The paradoxical enthusiasm of the unconventional hot-head for the conventional, for that 'iron cloak' which he had, according to his own words, donned with such reluctance, was destined to bear very different fruit; neither classic nor romantic but realistic, born from nature and warm with life. Janá-

---

*) In a letter to Zdeňka written on 20 May 1880.

ček was certainly far from wasting his time when the year before he had begun noting down what later became known as his melodic curves of speech*) and it may be said to be symbolic that, having left Vienna early in June, thus renouncing his right to a formal diploma, (although Krenn drew up a certificate testifying that he 'justified the very best hopes', and at roughly the same time the Leipzig *conservatoire* sent him a formal certificate which—all things considered—was quite good), he went to stay with his uncle Jan in the little village of Znorovy in the Slovácko district of south-eastern Moravia.

---

*) According to an interview given by Janáček to the magazine *Literární svět* (Literary World) of 8 March 1928.

(7) First Years of Married Life

Janáček now returned to Brno for good and took lodgings, cheaply as usual, with the Freyschlag family opposite 'The Blue Lion'. He at once threw himself wholeheartedly into both his teaching of music at the Teachers' Training Institute and his directorship of the Old Brno Choir. His studies being at the end, he now announced his engagement to Zdeňka Schulzová, on 1 July 1880.

Happiness, so long sought after, seemed now to lie within reach, when a new problem reared its head: the difference between Janáček's political and social background and the patrician, glass-house atmosphere in which Zdeňka had been brought up. She herself mentions this*) when referring to the one and only journey made with her parents at the age of 12 to visit her relations in Feldkirchen and Munich, most of her other contacts with coutry life being stolen glances through the window. In addition she had been brought up to use a foreign language—German. In spite of his nationalistic feelings, Janáček, it should be stressed, was no chauvinist, although his future father-in-law was later to give 'his national fanaticism bordering almost on insanity' as one of the reasons for requesting Janáček's transfer from the Teachers' Training Institute. Janáček simply could not bear the idea of foreign domination—in this case German—which meant that he turned his hatred against everything German in his usual uncompromising way. (He even refused to go—but only in Brno—to the German theatres and concert halls, and not until the German domination of the town council had come to an end would he even go in a tram.)

On the other hand, there is absolutely no indication either in Leipzig or Vienna of his ever having been the cause of any kind of nationalistic incident. He spoke German with Zdeňka during the first years of their acquaintance and wrote to her from Leipzig and from Vienna in German. He can scarcely be accused of chauvinism if, after becoming officially engaged to her, he insisted on their speaking Czech. This presented no difficulties to Zdeňka who knew Czech and considered communication with each other in that language as natural, even inevitable. Mrs Schulzová, however, and especially Mrs Schulzová's mother who sometimes stayed many months with her daughter, knew no Czech whatsoever; and although they were both sincerely fond of Janáček, they never ceased reproaching Zdeňka for daring to use a language 'fit only for servants'.**)

This attitude stirred up antagonistic feelings in Janáček, the descendant of poor weavers and village schoolmasters, and caused a certain tension in his

---

*) *Zdeňka Janáčková*, p. 3.
**) *Zdeňka Janáčková*, p. 14.

relations with Zdeňka which almost brought the engagement to an end, especially when Mrs Schulzová began insisting on the wedding ceremony being conducted in German. At a later date, Zdeňka surmised that in this way her family had hoped to prevent the wedding altogether, although she had answered the prophecies of inevitable unhappiness with Janáček—'partly out of deep love, partly out of childish stubbornness'—with the same touching words, 'rather unhappy with him than happy with someone else'. The ever-changing, unpredictable ferment of Janáček's personality brought to her life 'such a quantity of new exciting artistic experiences' that he soon became the axis around which all her thoughts revolved.

Zdeňka's father found the couple a pleasant four-roomed flat on the first floor of a corner house 46 Měšťanská Street and bought not only the furniture but also an excellent Ehrbar piano, which Janáček himself chose. Nevertheless, his distaste for Zdeňka's parents, and especially her German relatives, was not lessened and it even clouded the wedding day which the Schulzes would have liked to postpone until 30 July 1881, when Zdeňka would have reached the age of 16. The constant tension served rather to hasten the event, however, and the marriage was 'celebrated' on 13 July, the blushing bride feeling 'like being dressed for her own funeral'—the weather was glorious, there was music played by members of the German theatre, Zdeňka wore pink, but to the Schulzes' horror Janáček turned up in the ostentatiously patriotic black tunic of the Sokol movement.*)

The honeymoon, however, began in a more hopeful mood. Janáček took his young bride to Obříství to her Czech grandfather (on her father's side), then to Prague, where he introduced her to Ferdinand Lehner and to Dvořák, who made no effort to conceal his surprise on seeing 'the child his friend brought with him'. Dvořák went with the couple for an outing to Karlštejn castle and the distinguished baritone Lev showed them over the newly-finished building of the National Theatre, which soon after, as Janáček heard with horror, was completely destroyed by fire. After spending some days at Kutná Hora and returning for a week to Brno to celebrate their housewarming in their new flat, which Zdeňka's parents had had decorated in the meantime, they went to Znorovy to visit Janáček's uncle Jan; here Zdeňka, dressed up in a Znorovy peasant costume, took part in a festival of folk art at nearby Strážnice. From there Janáček took his wife to Velehrad, and showed her the neighbouring castle of Buchlov as well as his native Hukvaldy. Their honeymoon ended with a visit to the ageing Father Křížkovský at Olomouc.

The ill-feeling existing between Janáček and his father-in-law did not prevent director Schulz trying to further Janáček's private and public interests. This could be seen especially when Janáček began making plans to realize his old dream of founding an Organ School in Brno — a project which he had confided to Zdeňka in a letter from Leipzig (29 November 1879) and which he had had in mind when he went to study at the Organ School in Prague. Now, with his training completed, he was impatient to begin, and since every school

*) *Zdeňka Janáčková*, p. 19.

had to be run by a corporation, the first step was the foundation, on the Prague pattern, of the Society for the Promotion of Church Music in Moravia. The first general meeting took place on 23 November 1881, and at the first board meeting held on 7 December Janáček was elected director of the new school and the organization of studies and the curriculum were settled. Teaching began in September 1882. Janáček taught theory of music, Jan Kment, organist of Old Brno Monastery, organ playing; Jan Nesvadba, singing and church ceremonial. The necessity for such a school may be judged by the fact that among the students there were some over 40 years of age. Typical innovations were classes in psychology given by Emilian Schulz and a somewhat original system of terminology which Janáček had invented while in Prague. The school had no premises of its own and it was again Schulz who came to the rescue by offering the temporary use of the Teachers' Training Institute. This not only saved rent but also gave the students the benefit of the Institute's organ.*)

However, there were more pressing assignments for Janáček. During his absence in Leipzig and Vienna, the Beseda Choral Society had been directed by his friend and admirer Berthold Žalud, who far from considering himself Janáček's successor had acted merely as his substitute. He made no attempts to alter Janáček's choice of repertoire as Janáček himself saw at a concert on 6 January 1880, which he had attended during his Christmas holidays, when Dvořák conducted his Second Slavonic Rhapsody and his Symphony in F Major. Žalud, who died in 1886 of tuberculosis, had neither Janáček's immense driving energy nor his experience with orchestras. No wonder, therefore, that Janáček was, while still in Leipzig, re-elected director of the Beseda. After some hesitation, Janáček accepted this post on condition that Žalud was to be responsible for the entertainment side while he himself would devote himself entirely to the artistic events. So as early as 22 June, after his return from Vienna, Janáček conducted the Beseda on the occasion of the Emperor Franz Josef's visit to Brno. The programme, needless to say, was provocative: Tovačovský's *Vlasti* (Fatherland), and Javůrek's *Na Moravu* (Moravia).

The main composer in the society's repertoire was Dvořák. Not a single Beseda concert took place without including one of his works, and the two largest-scale cantatas which Janáček was to perform within the next eight years were Dvořák's *Stabat Mater* (2 April 1882)**) and *The Spectre's Bride* (29 April 1888). Smetana was also well represented by two performances of *Vltava* (1882) and *Vyšehrad* (1886) although he was less popular with the Beseda members. Other works performed were by Fibich, Brahms, (*Schicksalslied* and other works), Schumann (*Nachtlied*), Tchaikovsky, Saint-Saëns and Liszt. (Janáček, typically enough, chose Liszt's *Mazeppa*, with its Russian theme, and had the poem by Victor Hugo on which it is based recited at the performance.) As a former member of the Old Brno choir he did not forget the

---

*) The practising of the future organists so disturbed the future teachers that Janáček was soon obliged to move the school into two very dark rooms in Starobrněnská Street, and later into the flat in Česká Street of his cousin, Dr Dressler.

**) It is interesting to note that Janáček expected Hanslick to come from Vienna for this performance.

old masters of vocal polyphony nor, of course, Křížkovský. He also attempted to revive the chamber music concerts, which he had organized in the pre-Leipzig days with the help of Mrs Wickenhauser-Neruda. Being now a married man, he could scarcely continue collaborating with this lady as before, all the more as their relations had been not only artistic, even though she was 20 years his senior. Unfortunately Janáček failed in his attempts to revive these concerts; but he was successful in creating a permanent group of instrumentalists and in securing young musicians for orchestra and choir by establishing a school of singing and violin playing within the Beseda organization as planned in 1877*) and at the end of September 1882, shortly after the Organ School had begun its first term, the Beseda school also began functioning under Janáček's directorship.

At the same time, an event occurred in Brno which was to be the cause of an important change in Janáček's life, drawing his interest for the first time in the direction of opera, firstly as an observer and later as a creator. On 6 December 1884, a performance of Kollár's play *Magelona* was given to celebrate the opening of the first Czech theatre in Brno.

Even after this event there was no permanent company attached to the theatre, and the standard of the various companies who made their appearance for the few winter months was not very high. Now and again a name appeared which was later destined to become famous as, for instance, Karel Kovařovic, then aged 23, the future director of the Opera at the National Theatre in Prague; Karel Weiss, the future composer of *Polish Jew*, the actors Eduard Vojan and Hana Kvapilová. One can guess the conditions in the first Czech theatre in Brno from the fact that the 'orchestra' consisted of only 12 players, until Kovařovic (during the 1885—1886 season) managed to extend the number to 18. It was he who insisted too on conducting from a rostrum, for until then the conductor had directed the orchestra sitting at a harmonium, playing the parts of the missing instruments.

Under these conditions it is understandable that Janáček was not attracted to write for this theatre; but he felt it his duty to foster its development. On 24 November 1884—just before the opening of the new theatre—Janáček instigated the launching of a periodical by the Beseda, to be called *Hudební listy* (Musical Letters), which, among other things, was to publish notes on events in the new theatre and was to appear several times a month, at least while the theatre season lasted. Janáček, always willing to take up his pen whenever he saw the artistic need, supervised the musical side, signing his reviews with a triangle, △. Jan Herben, a distinguished folklorist and man of letters, became the paper's Prague theatre correspondent. Thus during 1885—1888 Janáček extended the scope of his activities into no less than ten different undertakings: teacher of music at the Teachers' Training Institute, from 1886 teacher of singing at the Old Brno Junior High School, director and professor of the Organ School, director and teacher at the Beseda school of music, choir-master of the Beseda, editor of *Hudební listy*, choir-master at the Old Brno Monastery and—composer. All this with a single purpose in view: to awaken the rich but dormant musical resources of Moravia.

---

*) see pp. 59, 60.

Unfortunately Janáček's collaboration with the Beseda was again a short one. The contrast between his unyielding personality and the easy-going conservatism of the board and members of the society was too great. Antagonism broke out openly for the first time after the anniversary concert on 12 December 1880, when Janáček conducted, among other pieces, his new choral work Píseň v jeseni (Autumn Song) and again after a chamber concert on 6 January 1881, when he included—with the board's approval—his Violin Sonata, composed in Vienna, and his Minuet for Clarinet and Piano. These two concerts provided a welcome opportunity for his adversaries to wound his pride where it was most sensitive: whereas the board had once thanked him for allowing them to perform his works, they now accused him of thrusting his compositions upon them and spending too much time on their rehearsal. Janáček could scarcely do otherwise than tender his resignation.

Nevertheless, it was soon discovered that there was no one to replace him, and after one year a newly-formed board invited him back with due honours. His triumph was shortly crowned by his extremely successful performance of Dvořák's *Stabat Mater*. The society now showered him with attentions, but it was not long before enthusiasm began once more to slacken and Janáček found himself obliged to include more and more blue-boys and student teachers to counter the lack of interest by the members. Many complaints were made about deficits in the concert budget, although Janáček was able to prove that the society's entertainment activities also showed a deficit both from the monetary and the cultural points of view. As a result, the board requested Janáček for the second time to take over the supervision of all the Beseda activities including light entertainment, for an extra 200 guilders per year. But the incorruptible Janáček again refused and on 1 June 1888, once more resigned his post of choir-master. The board continued to negotiate with him but all that Janáček offered to do was to prepare and conduct a performance of Dvořák's oratorio *St Ludmila*. The board then nominated the operatic tenor Josef Kompit to the post of choir-master (14 January 1889). Janáček continued to direct the Beseda music school but when, on 2 June 1890, the board decided to accept a later offer made by Kompit to conduct Dvořák's *St Ludmila*, Janáček, deeply hurt, resigned his directorship of the music school and Kompit succeeded him there as well. In addition to all this, Janáček's departure from the Beseda brought the paper *Hudební listy* to an end.

Everything, with the exception of the Organ School, now seemed doomed to failure. Janáček never again accepted any leading post in the Beseda or in any other choral society, and yet the ten years of his leadership were sufficient to lay the foundations of a tradition which has lasted up to the present day.

In the meantime, on the eve of the inauguration of the Organ School, a crisis in Janáček's private life came to a head—a crisis which could not be averted either by the birth of his daughter Olga on 15 August 1882, or by the devotion of his brave 17-year-old wife who, only a day before giving birth to their child, consented willingly to their move into a new flat at 2 Klášterní (now Mendel Square). On the contrary, Janáček's undisguised disappointment at the child not being the longed-for son*) completed the mutual

*) *Zdeňka Janáčková*, p. 31.

79

estrangement. The atmosphere became so tense that every word was interpreted as malignant. When Janáček announced that he wished to bring his old mother into their flat, Zdeňka saw no alternative but to make room for the older woman by returning to her parents. Refusing all offers of mediation which the Augustinian friar Anselm Rambousek attempted on Janáček's behalf, Zdeňka, after a formal separation and with implacable finality surprising in one so young, ordered not only all her furniture to be taken away from the flat, but even the piano which had been part cf her dowry. On 2 March 1883, when these drastic measures were being carried out by the caretaker of the Institute under the supervision of Schulz himself, a scene took place between the director and his teacher that made further contact between the two almost impossible.*) Thanks to the wisdom of their superior, the school inspector Vincenc Prousek, their quarrel was settled in June by forcing both sides to accept an 'armed truce'.

After a separation of more than two years the young couple came to terms once more and again it was Janáček who made the first move. He began by greeting her whenever he saw her. Then he sought permission to see his child once a week and in particular to escort Zdeňka to the theatre (only to the door, since at that time there was as yet only a German theatre in Brno) and home again—but only to the doorway, as if he were courting her for the first time. At last in the summer of 1884, she went back with her little daughter to her husband. A visit which they made during the holidays to the Gleichenberg spa in Styria finally sealed their reunion.

On 16 November 1884, having spent two years with her daughter Eleonora (Lorka) at Švábenice near Vyškov, Janáček's mother died at Hukvaldy—the mother whom even after Zdeňka's departure he had not dared to take into his household. Janáček, perhaps still secretly resentful at Zdeňka's refusal, again sank into a mood of sullen reserve.

On 16 May 1888, the much-desired son was born and like Olga was given a Russian name—Vladimír. Although delicate at first he grew into a fine little boy with his father's dark eyes, fair hair, dark eyebrows and soft skin. He laughed and sang the whole day through and Janáček noted eagerly the first signs of his musical talent, his tuneful singing and his interest in the piano. He would carry him about in his arms assuring everyone that he would become a musician.

But in October 1890, Olga caught scarlet fever and five weeks later, when she had almost recovered, little Vladimír caught it from her. The illness developed rapidly, meningitis set in and the boy, the hope and pride of his parents, was gone within two days—on Sunday morning, 9 November, aged two and a half years. With him also died Zdeňka's last hopes of married happiness.

Simultaneously, a third crisis came to a head, the crisis of Janáček the artist, which was probably largely responsible for the crisis in his family life. Although Vienna did not rob him of his faith in his own talent, it doubtless undermined his faith in the classically oriented course which his development was taking.

---

*) See Štědroň's article 'Leoš Janáček at the Teachers' Training Institute', *Rytmus*, vol. 12, No 9—10.

Proof of this is the fact that for four years after returning from Vienna he almost completely abandoned composing.

It is true that in September 1880 he wrote one work for mixed choir, AUTUMN SONG (a setting of the poem *Zpěv v jeseni* by Jaroslav Vrchlický). But the complaint from the board of the Beseda society that he was devoting too much time to his own works and especially to this particular work, although it was written to celebrate the twenty-first anniversary of that organization, was not an encouragement to compose.

Neither did the composition itself give him much encouragement, since official festive works were never his forte. The subject of the poem, reminiscent of the meditations of Victor Hugo or Lamartine, set him an almost metaphysical task ('My soul like a vine twines up the tree of humanity towards Heaven's limpid blue...'). But even the final invocation to nature ('Oh Nature, I am thine'), which Janáček later on in his life understood so well, did not help him to do justice to the poem. (He succeeded only much later in his ETERNAL GOSPEL, to words by the same poet.) The AUTUMN SONG, perhaps on account of the inherent solemnity of the poem, reveals the superficiality of Janáček's attempt to convey the solemn mood, helping himself out with quotations from Smetana. His carefree declamatory style lacking, as yet, its future originality was ill suited to the exquisite diction of the poem, and the inertia of his harmony had none of the strength of his later, gradually tensioned constructions.

The four-year silence which followed does not mean that Janáček had given up his creative struggle. But his efforts had so far produced no tangible results. When his wife, recalling the beginnings of his work on the opera ŠÁRKA (1887), says 'It was not a happy period. He was very dissatisfied with himself and tore up a great many things,' this was no doubt even more true in those 'lean' years. Be that as it may, not until 1884 did Janáček the composer again present himself to the public by publishing, at the Benedictine Press, TWO COMPOSITIONS FOR ORGAN; but they may be said to represent a search rather than a discovery.

Janáček came nearer to his true aims by returning to folk themes, as in his choral works KAČENA DIVOKÁ (Wild Duck) and especially in his FOUR MALE-VOICE CHORUSES. To this group may be added, as being similar in theme and presumably of the same date, the newly-discovered choruses, NA KOŠATEJ JEDLI (In the Spreading Fir Tree) and NA PRIEVOZE (At the Ferry).

Janáček composed the mixed-voice chorus, WILD DUCK, for a school song book, published in 1885. It is well above the usual level of such music and yet never exceeds the ability of those for whom it was intended, with the possible exception of the low E flat in the basses in the last bar. It is a touching and simple story of a duck shot and wounded who has done no harm, whose young 'drink the muddy water, eat the gritty sand'. It is a setting of a folk song, although all that remains of the original melody as taken down by Sušil is the rhythm ♩ ♩ |♪♪♪♪ (and that only partly).

Neither are the original words adhered to exactly, but to obtain greater compactness Janáček in most cases has made two verses out of every three, dividing the central verse between the one preceding it and the one following it. Janáček omitted, perhaps for educational reasons, the rather dramatic verse in which the duck calls for revenge on her destroyer.

The first known public performance of this work was conducted by Janáček himself at a concert given by the high schools of Brno on 17 March 1901.

The male-voice choruses, NA KOŠATEJ JEDLI and NA PRIEVOZE, both settings of folk poetry, one Moravian, the other Slovak, were brought to light in the following manner. Some time ago the Brno University Library took over the archives of the late Josef Kozlík (1862—1924), a teacher in the little town of Bílovice nad Svitavou. Among various pieces of music the librarian Dr Vladimír Telec discovered, in October 1956, the undated scores of two unknown choral works. The manuscripts were in Kozlík's hand but the composer was given as Leoš Janáček. After careful examination by Dr Jan Racek and Dr Bohumír Štědroň, the works have been proved beyond doubt to have been composed by Janáček with whom Kozlík studied at the Teachers' Training Institute sometime around 1880.

The simpler of the two choruses, IN THE SPREADING FIR TREE, which Racek and Štědroň consider to have been written about 1877—1880, is a setting of a folk poem taken down by Sušil with the title *Láska a závist* (Love and Envy) and bemoans, in seven verses, a lost love. As usual, Janáček combines the verses in couples and for this reason is unable to use the original melody which is a very old one and complete in itself:

As the first part of each couple is left in the original key:

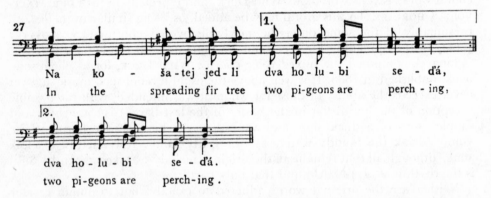

while the second makes a bold modulation (from G minor to F sharp minor), and as there are an uneven number of verses, the fourth and final repetition of the first part rounds off the piece in the tonic key. It thus becomes a kind of incipient rondo—Janáček's favourite form.

The folk ballad AT THE FERRY also tells a tale of frustrated love and was apparently composed sometime between 1883 and 1885. A girl is hurrying to bandage the head of her lover who is returning wounded from the wars. But she cannot reach him because she does not have enough money to pay the ferryman and in the meantime the young man dies. Janáček once again couples the verses, but this time the link follows a different pattern—that of the binary form, with the first part worked out in imitation and expressing poignantly by the suspended major seventh and the trembling triplets the urgency of the girls' imploring call to the ferryman:

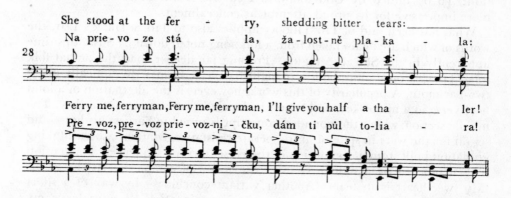

Four male-voice choruses, VÝHRŮŽKA (The Threat), Ó LÁSKO (Ah Love), ACH, VOJNA, VOJNA (The Soldier's Lot), and KRÁSNÉ OČI TVÉ (Your Beautiful Eyes), were probably written during the first half of 1885. The first three are settings of folk poetry, whereas the words of the fourth chorus are a poem by Jaroslav Tichý in imitation of Vítězslav Hálek; this might explain a certain similarity in the music to that of Karel Bendl, generally recognized at that time as the most fitting interpreter of Hálek's poetry.

In two verses containing only very slight metric differences, the poet praises the lovely eyes which cast on him their gentle light throughout the storms of life and which will shine even in the hour of his death. Janáček has here strictly adhered to the words in each verse and a dramatic passage in F minor is followed by a soothing change to A flat major where he uses the tenors *divisi* in 3.

Very different in character from this romantic effusion are the other choruses. The words of THE THREAT are taken from an East Moravian folk song *Ej, pravím, synku, pravím tobě* (Listen to me, my lad) which Sušil included in his collection of Moravian folk songs. Janáček's setting, however, is not only independent of the original melody but also brings out a deeper meaning in the words. 'The words could have been so easily misinterpreted,' writes Helfert, 'to mean the mere derision by a girl of her unfaithful lover. She decides to let him go and looks forward to the day when she will hurt his feelings and make him a laughing stock by going happily with another boy. But Janáček feels that under the surface of derision lies a barely definable mixture of sorrow, regret and compassion. Thus Janáček's musical interpretation transforms a simple, apparently derisive poem into a ballad about the parting of two lovers.' This work reveals a much more mature Janáček also in its musical structure. The first eight-bar verse is built up from a two-bar phrase which is gradually developed to the point where on the words 'And when one day I go to church' the melody leaps up defiantly to a third above the original melody—a device typical of folk singing, only to abate to a frightened *pp* unison on the words 'Then the priest will join our hands' (with the rival wooer). It modulates to an ostentatiously radiant D major at the words 'With the ties of love alone', but on the very word 'love' the symbolic descent to a cadence in B flat major suggests something self-deceptive, the whole concluding with solemn resignation: 'To be untied by God alone in Heaven.' A miniature drama, all the more impressive for its proud attempt at concealment.

What has been said of THE THREAT applies also to THE SOLDIER'S LOT, the words of which are again taken from a folk song noted down by Sušil, this time apparently in the Slovácko region. Probing far deeper than the actual folk song, Janáček once more builds an eight-bar verse from a rhythmically gritty two-bar motif. A peculiarity of this work, however, is the alternation of a loud fiery verse in a minor key, with a soft melancholy variant in a major key. The middle section, where the wounded conscript is urged to harness his horse and set off for the wars in spite of his desperate resistance, contains a breathtaking gradation built from a diminution of the verse in rising sequences. The tension is then relieved by a sudden change to a mood of compassion at the words 'My sweetheart is in tears'. Another variant concludes—by way of a short recapitulation—the work on a note of quiet resignation ('I must leave my beautiful sweetheart').

In contrast to these two choruses, AH LOVE may be said to be half-way between a straight choral arrangement of a folk song reminiscent of Janáček's earlier choral works, PLOUGHING and I WONDER AT MY BELOVED, and an original setting of a folk poem, similar to THE FICKLENESS OF LOVE, THE DROWNED WREATH, NO ESCAPE FROM FATE, and, in particular, the two works just discussed. AH LOVE is a partially literal, partially free version of a folk song which had deeply impressed Janáček when, as a fatherless child, he had spent his holidays at Znorovy with his uncle Jan, the local parish priest. 'I have remembered the tune of one superb song to this day. The long, long last note of each verse reverberated over the countryside, vanishing into the meadows and wooded banks of the softly flowing Morava.' This tune is identical to a particularly attractive version of the song *Ej lásko, lásko, ty nejsi stálá* (O love, love, you are not constant) from Kuželov in the hills east of Strážnice. This is the rhythmically free way Janáček wrote it down:

29

Janáček included this tune in his earlier choral work, THE FICKLENESS OF LOVE, where it appears in the third verse in combination with the melody of the first verse. He also included another version of this tune as No. 1 in the BOUQUET OF MORAVIAN FOLK POETRY IN SONGS for voice with piano accompaniment. In the present choral setting Janáček uses the 7/4 time signature for the rhythm, which together with the melody represents a sort of free imitation of the folk song. The fickleness of love is expressed by an unsteadiness of tonality, each of the two verses consisting of two basically similar phrases, the first of which drops from B major to A major while the second returns to B Major.

The wealth of unusual traits in the three folk poetry choruses caused Prague musical circles and publishers to take a rather evasive attitude, and so the Brno performances of 1886 and 1889 were not followed by a Prague perform-ance until 1906, when they were sung by the Hlahol Society with Adolf Piskáček conducting. Even Dvořák, to whom the cycle was dedicated, expressed his doubts quite openly in a letter of thanks written to Janáček on 13 September 1886: 'Let me tell you frankly that I found many passages and expecially the modulations rather startling. I was dismayed…' His sense of justice makes him add, however: 'But having played them through once, twice, a third time my ear became accustomed to them and I thought to myself, after all, why not. But we could find plenty to quarrel about.' However, he goes on to point out: 'They emit a truly Slavonic spirit, they are no *Liedertafel,* and they contain passages that will have magical effect.' Dvořák did not live to hear the cycle performed; however, the following passage from the third chorus:

30

must surely have been at the back of Dvořák's mind when he was writing the warning chorus of the water nymphs in the third act of his opera *Rusalka.*

(8) Janáček's First Opera

Having made a start in these dramatic choral works, especially in THE THREAT, it was not long before Janáček the dramatist brought forth a fully-fledged work for the stage—the inauguration of the Czech theatre in Brno doubtless providing new impetus. About a month after this memorable occasion—at the beginning of January 1885—Janáček outlined in his diary a synopsis for a romantic opera based on Chateaubriand's story *The Last Abencerage,* which probably attracted him in Leipzig, where he heard the overture to Cherubini's opera based on the same story.

According to Janáček's notes the opera would have followed these lines:

Act I. Aben Hamet, the last of the Moorish family of the Abencerages, meets in Madrid, whither he has returned unrecognized from banishment, the beautiful Doña Blanca. They fall in love, although Doña Blanca is betrothed to someone else.

Act II. Blanca's brother Carlos rebukes her and a duel with Aben Hamet ensues. Aben Hamet discovers that Doña Blanca is descended from the family who exterminated his ancestors, reveals his identity, relinquishes Blanca and returns into exile.

Act III. Doña Blanca is dying of grief at Aben Hamet's grave near the ruins of Carthage.

The conflict between the dictates of the heart and the categorical imperative of family and tribe probably aroused Janáček's interest in this story, but the events were so remote in time and place that it is not surprising that he soon abandoned it. He had, besides, come to know Julius Zeyer's *Šárka,* where a similar conflict including the heroine Šárka dying of grief is the richer for the lovers' eventual change of heart and has the added advantage of taking place in a Czech legendary setting.*) Unfortunately, Zeyer, who had originally written this story in most impressive verse as part of his cycle of poems *Vyšehrad,* was less successful with his dramatic version, as the following synopsis shows:

The legendary Princess Libuše has died and Přemysl her husband is now ruling on his own. But the bereaved maidens of Libuše refuse to accept the loss of their former power, and revolt. They are led by Vlasta although Šárka is the most warlike among them just as Ctirad is among their male opponents. Ctirad goes to the ruined castle of Libice, where Přemysl and his men have

---

*) This play was brought to Janáček's notice in 1887 by Karel Sázavský, music critic and art correspondent of the fortnightly review *Česká Thalie* in which Zeyer's *Šárka* was published in instalments: first act, 1 January, second act, 15 January, third act, 1 February 1887.

gathered, with a message from his father Dobrovoj ordering him to take from a vault (at the back of the stage) the magic shield and club of Trut, which will secure victory for the men. With shouts of 'Let us to Děvín (Maiden Castle)! We the masters, slaves no more'! (words which only in 1919 were especially added, at the composer's request, by F. S. Procházka), they rush into battle without even waiting for the miraculous weapons. Ctirad, left alone, seems equally in no hurry to take them from the vault and muses dreamily of forests, nightingales and the moon, only to be roused by the clamour of Šárka's maidens arriving. No sooner has Ctirad hidden himself in the tomb behind the throne on which the dead Libuše is sitting with a golden crown on her head, than Šárka enters. Accusing Libuše of having 'bowed her head before a man', she stretches out her hand for the crown which she knows to have magic powers and which will secure victory for Vlasta. But Ctirad steps forward and stops her with Trut's magic club. Libuše sinks through the floor and Šárka takes her leave, secretly vowing vengeance, while Ctirad, captured by her beauty, is torn by conflicting emotions.

In the second act, Šárka also struggles against her burgeoning love for Ctirad. She conquers it and allows herself to be tied to a tree, deep in the heart of the forest, in order to delude Ctirad, who is returning that way with the two weapons, into believing that she has been punished by Vlasta for not fulfilling her task. She gives the signal to the concealed maidens by blowing her horn and only when Ctirad has been killed, does she despair of her action.

In the third act, Přemysl and his men forgather full of dark forebodings at Vyšehrad. Suddenly the golden gate is thrown open and Ctirad's body is borne in on a hearse. The men urge immediate revenge, but Přemysl, for reasons not explained, holds them back with the order, 'First let the scarlet flame engulf him and set our blood on fire'—probably to give Šárka the chance, which she promptly takes, of returning the stolen magic weapons and leaping to death on Ctirad's pyre.

With its profligate use of mythology, symbolism and magic, this was hardly a subject to appeal to the realist in Janáček. It was, in fact, at Dvořák's suggestion that Zeyer had in 1878 written the play. But even Dvořák, a man of a relatively uncomplicated personality, eventually rejected it after three years of wavering. And yet, Janáček's choice of this romantic material is not altogether surprising. Beside the fact that he was a newcomer to operatic writing, obliged to use what material was available, there was the deeper motivation of the character of Šárka—her sudden change from violent hatred to pure love, from disdain to self-sacrifice—so dear to all romantics—so old as love itself. Neither does the plot have to revolve around a war between women and men (whether in the tragic form of Heinrich Kleist's *Penthesilea* and Zeyer's *Šárka* or Aristophanes' satirical *Lysistrata*). Such a theme may spring with equal force from personal relationships, as in the various *Armidas*, in *Tristan*, in *Dalibor*, perhaps even in *Don Giovanni*.

Then there were the descriptive passages which Janáček later recalled with gusto ('The gloomy forests reeking of moss'). But it was the fatal, tragic eroticism which attracted him above all.

Characteristic, too, was his reading of a deeper meaning into the collective drama of *Šárka* than the mere revolt of Libuše's followers against the men—he saw in it 'the revolt of disgusted femininity against the physical serfdom imposed by men.' (In this way Janáček once expressed himself to me when distinguishing between the allegedly misguided, empty *Šárka* of Fibich and his own work when, after having waited 38 years for its first performance, it was produced in Brno and Janáček, to compare the two, went to hear Fibich's *Šárka* at the National Theatre in Prague for the first time.) Unfortunately there are no revolutionary morals in Janáček's ŠÁRKA either, since the single reproach to Libuše that 'she has bowed her head before a man' is not sufficient to bear them out. As often happened, Janáček tended to read meanings into his works which he had not originally put in them.

Janáček lost no time in starting work on Zeyer's libretto, sometime in February 1887. He worked with such enthusiasm that within about five months he was able to send Dvořák (from the health resort of Cukmantl, now Zlaté hory, in the Jeseníky mountains) the vocal score of the complete opera for his opinion. Not until Dvořák had personally given him his opinion on 29 September, 'rather favourable' (Dvořák only wanted, as usual, 'more melody'), did Janáček approach Zeyer for permission to use the libretto. Zeyer was doubtless embittered by Dvořák's rejection, and he hoped that Dvořák might change his mind and use the libretto after all.*) He may also have mistaken Janáček's modesty for lack of serious intent, and disapproved of the alterations Janáček had made in the libretto, including the removal of over-romantic elements. In any event, on 10 November Zeyer refused Janáček permission to use the libretto with the odd consolation: 'Your music, I presume, will not be wasted, since you can use it for something else.'

In spite of the opera being as good as buried alive, Janáček, in the first half of the following year, carried out extensive alterations, probably following Dvořák's advice, and scored the first and second acts. Having done this, even he gave up. However, in contrast with his indifference to his next opera, THE BEGINNING OF A ROMANCE, Janáček never resigned himself to the fate of his ŠÁRKA, although the circumstance which led to the revival of his interest was accidental: 'I was looking for something in a chest and found the first and second acts of my ŠÁRKA. I had forgotten that the score existed,' he wrote on 14 January 1918 to Madame Horvátová, his Prague friend and interpreter of Kostelnička in JENŮFA. In October 1918, Janáček applied to the Czech Academy, to whom the poet Zeyer who died in 1901 had willed his rights, for their authorization, aptly adding to his request a dedicated copy of the score of JENŮFA, which had just been published after its tremendous success in Prague and Vienna. Thus he easily obtained what the poet had refused and began another revision of the opera (his pupil, Osvald Chlubna, was to

---

*) As late as 15 April 1889, the poet J. V. Sládek told Zeyer that Dvořák had again become enthusiastic and only now felt himself 'mature enough' to tackle the libretto. Since Dvořák by that time knew of Janáček's ŠÁRKA, and showed a sincere regard for Janáček, the fact that as late as 1896 he was still 'about' to make an opera out of Zeyer's *Šárka* can only be explained by his feeling sorry for the distinguished poet in whom he moreover found a fervent admirer of his work (see also Šourek's book, *Dvořák in Letters and Reminiscences*). In the end, Dvořák did create his own '*Šárka*', complete with magic shield, when he wrote his opera *Armida*, the libretto of which is by Jaroslav Vrchlický.

complete the scoring first in August 1918 and then in January 1919), making further improvements yet again in 1925 when its production in Brno seemed in the offing. It was eventually produced there for the first time on 11 November 1925.

From the musical point of view, it is the second version of 1888 which presents the most important changes. In it, Janáček cut out the academic, yet untidily constructed overture, replacing it with an introduction based on a theme in parallel thirds which is, according to his own words of a much later date, 'associated with the character of Přemysl':

He also cut out (besides many repetitions in the words of the chorus throughout) the whole of the introductory male chorus. On the other hand, he developed the introduction to Act III and thoroughly revised the voice parts on which he had made unusually heavy demands, for instance Šárka, who had been expected to 'cascade' from D sharp two octaves above middle C down to low G sharp.

The wild flame of my hatred consumes me, I thirst
for the blood of this proud man who thwarted my great designs.

After he had obtained permission to use the libretto, he wrote a new short overture which, like the 1888 introduction, leads straight into Přemysl's aria, and altered the voice parts to correspond more to the methods of expression which he had by then worked out for himself.

One example, showing how Janáček developed from formalistic repetition to dramatic methods of expression psychologically more in keeping with the characters, occurs in the second act. In the original version, Šárka repeats the whole sentence 'Then she ordered me to be bound and slain,' while in the revised version of 1918 she repeats only the most dynamic and telling part, 'Bound and slain'. Again, in the first and second acts, he made many improvements in the scoring—without changing the structure—with livelier rhythmic figures and with more variety in the alternation of instrumental registers, and he continued to make cuts until the first and longest act lasted less than half an hour, while the second and third acts occupied just over a quarter of an hour each. Thus the opera is hardly long enough to fill a whole evening and what has sometimes been called Janáček's 'Wagnerian' opera is, in fact, a model of conciseness.

This first operatic work displays Janáček's development in a nutshell. 'Everything in it is akin to my latest work,' he declared at a later date. In it may be observed, as in some of his early choral works, his predilection for uneven metres, for quintuplets derived from speech melodies or quadruplets in 3/4 bars, his love of lingering on the first inversion of the mediant chord which often changes an otherwise Tristanesque motif into one typical of Janáček:

This and the following examples also illustrate his liking for three-bar phrases in 3/4 or 9/8 time, or their equivalent in 9/4 time:

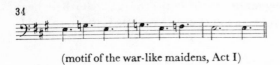

(motif of the war-like maidens, Act I)

Then there are, already at this early stage, those anguished diminished-third steps coupled with the excitement of runs, and triplets squeezed into two beats of a 3/4 bar:

those typical little figures fervently reaching out to their end note:

Aľ vzní - tí   na - ši krev

Let it inflame our blood

Thanks to you, Heaven, we give

Buď ne - be,   to - bě   dík!

even the characteristic melting down and remoulding of motifs heard perhaps unobtrusively at first, as for instance the seemingly unimportant quintuplet introducing Ctirad:

which are later developed into a sort of monothematic pool of Leitmotivs or, at least, of motto elements to be used throughout the work.

In particular, we already find the swelling gradation brought about by the rising repetition of a melodic curve:

There is even a foretaste of some of his great works, for instance TARAS BULBA (Ex. 39), GLAGOLITIC MASS and THE HOUSE OF THE DEAD (Ex. 34, 35). And perhaps a hint of his future naturalism. It is, therefore, all the more surprising that in Act III Janáček forgoes the possibilities of 'tone painting' at the moment of the opening of the golden gate or the firing of Ctirad's funeral pyre, in favour of some markedly ascetic writing.

Altogether Act III differs considerably from the other two, owing to the static character of its action. It shares its oratorio-like style, as illustrated in Ex. 42, with Fibich's *Šárka,* composed ten years later (first produced in Prague on 28 December 1897), which tackles the funeral scene in a similar vein. The forerunner of both *Šárkas* is, of course, Gluck's *Orpheus,* an opera Janáček was much preoccupied with at the time, since he was thinking of producing it in Brno.

42

Weep, oh maidens, shed your tears!

Janáček's ŠÁRKA, however, forms a less satisfying whole than Fibich's, not only because Fibich was much more at home with the romantic story and had developed further as a composer at the time he wrote it, but also because he was relatively better served by his librettist, Anežka Schulzová. This becomes particularly apparent in Zeyer's last act where there is nothing left of dramatic conflict, the voluntary death of Šárka being merely the aftermath of Act II. Janáček's ŠÁRKA remains interesting mainly as being one of the most important testimonies of his development.

The thematic material of ŠÁRKA is closely related to that of the ADAGIO FOR ORCHESTRA composed about 1891*) and rediscovered in the same chest as ŠÁRKA in 1918. A more suitable title and more in keeping with the music of this five-and-a-half minute work would be 'Dramatic Overture'. It is in fact nothing more than another 'Leonora' to ŠÁRKA. Only the first and last sections are Adagio and grow from a descending theme in the minor key:

43

while the middle section is livelier and in the more compressed 2/4 rhythm. The yearning melody surges first into the tonic major and finally to the typically Czech, Smetana-like conclusion:

44

This melody which is none other than Ctirad's motif from the first act of ŠÁRKA is then abruptly interrupted by the entry of the main theme, which

*) According to Štědroň's catalogue.

might be interpreted as fate pronouncing its veto. The two contradictory themes (including their various rhythms) seem to oppose each other until, after an exciting passage in semiquavers, the tragic theme is victorious and the work ends with a distant echo of the tragic theme in the horns.

Altogether it is a work of Faustian brooding though not particularly original. Its Faustian origin (see, for instance, Wagner's 'Faust' Overture and Brahms's 'Tragic' Overture said to have originally been an overture to *Faust*) is borne out by the key in which it is written—D minor; the only D minor in the whole of Janáček's output.

This ADAGIO should perhaps be given a special place in Janáček's work as having a deeper meaning: considering the time at which it was written and the sudden anti-climax which overtakes the optimistic building up of the middle section with its symbolic quotation of Ctirad's theme, it may be assumed that this work was written under the stress of a tragic circumstance, which could have been the death of Janáček's second child, Vladimír.*)

---

*) However, a work which is known to have been composed not long after Vladimír's death in November 1890, is the SUITE FOR ORCHESTRA, op. 3, completed in January 1891 (q.v.). K. J.

(9) Interest in Folk Music

The crisis which began in Vienna and continued for eight years afterwards, the wavering of Janáček the composer between romanticism and folk music (it is notable that he never returned to classicism) was, in 1888, definitely resolved in favour of folklore. In the meantime a person had come into Janáček's life, who encouraged him to identify himself once more with his own people, a person who helped to initiate one of the most essential periods in Janáček's development, a period which may be called 'ethnological' with a deeper meaning than the mere descriptive sense of the word implies. This person was František Bartoš (1837—1906), the most important of Sušil's successors in the field of collecting Moravian folk songs. Janáček's interest in folk music had been aroused at an earlier date as we have seen in his choral works. On 30 January 1882 he had given a lecture on folk songs at the Brno Reading Society where he and his wife were frequent visitors when they were first married. But it was Bartoš who first induced Janáček to make a closer study of folk songs in their natural setting. In short, Janáček, who until then had let folk songs come to him, now went in search of them.

Janáček probably first met Bartoš as early as 1876 during his temporary collaboration with the Vesna Women's Choral Society, of which Bartoš was a committee member. Closer co-operation between the two evidently began in 1886, when Janáček was appointed teacher of singing at the Junior Old Brno High School where Bartoš had been a professor since 1869 and was to become director in 1888. Since Bartoš was not a musician, he was seldom able to note down more than the words of the songs; thus the acquisition of a collaborator as distinguished as Janáček was all the more valuable.

They set out in 1888 for Hukvaldy (the first time Janáček had gone there since his childhood) and the surrounding Lachian and Valachian villages such as Čeladná, Kunčice under Ondřejník, Tichá, Mniší, Sklenov, Rychaltice, Karlovice, Polanka south of Vsetín, Jasenice near Valašské Meziříčí, Petřvald and many more. Janáček took down not only the words and the tunes and their accompaniment on the cymbalom, bagpipes and other instruments, but also the dances and the way they were danced. He made a special point of not organizing special performances but of catching the peasants unawares as they danced and sang. He recollected: 'At Harabiš's Inn, in the Ondřejnice valley, with Father Vladimír Šťastný we watch the changing patterns of the Lachian dances: *Troják, Požehnaný, Dymák*, etc. The gamekeeper's maid knows them particularly well. This was the origin of my LACHIAN DANCES and my HUKVALDY FOLK POETRY IN SONGS.'*)

---

*) Apart from the 'gamekeeper's maid' herself — Žofka Havlová, who sang for Janáček and played him such dances as *Požehnaný, Pilky, Kyjový* and *Dymák* on her accordion, the composer

The LACHIAN DANCES were the most important fruits of Janáček's first pilgrimage in search of folk songs. They were not originally intended to be a set of six dances as we know them today, but were composed separately and were called VALACHIAN DANCES. Janáček at first apparently thought the Hukvaldy district (Lachia) to be part of the mountainous Valachia to the south of it.

The first two dances (STARODÁVNÝ I and PILKY, which appeared jointly in print in 1890 as op. 2) were performed at a concert of folk music given by the Vesna Choral Society on 21 February 1889. For this concert, Janáček had rehearsed not only the musical part, but also—with the help of the ballet master Šimůnek—the choreography. It was there, presumably, that he met Mrs Lucie Bakešová (1853—1933, daughter of the archælogist and ethnologist Jan Wankl), whom the Vesna Society was fortunate enough to retain as a dance coach. This society, founded in 1870 as a women's choir, had developed—largely due to Bartoš's efforts—into a girls' college with a keen interest in Moravian folklore.

At this same concert, where two LACHIAN DANCES were played and danced, Mrs Bakešová also presented a Valachian dance called *Královničky (Little Queens)* danced on that occasion by 54 girls wearing the costume of the Highland village of Hrozenkov. This ancient ritual dance of pagan origin, which was still being danced in the last century at the time of the summer solstice, consists of a Queen and a King (also danced by a girl) who dance from house to house to the songs of their companions and collect presents symbolizing, it seems, sacrifices to the sun. Janáček was so captivated by the *Little Queens* that he decided to compose a large-scale work on the subject in seven sections for choir and orchestra and he wrote to the poet Svatopluk Čech, asking him if he would care to arrange the folk text for him. The poet never got down to it and so Janáček composed at least a piano accompaniment to the ten songs.

As a further result of Janáček's meeting with Mrs Bakešová she was entrusted with the choreography, on 7 January 1891, of four more of his LACHIAN DANCES: STARODÁVNÝ II, POŽEHNANÝ, KOŽUŠEK* and ČELADENSKÝ. In addition, he collaborated with her and two other collectors, Xaverie Běhálková from Tovačov in the mid-Moravian lowland region of Haná, and, later, Martin Zeman from Velká in the Slovácko region, in publishing between 1891 and 1893 three volumes of NATIONAL DANCES IN MORAVIA. This publication consisted of 23 dances (nine Lachian, eleven from the Haná region, two Highland ones and one from Slovácko) arranged for piano solo; the first twelve were also arranged, with some embellishments, for piano duet. And in the dance songs, the voice part or at least the text was also given.

The most important result of the concert on 21 February 1889, however, was the presence of Augustin Berger, ballet master to the Prague National Theatre, when the performance was repeated on 2 March. Berger was sent specially by F. A. Šubert, director of the National Theatre, to whom Janáček

gained much from the cymbalom players Jan Myška of Petřvald and František Klepáč of Kunčice. The former played him two versions of the *Starodávný* dance, the latter the *Čeladenský* and other dances.
*) Later omitted

had offered his VALACHIAN DANCES shortly before. The Prague company was preparing Karel Kovařovic's three-act ballet *The Tale of Happiness Found* for which Ladislav Stroupežnický had written a scenario, and Berger needed to include in it some Moravian dances. Berger had persuaded Kovařovic himself to arrange ten folk dances, and as luck would have it the *Little Queens* dance was among them. But since they did not appeal either to Šubert or Berger, the offer of Janáček's folk dances was very welcome to them. As Berger's report from Brno was favourable, Šubert proposed to Janáček that they should be inserted in Kovařovic's ballet. Janáček, naturally, rejected the proposal, and Kovařovic's ballet was performed on 6 April 1889 without the VALACHIAN DANCES. At the same time, however, Janáček offered to write a ballet of his own, which would include all the dances and would be entitled *Valachian Dances—an Idyll*. The story was set in Hukvaldy at the time of the Empress Maria Theresa, and Janáček submitted a sketch to Berger with the following synopsis:

The Burgrave of Hukvaldy is holding a feast in honour of an officer who has arrived at the castle, leading a recruiting party. The festivities are suddenly interrupted by two terrified youths, Vojtěch and Václav, who dash in to implore the Burgrave's wife to protect them from a pursuing press-gang. One of the youths is to be conscripted, but the choice is difficult as they are twins and are both engaged to be married. The officer capriciously decides that they shall dance for the choice. This proves to be no solution as they outdo one another. Lots are drawn and the choice falls on Vojtěch. General commotion and commiseration ensue, until the clumsy Janek, who is scorned by all the girls, boastfully pushes himself forward in the hope of being made a soldier. The Burgrave's wife, moved by the ardent love of Anežka and Vojtěch, asks the officer to substitute Janek for Vojtěch. The officer, out of gallantry, complies with her wishes, and all ends in general merrymaking.

The story was amusing and eminently suitable for a ballet. Apart from the possibility of creating numerous purely decorative dances, dancing itself takes its place as an essential part of the drama with the effective contrast of the dance contest between the two brothers and the antics of the clumsy Janek. In addition local colour was to be emphasized by using peasant musicians, including a cymbalom player. The subject 'appealed greatly' to Berger, and, on the whole, to Šubert as well. Nevertheless, on 24 September of the same year the management of the Prague National Theatre returned the score to Janáček 'for artistic reasons' and performed just a few of the dances later, and those only separately.

Suddenly there came an unsought for opportunity from a different quarter. A Jubilee Exhibition was being prepared in Prague for the summer of 1891, at which, for political reasons, the Czech organizers wanted the Bohemian and Moravian exhibits to be outstanding. All at once, the directors of the National Theatre promptly commissioned the author Jan Herben to write a scenario to Janáček's dances. Herben completed the task within two days without knowing the music, while Janáček rapidly added to the dances, by composing some extra Highland and Haná ones in particular, without himself knowing Herben's scenario. This was how the ballet RÁKÓS RÁKÓCZY, Janáček's first scenic work after ŠÁRKA, came into being.*)

RÁKÓS RÁKÓCZY, in fact, is not a ballet (its subtitle was 'Scene from Slovácko') but a collection of folk dances and songs, some solo, some for chorus. The figure of Rákóczy has nothing to do with the famous leader of the Hungarian revolt against Vienna at the beginning of the eighteenth century. He is an ordinary impostor who wishes to marry the daughter of a rich Moravian landowner and therefore pretends to be Count Rákóczy of Nové Zámky.**) In order to pay his wedding expenses, he borrows heavily from Schmule the Jew. But even at the height of the nuptial celebrations, the bride Katuška cannot forget her true lover Jan, presumed killed in the war. But Jan returns at the very moment when she is being led to the altar. Rákóczy is denounced by a crippled old veteran as an impostor and sent packing. The wedding is then resumed with Jan as the rightful bridegroom.

As is clear from the circumstances of its origin, this one-act work was written mainly to popularize rather than to present correct versions of the dances, since the songs and the dances of Lachia and other Moravian regions are linked together quite haphazardly. Slovácko is the only region not in fact represented here by any really characteristic dance.***)

In this work (as also in his one-act opera, THE BEGINNING OF A ROMANCE, similar to it in more than one respect) Janáček made abundant use of folk material, but his personal touch is not entirely absent, as for instance in the lovely violin ostinato in the song *Vyletěla holubička* (A Little Dove Took Flight), in the closing chorus *Komáři se ženili* (The Mosquitoes' Wedding) which could fit straight into the much later NURSERY RHYMES, and, of course, in the LACHIAN DANCES proper.

Despite its narrow purpose and somewhat fumbling orchestration, it enjoyed extraordinary success at its first performance at the Prague National Theatre on 24 July 1891. Josef Merhaut, writing in the paper *Moravská orlice*, hailed this unpretentious little work as a 'Slavonic national ballet'. In fact, RÁKÓS

---

*) Janáček and Herben, who had known each other for years, must have come to some agreement beforehand, since the story of RÁKÓS RÁKÓCZY is almost identical with another ballet scenario, which Janáček had made a note of in his 1889—1900 diary and which was called *Pod Radhoštěm* (At the Foot of Mt. Radhošť). The synopsis was as follows: Katuška and Tomeš are in love. A dashing 'tourist' drives Tomeš into a frenzy of jealousy. Believing Katuška to be unfaithful, he decides to kill himself. At the critical moment, however, he sees her escaping from the tourist's advances by bravely crossing a flooded torrent. The unwanted wooer gets a thorough soaking.

This story was, in its turn, none other then a farcical variant of Vítězslav Hálek's previously mentioned *The Girl from the Tatras* with the difference that in Hálek's semi-autobiographical story, the tourist, apart from being described as a congenial person, actually rescues the drowning couple.

**) In the musical magazine *Hudební rozhledy* (Musical Outlook) of 1954, p. 645, Karel Tauš quotes a plausible reason for the choice of the name 'Rákóczy' given by František Brábek, reader in Hungarian at Prague University: 'When the male line of the Rákóczys came to an end (1780), several adventurers claimed to be the heirs of that rich and illustrious family.'

***) The ballet was given only during the Jubilee Exhibition, and in a letter to the Czech Academy written in 1891, applying for a subsidy for his studies of folk music, Janáček cites these dances as one of the results of his previous studies.

Rákóczy is as far from being a Slavonic national ballet as its operatic counterpart—The Beginning of a Romance—is from being the genesis of Moravian national opera.

Janáček composed The Beginning of a Romance between 15 May and 2 July 1891, that is, almost simultaneously with Rákós Rákóczy and three years after Šárka. The libretto in verse by Jaroslav Tichý (real name František Rypáček, a Brno professor) was taken from a short story by the woman writer Gabriela Preissová. The libretto is interesting only in that it brought Janáček into touch with Preissová with whom he was later to win his first and perhaps his greatest victory in the dramatic field. It was also Janáček's first operatic excursion into the realm of ordinary country people, though it was a superficial exploration, as in Rákós Rákóczy. Country people were seen in it through the eyes of a romantically inclined town dweller, or through the eyes of other composers' operas—they were people who had nothing in common with those soon to be depicted by Janáček and Preissová in Jenůfa.

A young cavalier, Adolf, is flirting with Poluška, the daughter of a shepherd, Jurásek. Mudroch, a gamekeeper, betrays them to the girl's parents. Surprisingly, he then springs to their defence, and even persuades Jurásek (first making sure that he won't be found out) to go to Adolf's father to beg his consent to the marriage. Good old Jurásek agrees, and tries to prove the honesty of Adolf's intentions by showing a miniature portrait which the young man has presented to Poluška. The old Count takes his son's escapade with the village beauty surprisingly lightly, but the moment he hears the word wedding, he turns his aristocratic back on Jurásek. Meanwhile, the young man has switched his affections to the young Countess Irma, while Poluška, suddenly awakened from her dreams, makes a hasty return to her village swain, Tonek. Her task is simplified by the fact that he is too busy singing folk songs to have time for any concrete suspicions or to ask her one or two awkward questions. None of which prevents him from joining with the other participants of the romance in their final moralizing (freely adapted after Mozart): 'So it should always be, let only equals join together.'

It is a jolly tale of eighteenth-century *naiveté*, but very weakly constructed. Mudroch's plan is obviously doomed to failure since long before he divulges it, the *entente cordiale* between Adolf and Countess Irma has been concluded, making it impossible for any further matchmaking by Poluška's simpleminded parents to create suspense. The language fares no better and the peasants are made to talk in versified literary Czech, while frequently breaking into songs in a Slovakian dialect. The general impression is not of country people but of stately townsfolk decked out for a fancy-dress ball.

There is no realism in the drawing of any of the characters. Old Mudroch is very closely related to Old Řeřicha in Dvořák's opera *Tvrdé palice* (The Stubborn Lovers), while Poluška and Tonek are the obvious copies of Lenka and Toník in Dvořák's opera. Similarly the young cavalier with a weakness for village beauties is a younger cousin of the squire in Dvořák's *Šelma sedlák* (The Cunning Peasant). But even *Le nozze di Figaro* is never very far away. The only contemporary touch is the stressing of favourable native traits of character as against 'foreign' ostentation—a typical Janáček touch, to be found—apart from THE BEGINNING OF A ROMANCE—in RÁKÓS RÁKÓCZY and the roughly-sketched AT THE FOOT OF MT. RADHOŠŤ.

Like the libretto, the music also reaches far back in style to the *Singspiel*—although much use is made of Leitmotivs—alternating self-contained sections with passages of recitative. And, as with the characters, the music is closely related to Dvořák's middle period. For instance, the theme of Adolf's flirtatious feelings for Poluška:

identical to that of his feeling for Irma, is reminiscent of the aria 'Let us Say Goodbye' from Dvořák's *The Cunning Peasant*. Also Poluška's manner of confessing to her parents is entirely Dvořákian:

while the combining of the parents' theme with that of Mudroch (when Poluška sings 'Maybe my parents will appear') is like a combination of Dvořák with Janáček:

On the other hand, Tonek's love theme, which is derived from these themes, is pure Janáček:

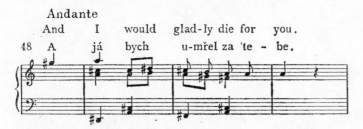

which, in its turn, is reminiscent of the well-known motif (see the bracketed notes, also in Ex. 47) from one of Smetana's Czech Dances for piano, *Slepička*

(Little Hen), when it appears in diminution after Adolf's question 'Have you a lover yet?':

and even:

The dance-like stylization in the manner of a *furiant*, especially when used to stress defiance in the dialogue, is in keeping with the Smetana—Dvořák tradition and is soon to appear in perfect examples in JENŮFA. (The word *furiant* as used by the Czech peasants means a person with blustering, self-assured, provocative manners—behaviour rather typical of the Czech farmer which was often a mere mask hiding trouble and pain. Smetana used this dance in 3/4 time in *The Bartered Bride* and Dvořák followed his example in the Scherzo of his Symphony in D major.)

Another point worth mentioning is the motif developed from that illustrated in Ex. 45, expressing Poluška's pangs of conscience following Adolf's question, 'Have you a lover yet?':

Janáček reveals his flair for characterization by reintroducing this theme when Poluška refutes Tonek's reproaches pretending not to understand ('Go, you keep nagging'), while the music clearly shows that she understands only too well.

Finally, there are some fine examples of Janáček's witty characterization as, for instance, his deriving the somewhat tatty, blasé theme of the count:

from his words:

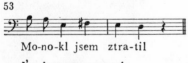

Mo-no-kl jsem ztra-til

I've lost my monocle

as if wanting to express in this charming little *pars pro toto* that count = monocle.

100

For such an unpretentious work, the orchestra is rather large, and includes tuba, cor anglais, bass clarinet, 'lyra' (Glockenspiel) and harp. However, the orchestration is full of typically Janáček touches, as, for instance, the interesting use of the harp (Ex. 49) or the combining of low bassoons with high strings.

There can be no doubt that THE BEGINNING OF A ROMANCE, compared with ŠÁRKA, represents a falling-off in creative effort, and the work as a whole—including the independent overture—gives almost no indication of the future composer of JENŮFA. Not even Janáček's dramatic instinct, apart from a few passages such as those mentioned above, could save him from frequent superficiality (largely due to the weakness of the libretto). This is demonstrated, for instance, by his use, at the time of Poluška's disappointment in love, of the same contented motif which accompanied her flirtation with Adolf.

In addition to the unevenness of the work, a most un-Janáček-like monotony may be explained by his lack of enthusiasm when writing this music. The numerous sketches bear witness to his struggle with the story and the number of torn-out pages show how little satisfaction he derived from it: 'THE BEGINNING OF A ROMANCE was an empty farce. To force upon me, in 1894, folk songs, was sheer bad taste, after ŠÁRKA of all things!'

In defence of the 'folk songs' it must be said that the words follow the action quite suitably—for instance, Tonek asking his jealous questions is accompanied off-stage by the folk song *Zaslíbila věrnost na věčnú věčnost* (She promised her faithful love for ever). In a sense, this could be considered as a preparation for the astounding contrast between the action and the seemingly haphazard folk-type tunes in KATYA KABANOVA, ADVENTURES OF THE VIXEN SHARP EARS and, especially, in THE HOUSE OF THE DEAD, all naturally on a much higher artistic level.

RÁKÓS RÁKÓCZY was performed in Brno in 1938, ten years after Janáček's death, in an arrangement by Rudolf Walter with the title, originally given it by Janáček, *The Count of Nové Zámky*.

Janáček offered THE BEGINNING OF A ROMANCE to the management of the Prague National Theatre on 18 January 1892, but the score was returned to him on 2 May of the same year and not even the revisions that Janáček carried out, nor the fourth Brno performance (as late as 10 February 1894, conducted by the composer) which was attended by the conductor Mořic Anger sent by the National Theatre especially to hear the work, did anything to alter the negative attitude of Prague.

Nevertheless, Moravia could boast of having produced for the first time an operatic work by a native composer and Janáček was enabled to see one of his operas performed on the stage, thus gaining much valuable experience. Incidentally, this was the first and last occasion on which Janáček took the baton in his hand to conduct an opera.

Fortunately, the most interesting ideas in these two minor works found their way into two important orchestral compositions; the LACHIAN DANCES, which had originally been written separately, and the SUITE FOR ORCHESTRA.

(10) The 'Lachian Dances'

The incentive for Janáček's collection of folk dances came from Bartoš, but his decision to treat them symphonically was doubtless due to Dvořák's influence, especially as he knew and had performed the *Slavonic Dances* in Brno. Nevertheless, in the LACHIAN DANCES, Janáček's personal style is firmly established, even though some passages are akin to Dvořák—for instance the first episode of No. IV (STARODÁVNÝ II) which is reminiscent of a Dvořákian *dumka*.

Janáček's dances, in spite of the care he took with the polyphonic working out of his material, lack Dvořák's brilliance. This is particularly true of the orchestration, despite much that is interesting, such as again the unusual use of the harp as in the above example. Apart from their musical charm, they are of particular value in that they represent—like Smetana's *Czech Dances*, although more consistently—genuine folk dances from specifically defined areas. When collecting them, Janáček noted down the steps, as well as the music. He even persuaded his wife, and later his daughter, to learn the dances on the spot, so that back at home they could refresh his memory when he was composing them.*)

Janáček's insistence on adhering to the correct rendering of the dances whether they were performed publicly or merely on social occasions is borne out by his letter addressed to the ladies of the National Union (*Národní jednota*—an association for the advancement of Czech minorities) in Olomouc. The club was giving a costume ball under the supervision of Mrs Lucie Bakešová on 11 January 1889, at which traditional Moravian folk dances were to be danced. Janáček points out in the letter that in the STARODÁVNÝ I two dances are alternated—the real *starodávný* (meaning 'old-time dance'), a processional wedding dance performed around the fire, and a 'kerchief dance' (*šátečkový*), also known as 'ribbon dance' (*pentličkový*). Janáček describes the step to be used in the opening which is based on the folk tune *Zabili Matuška* (Matthew has been killed), as a marching one similar to that of the polonaise:

---

*) Janáček himself never danced, according to all who knew him, strange though it may seem in one so elementally rhythmic and vital. In this abstention Janáček surpassed even Beethoven who had danced occasionally in his youth, although he did not keep time very well.

102

55

The undulating second subject calls for the dancers to turn on the spot:

56

In the second section, which is the 'ribbon dance':

57

and its variant on the dominant leading to the recapitulation, the dancers continue with their marching step but raise their hands holding the ribbons:

58

In the 2/4 Allegro and the subsequent corresponding passages, the dancers are to perform 'free turns with arms raised', and in every subsequent 'più mosso' 'quick turns'.

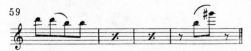

59

It should be noted that these directions are not altogether binding, for the simple reason that almost every village cultivates, with its own costume or, at least, its own variation of its colours, its own musical version and choreographic pattern of each dance, as well as sometimes calling the dances by different names. Moreover, different dances were very often danced to the same music. This is why Janáček himself mentions the following tune—No. 1871 of Bartoš's collection, called *Kyjový* ('a club dance')*) from the village of

*) The 'club' of the title is really a staff decorated with ribbons. One dancer stands with this 'club' in hand in the middle of a double circle—the outer one of girls, the inner one of boys. When he raises the stick the music begins and the slow section is played over and over again while the dancers, clapping their hands on every downbeat, circle round in waltz step; boys to the right, girls to the left. The central dancer moves parallel with the inner circle, swinging the stick above his head. When he has chosen his partner he drops the stick on the floor, takes his girl, and all dance a quick polka which the musicians strike up as soon as the stick has hit the ground. The odd boy out must then pick up the stick, swing it over his head and thus give the signal for the musicians to put an end to the polka and begin once more with the slow waltz. The boy who is left with the 'club' at the end of the dance is carried by the other boys to the musicians whom he must pay. (Vincenc Socha: *Lidové tance na Lašsku* (Folk Dances of Lachia) Vol. I., p. 17).

Kozlovice near Hukvaldy—as the original model for his own *šátečkový*:

60 Adagio

But in spite of some explicit dance patterns on which they are modelled, the LACHIAN DANCES, as far as their music is concerned, are far from being only interestingly harmonized orchestral transcriptions of folk music. This is proved beyond doubt by comparing Janáček's work with the original dances: whereas the original dance is repeated melodically and harmonically unchanged except for some figurative decoration, Janáček—generally at every second statement of the tune—varies the harmonic basis and imbues the melody with new colour. He is fond of alternating the original tonic version, which might be called consonant, with a version in the broadest sense dissonant, based as a rule on the dominant or leading-note seventh chord which can serve as a bridge leading to the recapitulation. This is the case with the STARODÁVNÝ I where the lively 'kerchief dance' leads back to the reprise of *starodávný*.

The dance POŽEHNANÝ (Blessed) is again based on a tune from the village of Kozlovice, which he included in Bartoš's collection (No. 1865) in the following version (unfortunately giving neither the words nor the conclusion):*)

61

Janáček in his POŽEHNANÝ made use, note for note, of the tune he had originally taken down. However, he adds an eight-bar coda in which, after a contrasting digression into G minor, he teasingly evades returning to B flat major and unexpectedly resolves the dominant of B flat by means of an interrupted cadence into G minor, the note G being also in the melody. This typically Slavonic mixing of major and relative minor, which is also one of Dvořák's peculiarities, here takes on a new aspect—very typical of Janáček.

The dance which departs furthest from the original is the third, DYMÁK (Bellows Dance) many variants of which exist with names like *kovárna* (smithy), *kovář* (blacksmith) and so on. In it a boy kneels on his right knee, puts his left fist on his left knee and with his right fist strikes it as with a hammer.

---

*) A similar tune is included in *Valašské pěsničky* (Valachian Songs) Vol. III, No 105, a collection by J. N. Polášek and A. Kubeša. Here the tune has the words: 'He felled the beech tree by the stream' *(Stínal bučka u potúčka)*, and is equally called *Požehnaný*. This is a nuptial dance in which a boy dances with two girls giving them alternately his 'blessing' *(požehnání)*. Each of the girls either turns on the spot or kneels down with the palms of her hands pressed together as in prayer. Janáček underlined the nuptial character of the dance by adding bells and organ or harmonium.

A girl stands on her toes in front of him and gently rocks from side to side, lifting and lowering her apron to suggest fanning a fire. To a sudden change of tempo, the boy springs up and they dance a quick polka.

The original melody is, once again, from Kozlovice:

62

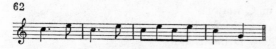

and is included in the Janáček—Bartoš collection as No. 1868 under the title *Kovář* (Blacksmith); no words are given. In this dance Janáček used only the characteristic rhythm of the third bar—apart from the alternating contrasted tempi, so typically Slav (and especially Dvořákian—compare his *dumkas*) — with its rough-hewn melody which he turns into a veritable symphony of the smithy.

The fourth dance, STARODÁVNÝ II, the only one which was not included in RÁKÓS RÁKÓCZY, is based on the folk song *A já zarmucena* in which a girl sings about her grief. Janáček included it in Bartoš's collection but unfortunately gave only the first three words 'And I (am) dejected':

63

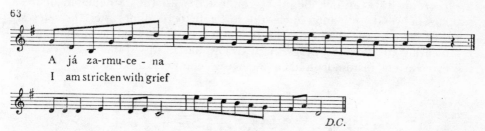

A já za-rmu-ce - na
I am stricken with grief

He uses the first four bars almost note for note. However, they do not reappear in the course of the composition, except in an E minor variant after the first episode in tonic minor (quoted in Ex. 54). And since the rest of the episodes are in minor keys as well, the whole dance—unlike STARODÁVNÝ I—is elegiac in character brightening up only towards the end.

The fifth dance, ČELADENSKÝ, seems to have been so named by Janáček because he first came across it in the village of Čeladná where it is usually called *kašper* (fool), *mynarsky* (miller's dance) or *žebrok* (beggar) after the song sung to it:

64

Ztra - til že - brak ka - be - lu, tra - la - la la - la,
kdo ju na - šel, vraľ mu ju, tra - la - la - la.
A ja mu ju ne - vra - tim, ra - či mu ju za - pla - tim.

A beggar lost his satchel, tralalala,
If you find it, give it back, tralalala.
'I won't give it back to him,
I'd much rather pay for it.'

105

Janáček uses the whole melody exactly as he had noted it down (Bartoš, No. 1864). As in Požehnaný, there is only one musical idea, but the alternation of a 'consonant' version of it with a 'dissonant' one, mentioned above as one of Janáček's favourite techniques, is here particularly graphic. Čeladenský is the most brilliant of the set and with its fiery abandon is reminiscent of Dvořák's Slavonic Dance No. 15 in C major.

The final dance, Pilky (Saw Dance), is worked out on much the same pattern. The original (Janáček uses it in D flat major):

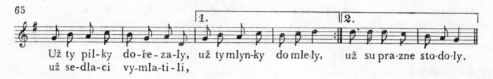

Už ty pil-ky do-ře-za-ly, už ty mlyn-ky do mle-ly, už su pra-zne sto-do-ly.
už se-dla-ci vy-mla-ti-li,

Now the saws have finished cutting,
Now the mills have ground the corn,
And the farmers done their threshing,
Empty is now every barn.

is, according to František Bonuš,*) connected with the bringing in of fresh supplies of wood for winter fuel—the last job to be done after the harvest. And, in fact, in the Těšín district it is apparently danced with movements representing the sawing of logs. As if to emphasize this, Janáček, as early as the first variant in minor, adds a 'swinging' countersubject:

From this countersubject is then derived the fast middle section (once more a *dymák,* as is indicated in the first edition). And it also ends the dance and the work itself.

One would suppose that a work as popular, in the best sense of the word, as this would have been successful and that ballet companies and organizers of so-called popular concerts would have been interested in performing it. However, apart from the 1891 Prague performance where it formed a part of Rákós Rákóczy, it was not produced until February 1925 when it was shown at the Brno State Theatre, while its first performance on the concert platform, apart from a performance given by an amateur orchestra in the little town of Písek in 1925, took place on 21 February 1926, when the Czech Philharmonic orchestra conducted by František Neumann played it in Prague.

The reason for this was typical of so many Janáček's works: no one knew of its existence.

---

*) *Lidové tance na Lašsku* (Folk Dances of Lachia) p. 34. The dance steps are also given.

(I I) Suite for Orchestra

THE SUITE FOR ORCHESTRA, opus 3, which should not be confused with the earlier SUITE FOR STRINGS, was completed in January 1891, four months before Janáček started composing the opera THE BEGINNING OF A ROMANCE. Janáček originally called it Piece for Orchestra, opus 3*) and it was not until 1924 that he changed the title. It was not performed until September 1928, after Janáček's death, at a Brno exhibition of 'contemporary culture'. In comparison with the earlier SUITE and the IDYLL, it marks a futher step towards a complete discarding of his earlier academic tendencies (to which he was to return in a different way).

The LACHIAN DANCES prepared the way for the SUITE, and one of them, the POŽEHNANÝ, reappears in an extended form but without bells and organ, as its third movement. The other thematic material is, for the most part, identical with that of the above-mentioned opera. Thus, apart from the inclusion of the POŽEHNANÝ, this work might well be called Suite from the opera THE BEGINNING OF A ROMANCE.

The main idea of the first movement grows out of three motifs, the first of which is identical with Poluška's pangs of conscience motif (Ex. 51), while the second is Tonek's love theme in diminution (Ex. 49). This theme reappears in the course of the movement in the clarinets in its original version (Ex. 48). The third motif:

accompanies Tonek's first entry in the opera. All this leads naturally to the conjecture that numerous sketches for THE BEGINNING OF A ROMANCE must have existed before the SUITE was composed.

The second movement (Adagio, in C minor) begins in the oboe with a wistful melody of strong Moravian flavour, imitated canonically in the horn:

---

*) Janáček, strangely enough, has no op. 1; STARODÁVNÝ and PILKY are op. 2 and with this SUITE the numbering ends.

This melody appears again in a number of other works, notably in the piano cycle IN THE MISTS (Ex. 180), in the fifth movement of the SINFONIETTA (Ex. 400), in JENŮFA (as the guilt motif), in the cantata NA SOLÁNI ČARTÁK, and of course, in THE BEGINNING OF A ROMANCE, also as a kind of guilt motif, since it is to this tune with its Dvořákian continuation (Ex. 46) that Poluška confesses to her parents. From the same scene of the opera comes also the cello motif in the middle section of the second movement:

69

The fourth movement, which is the last, shares its two basic motifs—one, a trumpet fanfare, strikingly masculine:

70

the other, rather feminine:

71

with the original introduction to the opera and the subsequent reapers' chorus.

The practice of borrowing from his own work—quite frequent at this stage of Janáček's development—in no way detracts from the quality of the SUITE. On the contrary, one should be grateful that in this way something at least of his second opera has been saved. The POŽEHNANÝ dance is, in itself, so charming that one is delighted to meet it again. When listening to the intoxicating last movement—at once a march and a dance with its rich, swirling figuration and trills—one can visualize the swaggering steps of the boys or the graceful turns of the girls in a whirl of bright coloured embroidery, flowing ribbons and a joyful mood of carefree youth.

108

(12) Occasional Works

Among other compositions connected in one way or another with THE BEGINNING of a ROMANCE is the mixed-voice chorus NAŠE PÍSEŇ (Our Song). In its original form it might be called an unpretentious counterpart to Smetana's *Czech Song*. The words are by an unknown author and recount how songs accompany the various phases of a human life, beginning at the cradle. Janáček wrote this buoyant patriotically revivalist part-song, half march, half polka, during the first half of 1890. On its completion, however, he incorporated the melody into his one-act opera THE BEGINNING OF A ROMANCE where it forms the concluding moralizing chorus. Janáček used this melody for the third time in his mixed-voice chorus (with piano accompaniment), the words of which are a Silesian folk song, *Sivy sokol zaletěl* (The ashgrey falcon flew away). OUR SONG shows Janáček's virtuoso skill in writing for mixed-voice choir even if from the point of view of originality it is a step back.

The reasons why Janáček's work during those years was a somewhat mixed bag of compositions, were the manifold demands made on him by Brno life. Although he had left the Beseda Choral Society, he was kept busy writing such things as HUDBA KE KROUŽENÍ KUŽELY (Music for Indian Club Swinging) written in the spring of 1893 for the Sokol gymnastic association, COŽ TA NAŠE BŘÍZA (Our Birch Tree) to words by Eliška Krásnohorská and written on 18 April of the same year for the Svatopluk Choral Society, also the choruses HOLUBIČKA (The Little Dove) and LOUČENÍ (Leave-taking) to words by the same woman poet, JARNÍ PÍSEŇ (Spring Song) written in 1897 for the Vesna Society and SLAVNOSTNÍ SBOR (Festive Chorus) written in December of the same year for the Old Brno St Joseph's Union.

The MUSIC FOR INDIAN CLUB SWINGING consists of five pieces in march time, each one beginning with a traditional two-bar fanfare. Equally traditional is their *ABA* form, while the Smetana-like trio in minor, shared by all five pieces:

originates, by way of diminution, in the folk-style melody in major used in the principal section of the third piece:

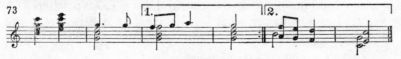

This, in turn, is reminiscent of the second half of the Slovácko song *Zítra sa*

já vydávat mám (I am to marry on the morrow) which should be compared with the 'feminine' motif (Ex. 71) from the last movement of the SUITE FOR ORCHESTRA:

74

The Silesian branch of the Sokol gymnastic association to whom Janáček—himself an enthusiastic member from 1876 until his death—dedicated these pieces, performed them in 1893 at their annual display in Brno. They were again performed in 1895, at the Third National Sokol Rally in Prague.

More important, musically, are the three male-voice choruses to words in the style of folk poems by Eliška Krásnohorská, Smetana's librettist. In the first chorus, OUR BIRCH TREE, she compares the trembling of birch leaves to the palpitations of the heart. Janáček sets the words in two identical verses, simple but affecting in style, his characteristic three-bar phrasing alternating fortissimo with pianissimo and with anxious pauses in the tenor part.

The other two choruses, THE LITTLE DOVE and LEAVE-TAKING, until recently unknown even by name, were discovered in the following manner. In 1940, Dvořák's biographer, Otakar Šourek, found a male-voice chorus by Janáček entitled ŽÁRLIVEC (The Jealous Man) among Dvořák's papers. The chorus, which was marked 'No 3' was obviously supposed to form the third piece in a cycle which Janáček had presumably sent to Dvořák for his opinion. The other two were not found until much later, when Dvořák's son came across them among his father's papers, and on 1 September 1956, the Moravian Teachers' Choral Society conducted by Jan Šoupal performed THE LITTLE DOVE and LEAVE-TAKING, the putative missing numbers 1 and 2.

Both these works (ŽÁRLIVEC will be discussed at a later juncture) are constructed—as is often the case with Janáček—from a one-bar rhythmic phrase. The subject of both is, in fact, leave-taking. In the first, the dove implores her apparently unfaithful mate to come back to her. He would reply if he had not 'silenced tumbled down to earth in blood'. Janáček divided the four verses of this ballad into two sections, setting the first and third verses in the same way, while the second and especially the fourth verse are gradated by striking enharmonic progressions such as the following:

75

Similar progressions are employed in the chorus LEAVE-TAKING where, for instance, the words 'Leave with me what sorrow aches your little heart' are set thus:

The reproachful entreaty, in this case in a single verse, builds up to a climax—first in full force and then in a conciliatory pianissimo—on the words 'God give you happiness, my dearest soul'.

While the rather antiquated vocabulary of Eliška Krásnohorská lags behind the poetic content, Janáček's musical vocabulary with its harmonic and polyphonic wealth, raises the poems to a higher level.

The same type of revitalized though essentially fashionable romanticism of these works and the earlier ROMANCE for violin and piano, the choruses KRÁSNÉ OČI TVÉ (Your Beautiful Eyes) and OUR SONG, and also of THE BEGINNING OF A ROMANCE (in contrast to the evergreen sincerity of the romanticism of ŠÁRKA), is again apparent, four years later, in Janáček's JARNÍ PÍSEŇ (Spring Song) for high voice and piano. However, this work is of considerable interest as it is his only solo song which has survived. (He planned a song cycle of which SPRING SONG was to have been a part, but nothing came of the plan, and he only revised SPRING SONG later—q.v.). It is a setting of a poem by Jaroslav Tichý, the librettist of THE BEGINNING OF A ROMANCE, and was first performed by the young students of the Vesna*) Society's College for Girls on 6 March 1898 in Brno. The three double verses and coda are in the spring-like key of E major (with the exception of the second section of each verse which is in D flat major) and from the very first arpeggio seventh chord F sharp—A—C sharp—E, a spring-like exuberance may be sensed, even though three identical verses become a trifle wearying. In the same year 1897, Janáček was soon to write a very different 'spring song' in his cantata AMARUS.

In December of that year he then wrote SLAVNOSTNÍ SBOR (Festive Chorus) for male-voice choir to words by Father Vladimír Šťastný, the priest in whose company Janáček had first seen the Lachian dances danced in their original surroundings. This song (in 6/4 time, E flat major) was first performed by the students of the Teachers' Training Institute at the ceremonial unfurling of the St Joseph's Union's flag, conducted by Janáček. Little more can be said of it than that the words are set smoothly and adequately.

---

*) Vesna, in Slavonic mythology, was the goddess of spring.

$\left(13\right)$ Folk Songs

The minor compositions, for the most part of a romantic nature, discussed in the foregoing chapter, certainly do not mean that Janáček had abandoned the idea of a realistic style based on folk elements. They could be regarded as a summing up of the past, leaving him free to continue his search for self-expression with renewed vigour. A new spur was given to his activities by the preparations going forward in Bohemia and Moravia for the Ethnographic Exhibition planned to be opened in 1895 in Prague. He met the organizers of the exhibition, in particular the aesthetician Otakar Hostinský and the ethnologist Čeněk Zíbrt, and gained valuable knowledge from their acquaintance.

A preparatory committee was formed in Brno in 1892, presided over by František Bartoš, and Janáček threw himself into the enterprise with his customary enthusiasm. It was at his instigation that a concert of the music of Slovácko took place in Brno on 20 October 1892, at which peasant musicians and dancers from the town of Velká took part. Even though this impromptu performance was not entirely successful when removed from its natural surroundings, Janáček remained undeterred and when, in February 1894, he was invited by the Prague Central Exhibition Committee to take charge of the Moravian section, he made a special point of getting together peasant musicians and dancers from all parts of Moravia and Silesia, including, in particular, 'the king of all living fiddlers', Trn—again from Velká, and dancers from the Lachian village of Kunčice and from the Valachian village of Polanka, with their cymbalom player, Jan Myška.

He engaged Mrs Lucie Bakešová to organize the dancing part of the exhibition programme and himself travelled tirelessly up and down the country persuading the musicians to practise and rehearse (he was responsible for bringing out a comprehensive publication entitled *Slavnosti a obyčeje lidové z Moravy* (Traditional Customs of Moravia). When the great day of the opening of the exhibition came, he marched in his Sokol tunic at the head of his folk artists through Prague, from the Žofín Island to the exhibition grounds in Stromovka Park, and Mrs Janáčková recollected in her memoirs how she and her daughter Olga, then 13, who was seeing Prague for the first time, 'felt very proud of their Papa'.

Janáček realized that his most important ethnographic task was to preserve for posterity the folk songs and dances which he noted down on his travels with František Bartoš or which were brought to his notice by other trustworthy workers in this field. With this purpose in view, he and Bartoš had edited in 1890 a collection of Moravian, Slovak and Czech folk songs which they called KYTICE (Bouquet) and which contained 195 tunes and poems mostly from collections already published by Bartoš such as *Nové národní písně s nápěvy*, Brno 1882—the so-called *Bartoš I*, and *Národní písně moravské nově nasbírané* (Folk

112

A view of Hukvaldy church.

Janáček's birthplace in Hukvaldy—the building was later restored. Janáček was born there on 3 July 1854 in a room in the front part which was originally an ice-store. *Škola* on the façade means school.

Amalie Janáčková, née Grulichová (1819—1884)
—the composer's mother.

Pavel Křížkovský (1820—1885)—a great choral composer, Janáček's teacher and benefactor at the Augustinian monastery in Brno.

Mendel Square in Old Brno with the Augustinian Monastery on the left.

An unusual likeness of Janáček—a photograph taken in 1874 during his lean years.

Janáček with his wife in 1881 shortly after their marriage.

Janáček in 1904.

Janáček's daughter Olga (1882—1903) before leaving for Russia in 1902.

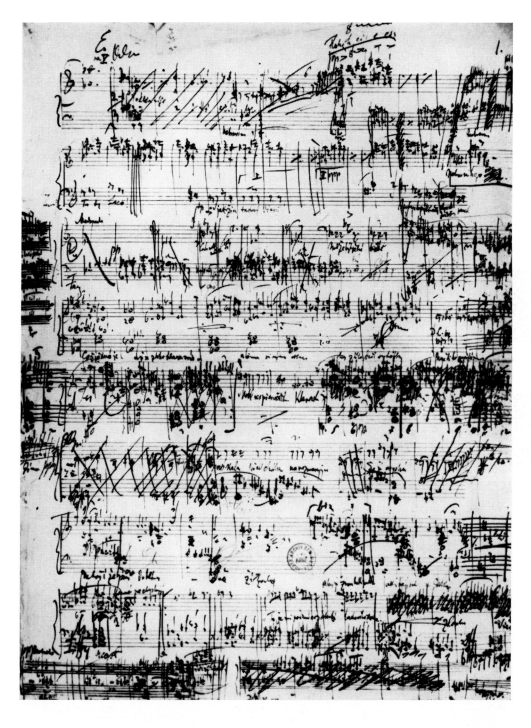

Part of the short-score sketch, in Janáček's own hand, of the opera Jenůfa, which Janáček began composing in 1894 and which he completed four days before his daughter Olga's death on Thursday 26 February 1903.

Karel Kovařovic (1862–1920), musical director of the Prague National Theatre Opera. He conducted the first Prague performance of JENŮFA.

Dr Max Brod (1884–1968), a Prague author and critic who was Janáček's first biographer and translator of his vocal works into German.

The 'Greek Villa' in Brno—Janáček's Organ School moved there in 1908 to be transformed in 1919 into a *conservatoire*. It now houses the Janáček Museum.

The Director's house in the grounds of the Organ School. The Janáčeks lived there from 1910 until the composer's death in 1928.

Songs of Moravia Newly Collected), Brno 1889—known as *Bartoš II*, or from the collections of František Sušil, K. J. Erben and Ján Kadavý. The interesting thing about the BOUQUET is that for the third edition—as had been the case with the Bartoš collection of 1889—a comprehensive introduction was written jointly by Janáček and Bartoš, in which the various characteristics of the songs are analyzed with surprising penetration.*)

The most interesting result of this collaboration was the comprehensive work, NÁRODNÍ PÍSNĚ MORAVSKÉ V NOVĚ NASBÍRANÉ (Folk Songs of Moravia Newly Collected) in two volumes, published by the Czech Academy in 1899 (Volume I) and 1901 (Volume II), the so-called *Bartoš III*—misleadingly so, and not to be confused with the earlier volume of the same name which was the work of Bartoš alone.

These volumes contain 2057 songs, some of which were supplied by other collectors, mostly by Martin Zeman from the town of Velká, who had studied at the Prague Organ School, and whose sister, Mrs Kateřina Hudečková, was a well-known singer of folk songs. Here the preface was entirely the work of Janáček and is a particularly comprehensive discourse (136 pages) on 'The Musical Aspects of Moravian Folk Songs'. This is certainly one of the most valuable dissertations ever written on the subject of folk songs. It is unfortunate that Janáček's self-made terminology, fragmentary style and habit of building on unclear or unexplained premises makes the reading difficult.

Janáček maintains that every folk song, even if 'its entire shape' has not developed from the words, will have originally 'grown from the cadence of the speech'. This, to him, is proved by the peculiar character of the rhythmic patterns which on account of their extraordinary variety 'cannot always be fettered with regular time', unlike tunes intended for social dancing, which make a virtue of it. Moravian folk songs are held together by their words, and for this reason, 'it is an impossibility for a tune to have been composed first and words added to it afterwards.'**) However, the same words assume various 'melodic curves' (*nápěvky*—these are Janáček's 'speech melodies', central to his method of composition) and take on a different melodic and rhythmic slant according to the context in which they are spoken and the different shades of their meaning. Thus the alert mind of the Slovaks expresses itself in speech melodies which avoid even beats, as in this tune from Slovácko:

77

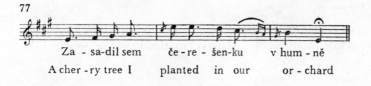

Za - sa-dil sem če - re - šen-ku v hum - ně
A cher - ry tree I planted in our or - chard

---

*) It may be safely assumed that Bartoš's contribution came to an end after the short introductory section where the authors refer to themselves in the plural. For the rest, apart from the peremptory singular, the bold concluding statement, 'If Gregorian chant exercised such an age-long and decisive influence on the development of Western music, I am convinced that the Slavonic song will in a similar way influence composing in the future,' shows that it is certainly the work of Janáček alone.

**) Janáček however does not answer the question of how further verses come to be added to the tunes.

Compare this tune with an analogous one from Těšín in the north east on the Polish border:

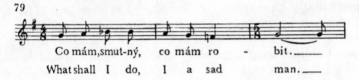

78

Na-sa-dil jsem ja-blo-ne-čku v hum-ně
An apple tree I plan-ted in our or-chard

Similarly, in Slovácko social dances, where the musicians must get a regular rhythm going, they enliven it by off-beat accents ♪♩ ♪♩ which relieve the monotony. These accents are nothing more than a variant of the Slovak crushed-note rhythm ⌐⌐. . smoothed out for dancing purposes.

Janáček also analyzes the structure of the songs and comments on many points, for instance, the prolongation of the normal two-bar phrase, as in the melody:

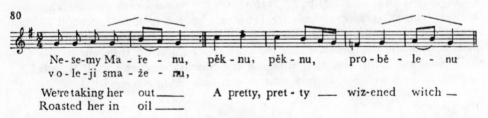

79

Co mám, smut-ný, co mám ro - bit.___
What shall I do, I a sad man.___

where the two final semiquavers are prolonged 'under the weight of mental reflection'.

Certain peculiarities in the melodic line are caused by characteristics of the dialect. Thus, the Lachian emphasis on the penultimate syllable*) is responsible for the 'convex melodic curve'   in this Passion Sunday song from the neighbourhood of Příbor:

80

Ne-se-my Ma - ře - nu, pěk-nu, pěk-nu, pro-bě - le - nu
vo-le-ji sma-že - nu,

We're taking her out___ A pretty, pret-ty ___ wiz-ened witch ―
Roasted her in oil ___

A trait which Janáček considers characteristic of Moravian songs in general is the so-called 'Moravian modulation', that is, to the key one whole tone lower — a favourite in minor keys:

81

Fiddlers, fid-dlers are you play - ing, fiddlers, fid-dlers are you playing,
Mu - zi - kan - ti, co dě-lá - te, mu - zi - kan - ti, co dě-lá - te,

etc.

*) In 'standard' Czech it always falls on the first syllable.

114

However, as in most cases cited by Janáček, the modulation is in effect no more than an intermediary between the minor key and its shift up a third, so common in folk singing:

82

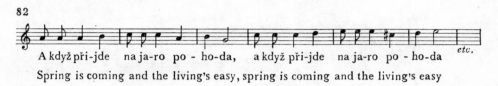

A když při-jde na ja-ro po - ho-da, a když při-jde na ja-ro po - ho-da *etc.*

Spring is coming and the living's easy, spring is coming and the living's easy

On the other hand, songs in major suggest rather the Mixolydian mode (with lowered seventh) than a modulation:

83

Ně - sko - ro, dě - ve - čko, ně - sko - ro li - tu - ješ,

Too late, my lit - tle girl, too late to be sor - ry

ach dy už na ru - kách dě - ťát - ko pě - stu - ješ.

Now that you're, in your arms, crad - ling a ba - by.

Janáček goes on to explain how folk songs were simplified when adapted for church use, and how accompanying instruments exacted melodic and harmonic changes. Some fiddlers liked one key, others another. Vladimír Úlehla, in his book *Živá píseň* (The Living Song), writes about what he calls the 'Moravian scale'—a melodic minor scale, identical up as well as down, starting and ending on the dominant (e.g. E—F sharp—G sharp—A—B—C—D—E). And then there were the special tunings of individual pipers' instruments, and the influence of the instruments of the typical village band: the first fiddle, *primo*, and one or two *contras* (fiddles), the double-bass (hung to a strap round the player's neck so that he could walk and play at the same time), the cymbalom, and the bagpipes, later replaced by clarinets. The possibilities of the bagpipe were limited. It had a relatively small number of 'free' notes (the pipers in their jargon called them 'flies') one of which, supported by the drone, tended to 'bend to itself all the other notes' (see Ex. 86). All these things caused the tonal simplification of the songs, the bagpiper playing either in 'the lower', which is the basic key (in Moravian bagpipes usually C major) or 'the higher', that is a perfect fourth above. On the other hand, the *primo's* florid embellishment of 'notes safely anchored in the melody' had the reverse effect of bringing the Slovácko folk singers to imitate the accompaniment by inserting their own vocal flourishes.

The methods of the village band are well illustrated by Janáček in the following *starosvětská* (old-time song) from Slovácko:

Young man, don't throw away,
Don't throw away your gold.
Once you have lost it all,
How will you get your bride?

At first, the fiddlers feel their way gingerly along, doubling the vocal line. But as soon as the words come to an end, the first fiddler strikes up a free interlude, paraphrasing the tune from as far back as he can remember—in this case, bars four to ten.

In the second verse the musicians gain confidence and play about with the tune, the leading fiddler richly embroidering it and again adding his interlude:

85

Finally, over the note A which has 'bent to itself all the other notes' (see
page 115), and 'like a shaft of sunlight piercing dark clouds', the piece is
brought to a bright conclusion in a major key:

86

Janáček's interest in the authentic instrumental accompaniments to folk
songs prompted him to write his piano accompaniments to Moravian folk
songs in a similar, though simplified vein. After the publication of the BOUQUET
he harmonized 15 probably in 1892, and about 1902 a further 38 songs
from the BOUQUET. All 53 were published under the title MORAVSKÁ LI-
DOVÁ POEZIE V PÍSNÍCH (Moravian Folk Poetry in Songs). In the meantime,
Janáček wrote in 1898 another collection, UKVALSKÁ LIDOVÁ POESIE V PÍS-
NÍCH (Hukvaldy Folk Poetry in Songs), 13 songs with piano accompaniment
dedicated to the Hukvaldy Circle called 'Pod akátem' (Under the Acacia Tree).
A year later Janáček arranged six of the songs for mixed choir especially for
the singers of his native village. The 1949 edition of them bears the title
Ukvalské Písně (Songs of Hukvaldy).

As Janáček's harmonizations differ considerably from those of other Czech
composers, for instance Vítězslav Novák and his school (Václav Štěpán and
Ladislav Vycpálek, although each of these have their own very personal
approach), they are worth examining more closely.

117

Before doing so, however, it is necessary to remind the reader that Czecho-slovak folk songs are divided into three main groups according to the three regions from which they originate. In Bohemia, a country hemmed in on three sides since time immemorial by the German element, and from the beginning of the Luxembourg dynasty in close cultural contact with France and Italy, the music, in spite of its originality, is Western European in feeling; its pre-vailing diatonic major and minor and its metric symmetry corresponds to the active, uncomplicated, optimistic, orderly mind of the Czech people, which found its most eloquent expression in the works of Bedřich Smetana.

In Moravia, especially in the east and south, (partly due to less influence from foreign culture) much has been preserved in the songs from the time when this region was the centre of the Great Moravian Empire. The frequent appear-ance of Greek or church modes besides bars and phrases of uneven length, give the Moravian songs something in common with Russian folk songs and church chant. Moravia together with Silesia in the north may be said to form a musical bridge to the East.

Finally, there is the highly original folk music of Slovakia, containing elements of an oriental character which were brought there from Hungary and even seeped through, by way of Slovácko, to some parts of Moravia. Thus the Czech songs are characterized by a prevalence of the major scale, while the songs of Slovakia and Moravian Slovácko present variants of the minor scale; examples are Úlehla's 'Moravian scale' (see page 115), or the Dorian scale with raised fourth (A—B—C—D sharp — E—F sharp — G—A) used by Vítězslav Novák to give some of his compositions their Slovak colour, or the 'Gypsy scale' — harmonic minor with raised fourth (A—B—C—D sharp — E—F—G sharp — A). This, combined with free rhythms, romping entries crashing in with heavy upbeats or joining in with groups of ornamental notes, and then the nostalgic prolongation of the end, is carried further in Slovak than in Moravian songs. It has nothing to do with church monody, being derived from Oriental influences which, however, are in complete agreement with the *genius loci*— the temperament of people living in sunny, wine-growing surroundings.

The origins of Moravian folk songs are closely linked with those of Slovakia on the one hand and of the Haná region on the other; the Haná songs, in turn, are related more to the Czech and Silesian songs (the latter again influenced to a certain extent by the songs of Poland). Janáček, as an arranger of folk songs, found himself with an exceptionally rich field of activity, and although he was never again to use actual folk songs in his own compositions— except in three cases where the use was justified by symbolism—he continued throughout his life to be preoccupied with them. His efforts to reproduce the authentic accompaniment perhaps account for his arrangements being so remote from the conventional style of harmonization used by earlier arrangers, or from the over-sophisticated one which is an easy trap for modern arrangers to fall into. Nearest to Janáček in this field was Vítězslav Novák, who also noted down Moravian folk songs in their natural surroundings. It was in 1897 that he was introduced to Janáček in Brno by one of Janáček's successors at the Beseda Choral Society, Rudolf Reissig, and the acquaintance was renewed the following summer at Hukvaldy.

118

Vítězslav Novák's accompaniments are also an attempt to reproduce the original folk instruments, for instance the cymbalom with its arpeggios and the fiddles with their embellishments of the tune. However, whereas Novák varies the accompaniment of each verse and inserts short interludes derived from the song itself (as well as adding some introductions and conclusions), Janáček, even in his later collections, always leaves the accompaniment the same for all verses, seldom writes interludes and hardly ever introductions or conclusions. From this it might appear that his only concern was to exemplify bare types, yet he treats his own folk-like songs in the same way, for instance the chorus *Daleko široko* (Far and Wide) and the bridesmaids' song in JENŮFA, Kudryash's song from KATYA KABANOVA, and Harašta's song in ADVENTURES OF THE VIXEN SHARP EARS. However, there are in these instances never more than three verses, and in the first example a long interlude removes any possibility of monotony. This cannot be said, though, of the otherwise lively and amusing folk song *Svatba komáři* (The Mosquitoes' Wedding, MORAVIAN FOLK POETRY, No. 49) where the same four-bar phrase is repeated unaltered ten times. Since every other time this phrase has to serve as an end to a verse of the text, a cadential differentiation of the harmony would be welcome. Janáček's self-restraint in this matter is all the more difficult to understand since the folk musicians, as he himself explained, did exactly the opposite.

Another controversial point in Janáček's arrangements is his harmonization of modes in a modern way (all the more surprising since he makes a prolific and effective use of modes in the most Moravian of his operas, JENŮFA, where, for instance, a passage in the Phrygian mode occurs between the verses of the chorus in folk song style, *Far and Wide*). He does not harmonise the Lydian beginning of the folk song *Sirota* (The Orphan, MORAVIAN FOLK POETRY, No. 34), as Lydian, say for instance:

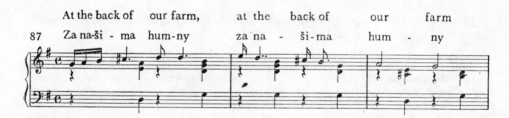

but, in fact, interprets the raised fourth at the beginning as a modulation to the dominant D from which he modulates back to the tonic G, in the following manner:

119

Janáček justifies this by stating that 'As to the key, they (the village band) play in an entirely modern way; major or minor.' Nevertheless, on the same page of FOLK SONGS OF MORAVIA NEWLY COLLECTED he quotes a harmonic scheme which he heard the musicians of Velká using to accompany the song *Před vaší je zahrádečka* (In front of your house there is a little garden):

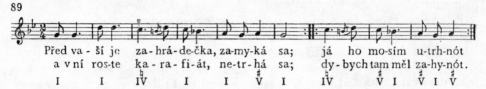

89

Před va - ší je   za - hrá - de - čka, za - my - ká   sa;   já   ho mo - sím u - trh - nót
a v ní ros - te   ka - ra - fi - át, ne - tr - há   sa;   dy - bych tam měl za - hy - nót.

I   I   IV   I   I   V   I   IV   V   I   V   I   V

Your house has a little garden which is kept locked;
There grows in there a carnation which is ne'er picked;
That carnation must be mine
Even if I were to die.

To remove any doubts he adds, 'The remarkable thing was the major triad accompanying the C in the third and seventh bars,' that is to say, the Dorian subdominant C major instead of the normal C minor, and this without the melody leaving no alternative to the musicians.*)

The many peculiarities of Moravian folk songs certainly cannot be explained away by the modes—for some of the melodies really modulate. On the other hand, many of the older songs came into being at a time when the modes were in general use and should therefore be harmonized accordingly. This does not mean that there is no intermediary type, neither modal nor strictly diatonic in feeling—moreover, even fastidious arrangers of folk songs, and Novák is no exception, often prefer nowadays to at least end their arrangements with a conventional cadence.

Janáček does not bind himself to any 'authentic' method of accompaniment,

*) Janáček's point of view is contradicted by another collector of Slovácko folk songs, Vladi-mír Úlehla, who says, 'The harmonies used by the musicians of Strážnice were never character-istic of gypsy music. Modes were never discarded in favour of the common major and minor.' (*Living Song*, p. 184). The names of the modes were naturally unknown to the peasants (even Berlioz admitted that it was a musicologist who pointed out to him his use of modes in *L'Enfance du Christ*) but they had their own way of referring to them, as for instance 'playing in the thin key' (p. 55), and they used to tune their bagpipes in the Lydian and Mixolydian modes (p. 220). In any case Janáček himself, in his later collection MORAVIAN FOLK SONGS for piano, harmonizes a song (No. 2) which is almost identical with *The Orphan*, keeping this time to the Lydian mode:

I'd like to sing a song from the top of Javorina

90   Keď si já za - zpí - vám   na vrch Ja - vo - ri - ny,

and rightly so, for arrangements which set out merely to imitate the folk players, cannot be any more successful than those of an 'urbane' fashion (whether conventional to the point of banality or, on the contrary, artificially ingenious). To elevate realism to a higher level, it is necessary to recreate or convey above all the spirit of the song in all its varying moods, and in pursuit of these ends, no suitable methods of composition should be renounced even though peasant musicians were not consciously aware of them (such as motivic work, imitation, pedals in different parts—although bass pedals were, of course, known to pipers). Janáček, writing on this point in the introduction to MORAVIAN FOLK POETRY (and also in the preface to the two-volume Janáček—Bartoš collection) says: 'For some songs the only accompaniment is the wind with all the living voices of trees and bushes, empty fields of stubble or succulent green grass; songs which require neither bagpipe nor cymbalom nor fiddles with their embellishments. What an unlimited source of ideas for accompaniment!' Later he said of his own methods: 'I find a characteristic figure of the song and with this I harmonize it—accompany it.' He follows this method mostly in his later collections, for instance in the song *Na slatinských lukách* (The Meadows of Slatina) in his TWENTY-SIX FOLK BALLADS *(Dvacet šest balad lidových)* where the entire accompaniment is worked out from an embellishment of the first bar (or half-bar):

Accompaniments similarly worked out are to be found in Nos 4, 7 and 8 in his SLEZSKÉ PÍSNĚ (Silesian Songs) of 1918 or in as early a collection as his MORAVIAN FOLK POETRY—for instance in the song *Pomluva* (Calumny, Vol. II, No. 33). No. 25 in the same volume, *Budíček* (Reveille—meaning the kiss with which the lad wakes his sweetheart) boasts a canonic accompaniment:

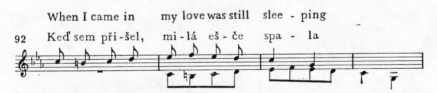

Janáček shows himself to be a commentator as well as a collector by the titles, some of them humorous ones, which he gives to these songs. Some of the titles are taken from the Bartoš collection and were possibly invented by Bartoš, some from Sušil's large collection. It is interesting that in his later collections Janáček called the songs by their first lines—which makes them easier to look up—or else simply numbered them. An original touch, typical of Janáček the commentator, is the occasional word-painting, as for example in the figure suggestive of galloping in the song *Koníčky milého* (My Lover's

Horses, Bartoš II, No. 18) or the hooting owl in THE ORPHAN (bracketed notes in Ex. 88) almost identical with the motif from ADVENTURES OF THE VIXEN SHARP EARS to the words in the marriage scene 'If you knew what I've seen', or in the love scene of the third act; and even in *The Little Night Owl Kept Hooting* from the piano cycle THE OVERGROWN PATH.

Janáček's work as an arranger of folk songs played an important part in awakening his Moravian awareness and in the development of his personality as a composer. He himself once gave a reason for spending so much of his time on folk songs, in an article entitled 'The Music of Truth' (*Lidové noviny*, 16 December 1893), in which he said: 'In this way I purify my musical thought.'

(14) Journey to Russia

It has already been stated that Janáček achieved full artistic self-realization by identifying his personality with Moravian peasant life and by studying the traditional songs, dances and customs of his native province. The position of Moravia in the original unified Slavonic culture, with its language written down and promoted by Cyril and Methodius, has also been explained. It was therefore inevitable that Janáček, in his search for the roots of this culture, should sooner or later undertake a journey to Russia.

The idea had been maturing in his mind for many years. He had begun to learn Russian while still studying with Skuherský and, characteristically, he had originally intended to study in St Petersburg, although it was partly his admiration for Anton Rubinstein, both as pianist and composer, which had prompted him to go there. His desire to know Russia, 'the mother of all the Slavs', as he put it, was further increased by his friendship with Dvořák, who was giving expression to his own Slavonic sympathies in his *Slavonic Dances* and *Rhapsodies*, his *Legends*, his opera *Dimitri*, his *Dumkas* and, to a certain extent, in his oratorio *Saint Ludmila*. Janáček's younger brother, František, had settled in Russia (St Petersburg) and it is not surprising that the future composer of KATYA KABANOVA should follow him there. In 1896, an unexpected opportunity arose in the All Russia Industrial and Art Exhibition which took place in Nizhny Novgorod in the summer of that year.

On Saturday 18 July Janáček left Hukvaldy and travelled through Studénka, Bohumín, Warsaw, Grodno and Vilno, reaching St Petersburg on 20 July. At the end of the first day he wrote in his copy of *Russian in Nine Lessons*: 'Twelve o'clock at night, *Granitsa*. At last the feeling of a Slav state. What lads these railwaymen! Clean, tidy, obliging, polite. Throughout Galicia I was depressed. Now I am jubilant: awaking, resurrection! I shake off slavery. Russia, here I come!' In Warsaw he made a further entry: 'The first sounds of folk music: a whistle from where horses are grazing.' In St Petersburg, where he spent a week, the future composer of ADVENTURES OF THE VIXEN SHARP EARS went to the zoo (as he did later in Berlin and in London) where there was an open-air theatre, which he also visited. During the days which followed he saw two cathedrals, St Isaac's and Kazan, where he attended an ordinary Russian Orthodox service and a service for the dead. He went to Pavlovsk and the islands of Yelagin ('an enchanting resort') and Krestovsky. On 23 July he noted: 'The sea, the sea! A vast surface spilt over with silver meets the blue sky in the far distance! A dark circle on the left and on the right cuts off the sea from sight. St Petersburg disappears behind me, it has sunk into the steel-grey sea.' He reminisces: 'Four hundred years ago, a Hussite captain, Jan Čapek of Sány and Hukvaldy, stood on this coast and he and his soldiers filled their flasks with sea water which they took back to Hukvaldy as proof that they had reached the sea.' Janáček also 'bashfully' filled a bottle with sea water and took it back to the Hukvaldy school.

On the night of 27 July he went to Moscow and the next day (again travelling by night in order not to lose a single moment) arrived at his destination—the famous old town of Novgorod. He found the ethnological part of the exhibition, insofar as it concerned the ethnology of Russia, disappointing, but was compensated by 'the beautiful Central Asian section showing also Russian contacts with Central Asia.' 'What do I see! A travelling Russian school for the far-away Asian regions. How proud and happy I am to think that a Slav nation is also spreading culture.' Although Novgorod fascinated him ('It is beautifully situated... more striking than St Petersburg') with its 'forest of masts at the junction of the Volga and the Oka,' he had that night to return to Moscow where, on 29 July, he visited the Kremlin. 'God, a fairy-tale! Those lovely blues and greens of the towers snuggled together. The inside—the wonderfull view: from here Moscow is a sea of towers—1600!'

With a heavy heart he began his return journey that same evening, travelling through Smolensk, Brest, Warsaw and, after a detour to Częstochowa, arrived home in Hukvaldy on Saturday 14 August after exactly two weeks.

Fourteen days is much too short a time to cover such a distance. He went to only one concert (dedicated to Rubinstein's memory), and there was no opera during the summer holidays. Neither did he meet any Russian composers who were away for the summer and who seemed to him, 'an unknown man', to be 'magnates'. But he eagerly absorbed the sounds of Russia, which he heard on the quays and in the market places. How thoroughly he understood the mentality of the people he saw there, was to be revealed later in some of his operas.

On his return to Brno he founded a Russian circle, with Dr Veselý and the publisher Joža Barvič, and turned his energies to studying the language which he soon spoke fluently and in which he wanted to compose a whole opera.

A few months before going to Russia, Janáček wrote HOSPODINE POMILUJ NY (LORD HAVE MERCY UPON US), a church composition which is so impregnated with the spirit of the music of the Russian Orthodox Church, that it is difficult to believe that he wrote it before his journey. The work is a paraphrase of the oldest Czech trope *Hospodine pomiluj ny*, attributed to the tenth century bishop, St Adalbert. It is set for a quartet of solo voices, two mixed choirs, organ, harp, three trumpets, three trombones and two tubas. Thus they comply neither with the Russian Orthodox tradition (purely vocal) nor with Witt's reform. However, this is compensated for by the use of orchestral instruments (including the organ and the harp) in an almost psalmodie way and in the character of a litany repeating single notes or chords, mostly a 6/4 chord which Janáček considered to be harmonically independent and with which he begins and ends the composition. All seven verses use the opening theme of the first verse in imitation:

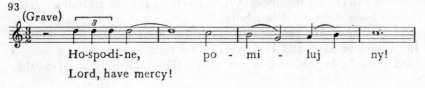

93
(Grave)

Ho-spo-di-ne, po - mi - luj ny!
Lord, have mercy!

124

Janáček does not use the oldest known version of this melody, but more or less that used by Dvořák at the beginning of the third part of his oratorio *Saint Ludmila,* although the joyous mood of Dvořák's setting is very different from the constraint of Janáček's work. (Another Dvořákian influence might be said to come from the psalmodic choruses of his opera *Dimitri.*)

The monotonous intoning which passes from group to group suggesting a multitude of worshippers, combined with the slow gradation falling back to pianissimo and the mystical-sounding insubstantiality of the second inversion chords make this an original and striking work. The dynamic and harmonic climax on the words *Dej nám všem, Hospodine, žizň a mír v zemi* (Give to us all, O Lord, life and peace on earth) is perhaps somewhat too reminiscent of the Faith motif in Wagner's *Parsifal* in its descending sequence.

The significance of this work (first performed on 19 April 1896 by the mixed choirs of the Teachers' Training Institutes in Brno, with Janáček conducting) lies in the link it forms in the chain of Janáček's 'Slavonic' sacred music, which begins with his harmonizations for Lehner's hymnbook and continues, in 1901, with THE LORD'S PRAYER, leading eventually to the GLAGOLITIC MASS. It is also his first religious work in which he allows himself to treat the subject in a less impersonal manner than before.

However, a more independent subject offering wider possibilities of treatment was necessary to enable Janáček to give full expression to himself in this field. For this he found a poem by Jaroslav Vrchlický, to which he composed his cantata AMARUS completed in the spring of the following year, 1897*).

It is the story of a young monk who pines away and dies of longing for love and life, a theme which was bound to captivate Janáček because of the special bearing he felt it to have on the circumstances of his own youth. He admits as much in a letter written in 1924 to the teacher and choir-master František Linda, where he says, '*Amarus*? The Queen's Monastery of Old Brno, the gloomy corridors, old church, gardens, my poverty-stricken youth, loneliness and homesickness—Amarus himself knew them all only too well. Vrchlický's words contain all the longings of youth. In them spring and youth meet.'

Amarus (meaning 'bitter, acrid'), compelled to become a monk because of his mother's wrongdoing and subsequent local prejudice, implores God one moonlit night to reveal to him the hour of his death. An angel whispers in reply: 'The night you forget to refill the lamp before the altar.'

Years pass. One evening Amarus sees two lovers praying in the church. Forgetting that he was about to pour oil into the sanctuary lamp, he follows the couple out of the church, as if hypnotized, and sees them in a secluded corner of the churchyard embracing under flowering lilac. In the morning the monks find the perpetual light extinguished and Amarus lying dead on his mother's grave.

---

*) Not 1898 as stated by Helfert in *Pazdírek's Music Dictionary*. This is proved by a letter dated 8 June 1897 in which Vrchlický writes to Janáček: 'I am convinced that you have succeeded in it (AMARUS) entirely', and also from a criticism of a vocal work, the title of which is not mentioned but which can be no other than AMARUS, written by Dvořák at Janáček's request on 21 May 1897. Incidentally, in the same year 1897, this poem was set by another Czech composer, J. B. Foerster, as a melodrama.

Janáček's setting is in five movements. In the first (in A minor) the clarinets and cellos play a measured, melancholy accompaniment (1a) to the main theme (1b) which begins in rebellious mood. However, on reaching the trill on its culminating A, it seems to sink in resignation like a wounded creature and falls in a solo arpeggio to its low, soft concluding notes as if presenting the tragedy of Amarus in a nutshell:

The first movement, in which the narrator is partly the baritone solo and partly the mixed choir, is joined to the second movement (in A flat minor) without a break. The last two bars of the first movement anticipate the following nostalgic tune (to the words 'He was tall, pale and always lost in thought') on which the second movement is based:

This movement contains Amarus' entreaty to God (in the tenor solo) and the angel's reply (first in the soprano solo, and, later, in the choir which alternates canonically with muted trumpets under a high harmonic pedal in the cellos).

The interval of several years which elapse before the fateful day is indicated by the formal separation of the third movement which is in ternary form. The first and third sections grow from these two motifs (bracketed):

which—especially the lower, chromatic variant—seem to foretell the fateful resolution, while the lyric tunefulness of the middle section:

describes the happiness of the lovers. Typical of Janáček, and here dramatically justified, is the transference of the part of the narrator at this point from the baritone soloist to the tenor one—the tenor solo having earlier represented Amarus himself in direct speech. The choir joins in with whispered but agitated repetitions of Amarus' words: 'There they sat, the happy ones.'

The fourth movement (in A minor) is again in ternary form. The first section is based on the narrator's motif (now back in the baritone) to the words 'Today Amarus left the lamp unfilled':

The second section is based on the melody to the words: 'There in the church yard he was lying on his mother's lonely grave':

In the church yard he was lying

The third section consists of an abbreviated orchestral reminder of the first, except for its conciliatory-sounding ending in major.

The final movement is unusual in that it is marked 'Marcia funebre' but is, in fact, in a major key (like its famous predecessor, the funeral march from Handel's *Saul*) and possesses a strangely exultant quality. In that it is surely unique. It leaves one wondering what Janáček had in mind. Does it suggest Amarus's joy on the verge of eternal bliss? Such sentiments were foreign to Janáček's philosophy. The need for contrast? This alone would not have satisfied him. In my opinion this movement (somewhat similar to the *Intrada* finale in the GLAGOLITIC MASS) may be interpreted as an epilogue in which Spring compensates the dead Amarus for what it was bound to deny him when he was alive.

It opens with a four-note ostinato in the bells and horns:

which is, in fact, a major version of the accompanying ostinato from the beginning (see bracketed notes in Ex. 94) with added triplets in the cellos. The ostinato continues in the central 'trio' where it is joined by a yearning spring-like melody:

101 *p dolce*

A hushed reminder from the choir, 'Amarus they called him':

102

ppp

which is based on the falling motif introduced originally by the orchestra (see Ex. 94, 1b), and the 'rebellious' motif (now quietened with mutes) with its arpeggio suggestive of resignation, bring the work to a conclusion redolent of an Old Slavonic service for the dead.

When considering the orchestration of the work, it is worth mentioning that apart from the operas, AMARUS is the only composition in which Janáček used the gong. It suggests a distant, sombre bell accompanying the words 'Next morning when the monks gathered for prayers, they found the sanctuary lamp extinguished.' The organ is not used at all and there is not the slightest suggestion of what could be called church-music style.

AMARUS was first performed by the choral society *Moravan* in Kroměříž on 2 December 1900, rehearsed by Ferdinand Vach, *Moravan's* chorus master and professor of singing at the local Teachers' Training Institute, but conducted at the concert by Janáček. Vach had refused to perform the work on account of inadequacies in the orchestra. Before this concert, Janáček conducted, on 20 March 1898, an otherwise unknown funeral march in Brno. It was, no doubt, the final movement of AMARUS, which it is possible to perform without a choir. In Kroměříž, neither the presence of an oboe player and a bassoon player called in from Brno, nor some exhausting rehearsals lasting into the early hours, could bring the local amateurs to master their orchestral parts. As Janáček recalled some years later: 'Oh, that I ever took up the baton to conduct AMARUS at Kroměříž! I regret it to this day. AMARUS floundered, butterflies flew out of the orchestra and choir...' And this in spite of the fact that, on Vach's advice, he had transposed the A flat minor first movement into the simple A minor. If this is true (as we can see from the traces of the seven flats scratched out in the manuscript of the first movement), Janáček must have decided that the transposition did not harm the work, since he kept to it in all his subsequent performances. Moreover, it strengthened the overall unity of it, since the final movement ends in A minor with a quotation from the opening of the work. As regards the difference of key between the first movement (A minor) and the second (A flat), this is not only smooth, but it may also be a deliberate device symbolizing the insurmountable conflict in Amarus's soul.

Be that as it may, Janáček's AMARUS seemed to be doomed to the same fate as its hero, since 15 years passed after the unfortunate première at Kroměříž before it was revived, or according to Janáček, 'before it was allowed to be performed'.*) The revival took place in Brno, conducted by Ferdinand Vach, with more competent performers than earlier in the small town of Kroměříž. In the meantime (in 1901 and 1906) Janáček had made some revisions, and AMARUS now took its place as one of his most successful works. Above all, however, it is the work which forms the link in his creative development between the early scenic works, RÁKÓS RÁKÓCZY and THE BEGINNING OF A ROMANCE, and JENŮFA. Naturally, his absorption by folk songs and folk poetry, ranging from his simple settings to the free inclusion of folk elements in his LACHIAN DANCES, helped to prepare him artistically for the composition of JENŮFA as far as the general milieu was concerned; but, more importantly, in AMARUS, the peak of his choral writing up to that point, Janáček showed himself ready to tackle in a mature way the innermost feelings and desires of an individual human being thrown entirely upon his or her own devices.

---

*) Stanislav Tauber: *Můj hudební svět* (My Musical World), p. 67.

(15) Preludes to 'Jenůfa'

In the meantime, however, Janáček wrote several works directly foreshadowing Jenůfa. The first is the piano composition Ej danaj, completed on 2 April 1892, although discovered only in 1948, which he wrote under the influence of the fiery Moravian dance of that name from Slovácko. In the main theme it is surprising to recognize the *odzemek* dance from the first act of Jenůfa: Even more surprising, however, is the appearance of the same melody in the not much later work for mixed choir and orchestra Zelené sem sela (Green I sowed, red I shall reap) which Janáček himself conducted on 20 November 1892 but which, once again, was rediscovered only after his death. In this work, the instrumental version of the tune:

alternates with this related one in the choir:

Green I sowed, red I shall reap,
Tell me, my lad, who's taking you from me.

which in turn is similar to the chorus *Far and Wide* in the first act of Jenůfa. The folk text leads to a further comparison with the two known versions of the folk song *Zelené sem sela* (one in minor, the other in major), which shows that Janáček's main motif, especially in its minor form as quoted in Ex. 103, is almost identical with the opening of the folk song in minor (Bouquet No.19).

Green I sowed, red I shall reap,
Tell me, my lad, who's taking you from me.

while the last two bars match the ending in the major version of the folk song (*Folk Songs of Moravia Newly Collected*, Bartoš—Janáček, No. 666):

106

Green I sowed, Green it grew
When my sweetheart Went away and left me.

In this way Janáček moulded the related thematic material of the two folk versions into a third, faster one, using the unaltered words of the song in minor which describe a girl's anguish at her parting with her lover. In JENŮFA, however, he was bound to develop the material farther, and to provide his more lively tune with more mettlesome words better suited to the dramatic moment. For this purpose he chose the words of the folk song *Far and Wide* (*Folk Songs of Moravia Newly Collected*, Bartoš II, No. 837.) With what unerring instinct he carried out the gradual conversion of this song, may be judged by the perfect homogeneity of the final version.

If these two works may be classed as preliminary studies for JENŮFA, the male-voice chorus VÍNEK (The Garland, 1893) could be classed as its parallel, dealing with the Jenůfa—Števa drama. But even judged on its own merits, VÍNEK is one of Janáček's most powerful choral compositions. In it he uses not only the folk poem, but also the folk melody in its entirety. Apart from the fact that Janáček himself indicated that PLOUGHING, THE GARLAND and THE EIDERDOWN were folk songs, not even he could have produced a song of such old-time ingenuousness as the following Mixolydian melody:

107

Up on the Bruntál hillsides   And his little sweetheart —
There is a lad sowing peas.   She's driving home the cows.

Such borrowing from folk material enabled Janáček to show how a folk song can be shaped into an entirely individual work of art or even into a miniature drama.

The first verse follows the folk original and even imitates the peculiarities indulged in by folk performers by giving the first phrase (moderato) to solo tenor.

131

The second verse begins similarly ('She closed the gates'), but the next words ('She wept bitterly: I wish I had never known you') are set in Janáček's own individual manner, enlarging the accompanying figure E—D sharp into a touching new 'legato dolce' melody:

which then suddenly modulates from C major (by means of a sequence with the parts inverted) to the remote E flat major, thus illustrating the emotional content of the words. Almost before the choir concludes the girl's sighing words they are overridden by the first tenors with the swaggering words 'He flung down four hundred, flung it on the table' which are set to the original melody including the subsequent words 'For you, my sweetheart, for your love!' While the lad (a true forerunner of Števa) is drunkenly repeating his cynically 'magnanimous' offer, it is now the girl's turn to break in with 'You could fling down three times more, nothing can repay the green garland that's gone.' These words are then repeated in a yearning dolcissimo with a captivating modulation to a 6/4 chord of B flat major, returning through D flat major and the dominant ninth of A major back to the original key. The closing words are reproachfully repeated in a stabbing rhythm.

There are two further compositions which are particularly closely connected with JENŮFA. Both may be said to reproduce the Jenůfa—Laca drama. They are the male-voice chorus ŽÁRLIVEC (The Jealous Man) and the symphonic poem ŽÁRLIVOST (Jealousy). The chorus was finished on 14 May 1888 shortly after the opera ŠÁRKA. As already mentioned, Janáček sent it off to Dvořák asking for his opinion and it was only discovered in 1940 by Otakar Šourek among Dvořák's papers. The symphonic poem was finished on 31 December 1894 as the first part of JENŮFA. Janáček originally intended it to be a 'real' overture and a literally programmatic one, as he made clear in his article 'The Introduction to Jenůfa' which he published on 10 November 1906 to coincide with the first concert performance of ŽÁRLIVOST in Prague conducted by František Neumann.

Both works are based on the brigand's song *Na horách, na dolách* (In the hills, in the valleys) which Janáček knew from Sušil's collection, which he included in his BOUQUET (using the title *The Jealous Man*) and which he later harmonized for his collection SONGS OF DETVA (TWENTY-SIX FOLK BALLADS). In it a wounded brigand begs his girl to hand him his 'glistening sabre'. He wants to see in it his cheeks growing pale. She complies with his wish but, suspecting treachery, jumps out of his reach. The brigand, dying, then admits:

'Whoever gave you that advice
Loved you truly.
I would have cut your head off
Rather than let another love you
When I am gone.'

In the chorus THE JEALOUS MAN, Janáček uses only the most dramatic parts of the poem. He contracts the original 12 verses into three large sections. The first (in 3/4 time) describes, in indirect speech, the situation. The second section is a more vehement 6/4 with more marked rhythm, and it describes the actual action. The third section, the music of which is identical with that of the first section (except for the end) forms both the girl's and the brigand's epilogue. The chromaticisms of the first and third sections, with their daring enharmonic modulations, are descriptive, firstly, of the sufferings of the wounded man and the girl's compassion, and later, of her trembling after her narrow escape from death; this is effectively contrasted with the clear-cut robustness of the middle section and the brigand's last words.

In the overture JEALOUSY there is a quotation from the chromatic melody of the chorus:

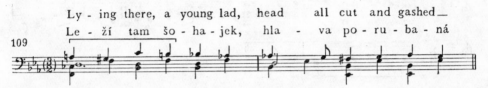

together with two quotations from the original folk song, the first of them a highly unsymphonic one:

and clearly the source of the terse brass motif accompanied by five strokes on the kettledrums:

with which the overture opens in minor and equally abruptly ends in major.

It may seem surprising that no overture is ever printed in any of the editions of JENŮFA. The reason is not far to seek: musically, the inclusion of this overture would anticipate the prelude proper with something dangerously similar—both pieces are in 6/4 time, both marked 'Allegro' and both are in a minor key. On the other hand, the similarity between the ballad and Laca's act of jealousy, by which he disfigures his loved one's cheek in order to make her repugnant to Števa, is, no doubt, characteristic. However, despite these thematic relationships with the folk ballad and with Janáček's choral song, and despite the care with which details of tone-painting have been carried out—in Janáček's own words 'the vexatious buzzing of troublesome flies' (using the motif from THE JEALOUS MAN quoted in Ex. 109)—the music cannot be said to describe the action of the ballad very clearly. Karel Kovařovic was quite right when he decided to omit the overture at the memorable Prague première of JENŮFA in 1916, though he did play it at a concert in Brno on 13 October 1917 during a tour of the National Theatre Orchestra. Kovařovic also did not hesitate to advise Janáček not to include the overture in the printed score, saying that musically it had nothing in common with the opera, except the title. According to a statement made by Janáček's pupil, Jan Kunc, who was present at the original Brno première of JENŮFA, the overture was not played even there.

Although it can hardly be made a component part of JENŮFA, it forms, like THE JEALOUS MAN, an interesting complementary work to the opera. On account of this and of many exquisite details, such as the moving harmonic progression of the coda (the last sighs of the dying brigand):

it deserves to be heard more often on the concert platform. In fact, works like these preliminary studies and parallels occupy a place of the utmost significance in the creation of Janáček's operas.

It is now time to turn our attention from these 'preludes' to the opera JENŮFA itself.

$\left(16\right)$ Jenůfa

There are works of art in which the creative effort, the boldness and novelty of the ideas, and the virtuosity of the technique are most admired; there are others in which the artist seems to express what has long been slumbering through the ages in the womb of eternity, works of art which seem to be giving a self-evident expression to nature, time and a people. Among the latter type belong Smetana's *Bartered Bride* and Janáček's JENŮFA, a tragic Moravian counterpart to Smetana's opera. (Max Brod aptly calls Janáček, 'Smetana in the minor key'.)

Yet it would be a mistake to suppose from the seemingly unpremeditated spontaneity of these two works that they flowed, ready-made, from the pens of their creators. On the contrary—just as Smetana reworked his *Bartered Bride* more than any other of his operas (although within a very short period), Janáček worked on JENŮFA (about 1894—1903) longer than on any of his other dramatic works, with THE EXCURSIONS OF MR BROUČEK as the only exception due to his troubles with the libretto.

The impression of freshness and originality in both operas does not come from creative speed and facility but from the perfection of the final result, from the ideal balance of the component parts: the form and content, the idea and the dramatization, the details and the whole, artifice and simplicity. This often gives the impression, in both works, of a merely superior form of folk art. In addition the choice of subjects, although fundamentally dissimilar, charmingly succeeds in capturing the milieu where national characteristics have been preserved in their most genuine form: the world of the country people. Moreover, in JENŮFA, apart from the folk element, there is (in the figure of Laca whose deprivation must have had autobiographical connotations for Janáček just as AMARUS had had earlier) a strong social element, combined with deep feelings of intimate understanding expressed in the moving figure of Jenůfa herself, through which Janáček poured out his love for his afflicted daughter, Olga. Here the three main elements of Janáček's inspiration are found united in their most complete form, and it is hard to tell which of the three is expressed more beautifully and sensitively.

This sudden attainment of creative unity—especially when compared with the two previous scenic works based on folklore—may seem at first to be inexplicable. And yet—as has been pointed out—the birth of JENŮFA had been heralded since as far back as the summer holidays of 1875 when Janáček came into contact with the folk music of Strážnice, Velká and other places for the first time. This is evident in his small-scale choral 'dramas' on folk subjects, such as THE THREAT or THE SOLDIER'S LOT. During these years he began jotting down the melodic curves of speech which later became known as his *nápěvky*, speech melodies. He was also collecting and harmonizing folk songs and dances which led to the LACHIAN DANCES, the SUITE FOR ORCHESTRA and, eventually, to those works which may be classified as 'preludes' to JENŮFA. Then there was his journey to Russia, his old hymn LORD HAVE MERCY, and the semi-autobiographical AMARUS. Even the weaker works such as RÁKÓS RÁKÓCZY and THE BEGINNING OF A ROMANCE played their significant part in enabling him to discard some evident errors. Thus it only needed such an impulse as the story of Moravian peasant life by Gabriela Preissová to set in motion all Janáček's creative powers, all his pent-up experiences, his conscious and subconscious sources of inspiration which combined to produce this great and original work.

It is not known exactly when Janáček first came across the play by Gabriela Preissová (1862—1946) produced under the original title *Její pastorkyňa* (Her Step-Daughter) first in Prague on 9 November 1890 and, later, in February 1892 in Brno. Perhaps it was first brought to his notice at a lecture which Gabriela Preissová gave in January 1891 at the Vesna Society about her plays from Slovácko peasant life. From dates jotted down in Janáček's copy of the play, it may be assumed that he had read the first act, at the latest, by 18 March 1894, the second act by 17 January 1895 and the third by 11 February of the same year. According to another note made in his copy of the play, however, it is evident that the overture JEALOUSY had been completed by 31 January 1894 and it may be assumed that before that date he had known the whole play from seing it performed and that, while reading it, he was already thinking about the libretto.

Unfortunately there are very few dates concerning the course and especially the beginning of the composing of JENŮFA. When, in 1917, Otakar Nebuška was preparing the second edition of the vocal score, he asked for some details in this respect from Janáček who replied in a letter written on 22 February 1917, which is so characteristic of him that it is given here almost in full:

'Dear Friend,

Here is everything that can be found out from the old manuscript of JENŮFA:

1) My copyist, J. Štross (once an excellent oboist at the Prague *conservatoire* when D. Weber was the director) put in nothing except the date he finished the first act of the vocal score; but I rubbed it out. I do not know why.

2) The copyist finished the second act of the vocal score on 8 July 1902.

3) The third act of the vocal score he finished with the words 'end of opera', 25 January 1903, 3.30 p.m.

I write the full score first and then make a vocal score; the work of the full score was therefore finished earlier. Between the first and second acts there was a long pause. I was working with František Bartoš on the folk songs published by the Czech Academy (FOLK SONGS OF MORAVIA NEWLY COLLECTED).

Our maid (!) remembers that during her second year with us I began composing JENŮFA. That means in 1896. For me, composing was then a matter of stealing time. Being choir-master and organist, teacher of music at the Teachers' Training Institute, director of the Organ School, conductor of the Beseda Society concerts—my daughter on her death bed—and having to live; it all made composing difficult and little of it was done. That is also why I remember only with difficulty.

There might be a date hidden somewhere in the first copy of the score: I cannot lay my hands on it. The original score I do not have at all.'

A further, although equally elusive clue, is an unsigned article (most probably by Janáček himself) in the programme for the Brno première, in which stress is laid on the novelty of the use of prose, pointing out that although the French composer, Alfred Bruneau, used prose in 1897, Janáček had done so on his own initiative guided by the principle of truth as revealed in the melodic curves of speech. And that the French composer preceded him only in the date of performance, since, in 1897, the score of JENŮFA 'was already in the process of being copied.' 'In the process of being copied' are the operative words here—they clearly referred to the first act.

Dates concerning the composition of the second and third acts are more exact and, according to a speech melody which Janáček wrote down on the envelope of a letter from his daughter Olga, dated 30 December 1901, it may be presumed that he did not begin composing the second act until November or December 1901. On 17 April 1902 he wrote to her at St Petersburg where she was visiting her uncle, František Janáček, and where she was to fall fatally ill: 'I work as much as possible in order to finish the second act before the summer holidays.' And in a further letter headed only 'Sunday, 6 p.m.' and, according to Helfert and judging by other circumstances, written either on 14 or 21 July 1902 he reports to Olga: 'Just finished the second act.' At the end of his copy of Gabriela Preissová's play he wrote: '18. 1. 1903, third week of my poor Olga's fearful struggle with death. It is finished.' And there is another note in pencil: '9. 11. 1902 Sunday'—perhaps the date when he began to write the third act. All the dates referring to the composing of JENŮFA fall on a Sunday—probably the only day of the week when Janáček overburdened with work could, except when he worked at night, concentrate on his composing.

Thus at last a truly Moravian national opera came into being which is, at the same time, the peak of Janáček's entire operatic production. If he called ŠÁRKA 'a passionate introduction', JENŮFA is passion itself. The parallel between Laca's act of jealousy and that of the brigand in THE JEALOUS MAN who would rather have killed his sweetheart than leave her to someone else, has already been pointed out. Other figures in the drama behave no less passionately than Laca—even humble little Jenůfa, seduced by the reckless Števa; even the stern Kostelnička who kills Jenůfa's child believing she will thus save the honour of her step-daughter. Let us glance at the synopsis:

Act I. A hot summer afternoon disturbed only by the sound of the mill-wheel represented by the 'icy-toned' xylophone. Jenůfa waits anxiously for her Števa, sometimes gazing in the direction of the recruiting station from which he is due to return, and sometimes at the millrace, imagining the water to be whispering where her shame will lead her 'if her lad has been conscripted into the army'.

Yet she gives others so much happiness: with shouts of joy and waving a crumpled copybook over his head, the shepherd boy runs 'down the steep slope'*) delighted that 'at last he can read: Jenůfa has taught him.'

---

*) As described by Gabriela Preissová, this is more apt for a shepherd boy than Janáček's direction, making the boy run out of the mill and back again.

Števa's step-brother, Laca, who has been cutting a switch with his jack-knife and jealously observing Jenůfa's anxiety, suddenly pulls her kerchief over her impatient eyes. Soon the good foreman of the mill announces that Števa has not been recruited.

Then Števa himself comes arm in arm with the recruits and obviously having had too much to drink. To Jenůfa's timid reproaches he brags about his mill and the posy he has been given by another girl; yet he drags Jenůfa into the dance which becomes more and more wild.

Suddenly an elderly woman with stern features, wearing the dark dress of a widow and until now unnoticed, comes forward and stops the merriment with a single gesture: she is Jenůfa's step-mother, called Kostelnička because she is the warden of the little church (*kostel*) and represents the highest moral authority in the village.*) Ignorant of the fact that Jenůfa is expecting Števa's baby, Kostelnička seals her doom by forbidding Jenůfa and Števa to marry until 'a year of trial' during which Števa must remain sober.

Jenůfa, left alone with Števa tries to make him realize his obligations. Števa assures her that he will never 'leave it at that', praising with lewd obstinacy her 'rosy cheeks' while waving in front of her the posy from another girl, until the old grandmother comes and leads him away to bed.

Laca, who has been watching the whole scene, picks up the love token that Števa has let fall and makes fun of Jenůfa, but when she challenges him with the words 'Števa will always be a hundred times better than you' and refuses to buy the posy from him for a kiss, Laca in a fit of jealous rage slashes her 'rosy cheek'—evidently her only attraction for Števa. Immediately he falls in desperation at her feet, clasping her knees, and a nearby servant-girl tries to explain everything away as an accident. But the foreman does not need to declare the fleeing Laca guilty: 'You did it to her on purpose.' He is running away from himself.

Act II. Jenůfa who in the meantime has given birth to a son, has been ordered by Kostelnička to stay for many months hidden behind closed shutters,**) while everyone is told that she has gone to Vienna to work as a servant.

---

*) For a clarification of the somewhat complicated family relations of the main characters in Jenůfa the following 'authentic' family history is taken from the original play and the later novel of the same name, *Her Step-Daughter*, by Gabriela Preissová:

Old mother Buryja has had two sons (both dead before the action of the opera begins); the elder of these, the miller, married a widow with one son, Laca (Ladislav) Klemeň, and with her had a son, Števa (Stephen). The younger brother, Tóma (Thomas), a spendthrift, had, by his first wife, a daughter Jenůfa (Genevieve), and after his wife's death married Kostelnička, whose name then was Petronila Slomková. Thus Jenůfa is in fact the step-daughter of Kostelnička, rather than her foster-daughter; Laca is Jenůfa's step-cousin and also the step-grandson of old mother Buryja. Števa is Jenůfa's cousin and the grandson of old Buryja. Under these circumstances Števa naturally enjoys more privileges—the entire mill will one day be his—while Laca has only a small inheritance from his own father.

In Act I Jenůfa has, for some time (since the death of her uncle, the miller Buryja), been lending a helping hand at the mill. In Act II she is 'at home' with Kostelnička, i.e. in the lonely cottage by the river in which (and not in the millrace) Kostelnička drowns Jenůfa's illegitimate child.

**) Although outside shutters are unknown in Slovácko (they would hide the stylized flowers

At last Kostelnička asks Števa in and begs him to marry her step-daughter 'according to God's Law'. But Števa has lost interest in Jenůfa, now deprived of her beauty, and becomes more and more alarmed by the severe Kostelnička who hates him more than ever before since she must debase herself in front of him. Besides he has become engaged to Karolka, the daughter of the rich village mayor.

Laca, on the other hand, is now more and more insistent in asking Kostelnička for Jenůfa's hand in marriage. But he momentarily wavers when Kostelnička tells him that Jenůfa 'a week ago gave birth to Števa's son',*) Kostelnička then blurts out that the child has died. Caught in her lie and tortured by false family pride, she is driven to drowning the child, telling Jenůfa that it died while she lay for two days in a fever. Jenůfa, shattered and bowed down with shame, accepts the offer of the high-minded Laca. Kostelnička gives them her blessing, cursing Števa and his future bride. But she is haunted by the curse of her crime and her blessings change to shrieks of terror when the moaning wind forces open the window 'as if death himself had peeped in.'

Act III. Wedding 'merry-making', though, for Kostelnička, far from merry, is in progress during a morning in late winter. She is still more haggard than in Act II and supports herself and her gnawing conscience only with the utmost effort. The catastrophe is now at hand. As she lifts her hands in order to bless Jenůfa and Laca before they leave for the church, shouts are heard. Men from the brewery, out cutting blocks of ice, have found a baby, frozen solid, with a red cap on its head. The last words are enough to make Jenůfa realize that it is her child, 'Števuška' (Little Stephen), and send her tearing through the crowd heedless of Kostelnička's imprecations, while Števa, whose own wedding is set for a couple of weeks later, watches petrified. Laca drags the deathly pale Jenůfa indoors, thinking she is merely raving but she guilelessly admits that the baby is hers, and only the fearless intervention of Laca saves her from the fury of raised fists.

At this moment the guilty Kostelnička comes forward confessing her murder of the child, begs Jenůfa's forgiveness and resignedly gives herself up to the law, while the shallow but still unspoiled Karolka renounces Števa.

Jenůfa leads her step-mother compassionately to the door and then asks Laca to leave her to her fate, but Laca, infected with her bravery, takes her hand in order to lead her into a better life. Only now does Jenůfa feel that she knows true love, 'the greater kind which pleases God'.

This is the action as it takes place in the opera, that is to say with the few cuts and additions made by Janáček. In Act I, for instance, he left out the scene in which the village mayor is scolded by his nagging wife—an incident

---

painted round the windows), shutters are set into the windows from inside. When Kostelnička asks Jenůfa at the beginning of Act II, 'Why do you go praying to the shutter?', she means the Madonna hanging, according to the author's note, near the window (which at the same time enables Jenůfa to peer through a crack in the shutter and see whether Števa is coming or not).

*) In spite of this, he is not anxious, like Števa, to escape. Kostelnička misinterprets his questions as a refusal.

which would have endangered his authority as an officer of the law in Act III. In Act II he left out the unnecessary scene of the peasant woman Kolušina and, in Act III, transformed her into the needy but faithful *pastuchyňa,**) a beautifully conceived character of an ordinary woman; and he made successful cuts throughout the dialogue.

Janáček's own additions are the song at the arrival of the recruits, 'Everybody's getting married', with its typical ♩♪ ♩♪ rhythm in the accompaniment of the village musicians and with its original folk words, although it is only an echo of the original folk melody. Janáček replaced Gabriela Preissová's 'song for Jenůfa' by his own fiery song, clearly based on the folk song *Far and Wide***) — perhaps too daring for the chaste Jenůfa. Similarly he replaced the *skočná* dance prescribed by Gabriela Preissová with the more locally typical and virile *odzemek* dance. He also provided his own melody for the bridesmaids' song in Act III to folk words given by Gabriela Preissová. An important addition (apart from the choral interjections, for instance, 'What a hard woman she is!') is the quartet with chorus in Act I, 'Every couple'.

These alterations improve the dramatic impact of the story. In fact, without these touches (which gradually matured in Janáček's mind) and the musical setting, the work could scarcely have become as popular as it did. This in no way diminishes the very original contribution and merits of the librettist.

Gabriela Preissová, *née* Sekerová, was not Moravian by birth. She was born in 1862 in Kutná Hora in Central Bohemia and moved to Slovácko only after marrying, at the age of 28, an official at the sugar refinery in Hodonín. It is therefore surprising that she was able in less than a year to acquire a working knowledge of local dialect and life as is shown in *Her Step-Daughter*. In spite of remaining a romantic idealist (although reared on the influence of the Russian realists) she created in *Her Step-Daughter* a gallery of characters that could hardly be more real, and a story that could not be truer to life.

This makes it possible to refute the accusation that Janáček was indulging in *verismo*. I will not deny that this drama, taking place as it does in the most passionate part of the land rich in wine, is, not only of all Janáček's operas, but of all Czech operas in general, the nearest to verism, if only by its southern atmosphere. Števa, with his liking for girls and wine, with his alternate boasting and helpless timidity, is like a fair-haired counterpart of Turiddu in *Cavalleria Rusticana* which Gabriela Preissová may well have known, at least in its famous short story version or as a straight play by Giovanni Verga.***) But irresponsible Turiddus and seduced Santuzzas exist outside Sicily, and realism was certainly not born only with Italian verism. Janáček's musical verisimilitude also is southern in temperament and contains some typical veristic traits as, for instance, the insistent repetition of a note or chord, or

---

*) *Pastuchyňa* — female inhabitant of *pastuška*, originally the village shepherds' cottage, in more recent times the communal poorhouse.
**) See p. 130 ff. of this book.
***) *Cavalleria Rusticana* was first produced, as a play, with Eleonora Duse in 1883, and, as an opera by Mascagni on 17 May 1890 in Rome — only a few months before the play by Gabriela Preissová.

the heavy accentuation as in Ex. 115. However, such instances may already be found in Verdi whose work was certainly known to Janáček. Janáček in any case had no need to bring such effects from Italy: Slovácko provided him with sufficient examples.

It may be said that both the music and the action of JENŮFA touch the limits of endurance (as is the case later, in a rather different sense, in THE HOUSE OF THE DEAD), even if some of the grisliest moments take place off-stage or are only recounted (the drowning of the baby in JENŮFA, the torture of Petrovich and poor Akulka's life story in THE HOUSE OF THE DEAD). There is nevertheless this fundamental difference between *verismo* and Janáček: Janáček's drastic scenes never become aims in themselves. It is sufficient to compare the finale of JENŮFA (or any other of Janáček's operas) with the finales of these veristic operas: whereas the verists (in contrast also to Verdi!) abandon us under the fresh, raw impact of the catastrophe, one could almost say, with a knife still in the victim's back, Janáček heals all wounds with a liberating, uplifting catharsis.

Janáček is sometimes blamed for his principle of the melodic curves of speech, put into practice independently for the first time in Jenůfa (see Introduction). It is now known that he never succumbed to the dangers of mere naturalism and mosaic-like disjointedness. Even his most ordinary jottings were no mere 'photographic' reproductions of speech, because each of them contains a scrap of his own personality, perception and experience. Time and time again he probed to the core of a word, releasing hidden treasures of musicality and proving himself to be a unique master of the art of drawing out, within the space of a few bars, or even a few notes, undertones of poetic beauty in both language and music.

How much real music is contained in Janáček's speech melodies is proved by their thematic and associative possibilities, as has been pointed out in the Introduction. Many of the secondary themes in JENŮFA, as well as the single Leitmotiv of the opera, are developed from melodic curves of speech; this Leitmotiv, progressing throughout the work, might be called the 'theme of guilt'.

In scene 5 of Act I it appears in this conciliatory guise:

113 JENŮFA

Du - ša mo - ja, Šte - vo, Šte - vu - ško!

My love, my heart, Šte - va, . Šte - vu - ška!

Earlier, it appears in a quicker, distraught rhythm, suggesting the wild pangs of Jenůfa's conscience. But in Act II it underlines the fear of the guilty Števa that he would have to meet Jenůfa face to face, and in Act III it is used in a low, dark register to accompany Kostelnička's 'Oh, what torture, sleep gives me no rest, I must keep awake and somehow live it through.'

Besides this Leitmotiv, there is another Leitmotiv element showing some interesting dramatic and psychological variants. It is a run of four descending notes derived once more from a melodic curve of speech—Kostelnička's horrific 'Look, look at her—Kostelnička' in Act II, just before the murder of the child. It re-emerges later in the Act in the ponderously wretched yet hopefully diatonic quavers to Kostelnička's words 'Let me bless you, may God keep you...' accompanied in the orchestra by the same notes almost joyfully speeded up to semiquavers:

114

At Kostelnička's words referring to Števa, 'Woe to him and me', it changes again to a moaning chromatic figure which reappears in Act III at the moment of consternation over the drowned baby in a piercing chromatic staccato in the trumpets.

In this connection I would like to point out the extremely touching reminiscence in the cor anglais of Števa's declaration of love to Jenůfa in Act I. This reminiscence accompanies like a quiet reproach her sigh in her monologue in Act II ('Števa has not come yet, and he will not come') which, at the same time, is an example of the power of music to underscore the text symbolically. It would be unwise not to make full use of such possibilities.*)

Another of Janáček's peculiarities in connection with the melodic curves of speech, especially in JENŮFA, is the frequent repetition of words or even whole sentences, and it is interesting to note that while Janáček was often reproached for his principle of the melodic curves of speech as being naturalistic, he was also blamed for these repetitions as being antiquated formalism. Any unbiased listener will admit that in JENŮFA, where all the main characters are bowed down by the weight of their painful thoughts which would not leave them, these repetitions have a definite psychological effect.

However, the artistic reason for them is not only to be found in the sphere or expression, but also in the sphere of construction—because, as has been pointed out in the Introduction, Janáček set Gabriela Preissová's realistic drama, with only a few alterations, in prose and dialect—in the same way as Debussy wrote *Pelléas et Mélisande* to prose and Richard Strauss, *Salome*. However, Strauss and Debussy had the advantage of poetic prose unthinkable in a village drama. Because music needs a certain symmetry as a means of development and balance, and in vocal music especially, as a means or achieving a singable melodic line, Janáček used repetitions as a substitute for verses.**)

---

*) The same variant appears once more, most poignantly when Jenůfa sings 'I have neither wealth nor honour' at the end of Act II and, again, in her 'You see, Števa, this is your true love', in Act III. An equally eloquent reminiscence is the tragic reminder of Jenůfa's lullaby in her dirge 'He is dead' in Act II.

**) It is interesting to note that both Maeterlinck and Wilde (and long before them Shake-

The part played by this process in the building up of the melody may be clearly seen when the same phrase is visualized without its symmetrical completion. For instance, Laca's 'He sees no more in you than your rosy cheeks' in Act I, or Kostelnička's 'I was so proud of you'. However, the determining factor is always the expressive power of each phrase and its corresponding speech melody.

In any case these repetitions are not always mere duplications but often they bring a change of mood (as in Laca's 'You could have seen how much I love her' where, under the suspicious look of the foreman of the mill, his bragging breaks down into an unwitting, humble admission; or, on the other hand, it may build up a gradation of similar effect as in Laca's melisma at his third repetition of 'our wedding' in Act III: 'I asked Števa, it's only proper, to our wedding, to our wedding, to our wedding!')

There is another point on which Janáček deviates from all operatic tradition: whereas a 'proper' operatic composer sees to it that his sentences have as many masculine endings as possible,*) Janáček, throughout JENŮFA, has hardly any masculine endings in the voice parts, not even where the words make it possible; on the contrary, he almost always ends on an unaccented beat and even stops abruptly just before reaching an accented one. This avoidance of the safe port of heavy beats even at the beginning of a phrase (as in Jenůfa's pitiful 'There's going to be reproaches enough from mother...' in Act I, reh. No. 61) gives Janáček's music its own peculiar atmosphere of unfulfilled, choking emotion. It does sound disjointed to those unaccustomed to his music, but it is also the secret of his disturbing and exciting impact even on those who find him irritating. Janáček's music sometimes produces conflicting emotions in one and the same listener—but it never produces indifference.

From the harmonic point of view, JENŮFA introduces into Janáček's work an innovation which later became typical of all his music: the frequent use of church modes, which may also be called Slav modes, since they penetrated Slavonic folk music through the Greek Orthodox cult—mainly Russian and Southern Slav music but also, as has been pointed out, the folk music of Moravia. He particularly favoured the Dorian mode (minor, but with its 'optimistic' major sixth) just as his most cherished keys, D flat major and A flat minor, stand in Dorian relation to each other. For instance, the introductions to Act II and III begin in the Dorian mode, as does also the ensemble 'Every couple of lovers has some troubles to bear' (in Act I) which, however, ends in the Phrygian mode (with its flattened second degree). This, too, plays an important role in JENŮFA, for instance in Laca's 'You, Granny' at the beginning of Act I, in the ritornellos of the chorus 'Far and wide' also in Act I, in Kostelnička's 'Jenůfa, unhappy girl' in Act II (reh. No. 51) and in Act II's opening motif:

---

speare in *Othello*) achieve special effects by repeating whole groups of words in the form of a question. In Janáček's later choral works, MARYČKA MAGDÓNOVA, SCHOOLMASTER HALFAR and THE WANDERING MADMAN, repetitions of text are also used in the form of insistent questions turning the lines into dramatic dialogue.

*) See Otakar Šourek, *Antonín Dvořák*. The librettist, Jaroslav Vrchlický, complains when Dvořák demands for his *Armida* the maximum of monosyllabic words to end his verses: 'Where am I supposed to find them (in a polysyllabic language like Czech)?'

while towards the end of the opera the Mixolydian mode with its flattened seventh predominates. The whole-tone scale appears in Act II as an expression of the apathy of the tormented Jenůfa: 'But now, it is as if my life was ending' (rehearsal No. 93).

Needless to say, just as Janáček avoids the usual conclusion on an accented beat, he also avoids the 'Old Lady's embrace' of the dominant-tonic cadence. Nevertheless, dominant pedals, such as the dramatic 'Stone her' (in Act III), or dominant endings of individual scenes or sections are not absent, and it is a peculiarity of JENůFA that these harmonic functions are assigned almost always to the dominant of A flat (G sharp) which is the tonal centre of the whole opera. It makes its appearance before the opening phrases of old mother Buryja and Laca in Act I, twice before the recruits' song (note here the engaging diversion into C major in the repeat), while the xylophone pedal on C flat (the tonic third in A flat minor)—when it is changed into B (the dominant ninth in D) after Števa's departure—is an example of Janáček's beloved modulation by means of a pivot common to both keys. In Act II the dominant of A flat (G sharp) rules over the scenes between Kostelnička and Števa and, later, the end of the act in the presence of Laca, then in Act III the entrance of the village mayor or Kostelnička's 'How will it be, up there?' soon afterwards (two bars before reh. No. 10). There are many other examples. In some cases, however, the dominant is followed by the expected tonic as, for instance, at the touching moment in Act III (three bars before reh. No. 50), where Kostelnička falls on her knees to speak directly to God. But the conspicuous resolution of dominant to tonic as practised, for instance, by Richard Strauss in an almost wasteful manner is found in JENůFA only once—just before the very end of the work where its effect is then all the more impressive.

To extol the special musical charms of JENůFA would be superfluous and would mean quoting the whole opera. There are many highlights, from Jenůfa's opening prayer to the Virgin; the orgiastic dance of the recruits; the eerie introduction to Act II punctuated by sudden fortissimos; to the moving viola solo accompanying Jenůfa's caressing glance at her sleeping baby; the shattering end of Act II; the wonderful introduction to Act III which, if not played too fast, captures so well the mood of the 'merry-making' under the cloud of the events leading up to it; the bridesmaids' interlude, and the agitation on the discovery of the drowned baby followed by Kostelnička's confession; and the catharsis of the finale when heaven itself seems to be opening.

For all that was contained in his music, Janáček had to pay dearly. 'I would tie up JENůFA with the black ribbon of the long illness, pain and cries of my daughter Olga and my little boy Vladimír,' he said. The sad fate of little Vladimír, who might have inherited his father's musical talent, has already been mentioned. As for Olga—from her earliest days her parents feared for her life. Although she was not musically talented which, in the beginning, grieved Janáček, she was clever and possessed an extraordinary memory, which made her an outstanding pupil at school. From earliest childhood, she also showed an exceptional talent for the theatre, liking nothing better than to recite and act, despite her small voice. Her parents—so strong was the tradition in the Janáček family—wanted her to be a teacher, or at least a private teacher of Russian. 'But fate had its own terrible plan,' wrote Mrs Janáčková. In February 1888, when only five, Olga, as a result of many attacks of tonsilitis, developed rheumatism of the joints and pericarditis, both of which recurred in 1894. Although, after several months, she recovered, she was left with a weak heart and delicate constitution and much of the fun of childhood—running, skating, swimming—had to be strictly forbidden.

When she left school she began preparations with Maria Nikolayevna Veveritsa, a Russian living in Brno, for the state exams in Russian and she joined the Russian and later the French circles at the Beseda Society with her father, and attended the Vesna Society with her mother. She grew into a pretty, slim girl with long, copper-coloured hair and blue eyes, which, however, held a look of dark foreboding even when she laughed. Now that it appeared no longer necessary to prohibit her from dancing, she began to attend balls, but this was also to have its fateful bearing on her life.

On 11 February 1900, a ball was organized to celebrate the founding of a women's home, where Olga took part in the display of dances of the various Slav nations, her father conducting the orchestra. Among the dances were Chopin's Polonaise opus 40, a Czech polka and the Lachian POŽEHNANÝ and Janáček even composed specially for the occasion a SERBIAN KOLO and a RUSSIAN COSSACK DANCE based on a song sung to him by Mrs Veveritsa. During the evening, a young medical student, the son of Olga's former piano teacher, began paying her special atention to which she was certainly not averse. Her parents did not approve, however, and her strict father forbade her to see young Vorel. Olga, at first, could not forget him, not even when he left for Vienna to continue his studies. However, after a year and a half, she wrote to him to say she was breaking off all relations. The result was alarming. The frantic young man threatened to come and shoot her.*) It is not surprising that Janáček welcomed the suggestion of his brother František, who spent the holidays of 1901 at Hukvaldy, that Olga should go and visit him in St Petersburg. It was at the same time an excellent opportunity for her to brush up her Russian before her exams and despite the instinctive misgivings of his wife, Janáček left with Olga on 13 March 1902 for the distant town on the marshy banks of the Neva. A few days later he returned alone and all seemed to be well; but in less than two months a message came that Olga was in hospital with typhoid fever. She made a gradual recovery but in June had a relapse. Janáček, who was finishing the second act of JENŮFA, immediately left with his wife for St Petersburg. About seven weeks later—in the middle of July, Mrs Janáčková was able to bring Olga home. Her husband, who had

---

*) *Zdeňka Janáčková*, p. 63.

in the meantime returned to Brno, met them in Warsaw and they travelled straight back to Hukvaldy. During the journey, Olga's condition deteriorated and when they were changing trains at Studénka they were obliged to carry her. Her heart was failing her, liver and kidney diseases were disfiguring her slim figure, she had a new attack of rheumatic fever which prevented her from walking and in this state she once more reached her beloved Hukvaldy. At the end of the summer holidays she developed severe bronchitis. After her return to Brno where she was attended by Janáček's cousin, Dr Dressler, she recovered sufficiently to be able to set out for a short walk one sunny October day with her mother to a park in Brno. But after a few hundred paces she had to admit that she could go no farther. It was her last outing.

After a sad Christmas with his family, for which Olga was still able to decorate the Christmas tree, Janáček left for Hukvaldy to gather strength for finishing JENŮFA, and Olga was able to enjoy a visit from the old Schulzes. Soon afterwards she developed dropsy and could neither sit up nor lie down for pain. Outside it was Shrovetide once again, the time of carnival and another ball at the Beseda, and the silent night was disturbed by the merry rattle of carriages. On Sunday 22 February Olga was, at her own request, given the Last Sacrament by Father Augustin Krátký, who did not even allow candles to be lit for fear they might affect her breathing. 'In the afternoon we all sat round her,' wrote Mrs Janáčková. 'My husband had just completed JENŮFA. All the time he was working on it, Olga showed great interest. Now she begged him, 'Daddy, do play me JENŮFA. I won't live to hear it.' Leoš sat down at the piano and played. I could not bear it and left the room.' The following days were spent in leave-taking, of her friends, of the faithful Máŕa (the housekeeper Marie Stejskalová), and to each Olga left a small token of remembrance. Even the Schulzes were allowed to come from Vienna. At the request of the dying girl all the windows were thrown open so that she might breathe more freely. On Thursday 26 February at dawn, the rhythm of her breathing suddenly changed, and at 6.30 in the morning it stopped altogether. Olga died within sight of her twenty-first spring. On the following Saturday, the funeral procession, followed by the whole town, left the church of the Old Brno Monastery where Olga's father had begun his life in Brno. In April of that year, Janáček composed in memory of his daughter, who, according to his own words, was for him Jenůfa personified, a work for mixed-voice chorus and piano, entitled ELEGY ON THE DEATH OF DAUGHTER OLGA, a setting of Russian words by Mrs Veveritsa, and on the first copy of the vocal score of JENŮFA he wrote in Russian: '18. III. 1903. To you, Olga, in your memory.' Janáček's most famous work will carry the dedication forever.

(17) The First Battle for 'Jenůfa'

The writing of JENŮFA, especially the second and third acts, was undertaken under conditions of severe pain and stress. Nor did the skies clear even when the work was finished. Soon after its completion, Janáček sent the full score and the manuscript vocal score to the National Theatre in Prague—mainly because the Brno Theatre, with its incomplete orchestra and other limitations, had not the necessary artistic means at its disposal for producing such a work. After waiting a month for a reply, he wrote diffidently to Karel Kovařovic who, from 1900 until his death on 6 December 1920, wielded almost unlimited power at the opera of the National Theatre—diffidently ('I am afraid of writing to you') for a very good reason. Janáček was fully aware that Kovařovic would not have forgotten the biting criticism of his opera *The Bridegrooms,* composed when he was only 21, which Janáček had published in his paper *Hudební listy,* on 15 January 1887, not to mention Janáček's criticisms of Kovařovic's ability as a conductor. Kovařovic, on the other hand, had during his Brno season in 1885—1886 written warmly in the same paper about Janáček's jubilee concert with the Beseda. Kovařovic did not even reply to Janáček personally but in April 1903 sent a message through the director Gustav Schmoranz—not surprisingly in the negative and without giving any reasons. The refusal, although obviously dictated at least in part by personal motives, was a blow to Janáček's artistic confidence (according to Jan Kunc and Mrs Janáčková he 'wept bitterly', blaming himself for being no good).

There was now nothing for it but to leave the first performance to the small Brno Opera company which, however, was fortunately in the hands of Janáček's talented and faithful pupil, Cyril Metoděj Hrazdira (1868—1926), a fervent Moravian nationalist. (He himself wrote the opera *Ječmínek* (King Barleycorn) based on a Moravian legend and produced in Brno shortly after JENŮFA, on 3 March 1904.) JENŮFA was produced by Josef Malý and the sets were designed by the well-known Slovak architect, Dušan Jurkovič. The cast was such that the National Theatre itself could hardly have done better: Kostelnička—Leopolda Hanusová-Svobodová, Jenůfa—Marie Kabeláčová, Laca—director Alois Staněk-Doubravský, Števa—Bohdan Procházka, Old mother Buryja—Věra Pivoňková, the Foreman—Karel Beníško. In fact, Procházka, under his stage name of Theodor Schütz, and Pivoňková later became members of the National Theatre company and Beníško a member of the Plzeň opera house.*) On 8 October 1903 the management of the Brno theatre sent

---

*) Janáček praised Hrazdira's qualities as a conductor in a letter to Artuš Rektorys (18 Nov. 1907) in which he related how Hrazdira was obliged to leave the theatre suddenly in 1907 because of repeated conflicts with the soloists. Janáček admitted that Hrazdira was eccentric but made it clear that in contrast to his successor, Bedřich Holeček, he 'could not deny that

for the scores of JENŮFA and on 12 November rehearsals began. Almost at the last minute, during the first full rehearsal of Act I, the prospects for the first night 'were badly shaken' by an 'unpleasant quarrel between the director and the conductor' combined with a disturbance in the orchestra caused by one of the trumpeters who had drowned his sorrows too thoroughly in drink after being reprimanded, and whose insubordinate behaviour spread through the whole orchestra. But all this merely gave credit to the old theatrical super-stition that 'the more stormy the rehearsals, the more stormy the success.'

The reception of JENŮFA at its first night on 21 January 1904 in the modest Na Veveří Theatre could scarcely have been more enthusiastic. The composer, pale and exhausted, who followed the performance from the wings, was called after the first act and again after Act II. 'The dramatic crisis of Act III—the wedding day ending in the discovery of the murdered baby; the typically Slav confession of Kostelnička and the ending itself completed the success,' writes Jan Kunc. 'The applause was incessant. Janáček had to take curtain after curtain, as also did Gabriela Preissová from her box. The students cheered and led Janáček, borne on the shoulders of the soloists still wearing their costumes, to the Beseda Society where a party was held.'

The press also received the work with unreserved praise, especially the Brno critics, who recognized in JENŮFA the first realistic Moravian opera. The Prague press was also favourable, especially the influential Emanuel Chvála, critic of the paper *Národní politika* (National Politics). Strengthened in his belief in his own work, Janáček again wrote to Kovařovic on 19 February this time with more insistence and confidence: 'I am not basing my renewed request on flattering criticisms from the press of Prague and Brno. I am only deploring the injustice of your refusal of JENŮFA.

'I complain as a Czech composer who cannot get himself heard. Because of Moravian style of the work? This has been misunderstood. More for its highly important principle of individual naturism*) in the melody which, as has been seen, did not miss its effect, and met with understanding.

'The score naturally needed some adjustments. These I think have disposed of the objections that were made.'

Kovařovic in his answer of 3 March denied the accusation of being unjust and referred to 'very serious reasons' which, however, he did not specify. Yet he promised to come to Brno to see a performance. Janáček waited from one performance to another. The management sent altogether nine invitations to the mighty man who still did not come. Janáček, writing at this time, says 'The orchestra of our local theatre is getting more and more depleted.**)

Hrazdira conscientiously led the company to a high and definite goal.' And whatever he produced was given 'a true and fitting form'.
*) Janáček used the term 'naturism' here and at other times to counter the accusation of 'naturalism'. The term 'naturism' was already used by Alfred Bruneau, mentioned earlier, for his own realistic style.
**) Janáček wrote in a letter to Dr Jaroslav Elgart, an executive of the Brno theatre company, dated 31 July 1908: 'There were no flutes on the first night of JENŮFA, and, throughout, many of the orchestral colours were missing. Dr Hynek Kašlík mentions (in his 'Karel Kovařovic's Retouching of Janáček's JENŮFA'), that at that time the wind instruments were completed by

The new director, František Lacina, gave the horn and trumpet players notice because they were not needed for the summer season.' In his letter to the actress Hana Kvapilová, wife of the drama director of the Prague National Theatre, Janáček complains during April 1904, 'I never go near the theatre—I cannot bear to hear my work in such a state. What will a guest, who does not wish me well, think of such a performance?'

Not until the following season, on 7 December, did Kovařovic at last make the journey to Brno—only to persist in his negative attitude. But when soon afterwards he accepted and, in 1906, produced Josef Nešvera's conventional opera *Radhošť*, Moravian only in its mythical setting and costume, the editor of the Prague paper *Čas* (Time), Jan Herben, published an article on 19 October 1906 in defence of JENŮFA. (Jan Herben has already been mentioned in connection with Janáček for his collaboration in the magazine *Hudební listy* and the ballet RÁKÓS RÁKÓCZY.) Kovařovic remained unshaken, especially as his self-assurance had just been boosted by the fact that in the negotiations for the renewal of the contract between the board of sponsors and the National Theatre company, his name had proved to be the trump card. Not even the Prague performance of Janáček's overture JEALOUSY at a concert given by the Czech Orchestral Music Association on 14 November 1906 conducted by František Neumann (also a Moravian and at that time conductor of the Frankfurt Opera House) nor, four days later on 18 November, the performance of Janáček's new cantata LORD'S PRAYER given by the Prague Hlahol choral society conducted by Adolf Piskáček, could alter Kovařovic's attitude; perhaps because neither of these performances was quite successful. 'I was depressed by the performances of the overture and of the LORD'S PRAYER', wrote Janáček on 20 November to Rektorys.*) The performance of JEALOUSY lost much from mistakes in the newly-copied parts**) where important dynamic indications had been left out. And in the case of the LORD'S PRAYER, the conductor was so overworked that Janáček himself had, at the last minute, to take the final rehearsals.

Hrazdira in the meantime revived JENŮFA and on 25 September 1906 the Brno company performed it in Ostrava before giving it twice more in Brno in October. After that, indefinite silence followed—partly, no doubt, as a result of the change in conductors.

These many disappointments were incapable, however, of paralysing Janáček's creative energy. On the contrary, in order to be able to devote more of his time to composing, and, at the same time, to rid himself of the 'stultifying influence of chewing over the rudiments of music', he resigned at the end of October 1903 as a teacher of singing at the Teachers' Training Institute, and

members of a military band and that the strings were reinforced by amateurs. The casting of the singers was also soon to suffer from the fact that Marie Kabeláčová was ruthlessly given notice on grounds of ill health, and the part of Jenůfa had to be taken over by Růžena Kašparová, whose voice was too small for the part and who had originally sung the part of Karolka.
*) Artuš Rektorys, although closer to the Smetana camp, was from 1906 till 1919 the most loyal of Janáček's mediators in Prague and supported his efforts by starting, among other things, in 1906, a Moravian column in the music magazine *Dalibor*, of which he was editor.
**) This seems to indicate that the overture had not been performed in Brno.

asked to be pensioned off. He had ceased to be *regenschori* (choir-master) at the Queen's Monastery earlier (according to Mrs Janáčková's memoirs, as early as 1888, or in 1891 according to Metoděj Janíček's letter of 22 February 1917 to Otakar Nebuška). After a year's leave on grounds of ill health, he received his pension and might even have changed his post of director of the Organ School for something more important: directorship of the Warsaw *conservatoire*, at that time still Czarist. How this came to be offered to him is one of the mysteries of Janáček's life.*) Certainly the impulse did not come from Janáček but from the other side.**) And, not from the Poles but from the Russians. This is confirmed by Janáček's article in the Polish musical magazine *Muzyka* of May 1926, 'My Reminiscences of Poland—Two days in Warsaw', where he wrote: 'It was in 1904, late in the evening, when I arrived in Warsaw for the first time in my life.***) I had been invited by governor general Skalon... The *conservatoire* was in a state of strife, the cause being the line of study and the language to be used. As a compromise could not be reached, the Russians turned to me with the offer of the post of director. They mentioned their internal difficulties and the necessity of teaching in several languages.†) But these difficulties did not deter me... I was full of enthusiasm, eager to work, and I felt great sympathy for Poland and the Polish people as soon as I set foot in their capital on the banks of the Vistula. In the early morning I attended a meeting of the governors of the *conservatoire*. To my surprise I found them to be mainly military persons. I presented them with my plans both for teaching and for administration. The assembled gentlemen took note of what I said. Next day I was invited to talk privately with Skalon who probably wished to probe my political loyalty to Russia and the Russians.'

In this respect the choice could not have been better. At the same time Skalon thought Janáček acceptable also to the Poles, on account of his long-standing connection with the Polish musical world. As far back as 1886, Janáček had organized two concerts at the Beseda Society for the ten-year-old Polish pianist, Josef Hofmann, conducted by the boy's father, Kazimierz Hofmann, and in his magazine *Hudební listy* (Vol. III) he published regular surveys of Warsaw musical life by a Warsaw correspondent who signed himself -aa-. In addition, Janáček made use of his stay in Warsaw in 1902 to make contacts with local musicians and, as will soon be seen, had already been in touch with Polish art as a composer.

---

*) According to Adolf Vašek's *Po stopách L. Janáčka* (In the Steps of Leoš Janáček), p. 119, Janáček explained this to the composer Stanislav Goldbach as being the result of the success of his choruses during the Moravian Teachers' Choral Society's tour of Russia. This choir, however, did not go on its first tour of Russia until 1913.

**) This is evident from an undated letter written, no doubt, in 1904 to Mrs Kamila Urválková (of whom more later) shortly before the first night of JENŮFA, in which he tells her 'I have been offered the post of director in Warsaw. I asked them to give me time since I cannot think of anything now.'

***) This is not strictly correct as Janáček was for a short time in Warsaw in July 1902 when he went there to meet his wife returning with Olga from St Petersburg.

†) In particular, in the official Russian language, just as German was also used at the Prague *conservatoire*.

The final discussions were held about 1 May 1904, the day his beloved composer, Antonín Dvořák, died. This is what Janáček says about the affair: 'Warsaw: symphonic concert. Suddenly the conductor*) announces the death of Antonín Dvořák. The audience rise. The Hussite Overture is inserted in the programme.

'I missed my appointment with the governor general. I understood "at one o'clock" and it should have been at eleven. The Russo-Japanese war broke out,**) and I, instead of becoming director of the Warsaw *conservatoire*, remained director of the Brno Organ School.'

This was, however, the best thing not only for the Brno Organ School but also for its director. In the conditions prevailing at that time in Warsaw he would have found himself in too delicate a situation where he would not for long have been able to satisfy both sides.

Of more interest is Janáček's contact with Polish culture which opened a new phase in his participation in the musical life of Brno and also in the sphere of church music.

---

*) Emil Nikolaus von Rezniček (1860—1945), renowned German conductor and composer of Viennese origin who, for seven years, worked in Prague and later settled permanently in Berlin. Of his numerous works his opera, *Donna Diana*, first performed at the German Theatre in Prague (1894), was the most successful.

**) This had happened already on the night of 8 February of the same year!

$\left(\text{I}8\right)$ Sacred Music

In the spring of 1901 the committee of the recently founded women's home, where Mrs Janáčková and Olga were actively engaged, decided to stage a scenic version in the form of *tableaux vivants* of the cycle of seven pictures by the Polish painter Josef Krzesz-Męcina (1860—1934) entitled *Lord's Prayer* which had been lent to the governors (as reproduced by the Polish journal *Tygodnik Ilustrowany*) by a certain Brno teacher. Janáček was asked to 'make musical illustrations' to the pictures, which he did in May of that year. Thus what might be called an unintentional sacred parallel to Mussorgsky's *Pictures at an Exhibition* came into being—Janáček's LORD'S PRAYER for mixed voice chorus, harmonium and piano, rearranged in 1906 for organ and harp, the classic instrument of the psalms. Janáček originally called the work *Moravian Lord's Prayer*, but later deleted the word 'Moravian' since its only justification was the national fervour of the composer of the cantata.

LORD'S PRAYER was given, complete with the *tableaux vivants*, soon after its completion, on 15 June 1901 in the Brno theatre where it was conducted by Janáček and directed by Josef Villart of the Josef Kajetán Tyl amateur theatre group. The idealistic conception of Krzesz's seven pictures corresponding to the seven parts of the prayer was, beside being turned to realism, reduced to five *tableaux* by combining the first two and the last two. In the first (according to an explanation published in the paper *Lidové noviny* on the day of the first performance), 'the fervent prayer of a believing people mingles with the soft chime of the village bell'. This *tableau* begins with a canon which appears a little too early and, in fact, was composed and added only later. It is at the octave between the basses and contraltos, to the humble invocation:

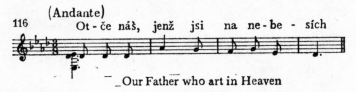

Our Father who art in Heaven

over a dominant pedal with an ostinato-like upward surge on the harp suggesting, perhaps, an imploring glance to heaven or the ascending smoke of incense; this leads to a bell-like motif, this time symbolically descending:

on which is built the middle section with its fervently insistent tenor solo

'Thy kingdom come'. This is followed by a shortened recapitulation of the opening without the voices, again on the expectant dominant of A flat on which it also ends. The second *tableau* ('Family with the child') introduces the words, first solo and then in the choir, 'Thy will be done' in a terse B flat minor and is (again symbolically, as if to express the single will) based on a single melodic idea expressing resignation to God's will. In strong contrast is the defiant conception of the following *tableau*. ('The villagers sing gaily in the field at the harvest. Suddenly a storm*) breaks and in one stroke all that has been achieved with toil and sweat is destroyed. Desperate cries to Heaven are heard as though the storm raged in the people themselves.') The prayer 'Give us this day our daily bread', pronounced by the whole choir and gradated over a restless ostinato figure to the pressing cries 'Bread, bread' is reminiscent of the massive scene in front of the cathedral of Basil the Blessed in *Boris Godunov* where the hungry crowd cries to its Czar with almost the same words—'Give bread, give bread', a scene which Janáček could not have known since it was neither performed nor published during his lifetime. In the fourth *tableau* ('Quiet prayers for the forgiveness of sins') which follows without a break, the words 'Forgive us our trespasses' are contritely presented mostly in solo voice and solo instrumental parts. The fifth *tableau* ('A tired mother overcome by lack of sleep leans over her sick child. A thief who has broken into the room stands behind her with hand raised to kill her.') contains insistent ostinato quavers in the basses:

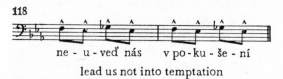

118

ne - u - veď nás   v po-ku - še - ní

lead us not into temptation

which suggest a warning against evil in ourselves and in others.

This too-seldom performed work lasting about 14 minutes reveals the meditative qualities of its creator and his ability to merge into one the Christian prayer and his own social feelings and human compassion.

In contrast to this work, the third *tableau* of which anticipates Janáček's social revolutionary period at a later time in his creative development, his other religious compositions of this period are purely ecclesiastical in character. They are VENI SANCTE for male-voice choir (in two versions) written about 1900, ZDRÁVAS MARIA (or rather, *Ave Maria*) for mixed choir, tenor solo and organ (also arranged for soprano, tenor, violin and organ or piano) and FOUR OLD CZECH SACRED SONGS from the Příbor Hymnal, consisting of the following Christmas carols: 1 *Slavně budem zpívati* (Rejoice and sing), 2 *Narodil se syn Boží* (The Son of God is born), 3 *Kristus syn boží* (Christ the Son of God), 4 *Prorokovali proroci* (The prophets have prophesied) in the Mixolydian mode. The first two are composed for three-part mixed choir, the others for four-part mixed choir. The AVE and the carols, both from about

---

*) A Brno addition.

153

1904, are closely related to folk music. The Ave Maria also anticipates in an interesting way certain motifs of the Glagolitic Mass, like for example:

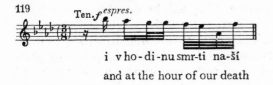

119

Ten. *f espres.*

i v ho - di - nu smr-ti na-ší

and at the hour of our death

Janáček's Unfinished Mass of the spring of 1908 offers an interesting glance into his creative workshop as well as his composition class at the Brno Organ School. Janáček's pupil, Vilém Petrželka, who discovered the fragment among his own papers and edited it, wrote a commentary to accompany its publication in which he says: 'Janáček's Unfinished Mass was not the work of his pupils but an example which he dictated to demonstrate how to set religious words. He advised us: 'Write Latin but think Czech'—a remark typical of Janáček in general and of his Unfinished Mass in particular. Among my papers and those of my fellow students I found a complete *Kyrie, Agnus Dei* and an unfinished *Credo* of which about two-thirds had been written.

'Every bar of this Unfinished Mass'—continues Petrželka—'exhales Janáček's dramatic powers and his power of brilliant invention, especially the impressive *Credo*.' Petrželka decided to complete the *Credo* and the three sections were then performed first with organ accompaniment on 7 March 1943 at the church of SS. Cyril and Methodius in Brno, conducted by Karel Hradil, and then, on 1 March 1946, in Petrželka's orchestration, by the Czech Philharmonic Orchestra conducted by Rafael Kubelík.

'The dramatic veracity', adds Petrželka, 'of Janáček's approach to the setting of the text of the Mass is best illustrated by his remarks as to programme and mood. Thus for instance, the *Kyrie* bears—instead of a tempo indication—the words 'in very sullen mood'. Janáček called the theme, sung by the choir in the *Kyrie,* 'the theme of anguish'. The orchestra brings in the motif of guilt—very softly, since guilt remains hidden deep in the soul. There is an interesting remark attached to the *Agnus Dei:* 'The concluding accompanying figure was directly inspired by a memory of chimes.' Another remark concerns the *Credo* which was 'developed from the speech motif of the words *Credo in unum Deum*—its shape remains always the same because strong and steadfast faith is always the same. That is why it also remains in major while only the harmony changes.' These few remarks show the keenness and depth of Janáček's inspiration.

Although these 'exercises' are interesting from the artistic point of view, they can hardly be called suitable examples for explaining the technique of composing a Mass to students—they contain even less polyphony than Janáček's secular compositions.*) And some of the soaring lyricism, for instance the Verdi-like or Berlioz-like passages such as the *Crucifixus* in the *Credo:*

---

*) 'The teaching of counterpoint and polyphony in general was rather poor at the Organ School,' says Jan Kunc.

154

does not even suit the words unless their sweetness should be taken as an expression of the loving self-sacrifice of Jesus Christ. The *Agnus Dei* is a precursor of the *Agnus* of the GLAGOLITIC MASS insofar as it is sung very softly by the choir *a cappella*. But it is, with its cursory treatment of the words *Dona nobis pacem,* too short, especially since it concludes the work. However, our thanks are due to Petrželka for publishing this fragment and Janáček's remarks and thus saving them from oblivion.

PART TWO (1903 · 1918)

(19) Teacher and Theoretician

Let us consider here Janáček's work in the fields of teaching and theory of music in general, especially since at this time his opinions were in the process of crystallizing.

Until 1903, his teaching was of two kinds. From early morning until four or five in the afternoon he taught choral singing, violin and organ at the Teachers' Training Institute, first for five, later for seven guilders per month; in the early evening he taught theory and composition at the Organ School. The former tuition with its 'constant chewing over the rudiments' he endured only to earn his living. Yet he threw himself into it with his customary sincerity as can be seen from his articles published in various magazines in which he discussed professional matters. For instance, in his article 'Základové, jimiž se řídí vyučování hudbě na slovanských průpravách učitelských' (Rudiments of the Teaching of Music in Slavonic Training Schools for Teachers) in *Cecilie* (1877), the then 'formalistic' Janáček argues that 'all pleasure is derived from proportion (relationships between pitch, rhythm and suchlike) and form, and in his article 'O vyučování zpěvu v I. třídě školy národní' (Teaching of Singing in the First Form of Elementary Schools), he gives the original advice that reading should be taught with the aid of singing. In his pamphlet 'Návod pro vyučování zpěvu' (Instructions for the Teaching of Singing) published in Brno by A. Píša in 1899, he says nothing about voice production—in this respect he adhered to the methods of František Pivoda—but expounds musical training from the point of view of rhythm and conducting, intonation, dynamics and expression. But even here it is incomplete in that it, for instance, leaves out ornamentation almost entirely. Even this book, however, bears on every page the stamp of Janáček's original personality as can be seen from the introduction entitled 'The Starry Sky' with this warning against the nebulous treatment of music:

'The Milky Way stretches over the heavens in a huge veil of glittering silver. The light of innumerable little stars merges to form a single shining sea. Only when the eye accustoms itself to the sight can it distinguish each small star twinkling with its own silvery gleam.

'Similarly infinite is the abundance of music. It envelops the mind of the layman in a dense fog like the rising waves of a storm and, before each particular note can be perceived on its own or in relation to other notes, much genuine teaching is necessary!'

For teaching performers Janáček made much use of the solo singing of folk songs (especially those from his BOUQUET) because above all he endeavoured to instil in the future teachers a love of folk songs which they would then pass on to the children in schools. Janáček always became most enthusiastic when lecturing on these two subjects—folk music and children.

The other type of music he chose was generally sacred music, with a marked preference for Liszt. He even arranged Liszt's Organ Mass for teaching purposes—for mixed choir and organ. As we have seen, he made his own contribution to all the different types of music: in the realm of folk music— apart from the BOUQUET—the mixed-voice chorus THE WILD DUCK; in the realm of sacred music, the offertorium CONSTITUES and his arrangement of the hymn LORD, HAVE MERCY UPON US; and in the realm of secular music, in 1877, THE FESTIVE CHORUS for the laying of the foundation stone of the new Teachers' Training Institute, performed on that occasion by his pupils.

Needless to say—just as the case had been with the Svatopluk Society and the Beseda Society—relatively few works were studied, but those very thoroughly.

Janáček was more in his element at the Organ School. There he was his own director and could more easily carry out his plans. From the beginning he had insisted that every student should acquaint himself with subjects other than his own particular speciality. And he himself, even after his sixtieth birthday, never ceased studying subjects connected even only marginally with music, for instance philosophy, psychology and aesthetics: he was an assiduous reader of the classic Czech aesthetician Otakar Hostinský, also of Wilhelm Wundt and his pupil Ernst Meumann (1862—1915), also Robert Zimmermann, Marie Jean Guyau (1854—1888) who stressed the sociological importance of art, Theodor Lipps and R. H. Lotze. And in phonetics he read the Norwegian Slavist Olaf Broch,*) P. Rousselot, the founder of experimental phonetics, and the Czechs Josef Chlumský, Antonín Frinta and the father of modern Czech philology Jan Gebauer.

Janáček went even further by endeavouring both to contribute to their theories and to formulate his own. If it is surprising that with all his teaching he still found time for such studies, it is even more surprising that besides his theoretical interests often passionately pursued, and his hobbies**) he still found time and the necessary freshness and naivety for composition.

But as Herbert Eulenburg says in his book *The Immortal Mortals* about Raphael, '*Naiveté* as part of a divine youthful strength which is either given or not to artists, cannot be changed, not even by all the learning in the world. It is a force that is active in an artist endowed with it, from early childhood until old age.' Janáček himself once said: 'It is feeling that makes a composer; not so much the scientific but the musical sort of feeling.'

There is plenty of evidence in his theoretical works that Janáček the musical poet and Janáček the musical theoretician very often came into serious

---

*) 'In Broch's Slavonic phonetics I like best his commentary on groups of phonemes common to all Slav nations. In these I see certain common emotional characteristics.' Janáček's article 'Ticho' (Silence), *Lidové noviny*, 26 August 1919.

**) One can certainly call a hobby his Hipp's Chronoscope which he obtained from Vladimír Novák, professor at the Brno College of Technology, and which he carried everywhere with him to measure the duration of *nápěvky* (speech melodies) 'to the tenth of a thousandth of a second' —surely only *ex post facto* and, therefore, approximately, since Janáček did not approve of recording speech melodies by prior arrangement.

conflict, and that the latter usually prevailed even in works whose title might lead the reader to expect communications of a truly revealing character. For instance, in the essay 'The Thought Processes Involved in Composing' (*Hlídka*, 1916), Janáček, with the help of complicated diagrams and cubes, illustrates the intensity and duration of a schematic harmonization of a simple *cantus firmus* and a straightforward setting to music of a short passage from the Bible by various pupils of his class, merely to prove that in this intellectual task, which in the case of the *cantus firmus* harmonization could not even be called composing, they were able to work quickest at the beginning and at the end of the exercise.

Janáček's purely theoretical writings are concerned mainly with harmony, since in this field he achieved, on the basis of his studies with Skuherský and the work of Helmholtz (*Lehre von den Tonempfindungen*), his most striking results. In 1887 he wrote a treatise on the 'Concept of Tonality', ten years later, on the 'Formation of Concords and their Progressions' and in 1912 he published *Úplná nauka o harmonii* (A Complete Harmony Textbook) which, in the second edition (1920) he supplemented with discoveries from Wundt's *Principles of Physiological Psychology* and their relevance to harmony.

The book is far from easily intelligible and Janáček confuses the reader unnecessarily by his notorious imprecision in terminology, giving different meanings to traditional terms and even inventing his own ones. What, to him, is a ninth chord is, in fact, a triad with an added ninth or an unresolved suspension; similarly an 'eleventh' chord is an unresolved suspended fourth over a triad with neither a seventh nor a ninth present; his 'thirteenth' chord is in reality a seventh with an added unresolved suspended sixth:

121

Similarly he calls the following progression:

122

that of a seventh chord followed by a sixth chord, whereas it is merely a resolution of a suspension. On the whole he almost always sees independent chords where there are only suspensions, and this seeming simplification becomes an absurd complication as it vastly increases the number of basic harmonies.

When teaching harmonic progressions, Janáček based his explanations on Helmholtz's finding that 'a tone, after its end, goes on sounding for a further tenth of a second in one-tenth of its original strength.'*) The lingering on of

*) Janáček's definition, as it appears in his 1876 autobiographical sketch. In his *Harmony* it is expressed somewhat differently: 'The continuation of the sound lasts up to three-tenths of a second, diminishing in one-tenth of a second to one-tenth of its original strength.'

the 'quasi perceived' sound of one chord mingles with the start of the sound of the next one—the actual 'perceived' chord—with the result that there occurs momentarily what Janáček called *spletna*—a tangle. Its unravelling, the' freeing of the new chord from the 'quasi perceived' sound of the preceding one lends chord progressions their beauty, gloss and character. To Janáček, the most important to look for was 'the effect of the tangle and of its disentanglement according to formal esthetic precepts.'

There are only two possible interpretations: he either meant the actual acoustic fading out, although the length of this phenomenon varies according to space, type of instrument, pitch and so on; in which case the mingling with the following sound when it does not belong to the same chord will result in an unpleasant rather than an exciting sensation; or else, he meant the continuation of the sound in the ear caused by the movement of the otoliths and other parts of the labyrinth. He says nothing about it in his texbook, but he did favour the second possibility in his article 'A New Trend in Musical Theory' (November 1894). In either case, however, he does not explain why the same effect should be produced (in a person possessing a musical imagination) when music is being merely read or when both chords are separated by a rest. Do not harmonic progressions have in this situation the same beauty, gloss and character? Do they not produce the same tension? At the beginning of Beethoven's *Coriolan* Overture, to take a simple example, the chords are separated not only by rests of more than three-tenths of a second's duration, but also in each case by two bars of neutral unison on C. This, far from diminishing the tension, increases it immensely by the almost agonizing postponement of the final resolution. The explanation is simply the continuation of the sounds in our memory, and neither rests nor a score heard only in the mind can prevent the impression of the 'tangle' in the inner ear. The theory presents nothing new as it is self-evident that in a sequence of two chords or only just two tones, the impression made by the second is dependent on its relation to the first and on their relation to the tonic (here memory plays a part even longer than three tenths of a second!), and on the speed with which they follow each other.

Even harder to concede is Janáček's assertion that the 'quasi perceived' sound in relation to the 'perceived' one explains why we expect a chord to resolve to a particular one—the mystery of the ear's demand, after, say, a triad on the fifth degree of the scale (the dominant), for a triad on the first (the tonic). The jump up of a fourth in the bass:

123

involves, according to Janáček, the simultaneous sounding of the 'perceived' note C sharp in the bass of the tonic chord, with the 'quasi perceived' note B sharp in the soprano. The resultant 'seventh' dissolves in an instant into the octave thereby completing what the ear has been asking for. Janáček takes care

162

not to say 'major seventh' for, indeed, a minor seventh has, as we know, the opposite tendency to fall. Moreover, the ear demands the tonic as soon as the dominant has been sounded, and not when the so-called 'tangle' takes place later. Neither is the harmony book methodically arranged. Many of the footnotes containing examples and formulae have no connection with the subject under discussion and, mixed into the text, are passages on conducting, giving, out of the blue, patterns for beating even time (p. 263) but omitting to give those for uneven time. In the section on modulation there is no mention of the basic principle of pivot chords common to both keys or at least to the intermediary keys. The speech motif ♩ is for him a theme.

Slá-va

Glory

On the one hand he overburdens the reader with too many complicated technical terms, on the other with esoteric, poetical explanations devoid of all technical definition. For instance, when discussing chromatically altered chords, he says: 'There are passages of lapidary harmonic plasticity deeply cut, of broadly secure tonality, passages of heightened tension before a cadence or after an interrupted cadence—passages which cannot tolerate musical wit, but whose depths are a repository of truth. It is in these passages that we find the bright luminosity of the dusky gloom of chromatically altered chords.' He even gives unconvincing or even faulty harmonic examples of his own.

However, the tangle theory makes the book extremely typical of Janáček, since the intersection of two or more impressions is one of the main characteristics of his music—a trait which is also found in Janáček the dramatist.

If Janáček's written deductions are unmethodical and hard to understand, one can hardly suppose that his oral teaching fared any better, although, by requesting his pupils to repeat *verbatim* each of his definitions,*) he enabled them to give mechanically satisfactory answers even when they did not know what they were talking about. When the student failed to answer correctly 'Janáček gave us no help, merely calling one after another from his seat and making him sit down again. If none could satisfy him he often ran all of a sudden from the room,' wrote Jaroslav Kvapil,**) one of his most talented students. Probably they had been guilty of no more than not being able to guess that the correct answer to the question 'How does this chord sound?' was 'Like the crackling of a fire.'***)

But Janáček became enthralling when he talked about music purely from the point of view of its expressive power. Pavel Haas, writing about his two years, 1920—1922, in Janáček's master-class for composition, tells us:†) 'He never talked much but often repeated his creed in order to become intelligible to everyone. His short sentences were often glaringly contradictory, and yet his powers of persuasion were as strong as his beliefs.

---

*) Jan Kunc: 'Leoš Janáček', *Hudební revue* IV (1911), p. 186.
**) 'Leoš Janáček, Director of the Organ School', *Hudební rozhledy*, Brno, I, p. 39.
***) Robert Smetana: *Stories about Janáček*, p. 91.
†) 'Janáček the Teacher', *Hudební rozhledy*, Brno.

'He crammed familiar feelings and impressions into completely new forms and made everyone feel they were being faced with new discoveries.

'His immense love of life and nature welled up with his every word.' Haas continues: 'He worked ceaselessly to instil into us his passionate love of folk music. He gave both classes and individual lessons. His classes were mainly devoted to lectures on phonetics and complex reactions, musical forms, opera, orchestration and other topics.*) Where he was in his element, his explanations were unique, for instance, his words became a rising tide when he talked about gradations—what new worlds were opened to our minds. On one occasion he spoke about a gradation which at the point of climax spills over into a single pianissimo note; an unstanchable flow of music heading for a chilly, terror-stricken moment.'

Occasionally, especially during individual lessons, he would be betrayed by his own erratic temperament. 'He would ruin, with thick, black criss-crossings, the wearying work of some scared young student and, next day, fly into a rage over his own illegible hieroglyphs and bring back to life notes which he had originally sentenced to death.'

Another quality which captured the hearts of his students was the sincere personal interest he took in their welfare. 'Janáček took care of us like a father,' to quote, once more, Jaroslav Kvapil. 'He knew everything about each one of us and, if we fell ill, he used to go to our digs**) to see if we needed anything— a rather awkward situation sometimes, especially if the illness was not serious enough to detain the student at home***), in which case there would be a row the next day at school and the culprit would be thrown out of Janáček's class—not for long, however. Janáček's tempers soon calmed.'

When he himself fell ill, he sent for the students to come to his house so as not to deprive them of their lessons. He even provided meals for the poorest of them.

As the years passed, his teaching at the Organ School began to wear him out. 'I am depressed,' he wrote to Kovařovic on 30 September 1918. 'I stumble around the school like a bumble-bee trapped between the double windows who cannot find its way out into the free air.' He could scarcely remain indifferent to the fact that most of his more talented students left to finish their studies with other composers, in particular with his greatest rival, Vítězslav Novák. Yet he bore them no grudge and each one was conscious of the debt

---

*) In the later years Janáček also taught opera composing—in 1920 he worked with the pupils of his master-class on the comedy *Dyevichy perepolokh* (The Girl Scamp) by the Russian dramatist Viktor Krylov (1838–1906)—an innovation and one of the most positive aspects of his teaching activities.

**) Or send his housekeeper Mářa (Marie Stejskalová) who faithfully served the Janáček family from 1895 until Mrs Janáčková's death in 1938.

***) Or—even more awkward—if the student was indeed detained at home but was caught there playing cards, as happened to František Rybka. But this one-time 'gambler' went on to settle in America and there become a distinguished organist who kept in cordial and fruitful contact with Janáček. Other students used to take advantage of Janáček's unreliable memory by showing him the same work twice or even more often. Janáček's memory was the cause why he almost never quoted his own themes in their correct shape or, at least, their correct key. For instance, in his article 'Scestí' (Crossroads) in *Listy Hudební matice*, Vol. 4 (1924), he misquotes the dawn theme from Act I of ADVENTURES OF THE VIXEN SHARP EARS.

they owed him since in spite of the dubious aspects of his teaching he endeavoured to draw out the personality of each student as much as possible. To be in daily contact with an artist of Janáček's stature was certainly an asset.

As in every music school, public concerts were part of the curriculum. And as the professors also performed at these concerts, Janáček was able to use these evenings for the premières of his own works; for instance, the cello composition FAIRY TALE.

However, at the turn of the century a new institution came into being in Brno which gave further scope to Janáček for performing his works (e.g. his PIANO SONATA, FOLK NOCTURNES and PIANO TRIO) and generally enabled him once again to take an active part in the burgeoning musical life of the city. Round the New Year of 1900, the architect Dušan Jurkovič and the builder Antonín Tebich (the owner of the very popular wine cellar known as 'Tebich's Den' at the back of the future Brno College of Technology) founded the Friends of Art Club consisting, from 1904, of three separate sections—music, literature and art. The first chairman of the club was the director of the Vesna Society, František Mareš, and Janáček soon joined forces with him, becoming a member formally in 1904. On 22 February 1909 he became chairman, a post he held until 18 February 1911 when he was succeeded by his fervent admirer, a medical man and developer of Luhačovice Spa, Dr František Veselý. The important part played by the club under Dr Veselý in propagating Janáček's work will be seen later.

Janáček continued to be highly influential in the Club even after he ceased to be chairman, despite the fact that his ideas were sometimes rather curious. Once, for instance, he suggested that the Club organize a chamber concert of Mozart's compositions with the performers (the Ševčík Quartet) in Rococo costumes,*) and when his pupil, Jan Kunc, prevented 'such a masquerade', Janáček, like a 'thundering god', peremptorily expelled him from the Club.

Janáček was particularly fond of arranging 'programmatic' programmes with one common theme. For instance, his SPRING SONG was not only performed on but specially revised for an 'Evening of Spring Songs' at the Club on 9 April 1905. The programme on that occasion (as indeed on similar other occasions) was not limited to one genre, since the idea was to give as much scope as possible to a charming visiting artist, the Russian violinist Elizaveta Shchedrovich. Similarly on 15 December 1907 the first performance of Janáček's FOLK NOCTURNES took place at an evening entitled 'Nocturne' which included two other works representative of the genre, Chopin's Nocturnes in B major and C minor.

This period of Janáček's renewed public activity is marked by his rare appearance as a conductor on 4 March 1909. The tenor, Stanislav Tauber, as one of the soloists who took part in this concert (as well as the soprano, Marie Calma-Veselá, and others), has recounted some delightful anecdotes which complete the picture of Janáček the conductor.**)

---

*) According to Vítězslav Novák who recounts the story in his *O sobě a o jiných* (About Myself and Others), p. 92.
**) Stanislav Tauber: *Můj hudební svět* (My Musical World), p. 68.

'Vach had prepared a performance of Gounod's Oratorio *Mors et Vita* with the enlarged choir of the Organ School.*) Before the end of rehearsals he fell ill. Janáček could not wait for his recovery and was loath to leave the work unperformed. He therefore decided to conduct it himself. He had apparently not wielded a baton for 15 years. The singers had the darkest forebodings and were also afraid of his temper. But they were mistaken. Janáček behaved with the utmost correctness at each rehearsal. If he was to appear before the public after 15 years as a conductor**) it would not be an ordinary concert but a 'festival'. All the former students of the Organ School were invited to take part in the choir and orchestra. They were given the music to take home and learn and young Klička, who had just won his laurels in England, was asked to play the harp.

'When we were having lunch together during the preparations, Janáček declared enthusiastically: "I want to have it big. There are four trumpets, but I will have seven."

'While nowadays the orchestra usually sits in front of the choir, on that occasion it was behind it and only Václav Klička was to sit with his harp next to the rostrum. The dress rehearsal was progressing peacefully when suddenly Janáček tapped his desk and ordered: "The harp alone, please." This was a surprise to us and Klička's face showed his evident distress. Didn't he know his part? The harp began alone and Janáček conducted for about 12 or 15 bars, then he stopped him. We waited for his criticism, but he only lifted his striking white head and called to the orchestra***): "Gentlemen, did you hear it?" "We did," they answered in unison. "Now, will you kindly play in such a way that you hear it again."

'In the same Oratorio, as sometimes happens during a long upsurging melody, the musicians were unconsciously adding an undesirable crescendo. After a few bars Janáček stopped them, but instead of telling them in the usual way, he said: "When a man walks uphill he breathes harder and harder. If he did not, he would be doing himself an injury. We will now do ourselves such an injury.'

The concert was a triumph for the conductor and yet it was Janáček's last public appearance on the rostrum.

---

*) Ferdinand Vach was at this time professor of choral singing at the Organ School.
**) This is not exactly true, for Janáček conducted the première of his cantata LORD'S PRAYER in 1901.
***) The band of the 8th Infantry Regiment.

(20) 'Destiny'

The rejection of JENŮFA by the National Theatre in April 1903 did not deter Janáček from making further theatrical plans. Without waiting to hear it performed he asked the Brno writer Josef Merhaut, in June of the same year, to make an operatic libretto out of his novel *Angelic Sonata*. This is the plot:

Hřivna, a young *ingenieur* and patriot, has been living in Brno for five years with his pretty and devoted wife who, however, is still childless. One of Hřivna's hobbies is open air photography. He becomes so obsessed with it that he takes pictures of anything he comes across. One day he takes a picture of a house near Brno, without noticing its seductive owner, a rich German woman, who is sitting in the garden at the time. The bored beauty, whose husband spends most of his time travelling, sends her maid to ask the unknown photographer to give her one of his pictures and in return promptly gives herself to him. Although Hřivna increasingly feels the emptiness of this love-making without love, he cannot resist hurrying back every evening to the passionate arms of his mistress. His wife soon suspects what is going on and a dramatic scene takes place ending in a complete break between the two. However, tormented by her conscience and gradually convinced that her barrenness makes her partially responsible for her husband's unfaithfulness, Hřivna's wife decides to make a pilgrimage to the church on the mountain of Hostýn (at the westernmost tip of the Carpathians in Moravia). Her husband, who has long since given up his empty flirtation, also decides to make the pilgrimage and, standing before the Virgin, he finds forgiveness. A new wedding night in the clear mountain air seals the reunion, and a child is subsequently born. After a year of complete happiness the baby suddenly dies and the feeling that this is God's punishment for Hřivna's unfaithfulness, which at one time affected the body and soul of the future mother and with it the health of the unborn child, throws a dark shadow over the couple once more. Once again the crisis is overcome by the wife's devotion, and the music (Angelic Sonata) affirms their solemn resolve to start a new life.

According to passages marked by Janáček in the book and according to his synopsis for Acts II, III and IV which he jotted down in his school notebook (Act I was to consist of the adventure with the rich German beauty), it is likely that apart from obvious social contrast between the destitute poor and the idle rich, Janáček was mainly attracted, according to Dr Theodora Straková,*) by the idea of the loss of the child which he himself had just

---

*) 'Janáček's Operatic Themes and Fragments', *Musikologie III*, p. 427.

167

experienced for the second time, combined with the theme of guilt, punishment and the urge for a public confession—so typically Slav—which had given
birth to the most striking moment in JENŮFA. He may also have seen part of
his own conjugal life in the story. In any case he took the story seriously and
even went so far as to visit Hostýn. But Merhaut was not interested in returning
to a work which he considered over and done with. Then Janáček found
a substitute subject straight from life when he was spending the summer
holidays of the same year (1903) at the spa of Luhačovice. There he met the
attractive young wife of the forest superintendent on the estate of a certain
aristocrat at Zaháje near Dolní Kralovice in Central Bohemia—one Kamila
Urválková.

'She was one of the most beautiful of women,' remembers Janáček excitedly
— a man in his seventies*). 'Her voice was like that of the viola d'amore. The
watering room at Luhačovice was in the full glare of the August sun.

'Why did she walk about with three glowing roses and why did she tell the
story of her young life?

'Why was its end so strange?

'Why did her lover disappear without trace?

'Why is it that, to the other, the baton is a dagger?

'A work of tearful drift and of womanly diction. It was given the title
Destiny—Fatum.'

Originally it was to have been called Red Roses—perhaps an allusion to the
roses which started Janáček's acquaintance with the mysterious beauty**),
also The Star of Luhačovice—as a tribute to Mrs Urválková, or also, Blind Fate.

Another, no less mysterious hint of a story from life which was giving birth
to the new opera, may be found in a letter written by Janáček on 9 January
1917, 12 years after the completion of the work, to the poet, František Serafín
Procházka, when they were working together on the libretto of THE EXCURSIONS
OF MR BROUČEK. Wanting to add to DESTINY an overture which would bear
a similar relation to it as JEALOUSY bore to JENŮFA, Janáček asked him to write
sa motto a romance approximately as follows: 'Two young people fall in love
with each other. She rich, he poor, an artist—a composer. They do not succeed.
She is married off to a rich farmer.

'He avenges himself by exposing her in his work—an opera—as a naked lie;
he tears from her all that was genuine. Her husband renounces her. A simple
ending: the young couple meet again in a certain spa. The event is real and
happened in Prague in the district of Vinohrady—but with more serious
consequences.'

The story, so far as it goes, is true: the conductor and composer Vítězslav
Čelanský (1870—1931) wrote an autobiographical one-act opera, Kamila,

---

*) In Veselý – Janáček, p. 94. On p. 69 of the same book Janáček reminisces about Luhačovice
as 'an annual congress of beautiful women'. Apart from the importance of the spa for the treatment of his rheumatism, Luhačovice with its delightful surroundings on the southernmost
slopes of the Beskydy Mountains, became Janáček's dearest and artistically most fruitful
summer retreat second only to Hukvaldy.

**) According to the memoirs of Mrs. Janáčková (p. 87), on the initiative of Mrs Urválková.
She, touched by Janáček's loneliness and sad look (half a year after Olga's death), had the
roses sent to his table.

which was performed in the autumn of 1897 at the National Theatre in Prague. In it, the heroine is described as a flirtatious coquette who, having awakened serious hopes in the young poet Viktor*), accepts with equal complaisance the advances of a young lieutenant, not knowing that he is, at the same time, arranging for a nocturnal visit to her maid. When the affair is exposed by Kamila's brother, she turns in repentance to Viktor who laconically renounces her forever.

It is obvious**) that the Kamila of this story was none other than Kamila Urválková, whose maiden name was Schiller, the daughter of a rich baker in the Hybernská Street of Prague, who owned a house near the capital in Dobřichovice, in the garden of which the action of *Kamila* takes place. She was the sister of the poet Egon Schiller who appears in the opera, interceding on behalf of Viktor.

We have no right to judge the quarrel, but in Luhačovice Kamila Urválková certainly succeeded in persuading Janáček that her former suitor had wronged her in his opera. And so, Janáček attributing to the composer of the one-act opera pangs of conscience which Čelanský probably never felt, created a kind of continuation of *Kamila*, and Mrs Urválková became, under the name of Míla***) the heroine of a second opera, Janáček's DESTINY. Čelanský, by a curious twist of capricious fate, nearly became the conductor at its première.

Immediately following the village drama, JENŮFA, Janáček, who hardly ever repeated himself, thus set to music a story from entirely different milieus— the fashionable world of a spa and that of artists—and, after using a prose libretto in the Slovácko dialect, now wanted a libretto in verse, as he himself requested from his new librettist Fedora Bartošová†). Nevertheless the only trait that JENŮFA and DESTINY have in common is the suffering of the heroine for a past lapse. The essential difference between them is the standard of the writing in the librettos, both from the dramatic and the stylistic point of view. It has to be said in fairness that the authoress of the libretto to DESTINY was a 20-year-old friend of Olga and a teacher at the Vesna Society's College for Girls, and that the shortcomings of the opera cannot be attributed entirely to her inexperience, since she was only carrying out Janáček's wishes.

---

*) Viktor is Vítězslav in Czech.
**) Čelanský's widow, Mrs Marie Čelanská, has confirmed it.
***) Originally under the even more transparent name of Míla Válková.
†) On 12 November 1903 he wrote to her: 'I have in mind the kind of verse Pushkin uses in *Eugene Onegin*.' According to Dr Theodora Straková's study 'Janáček's opera DESTINY' (Acta Musei Moraviae, XLII, 1957) the influence of *Onegin* goes further: apart from the name Lensky (Čelanský in disguise), there is the unexpected meeting of the lovers after several years, reminiscent of Tatiana's meeting with Onegin at the ball in St Petersburg. And the original scenario for DESTINY also contained a letter scene. It is interesting also that Kamila Urválková, the real heroine of DESTINY, signed her letters to Janáček 'Tatiana' — the name he apparently gave her himself.
Dr Straková also points out the influence of Charpentier's *Louise* which Janáček had seen at the National Theatre in Prague shortly before, on 21 May 1903: 'Following Charpentier's example Janáček wrote a libretto himself which he called, in the first copy, *Fragments of a Novel from Life* and, like Charpentier, called the first version a *roman musical*. It may be added that the choice of artistic milieu (similarly that in the first part of THE EXCURSIONS OF MR BROUČEK) could also be linked with *Louise*.

169

The story is as follows:

Act I takes place on the promenade at Luhačovice. A waltz, typically Janáček in character, is heard. After a chorus in praise of the morning sun, the painter Lhotský offers the much-courted Míla (or Mína—the authors could not make up their mind) a bouquet of roses.*) The composer Živný (Life-Giving), Míla's former lover, appears. 'Have you come for your child?' she asks him when they are left alone. Their conversation is interrupted by the calls of the schoolmistress, Miss Stuhlá (Rigid): 'Come to the rehearsal, ladies,' while the others prepare for a day's outing. A Dr Suda, brandishing an umbrella, calls: 'Here, our banner!' and the 'gay young things' busy themselves tying ribbons to the umbrella (red, white, and blue, the 'patriotic' colours). Lhotský's cry: 'Eat, eat, let us be healthy!' is followed by a general request for lunch, only moments after 'the morning sun'. The whole high-spirited crowd set out, led by a bagpiper and fiddlers, singing another song about the sun.

Živný and Míla return to the empty stage, but their second dialogue throws no more light on the situation except for hinting that Míla was betrothed to a 'beau' of some sort but gave herself to Živný after seeing him conduct his own opera—with the result that she left Prague and went off to the country to give birth to a child. Živný's remark, 'I have believed slander,' suggests yet more mystery. No attempt is made to clear it up, however, and when, at dusk (a quarter of an hour after dawn) the party return in pairs from their outing, Míla declares: 'I am yours and our child also,' her only worry being the effect her expiatory decision is going to have on her mother. And indeed, the mother, hearing that her daughter has gone off with Živný, exclaims in horror, 'No, no, sheer disaster,' and duly becomes insane (during the interval between the first and second acts).

In Act II Živný and Míla are poring over the score of the opera in which he has expressed the confession of his love. It is an odd work: 'The opera is complete,' he says, 'but without the last act.' Why? The explanation is given in Živný's self-accusation:
'Oh baseness of all baseness!
Your heart I wanted to wrench from your breast,
Expose its wounds
And let my laughter chime its hard derision.
To human judgement expose you as lie personified
With Fraud's deceitful shield
With smiling Falsehood's ruse
A few moments of lust —
And to another you were said
To have sent your soul, your kisses and your love.
'A lie, a lie,' cries Živný tearing up the pages of his score. 'Cursed suspicion born of insanity.' But even this speck of light is obscured by Míla's own words,

---

*) Dr Straková thinks that Lhotský who in the original version played a much more important part in the plot, was intended to be the Slovácko painter Joža Úprka who lived in the village of Hroznová Lhota (Lhota, adj. Lhotský) and that the name Mína was suggested to the authors by a similar character in Jaroslav Hilbert's play, *Vina* (Guilt).

170

'You know I am guilty.' To complete the confusion, Míla's insane mother who appears, cursing Živný for carrying off Míla and fearing that he only wants to rob her of her gold, not only throws herself out of the window but drags her daughter with her! 'Strike harder, pallid lightning!' cries Živný...

Approximately the same words are then picked up at the beginning of Act III by a chorus of Živný's *conservatoire* students who, in his absence, have been singing the last scene of his unfinished opera. Živný, when delivering the score with its missing last act, mysteriously points out to the management of the theatre that the last act 'is in the hands of God where it must remain'. The opera, therefore, is to be performed unfinished. It is also made clear that the hero of Živný's opera, the composer Lenský, is none other than Živný himself. (This opens up further interesting prospects: since Lenský, as we know, has written an opera in which he indicts his mistress in the same way as Živný, the reincarnation of composers could go on for ever.) In the meantime Živný appears and his pupils insist on him explaining about Lenský. To the accompaniment of a gathering storm outside, Živný tells them indirectly about his tragic romance with Míla. When he recalls her beauty, Doubek (the child of their love) calls instinctively for his mother and simultaneously the classroom is struck by lightning. When the pupils come to themselves they hear the stricken Živný raving on the floor: 'That is her cry! Can you not hear it?' and his pupil Verva adds: 'That perhaps is the music of the last act!' Now one would expect the curtain to fall. But it is not to be. Živný catches Verva's remark, adds abruptly: 'Of the last act? That is in the hands of God where it must remain.' After which he lets himself be led away by Doubek. Thus an impression is created of a missing last act in DESTINY itself.

This should suffice to show with what a bizarre and extravagantly romantic libretto, in spite of its realistic setting, Janáček chose to follow the clearcut story of JENŮFA.*) The extent to which he was carried away by the story can be seen by the fact that in the autumn of 1903, straight after returning from Luhačovice and in the midst of exhausting preparations for the première of JENŮFA, he began sketching the scenario and sending it piecemeal to Bartošová who was then teaching at Sudoměřice nad Moravou, asking her to put it into verse as quickly as possible, without giving her a chance to get to know the whole story. He himself set the versified bits as soon as he received them from Bartošová. In this way he finished Act I in April 1904 and completed the opera by mid June 1906, although many revisions were to follow—for instance, the character of the insane mother was not added until after the completion of the first act.

The conception of the work is not without dramatic impact, with its contrast of the carefree couples returning from the outing at the end of Act I, and the tragic love of Živný and Míla which hints at a later, similar scene in KATYA KABANOVA. The crucial problem of the play is the right of an artist to expose in public the private and intensely personal experiences of other people. Even

---

*) It was by no means a *faute de mieux:* 'Flowing, melodious verse, so fresh, new,' he praised the libretto delightedly. 'Not only are all the main characters absolutely clear, but also the episodes; great monologues next to so much real life that they become tolerable.'

disregarding the instances of those who desire nothing more than to become the object of notorious indiscretion, it cannot be denied that a certain *sacro egoismo* made possible the creation of some of the most beautiful works of art. One thinks of Goethe, who disclosed much of the private life of Charlotte Kestner and her husband, and who included in a sonnet the surname of another mistress, Minna Herzlieb, split into its two component parts, (*'Lieb Kind! Mein artig Herz!'*) not to mention his making Frau von Stein into the negative character of the Queen of the Night in his continuation of Schikaneder's *Magic Flute*.

In the case of DESTINY the problem is complicated by the fact that the hero not only exposes the lapse of his wife, but that in so doing he deprives it of its inherent justification by harbouring unjust suspicions of spiritual fraud, of some kind of erotic *reservatio mentalis* such as D'Annunzio describes in his novel *Piacere*. Unfortunately the strong dramatic embryo is almost entirely obliterated by banalities and unpleasant elements such as the mother's insanity. Moreover the cause of her madness is not clear since her daughter's sin is expiated by her union with her lover and since Živný's character gives no reason for her madness either.*) The most life-like character, except for his unfortunate ending, is the composer Živný through whom Janáček no doubt expressed many of his own thoughts: Živný's two confessions about his work— in Act II to his wife, and especially in Act III to his pupils—are most moving. Míla, the enchanting woman of the world in Act I, the humble mother and wife in Act II, is almost of equal interest, apart, again, from her embarrassing end. The precocious child, Doubek, is sophisticated beyond his years, and the rest of the many characters in Act I are completely shallow, lacking even any satirical purpose.

The work becomes no more convincing by virtue of Janáček's untiring insistence on it being true, nor is it helped by the mysterious choice of title which attributes almost everything to fate, destiny. This conception was, however, very dear to the tragedian in Janáček, as may be seen in the part played by fate in KATYA KABANOVA, THE DIARY OF THE YOUNG MAN WHO DISAPPEARED and, less overtly, in THE HOUSE OF THE DEAD.**) But in these works fate brings its victims convincingly to the verge of temptation to which they cannot but succumb in situations where love or hatred break all fetters and the highest price has to be paid. Not so in DESTINY. Apart from the possibility that Mrs Urválková probably enjoyed flirting with the word 'fate' in front of Janáček, everything in the opera is ascribed to it because the lovers

---

*) Dr Straková points out (*op. cit.* p. 149): 'Janáček saw the reason in her almost pathological avarice and saw the conflict from the social point of view. He even contemplated studying such a case in an asylum.' He did not find one either in Brno or in Prague. In his 1907 synopsis of DESTINY, he wrote: 'I happen to remember an old woman who lived in Žitná Street in Prague. She went mad and her daughter lived with an artist sharing his beggarly destiny.' Perhaps this is what Janáček is referring to in his letter to Procházka when he mentions 'more serious consequences'. But even here money is not stated to be the cause. In any case, such sudden madness would necessitate a greater and more material catastrophe than Míla's marriage to the artist whose hospitality she is constantly enjoying and who, according to Janáček's own instructions, lives in an elegant apartment with two servants (Jean and Nána).
**) This does not mean that Janáček was a passive fatalist. 'We form our Destiny ourselves,' he wrote on 9 October 1903 to Mrs Urválková.

have no other antagonist, Míla's former beau does not even appear and the insane mother is really no more than the voice of their conscience—a rather unnecessary voice at that, since the crisis comes from a different quarter: the conflict between Živný the man and Živný the artist who cannot finish his opera. It is more a tragedy of conscience than of fate.*)

Fortunately Janáček's music stands high above the libretto in quality—or perhaps unfortunately, since the question of DESTINY's own destiny is thus made more agonizing. The fact that the score bears all the characteristics of Janáček's style is not surprising for a composer who had already written JENŮFA, even if the faulty construction of the libretto has caused some flaws in the music itself, for instance, a certain long-windedness in Act I on the one hand and its all-too-abrupt ending on the other. But these and similar minor flaws, such as unnecessary repetition which does not have the same effect as in JENŮFA, can on the whole be removed by cutting. For the rest, the music of DESTINY is so rich and inspired not to say almost shattering in places, that it may be classed among Janáček's most powerful and beautiful works.

At the same time, DESTINY represents an important development in Janáček's style if only because of its harmony. In it appear for the first time his fourth, fifth and ninth chord formations (see Chapter 19) which later became so typical of his work. It introduces the period of consistent monothematicism, although hints of this may be found as early as ŠÁRKA. Groups of related motifs emerge like planets circling with their satellites round the sun common to them all.

The first of these groups is actually formed from the motif of the sun representing in a wider sense the lust for life.**) It seems to scintillate in Act I at Míla's words, 'I want to get sunburned.'

124

*) Dr Straková (*op. cit.* p. 135) points out that Janáček chose the title DESTINY for a number of reasons, among others because he saw in the love which dominates the lives of the two lovers and eventually reunites them a fateful motive force, and because he saw in Míla's insane mother 'the guardian of the social order'—some sort of cruelly-punishing Fate in the ancient Greek sense (*ibid.* p. 158). To support this, however, the guilt of Živný and Míla would have to be much graver and the paying of the penalty by death in Míla's case less accidental. Besides, Míla's supposed guilt was of quite a different nature. I cannot therefore agree with Dr Straková when she says that the introduction of the mad mother (which Janáček decided upon only in April 1904 after otherwise completing Act I) represents a decisive step taken by Janáček 'who saw in her the proper antagonist to wreck the happiness of Živný's and Míla's married life as had been done by her seducer some years earlier' or that 'he thus obtained, after a long creative struggle, a unified dramatic libretto'. In fact there can be no question of unity since the mother diverts attention from the main problem instead of focusing it. If Míla's supposed seducer had reappeared (in which case the title DESTINY would have been more apt)—as did the seducer in Jaroslav Hilbert's play *Guilt*—the reawakened suspicions of Živný could have led to her death.
**) In this respect it is interesting to read Jan Kunc (*Hudební revue*, Vol. IV, No 3), who says of Janáček's intentions: 'He carried out successfully in music what Antonín Slavíček depicted in painting—the mood, at a health resort, of scorching sun beating down in a deluge of light.'

It appears again, warningly, when Míla's mother hears of her daughter's departure with Živný, and flares up again to Lhotský's words, 'The sun which we have praised':

125

It soon appears again in the glockenspiel when the youngsters are teasing each other for a kiss.

In Act II it underlines, symbolically and in a distorted form, the derision of the insane mother, and in Act III it resounds majestically when Živný sees the vision of the 'silver gate of lightning':

126

It has to be borne in mind that in Janáček's music the motif almost never returns in exactly the same, original shape. Thus the second group, related musically (see the bracketed notes) as well as in content, is centred on a thoughtful 'family' motif of the Živnýs:

127

After appearing first at the beginning of Act II, it then undergoes these variations:

128
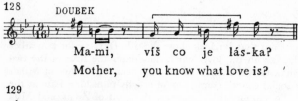

DOUBEK

Ma-mi,   víš co je lás-ka?
Mother,   you know what love is?

129

again, in the following form:

130

during Živný's reminiscence in Act III.

The third group is centred on the motif:

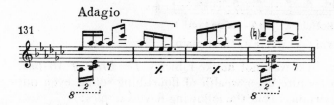

which, in Act III, appears in diminution:

and is then touchingly altered:

Among some of the independent motifs, a dramatic part is played by the speech melody to the word *fatum* (a descending fifth):

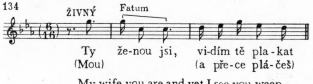

Then there is a painful-sounding melody which accompanies the unexpected meeting of the lovers:

and which reappears for Živný's confession in Act III, while its sextuplet upbeat plays an important part in Act II right up to its precipitate end. In Act III a minor 9th chord plays a significant part as a dramatic motto appearing every time storm is mentioned. Also important is the prophetic-sounding unison of the pronouncement concerning the missing last act:

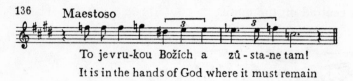

136 Maestoso

To je vru-kou Božích a   zů-sta-ne tam!

It is in the hands of God where it must remain

This motif ends the opera in a way not unlike Fibich's *The Bride of Messina*.

Janáček knows how to conjure up a wealth of flourishing sound even out of motifs of transitory importance as in the following few examples:

Act I:

137

dolce

138

139 *)

pp

Act II:

140 *dolce*

sf

I have dwelt at considerable length on the thematic aspects of DESTINY because its vocal score has not been published yet and, in particular, to provide the reader with examples showing the extent of innovation in Janáček's work after JENŮFA had been written.

As already mentioned, DESTINY was to encounter even more difficulties than JENŮFA in its early days. The modest Brno Theatre, thanks to some members of its board of directors (the writer Merhaut, the executive Elgart and especially the conductor Hrazdira), showed sincere interest soon after its completion in June 1906. But, at that time, the opening of the new Vinohrady Theatre in Prague had just been announced for 24 November 1907 and

---

*) This motif is identical with the basic motif of his offertory CONSTITUES which Janáček rewrote on 15 July 1903. That was shortly before the summer holiday which led to the writing of DESTINY (see Ex. 13).

176

Janáček, on the advice of Rektorys, decided to try to have DESTINY produced on this better-equipped stage. When the designated head of the new opera company—the same Čelanský who wrote DESTINY's precursor *Kamila*—assured Rektorys that the moment Janáček offered the work it would be automatically accepted, Janáček, feeling perfectly confident, revoked his promise to the Brno Theatre and only then officially offered DESTINY to the Vinohrady Theatre on 29 May 1907. Unfortunately Šubert, the director, immediately demanded to see the libretto, and Janáček suddenly lost confidence: 'I am afraid of the critical spirit of the *writer* Šubert,' he confesses to Rektorys on 8 June and, on 11 September, he begs him, 'Please do not forget to stress (to Šubert) that the story is actually true.'

At the same time he addressed a request, again on Rektorys's advice, to the writer Dr František Skácelík for a hasty rewriting of the libretto. At first Skácelík agreed but, on 27 September, declined, observing, 'The complete rewriting, which seems necessary, would take at least half a year and, under the present circumstances, since the music is written, would make little practical sense.' He went on to add, 'The material itself is very good but it needs a poet and a professional theatre man.' The following year (1908) the Brno company once more asked to produce the work. Although Janáček did not actually refuse, he insisted that the Brno performance should follow the Prague performance. But in the following spring Čelanský left the Vinohrady Theatre and Janáček found himself deprived of his main support. For years afterwards nothing happened: occasionally the opera was announced but never performed. Finally, in the autumn of 1913, Čelanský returned to the Vinohrady opera company for a single season. But all he did was persuade Janáček to withdraw the charge against the directors of the theatre, which the embittered composer had made after seven years of hopeless frustration. At the beginning of July 1914 the Brno Theatre company once more came forward with an offer made through the designated producer of DESTINY, Karel Komarov; this time Janáček accepted. However, on 28 July the First World War broke out reducing the importance of theatre to a mere trifle, the theatres found themselves *vis-à-vis de rien* and there could now be no question of producing a work with such a problematic plot.

Once more, in 1917, Janáček, by then the renowned composer of JENŮFA, begged the poet Jaroslav Kvapil to rewrite the libretto, again to be politely answered in the negative. And when a year later Max Brod, a new and devoted advocate of Janáček's music, also refused, Janáček finally gave up. DESTINY remained unperformed for many years till Brno gave it a broadcast performance in 1934 conducted by Břetislav Bakala, and a concert performance in 1954.

In my opinion a work with so strong a basic idea must potentially be suitable for stage production. Yet it is undeniable that the dialogue needs rewriting in such a way as to give this idea more scope and remove at least the most disturbing elements of diction. In Act I several cuts are badly needed, for instance, Živný's *plat du jour* prosaically interrupting his fateful dialogue with Míla. In Act II and at the end of Act III the action needs some revision, at least from the production point of view: mainly the prevention of Živný's incongruous revival at the end of the work. Well produced, much of Janáček's 'boldness' could be smoothed out without too much alteration and the true

177

value of the stylized versification realized—the opera, in my opinion, should perhaps be produced as unrealistically as possible, or rather, over-realistically in an expressionist style, and be made into a fantastic nightmare. In this case the spa characters would become satirical, and the mad mother bearable, and the *deus ex machina*, lightning, might fit more convincingly into the action. A distinct plus of the libretto is the well-thought-out and poetic preparation*) leading up to the thunderbolt in Act III: it begins lightly in Act I with the sun worshippers, continues with Živný's 'Strike harder, pallid lightning' and the chorus of his students (end of Act II and beginning of Act III) and eventually, in Act III, establishes the heavy, expectant mood before the storm.

DESTINY was twice performed on the stage on the occasion of the thirtieth anniversary of Janáček's death. The first of these performances took place on 25 October 1958 in Brno where František Jílek conducted Václav Nosek's arrangement. The second took place the following day in Stuttgart in an arrangement by Kurt Honolka. Both versions had advantages in certain details but both made similar, deep, not really necessary and therefore detrimental, inroads into the structure of the work. Both began with the first half of the *conservatoire* scene after which the first and second acts followed as flashbacks as if recounted by the hero. The second half of Act III formed the conclusion.

This type of arrangement may be justified, since Janáček himself, while working on DESTINY, wanted to arrange the plot in this way. But Bartošová rightly guessed that Živný—who is not telling his own tale but the story of his opera hero—would have to be called Lenský in the flashbacks. She therefore began making appropriate changes throughout the libretto, contrary to Janáček's wishes, since he probably felt that this would obscure the story's autobiographical relationship to Živný. Be that as it may, he finally decided to make no structural alterations. To my mind the production by the Janáček Opera company of Brno should have adhered more closely to the original, especially as it was the first performance of its kind in the composer's native land and as the more serious flaws were left untouched (in particular the tragicomical ending of Act II). They contented themselves with making Živný prophesy optimistically that little Doubek 'will finish my work'. And yet, Živný, true to the original version, goes on to declare that the last act 'is in the hands of God where it will remain...'

The advantage of Honolka's arrangement was that he turned Konečný, who is only vaguely mentioned in the original, into the rich suitor chosen for Míla by her mother. This gave Živný a real antagonist and made Živný's spoiling of the marriage a more plausible reason for the mother's pathological hatred of Živný. Another improvement in Honolka's version was that the mother was not insane. A madman is an irresponsible person. He becomes a dramatic figure only when his affliction becomes an indictment of the irresponsibility of others (like Marguerite in Goethe's *Faust*) or if the author needs his irresponsibility in order to say what others are unable to express (like Yurodivi in *Boris Godunov*). Here, neither alternative applies. Honolka

---

*) This was Janáček's own idea (see *Janáček—Rektorys*).

178

made the mother, at the end of Act II, try once more to persuade Míla to return to Konečný, which led to the necessary culmination in the conflict. The tragic impact of the ending was heightened by the fact that Živný died just after seeing the vision of his wife which had given him new creative strength.

Unfortunately, Honolka omitted the main motivation of the plot: Živný's groundless accusation of Míla's unfaithfulness and thus his own self-accusation—that he has wronged her in his work—which is the real reason why he cannot finish his opera. Honolka instead suggested weakness and lack of talent on the part of Živný, and even added such trivialities as the noise of neighbours' pianos and other circumstances preventing Živný from concentrating. Honolka's version of Míla's death seemed no less accidental: Živný, trying to hold Míla back from her mother whom he was turning out for intriguing with Konečný, struggled with Míla, who, disengaging herself in the scuffle, knocked her head on the piano and fell dead.

The problem of DESTINY remains unanswered even after these two productions. The answer might be to add to Honolka's positive alterations:

a) a solution to the catastrophe at the end of Act II, perhaps making Míla, driven by Živný's re-awakened suspicions, end her own life;

b) a clarification of the question of Míla's supposed sin and the related problem of the wrecking of Živný's creative and family life. Míla's past lapse cannot be as sufficient a reason to motivate the action, as her alleged unfaithfulness to Živný during their life together. The fact that Janáček himself occasionally lost this main thread of the story makes no difference.

As can be seen, producers have a difficult task before them. But even as it stands, DESTINY occupies an important place in Janáček's development as being his first opera 'in city clothes' from which there issued THE EXCURSIONS OF MR BROUČEK and THE MAKROPOULOS CASE. DESTINY is their precursor in a further sense, for in it Janáček exhibits satirical tendencies for the first time.

$\left(21\right)$ Later Folk Songs

JENŮFA was the culmination of Janáček's work in the field of folklore, and, like Smetana after *The Bartered Bride*, he never again wrote an opera set folkloristically in a narrow locale and performed in folk costume. Yet he continued to collect folk songs and dances. During Whitsun 1904, at the invitation of the teacher Alois Král, he went to the Slovácko villages of Březová and Strání to see the old sword dance called *pod šable*. He was so thrilled by it that he made plans to bring the dancers with their piper to Brno*). In July 1906 he went to the villages on the river Ostravice where he noted down many songs with their cymbalom accompaniments, in August 1907 he did the same on the slopes of the mountain Radhošť, and during his holidays in 1907 around Jablunkov—all in the north-eastern corner of Moravia.

In 1909 Janáček wrote about some of these excursions: 'Like an intruder I penetrate searching for folk songs from the country around Bílá (in the Beskydy Mountains, across the border) to Makov and Turzovka in the country ruled by the Hungarians (Slovakia). I remember my host, murdered by the Hungarians. I escape the Hungarian *gendarmes* through the Karlovice Pass.'

In 1915 he made a second intrusion 'with a double span of horses', to bring back a bagpiper from Nové Mesto nad Váhom.

Unfortunately the originator and faithful companion of these quests, František Bartoš, could no longer take part. Janáček recalled many years later: 'At Mlatcova I read aloud to the sick man my introduction to the large volume of songs.**) The Czech Academy was publishing it. On the road to Zlín we said good-bye for ever.' Bartoš died soon after, in 1906, at Mlatcova in the heart of his native Slovácko.

In the meantime Janáček's reputation as an authority on folk music continued to grow. In 1903 he organized, in Moravia, the folklore section for the Pan-Slavic Exhibition in St Petersburg. When the Austrian government, disturbed by the growth of the folklore movement among the Slav nations within the empire, made an effort to bring these trends under its control by bringing them under the umbrella of *Das Volkslied in Oesterreich*—a folk-song collection planned by the Universal Edition of Vienna—Janáček accepted the chairmanship of the working committee for the Czech folk song in Moravia and Silesia (today, the State Folk Song Institute in Brno) with the sole desire of thwarting the ulterior political motives of the Austrian government. From the first he strove to have the Slav songs published in their original languages, and when during the war, in 1917, the Austrian government ordered all the

---

*) See Janáček's article 'Pod šable', *Lidové noviny*, 29 April 1911.
**) He is referring to their combined work, *Folk Songs of Moravia Newly Collected*.

180

collected material to be sent to Vienna 'for safekeeping', Janáček foiled this plan.

Naturally, he did not hesitate also to express his dissent in purely technical matters. When, for instance, Dr Josef Pommer, an influential member of the Austrian committee for folk song, published in 1906 his pamphlet *Anleitung zur Sammlung und Aufzeichnung von Volksliedern* in which he advised collectors to note the songs down in simple keys such as C, D, F or G, Janáček replied in an article 'Collecting Czech Folk Songs in Moravia', which appeared in the magazine *Dalibor*, that the songs should be taken down exactly as they were sung, arguing that the key is characteristic not only of the mood of the song but of the character of the singer himself. He based his arguments on the theory that 'the cradle of the song' influences its form. In accordance with this theory, Janáček, for instance, included in his introduction to the collection MORAVIAN LOVE SONGS of 1913 photographs of the singers and the countryside around Makov near Čadca in north-western Slovakia.

He continued to be interested in folk music also as a composer and already during the work on DESTINY he wrote, in 1904, his ČTVERO MUŽSKÝCH SBORŮ MORAVSKÝCH (Four Moravian Male-Voice Choruses) full of a tangible, spontaneous sense of humour.

This group of choruses was dedicated to the Moravian Teachers' Choral Society founded shortly before by Ferdinand Vach and soon to become a perfect vehicle for Janáček's genius, enabling him to give full rein to his inspiration.*) These four choral works were not only dedicated to Vach's choir, but its existence influenced, at least partially, Janáček's technique, though it is uncertain whether all were written after Janáček had become acquainted with this fine body of singers. According to Vach**) Janáček did not at first show much interest in it 'until he accidentally heard us in 1904, I think it was in the town of Veselí in south-east Moravia. He was very surprised and straight away he sent me an interesting letter and two choruses—DEŽ VIŠ (If You Knew) and KLEKÁNICA (The Evening Witch).'

In fact these two choruses (both to words by the poet Ondřej Přikryl, in the Haná dialect) present no particular problems apart from the strenuous demands, common to the other two choruses as well, made on the first tenors,

---

*) It is perhaps symbolic that the first concert given by this choir, made up originally of Vach's pupils from the Teachers' Training Institute in Kroměříž but soon enlarged to a permanent number of 60 singers by the inclusion of his former students from all over Moravia, was on 3 July 1903, Janáček's birthday. The future development of the Moravian Teachers' Choir is best shown by simple dates: 1904, first appearance in Brno, 1905, first appearance in Prague, 1906, first time abroad in Germany with the result that the Leipzig publishers Forberg began in the same year their collection *Männerchöre aus dem Repertoir des Sängerbundes Mährischer Lehrer*; 1907, a visit to Belgrade and again Germany; 1908, France (Paris, Nancy); 1913, Russia (St Petersburg, Moscow, Kiev). After the war in 1919, London, Paris, Switzerland; 1923, Italy; 1925, South-East France and Northern Italy; 1927, appearance at the Musical Exhibition in Frankfurt; 1928, Berlin, Warsaw, Yugoslavia, etc. Thanks to the enthusiasm of its members (for every rehearsal, whether in Brno or Přerov, they have to travel a total of 7000 kilometres) and to the fact that they found adequate successors to Vach, the Moravian Teachers continued to maintain their high standard.

**) Ferdinand Vach, 'Memoirs', *Hudební rozhledy*, Brno, Vol. I. (1924/25), pp. 38, 39.

and the enharmonic modulation from F minor to E major at the touchingly tender beginning of the third verse of IF YOU KNEW ('If you knew that I love you more than the whole world'). THE EVENING WITCH is a humorous counterpart to Dvořák's tragic symphonic poem *The Noonday Witch*. A daughter makes fun of her mother who used to warn her not to go out after dark, i.e. after angelus, or the evening witch might catch her. The girl paid no attention and got caught—by a 'handsome lad'. The humorous effect, accentuated by Přikryl's Haná dialect, is heightened even more by the eerie chime-like notes:

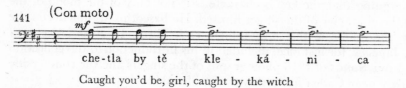

che-tla by tě   kle - ká - ni - ca

Caught you'd be, girl, caught by the witch

by the quasi-balladic harmonies, rhythms and exciting pedal notes—all spiced with an augmented (Lydian) fourth. The daughter's memory of the 'happy ending' gives Janáček an opportunity to bring in a mellow section at the beginning of the last verse, after which—as in the previous chorus—the conclusion appears with all the more buoyancy.

Much greater demands are made on the singers in KOMÁŘI (Mosquitoes) (a setting of folk words which Janáček had used before in RÁKÓS RÁKÓCZY and which he arranged in his MORAVIAN FOLK POETRY).*) The voices wind their way through a narrow lane of chromatic keys, B, B flat, G sharp, G, G flat and so on, to the words 'the gnat lies in the chamber, his lady fly weeps in the yard outside'. And since they enter alternately and in imitation, the harmony is scarcely intelligible.

The fourth chorus, ROZLOUČENÍ (Parting), is again based on a Moravian folk song, *Zhůru cesta, dolů druhá, rozlučme se spolu, milá* (One road leads high, the other low, let's say goodbye, my love) which was also noted down by Sušil. Janáček in this setting in straightforward ternary form (*ABA*), in which the middle section is built up from the quaver counter-subject of the outer sections, maintains the typical Moravian character of the original.

Although none of these four works reach—nor do they try to—the spiritual depth and power either of the earlier choruses such as THE THREAT or THE GARLAND or of the later choruses to words by Petr Bezruč, they represent an important and attractive stage in the development of Janáček's choral writing.

Janáček produced several equally delightful folk-song harmonizations during this period: his FOLK NOCTURNES and SIX FOLK SONGS; the humorous KRAJC-POLKA published on 17 February 1912 in the literary supplement of the paper

---

*) Among Janáček's papers was found (and, soon after, lost again) a sketch entitled THE MOS-QUITO for violin *sul ponticello* and piano. Considering the part played by gnats, flies and midges in the prelude JEALOUSY (see p. 133), in the FAIRY-TALE for cello (see p. 198), in ADVENTURES OF THE VIXEN SHARP EARS, in the CONCERTINO (see footnote on p. 304) and by fire-flies in the third song of THE DIARY OF THE YOUNG MAN WHO DISAPPEARED, not to mention the 'flies' in the jargon of the folk musicians (see p. 115), it might be tempting to make a really high flown (!) musico-entomological study of this subject. Keen musicologists please note!

Lidové noviny, and PERINA (The Eiderdown), a male-voice chorus composed about 1914.

The LIDOVÁ NOKTURNA (Folk Nocturnes), subtitled 'Evening songs of the Slovak people from Rovné', are written for 'folk duet' (female) and piano. They were written in 1906 based on Janáček's notes, and were first performed at the Friends of Art Club in Brno on 5 December 1907. Adolf Piskáček published, in the music magazine *Dalibor* on 25 May 1906, an authentic explanation given to him by Janáček who had gone to Prague to hear Strauss's *Salome* at the German theatre: 'I have discovered something new in folk music, something quite extraordinary. The best title for it would be 'Nocturnes'. These are strange songs for more than one voice with very interesting harmony. I took them down during wanderings through regions still unexplored by collectors. I cannot mention them without getting excited. In the evening after sunset, girls meet at the back of the cottages and one of them, the best singer, stands in front of the others leading the singing. She sings the first line and the others join in, holding hands, with an unusual melody which carries over the hill tops, falls into the valleys and dies away in the distant dark forest.'

The collection ŠEST NÁRODNÍCH PÍSNÍ (Six Folk Songs), as sung to Janáček and a Brno folklore researcher, Františka Kyselková, by Eva Gabel (a Slovak woman from Velká Slatina working at the time as a labourer at Modřice south of Brno), was arranged for solo voice and piano not later than the beginning of December 1909. Both the NOCTURNES and these SIX SONGS keep less strictly in their accompaniments to the folk style, although there are some typical instances of ornamentation and of imitation of the cymbalom. But at the same time Janáček develops the accompaniments motivically, sometimes in diminution (first and fifth NOCTURNE), sometimes by adding a counter-melody in a high register (second and fifth NOCTURNE); in the last of the SIX FOLK SONGS he even writes a free canon. There is also some tone painting (in the first song a horse ride, in No. 3 the sweep of a scythe, and in the seventh NOCTURNE the flight of a swallow), yet the spirit of the folk song is, in every case, preserved.

The same may be said of the miniature KRAJCPOLKA based on a Moravian dance-song taken down by Františka Kyselková.*) It is similar to the Czech song *Ztratila jsem kanafasku* (I've lost my apron) which Janáček used in RÁKÓS RÁKÓCZY and which is therefore an unintentional example of the extent of his development since.

THE EIDERDOWN is one of Janáček's very few choral arrangements in which the folk song remains quite unaltered—except, in this case, that it is in quick 2/4 time, more in keeping with its humour, whereas Dr Jan Poláček**) took it down in 3/4 time and marked it 'slowly and sostenuto'. Janáček heightens the effect of the humorous words (listing all the fine deeds an eiderdown can accomplish) by stressing the final point of each verse with a typically caustic diminution or a teasing pause in the bass as a saucy afterthought.

---

*) *Krajcpolka* (from the German *Kreuzpolka*, or cross-polka) is an old dance in 2/4 time. It can be danced to any polka music, and combines the steps of a square dance with those of the conventional, round polka.

**) *Slovácké pěsničky* (Songs of Slovácko), II; the song, according to Dr Poláček, comes from Kopanice—smallholdings on poor soil in the hills around Starý Hrozenkov overlooking the Slovácko district.

(22) Social Motifs

Despite his persistent enthusiasm for folklore—for the art of the people, Janáček could not fail to realize that a change was taking place in the people themselves. Under the growing pressure and levelling influence of modern civilisation and foreign industrial capital, the country people were discarding the attractive obsolete national costume of their ancestors and were exchanging work in the fields and on hand-looms for work in factories and mines. Yesterday's free and bragging individual became one of the innumerable thousands who often found themselves faced with the dilemma of either forsaking their nationality or losing their livelihood. The realistic Janáček could not for long hold himself aloof, for the people's struggle for a livelihood was in itself a struggle for national survival.

These changing conditions ushered in a new phase of his work, his revolutionary phase. The event which inspired the first of these works could scarcely have been more dramatic or impelling. On 1 October 1905 the Brno Germans organized a rally of Germans from throughout the Empire as a protest against the Czech request for the setting up of a Czech university in Brno. The Czech population retaliated with its own mass meeting on the same day. Clashes occurred and, at the request of the then German town-council, not only the police but, on the following day, the army were also called out to intervene. They were ordered to clear the Beseda Society building, at that time the rallying point of the Czechs of Brno, and during the operation (on 2 October, in fact) a 20-year-old workman in the joinery trade, František Pavlík, was wounded by a bayonet and died in hospital afterwards.

These events created such a tumult in Janáček's mind that he sat down and wrote a piano work in three movements with the title, STREET SCENE 1 OCTOBER 1905. The first movement, *Foreboding,* may be called a ballad in which a disturbed diminution of its third and fourth bars:

142

forms itself into the insistent accompaniment of the second subject:

143

and—compressed into a quadruplet—into the development.*)

184

The second movement, originally called *Elegy,* later *Death,* begins like a quiet dirge in the style of a funeral march, derived from the second bar of *Foreboding,* with the typical Janáček rests on all the accented beats:

The gradation of its dotted rhythm and the fortissimo recapitulation suggest a crushing accusation which finally fades away to a disconsolate conclusion in pianissimo, the brevity of which makes the loss of the conventional finale movement even more strongly felt. During the final rehearsal for the first performance of this work at the Friends of Art Club in Brno on 27 January 1906 Janáček suddenly seized the music of the finale from the horrified performer and burned it on the spot, apparently because he was depressed by the other, more attractive novelties on the programme—Josef Suk's *Spring* and Vítězslav Novák's cycle *My May.* And so Ludmila Tučková, a professor at the Organ School, was on the night able to perform only the first and second movements. After a second private performance in Prague Janáček threw the two remaining movements into the Vltava. ('They did not want to sink. The paper bulged and floated on the water like so many white swans.') Fortunately the soloist, after her experience with the third movement, had made a second copy of the other two movements, thus saving them from destruction. Later, Janáček even gave permission for their publication.

They are rather unpianistic in style (in places the work sounds more like the piano score of a symphony) although there are some pianistic effects such as the thematic figuration in the first movement, sounded pianissimo over a sustained chord struck fortissimo and held by the pedal. The work has probably more importance as an idea rather than a composition. In any case it made the honorary doctorate which Janáček was to receive later from the Czech University of Brno, for which he stood up in 1905, doubly deserved.

By far the most valuable fruits of this stage in Janáček's development were the result of his discovering (not later than 1906) the poems *Slezské písně* (Silesian Songs) by Petr Bezruč. This pseudonym concealed a humble Brno post-office clerk, Vladimír Vašek, who, in his poems from the troubled Těšín district had, since 1899, been attempting to rouse the national and international conscience in favour of his own compatriots and against the denationalizing regime of the 'Marquis Gero'—the notorious Archduke Frederick.**) His words could scarcely have fallen on more fertile soil, for Janáček was akin to Bezruč both in origin and in social background. (The spiritual relationship

---

*) The sonata form of this movement contains one peculiarity in that the second subject in G flat major (relative major of the tonic E flat minor) reappears in the recapitulation not transposed to the tonic key in the usual way, but in its original G flat major accompanied by the tonic E flat minor.
**) The real Gero was a historical figure of the tenth century—a German war-lord who crushed Slavonic tribes settled between the Elbe and the Oder.

of these two 'tribunes of the people' is best expressed in a letter written by Janáček on 31 October 1924, thanking Bezruč for congratulating him on his seventieth birthday: '...you were the only one of that large artistic collection of writers, painters, sculptors, etc. who peeped into the lane throbbing with sound, and there you found me. Apparently we once stood next to one another,*) without knowing. I feel so near you and yet we have never met. Your words came at the right moment and I brought to them a musical storm of wrath, despair and pain... Thus we have shared many moments—with one and the same thought... It is impossible to separate us.') They were closely related not only in their thought but also in their technique. It was a technique which drew its main power from relentlessly repeating, like an indictment, the most meaningful words and images.

Janáček, using Bezruč's works, composed his three supreme choral works, KANTOR HALFAR (Schoolmaster Halfar), MARYČKA MAGDÓNOVA and 70,000 in the space of—ignoring later revisions—four years. They form an unintended trilogy, and represent three milestones, three revolutionary acts in Czech choral writing, deeply significant in music as well as in content, whose power can still be felt, despite vastly changed conditions and inevitable anachronisms. 70,000 and MARYČKA MAGDÓNOVA had been set by other composers**) but, while these have faded into oblivion, Janáček's settings have become three national monuments. Max Brod considered Janáček's SONGS OF HRADČANY to be the counterparts of Smetana's *My Country*. I consider the parallel to be more apt in the case of these choral works.

MARYČKA MAGDÓNOVA was the first of the trilogy to be performed—on 12 April 1908 at Prostějov and 26 July of the same year in Prague, both performances by the Moravian Teachers' Choir. It was in fact the second to be written: the first version dates from autumn 1906, the second, a quite different version, from spring 1907.***)

The heroine, Maryčka Magdónova, a miner's daughter suddenly orphaned, finds herself with her younger brothers and sisters to care for. Her father Magdón paid a visit to the tavern after work and 'on the way home, his skull split open, fell into the ditch' (Bezruč does not idealize the comradeship among his fellow countrymen). The mother had been crushed under a coal-wagon. The children cry from hunger and cold and Maryčka Magdónova decides to go gathering sticks in 'Marquis Gero's' wood. She is caught and marched to Frýdek by a *gendarme*. To avoid shame and derision of the Frýdek burghers, she throws herself into the wild Ostravice and is drowned.

Janáček set this ballad in its strophic form with the verses divided by a repeated refrain. The verses, joined into pairs, flow calmly while recounting

---

*) During a performance of MARYČKA MAGDÓNOVA in Brno on 15 November 1908.

**) Janáček composed MARYČKA MAGDÓNOVA after hearing the melodramatic setting (declamation with musical accompaniment) by Karel Moor, and 70,000 after hearing Jan Kunc's setting for choir and orchestra which, according to Janáček, was not sufficiently realistic (Jan Kunc, in *Listy Hudební matice*, IV).

***) MARYČKA MAGDÓNOVA is of further interest in that it was the first of the three to bring Janáček international fame since on 27 April 1908, before its Prague performance, the Moravian Teachers' Choir sang it in Paris where they also performed Janáček's IF YOU KNEW and THE EVENING WITCH.

the circumstances of the action. As the action gathers momentum the verses broaden out; themes and words separate, cross each other and interchange (only the conclusion of each verse, usually on the name of the heroine, remains unchanged as though erecting her monument) until, in the verse describing the rapacity of the overflowing river and the final catastrophe, a new motif is introduced while the accompanying voices repeat startled cries 'Ostravice'. This new motif, sharply ascending, seems to foretell what is to come, and a rubato sextuplet, falling precipitously from the high, dissonant notes of the tenors with the words 'her black hair caught on the rock', announces tersely: 'It is ended.' In touching contrast is the quiet, simple conclusion, describing Maryčka's flowerless grave in the corner of the cemetery where suicides are buried.

Adolf Vašek gives 1905 as the year in which the first version of SCHOOL-MASTER HALFAR was written. Helfert, in *Pazdírek's Music Dictionary* states 'before October 1906'—perhaps because the copy from which the Smetana Choral Society of Plzeň gave the first performance of the original version on 27 May 1911 is dated '28. X. 1906'.*) According to Max Brod, however, the final version was completed in 1917, which is borne out by the late date of its first performance—3 August 1918, by the Moravian Teachers' Choir at Luhačovice. Bezruč's poem seems to have been based on a true event. (Halfar's brother, Alfréd Halfar, also a teacher, introduced Janáček to some local songs at Sedliště in the Těšín district in 1893.)**) The Halfar of the title is an assistant teacher. 'A good, quiet lad. His only fault—he spoke Czech in Těšín.' This under 'Marquis Gero' was unforgivable. In vain he waits for a teacher's place and he loses his fiancée who does not care to wait ten years. But he persists in teaching 'according to God's law' even after his superiors have decided to make the school Polish. One evening he is found hanged from the apple tree. At last he has found his place—likewise in the suicides' corner of the graveyard.

The work is in three differently constructed verses, the two sections of each corresponding to their two different motifs: the first, a melody in equal crochets with a counter-melody in quavers, both seeming to circle round one note:

145   Moderato

Kan - tor   Hal - far   byl   hoch   do - brý

Tea - cher   Hal - far   was   a   good   lad

as though Janáček wanted to express the hero's monotonous life, his endless waiting. The second, more dramatic in character:

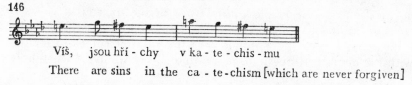

146

Víš,   jsou hří - chy   v ka - te - chis - mu

There   are sins   in the   ca - te - chism [which are never forgiven]

---

*) See article by Antonín Špelda: 'Janáček and Plzeň'. Prague *Hudební rozhledy*, Vol. VII, p. 646.

**) Jaroslav Procházka: *Lašské kořeny Leoše Janáčka* (Lachian Roots of Leoš Janáček), p. 98.

expresses the adversities of Halfar's life and, eventually, his answer to them—suicide. The announcement of Halfar's death gives Janáček an opportunity for one of his subtlest strokes. While the tenors describe the distant bells ringing angelus in the summer evening, the basses break in with 'The girl rushes into the darkened room'. The tenors then announce canonically 'Schoolmaster hangs from the tree', and Janáček adds an extra dramatic touch by repeating in the basses 'Schoolmaster? Schoolmaster Halfar?' 'And we seem to see the men in the tavern, with their pipes in their mouths, turning towards the door,' writes Křička,*) comparing this place with an analogous scene of alarm in Act III of JENŮFA. The tragic point of the poem is emphasized with special beauty by the use of a quiet adagio version of the motif from Ex. 146 but in resigned even crotchets describing Halfar's funeral 'devoid of any prayers'. But I think the supreme moment comes at the conclusion where, with the work firmly anchored in A major (at least, during the opening section of each verse) Janáček repeatedly puts off the tonic chord until finally coming to rest on it to the words, 'and so Halfar found his place'.

Jan Šmolík has pointed out**) the similarity of the motif 'There are sins...' (Ex. 146) and its variant:

147

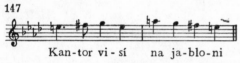

Kan-tor vi - sí   na ja-blo-ni

Teacher's hanging from the apple tree

with the national anthem of the Austrian Empire which stands accused alongside 'Gero' in the work. Šmolík also draws attention to Janáček's dramatizing of the poem in all three of these choral pieces as well as later in THE WANDERING MADMAN by changing them into dialogue. In MARYČKA MAGDÓNOVA, for instance, Janáček changes Bezruč's question, 'Hochfelder the Mayor saw you gathering sticks in the wood, will he keep silent?' into the following dialogue:

Maryčka: Hochfelder, the mayor, saw me gathering sticks.
Questioning voice: What do you say? Hochfelder saw you gathering sticks?
Maryčka: Will he keep silent? Will he keep silent?
Questioning voice: He saw you!

The third chorus of the Bezruč trilogy is 70,000. The title refers to the last 70,000 who have not yet abandoned their native tongue for a loaf of bread but are faced with the necessity of doing so. To express this tragic dilemma, Janáček evolved a yet more complicated means: to the choir who are, so to say, speaking for the living crowd he adds a male-voice quartet representing the 'soul' of the helpless people just as the quartet of violas is used later in THE FIDDLER'S CHILD. The effect is most striking when, in the middle of the second verse in a minor key, the quartet comes in for the first time with the anguished question, pianissimo: 'May we live?' when only

---

*) In *Listy Hudební matice*, Vol. IV (1924), p. 133.
**) In his collection of studies: *Leoš Janáček*, p. 101.

'seventy thousand of us are left', followed by the desperate solo tenor's 'Only live, only live!'

The work (in 2/4 time) is basically in ternary form but built from a single melodic idea, in particular its opening leap of a third stretching later to as much as a ninth. The first section opens just like the other two choruses, with a melody in slow swaying crotchets:

Se - dm - de-sát ti - síc je nás před Tě - ší - nem, před Tě - ší - nem
Seventy thousand are we around Těšín

which reappears later in a shortened form. In the second section ('seventy thousand graves they are digging for us around Těšín!') the melody suddenly turns to an agitated presto, the intervals compressed into diminished thirds, while 'Only live' suggests, according to Max Brod, the 'endless longing for light and life'. Here, the pounding of the incomplete triplets to the words 'Marquis Gero' symbolizes the accusations of the helpless. One does not notice the technical device of a three-part fugato four times exposed by the way of, on the whole, literal transpositions at the fifth without any additional polyphony. After their short weary reflection, the future inhabitants of the graves realize the horror of their situation, and a mood of feverish agitation invervenes, accentuated by the desperate-sounding solo tenor on high C ('Only live') which leads to a stretta in polka rhythm on the same theme, to the cynical call 'Give us seventy thousand barrels, then half of us shall become Germans, half shall become Poles.

70,000 is perhaps one of the most moving choruses ever written, the effect of Janáček's music being to keep the listener in suspense, an effect which Max Brod attributes to 'the turmoil of passionate revolt, the eruption of infinite grief and strength accumulated through centuries of oppression.'

Even a composer of Janáček's stature did not master this subject at the first assault. The original version was completed in December 1909. He rewrote it in 1913 in which form it was performed (4 April 1914), not by Vach who singularly enough had returned it to the composer as unsingable, but by the Prague Teachers' Choral Society conducted by František Spilka to whom the work was dedicated. Its success in Prague was immediate.

$\left(23\right)$ 'The Fiddler's Child'

Janáček, having protested in his previous works against foreign national and social oppression, now began attacking his own people—the collaborators and the imitators of the oppressors, and the parasites. While still working on the Bezruč trilogy he began planning a number of other revolutionary works, this time based on the writings of Svatopluk Čech. It was not his first encounter with this poet, as he had once asked him to arrange the *Little Queens* dance— a request which had not been granted. Now Janáček began studying Čech's *Písně otroka* (Songs of a Slave), evidently intending to make them into a cantata. This is born out by a copy of the poems (tenth edition, 1895) which had belonged to Olga and which she had left to the Hukvaldy Reading Circle (which also proves that Janáček was planning the cantata before her death). In this copy, some of the poems, for instance Nos 1, 5, 8, 10, 15 and 18, are marked with numerous motivic glosses. (Janáček always began work by jotting down speech melodies for the most striking sections of the text.) The ironic hymn to the boot-lickers (No. 13) is marked at the words 'God's will made us a doormat for His boots'; poem No. 15 at 'I have found the world could offer enough modest pleasures to all if lazy parasites did not need to thrive on their toil'; poem No. 18 at 'Break out, storm, in all your might and terror' and so on.

Despite all these preparations the work was never written. Perhaps Janáček found the style of the poems too romantic and picturesque. However, in 1912 he found among the works of Čech a subject much more to his liking— *Šumařovo dítě* (The Fiddler's Child). Čech's story is as follows:

An old fiddler has died. The village takes charge of what is left: his fiddle on the peg and his child in the cradle. An old woman is told to keep watch during the night. At midnight she has a strange vision. The dead fiddler stands at the cradle luring the child by his playing to another, better world where it will neither die of hunger nor sell its soul like its father. The old woman drives the apparition away by making the sign of the cross at the very moment when the fiddler kisses the child. She then falls asleep. In the morning, when the village mayor arrives, he finds the fiddle gone and the woman rocking the child's corpse.

This subject appealed immediately to the composer, himself the son of a poor village *kantor* (school- and music-master). Moreover, the plot was clearly intelligible and had the advantage of the participation of one of the most expressive of musical instruments. In the event, Janáček wrote a symphonic poem which is rather less intelligible, though he wrote an exhaustive programme of it in the *Hudební revue**) for the projected first performance

---

*) Vol. VII Nos 4—5.

in 1914 which did not take place. He describes the main themes and their relation to the plot, and gives the valuable hint that 'the theme, as a means of expression, is tied to a certain instrument from which it does not deviate in its development—except perhaps to related instruments which add more shadow or light.' In other words, 'A certain instrument is the bearer of the same and, often, only musical mood'—in contrast with Beethoven, for instance, in whose trios and sonatas Janáček objected to the constant shifting of the theme from one instrument to another.

Thus, for instance, the quartet of violas*) expressed for him throughout the work the souls of needy people living out their bitter lives in the village poor-house—similar to the four solo voices in 70,000 with their anguished refrain 'May we live?'. Janáček continues: 'The solo violin is everything the old fiddler was. He pines in it:**)

149

rejoices in it:

150

lures his child away:

151

and promises it golden dreams:

152

The oboe weeps the few whimpers from the sick child:

153

'The village mayor is almighty. The village is full of his presence. All bow to his will. His step is measured by the cellos and double-basses:

154

---

*) Janáček wanted not four solo violas but 'eight good players' (*Janáček—Ostrčil*, p. 21).
**) For the sake of interest I have left the music examples in their earlier version as quoted by Janáček.

'while the awe he inspires is the same motif in the bass clarinet, and his harshness, in the trombone.' Just as 'the whole poorhouse trembles at his arrival, so his motif spreads throughout the orchestra.'

The poem is printed in full at the beginning of the score. Janáček, however, has the fiddler still alive at the beginning of the poem, and lets the child fall ill first, basing this adaptation on a hint at the end of the poem that the old woman (whom he omits completely) has merely imagined the apparition. His quartet of violas indicates that the old fiddler does not live alone but that the poorhouse is full of wretched people. This gives the work a broader social significance. For the same reason Janáček extends and accentuates the part played by the village mayor. The thought of him constantly disturbs the inhabitants of the poorhouse with his theme in its broader, prying form:

or its startled diminution:

The terrifying appearance of the fiddler's motif, originally a happy one, in the timpani:

tells him of his approaching end at the very moment when the child's illness announces itself. The mournful Adagio in C sharp minor (under a high violin harmonic) indicates, although rather disjointedly, that the fiddler is dead. The agitation caused by this event brings in the village mayor. His initial surprise (fermata) changes to harshness, and when he departs, the terror of his visit (his motif, solo, in the bass clarinet) changes into a fervent prayer to Mercy (a beautiful espressivo played by half the violas above an agitated tremolo of the other half with sharp chords on the last semiquaver of each bar).*) After the whimpering of the sick child in the oboe, the ghost of the child's father appears, luring it with 'wonderful dreams' until, in the last bars of his solo (over the more and more insistent motif of the village mayor):

---

*) Janáček in a letter written to Otakar Ostrčil, the first conductor of THE FIDDLER's CHILD, on 6 November 1917 calls this the 'falling asleep motif', although it sounds more like 'overcoming sleep' and, in his effort 'to link its elements as closely as possible but with the softest possible breath', he writes that he intends to add the celesta in unison with the flutes. He thinks that the celesta's tone 'like gleaming eyes would be most characteristic.'

he clasps it in his arms, while the village mayor rushes in as if drawn by an unearthly power and gazes at the tragedy he and his like have brought about. He may even show his regret; he was, after all, acting according to the rules.

For many years the fate of this work was as sad as its theme, although Janáček seems to have written the work and sent it to the Czech Philharmonic Orchestra at the request of its chief conductor, Dr Vilém Zemánek. The official reason for cancelling the performance arranged for 15 March 1914 which Janáček should have conducted was 'the composer's illness', but in reality insufficient rehearsals had been reserved for the unusual new work. In the summer of that year The Friends of Art Club in Brno arranged to have the score published on the occasion of Janáček's sixtieth birthday, and for this purpose he made some changes in the score, but the first performance did not take place until 14 November 1917—after the Prague success of JENŮFA—with Otakar Ostrčil conducting the Czech Philharmonic Orchestra. The work is still a rare guest at symphony concerts. The first performance outside Czechoslovakia was given in London by the New Queen's Hall Orchestra conducted by Sir Henry Wood in October 1923.

Janáček now began working on a third subject from Svatopluk Čech: this time in the field of opera. Before completing DESTINY he had been feverishly searching for a subject for a further opera. In April 1904, and again in August 1907, he had been considering another Slovácko drama by Gabriela Preissová, *Gazdina roba* (The Farmer's Woman) despite the fact that Josef Bohuslav Foerster (1859—1951) had already used it as the libretto of his opera *Eva*.

Towards the end of April 1904 Gabriela Preissová herself offered Janáček her one-act play *Jarní píseň* (Spring Song):

A young girl worships an elderly artist who, inspired by such love, composes a Spring Song. Seeing, however, that the girl because of him refuses a young suitor, he leads her into the younger man's arms and the Spring Song becomes theirs.

In June 1905 Janáček was considering writing a fairy-tale 'national' opera, *Honza hrdina* (Johnny the Hero) with a libretto by Karel Dostál-Lutinov, consisting of charming verses in folk style but with rather naive patriotic scenes. Nevertheless, Janáček, at the request of the librettist, went to see the pilgrimage to the chapel of St Anthony of Padua near the Slovácko village of Blatnice, and the fair traditionally connected with it, where he jotted down, on his copy of the libretto, various melodies he heard there, for instance that of a shepherd's long horn:

a barrel-organ, and 'the dark full-sounding bells of Blatnice'. In the end, however, he abandoned the idea.

In November 1906 Quido Maria Vyskočil offered Janáček his Easter mystery play *Duše zvonů* (The Soul of the Bells). At the beginning of 1907 Janáček was considering the amusing historical comedy *Paní mincmistrová* (The Mint-master's Wife) by Ladislav Stroupežnický. No sooner had he written a few sketches for the first scene than he began to turn his thoughts to Tolstoy's *Anna Karenina*. Between 5 and 29 January 1907 he began writing an opera on this story directly to a Russian text, intending it, it seems, for Russia. He may have put his hopes in that country after having been continually neglected at home. However, in spite of some interesting sketches, especially for the characters of Levin and Kitty, the work was left as a small fragment.*)

In July of the following year (1908) Janáček began considering another folk drama in costume, *Maryša*, by the Brothers Mrštík, but the authors refused to give their permission. Thus after four years of seeking and broaching various subjects (mostly of a realistic character) he found himself no further forward.

Suddenly, in 1908, he decided to compose a satire on the bourgeois pettiness in the midst of which he lived. He chose *The Excursion of Mr Brouček to the Moon* by Svatopluk Čech**) to which was added, during the war, in 1917, the more serious satirical story, *The Excursion of Mr Brouček to the Fifteenth Century*.

Before following Janáček as far as this, however, it is necessary to turn to some lesser works which were written in the meantime but which give no less eloquent testimony to the greatness of his art. Apart from impersonal works with national, social, or religious aims, Janáček, like Smetana, was constantly urged on by the necessity of creating works of an intimate character. These were, above all, personal confessions from which he sought either healing relief as in the witty FOUR MORAVIAN MALE-VOICE CHORUSES and the amorous skit ČARTÁK ON THE SOLÁŇ, or the expression of happy or sad memories as in THE OVERGROWN PATH and IN THE MISTS, or the invigorating influence of folklore and the old epic tales of the Slavs which gave rise to the FAIRY-TALE for violoncello and piano.

Such intimate works allow us a glimpse of his private life at this time.

---

*) See Dr Gracian Černušák: 'Janáček's Anna Karenina', *Lidové noviny*, 9 August 1936.
**) As early as 1887 when he was composing the romantic ŠÁRKA, Janáček had published, in his *Hudební listy*, a scene from Čech's novel in which Mr Brouček flees for his life from a concert after hearing a composition called *Storm* by the famous Lunar composer, Harpwarp Thunderbolt.

$\left(\underline{24}\right)$ Intimate Episodes

The first of these works to be written was the piano cycle THE OVERGROWN PATH which Janáček began, at random, at the time of writing JENŮFA. Some of these small pieces, moreover, were originally not even intended for the piano although, with the exception of some tenuto chords marked crescendo, they are eminently suited for it, and are today regarded as an innovation in piano music. They were written for the harmonium, and were published as such in the 1901—1902 volume of a periodical collection for that instrument called *Slav Melodies* edited by Emil Kolář at Ivančice u Brna. The dates of publication are given by Dr Jan Racek in his preface to the complete edition (published by *Hudební matice*, Prague, 1947). These earlier pieces in the first set of ten were OUR EVENINGS, A LEAF GONE WITH THE WIND, THE LITTLE NIGHT OWL KEPT HOOTING, OUR LADY OF FRÝDEK, and GOOD NIGHT. A further five, COME WITH US, THEY CHATTERED LIKE LITTLE SWALLOWS, WORDS FAIL, SUCH INFINITE ANGUISH, and IN TEARS, composed definitely for piano, were completed by 1908, since in that year Janáček was discussing the publication of the whole first set.

In the shorter second set of five, Nos 3 and 5 were also apparently written about 1902, but Nos 1, 2 and 4 about 1911 at the latest. Of these only No. 1 was published during Janáček's lifetime (and then only as a supplement to the paper *Lidové noviny* of 30 September 1911). The five pieces of the second set, unlike those of the first, have no titles and differ considerably in style, especially the experimental No. 4 with its nearly atonal cadenzas over sustained harmonies—a peculiarity which Janáček employed at about the same time in the piano sonata fragment STREET SCENE 1 OCTOBER 1905, and which is obviously meant to represent an effective application of his principle of harmonic tangles. It is necessary to stress, however, that even the pieces with characteristic titles have their definite musical structure, mainly ternary (*ABA*) or rondo form (*ABACA* or *ABABA*). The whole cycle forms a single stream of reminiscences of Hukvaldy, Janáček's youth and of his daughter Olga. The irretrievable nature of what memory brings back is no doubt the deeper meaning behind the cycle's title which has its models in Moravian folk poetry. There is a wedding song from the Těšín district, in which the bride laments *Ej, zarost mi, zarost drobnú jatelinú ku mamince chodníček* (The path to my mother's grown over with weedy clover).

A separate analysis of each of these delicate, modest pieces, Janáček's first 'Intimate Letters', is unnecessary. Their charm is intimated by their titles.*)

---

*) Janáček, like Schumann and Debussy, gave titles to these pieces only after their completion, in the definitive piano edition of the first set, in fact, published by A. Píša in 1911 in Brno (Ludvík Kundera in *Musikologie III*, p. 316).

But it is perhaps worth pointing out that the last three notes of the original irregular phrases of the main theme in OUR EVENINGS:

(which happens to be related to the melody of the somewhat analogous 'Promenades' in Mussorgsky's *Pictures at an Exhibition*) are developed into a seemingly new, chirping motif:

This is then beautifully combined with a variant of the main melody in the second, dolcissimo episode. Also worth mentioning is No. 3 (COME WITH US) where the second phrase of the opening polka which suggests, perhaps, girls dancing arm in arm, is quickened by diminution as if the dancers were playfully running away; or the next piece, OUR LADY OF FRÝDEK, where the litany-like melody heard *z dálky* (from afar) and reminiscent of the humble singing of women pilgrims:

is almost identical, especially in its subsequent variants, with the main theme of Janáček's vocal work AVE MARIA composed a little later:

In OUR LADY OF FRÝDEK the melody alternates with dark, pensive chords as if the composer himself was conversing directly with the Lord (or, by staying silent, plaintively accusing Him).

Finally, let me mention the charming Lydian effects in No. 7 (GOOD NIGHT) with its airy, floating off-beats.

For the rest, I shall limit myself to those of the pieces that lend themselves easily to erroneous interpretation. A good guide to Janáček's own intentions is the descriptive commentary which he sent, on 6 June 1908, to the music critic Dr Jan Branberger*) who was music editor for the publishers B. Kočí

---

*) Janáček's complete letter was published by A. Rektorys in the Janáček number of the Prague *Hudební rozhledy*, Vol. VII, p. 639.

and who wanted to print the seven pieces Janáček had written at that time, in their original form, rather different in some respects from that in which we know them today.

In his letter, Janáček describes No. 2 (A Leaf Gone with the Wind) as a 'love song'; No. 3 (Come With Us), rather enigmatically, as a 'letter filed away for good'; and No. 6 (Words Fail) is supposed to express 'the bitterness of disappointment'—the change of the last notes of its mournful three-bar theme into a startled diminution:

is evidently not, as Max Brod thought, 'the comic interruption of a loquacious woman'.

Janáček was clearly thinking of No. 8 (Such Infinite Anguish) when he wrote: 'Maybe you will sense tears in the penultimate piece. The premonition of certain death. During the hot summer nights that angelic person*) lay in such deathly anguish.'

It seems that the last piece of the first set, The Little Night Owl Kept Hooting, was bound up with similar memories. Its 'confident song of life, full of trust' (the chorale-like melody in E major) alternates incessantly with the 'ominous motif of the owl'**):

It is therefore not surprising that although 'there is distress beyond words' in these pieces, Janáček said of the memories they recall: 'They are so dear to me, I don't think they will ever end...'

The inspiration for his next chamber work came from Russia. In 1908 Janáček completed a Piano Trio based on Tolstoy's *Kreutzer Sonata*. He probably destroyed it, but resurrected it 15 years later in the form of a String Quartet. Thus his first extant work of its type and at the time his most developed chamber composition is the three-movement Fairy-tale for cello and piano, originally entitled *The Story of Czar Berendey*. It is based on an epic poem of the same name by Vasili Andreyevich Zhukovsky (1783—1852) and its complete title runs: *The tale of Czar Berendey, of his son the Czarevich Ivan, of the intrigues of Kashchey the Immortal and the wisdom of the Princess Marya, Kashchey's daughter*. The story is as follows:

Czar Berendey unwittingly promises his new-born son in ransom to Kashchey the Immortal, Ruler of the Underworld. When the Czarevich Ivan

*) No doubt Olga, who spent the last summer of her life (1902) in Hukvaldy.
**) Superstition has it that it is a bad omen to hear the hoot of the Little Night Owl, *Athene noctua noctua*, which Janáček wrote down with his customary accuracy. K. J.

grows up and is told by his father about the fateful promise, he bravely sets out alone to meet Kashchey. One evening he comes to a lake on which he sees 30 silver ducklings and, on the bank, 30 white gowns. The Czarevich steals one of the gowns. The ducklings swim to the shore, 29 of them putting on their gowns and turning into beautiful maidens. The thirtieth searches in vain for her gown. At last the Czarevich takes pity on her, gives back her gown, and she changes into a maiden more beautiful than any of the others: she is Marya, daughter of Kashchey himself. They fall instantly in love. With the help of princess Marya who takes on various disguises, even turning herself into a fly, Czarevich Ivan successfully accomplishes two tasks set him by the Ruler of the Underworld. The two then escape on horseback, evading the pursuit of the sorcerer Kashchey but not the intrigues of a neighbouring Czar and Czarevna who try to marry Ivan off to their own daughter. The forsaken princess Marya changes, in her grief, into a blue flower. However, on the eve of Ivan's marriage, a kind old man releases her from the spell, Ivan remembers her and leads her back in happiness to his father's house.

An attempt to trace this story in Janáček's sonata (with the possible exception of the first movement describing, perhaps, the lake episode) shows how wise Janáček was to shorten the original title to FAIRY-TALE. However, the youthful freshness and the tender mood of the musical material portray, no doubt, the main hero and heroine, Ivan and his bride. The Czarevich is symbolized by the fanfare-like pizzicato of the cello, which alternates with the first movement's opening melody—a gently curving one in G flat major:

The second section is marked by the canonic dialogue between the two instruments suggesting the betrothal of the two young people:

It is of interest, as Jarmil Burghauser has pointed out,*) that 'this passage is, both by its nature and by its use of melodic material, patently akin to the famous brass imitation at the end of JENŮFA, and it should be pointed out here as proof of Karel Kovařovic's musical perception, for it was he who added this imitation to JENŮFA. It was not a cheap effect, and it shows that Kovařovic, after his prolonged coolness towards Janáček, came to penetrate the character and style of Janáček's work, so that his alterations bear the marks of Janáček's technique of composition.

This 'love duet' gradually quickens to a wild gallop over broken off-beats

---

*) *Musikologie III*, p. 226.

(the pursuit of the fleeing lovers?) only to be cut short by a chromatic run
in contrary motion. A shortened and quickly subsiding return of the 'love
theme' (this time in the piano alone without the canon) concludes the movement. The missing recapitulation is yet another indication that the form of
the piece was dictated by programmatic rather than 'absolute' considera-
tions.

The second movement begins with another dialogue in canon between
the piano and the cello in which a playful motif:

is soon answered by its slower, more lyrical variant:

The interplay continues with the lyrical version of the motif being stirred by
intensified harmonies and entries of the original bustling motif and, later, even
by the appearance of the 'fanfare' motif from the first movement. The climax
is reached when the lyrical motif appears in the cello accompanied by majestic,
harmonically enriched arpeggios in the piano:

Then the first motif returns in its original, playful form. But it soon gets slower
and softer as if in disappointment, bringing the movement to an end like
a dissolving dream once again.

The same applies to the third and last movement, although it, too, opens
with a youthfully heroic theme. This theme is so Russian in its character
that even such a close observer of Janáček's work as Jan Kunc described
it in his critique after the first performance as an authentic Russian folk song
(an opinion which he was obliged to correct the following day at Janáček's
request):

The 'dissolution' at the conclusion of each movement heightens the fairy-
tale atmosphere, and the charm is enhanced by Janáček's ability to enter

completely into the spirit of the old Russian epic tales; in this respect he is second not even to native-born Russians such as Rimsky-Korsakov or Stravinsky who, incidentally, composed his *Firebird* in the same year 1910. Nor does Janáček lag behind them in the magic of his sound, and in his soloistic use of the instruments, allied with the programmatic significance he gives them— their poetic symbolism in the FAIRY-TALE, just as in THE FIDDLER'S CHILD later. In the FAIRY-TALE the cello speaks throughout for the young Czarevich while the piano for the beautiful princess.

It should be pointed out that the version under discussion, which differs from the original one completed on 10 February 1910 and performed on 13 March of that year by Rudolf Pavlata (cello) and Ludmila Prokopová (piano) in Brno, is the rewritten version of about 1923. This was first performed by Julius Junek (cello) and Růžena Nebušková (piano) on 21 February 1923 at the Prague Mozarteum.*)

Several months after finishing the FAIRY-TALE, this dream-like vision of happiness, Mr and Mrs Janáček were at last able to move on 2 July 1910 from their large but primitive flat in Monastery Square to a respectable dwelling. Three years previously, the Society for the Promotion of Church Music bought, at Janáček's suggestion, a house from a certain business firm at the corner of Kounic (Giskra) Street and the present-day Smetana Street, and the Organ School was subsequently moved there from Jakubská Street. The house was known as 'the Greek villa' on account of its architectural style, and had originally been intended to house the Russian consulate. Janáček then had another good idea. His wife insisting that, for reasons of his health, they move to a house with a garden,**) Janáček suggested that the Society should build,

---

*) The changes are not nearly as drastic as those made, for instance, in the later VIOLIN SONATA, and mainly concern the middle section of the first movement('Un poco più mosso ²/₈') which was originally quite different and led into a shortened recapitulation (later omitted) and coda. Otherwise the changes are minor, for instance, the original arco of the initial Czarevich motif was changed to pizzicato, etc. It appears that the PRESTO FOR CELLO AND PIANO composed, according to Štědroň's catalogue, about 1910, represents a sketch for the second movement of the FAIRY-TALE. This theory is supported by the comparison of its main theme:

172

as well as that of the trio which is derived from it:

173

with Ex. 168.

**) During the holidays of 1909 Janáček undertook so drastic a cure for his shattered nerves at Tišnov near Brno and lost weight so rapidly that he developed heart trouble when he returned to Hukvaldy. ('I no longer saw the world in such a rosy light,' he admitted in a letter to Rektorys.) His Brno doctor, Dr Dressler, insisted that he should find a house nearer to the Organ School so as not to have too far to walk to work and to recreation.

in place of the useless stables in the garden of 'the Greek villa', a house for the use of the director of the Organ School who would pay them rent. This is how Janáček's so-called cottage came into being—the retreat where he lived and worked till the end of his life, looked after by his wife and his housekeeper Máŕa, and with Čert and later, Čipera for company. Čert (Devil) was a black poodle, and Čipera (Frisky) was a bitch in whose honour Janáček began, in his last years, to compose a piano piece. Yet he can scarcely have left his old flat without mixed feelings. It was there that ŠÁRKA, AMARUS (the flat's windows gave onto the monastery walls of his own youth), JENŮFA and the Bezruč choruses had come into being. There, too, his little Vladimír and his beloved Olga had breathed their last.

When the new house was in order, the Janáčeks went on their holidays. He, first to the spa of Teplice nad Bečvou in northern Moravia for his heart, from where he joined his wife at Hukvaldy. This time it was not a happy place to return to. His brother František who had returned from Russia and bought and converted a peasant cottage in Hukvaldy, died of cancer on 20 December 1908 at the early age of 52, and his sister Josefka was ending an uhappy marriage with a husband 25 years her junior.

The new home in Brno was to bring the Janáčeks 'a quiet time full of peace.'*)

Their acquaintances included the painter and photographer J. L. Šichan (Janáček's witness at his wedding) and the medical man, Dr František Veselý and his wife, the writer and singer Marie Calma-Veselá, and they went out very occasionally to meet them at the Bellevue or Slavia coffee-house. Their home life was all the more intimate. 'Especially beautiful were our evenings,' continues Mrs Janáčková in her memoirs, showing that if she was not capable of giving, she was at least able to take—that, too, can be a gift sometimes. 'We used to read or else I sat at my work and he used to pace up and down the bedroom and we talked. Mainly about his work. He was always full of ideas about furthering the musical life of Brno. At that time he had long been studying Wundt's *Psychology of Nations* which helped him, he said, in his study of phonetics. Sometimes he gave me long lectures on musical theory. I always asked when I did not understand and he was always willing to explain. He had moments when he seemed to be overflowing with the desire to talk about his work.' (When actually working he was not to be disturbed—if he was, he could be 'very cross'.)

'I had to be mentally ready in order to keep pace with him, flexible in order to adapt myself to his moods and his ideas. I was aware of it and it gave me pleasure and made me develop. I looked forward to those evenings as to the most beautiful thing the day could bring me.'

The first composition to be written in the new home was the Valachian nocturne for men's voices and orchestra ČARTÁK ON THE SOLÁŇ. It came about in the following manner:

During the autumn of 1910 Janáček went to the town of Prostějov in central Moravia to see its new cultural centre, which included a good theatre. There

*) *Zdeňka Janáčková*, p. 95.

he attended a rehearsal of the male choir Orlice which sang some of his choruses.

For the fiftieth anniversary of this choir in 1912, the committee at the suggestion of Vilém Steinman (conductor of the Orlice and also of the women's choral society Vlastimila) decided to ask Janáček to compose a special work, and even selected some suitable festive poems by Martin Kurt (the pen-name of Dr Max Kunert), a poet who drew on social and local Valachian themes.

Steinman was sent to Brno just before Christmas 1910 to present the texts to Janáček and to discuss the whole matter with him.

Janáček immediately discarded the festive poems but when Steinman pointed out Kurt's ballad ČARTÁK ON THE SOLÁŇ Janáček was so struck by it that in Steinman's presence he began hastily jotting down in pencil the scheme of the composition; it is still preserved in Steinman's copy of Kurt's poems. It says a great deal for Janáček's prompt imagination that in composing the piece he scarcely had to change anything of this original sketch except for leaving out one of the verses in the middle section. He adapted the poem by repeating each line, with the exception of the first one, in the time-honoured flashion of Old Slav folk poetry, whereby the repeated line ushered in each new couplet. Similarly, the original sketch saw the definitive reversal of the order of the last lines so as to concentrate all the action in the middle section and end the work in a quiet evening mood. On 24 April 1911 he sent the completed score to Steinman with a dedication to the Orlice choir of Prostějov where the work was performed on 13 March 1912 conducted by Steinman. The choir went to the expense of fulfilling Janáček's wish by engaging the military band from Brno with which he had three years previously performed Gounod's oratorio *Mors et Vita* with such excellent results. Janáček was present at one of the orchestral rehearsals in Brno but did not attend the Prostějov performance.*)

The story of the ballad takes place in an old smugglers' inn called Čarták n the Beskydy Mountains.**)

---

*) Perhaps he had been unable to go or perhaps there had been a misunderstanding similar to the one which occurred in 1920 and which is described by Stanislav Tauber in his book *My Musical World* (p. 71—72): 'I had been engaged by the Záboj choral society of Ostrava to sing in AMARUS. I arrived on a Saturday afternoon for the evening rehearsal. Members of the society were at the station and asked whether Janáček was travelling with me. I had not seen him. We waited until the train left. He was not there. We decided that he would probably arrive the next day in time for the afternoon concert in the theatre. He did not come. The conductor, Professor Rund, was obliged to seek all the information he needed abou tempi etc. from me. In the afternoon, after the concert, I returned to Brno. On Monday, on my way from school, I met Janáček. I greeted him but did not expect him to see me as he was walking gloomily with his eyes riveted to the ground. However, he followed his first indifferent "My respects" at once with a livelier "My greatest respects! You were in Ostrava. How did it go there?" "It was a wonderful performance, the choir well rehearsed, the orchestra good, the trombones fairly blasted the quintuplet…" "They blasted it, did they? That's good." (This had been one of his wishes.) "But, Maestro, they had been expecting you. On Saturday at the station, Sunday morning again…". "But, but, I wanted to go, but I wasn't invited." "How could that be?" "I got a letter from Professor Rund telling me that the committee was at the moment deciding to invite me, etc. But no invitation came."

**) The word 'čarták' seems to derive from the Hungarian for 'lonely hostelry'. The poet in his opening lines would have us believe that this inn was a squat, black eagle's nest in the clouds, when, in actual fact, it is an ordinary little inn on the none-too-steep Soláň hillside

The poet comes to the inn longing for his 'pale Vsacanka' (i.e. a girl, native of Vsetín) whom he has just left behind at Karlovice. From the lighted inn he hears the clanging of the cymbalom and in the doorway he sees the innkeeper's pretty daughter. He dances with her and later when the inn is steeped in darkness and the girl breathes blissfully in his arms, he forgets all about Karlovice and his pale sweetheart.

The composition consists of a quick section in dance rhythm wedged between two slow, evocative, more or less similar sections. There are two basic motifs symbolizing the two loves of the poet; one, over a soft C sharp pedal (in a kind of Dorian mode with a Lydian raised fourth), which could be called the motif of longing:

and two, the Soláň motif, which is introduced soon afterwards in the choir:

Na So-lá-ni Čar-ták,   čer-ná krč-ma sto-jí___

On the Soláň the Čarták,
It's a gloomy tavern

Soon the two are combined, as the ardent, yearning sixths of the clarinets underscore the boy's memory of his sweetheart:

Sbo-hem buď, sbohem buď   má Vsacan-ko ble - dá ___

Fare thee well,
My pallid Vsacanka

The mood is suddenly enlivened and the combination of the two musical ideas gives rise to the faltering motif of the wild dance-like middle section, brimming over with keen desire:

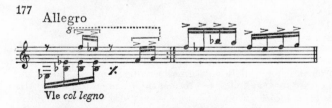

Vle col legno

where the frontier once ran between Moravia and Hungary, situated on that same road to the Karlovice Pass along which Janáček, according to his own words, had over a year earlier escaped from the Hungarian *gendarmes* (see p. 180).

Sustained trills, harp glissandos, the tantalizing languor of the triangle and the glockenspiel (first heard in the slow opening as if ringing a distant angelus but, in fact, preparing the sensuous change of mood), together with an exuberant augmentation of the title 'Na Soláni Čarták' in the basses, all combine with the fragmented variant of the motif of longing in the tenors:

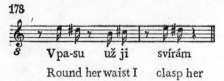

178

Vpa-su už ji svírám

Round her waist I clasp her

in an intoxicating bacchanal, the tempo of which is increased to presto. No less exciting is the languid reminiscence of the motif of Soláň, which then follows in muted horns:

179 (Andante)

This signals the return of the opening section which now describes the starry night in the Beskydy mountains. The motif of longing makes several prominent appearances before its dying notes bring this Valachian nocturne to its end, as startling as it is logical in typical Janáček fashion, on the last semiquaver of the bar with an unresolved cadence. There is no doubt that Janáček was inspired both by the passionate character of the poem and by its setting in his native region to write one of his most charming and yet least performed works. It lasts a mere seven minutes—but seven minutes bursting with ardent life.

During their holidays of 1912 the Janáčeks realized their long-standing wish and went, once again, to the seaside—not as in 1896 to the 'leaden' sea of the north near St Petersburg, but this time to the 'rainbow glitter' of the Adriatic.

They crossed the Alps to Rijeka and from there went by ship to Crikvenica.*)

'Sea. You can see the crustaceans down at the deep bottom. An octopus with its family of baby octopuses.

'Sun scorching the noonday beach. It is setting. A golden bridge reaches from shore to horizon.

---

*) The choice of this beautiful spot, the detailed planning of the journey and the reservation of rooms in a pleasant house with a balcony overlooking the sea was the work of Mrs Marie Steyskalová, director of the women's home in Brno, with which the Janáčeks (including Olga) had been associated ever since its founding at the turn of the twentieth century. (Mrs Janáček helped to keep a little orphan girl there.) The Brno home ran a children's holiday settlement at Crikvenica. However, Janáček used Mrs Steyskalová's plan only in part and, having explored Crikvenica itself, decided to keep his headquarters there for the rest of the three weeks' holiday.

'Tolstoy's three holy men could wander across it.

'The cool shade of Vinodol.*)

'Excursion to the Krk vineyards.

'Women worn out by work, easy-going fishermen.

'Passing by Rab.

'To Pula to see the Roman ruins, the amphitheatre.**)

'Storm at sea. (Janáček was the only passenger who remained on deck eagerly watching and taking down 'melodic curves' of the raging elements.)

'Trieste and its osterias (inns).

'White Ljubljana; the castle and its guardian—a Czech veteran.

'The lake at Bled with the little church and its bell which lures bridegrooms to girls.

'Mount Triglav with its golden crown appeared on the horizon.

'The Vindgar ravine with its wild cataract.

'At the end, a bad attack of rheumatism.'

The rheumatism did not come until after Janáček's return home. He was scarcely able to move from November until March, his feet and hands were so swollen. During these months he taught at home.

In the meantime, Janáček wrote another of his 'intimate confessions', the piano cycle IN THE MISTS. (It was written, perhaps, just before the attack of rheumatism, since Janáček entered it in a competition, the closing date of which was 1 November 1912.)***)

The four pieces in this new cycle have no names, but they are bound to the title they share by more than their 'misty' keys with five of six flats and their simple ternary forms: their connection is motivic and, therefore, programmatic.

In any case, to note the simplicity of their form is not to say that their musical content is simple. It is the heightened emotional pitch of this content that accounts for an even greater metrical freedom than in THE OVERGROWN PATH and for the frequent use of emotionally charged motivic diminutions as, for instance, in the middle section of No. 1:

*) A wood near Crikvenica.
**) In Pula on the Istra peninsula, which at that time was a big Austro-Hungarian naval base, Janáček saw warships for the first time. While the other members of the excursion paid a visit to the ships, Janáček refused the invitation on principle. On the other hand he enjoyed taking part in the Venetian type of fiesta on water and on land which took place every Saturday at Crikvenica.
***) In the same year—probably in the spring—Janáček had written another piano cycle, entitled SPRING SONG, his fourth work to be given this romantic title. The others were a lost song-cycle to words by Zusner, the SPRING SONG for voice and piano and the one-act opera to Gabriela Preissová's libretto which was never realized. It is perhaps no accident that the piano cycle SPRING SONG is lost.

or in No. 2, where the main theme, in a tender, resigned mood:

Molto adagio

181

alternates with its spectral-sounding diminution compressed even further by close imitation:

82   Presto

This is later joined by an urgent syncopated motif of the middle section. In No. 4 a similar figure of the central motif:

Andante
espressivo

183

turns into this steep, off-beat diminution:

184

Particularly closely related are the motifs in No. 3—those of the wistfully reconciled main section with those of the agitated central episode:

Andantino

185

dolente, appas.

186   Poco mosso

Moreover, the motif quoted in Ex. 186 reappears in No. 4 before the end in the following form:

187

ff espress.

which in its shape, its in effect enharmonically identical key, and its persistent, hammering triplet accompaniment A flat—F flat (G sharp—E) resembles the motif of the owl in the last piece of the first set of THE OVERGROWN PATH (see Ex. 165). Compared with its predecessor, the cycle IN THE MISTS does not contain a single moment of cheerful respite—it is one long struggle between resignation and newly felt pain—pain which gains the upper hand at the end. In my opinion the title IN THE MISTS should be interpreted as meaning not so much memories of childhood or impressions of nature,*) as the expression of Janáček's mental state at the time, in view of the petty indifference shown by the world at large to his work in general and to JENŮFA in particular. This interpretation is borne out by the cycle's close proximity to the pessimistic ballad THE FIDDLER'S CHILD and explains its thematic link with the most ominous of the pieces in the earlier cycle, THE LITTLE NIGHT OWL KEPT HOOTING.

The physical suffering which Janáček endured after completing this work returned in a different form during the summer holidays of 1913. On the advice of his doctor, Janáček went to the spa of Karlovy Vary in Bohemia (he would rather have gone south again but 'this Balkan theatre [of war] makes one feel uneasy'). He had scarcely completed the journey from Karlovy Vary to Mšeno in Bohemia, where he was to complete his cure, when he got erysipelas all over his body and had to be taken to hospital at Roudnice. When at last he returned more or less cured to Brno, he was so eager to get about that he began getting cramp in the legs and could not walk at all. Yet another blow was in store for him. The première of his opera DESTINY, which had at last in August 1912 been included in the season's announcements by the Vinohrady Theatre in Prague, failed to materialize, this time for good. The conductor Bedřich Holeček, who was not on friendly terms with Janáček ever since his Brno days, refused to rehearse the opera saying that the singers would ruin their voices. The directors of the theatre then decided to entrust the assistant conductor Adolf Piskáček with the opera but by that time the antagonism of the company had been so roused that he was unable to overcome their objections.

And Janáček? In the midst of these squabbles and while the Balkan war was waged between brotherly nations over the Turkish inheritance, he composed, at the end of 1913 and the beginning of 1914, his message of love and good will—his setting of Vrchlický's ETERNAL GOSPEL. His call to humanity which he had expressed one year earlier in THE FIDDLER'S CHILD now found even fuller expression in this cantata for soprano, tenor, mixed choir, orchestra and organ.

---

*) Is not Debussy's *Des pas sur la neige* more than the title suggests—steps in life, rather than mere impressionist tone-painting?

(25) 'Eternal Gospel'

The title THE ETERNAL GOSPEL—*Evangelium æternum*—borrowed from the
Revelation of John XIV, 6, was posthumously bestowed on the writings of the
Cistercian mystic Joachim of Fiore (d. 1201 or 1202) who, without considering
himself to be a prophet, believed himself able to interpret biblical prophecies.[*]
Vrchlický's poem (from the second volume of his *Frescoes and Tapestries* called
Mediaeval Legends) describes Joachim's vision of an angel bringing the Eternal
Gospel which foretells the coming of a 'Third Kingdom': after the Kingdom
of the Father and the Kingdom of the Son will come the Kingdom of the Spirit.
In other words, after the Kingdom of Justice and the Kingdom of Grace will
come the Kingdom of Love for all creatures, with St Francis of Assisi as its
'high priest'.

Although Vrchlický meant his poem sincerely enough, its subject was, no
doubt, more a stimulus for his imagination than a personal statement. Yet
out of his theologically muddled poem clad in the verbiage of Secession (which,
incidentally, has also left its mark on the libretto of THE EXCURSIONS OF MR
BROUČEK which Janáček was working on at this time and which, in part,
satirizes none other than Vrchlický), Janáček created a deeply-felt declaration
of faith in mankind, faith which runs like a red thread through his *œuvre*
right up to THE HOUSE OF THE DEAD. Janáček divided the poem into four
movements, the first three forming an entity and the fourth an epilogue beginning with Joachim's words 'All this spoke the angel unto me in the darkness
of night.' The solo violin and the solo soprano represent the angel and his
gospel of love while the solo tenor is Joachim of Fiore. The choir acts as
commentator.

The composition, which lasts about 20 minutes, begins with the majestic
ascent of an octave motif taking in the broken chord A flat—F flat—C—E flat
over a quiet pedal A flat:

This theme which, according to the composer, represents open arms longing
to embrace the whole world, is immediately answered by an anguished theme
in A flat minor combined with a tiny motif of a third airily leaping up an
octave like a wisp of a cloud in the heavens:

---

[*] It is worth mentioning that Joachim's *Eternal Gospel* containing the prophecy of the fall
of Papal power was adapted in 1527 by the Nuremberg poet-cobbler Hans Sachs, the hero
of Wagner's *Die Meistersinger*.

The rhythm of its accompaniment undergoes a transformation into a psalm-like unison:

The beginning is then repeated over the dominant to be answered by the solo violin with the tender, hopeful motif of the angel:

which Janáček then builds up to a climax, at the peak of which the orchestra stops completely (the choir does not sing in the first movement at all) while the solo tenor (Joachim) enters with the words 'Now it shall be as foretold in Revelation':

as foretold in Revelation.

This speech melody is taken up by the horns:

and leads through a stormy descent in octaves to this triumphal fanfare of three trumpets:

Its character is reminiscent of the introductory fanfare in the **Prologue** to Boito's *Mefistofele*. The fanfare is gradated at first, but then it subsides to bring the first movement to a close. In the second movement the announcement of the coming of the angel who is bringing a new gospel to the sinking humanity is accompanied by this agitated diminution of a motif derived from the theme of anguish (see Ex. 189):

195

This is compressed with the help of some high notes in the trumpets (up to high E flat!) and then expanded again into a seemingly new theme:

196

Je těž-ká mi-tra pa-pe-ži

The Pope's mitre weighs heavily

whose opening and concluding 4/3 chord (a subdominant triad over the dominant) is used throughout THE ETERNAL GOSPEL so often that it almost becomes a motto in itself. After building up to a big climax topped with the opening theme (Ex. 188) twice repeated and each time followed by a consoling phrase in the harp:

197

the third movement begins on a hushed note F and the same theme from the opening of the work is heard again. This time, however, it rustles softly as its tremolo *sul ponticello* rises higher and higher. It is repeated three times (symbolically, perhaps), interrupted each time by the piccolo with its fleeting diminution suggesting, perhaps, the blinding approach of the angel:

198

The angel intones his message of the coming of the 'Third and only Kingdom of the Spirit' and the choir answers with enraptured cries of *alleluia*:

199

Al - le - lu - ja

prepared beforehand in augmentation in the orchestra:

200

The choir then bursts out with a joyous repetition of the angel's words:

Říš lás - ky při - jde k nám.

201

Love's Kingdom will come to us

and then, buttressed by a triumphant fanfare, solemnly sings after Joachim
to an expanded form of the *alleluia* motif—perhaps too solemnly, considering
the essence of the inward-looking text:

202

Kri - stus   jen se   sklo - nil   ku člo - vě - ku,
Fran - ti - šek se   sklo - nil   ku zví - ře - ti.

Al - le - lu - ia

Christ was serving only human kind,
Francis served wild creatures, bird and beasts.

The fourth movement begins with a meditative variant of the theme of
anguish:

203
Andante

There is a mighty surge of the original opening theme, the orchestra stops,
and Joachim, once again in complete silence, proclaims: 'I, Joachim of
Fiore, prophesy the Golden Age.' The work ends with a joyful assurance of
the coming of the Kingdom of Love.

THE ETERNAL GOSPEL was first performed on 5 February 1917, after the
success of JENŮFA, by the Hlahol choral society of Prague conducted by
Jaroslav Křička. The first Brno performance was given in 1919 by the Beseda
Philharmonic Society conducted by Ferdinand Vach. In both towns it was
performed again in 1924 on the occasion of Janáček's seventieth birthday, for
which Janáček revised it, replacing, for instance, the three solo violins
by a single one. To give some idea of the strong impression the work made
even in its original form let me quote Ladislav Vycpálek (1882—1969),
himself a composer of fine cantatas, who wrote in an article in the *Hudební*

211

revue of February 1917: 'Janáček sees everything as drama... his ETERNAL GOSPEL is also a dramatic scene. I had the impression that the composition was taking place on the tops of high mountains in the glow of a few blood-red rays which pierced the darkness. Towering in the gloom—the ecstatic figure of the prophet who tells, on the wings of his voice flying to the dark unknown, of the coming of the Third Kingdom... Everything is, in a sense, unclear, indefinable by colour but full of ardour and of mighty gestures and apocalyptic ecstasy. It is a strange composition, but somehow it is intoxicating.'

(26) The Violin Sonata

Janáček's sixtieth birthday, 3 July 1914, passed almost unnoticed, though the faithful Friends of Art Club did at least publish the score of THE FIDDLER'S CHILD, and the Organ School put on a small birthday party with presents and speeches from members of the board, teaching staff and students. Janáček thanked them by giving everyone a day off and taking the professors with their wives out to a simple dinner in the Lužánky gardens and then back to his own little garden for wine and dessert.*) There was still no change in the attitude of the Prague National Theatre, and Joachim of Fiore's prophecy was once more to be discredited, since although the beginning of 1914 was marked by performances all over Europe of Wagner's *Parsifal* which had just ceased to be an exclusive property of Bayreuth (Janáček hurried to Prague to hear it), this was also the year which, on 28 July, saw the outbreak of war.

In the middle of July Janáček had gone to Hukvaldy, intending to travel from there with his wife to Crikvenica again and to Montenegro. This had now to be cancelled and instead he went alone to Luhačovice, having first ordered Miss Olga Vašková (Bezruč's sister), the secretary of the Russian Circle, to destroy all pro-Russian protocols and write inoffensive new ones. It did not occur to him to destroy his own correspondence with Russian personalities or with the fiercely nationalist Croatian politician, Stjepan Radić (nevertheless, this was secretly attended to by his wife). To Janáček, there seemed no cause for alarm, since news had arrived of Russian gunfire having been heard in Ostrava, while farther east, the Russians were said to be approaching the Carpathian Mountains and might even have crossed them.

It was in this mood of suspense while awaiting freedom that Janáček wrote the VIOLIN SONATA.**) It was not his first work of this kind. As a student he had written an unfinished one in Leipzig, and a second one shortly afterwards

---

*) Robert Smetana: *Stories about Janáček*. p, 58.

**) 'I wrote the VIOLIN SONATA in 1914 at the beginning of the war when we were expecting the Russians in Moravia,' wrote Janáček on 21 January 1922 to the musicologist Otakar Nebuška. This connection with the war is confirmed by the pianist Karel Šolc who rehearsed the sonata with the leader of the Czech Philharmonic Orchestra, Stanislav Novák, for its performance at the second festival of the International Society for Contemporary Music held in the first week of August 1923 in Salzburg. (At the actual performance the piano part was played by Václav Štěpán who had performed the sonata shortly before, on 16 December 1922, at the Prague Mozarteum with the leader of the Bohemian Quartet, Karel Hoffman. The actual first performance of the sonata took place in 1922 in Brno where it was played by the leader of the Moravian Quartet, František Kudláček, accompanied by Jaroslav Kvapil.) According to Šolc, Janáček insisted on the most agitated rendering of the high piano tremolo over the final appearance of the chorale-like theme of the last movement—he explained that it was the Russian armies entering Hungary. The Russians really did enter Hungary on 26 September 1914, but the rejoicing lasted just one week.

for Professor Krenn in Vienna (both are lost). Even this third sonata dates back to an earlier period because of one of its movements, the *Ballad*. The sonata passed through no less than three revisions and, curiously enough, the only movement to remain almost unchanged was the one which was not originally intended to be part of it, namely the *Ballad*, except that originally it ended in C sharp major instead of the less convincing C sharp minor of the final version; and that it was originally the third, and not the second movement.*)

The Russian atmosphere which pervades the work is all the more striking in view of its motivic affinity with the opera KATYA KABANOVA. That, however, was not composed until 1919—1921. For instance, the main theme of the first movement:

is almost identical, even in key, with the closing motif of the penultimate scene of KATYA KABANOVA:

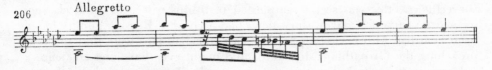

The main theme of the third movement (a kind of scherzo in 2/4):

is reminiscent of the *troika* motif and its variants in KATYA (see Ex. 266), and it is also worth mentioning that there is a similarity between the main theme of the finale (Ex. 211) and the main idea of the opening movement of the FAIRY-TALE (see Ex. 166)—another work with a Russian setting.

But let us take the four movements of the VIOLIN SONATA in turn. The first is introduced by a short solo improvisation on the violin developed from a diminished seventh chord over the dominant seventh of A flat minor, and foreshadowing the main theme by its use of the motif C flat—B flat—G (see bars five and six of the main theme, Ex. 204). A piano variant of the closing bars of the main theme:

---

*) For details see Štědroň's catalogue.

which, incidentally, is similar to the opening of the *Kyrie* in the GLAGOLITIC MASS, gives rise, at the end of the exposition, to a halting, weary theme:

In view of its character and brevity (only five bars as against the preceding 37) it can hardly be regarded as the second subject. It is perhaps better to look upon an earlier buoyant variant of the main theme, in the relative major of C flat, as the second subject, and upon Ex. 208 as the codetta. A more important part is played by this codetta theme in the development section where two of its forms are juxtaposed—the one agitated, the other plaintive. An earnest gradation ushers in the recapitulation, with the second subject in its regular tonic major of A flat. Then comes the surprise—the codetta theme, although it first reappears in the tonic key, shifts to D flat major in which the movement ends. In spite of this and in spite of Janáček's key signature of five flats, A flat minor must be regarded as the basic key of the movement and of the whole work. (The last two movements are in the same key despite the third movement's curious signature of six instead of seven flats and despite the finale's enharmonic, G sharp minor, notation.)

The second movement, the *Ballad*, alternates a lilting imitative version of the main theme in E major (later in D flat):

with an extended soothing melody of a typically Valachian atmosphere (one of the rare occasions when Janáček develops a melody to any great length):

The figuration which accompanies this middle section (a kind of nocturne) is once again derived from the main theme and it goes on to serve as the turbulent backdrop to a new tide of improvisation on the opening idea of the movement. A dreamy reminiscence of both ideas brings the movement to a close.

In the third movement there is some further ingenious development of material. The trio is derived from the descending motif C flat—B flat—A flat—which (see Ex. 206) previously punctuated, in two different guises, the main theme of the movement.

The main idea of the final movement is a typical Janáček juxtaposition of a *dumka* motif in the piano with a savagely energetic, yet evocative answer in the violin*):

The second subject in E major:

brightens the mood temporarily. But soon the two original elements return to dominate the development section and to lead to the majestic, liberating recapitulation of the *dumka* motif in the violin 'fortissimo sul G' under the high tremolo of the piano. The climax of the recapitulation sees the reappearance of the second subject which, however, fractures to bring the sonata resignedly to an end, with the contradiction inherent in its material unresolved. Thus the general character of the VIOLIN SONATA is in complete contrast to the lofty optimism of the FAIRY-TALE though both have their Russian connotations. The brightest part of the SONATA is, curiously enough, the *Ballad*.

This in no way detracts from the quality of the work. On the contrary, it is one more proof that Janáček let himself be guided by the inner logic of a work regardless of matters of effect, and if he felt slighted by the lack of interest shown by the violinist Jaroslav Kocián to whom he sent the sonata in 1915, he told the singer Marie Calma-Veselá**): 'I don't consider it to be an exceptional work but there is some truth in the second and third movements.' The same can certainly be said of the other two movements. And it also applies to the movement which was originally the last and which Janáček, in the final version, left out altogether, replacing it with what had originally been the second

---

*) Was this 'con sordino feroce espressivo' in the low register of the violin an evocation of the boom of Russian heavy artillery heard from afar? K. J.
**) *Janáček—Calma-Veselá*, p. 53.

216

movement (Adagio in G sharp minor) and, in place of the second movement, putting the *Ballad*.

This discarded movement contains a particularly beautiful main theme (con moto, tempo di marcia), most typical of Janáček both in the beginning where it seems to be softly breaking through morning mists:

213

and in the recapitulation, once again over a 6/4 chord, in a solemn hymn-like pleno.*)

This movement gave the sonata an interesting cyclic form because it quoted, before its end, the two ideas from the G sharp minor Adagio—the original second movement (compare Examples 211 and 212, although the energetic violin figure was originally calmer), and because the triplet figure which accompanies its main theme (see Ex. 213) played an important role in the first movement.

In any case the original version of the sonata deserves an occasional hearing (Jindřich Polášek, leader of the Brno Radio Orchestra, gave several performances of it), and the discarded last movement should be published. Janáček may have been a spendthrift, but we cannot afford to be squanderers.

---

*) It is interesting that this melody reappears in Janáček's BALLAD OF BLANÍK as the theme of the Knights of Blaník.

217

(27) Women's Choruses

Hopes of an early end to the war were soon frustrated and its protraction began to be felt by the civilian population; apart from the shortage of food, the number of students continually decreased and the Organ School subsidy was withdrawn. The director's salary was reduced to the small sum of 100 crowns per month which Janáček was fortunately able to eke out with his small pension from the Teachers' Training Institute. Janáček the composer was also indirectly affected since he wrote so much for male-voice choir. In fact, the song PERINA (Eiderdown), composed in 1914, was the last work he was to write for this 'instrument' for some considerable time, since the numbers of even the famous Moravian Teachers' Choral Society as well as all the other male-voice choirs were so depleted that they were obliged to curtail their activities. Ferdinand Vach consequently turned the situation to his advantage by forming a women's choir known as the Vach Choir of Moravian Women Teachers. Janáček, like Vach, turned his attention to this side of choral music and, just as the founding of Vach's original choir had acted as a source of inspiration,*) so the formation of this new choir acted on Janáček's creative imagination in a similar way. In quick succession he now produced five outstanding works for women's choir: VLČÍ STOPA (The Wolf's Tracks), a setting of a poem by Jaroslav Vrchlický from his *Epic Poems (Romances and Ballads)*, completed on 25 January 1916, HRADČANSKÉ PÍSNIČKY (Songs of Hradčany) consisting of three choruses to words by F. S. Procházka, probably completed on 1 February 1916, and the balladic burlesque KAŠPAR RUCKÝ to words by the same poet, completed on 12 February 1916. Just as Janáček embellished his latter male-voice choruses NAŠE VLAJKA (Our Flag) nad POTULNÝ ŠÍLENEC (The Wandering Madman) with a solo female voice according to the demands of the words, so in three out of these five choruses he added a solo instrument: for example the bleak piano in THE WOLF'S TRACKS and the flute and the harp in the almost impressionistic SONGS OF HRADČANY.

The ballad THE WOLF'S TRACKS tells of an old army captain who is out for the second night in succession searching a snow-covered plain for the 'wolf's tracks'. Finding nothing, he returns with the darkest forebodings to his home and in one of the windows sees the shadow of his pretty young wife in the arms of another man:

Is this kiss to last for ever? The captain
Lifts his loaded gun—a wild and wondrous thrill.
Oh! A shot rang out, a cry—now the snow plain's
Mute. Today the captain's found the tracks for sure.

---

*) See Janáček's FOUR MORAVIAN MALE-VOICE CHORUSES of 1904.

Janáček set this exciting drama in three sections, the first and the last (in C sharp minor, Janáček's ominous key) are born along on a soft melody:

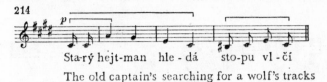

214

Sta-rý hejt-man hle - dá sto-pu vl - čí

The old captain's searching for a wolf's tracks

Its second element (see brackets in Ex. 214) is compressed into this prying motif as the captain's suspicions are roused:

215

whereas its first component reappears in a lyrical form (reminiscent of the second subject of the VIOLIN SONATA, Ex. 212) in the slower, ardent middle section:

The captain's youthful wife, a full and lovely rose

Je - ho mla-dá že-na, pl - ná krá-sná rů-že

216

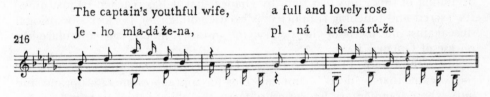

in which Janáček most eloquently describes the beauty of the lovelorn wife. In the frenzy of jealousy even the first component of the theme becomes highly charged, with its hammering upbeat and with the expanding arch of its outline (reaching the interval of a tenth after the shot has rung out). A short return to its original form signals the end of the work.

Once again, Janáček did not hesitate to adapt the poem a little. The most interesting change was the different meaning he gave to the captain's query, 'Is this kiss to last for ever?' In the poem it prompts the captain to deliver the fatal shot. Janáček, however, gave the line to a solo soprano, in slow tempo, after the shot as though he wanted to hint that the lovers passed, embracing, into eternity.

The SONGS OF HRADČANY hold a special place among these wartime women's choruses by virtue of their underlying nationalism which had even before the war made Procházka's poems very popular among the Czechs. (They had appeared in numerous editions since their first publication in 1904.) Yet they did not give as full a scope to Janáček's patriotism as did TARAS BULBA not long afterwards, and at best he could only brood in them over themes from the past.

The first song, ZLATÁ ULIČKA (Golden Lane) evokes the picturesque atmosphere of the poor, toy-like little houses in this famous lane along the nothern end of the wall of Hradčany, the Prague Castle. Legend had it that alchemists of the Emperor Rudolf II (of whom more will be heard in THE MAKROPOULOS CASE) used to make gold there. The song compares these houses with the splendour of the castle only a few paces away. The musical means that Janáček uses to illustrate this is the transformation of a a bright fanfare into a sad dolcissimo which brings the piece to a consoling end with these lines:

217

Víš-li chudá   u-li-čko ty,   že tam tráva   pu - čí,
zla-té jiz-by,   sí-ně ši-ré,   že jsou ještě   chud - ší?

Tell me, humble Golden Lane,
Do you know that grass grows
In the gilded, empty halls?
Humbler than you, they are.

This, no doubt, was the melody that Brod had in mind when he wrote: 'We have to go back to Schubert if we are to find similar skill in composing songs. At the very first hearing we feel this melody has not been invented, it is an archetype which has always been ready in the dream of the universe since the beginning of time, and it is only by chance that it has reached us just now.' Its 'sacred and touching simplicity' is excuse enough for Janáček's occasional sins against the metre of the poetry, for instance in the earlier fanfare-like phrase of GOLDEN LANE.

The second song, PLAČÍCÍ FONTÁNA (The Weeping Fountain)—weeping for the 'dream' that is 'dead'—contains solos for soprano or mezzo-soprano and flute whose fragmentary figuration suggests the play of the fountain.*)

The third song, BELVEDERE (with soprano and contralto solos), is a meditation on the events which took place at the summer palace of the title, from the time when the Royal Garden echoed with the notes of Queen Anna's harp, to the days of Rudolf II's insanity when, having been deposed by his brother Matthias, he bemoaned his fate in this lovers' retreat. The poet then prophesies that Belvedere, this 'poem in stone', will weather the storms of time unharmed since it was 'built by love' and, progressing somewhat boldly from sensual love to love of humanity, proclaims with a sigh: 'If only love would prevail, sweeping the land with her song, where would you be, my poor land, what miracles we might see!'

All three songs of this cycle exhibit, as Max Brod rightly points out, 'the true mood of women's choruses. They are treasures of gentleness and softly-spoken poetry, breathing of roses and enshrouding in melancholy the symbol of a great past—Hradčany.' They abound in Janáček's characteristic vocal effects such as octave doublings crossed through sometimes by other voices in measured legato figurations—a device favoured by Czech choral composers ever since the time of Křížkovský—pedal effects, *sfp* chords and others. Their

---

*) There is in the Royal Garden at Hradčany a fountain made of bell-metal, which is designed so as to emit a curious sound when it plays. It stands in front of the renaissance summer palace Belvedere built in the mid-sixteenth century by the Habsburg Emperor Ferdinand I for his Queen, Anna Jagieło. The fountain itself is the work of Ferdinand's bell-founder, Tomáš Jaroš. K. J.

charm is further increased by the use of the flute in No 2 (for descriptive effect) and the harp in No 3 (as an integral part of the story).

The harp part in No 3 opens with a variant of the three-note motif of the main vocal theme (Ex. 219), split by an octave leap:

Belvedere, a poem in stone submerged in flowers

The harp then goes on to develop this regal motif:

The dramatic story told in this poem gave Janáček full scope for employing all the means at his disposal in the spirit of a true finale, and he gradated them to the most forceful effect at the point of the prophetic line 'This poem in stone will stand for ever more.' After that, the quiet ending makes a doubly beautiful impression with its characteristic 'tangle' of moods: while the solo voice rises confidently with the words 'What miracles we might see', the choir only whispers 'My poor land'.

In contrast to the SONGS OF HRADČANY, Janáček composed, almost at the same time, another women's chorus to words by the same poet (F. S. Procházka), entitled KAŠPAR RUCKÝ. It describes the adventures of a fraudulent alchemist of that name in the services of Emperor Rudolf II, who in 1612 is sentenced to be quartered alive. On the night before his execution, however, he hangs himself in his prison cell. Yet the world is still not rid of Master Kašpar. The devil causes his soul to ride for 40 nights through the castle courtyards on a fiery goat, escorted by 100,000 witches and their cats. The ballad ends with the poet's declaration: if the devil wished to repeat the prank today, he would not be able to find enough goats to seat the enormous number of Kašpars among us.

Josef Plavec points out the relationship of this truly baroque ghost story to Mussorgsky's *Night on the Bare Mountain* as well as to Janáček's EXCURSIONS OF MR BROUČEK and THE MAKROPOULOS CASE. Janáček added a special atmosphere to this 'song from Hradčany' by humorously copying the ballad-hawkers' style, doubtless suggested to him by the poem itself which has a slow polka refrain and which begins in the style of an old popular ballad.

Janáček heightens the effect of the folk ditty by altering the poem's trochee

221

into a dactyl rhythm and giving a whole bar to the last unaccented syllable, thus exaggerating it in the true fairgound-singer's style:

I'm picking this olden tale   like a berry on the bush

Tr-hám ji jak ma-li - nu,   tu-hle sta-rou no - vi - nu

This crude characterization, though it is toned down by the use of the women's choir, cannot be held responsible for many other cases of declamatory high-handedness. Janáček does not hesitate to distort whole verses, intermixing them and their melodies, making them overlap, dissolve into one another, anticipate. But the effect of this procedure, as in his rebellious Bezruč trilogy for men's choir earlier (of which this chorus is reminiscent because of its free strophic pattern), is most enthralling. 'The turbulent humour, the sparkle and whirl of the interplay of the various lines makes one wonder how the composer himself can have escaped getting lost in the maze of his own creation as though all ten fingers had been writing simultaneously. And yet there is logic in the motivic work and in the many enharmonic modulations—an original, different kind of logic and construction,' wrote Jaroslav Křička.*)

The first performance in Prague on 6 April 1921 given by the Prague Women Teachers' Choral Society conducted by Method Doležil in the presence of the composer, was a tremendous success, and the work became this choir's *pièce de résistance* during its tour of Germany.

*) In the music magazine *Listy Hudební matice*, Vol. IV, p. 17.

$\left(\underline{28}\right)$ 'Jenůfa' Victorious

The time was approaching for JENŮFA and its composer to gain wider recognition. Although Janáček had done nothing for several years to promote this child of his own suffering, his admirers were not idle. One of the most faithful of these was the physician František Veselý, well known for his work during the years 1902—1909 in bulding up, with the help of the Slovak architect Dušan Jurkovič,*) the spa of Luhačovice. Janáček had known Dr Veselý since the 1890s when together they founded the Russian and Polish Circles and, in particular, the Friends of Art Club in Brno. This club, at the suggestion of Dr Veselý, published the vocal score of JENŮFA in the spring of 1908.

Dr Veselý was aided by the young writer Marie Calma (née Hurych) who was also a talented singer and who, in October of the same year, became his wife. He had introduced her to Janáček during the preceding summer at Luhačovice where she expressed keen interest in the opera JENŮFA. In her congenial Luhačovice home, she managed to induce Janáček to make peace with several people, among others with his former pupil Jan Kunc, the most influential figure, after Janáček, in the musical life of Brno. (Kunc never ceased being Janáček's admirer and propagandist and wrote the first penetrating study of the composer in two instalments for the *Hudební revue* of 1912.) The main fort to be captured was Kovařovic and the National Theatre. Dr Veselý addressed a request, in February 1911, to his medical colleague, Professor Jaroslav Hlava, president of the board of sponsors of the National Theatre, to arrange for JENŮFA to be performed.**) It was a favourable psychological moment to make such a move since shortly before, on 31 January 1911, JENŮFA had been put on in its third production in Brno, conducted by Rudolf Pavlata, and Janáček had again made some small corrections and cuts. Yet just this conscientiousness aroused Hlava's suspicions: 'Mr Janáček has revised his opera and would be ready to revise it again—this, I think, proves that it is not the *chef d'œuvre* you imagine,' he wrote in answer to Dr Veselý. 'He would do better to write something new...' He went on to say that the National Theatre had new works of more importance to put on, such as *Rainer the Painter* by František Picka, Piskáček's *Wild Barbara* and a non-existent opera by Vítězslav Novák. (Hlava mistakenly assumed that Novák's cantata *The Storm* was an opera.)

In March 1913 JENŮFA was being produced in Brno for the fourth time (conducted by Karel Winkler) and Dr Veselý was planning a new offensive against Prague for later in the year. Janáček again opposed the plan, declaring

---

*) Jurkovič's style combined modern architecture with Valachian and Slovak folk elements.
**) This measure was decided upon at the general meeting of the Friends of Art Club on 18 February 1911. Janáček was against it but was defeated.

proudly:*) 'Prague will soon be hearing THE FIDDLER'S CHILD and in the autumn, perhaps THE ETERNAL GOSPEL—that will suffice.**) You would do better to help Miss Dvořáková***) to a concert for the Prague Chamber Music Association. She plays my IN THE MISTS as it should be played.'

As neither the great success of 70,000 at its Prague première on 4 April 1914 nor the publication of the score of THE FIDDLER'S CHILD did anything to make Kovařovic alter his attitude, different tactics were now adopted. Karel Šípek, Kovařovic's intimate friend and librettist, used to spend his holidays at the spa of Bohdaneč near Pardubice in eastern Bohemia where Dr Veselý had in 1915 been appointed director. Marie Calma-Veselá took advantage of Šípek's presence there and managed to arouse his interest in JENŮFA. In the summer of the same year she approached the director of the National Theatre, Gustav Schmoranz, who was also staying at the spa, and sang for him Jenůfa's main scenes in private. Schmoranz was won over and persuaded Kovařovic to have one more look at the vocal score. However, the result—as he was obliged to admit to Šípek on 29 September 1915—was again negative. 'He considers the prayer and some of the monologues to be good—in fact all that follows the pattern of Slovácko songs. But he thinks the dialogues to be totally wrong. He says that, on the one hand, the composer adheres rigidly to the principle of reproducing faithfully the aural effect of the language as it is spoken in Slovácko, while on the other he makes the singers repeat, contrary to all true speech, passages of the text n number of times. It is, he says, an odd mixture of striving after 'novelty' in quite a novel way, with extreme primitivism.'

After this failure, the Veselýs, having returned for the winter to Prague, began making new plans. They obtained Janáček's consent and set out to organize a concert at the Moravian Beseda in Prague at which a condensed version of JENŮFA would be performed with an introductory speech by the composer plus, perhaps, IN THE MISTS, the PIANO TRIO (*Kreutzer Sonata*) and the new VIOLIN SONATA. The concert, however, proved to be unnecessary. At the beginning of November Šípek managed to persuade the renowned conductor Kovařovic to look through the full score of the opera once again. He then asked Mrs Calma-Veselá who had been encouraged by Janáček's laconic telegram 'Do break through!' to sing to Kovařovic some of Jenůfa's and Kostelnička's scenes, which she did on 7 December. Kovařovic was at last converted and promised to take on the musical direction of the opera himself, provided the composer would allow him to make some adaptations and cuts. Since he did not wish to negotiate personally with Janáček, the discussions were carried out by Doctor and Mrs Veselý. Janáček was so over-joyed by the acceptance of JENŮFA that the Veselýs had little difficulty in persuading him to agree to such 'trifles'.

There were still two obstacles to be overcome: how to dispel the doubts of the cautious board of sponsors of the National Theatre regarding the financial

---

*) In a letter to Dr Veselý dated 24 December 1913.
**) These two performances took place as late as 1917 when JENŮFA no longer needed their support.
***) A piano professor at the Brno Organ School.

success of the opera, and how to bring about a reconciliation between Kovařovic and Janáček. Once more the magnanimous doctor solved the first problem by personally guaranteeing the sale of the tickets for the first six performances and pledging himself to cover any financial loss. His wife took on the other task. Profiting by a visit Janáček made to Prague at the end of December, she pointed out to him the cuts which Kovařovic insisted on making. (Two of these she had saved by replacing, at Kostelnička's departure in Act I, the many times repeated 'Goodbye to you all' which irritated Kovařovic, with Gabriela Preissová's original words carrying on the plot 'Tomorrow morning you must go away, then people will not say you are after him.') The Veselýs then invited Janáček to their box to hear Smetana's opera *Libuše* which Kovařovic was conducting. In the interval at Mrs Veselá's suggestion, Janáček and Dr Veselý went round to see Kovařovic. The carefully engineered *rapprochement*—Mrs Veselá had, for instance, revealed to each composer in turn only the nicest things they were saying about each other—was a cordial success.

Many years of antagonism were forgotten; they were even said to have embraced. Janáček returned to the box well satisfied, remarking in his laconic way, 'It's done.'

The combined efforts of three people—the Veselýs and Šípek—had thus prepared the way for JENŮFA to the National Theatre where it rightly belonged. But, as Janáček's niece Věra Janáčková pointed out in an article published in the paper *Lidové noviny* on 2 March 1941, the instinct toward national unity during the war demanded the closest possible *rapprochement* between Czechs and Moravians. And what work could have been better suited to this mood than JENŮFA? No doubt that Kovařovic, who personally contributed so much by his unforgettable performances of Smetana's and Dvořák's operas, as well as by his own opera *Psohlavci,**) clearly felt it himself.

The Prague première of JENŮFA took place on 26 May 1916. It was not only unusually successful, but it was the point from which the opera, 13 years after its completion, set out on its journey round the world. The casting was, on the whole, exeptionally apt: Gabriela Horvátová—a distinctly original Kostelnička; Theodor Schütz—Števa in Brno, now in Prague a manly but sensitive Laca; Věra Pivoňková—old mother Buryja as in Brno; Arnold Flögl—the Mayor; in the part of the foreman of the mill, no less a person than Vilém Zítek; Kamila Ungrová—Jenůfa; Antonín Lebeda—Števa. The producer was Robert Polák.**) A further factor in promoting the success of JENŮFA, particularly abroad, was the appearance of a new admirer of Janáček's work. He was Dr Max Brod, of German-Jewish origin, who was born in Prague on 27 May 1884 (died 1968). Having taken his law degree at the German university in Prague, he worked for a time as a civil servant. After the First World War he worked in the press section of the Prime Minister's office and was music and

---

*) Members of the fiercely independent *Chod* people of the mountainous south of Bohemia, whose traditional job was to guard the frontier and whose emblem symbolizing loyalty and vigilance was a dog's *(Pso-)* head *(hlavci)*.

**) Under the influence of the success, one of the conductors at the National Theatre, František Picka, told Janáček that it was he who, after a cursory glance at the score, had influenced Kovařovic in his constant rejection of the opera. Probably, out of rueful enthusiasm, he ascribed to himself a bigger part in the wrongdoing than he had actually played.

drama critic of two Prague papers published in German: *Prager Tagblatt* and *Prager Abendblatt*. Apart from his interest in humanism, pacifism, in local topics on the history of Prague, and in the Jewish question, he was also attracted to the dramatic side of music and to art in general. (He composed a number of songs.) When Josef Suk, who had never written to Brod before and was never to write to him again, drew his attention to JENŮFA by sending him an impulsive postcard, Brod went to hear it at the beginning of November 1916 with the result that on 16 November he wrote in the Berlin *Schaubühne* an enthusiastic article headed *Tschechisches Opernglück*. Janáček read it and thanked Brod, thus initiating a friendship which had important consequences.

Max Brod had made successful translations of Vítězslav Novák's *Zvíkovský rarášek* (The Pixie of Zvíkov) and *Karlštejn* (Karlštejn Castle) and was to translate Novák's opera *Lucerna* (The Lantern) later, and Janáček, who had decided that he would have no one else but Brod to translate JENŮFA, made a special journey to Prague to arrange it. Brod, though overburdened with work, eventually agreed, persuaded by Janáček's straightforward belief in the importance of his participation. Brod also mentioned JENŮFA to Emil Hertzka, director of Vienna Universal Edition who heard JENŮFA in Prague on 4 March 1917 and was so delighted that he immediately decided to publish both the full score and the vocal score. Not less enthusiastic were the gentlemen who accompanied him and who were to judge whether the opera would be suitable for the Vienna Court Opera: the conductor Hugo Reichenberger, the composer Julius Bittner and, among other music critics, Richard Specht, the biographer of Gustav Mahler and Richard Strauss. (Richard Strauss had heard JENŮFA—again at Suk's suggestion—some months before, on the evening of Sunday 15 October 1916,*) after his afternoon concert with the Czech Philharmonic Orchestra.) Two days later Janáček wrote to Schmoranz thanking him for putting on that performance for the famous guest. 'I met Richard Strauss once more at the station before his departure. He had liked best the dramatic effect of the third act. I was right in thinking that for many, many Prague musicians Strauss' opinion was necessary. I won't deny I had feared him. His scalpel could have been deadly.'**) As the Austrian visitors found the work suitable,***) the acceptance of JENŮFA by Vienna now depended only on the approval of Brod's translation.

But unexpected difficulties arose just on this point since Reichenberger who was to conduct the work insisted on the words being in dialect, preferably Tyrolean. And although he was overruled, he made many changes in Brod's

---

*) Not, as the editor of the Janáček—Kovařovic correspondence states in his footnote on p. 43, on the occasion when he conducted *Elektra*. Strauss did, in fact, conduct *Elektra* at the National Theatre, but in June 1910. At the above-mentioned concert Strauss conducted, besides Mozart's 'Jupiter' Symphony and his own tone-poems *Macbeth*, *Don Juan* and *Death and Transfiguration*, Suk's *Scherzo fantastique*. Strauss heard JENŮFA (he arrived in the middle of the second act) from a box which he shared with Dr Vilém Zemánek, at that time conductor of the Czech Philharmonic Orchestra, and Gerhart von Keussler, conductor of the German *Gesangverein*.

**) Strauss qualified his praise when talking of the opera with Suk, saying that he admired the music but that from the technical point of view it was *'etwas manieriert'*.

***) Specht's opinion was published in the *Illustriertes Wiener Extrablatt* on 11 March 1917 — see *Janáček—Brod*, p. 24.

translation, altering the dialogue into 'dreadful operatic German' almost causing Brod to withdraw his translation.*)

As soon as these difficulties were straightened out, a new problem appeared, this time political. The nationalistic German members of parliament, Schürff, Weber and Wedra protested on 29 January 1918 to the Ministry of Culture against the production (after Smetana's *Dalibor*) of any further Czech operas at the Vienna Court Opera. This cloud was dispelled by the intervention of the Court itself, and the bills for the first night bore the memorable inscription *Auf allerhöchsten Befehl* (By supreme order). Emperor Karl was, in fact, intending to attend, doubtless for political reasons, but in the event he stayed away. The Empress, Zita, was pregnant and when the Court made discreet enquiries beforehand, the directorate of the Court Opera had to admit that the story of Janáček's piece was rather disturbing. That put paid to the Imperial visit.

The Vienna public, however, received JENŮFA at the first performance on 16 February 1918 with truly Viennese enthusiasm—Janáček had to take about 20 calls. Probably the best proof of success was the fact that the Vienna Court Opera (State Opera after 1918) continued to perform JENŮFA even after October 1918 when the Czech lands separated from Austria. Janáček remarked: 'In the tumult of Vienna, the colourful Moravian stage is like a red carnation buttonhole on a minister's tailcoat.'

The critics, as was to be expected, were divided. It is of interest, however, that the greatest understanding for this realistic Slavonic work was shown by the classically minded biographer of Brahms, Max Kalbeck (first translator of Smetana's *The Bartered Bride*) who wrote for the *Wiener Tagblatt*. The least perceptive was Richard Batka (in the *Fremdenblatt*) who, perhaps because he had been active in Prague for many years, seemed to have picked up some old prejudices against Janáček. And some critics, like Hedwig Kanner (In *Der Morgen*), attributed the success to the excellent production. People will go to hear this 'obstinate' opera, she wrote, because of Maria Jeritza's wonderful Jenůfa.

The performance was certainly an extraordinary one, although Max Brod complained that Reichenberger did not follow Janáček's instructions, and Janáček wrote on 1 February 1918 to Mrs Horvátová: 'He draws out my tempi', and complained of many musical distortions. Nevertheless, he conceded that Reichenberger was fond of the work. Reichenberger himself told Janáček: 'From director Gregor down to the last member of the chorus, everybody likes JENŮFA.'**) Janáček had also been annoyed with the producer Wymetal for not allowing the Viennese ballet master Hassreiter to go to Prague to see the *Odzemek* and other dances as performed at the National Theatre. Wymetal thought that the Viennese public did not know these dances well enough to notice any divergence from the original.***) But once rehearsals had started,

---

*) In some instances, however, Reichenberger should be given his due, e.g. at the end of Act II where he replaced Brod's '*Grad als ob der Tod reingeschnuppert hätt*' with the more common '*Grad als ob der Tod hätt hereingegrinst*'.

**) *Janáček — Horvátová*, p. 82.

***) *Janáček — Horvátová*, p. 52.

Janáček was full of praises. 'The production in Vienna is excellent. Every word is clear also from the gesture.' And after the first rehearsal in folk costumes he remarked 'What beauty of colour. All new and shining bright. The mill and the distant view of the hilly landscape. All in brilliant sunshine, almost enough to make even the audience perspire. The recruits on a garlanded horse. It is the kind of production which I longed for in Prague—in vain.'*) Unlike Brod, Janáček found the Kostelnička of Lucia Weidt 'excellent and in accordance with the producer's instructions', although she was very different in her working-woman sobriety from the Prague Kostelnička of Gabriela Horvátová whom Janáček also admired. (In Act I, Lucia Weidt came on as though straight from the fields, carrying a rake, and at the beginning of Act II she was doing the washing, splashing with the wet linen.) 'Your Kostelnička is aristocratic, hers is rough. You could learn something from her and she from you.'**)

Jeritza's Jenůfa? During the previous year Janáček had been trying in vain to persuade Emmy Destinn to sing the part at the National Theatre. 'Wouldn't you like to sing Jenůfa?—a woman who goes through purgatory and the whole range of human suffering and who in the end, dazed by the vision of God's goodness and justice, forgives those who wanted to stone her and even the one who drowned her baby. She remains firm and steadfast in the love to which even God gives his blessing. I know you would bring this conception of Jenůfa to life... until now the part has been merely sung.'

After hearing Jeritza's performance he wrote: 'I have at last heard and seen Jenůfa in my opera.'***)

The Vienna performance was the culmination of efforts begun by Janáček 14 years earlier when in the autumn of 1904 he had invited the director of the Vienna Court Opera, Gustav Mahler, through the good offices of the Czech minister Dr Pražák to hear a performance of JENŮFA in Brno. Mahler's answer to the then completely unknown Czech composer was in striking contrast to the attitude adopted at that time by the National Theatre. Mahler wrote:

Dear Sir,

As I have explained to Baron Dr Pražák, I am unable to leave Vienna at the present time, but as I would be very interested to get to know your work, I beg you to be kind enough to send me the vocal score with German words.

Yours

Vienna December 9 1904.   Mahler

As no vocal score with German words could be provided at that time, Mahler's request could not be fulfilled and the matter got no further.

The publication of the full score of JENŮFA by Universal Edition contributed significantly towards the success of the opera on the world stage. The adaptations made in the score by Karel Kovařovic are of interest, since it was in that

---

*) *Janáček — Horvátová*, p. 69.
**) *Janáček — Horvátová*, p. 69.
***) *Janáček — Horvátová*, p. 74.

form that it was published. (This is very little known since the modest Kova-řovic gave the fees he received for his painstaking revisions to the benevolent fund of the National Theatre orchestra and did not wish his name to be printed in the score.) After Kovařovic's death, Janáček denied outright all justification for the interference (especially when he discovered that Kovařo-vic's widow was getting a one percent royalty, which led him to assume that he was being cheated), in spite of the fact that he had authorized them. In a letter to his lawyer Dr Jaroslav Lecián, dated 30 October 1923, Janáček even went so far as to maintain that Kovařovic had used 'so much red ink' in the score of JENŮFA only in order to justify retrospectively his continual rejection of the work earlier. As a conductor who has conducted JENŮFA at the National Theatre where the original clean copy of the score with all Kovařovic's alterations exists, I have been able to make a careful study of these changes, trying out some of the original orchestration; and I must admit that in every case I ruefully reverted to Kovařovic's version. People have complained that Kovařovic romanticized the sound of Janáček's score. This could be said, perhaps, of the tremolos with which he replaced Janáček's rhythmic figures in some places, but there the original rhythm can easily be reverted to. But there is nothing romantic in Kovařovic's replacing of the trombones at many points (Janáček had them playing almost continuously) by the horns, thus making the trombones much more effective in the places where they are really needed. Kovařovic can never be accused of wilfully using red ink. His only creative addition as a composer in his own right is the imitative gradation in the brass section of the orchestra at the end of the opera where it perceptively and perfectly symbolizes Laca's and Jenůfa's newly-found love for each other. Or, shortly before, he for instance extends Jenůfa's grudging:

to the more florid:

One is tempted to say that Kovařovic, had he had more time, might have gone further. For example, the double-bassoon, to which Janáček gives only a few unimportant notes at the end of Act I, could have been used more effectively elsewhere and especially to support the crushing chords at the end of Act II.

Thus Kovařovic's modifications in JENŮFA may be cited as an example of the most considerate and relevant realization of a composer's intentions.

229

In the meantime—between 16 and 19 January 1916 when the great future of JENŮFA was beginning—Janáček refreshed himself by harmonizing some folk songs, among others the song he had used as a motto in JENŮFA and as a basis for JEALOUSY, namely the Slovak brigand ballad *Na horách, na dolách* (In the hills, in the valleys). The collection is called PÍSNĚ DETVANSKÉ (Songs of Detva) although only Nos 1—5 are from that region of Central Slovakia,*) the other three melodies being Moravian from Janáček's own BOUQUET.

A similar collection is PĚT NÁRODNÍCH PÍSNÍ (Five Folk Songs) from Moravia and Silesia for male-voice choir and piano, written, according to Štědroň, between 1916 and 1917. I believe that they are basically identical with the folk song arrangements for the Moravian Teachers' Choir which Janáček mentioned as early as 26 September 1908 in a letter to Rektorys**) where he remarks, 'Don't think they are mere harmonizations.' The Moravian Teachers, however, never received them. These five songs are, as it were, a male-voice counterpart to the FOLK NOCTURNES of 1906 for female-voice duet and piano. They too begin mostly with a solo (here taken by a tenor). There is, however, one fundamental difference: whereas in the FOLK NOCTURNES the choir comes in immediately after the opening solo and shares the melody with it in true folk style, in these five male-voice choruses the soloist sings the whole melody and only then the rest of the choir repeats it in a more or less free arrangement or repeats only its conclusion.

At a later date Janáček incorporated the SONGS OF DETVA and the FIVE FOLK SONGS together with the FOLK NOCTURNES and the SIX SONGS sung by Eva Gabel in a four-volume collection under the generic title of TWENTY-SIX FOLK BALLADS—a misnomer to a certain extent since only a few of the songs are balladic in character and even in these the balladic element does not predominate. A ballad which tells a dramatic story—especially when it contains many verses (here as many as 12) surely needs a changing, 'through-composed' accompaniment.

Just as the SONGS OF DETVA were written during the preparations for the first Prague performance of JENŮFA, during the preparations for the Vienna première Janáček wrote, between 15 and 25 January 1918, a further collection for solo voice and piano called SLEZSKÉ PÍSNĚ (Silesian Songs) from Helena Salichová's collection, because 'they breathe the new smell of earth...'

---

*) Janáček took them from the book *Detva by* K. A. Medvecký.
**) *Janáček — Rektorys,* p. 95

230

$\left(29\right)$ 'The Excursions of Mr Brouček'

Shortly after writing his choral burlesque KAŠPAR RUCKÝ, Janáček complet-ed the score of his large-scale operatic burlesque in two parts THE EXCURSIONS OF MR BROUČEK TO THE MOON AND TO THE FIFTEENTH CENTURY, one of his most typical and, despite the burlesque motif, most serious works. It is close-ly linked with the *Songs of a Slave* which Janáček intended to turn into a cantata and THE FIDDLER'S CHILD, not only because it shares with them the same author, Svatopluk Čech, who wrote the novels on which MR BROU-ČEK was based, but also because the criticism contained in all three was direct-ed against Janáček's fellow countrymen. Although neither Svatopluk Čech nor Janáček considered Mr Brouček to deserve the same heavy artillery as the slave drivers and their lackeys and imitators, he is not allowed to escape unpunished. If in a tragedy the hero pays for his guilt with his life, in a come-dy he pays with derision, and Mr Brouček, although in his dream he does indeed pay with his life, in reality he suffers the lighter type of punishment. Who is this 'hero' and what is he guilty of?

Mr Matěj (Matthew) Brouček is a late nineteenth-century landlord of Prague 'with not a ha'p'orth of debt to my name' who, falling asleep when drunk, imagines himself to be carried from the old Hradčany tavern, Vikárka, to the moon. Here he finds the inhabitants living exclusively on perfumes and dew.*) His own rough materialism is shown up in a most unfavourable light. He is like a Faust in reverse, who reveals his wretched stupidity when he comes into contact with the supernatural; or a pocket-size Falstaff who is flirted with by Etherea the 'merry Wife of the Moon', and teased by the moon dwellers. (In this respect it is interesting to note that Janáček at first wished his hero to be infatuated with Etherea—but, of course, only until he got to know what her gossamer body was made of. In the event, the unfeeling librettists would not even have him fall in love with the damsel Kunka in the FIFTEENTH CENTURY.)

Even worse does Mr Brouček represent his 'enlightened' age in the Hussite Prague of the fifteenth century on the eve of the decisive battle of Vítkov Hill. He refuses to fight with the united, though grossly outnumbered, Czechs against Emperor Sigismund's foreign crusaders by declaring 'Sigismund be damned, it's all the same to me, why should I fight him when he's done me no harm?' He refuses to be butchered. 'What's the percentage in that?' And when the Hussite 'Warriors of God' force a weapon, a nasty-looking three-pronged pike, into his hands he runs away at the first opportunity. Meeting

---

*) The moonmen are a satire in its own right upon high-flown artistic movements from seces-sion in art to symbolism in poetry.

some soldiers whom he takes for the enemy he falls on his knees and cries to them in German (with a Czech accent): '*Meine Herr'n!* I'm one of you! No Czech! No Huss! *Gnade!*' All of this does not prevent him from bragging later: 'I helped to liberate Prague—but keep it to yourself.' As a punishment he is to be burned alive in a barrel, eventually waking up to find himself inside a real barrel at the foot of the stairs at the Vikárka—the sole destination of his regular excursions.

Once again Janáček made no effort simply to choose an 'attractive' libretto, although the novel by Svatopluk Čech would make a good farce.*) Janáček stressed the moral issues of the story, especially since the character of Mr Brouček became a topical phenomenon during the First World War. When asked by the first Czechoslovak President T. G. Masaryk (to whom the work was dedicated) what contribution the Czech nation had made to the development of music, Janáček, the Doctor-of-Philosophy-to-be, replied: 'Besides indulging in rich tone it has begun to explore the philosophy of tone.'
What is the philosophy in the case of Mr Brouček?
'We see as many Broučeks in our nation as there were Oblomovs in the Russian nation.**) I wanted people to be disgusted by him, to want to destroy him and stifle him at first sight—but, in the first place, mainly in themselves. So that we may be reborn in the heavenly purity of our national martyrs. Let us not suffer for the Brouček part of our makeup as others suffer for the Oblomov in theirs.'
Convictions such as these, Janáček adds, prompted him to compose THE EXCURSIONS OF MR BROUČEK, especially the more ticklish and serious satire of the second part. And yet from the outset, while he was still searching for a librettist, the work was ill-starred. He approached several writers in vain and poor Mr Brouček was to tread a wearying path before he returned at the end of 1916 both from the moon and from the fifteenth century. This is best summed up by Janáček himself: 'The structure of Svatopluk Čech's story was taken up by Karel Mašek, it was the theme of Josef Holý's variations, the peg to hang Dr Zikmund Janke's additions on; František Gellner intervened with his wit, Jiří Mahen remained master of his own work (sic), Viktor Dyk carved out the work's motto, František S. Procházka intruded with his winning songs, Dr Max Brod added a touch of caricature. I might ask, for fun, in the words of the folk song:***)

> Wait a bit, stay and see,
> Count how many of us,
> See if we're all here.

---

*) The *Excursion to the Moon* was made into a farce spectacular by F. F. Šamberk with music by Kovařovic and into an operetta by Karel Moor.
**) Oblomov, the eponymous 'hero' of Ivan Alexandrovich Goncharov's mid-nineteenth century novel.
***) A Highland dance included under the title 'The Brigand's Funeral' in Janáček's MORAVIAN FOLK POETRY, Volume III, No. 52, and rearranged by the composer later for mixed choir and orchestra.

And yet he is pleased, adding 'How the voices rustle… All who have contributed, even if only by a single line, have done well.'

As a matter of fact, the history of the libretto for THE EXCURSION TO THE MOON is even more complicated than that of the equally anonymous libretto of Puccini's *Manon Lescaut,* and is a burlesque of its own. It is hardly surprising that Janáček, in a letter to Mrs Horvátová, vowed that he would never write another opera. The original librettist had evidently been Janáček himself, receiving a little help from Fedora Bartošová, who had worked with him on the libretto of DESTINY and whose literary talents he held in surprisingly high esteem. At the beginning of 1908 he took the libretto to the writer Zikmund Janke, a doctor he had met at the Luhačovice spa who, however, seemed unable to come up with what Janáček wanted. On the advice of Rektorys, Janáček then, in April of the same year, approached the humorist Karel Mašek. Mašek despite his pen-name 'Fa Presto' worked at it very slowly and in July gave up, arguing that the libretto deviated too far from the original novel which, in his opinion, was in any case unsuitable for stage adaptation. He suggested that Janáček should consult the opera translator and librettist, Josef Vymětal, but Janáček, after Mašek had definitely said 'no' in October, turned in early November to Dr Janke once more, then to the Mrštík brothers and finally to Karel Elgart-Sokol. When all had refused, he went to the writer Josef Holý. In the meantime, as he tells Rektorys in a letter dated 26 November 1909, he had been obliged to compose the first scene of the opera no less than four times owing to constant changes in the libretto. Although Holý did not care for the subject, he agreed to take it on, only to produce a sketch for a three-act ballet with songs, entitled *The Moon.* What is more, Holý—to Janáček's astonishment—had his sketch published at once. The composer now turned to the poet S. K. Neumann who on 29 April 1912 also refused. The Odyssey of the libretto, some of which was already set to music, had by now entered its fifth year. Neumann recommended Josef Mach, but Janáček went instead to František Gellner who agreed at first but then, after letting another year pass, wrote that he did not know what to make of the work and enclosed a mere handful of verses for songs which Viktor Dyk was later to cut out altogether. This is what Janáček meant when he wrote 'Gellner intervened with his wit'.

On 12 April 1913 Janáček finished the second scene and another long interval followed. In the autumn of 1915 Marie Calma-Veselá introduced Janáček to Kovařovic's librettist Karel Šípek who, although he was to become Janáček's devoted ally in the final struggle for having JENŮFA staged in Prague, advised him to drop the whole project and ask F. S. Procházka for a new libretto (perhaps on the subject of King Barleycorn) or to approach some other writer, for instance Ozef Kalda or K. M. Čapek-Chod. Yet Janáček remained firm and asked F. S. Procházka to adapt the fourth and final scene. This he did between January and June 1916, but Janáček was so dissatisfied with it that he decided to ask Jiří Mahen to rewrite the whole text, beginning with the final scene.

Mahen, after a month of arduous work, completed the passages Janáček had asked him for and delivered them to him, only to read in the paper

Právo lidu of 13 September 1916 that Janáček's Brouček (only the first trip, to the moon, of course) had been finished to a libretto by Viktor Dyk. To Mahen's astonished inquiry Janáček explained that his libretto which he had highly praised only a short time before, could not be used since in order to do so he would have to 'compose the opera all over again'. Janáček had omitted to draw Mahen's attention to the fact that the music to the first three scenes had already been composed. And since Viktor Dyk had according to Janáček 'approved the old text, changed nothing and added an end which he had worked out strictly according to Svatopluk Čech's book, Mahen must try to understand...'

The irate Mahen demanded an immediate return of his work, financial compensation for loss of time and Janáček's pledge that not a single word of his libretto would be used. Janáček made no objection to the first and the last of these demands (the second was more difficult); it was thus that Mahen's part in the libretto was annulled or, as Janáček described it, 'Mahen remained master of his own work.'

In the meantime, Viktor Dyk, who now had the additional problem of pacifying his colleague and friend, was faced with the almost impossible task of patching up a libretto to an opera which was musically almost completed. He set to work with little enthusiasm, and contrary to Mašek, protested that the libretto followed Svatopluk Čech's original too closely. His only reason for undertaking the work was sympathy for the composer, for his painful experiences with Jenůfa, which had only just reached their successful conclusion. All he could do was to smooth out some of the most obvious banalities in the diction. A further catastrophe was in store, however, since before he could complete his work he was arrested in November 1916 on a charge of 'high treason'. The task was once more taken over by the devoted and dependable F. S. Procházka who fulfilled it—accepting some suggestions from Max Brod—with such promptness that around the New Year Janáček could, after nine years, consider The Excursion to the Moon finished, and on 15 January 1917 could send the score of the last scene to the National Theatre.

But the opera was still not finished. On 24 March Janáček wrote to Rektorys: 'I see now that it is my duty to complete my work by adding Mr Brouček's Excursion to the Fifteenth Century'. On the same day he addressed himself once more to F. S. Procházka: 'A new era is at hand. It is just around the corner. What about holding up to it the clean mirror of the battle of Vítkov Hill?' Procházka liked the idea but would rather have waited until the 'new era' had actually arrived because, as he said, 'It is necessary to have a perfectly free hand in every respect. There is no free hand nowadays.'

Janáček, misunderstanding this condition, promptly accorded him 'a free hand', adding: 'I have sketched out a synopsis myself—but do whatever you like with it.' In the event, Procházka did not wait (the creation of the sovereign Czechoslovak state was another year and a half away) and got down to work. On 3 December 1917 the libretto was finished and the music only one day later, since Janáček was composing it bit by bit as he received the text from Procházka. Thus he wrote Act I between 5 May and 1 July, Scene I of Act II between the end of August and 18 September and on 1 December the whole work was finished except for Kunka's lament which Procházka added, at

Janáček's request, on 3 December and which he set a day later. Since he was, as usual, writing directly in full score, the orchestration was also virtually complete. However, Janáček was not able to send a fair copy to the National Theatre until 17 August 1918.

From this it is evident that the statement on the cover of the published vocal score concerning the libretto is correct only insofar as it attributes the words of the second part to F. S. Procházka, although even here Janáček made some alterations. It would be more suitable to style Viktor Dyk as 'editor' rather than 'author' of the first part, since no one was willing to put his name to the libretto of which one critic (Jindřich Pihrt) aptly remarked that it was a 'work created by nobody'.

Under these circumstances it was not surprising that the transfer of Mr Brouček from Svatopluk Čech's somewhat verbose and, in the fifteenth century part, authentic but plodding novel to the operatic stage was not entirely successful, even though Janáček was, in the end, satisfied with his librettists. Did the subject become less topical? Had the Broučeks died out? On the contrary, the Second World War and its aftermath drew out and fostered many a character worse than he was. Or did the music take the edge off the satire? Janáček may have had some doubts as the work progressed.

But I think there was no need for him to reproach himself, at least from the musical point of view; in fact, he carried out his task so well that the libretto can almost be reconstructed from the music alone. It is true, however, that he did not quite succeed in deriding Mr Brouček who, if only because of his name (*brouček* means 'little beetle') cannot seriously be despised since he cannot be taken seriously.

Besides, Mr Brouček's trip to the moon contains a basic illogicality: Brouček being the 'villain' on the moon, there is no 'hero' to balance him. The moon dwellers are supposed to represent, compared with Brouček's vulgar material-ism, some kind of sublime, supramundane world—yet, both in the novel and in Janáček's libretto, they are a caricature of themselves, ridiculing by their pretentious speech the literary and social eccentricities of the time. They so overwhelm us by their affectations that Mr Brouček, far from disgusting us with his down-to-earth materialism, gradually gains the better part of our sympathies; and when amidst the lunar witticisms he shouts, even if only in his dream, 'Mr Würfl (patron of the Vikárka Inn), roast pork, sauerkraut and dumplings (a staple of the Czech diet)!', this subconscious protest comes as welcome relief.

It was precisely this many-sided caricature which appealed most to Janáček. In an interview with Josef Pachmayer, editor of the daily paper *Venkov*, he said about the first EXCURSION (at the time when Viktor Dyk was collaborating on the libretto), 'The particular attraction of the opera will be the overdoing of every aspect of it, giving it a burlesque quality. If I can manage to carry this out in every direction, then I am sure I will produce something which has not yet been done in music.' He might have succeeded better if his caricature of sophistication had been more sophisticated itself as it is for instance in *Les Précieuses ridicules* by Molière.

The subject of Mr Brouček's trip to the fifteenth century presents more agreeable opportunities since it is concerned with more serious matters. Against

Mr Brouček's egoism and cowardice is ranged the self-sacrifice and fearlessness of the Hussites. This conflict, however, is again weakened even in Čech's novel by the mildly humorous use of medieval language and by the insertion of a long-winded argument among the Hussites over matters of dogma at the very moment when the enemy troops are crossing the Vltava in preparation for their attack on the city.

There is little dramatic purpose, either, in Domšík's death—all that is left is sympathy for the bereaved. One rather strange idea of Janáček's was to let the poet, Svatopluk Čech, appear in person after the transition from the Vikárka to the fifteenth century,*) just before Mr Brouček comes into contact with the Hussites. Janáček uses a direct quotation from the opening of Chapter 12 of the original novel, where Čech laments: 'Oh shining sun of that great historic day! Oh sun of our former strength, forever set, will you ever rise again to find a poet who will know how to greet you with burning zeal, and not with such petty caricature as I do?' At first this unusual detail caused considerable embarrassment among the surviving contemporaries of the late poet, but as time passed and the figure of Svatopluk Čech became more legendary, his appearance on the stage became less and less disturbing.

It is not surprising that many of the characters in both EXCURSIONS—apart from Brouček himself, the innkeeper Würfl, Málinka and her lover, the painter Mazal (Daubster)—are somewhat lifeless. There are too many of them and their appearances are too short for them to be developed. Janáček was aware of this danger and—as in ADVENTURES OF THE VIXEN SHARP EARS later— he joined a number of characters into three versions of one. (The same happens in Offenbach's *Tales of Hoffmann* and in *Julien* by Gustave Charpentier— a composer much admired by Janáček at that time.) Thus Mr Würfl becomes Wonderglitter (Čaroskvoucí) on the moon and the Councillor in the fifteenth century, while Málinka becomes the rapt Etherea on the moon and the chaste, true Kunka in the fifteenth century, Mazal is Starry-Eyes (Blankytný) on the moon and Petřík in the fifteenth century, the lunar artists Dreamy Cloud (Oblačný) and Harper (Harfoboj) become Vacek the Beard and Miroslav the Goldsmith in the fifteenth century, and so on. To some extent these connections are also emphasized even by the relevant motifs.

There is some confusion in the fifteenth-century part of the opera where Mr Brouček calls Vacek the Beard 'you, Harper', although Vacek is the *alter ego* of Oblačný, and Domšík 'Mr Mazal', although Domšík is really the Sacristan. It is neither the first nor the last of Janáček's inconsistencies. Originally, Domšík were indeed to be Mazal,**) but when Janáček added the part of Petřík, he left Mr Brouček's line unchanged. None of this, however, prevented Janáček from creating in this two-part story of his down-to-earth 'hero' one of his most fresh and original works. It was said of Schubert that even stones changed to music in his hands, and the same is true of the composer of DESTINY and the EXCURSIONS. Janáček's humour at that time was, as has been noticed in DESTINY, of a somewhat bizarre and prickly kind. It was (like

---

*) Originally, before Janáček decided to write the second part, Svatopluk Čech was to speak at the end of the EXCURSION TO THE MOON.
**) See *Janáček—Procházka*, p. 38.

the private humour of the deaf Beethoven) typical of a lonely and hurt man—
pained and painful.

But just as Janáček was capable, in his more serious works, of the utmost
tenderness beside barbaric wildness, here he created humour ranging from
the savage and premeditated to the child-like and spontaneous. There is
also some subtlety in the EXCURSIONS. For instance, at the moment when
Mr Brouček is flying to the moon he hears, as if from a great depth,
Mr Würfl's voice calling mechanically:

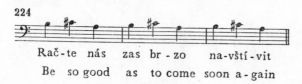

224

Rač-te nás   zas br - zo   na-vští-vit
Be so good   as to come soon a - gain

which is a variant of the initial motif of the opera; or the moon theme is
heard when Mr Brouček tries to make the Hussites believe that he has come
from Turkey (the land of the half-moon). The typical Janáček waltz is also
to be found in the EXCURSIONS, for instance in Part One (on the moon) in
both Act I (reh. No. 82) and in Act II (reh. No. 61) where it reaches abandon
of *Der Rosenkavalier* proportions, which is entirely appropriate to the story
and its historical period.

A new element of style which was to become typical of all the later Janáček
operas appears here for the first time: it is the regular alternation of a motif
at rest with its variant or another motif altogether, in motion. Otherwise
all the innovations of JENŮFA and DESTINY are used, but with greater freedom
and mastery, while Janáček displays to the full his capacity for changing, as
if by a sleight-of-hand, a burlesque into an exalted hymn. In spite of the
mosaic-like origins of the work, the overall form of each of the two parts is
one of a compact, homogeneous span of a poem in sound.

The first of these, THE EXCURSION TO THE MOON, falls into two Acts framed
by scenes at the Vikárka, rich in bohemian atmosphere and imbued with the
light of a full moon. How suggestive, for instance, is the beginning with its
dreamy C sharp pedal in the middle voices and the softly undulating octaves
of the outer parts. How the moon smiles teasingly in the bassoon theme:

225

p marc.

as if guessing what is to befall Mr Brouček. How masterfully Janáček handles
the first scene on the moon up to the entry of Etherea, first quoting the almost
folk-like motif of the earth (see Ex. 2), then the opalescent motif of the
moonmen (at reh. No. 58):

226 Adagio

then introducing the Calibanish bassoon motif of Mr Brouček:

and its ostentatious variant at Brouček's 'I've a three-storied house!'

Starry-Eyes' high-flown wailing:

and finally a reminder of Málinka's earlier, coquettish phrase:

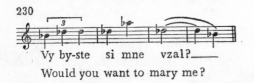

How irresistibly Janáček sends Mr Brouček away on Starry-Eyes' Pegasus while the lunar artists end their mummery with a subtly amusing hymn:

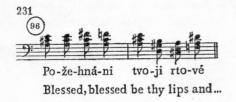

to be followed by a brief duet by Málinka and Mazal (back on earth and in genuine Italian style in octaves!) which is derived from it:

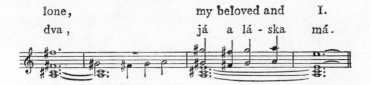

lone,   my beloved and Í.
dva ,   já a lá - ska má.

and which ends Part One. In the two final pianissimo chords, B flat major and A major, the moon seems to be whispering 'don't blame me'.

With what strength Janáček evokes (and how differently from Smetana, although using the same chorale tune *Kdož jste boží bojovníci*, 'You who are God's own warriors') the strength of the Hussites and the sweet taste of victory in a righteous cause. Janáček uses here two chorale motifs—one at the end of Act I of Part Two:

233

Slyš - te, ry - tie - ři bo-ží,
Har - ken ye Knights of God

the other in Act II:

234

and, also in Act II of Part Two, their march-like variants:

235

And how his music rejoices with his hero—perhaps unwillingly—at the words, 'I'm home, home, home again', finishing off the comedy with a grand farcical brio.

Even if Janáček failed to rouse as much disgust as he had intended, he added an excellent type to his collection of characteristic figures and left his listeners with much to ponder upon and much to enjoy.

(30) 'Taras Bulba'

The work in which Janáček expressed himself most significantly and un-
equivocally on the gigantic struggle of the First World War which was also
the struggle for the future of his nation, was the orchestral rhapsody TARAS
BULBA after Gogol's story which in turn is based on an Ukrainian heroic
tale. The idea had been in his mind, as proved by his glosses in his copy
of Gogol's book, since March 1905, and he gave his reasons for choosing this
early seventeenth-century tale full of old Slav heroism and colour: 'Not
because Taras Bulba killed his own son for betraying his people (First Part),
not for the martyr's death of his second son (Second Part), but because "there
is no fire nor suffering in the whole world which could break the strength of
the Russian people"—for these words which fall onto the stinging fiery embers
of the pyre on which Taras Bulba, the famous Cossack captain, was burned
to death (Third Part), I have composed this rhapsody according to the legend
as written down by N. V. Gogol.' He began writing 'this musical testament',
as he himself called it,*) not later than 1915—long, that is, before the collapse
of the Russian armies. The sketch for the work was possibly finished by 1916
and the definitive score, after endless improvements, was completed on Good
Friday, 29 March 1918.

I will try to describe the content, basing my remarks partly on Gogol's
story, partly on the explanation which after a performance in Prague, I was
able to prize out of the normally uncommunicative composer himself.

1. *The Death of Andri*

During their campaign against the Poles, the Zaporozhye Cossacks, among
them their captain Taras Bulba and his two sons Ostap and Andri, besiege
the town Dubno. Andri discovers that among the starving inhabitants of the
besieged town is a Polish noble's beautiful daughter with whom he once fell
in love in Kiev. Under cover of darkness he enters the town by a secret
underground passage in an effort to save her. It is at this point in the story that
Janáček's composition begins with a description of the conflict in Andri's
heart between his vision of the beautiful girl:

236

---

*) *Janáček — Horvátová*, p. 83.

and his fear of being discovered (portrayed by this agitated variant of the first bar over a menacing triplet figure in the bass):

237
Più mosso

while, according to the composer's own words, the distant sound of the organ and the warning bells express the prayers and the anguish of the besieged:

238
Allegro vivo

Wwind p

The bracketed motif is taken from the second bar of the original melody of longing. The fragmented rhythms in the woodwind then describe—again according to the composer—Andri's concern as he walks among the starved, ghost-like defenders, the entries of the agitated variant of the theme of longing (as in Ex. 237) suggesting Andri's searching for his beloved. He finds her house, and then—to a sudden burst of the same motif in the violins in unison—he throws himself into her arms. A passionate love scene follows, introduced by this blissful melody in the oboe:*)

239
Adagio

which seems to try to ignore the sounds of fighting from outside (cymbals over the bass triplets as in Ex. 237). However, pangs of conscience become more and more pressing (a menacing bass variant of the love motif itself) and the lovers repeatedly but vainly seek oblivion in their passion. The wailing chromatic ringing becomes more and more insistent and then suddenly, as if presented by the challenging motif of the trombones:

240

ff

Andri's father himself seems to appear terribly near.

A battle follows (developed from the trombone motif of Taras's challenge) in which at first the faithless son fights valiantly against his own people. However, when he comes face to face with his father, he lowers his gaze in shame,

---

*) It is interesting to note that Andri's theme of *unfulfilled* longing was scored for the nostalgic-sounding cor anglais.

and on his order dismounts and accepts death at his father's hand. As he dies he once more remembers his love while the relentless Taras gallops away into battle.

2. The Death of Ostap

After a short slow introduction where soft figurations on the harp are interrupted several times by a harsh ostinato of the strings:

a 2/4 allegro motif is introduced describing a new equestrian battle:

This time fate strikes at the loyal Ostap who is overcome by the memory of his brother's unhappy end. He is taken prisoner by the Poles and led away to Warsaw for execution (3/4 moderato with the ostinato motif in the bass and a sorrowful, typically Janáček melody in the violins in sixths). The Poles dance a wild *mazur* of victory, symbolically akin to the battle motif. The tortured Ostap (solo high clarinet over a fortissimo tremolo in the strings with muted trumpets) calls, in unbearable pain, for his father. Taras, who has forced his way through the crowd (bursts of the shortened sorrowful motif, in 2/8, earlier on) makes a larger-than-life appearance to the triplet figure (Ex. 237) from the first movement (trumpet blasts, this time evidently without mutes) only to disappear at once from the astonished throng.

3. The Prophecy and Death of Taras Bulba

Taras himself now meets a Cossack's end. After cruelly punishing the Poles for the death of his son, he too is taken prisoner when he lingers because he does not wish even his pipe, which he has dropped during his flight, to fall into the hands of the enemy. The Poles sentence him to death by burning. We find him nailed to a tree, pining for his lost freedom—Ostap's sorrowful, descending motif, a reminder of the last battle, answered by an ascending fragment:

alternating with its own plaintive augmentation. This is then developed into a mournfully majestic melody over undulating sextuplets in the lower strings, as though Taras were thinking, for the last time, of his leaderless warriors while the flames leap higher and higher:

244

Round him, the victorious enemy stamps out a wild *krakowiak* (which uses
the fragmentary semiquaver motif from Ex. 243). But Taras has the satisfaction
of witnessing (the motif of his challenge, Ex. 240, is triumphantly augmented
and the theme of suffering, Ex. 244, brightened as if in reconciliation) the
daring feat of horsemanship—a leap into the River Dniestr—by which his
warriors escape their pursuers. There is a sudden lull. Distant fanfares are
heard and Taras is left alone with his pain. In his last moments he has a vision
of the indomitable strength of his people; the bells and organ which in the
first part of the rhapsody represented the enemy calling and praying for help,
now swell to a majestic apotheosis of Russia. This is how the apotheosis is
developed:

It is introduced by a variant of the motif of suffering:

245

which is then, at the beginning of the coda, enlarged into an octave over
magnificent chord progressions in the trombones and the organ, and arpeggios
of the harps and cellos:

246

From its melodic continuation:

247

emerges this new intoxicating melody:

248

like the arch of rainbow of peace spanning the earth.

More deeply felt and more authentically national music than this can
scarcely be imagined. Janáček maintains the feeling of constant suspense
throughout its 25-minutes' duration, and only at the very end comes the
sensation of liberation. The work was an immediate success both at its Brno
première on 9 October 1921 when it was conducted by František Neumann,

and at its first performance in Prague where it was played in Janáček's 70th year by the Czech Philharmonic Orchestra conducted by Václav Talich on 9 November 1924. Even abroad, where the background of this 'Slav Rhapsody' as it was originally subtitled, could not be expected to commend it to the listener, it was no less successful which is proof enough of its musical wealth and its elemental expressive strength.

PART THREE (1918·1928)

(31) Patriotic Motifs

On 28 October 1918 the Czech and Slovak people—even before the signing of the official armistice—freed itself from the foreign domination which, for the Czechs, had lasted for 300 years and, for the Slovaks, 1000 years. Janáček's joy at the victory of the cause for which he had fought all his life coincided almost symbolically with the belated success of his work. He felt himself to be starting a new life and, having until now assumed the role of spokesman of the enslaved, he took upon himself the part of bard of the resurrected independent national life—in fact, of life itself.

He began by expressing his gratitude to those who had paid for the newly-acquired freedom with their lives. On 18 November he completed the male-voice chorus ČESKÁ LEGIE (Czech Legion)—a setting of a poem by Antonín Horák published in the paper *Národní listy*. This poem, appearing at a time of general exultation, caused an unusual stir. It is not surprising, therefore, that Janáček in his enthusiasm turned to this poem, overlooking the romantic naivety of some of its text (although he did leave out the most romantic passage later) and the fact that the Czech Legion never fought at the poet's chosen locale, the battlefield *Chemin des Dames*.

The setting of the words leans on the earlier Bezruč choruses, for instance, the suggestive 'scenic' refrain:

249

Na Chemin des Da - mes
At Chemin des Dames

recalls the refrain of the River Ostravice in MARYČKA MAGDÓNOVA. Similarly, the next phrase:

(Moderato)

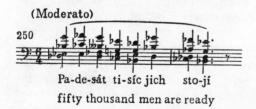

250

Pa-de-sát ti-síc jich   sto-jí
fifty thousand men are ready

which, at the mention of the Czech red and white flag, turns into a diatonic reminiscence of the Czech national anthem, is analogous to the chorus 70,000. There is, however, great sincerity in this poem and Janáček made the most of it by his masterly craftsmanship in choral writing.

The independence of his native land not only spurred Janáček to write patriotic works but also gave him renewed vigour in organizing and building up the musical life of the new state. He rejoiced when the newly-formed government agreed to the transformation of the Brno Organ School into a *conservatoire* on 26 September 1919, and to mark the occasion he wrote an article which was published in the daily paper *Lidové noviny* entitled 'Introductory Word to the Opening of the Brno *Conservatoire*', in which he stated somewhat paradoxically: 'It is impossible to learn to compose music.' And he continued: 'Create your own compositions. Keep the secret of your work and your inspiration. Do not clutter up your workshop with other people's work. Do not stifle it with an alien atmosphere. The field of exploration is the only field of learning.'

It was typical of Janáček to add: 'You will speak with a richer voice, you will harvest greater yields and attain a sweeter, headier tone if in your search you apply musical psychology.' And again: 'There can be no better way of taking the pulse of the nation than studying the motifs of its words. At the *Conservatoire* we want to contribute to the collecting of material for a vocabulary of the living Czech language. I want such composers who compose because they must; who overflow with sound but who also know how to keep silent.'

After all he had done for the establishment of the *Conservatoire*, and continued to do,*) it must have come as a shock when in March 1920, as the *Conservatoire* became a state institution, Jan Kunc was appointed director. This disappointment was not lessened by the fact that on 25 September 1919 Janáček was nominated Professor of the master-class in composition at the Prague *Conservatoire* with residence in Brno,**) nor by the fact that it would have been practically impossible for him to have combined these two posts without endangering his interests as a composer. His understandable bitterness reached a high point when the authorities, in the interests of a common *Conservatoire* curriculum, did away with his original and, perhaps, too idiosyncratic way of teaching harmony.

There was also the problem of chosing a new artistic director for the Brno Opera House which at last moved from the primitive 'Na Veveří' theatre to the excellent municipal 'Na Hradbách' one built in 1881 by F. Fellner and H. Helmer. It is amusing up to a point to note that Janáček, who, incidentally, accepted the membership of the Opera's board of sponsors after Independence only to resign in May 1920, consulted Karel Kovařovic on this matter. In a letter written in March 1919 he asked him in general terms whether, in his opinion, it would be better to 'put a renowned composer or a conductor at the head of an opera company'—a question all the more surprising since, generalities apart, the only person who could fill the bill both as an eminent composer and conductor was Otakar Ostrčil (1879—1935), then artistic director of the Vinohrady Opera in Prague. In fact the only question was that of specific individual qualities, whether such a person would make a good operatic director. Kovařovic could hardly answer otherwise than in this sense.

It was no coincidence, however, that Janáček couched his question in those

---

*) He tried, for instance, to engage Jan Kubelík as a violin teacher.
**) In addition he gave two lectures at the Prague *Conservatoire*: 'The Thought Processes Involved in Composing' in 1921, and on 'Naturalism in Composition' in 1923.

terms, since in a letter to Rektorys written on 31 May 1919 he mentioned that he was in favour of nominating František Neumann rather than Ostrčil because 'Ostrčil as a composer should compose and not tie himself down to conducting in a theatre.'

The post did finally go to František Neumann (born 1874 in Prague, died 1929) and neither Brno nor Janáček nor, for that matter, Ostrčil were to regret the decision: Ostrčil was soon to become opera director at the Prague National Theatre, and Brno acquired in Neumann an artistic director of great musical erudition and also a good organizer. Janáček found in him a faithful and sensitive interpreter to whom he could entrust each of his new operas (with the exception of his last—THE HOUSE OF THE DEAD—the posthumous première of which took place after Neumann's death). Neumann actually began his Brno career with a new production of JENŮFA on 23 August 1919.

Yet it was not only Janáček's faith in Neumann and the high standard of the company which led him to let his opera premières be staged in Brno. 'I can go to every rehearsal, I can see the designs for the costumes and see how they are made. I can make corrections, etc.,' he wrote on 12 November 1924 to Ostrčil. The fact that Janáček told Adolf Veselý, when he was planning to have the première of his HOUSE OF THE DEAD in Brno, that 'this, for me, is always a dress rehearsal,' does not belittle the importance of the Brno opera company. On the contrary, it shows that the Brno Opera was able faithfully to carry out his intentions.

After JENŮFA, Janáček offered Kovařovic and the Prague National Theatre THE EXCURSIONS OF MR BROUČEK. It presented numerous difficulties. The war was still raging and there were shortages of materials, especially textiles, for the sets and costumes. Moreover, the National Theatre could not find a suitable tenor for the tough caricature of the title role. (Janáček, curiously enough, was in favour of the lyrico-heroic tenor Otakar Mařák.) In fact most of the main parts were too high for the singers. Since, after JENŮFA, there could be no question of not accepting the EXCURSIONS, the actual production was postponed from one season to another. Janáček, it is true, contributed to the delay by deciding in 1917 to add the EXCURSION TO THE FIFTEENTH CENTURY, less than a year after he had offered the EXCURSION TO THE MOON to the National Theatre.

At last in November 1919 Kovařovic asked Otakar Ostrčil who had recently been appointed dramaturge to the National Theatre, to make a critical assessment of the EXCURSIONS. It is questionable whether Kovařovic acted wisely in shifting onto someone else the responsibility for accepting Janáček's work since this led inevitably to the impression that the shortage of material was not the only reason for the constant postponements of the EXCURSIONS.

When Ostrčil presented a favourable report (surprisingly for him, he preferred the burlesque moon excursion to the more serious Hussite part), Kovařovic, now ailing, entrusted the whole production of the opera to him. Janáček agreed to make some alterations, mainly to accommodate some rebellious singers,*) and the work was performed for the first time at the

---

*) Some further changes, as for instance, the enlarging of the chorus at Žižka's triumphal entry (Part Two, Act II, reh. No. 52 ff), were made after the first performance.

National Theatre on 23 April 1920, produced by Gustav Schmoranz with scenery by Karel Stapfer and with Mirko Štork, Vilém Zítek, Emil Burian, Václav Novák, Věra Pivoňková, Ema Miřiovská and Karel Hruška in the main parts. Although the opera was repeated ten times during the season, it was received with embarrassment rather than enthusiasm. Janáček celebrated the first night with only a small group of friends at the almost empty beer cellar 'U Bumbrlíčka'—surroundings more suitable for Mr Brouček than the composer.

Shortly afterwards, on 6 December 1920, Kovařovic, whose health had been undermined by constant antagonism from all sides, died of cancer. On 28 October, the second anniversary of Czechoslovak independence, he had appeared in the pit of the National Theatre for the last time. The work he conducted on that occasion was Smetana's *Dalibor*, by coincidence the opera with which he had, 20 years earlier, begun his activities as artistic director of the first Czech opera house. Janáček observed the illness of his former adversary with sincere concern. When he heard from Kovařovic that owing to ill-health he had entrusted Ostrčil with the EXCURSIONS OF MR BROUČEK, Janáček wrote to him, on 22 November 1919, 'If I could give you half of my health—it would not be much—but I would gladly do it,' and when Kovařovic died, Janáček wrote to Ostrčil, his successor: 'I write to you on the day of Kovařovic's death. I am deeply moved. How am I to retain what has been binding us for so long! We had known each other since our Brno days. Our first encounter was not happy, and from that time there were shadows between us and you know that more were cast even over Brouček.

'But let all be forgotten.'

'He worked himself to death and was a credit to the National Theatre. I, too was thankful to him in the end for my success with JENŮFA. I want to remember only what was good in him.'

If the EXCURSIONS OF MR BROUČEK gave Prague reasons for doubting Janáček (TARAS BULBA had not yet been performed), the same was the case in Brno after the first performance of the orchestral BALLAD OF BLANÍK (then called *The Knights of Blaník*) conducted by František Neumann on 21 March 1920, especially since the orchestra was not up to the standard demanded by this difficult and unusual work.

THE BALLAD OF BLANÍK composed at the beginning of 1920, is based on a poem of the same title by Jaroslav Vrchlický, taken from his collection *Peasant Ballads*, published in 1885. It is a modern version of the legend of the Blaník Knights as written down by Alois Jirásek in his *Old Czech Legends* and by Josef Kajetán Tyl in his play *Jiříkovo vidění* (Jiřík's Dream). The story is as follows:

Young Jíra who is something of a bookish peasant, instead of going to church on Good Friday decides to take a walk to Blaník Hill (near Vlašim, south-east of Prague), thinking, with an indulgent smile, of the legend according to which on Good Friday, during the singing of the Passion, Blaník discloses its secrets. Suddenly he sees the rock-face open. He follows a mysterious light through a long passage into a stone hall where, just as the legend says, he finds the patron saint of the Czechs, St Wenceslas, and his Blaník Knights, asleep and yet standing erect lined up for battle for the liberation of their country, their weapons at their feet and the banner of St Wenceslas overhead. Before Jíra realizes what is happening, the rock closes behind him with a crash—he feels faint and falls asleep. When he awakes, he can hear the Passion music again from the distance and the knights with their horses are still standing at the ready, but instead of weapons there are peaceful farming implements at their feet. Jíra quickly leaves the hill but when he bends over a stream to drink, he sees the reflection of an old man. Nobody in the village recognizes him—only the lark sings the same joyful song above the pleasant countryside.

The idea of the poem, that weapons of war should become implements of peace*), appealed to Janáček especially after the successful conclusion of the war, although the logic of the symbolism concerning the Blaník Knights should not be scrutinized too closely. It is, perhaps, a pity that the idea is treated with insufficient clarity and too briefly since the entire action is compressed into the space of eight minutes. The protagonist of the poem, Jíra, is a man who has become sceptical through much study. Jíra's theme:

which is derived from motifs heard earlier on in the work, suggests, by its high tessitura and freshness, a young man. His subsequent ageing may symbolize the painfully long time needed by humanity to achieve any sort of progress. The theme's closeness to the Valachian shepherd's song *Po valašsky od zeme, kdo ty kozy zažene?* (Strike up, play a Valach tune, who's to chase the goats away?) gives a clue to Jíra's peasant origin.

Disjointed fragments of Jíra's theme, such as this whole-tone one:

describe his erratic approach to Blaník Hill. A melody of religious character:

whose descriptive power is weakened by its irreligious harmony, suggests—or perhaps should suggest—the distant sound of the Passion music. The subsequent upsurge in the strings describes Jíra's astonishment at the sight of the

---

*) It is significant that at about this time Janáček was considering the composition of a choral setting of one of Bezruč's Silesian poems, *The Plough*.

Knights who are represented by maestoso chords of two harps (with horns added in the lower octave by Neumann):

254

The resemblance of the melody to the beginning of the folk song:

255
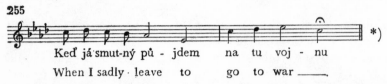

Keď já smut-ný pů - jdem   na tu voj - nu

When I sadly · leave   to   go to war _____.   *)

which has been pointed out by Jarmil Burghauser**), must be considered accidental, if only because of the majestic instrumentation that Janáček employs in this passage. It can scarcely be taken symbolically in view of the nature of the legend of St Wenceslas and his Knights***). Not even the dramatic moment where the rock closes with a crash is clear. Most probably it occurs at the end of the harp episode where the septuplets of the strings tumble downward without, however, reaching any emphatic conclusion. They should have, perhaps, reached an interrupted cadence since they are describing an abrupt change of situation. The theme:

256

(a variant of Ex. 252) is probably intended to suggest, with its insistent repetitions of falling thirds, Jíra's calls for help (not mentioned in the poem). And the harp and celesta glissandos before each of these 'calls' may suggest Jíra running back and forth, desperately searching for a way out of the stone hall. His subsequent falling asleep is depicted clearly enough in the languid fragments of his motif over a pianissimo tremolo in the second violins and later in the violas.

Janáček gives no indication of the long passage of time during Jíra's sleep,†)

---

*) Jan Kunc: *Slovácké písně* (Slovácko Songs), Ostrava, 1913.
**) *Musikologie III.*
***) There might rather be a symbolic link with the original last movement of THE VIOLIN SONATA, EX. 213.
†) Dvořák proved that music is capable of this in his symphonic poem *Holoubek* (The Wood Dove) by the gradual subsiding of the legato theme:

257

while its repetition suggests the tedium of the passing years, and at the same time its changing cadences hint at the ripening of time under the seemingly motionless surface.

but goes straight to the final part of the story—Jíra's awakening and his surprise at the changed implements of the armoured knights. Here Janáček found a beautiful way of suggesting this (although intelligible only to those who know TARAS BULBA). Apart from softening the outlines of the knight's motif (cf. Ex 254) by the use of legato strings, he makes it at one point almost identical (except for shifting the barline) with the melody of the apotheosis at the end of TARAS BULBA (see Ex. 248):

Once again—too briefly—the Passion music is heard over a tremolo pedal in the double-basses and timpani. The tremolo begins to rise while Jíra's increasingly agitated 'calls for help' are heard once more, topped by the clear sound of the bells (suggesting, perhaps, the penetration of daylight). Jíra finds his way out of the hill as his theme (Ex. 251) rings out in a joyfully concordant variant. His joy turns to horror, on the dominant ninth of A minor, when he sees his reflection in the stream. The mournful clarinet solo describes his disappointment: motifs of Jíra's youthful theme sink lower and lower, its staccato changes into a weary legato, the rhythmic pulse grows slower. Jíra now stands before us as an old man. However, he is reminded, in an allusion to the harp theme of the Blaník Knights, of the other great transformation of warriors into farmers, that he has been privileged to witness.

I have dwelt on the analysis of this short work because of its vague story-line and because it sets out to express too serious an idea for mere abstract listening even though its firm musical structure allows it. In my opinion THE BALLAD OF BLANÍK (performed for the first time 18 months before the earlier TARAS BULBA) will come to be regarded as one of Janáček's interesting experiments rather than one of the key works of his œuvre.

These lesser achievements were soon to be overshadowed not only by the first performance of TARAS BULBA but also by new compositions maturing in Janáček's mind at this time, thanks to the fact that he was inspired by subjects particularly closely linked with the nature of his genius and some intimate moments of his life. During the summer holidays of 1917 at Luhačovice Janáček met Mrs Kamila Stösslová for the first time.*)

Kamila Stösslová (née Neumannová) was then a 25-year-old Czech Jewish brunette from Písek in southern Bohemia. She was of medium height, full figured, with a dark complexion, black eyes and curly hair like a gipsy. Her husband, David Stössl, born in Lvov, was an antique dealer who was stationed during the war at Přerov in central Moravia and was able to assist the Janáčeks when food became scarce. After the armistice Janáček reciprocated by using his influence to prevent Stössl being expelled as an alien, and to secure permanent residence for him in Czechoslovakia.**)

In this way a friendship of a practical nature sprang up between the Janáčeks and the Stössls (although it had started—as once before in Luhačovice with another Kamila—with a bunch of roses, this time sent by Janáček). According to Mrs Janáčková it was David Stössl who was making the advances, being impressed by the newly-acquired fame of JENŮFA's composer. It should be made quite plain that if Mrs Janáčková, lacking—in spite of her good will***)— the understanding necessary for the wife of a genius, could be called a second Minna Wagner, on no account should it be assumed that Kamila Stösslová was a second Mathilde Wesendonk or Cosima Wagner. What Janáček admired most in women was an unspoiled nature and spontaneity, and he never sought, or at least never found, anything further.†)

It is certain that the young, light-hearted and temperamental Kamila (thanks to her unfailing feminine instinct, to the fact she did not meet Janáček too often since they were separated by the distance between Brno and Písek, and to the uncompromising jealousy of Mrs Janáčková) held Janáček under her spell longer than any other woman. Yet, she was never in love with the

---

*) According to Štědroň (Prague *Hudební rozhledy*, VI, p. 608) their first meeting took place at Hukvaldy in 1915, but a letter dated 5 August 1918 in which Janáček describes the beauties of Hukvaldy in order to persuade her to visit the village makes it doubtful whether she had been there before.

**) *Zdeňka Janáčková*, p. 134.

***) See p. 201.

†) The relationship between Janáček the composer and his wife, very unsteady to say the least, is described by Stanislav Tauber in his book *My Musical World* perhaps too cruelly, although no doubt truthfully, since he quotes Mrs Janáčková's own remarks made in his presence.

composer. It was not for the first time that Janáček lavished his whole heart on someone who in return for his actual, 'perceived' feelings—to use his own vocabulary (see Chapter 19, Teacher and Theoretician)—gave him only 'quasi perceived', fictional ones.

Yet from time to time he guessed the truth, since he wrote to Kamila: 'It is fortunate that only I am infatuated,' or when in January 1927 he invited his 'little weasel' to THE MAKROPOULOS CASE with the words: 'Come and see the cold one. You will see your own photograph.' His love for her is expressed most truly and touchingly in a letter written on 8 June of the same year: 'Yesterday I wrote to Zdeňka telling her all that binds me to you. An open confession. I think she will understand. She suspected more than is at all possible. Between you and me there is only a world of beauty and all is nothing but fantasy.' He continues: 'But this world of fantasy is as necessary to my life as air or water.' He was all the more convinced of this necessity since he now began producing his finest works, inspired by his love.

If it was true that love inspired his works, the reverse was equally true. Both intensified each other. All that Janáček wrote with Kamila in his thoughts led him to idealize her person until she seemed to him to be unique among women just as the works themselves seem unique to us. Yet this self-deception, if such it was, can seldom have given birth to a more sincere art—reflected not only in his music but also in his letters, for instance a charming one which he wrote to her on 25 November 1927, before the first performance of the GLAGOLITIC MASS*): 'Today I wrote a few lines to describe my cathedral.**) I have located it in Luhačovice. That's good, isn't it? Where else could it be but there, where we have been so happy. And it is high, this cathedral, it reaches up to the dome of the sky. And there are candles burning—the tall pine trees with lighted stars at their tops. And the bells of the cathedral? They come from a flock of sheep. Two people enter the cathedral, walking festively as though down a road paved with carpets—the fresh green grass. And these two want to wed. How strange—there are just these two. Come, priest! Nightingales, thrushes, ducklings, geese, make music! The Music General wants to marry the little dark girl, the tender, the sweet Kamila.—End of dream. You are asleep and I am raving about you...'

Janáček's attachment was strengthened by the fact that three subjects were maturing in his mind, in which the heroines could all be identified with Kamila and which—and this is a further paradox of his one-sided love—gave him the full possibility of showing the right of a woman to choose her love and happiness according to her own heart; subjects through which Janáček became also a spokesman of the moral revolution. These works were THE DIARY OF THE YOUNG MAN WHO DISAPPEARED, KATYA KABANOVA and the QUARTET inspired by Tolstoy's *Kreutzer Sonata*.

The history of the DIARY is a romance in itself: On successive Sundays, 14 May and 21 May 1916, the Brno paper *Lidové noviny* published an anonymous cycle of poems entitled 'From the Pen of a Self-taught Peasant' with the

---

*) There are almost 600 of these 'intimate letters'.
**) He is referring to his article about his GLAGOLITIC MASS, which he wrote for the paper *Lidové noviny*.

following editorial note: 'Some time ago, in an East Moravian highland village, J.D., a law-abiding and industrious youth, the sole object of hope for his parents, disappeared from home in a mysterious way. At first an accident or even a crime was suspected and the imagination of the villagers was kindled. Some days later, however, a diary was found in his room which disclosed the secret. It contained several short poems which eventually provided the key to the mystery. His parents had at first thought that the poems were folk songs and soldier's songs that he had copied out. But a court investigation later revealed their true content. If only for their moving and sincere atmosphere, they deserve to be saved from the dust and oblivion of court files.' There followed 23 poems (though number 14 consists of nothing but dashes) relating, in Valachian dialect, the romance of an honest farmer's son and a young gypsy girl. At first he resists the mute enticing of her eyes, but one day, after losing an axle-peg from his plough, he goes to cut himself a new one in the thicket even though he feels that 'the dark Zefka' will be there. He is sure (as he assures his oxen) that he will resist the temptation. But she speaks to him and sings him a 'sad song' about the bitter lot of the gypsies. Then teasing him for his shyness and his fright, she 'calms' him with the words 'I am not as dark as you might think. Where the sun cannot reach, I have lighter skin.' When she shows him, with amusement, 'how gypsy girls make their beds', his own words come true: 'What will be, will be, and no man can escape it.' The fate of the hitherto innocent youth is sealed. Every evening, despite pangs of conscience, he hurries to the thicket. He has to remain silent when his sister is robbed. And in the end he secretly leaves his home for ever. Zefka is waiting for him with their son in her arms.

Such a subject had an obvious appeal to Janáček, even though this *Carmen* had a happy ending. The power, sincerity and spontaneity, and depth of insight into the first emotional crisis of a young human being, show that the 'self-taught anonym' had nothing to learn even from the creators of such angelic characters as Elisabetta or of 'pure fools' like young Siegfried or Parsifal. Here, everything is only more simple and less pretentious. 'Siegfried only stooped to a bird', we could say misquoting Vrchlický, 'J.D. argues with his oxen and is even ashamed in front of them.' The familiar Valachian setting and dialect were certainly an added attraction for Janáček as was probably the mystery shrouding the author and hero of the poem, and Janáček, as we know, always loved a certain element of mystery.*) However, a year passed without Janáček doing anything about the poems. But, 'what will be, will be, and no man can escape it...' In July 1917 he met Kamila Stösslová and discovered in J.D.'s story a reflection of his own budding romance. (As late as 1927 he confessed to her: 'While writing the 'Diary', I thought only of you. You were Zefka to me!') He even expressed a wish to have the work published with a picture of Kamila on the cover with her hair down, and this was eventually

---

*) The leading Czech philologist, Professor František Trávníček, gives his opinion in Václav Tomsa's *Symposium* that the author of the *Diary* was Jan Misárek, a journalist born in Vsetín in 1861 who died in Prague in 1932 and who was the author of three remarkable Valachian short stories. He was a friend of Jiří Mahen, at that time literary editor of the paper *Lidové noviny*, who admitted to Trávníček that on several occasions he had mystified the public in a similar way.

borne in mind when the cover was designed. On 9 August 1917 Janáček made a note of the completion of the third song and the next day he wrote to Kamila: 'Regularly every afternoon several themes for the lovely verses about the gypsy love come to my mind. It might make a nice musical novel—there would be some of the atmosphere of Luhačovice in it as well.' However—driven by the necessity of finishing some of his older works—it was not until 11 March 1919 that he wrote to her: 'I have finished those songs about the gypsy girl', and even then there were final touches to be added, because on 25 June he again wrote that 'the black gypsy' was finished.

Two more years passed, however, before Janáček presented the DIARY to the public. The tenor, Audebert Koreček, one of the first to sing the DIARY, wrote in Václav Tomsa's *Symposium:* 'When the DIARY was composed Janáček was not yet so well-known as to see his compositions going straight into print. He kept his manuscripts in a wooden chest painted with Slovácko peasant designs. His pupil Břetislav Bakala used to rummage in it and sometimes discovered works which the composer had long since forgotten, for instance SUITE opus 3 and an ADAGIO FOR ORCHESTRA which Bakala, by analyzing the thematic material, ascertained to be an overture to ŠÁRKA.*) In this chest he also found THE DIARY. It had been lying there for more than a year, a bundle of sheets of white paper which, after careful sorting, could be divided into three groups. The first group consisted of pages on which Janáček, in quick strokes, had drawn staves in ink in order to take down his ideas—these pages show how many times he changed his ideas. He worked much at the piano and that is how the DIARY was written. He would play the accompaniment and sing the tenor part in a high falsetto. Then he would take down what he sang, in no way sparing the high notes. In further versions he lowered some of them but, on the other hand, in the final bars he twice takes the tenor up to top C, although in all the original sketches the voice went down to the middle register.

'In the second group there were sheets on which Janáček had drawn the staves in pencil and taken down in ink those versions which he selected from the first group. Only the third group, similarly laid out, could be regarded as something approaching a clean copy from which the copyist then prepared the work for the printer.'

But even that was not the final version. When Břetislav Bakala discovered the DIARY he asked his friend Dr Jaroslav Lecián to look over the tenor part. For a week they rehearsed several of the songs together, then went to Janáček to perform them, after which he again made some changes. It was in this version that the DIARY was published, and Janáček presented a copy to Bakala with the following dedication: 'As a souvenir for your having pulled it out of the chest, L. Janáček, Brno. November 23, 1921.' The title had clearly been suggested to Janáček by the commentary which had appeared in *Lidové noviny*, in which it was explained how the diary had revealed the secret of the vanished man.

Except for the first stanza and the last line of No. 10 Janáček set all the 23 poems in full, giving even the 'mute' number its proper place. The fact that

---

*) See p. 92.

there are only 22 numbers in the DIARY is caused by the joining of poems 10 and 11 so that Zefka interrupts her 'sad song' with her suggestive remarks while the trio of women's voices completes the action, changing the youth's direct speech into indirect speech. Dr Trávníček in Tomsa's *Symposium* reproaches Janáček for leaving out the first stanza of No. 10 and, in particular, the last line of the last stanza which, in a free translation, reads as follows:

'Oh, mighty and merciful God,
Before I leave this desolate world,
Let me experience, let me feel,
That I too have a native land of my own!'

According to Trávníček, this robbed the final stanza of its meaning. In my opinion, though, Janáček by ending the stanza with 'Let me experience, let me feel...' (repeated three times, fortissimo)—showed that this verse certainly had meaning for him, but a different one. And for similar reasons he left out the first stanza which, in any case, duplicated the second one.

In order to avoid a disjointed effect, Janáček, like the classical composers of variations, chaconnes, etc., linked some of the numbers *attacca* or used the same thematic material or similar figuration in some of them (e.g. Nos 4 and 5; 9 and 10) and when the story reaches its turning point, three of the poems, including No. 11, are linked together, forming a miniature drama. Nos 7 and 17 share the motto 'What will be, will be...', and Nos 12 and 13 are joint comments on J.D.'s surrender: in No. 12 are named the four things the youth will never forget (the dark thicket, the cool spring, the dark gypsy and her white knees); and No. 13 (No. 14 of the original, the 'mute' number consisting of dashes) is a forlorn piano soliloquy gradated, with its ostinato-like four-note motif, from pianissimo to fortissimo and back in another deeply moving drama (which did not prevent an enterprising publisher from branding this portrait of forlorn regret with the title *Intermezzo erotico*).

Apart from these obvious thematic connexions, there are melodic turns of phrase which keep reappearing almost symbolically. There is, for instance, the young man's descending quadruplet in No. 2:

gdy - by   od-jít chtě-la

if she went away (I would be happier)

which returns in No. 3:

(Bože,) stoj   mi   ku po-mo-ci!

(Dear God,) stand by me and help me!

and in No. 5:

261

O ní   sa mi zdá-lo
Of her   I was dreaming

always as an expression of tortuous preoccupation.
However, in No. 18:

262

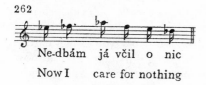

Ne-dbám já včil o nic
Now I   care for nothing

and especially in its final form in No. 20, at the youth's realization that
Zefka is pregnant:

263

Mám já panenku,   a-le po   po   po kolenka,
I have a maiden–(her skirt is lifting)   up, up, up to her knees

it becomes an expression of buoyant light-heartedness which for the moment
has replaced the youth's self-torture. This number is the only strophic song
in the whole cycle which otherwise relies mainly on repetitions or free transpositions of sections of the melody, often enlivened by shifts in the rhythm
also.

The piano sometimes doubles the voice, sometimes, for instance after Zefka's
Vítaj Janíčku (Welcome, Janíček) at the beginning of No. 9, imitates it, at
other times it anticipates the voice as, for instance, in No. 9 again, where it
hints at Zefka's *Co tak tady stojíš* (Why do you stand there), or telescopes the
motifs of the vocal line as in this excerpt from the chorus commentary in
Nos. 9 and 10:

(She sang a) sad song (which moved the heart)

There are many examples of word painting: In No. 1 the piano anticipates, with a fast descending run, the line *Pak vznesla sa přes peň* (She leaped
through the undergrowth); in No. 3 it sketches the glow-worms, and in
No. 4 the twittering swallows, in No. 11 the scent of buckwheat in bloom

259

wafting to the wood; and in No. 18 it supplies the crowing of the cock. But the piano part is vitally important not only for its expressive contribution but also as a foil that sets off the vocal line, and in the final song it is even reminiscent of the conclusion of JENŮFA (the heroic E flat major included), taking on an almost orchestral character.

It can easily be understood that for such a unique work—an intimate duo-drama for the concert platform—Janáček wanted a scenic interpretation. His directions are: 'To be sung in semi-darkness, if possible with reddish lighting to heighten the erotic mood, and the contralto (Zefka) should not appear on the platform until No. 7 is being played, and she should leave equally unobtrusively during No. 11. The three women's voices which describe the action at its fateful moments should sing off-stage and almost inaudibly.' Of these, quite rightly in my opinion, only the first and last directions are adhered to. An experimental performance of the DIARY on a stage with an orchestral accompaniment has been given. Janáček may have had a similar idea which he wisely abandoned. It is the sung word which gives the fantasy its fullest scope, the transposition into action of such an intimate and volatile work overburdens it without adding to its effect.

The DIARY OF THE YOUNG MAN WHO DISAPPEARED was first performed at the Brno Reduta on 18 April 1921 when the piano part and general presentation were in the hands of Břetislav Bakala. The Prague première followed on 10 December with Dr Václav Štěpán playing the piano. Berlin heard it on 21 September of the following year, when the piano was played by a native of Brno, Felix Petyrek, a pupil of Franz Schrecker, while the high tenor part was sung by Karel Zavřel, a member of the Brno Opera who had also sung it at the first hearing in Brno and Prague. Among other outstanding Czech interpreters of the tenor part were the soloist of the Moravian Teachers' Choral Society, Stanislav Tauber, and Josef Válka; and of the early interpreters abroad mention should be made of the Danish tenor Mischa Léon who, although knowing no Czech, took great pains to learn the part in the original language with Břetislav Bakala with whom he then gave the first performance in London (on 27 October 1922) and in Paris (on 15 December 1922).

(33) 'Katya Kabanova'

Another fate-ridden but strongly lyrical subject soon engaged Janáček's interest, this time in the field of opera.

In September 1916 he was considering Tolstoy's *The Living Corpse,* in one way strikingly similar to the DIARY. In it Fedya Protasov also breaks with convention and leaves with a gypsy girl.*) Janáček sketched out the score of the first scene (in the house of the Protasovs) in which the introductory bars:

are surprisingly like the introduction to ŠÁRKA (see Ex. 31). The work got no further, perhaps, as Dr Theodora Straková has pointed out**) because 'Tolstoy flatly and uncompromisingly subjects passion to the dictates of duty—an attitude which could scarcely have satisfied Janáček.'

At the beginning of 1918, Václav Jiříkovský, then a young assistant director of the Brno Theatre (who was to perish at the hands of the Gestapo many years later), suggested three Slav subjects to Janáček: *The Forester's Wife,* a tragic idyll by the Slovak poet Hviezdoslav, the heroic *Hasanaginica* by the Yugoslav playwright Ogrizović and *The Thunderstorm* by the Russian playwright Alexander Nikolayevich Ostrovsky (1823—1886) which he staged in Brno specially for Janáček's benefit on 29 March 1919.

Janáček selected *The Thunderstorm*—certainly in every respect the choice of his heart. The Russian setting itself must have awakened particularly fertile memories—memories of the Volga 'as white in the moonlight as Katya's soul', and the life on the river banks as he once saw it at Novgorod. He wrote on 10 January 1920 to Vincenc Červinka telling him that he proposed to use his translation of *The Thunderstorm* for the libretto; and in order to differentiate it from other *Storms* or *Tempests,* on Schmoranz's advice, he called it KATYA KABANOVA: 'There is much sadness and Slav tenderness and depth of feeling in it. May I find the right way to express it with equal intensity.'

There was the further attraction of again being able to identify the heroine with his beloved. 'My Katya grows in her. In her, in my Kamila! It will be one of my most tender works.' The opera, which may be called his *Appassionata,* was written without interruption. On 17 February 1921 the work was finished.

---

*) In Tolstoy's drama matters are complicated by the fact that the hero is married and decides to feign suicide. The ruse is discovered and Protasov shoots himself in court, to pave the way for the happier marriage which his wife had been planning after his supposed death.
**) 'Janáček's Operatic Topics and Fragments', *Musikologie III.*

The opera is set in a remote town on the banks of the Volga in the 1860s. Katya, married to the weakling Tikhon Kabanov, is dominated by his despotic mother Kabanikha. She falls in love with the cultivated Boris who suffers, in a similar way as she does, the whims of his uncle Dikoi, an inveterate drunkard. Despite the instigations of the light-hearted Varvara who is conducting an affair of her own with the young unmarried Kudryash, Katya resists temptation. When her husband prepares to go on a long journey, she implores him to change his mind or else to take her with him; but in vain. During his absence Katya succumbs to her desire. But it is not long before she begins to be tortured by her conscience, and she is driven to a public confession under the impact of a violent storm which she takes to be a sign of God's wrath. When even Boris has left her, she leaps into the Volga and is drowned.

Spiritually, the work is akin to the pure, youthful confessional tone of AMARUS and to the DIARY, and its mood reappears in Janáček's FIRST QUARTET inspired by Tolstoy's *Kreutzer Sonata*. The action and characters are closely related to *Gazdina roba* (The Farmer's Woman) by Gabriela Preissová (and thus to J. B. Foerster's *Eva*), a subject which Janáček had begun setting to music some 14 years previously but had abandoned because of its close similarity, as he thought, to JENŮFA. KATYA KABANOVA and THE FARMER'S WOMAN share the same despotic mothers-in-law Kabanikha and Meshyanovka (Kostelnička is not far removed from them either) whose weakling sons Tikhon and Mánek drive Katya and Eva to the same end—suicide. Of course, the meek (in my opinion excessively meek) Katya who takes the full weight of the guilt on herself is very different from the overwrought Eva.

At any rate Janáček, after a full 20 years, had once more found a subject worthy of his genius. After his experiences with the libretti of DESTINY and THE EXCURSIONS OF MR BROUČEK he chose, as with JENŮFA, a ready-made play. This did not prevent him, however, from making some radical changes to it. By leaving out scenes of purely documentary character and shortening others, he was able to reduce the original five acts to three—each with two scenes— and to concentrate on the spiritual core of the play. He also enhanced the intimacy of the atmosphere for Katya's reminiscences and confessions to Varvara which he placed in the Kabanovs' living room and which he followed with Katya's plea to Tikhon not to leave her at home alone with Kabanicha. By changing Tikhon's description from Ostrovsky's Act V, Scene I, into direct speech he gained an effective scene in which Varvara elopes with Kudryash to Moscow. Janáček cut some characters out altogether (for instance, the sinister old lady with two footmen who probably reminded him too much of Pushkin's *Queen of Spades*) or gave some of their lines to other characters.*) So for instance he gave Kuligin's speech in defence of electricity, together with his interest in mechanics, to the tenor Kudryash. This was probably in order to sharpen the contrast between progressive ideas of youth and the backwardness of old Dikoi, although the lines suit the character of Kuligin better—much more so than the impudent-sounding ditty, added by Janáček, which Kuligin sings

---

*) It is not clear what Janáček meant by his remark in a letter to Červinka (31 March 1921) 'I have compressed the mad lady into the evil woman of a few shouts.'

as he knowingly watches the lonely Katya in the last scene. Janáček also took away Kuligin's dramatic task of carrying in the drowned Katya with the accusing statement 'Here you have your Katerina', and gave it less appropriately to Dikoi who is as much to blame as Kabanikha herself.

These incursions into the sensitive structure of a self-contained work, despite Janáček's exceptional dramatic and musical sense, led to some inconsistencies. For instance, in Scene III, he allowed Kabanikha to sing her first line to her drunken friend off-stage ('Did you want something? Talk properly, don't shout!') in the middle of Katya's monologue, after her frightened 'Someone's coming!' Katya then reassures herself 'No, no! No one,' while Kabanikha in fact goes on talking outside the door.*) And Dikoi's answer ('Nothing in particular') comes a whole three pages too late in the vocal score. In another instance one need not object to Janáček making the drunken Dikoi fall amorously at Kabanikha's feet in order to emphasize her hypocrisy, although she, rather paradoxically, admonishes him: 'Don't torture yourself—but behave respectably.' Elsewhere, he let Varvara calm Kudryash during her rendezvous, with the assurance that Dikoi is with the old woman and that they are getting on very well together. Here Janáček overlooked the fact that she had just assured her lover that the old woman was fast asleep.**)

A more glaring oversight occurred when the composer, again departing from the original, made Katya flee from her home directly after her confession, while in the following scene***) which evidently takes place the same evening she describes her harassment at home following the confession; she tells Boris how 'they all reproach me for you'.

It is interesting to note the different functions assigned by Janáček and Ostrovsky to a mural painting of Gehenna in the arcade of the boulevard during the storm scene. Ostrovsky seems to have felt, rightly, that the audience would hardly consider Katya's infidelity to her pathetic husband as sufficient motive for her tragic act of repentance, and he omitted nothing which would reinforce it. Thus he inserted the passage concerning Gehenna mainly to suggest that the sight of Hell's torments was the direct and decisive motive for Katya's public confession. Did Janáček forget this time-bomb just when it was to explode? Or did he leave it out intentionally in order to make Katya confess for purely moral reasons? If that was the case, the storm itself should have been omitted.

The motivation of Katya's tragic end, even in Ostrovsky's play, is not flawless. Boris, her lover, lacks the stature to drive her, by his departure, to suicide as her only remaining alternative. He is simply 'a well-brought-up young man', according to the *dramatis personae*, colourless and indecisive (Varvara calls him 'boring' in the play), a true Oblomov, not much more than a well-bred version of Katya's husband Tikhon Ivanych.

---

*) The producer can, of course, help at this point by making Kabanikha step back from the door.

**) Max Brod corrected this and similar discrepancies in his translation.

***) Janáček himself confirmed this in a letter to Max Brod written in October 1921: 'Katya does not return home after the storm. She runs away and they search for her.' (But she may have her own reasons for speaking to Boris as she does. K. J.)

However, of all the libretti which Janáček worked upon, KATYA KABANOVA is the most integrated and musical, and it drew from him the greatest lyrical wealth. Only in JENŮFA (though in my opinion Katya's tragedy is artistically even purer and more fervent) did Janáček create music of such breathtaking melodic majesty which, nevertheless, is firmly and inevitably rooted in commonplace speech. One example is Katya's 'For me, mother, you are like my own' from Scene I, the melody of which forms one of the main thematic elements of the work. Or her 'Tisha, darling, if only you would stay at home or take me with you, I would so love you, I would so caress you' in the following scene, which rings out in Janáček's setting as pure poetry although it is, in fact, mostly prose.

The whole work is perfectly balanced in construction and in dramatic expression. The thematic material alone deserves a study of its own. Let me only point out the apparently effortless development of the simple harness-bell motif of Tikhon's departure, which with its pedal fifth evokes the brooding monotony of the Russian steppe while its brisk rhythmical movement suggests the motion of the Russian *troika*. Yet it remains dramatically neutral, reminiscent of the 'icy tone' of the xylophone in Act I of JENŮFA, so that it is in cold contrast to the rest of the spirited musical material:

The first eight notes of the motif acquire great dramatic importance. Just as Tikhon's departure seals the fate of Katya, so these eight notes spell fate—they are the motto of fate, introduced in the opening bars of the opera in the timpani in augmentation and off the beat. Eventually they play a terrifying role in the storm. Equally, the last notes assume a special significance at the moment of Tikhon's departure (Act I, Scene 2, reh. No. 23):

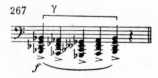

From the apparently unimportant middle-part motif comes, already in the introduction, another figure:

out of which develops, as soon as the curtain rises, the motif:

264

269

etc.

which in turn gives rise to:

270

and to:

271

Andante

and, by further development, to:

272

Finally, at Katya's first entrance, it is transformed into this shining melody:

Adagio

273

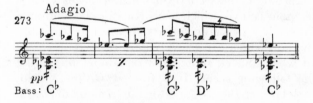

But this is not all; with the variant:

274

which is closely related to Ex. 268 and 269 and underscores each time the raging of Kabanikha, Janáček develops, in the departure scene, a further motif of fatal portent, with which he then concludes Act I:

275

Andante

In the same way we could follow, right from the opening of Act III, the

265

metamorphoses of seemingly unimportant figuration into this hymnic motif
of nature—nature as a tool in the hands of God:

and eventually into the 'sigh of the Volga' motif—a motif of atonement and
redemption in relation to Katya, and in the closing bars of the work a horrific
motif of guilt in relation to Kabanikha:

(wordless chorus off stage)

A close study of the score will reveal other examples demonstrating the skill
with which Janáček developed his material.

Although it is not surprising to find that the 66-year-old composer was so
complete a master of his art, the youthful fervour and lyricism which pervade
the whole opera must be particularly admired. While the first scene could
be considered as a balladic exposition, the second, in which Janáček creates
a passionate atmosphere of religious ecstasy which leads Katya to contemplate
the ecstasy of 'sin' and portrays her desperate efforts to avert temptation,
reaches heights of dramatic tension which can scarcely be surpassed.

This is perhaps the reason why Janáček shifted the remainder of the act
in Ostrovsky's original to the following scene. It is framed within a cold,
mysterious motif in thirds which later changes ominously into a mood of almost
stifling suspense. This is relieved only by the occasional hint at the ditty sung
later by the carefree Varvara, 'My Vanya is over the river', with its lusciously
swaying accentuation scored for four flutes and celesta.

Scene IV has a richer colouring which describes the rendezvous of the two
couples and contrasts the deep and fatal love of Katya with the natural and
openly physical love of Varvara and Kudryash. Only the beginning is gloomy,
a stealthy theme twice alternating with a lyrical variant, as if the philandering
Boris were equating Katya's image in his mind with some old-world romance:*)

After Kudryash's cheerful Cossack song, the meeting of Katya and Boris
begins in a guilt-laden mood, fundamentally different from that of the conventional operatic love scene. Thus the inevitable outburst of suppressed

feelings is all the more impelling. The passionate declaration of love, breaking at first into gasps of delight, subsides at last into a happy consonance of the two voices. Only the dark-sounding reminders in the double-basses bode ill. At the end comes the lovers' leave-taking, with a new outburst in the orchestra and a mysterious cadence in alternating major and minor.

How different is the second and last meeting of the lovers after the pilloried Katya's tortuous waiting. Now, when all has been confessed, there are no more feelings of uneasy indecision—only desperately boundless intoxication which abates after the words 'I have managed to see you once more', to be followed by the most beautiful melody without words in muted strings. There follow the absent-minded questions denied each time by a 'No, no! I wanted to say something else to you,' and finally there is Katya's last wish, sung to a soft tremolo and the 'sigh of the Volga' motif.

The somewhat characterless departure of Boris is followed, after an exquisite move to the dominant of A flat minor, by what is surely one of the most unpretentious and yet the most touching farewells to life ever composed. 'The birds will come flying to my grave, they will hatch their young, and the flowers will blossom—red, blue and yellow...'

And over the body of Katya, there stands the old Kabanikha taking care to 'observe good manners'.

---

*) It is interesting, although no doubt accidental, that this melody does in fact sound like a deliberate quotation from a period piece since it is almost identical, down to the triplet accompaniment, with the beginning of a romance from a very well-known opera—*Il Barbiere di Siviglia*:

279

The year 1921 in which Janáček finished KATYA KABANOVA, also saw the first performance of THE DIARY OF THE YOUNG MAN WHO DISAPPEARED (18 April), TARAS BULBA (4 October) and the première of the new opera (23 November) produced by Vladimír Marek, with Marie Calma-Veselá in the main part. At first it was coolly received but after several performances the audiences became increasingly enthusiastic, although the scenery of A. V. Hrska did not meet with Janáček's approval.*)

At the beginning of July, Janáček went on holiday to the High Tatra mountains in Slovakia, where he visited many lakes and colourful valleys. He wrote about them on 18 July in the paper *Lidové noviny* and included even examples of the *nápěvky* (melodic curves) of the Studený potok water-falls. The article ends: 'I would like to sing the majesty of these mountains, the soft tepid rain, the chilling ice, the flowers in the meadows, the snow fields. The bright peaks touching the sky and the ghostly darkness of the forests at night, the love call of the songbirds and the shrieks of the birds of prey. The dreamy silence of noon and the humming tremolo of a thousand insects.

'And the God-given barrier of our frontier!'

During the last days of the year, he finally found a house for himself in Hukvaldy. Until then he had always stayed with the gamekeeper Vincenc Sládek and his family (The 'Sládečeks'—little Sládeks—as he called them) immortalizing their children Lidka and Vincek by taking down innumerable 'melodic curves' of their speech and by writing about them in his articles. Now, having become 'rich', Janáček bought the cottage which had belonged to his brother František who died on 20 December 1908 and whose German-born widow had moved to Gliwice in Silesia.**) The cottage was situated in Podo-boří—a quiet spot between a game-reserve and Janáček's beloved Babí Hill. On the ground floor, facing the sun, Janáček made himself a study in which he put a richly inlaid writing desk from the estate of Count Pálffy which was given to him by Ferdinand Lehner, a carved writing-stand, and a harmonium at which he composed. The cottage had its own orchard and a small yard furnished with a seat and populated by hens who were

---

*) 'The Brno production looked coarse and tasteless— the period of the 'forties and 'sixties was not even suggested,' he complained to Ostrčil on 21 September 1922.

**) It is typical of the period that most of the Janáček brothers married Germans. Karel, the eldest, a patriotic teacher at Valašské Meziříčí and later head of a school at Krásné nad Bečvou, nevertheless married a German from his own district, as did Josef, a farmer at Zubří in Valachia, who outlived the composer by 30 years. Bedřich married, on 18 February 1914 at Aspang near Vienna, a German woman, Hedwig Schmied, became a German himself and brought up his four children as Germans. (Robert Smetana: *Stories about Janáček*, p. 74.)

to 'help' the perspicacious Janáček to compose his next opera. For Janáček now began work on a subject from animal life. This came about in the following way.*)

The arts editor of the paper *Lidové noviny* Dr Bohumil Markalous (pen name, Jaromír John) had the job of providing his paper, among other things, with illustrations. Suffering from a 'chronic shortage of decent pictures' he went one day to Prague to the studio of the painter Stanislav Lolek who was known to be equally fond of painting and of shooting. Lolek said that he had nothing, but the persistent editor noticed the edge of a drawing in a corner near the floor. He turned over the pile of sketches and discovered 'a comic hunting serial in the style of Wilhelm Busch, Pater Filucius or Hans Huckebein.'

After some argument the editor was able to return the same night to Brno with the pictures. The chief editor Arnošt Heinrich who despite the late hour was still in his office, decided to ask Rudolf Těsnohlídek (a writer and member of the staff of the *Lidové noviny*) to write verses for them. At first Těsnohlídek was unenthusiastic—the subject did not suggest verses to him. Finally he found the right approach after making a journey to the Adamov district north of Brno to study the dialect of the lumberjacks; and then he wrote the story in prose, and gave it the name of the attractive central figure, *Liška Bystrouška* (Vixen Sharp-Ears), originally *Bystronožka* ('Light-Foot', misread by the compositor and left as it was by Těsnohlídek). The story, with the illustrations, was brought out in instalments during 1920. Janáček was a regular reader of this paper which had, as has been seen, supplied him with more than one subject.

Janáček did not begin composing at once. 'Each of my operas has grown for a year or two without my hindering its growth by a single note. Each one gave me a long headache,' he said once, adding with a laugh: 'But I just played about with Bystrouška as though she had been tame.'**)

On 10 January 1922 he still wrote to Brod: 'My head is an empty shell, like after a fire. I don't know what to bite and chew. I dabble in folk songs and read Einstein. But the relativity of time and space is rather unsuitable for tones. We live by air and not by ether. We smell of earth, but at least we stand firm.'

The folk songs he refers to are the MORAVSKÉ LIDOVÉ PÍSNĚ (Moravian Folk Songs) for piano, written about New Year 1922 at the suggestion of the publishers *Hudební matice* (Music Foundation) which, in order to produce something for non-singing amateurs, decided to publish the folk songs arranged for piano alone, printing the words of the first verse with the melody and the other verses separately underneath. Despite being limited to the piano, this group of 15 songs is one of the most interesting of its kind. In them Janáček is relatively free from the 'authentic' folk example. He accompanies the tunes, placed in only eight of the songs in the top and in the rest in the middle parts or in the bass, with ostinato motifs, contrary motion (as in No. 12), imitation

---

*) As told by Jaromír John and Josef Rejsek in the Brno National Theatre Magazine, 5 May 1948.
**) *Veselý — Janáček*, p. 96.

and shifting rhythms—as in No. 6 which contains a pithy example of the so-called 'Moravian' modulation:

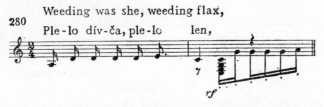

Weeding was she, weeding flax,

Yet in spite of these technical tricks and considerable freedom of harmony, the spirit of the folk song is perfectly preserved—with the possible exception of No. 4—in the Lydian G major. Here the modern conception, especially of bars seven to nine, ending on what sounds like the tonic:

Maryse, my Maryse, why d'you always tease me?
Why don't you, Maryse, please, open your door to me?

gives a conclusive character to an inconclusive verse. One is tempted to ask whether the otherwise so unconventional Janáček did not, in this case, throw himself into the arms of the 'Old Lady'.*)

To return to the opera; the 'taming' of Bystrouška had soon advanced sufficiently for Janáček to write to Brod on 22 August 1922 from his retreat amidst 'the peaceful solitude of the dreaming forests' of Hukvaldy: 'I'm writing the libretto for the ADVENTURES OF THE THE VIXEN SHARP EARS as far as I've arranged it. Roughly, all except the last act.'**) By the autumn the libretto was finished and Janáček started writing the music. He continued throughout 1923, and in January 1924 the opera was complete.***) On 3 April 1923†) Janáček wrote to Kamila: 'I'm composing like the devil catching flies—when he has nothing else to do. I caught Bystrouška for the sake of the forest and the sadness of old age.' But on 31 October 1924 Janáček invited Brod to the

---

*) See the allusion to Debussy in the Introduction, p. 22.
**) According to Robert Smetana (*Stories about Janáček*, p. 118), Janáček originally asked Těsnohlídek to write the libretto, but he refused. He did, however, help to put the final touches to it.
***) Adolf Veselý: 'The Path of a Work of Art' (*Lidové noviny*, 6 November 1924). According to Štědroň's catalogue, ADVENTURES OF THE VIXEN SHARP EARS was finished already on 17 March 1923.
†) i.e. at a time when according to Štědroň the opera should have been finished.

270

première of his 'best work', which took place on 6 November 1924 in Brno.

'For the sake of the forest and the sadness of old age...' but these were not the only things which prompted Janáček to illustrate in music an animal story which had for once been a writer's illustration to a draughtsman's original. The reason why he 'caught' the vixen was its tantalizing and intoxicating youthfulness and its essentially female nature which makes it a counterpart to all the male foxes in literature from Aesop's fables, the *Roman de Renard* and Goethe's *Reineke Fuchs*, down to the singing and dancing fox of Stravinsky. He 'caught' it—paradoxically—as a symbol of freedom amidst unfettered nature just as in THE HOUSE OF THE DEAD the symbol of freedom is 'the eagle, the Czar of the forests.' He also longed to give full expression to his admiration for nature which, until now, he had used only as a backdrop—dreamy in ŠÁRKA, AMARUS, THE EXCURSION TO THE MOON, THE SONGS OF HRADČANY or Katya's farewell to life; sinister as the overflowing River Ostravice in MARYČKA MAGDÓNOVA, as the gale in JENŮFA or the storms in DESTINY and KATYA KABANOVA. This time he wanted to sing the praises of Nature the regenerator which gave solace to the almost 70-year-old composer as he pondered upon mortality.*) Finally, the success of the Čapek Brothers' satire *The Insect Play* (first performed on 8 April 1922) may have given him the courage to write an animal opera.

His pattern of dramatization seems, on the face of it, simple. He chose the most important scenes from the original and made them into a three-act story, sung, acted and danced, with subtitles such as: 'How Bystrouška was caught', 'Bystrouška in the gamekeeper's yard', 'Bystrouška the politician', 'Bystrouška makes herself scarce', 'Bystrouška expropriates', 'Bystrouška's flirtations', 'Bystrouška's courting and love', 'How Bystrouška outwitted the dealer Harašta from Líšeň', 'How Bystrouška died', 'Little Bystrouška, the spitting image of her mother'. The attraction of the story is enhanced by a complete disregard for the logic of time and space and also by the attractive Líšeň dialect, used by the people and animals alike.**) The plot is as follows:

Act One. Scene 1. *A clearing in the forest.* It is a hot summer afternoon. The badger, peering out of his set, smokes a long pipe; midges and a dragonfly dance around. Suddenly they disappear. The gamekeeper enters. He has had too much to drink and decides to take a nap in the shade away from the sweltering heat. A cricket and a grasshopper dance nearby. Scenting sweet blood, a mosquito enters and dances round the gamekeeper. A frog tries to catch the mosquito, chasing it away. At this moment little Bystrouška rushes in, the frightened frog leaps up and lands on the gamekeeper's nose. Seeing a fox cub, the gamekeeper hurls himself at it and catches it. The little fox cub calls, 'Mummy, mummy', but the gamekeeper only laughs and carries his prey home: 'It will be fun for the kids.' The blue dragonfly returns to the clearing, only to find little Bystrouška gone.

---

*) Solace only in theory, since Janáček once cried out paradoxically: 'And if I didn't live, what would I care about the world?'
**) Líšeň is a village near Brno, famous for its poultry, on the edge of the large and picturesque Adamov forests where this opera takes place.

271

Scene 2. *The gamekeeper's lodge.* The dog Lapák (a male character, but sung by a mezzo-soprano) and Bystrouška are both lying by Lapák's kennel. The gamekeeper's wife grumbles that the vixen will only spread fleas, yet she does pour out some milk for her. Bystrouška licks her drink and whines. Lapák consoles her: his own life is so lonely, especially during the mating months of February and March, that he has taken to art and music. Every evening he sings melancholy songs of his own composition. But he only gets a hiding for it from the old man. Lapák does not know what love is. Bystrouška tells him that she does not have any experience in love-making either, although she has heard quite a lot from the starlings who nested near the den. They were always quarrelling and behaving in a scandalous fashion. One of them had an affair with a cuckoo and the starling's daughter was carrying on with a young raven. When Lapák, his imagination kindled by these examples, makes amorous advances, however, Bystrouška knocks him over and the dog crawls into the kennel. The gamekeeper's son Pepík enters with his friend Frantík to show off his vixen and he tickles her under the nose. Bystrouška growls and Pepík hits her on the nose with a switch. Bystrouška gets angry, bites Pepík in the leg and makes off for the forest but, like Lot's wife, out of curiosity she looks behind her, trips, and is recaptured by Frantík. The gamekeeper's wife runs out scolding and the gamekeeper boxes Pepík's ears and ties up the fox.

The light begins to fade. Interlude. Bystrouška whimpers in her sleep. At dawn Lapák wakes up, stretches and lectures the vixen for trying to run away. 'You should be like me! You shouldn't have run away.' The cock struts round: 'See, the justice of man. Miss Vixen here used to chase us. Now look at her,' he tells his hens. 'All because she lays no eggs! Lay eggs, work hard, and I will not desert you!' Bystrouška tries to set the hens against the cock who has sold his soul to man: let the hens destroy the old system and create a new world in which they will enjoy happiness and prosperity on an equal footing. But the hens cackle: 'Happiness without a cock?' So the vixen digs a hole in the rubbish-heap deciding to bury herself alive rather than see such backwardness. When the chickens gather curiously aroung her, the vixen suddenly leaps up and catches the cock. The hens weep for their cock, the gamekeeper's wife complains that she would have preferred a fox-fur muff and Bystrouška, hearing her words, bites through her rope, trips up the gamekeeper and makes off into the forest.

Act Two. Scene I. *The clearing as in Act I, Scene I.* The homeless Bystrouška peers enviously into the badger's set. The badger allows himself to be provoked by Bystrouška and her rabble who ridicule his haughty, possessive attitude. He strikes her and threatens her with the law, whereupon she retaliates by defecating in his lair. The badger cries: 'I am leaving this ungrateful flock,' and angrily runs away. The triumphant Bystrouška occupies the abandoned lair.

Scene 2. *The inn 'U Pásků'.* The parson with the voice and face of the badger finds the gamekeeper taunting the schoolmaster with a song about Veronika who had once been his love. The schoolmaster retaliates by asking how the vixen is faring. The crowing of the cock announces the dawn and the parson has to go home.

Scene 3. *In the forest.* A path leading uphill. A fence with a sunflower growing. It is dawn. The schoolmaster reminisces in a long drunken monologue. He stumbles uphill and falls. Bystrouška comes running out from behind the sunflower, and the schoolmaster mistakes her for Terynka with whom he has been in love 'for years and years'. He tries to embrace her but topples over the fence.

The parson appears, deep in memories of the girl he loved as a student, watched by Bystrouška from a thicket. He recalls the treacherously innocent eyes of the girl who got into trouble with the butcher's apprentice, and how he himself was then accused. Yet all is past and now he is left alone like a broom in a corner. The gamekeeper appears and shoots at the vixen, who bounds off. Only the two frightened men, the schoolmaster and the parson, remain.

Scene 4. *Outside Bystrouška's den.* A moonlit night. Bystrouška is resting blissfully. Suddenly there is a stir in the thicket and Bystrouška trembles at the approach of a male fox. The fox offers her his company for a walk since the forest is crawling with huntsmen. Bystrouška delightedly accepts and describes her struggle with the gamekeeper. The fox is impressed and when, in answer to his question whether she likes rabbits, Bystrouška enthusiastically answers in the affirmative, he vanishes to return with a rabbit in his jaws. During the ensuing meal the fox kisses Bystrouška on the ear, remarking: 'Have you never made love yet?' Bystrouška answers bashfully: 'Not yet, and what about you? A lot?' 'Oh, no,' replies the fox. 'Why?'—'Because I haven't yet found anyone I respect so much that I would give my life for her. But should I find anyone, then—then I would say: do you love me?' Bystrouška makes no reply and the fox embraces her fiercely. Bystrouška struggles: 'Leave me alone. I'm afraid of you.' The fox sadly lets her go. 'So run away and take my happiness with you,' says the fox. 'Ruin me! I don't want to live any more!'—'Really?'—'It's not your body, its your soul I love,' says the fox taking her in his arms, and they slip into the lair. This starts the owl and the jay gossiping maliciously. Some time later a tearful Bystrouška whispers her secret to the fox, who sighs: 'Well, if that's so, we must go to the parson at once.' The woodpecker sticks his head out of a hole in an old rowan tree and announces the marriage banns from his pulpit. Then the wedding party begins.

Act Three. Scene I. *At the edge of a thicket.* Harašta, a poultry dealer from Líšeň, is walking along a track when he sees a dead hare. He is about to pick it up when he notices the gamekeeper. The two start chatting and Harašta, on being asked how he enjoys his life as a bachelor, tells the gamekeeper that he has just found himself 'the best of wives—Terynka'. The gamekeeper accuses him of poaching. Harašta hotly denies the charge, arguing that he does not even pick up what he finds, and points out the dead hare. When the gamekeeper discovers the vixen's footprints, he sets a trap and departs sullenly. Harašta, on the other hand, is laughing softly to himself. He goes off in the opposite direction. Bystrouška enters with her cubs and sees the dead hare. 'Funny thing! A man was here but left the hare.' She sniffs at the chain of the trap and smells the gamekeeper's pipe. Even the cubs recognize the snare and scamper away. Harašta returns, carrying a basket of poultry on his back. Bystrouška pretends to be lame to lure Harašta away from his basket. Then she runs away and the old poacher as he pursues her trips and breaks his nose while the entire fox family fall on the chickens in the basket.

Harašta, in desperation, picks up his shotgun and shoots at random. And this time Bystrouška is hit.

Scene 2. *At the inn 'U Pásků'*. The gamekeeper tells the brooding schoolmaster how he followed a vixen's track but found the den empty. Then smiling cunningly he remarks that his wife will have a new muff after all. The inn-keeper's wife brings the news that Terynka has a new muff for her wedding. The schoolmaster turns away to hide his tears. The gamekeeper consoles him as best he can but suddenly gets up to go, remembering that his old dog, Lapák, is at home alone.

Scene 3. *The clearing as in Act One*. The sun is setting. Walking home through the forest and brooding over memories of his youth, the gamekeeper sits down for a rest and falls asleep. He dreams of his beloved animals—only Bystrouška is missing. He wakes up with a start only to see a little fox cub, the image of Bystrouška. He wants to catch it as he once did its mother, except that this time he wants to bring it up better. Instead, he catches a little frog, but it too is the grandchild of the frog he knew a year ago. The gamekeeper is overwhelmed by the miracle of perpetual rebirth.

This is the story which Janáček worked out with his usual disregard for sober logic. When for instance in Act II Bystrouška tells the fox about her flight from the gamekeeper's cottage, one naturally assumes that she is referring to the flight witnessed at the end of Act I. This assumption, however, leads to so many discrepancies that one finally consults Těsnohlídek only to find that she is referring to another, later escape not mentioned in the opera.

Yet Janáček went further than merely dramatizing the story. He made the poacher Martínek and the poultry-dealer Harašta into one character and made Bystrouška die at Harašta's hands. Těsnohlídek ended the story on a lighter note; 'I cannot find out how all this ended,' he wrote.

Janáček made Bystrouška's death all the more touching by showing her supremely happy with her cubs, and by giving to her and the fox the lines which in Těsnohlídek's story belong to a sparrow and his mate.

The most typical of his contributions was emphasizing the analogies of character between animals and people by linking some of the *dramatis personæ* of the human and animal worlds just as he had combined the real characters with those of the moon and of the fifteenth century in his Excursions of Mr Brouček. Thus he created the symbolic parallels: parson—badger, schoolmaster—mosquito, gamekeeper's wife—owl, cock—jay. In particular, there is the unexpressed parallel of Bystrouška and the mysterious Terynka who never appears on stage and who symbolizes tantalizing, flirtatious femininity.*) The nocturnal interlude in Act I, Scene 2, with its ensuing greeting to the rising sun is one of the most enchanting parts of the opera, during which the appearance of Bystrouška as a girl is evoked most suggestively and the lamentations of the fettered Bystrouška become the sighs of the fettered desire of a young girl. The schoolmaster returning late from the inn imagines

---

*) In Těsnohlídek's story, where she also does not appear directly, she is the light-hearted part owner of a travelling sweet-stall.

274

that he sees Terynka in Bystrouška teasing him from behind the sunflower (although back at the inn he was being taunted about a girl named Veronika), and the theme of Bystrouška-Terynka then accompanies the parson's memories of his youthful infatuation. Finally, the poacher Harašta claims the by then almost legendary Terynka as his bride. But there Janáček leaves us at a loss since if Harašta has on the one hand shot Bystrouška and is on the other, as we are told, marrying Terynka, even giving her a present of a muff made from Bystrouška's pelt, it is hard to find the symbolic link unless Bystrouška's death symbolizes, rather ploddingly, the 'moral end' of Terynka at the poacher's hands, and unless Terynka considers a present made out of her own skin to be a cause for pride. I am inclined to be suspicious of this kind of ingenious analysis even when it can be based on Janáček's own remarks.

Nor would I waste too much time on inconsistencies such as, for instance, the improbable invasion of the inn by the parson's 'new lodgers' which was to have been a forceful analogy, inserted at Max Brod's insistence, with the animal folk invading the badger.*)

Let us be content with the natural and obvious symbolism without obscuring the refreshing and unique charm of ADVENTURES OF THE VIXEN SHARP EARS. There is the delightful figure of the gamekeeper with his nose so saturated in alcohol that even a mosquito bites it at the risk of getting drunk, who, on the other hand, has a childlike sensitive heart in spite of his coarse language. (No one, not even Bystrouška, has very good manners in this opera.) There is the lovable schoolmaster with his timid visions of love; the parson-badger, essentially human despite his many weaknesses; and the irresistible, foxy rogue Harašta.

Above all, there are the animal folk. Bystrouška herself, with her childish curiosity and playfulness, her awakening animal rapacity and budding woman-hood, aware of her beauty for the first time under the gaze of her first suitor. How charmingly she expresses her surprise at her happiness ('Why should it be me?') and how simply their marriage ceremony ('Do you want me?'—'I do!') and the bliss of maternity ('How many children have we had so far?'); then there is her mate—good-looking and chivalrous; then the infatuated dog Lapák growing old with his master; the proud cock, with his short-lived glory, and all the gossips of the forest: the owl and the jay with their 'If you only knew... that our Bystrouška, like a common...'— 'With whom?'; the woodpecker receiving the erring couple with a superior 'I haven't got all day'; and the little frog and his great-grandchild who surprises the game-keeper with his disarming 'That wasn't me, that was my grand-dad, but he told me all about you.' It would be necessary to quote the whole of the ADVENTURES OF THE VIXEN SHARP EARS in order to savour its charm and yet the main thing would still be missing—the unique humour and fascina-tion of Janáček's score.

The music, like the libretto, gives rise to an endless series of conjectures

---

*) This stumbling-block may be avoided without omitting the inn-keeper's hint, by letting the inn-keeper sing instead of 'Your new lodgers are coming,' 'It is time for you to leave,' which can be taken to mean either his going home or his leaving for another parsonage. The 'invasion' and the cries of the chorus must then, of course, be cut.

regarding the various affinities and links it contains. It is perhaps worth pointing out the principal ones without over-estimating the importance of their analysis to an understanding of the work. ADVENTURES OF THE VIXEN SHARP EARS can be fully enjoyed without any technical understanding of its intricate structure. Janáček himself, in connection with AMARUS, wrote about analyzing music: 'To understand the words and feel in the sounds the magic of spring and love is enough for the work to have fulfilled its purpose. Any analysis of the material is a burden at the moment of perception.'

The first of the most important motifs to make its appearance in the opera is the little vixen's diffident theme:

It appears immediately afterwards in a combined variant:

and the motifs and melodies which follow may rightly be considered as being derived from it:

Little Bystrouška:

Malá Bystrouška:

Ma-mi, ma-mi!

Mummy, mummy!

Cha, cha, cha, cha!

Gamekeeper: Ha, ha, ha, ha !

---

*) Note the shift of the semiquaver motif over the barline which occurs at the point in the story when the gamekeeper captures Bystrouška. (It is used in this form again later in association with Harašta the poacher.) Note also how the motif vaults up at the end of the bar — Bystrouška vainly trying to free herself.

including even the lamentations of the gamekeeper's wife, accompanied in the orchestra by a riotous brio after the slaughter of the chickens near the end of Act I:

Bystrouška: Ha, ha, ha, ha!
Gamekeeper's wife: Oh, you beast!

One can go on finding analogies, for instance, between Bystrouška's motifs and those expressing the schoolmaster's phantasmic vision of his beloved Terynka (Ex. 288, Act II, 5 bars after reh. No. 31; and Ex. 289, reh. No. 35):

and the motif of the parson's meditation on the perfidious love of his student years (Act II, reh. No. 38):

There is, however, a convincing link between the motif in Ex. 284 and these motifs which accompany Bystrouška's telling of her human upbringing which she received at the gamekeeper's cottage ('I stole once...'):

this weeping phrase of the 'fallen' Bystrouška:

and its orchestral variant:

and this melody scored for the 'old' voices of the chorus (altos and basses) during the general merrymaking of the youngsters at Bystrouška's wedding:

295

Perhaps of still more importance is the elegiac melody of Scene 2:

296

referring at first to the imprisoned Bystrouška. Its first motif evolves into these prickly variants:

297

298

299

while its second motif which is more specifically Sharp Ears' own, represents, in its different guises, her misfortune:

300

Ou,   ou?

her growing up during the nocturnal interlude in Scene 2:

301

her determination after her escape (beginning of Act II):

302

her fawning:

303

In the middle scene of Act III it gives rise to the following motto of general wistfulness (after all, are not Sharp Ears and Terynka, individually or together, its main cause?) and its variants:

278

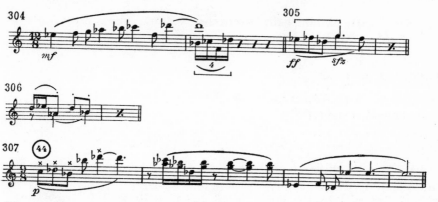

The first component of the twofold motif from the beginning of Scene 4 of Act II:

gives rise, on the one hand, to the tripping motif of the foxes:

and to the more emotive variant:

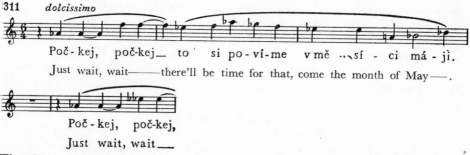

while, on the other hand, its second component provides the musical material for the wedding ballet.

A relatively less important part, since it is restricted to Act III, is played by Bystrouška's 'wife and mother' theme which is also an example of Janáček's 'musical rhyming' by means of repetitions of the text:

The theme reappears in the sad coda of Scene I of Act III after Bystrouška's sudden death, and again in the final apotheosis of perpetual rebirth.

The first appearance of Bystrouška's own cubs is marked by this gambolling tune derived nearly symbolically from the wedding music (compare the second half of Ex. 308):

312

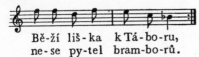

Bě-ží liš-ka k Tá-bo-ru,
ne-se py-tel bram-bo-rů.

There's a vixen with a sack
Of potatoes on her back.

Other light-hearted ditties include the gamekeeper's 'What has been, has been' in Act II, Scene 2, and the two songs sung by Harašta, 'When I wandered by' and 'When I by the green wood came,' both in Act III, Scene 1.

Nature inspired Janáček to a musical fecundity such as may otherwise be found only in his JENŮFA and KATYA KABANOVA. Moreover, of all his operas, ADVENTURES OF THE VIXEN SHARP EARS must surely emerge as the most lovable since it is the personification of his optimism—a carefree excursion of his fantasy—a Czech *Midsummer Night's Dream*.

Max Brod translated ADVENTURES OF THE VIXEN SHARP EARS into German. As he pointed out to Janáček in a letter dated 22 June 1925, it was not meant to be a straight translation but an interpretation or, more modestly, an adaptation. Brod had earlier, on 13 June, tried to prove the necessity for this: 'The more I work on it, the more I see that the libretto is rather poor and unclear and badly needs big changes in order to be suitable for the German stage. The expectations of the public are great and we must not disappoint them. I am taking great pains to liven up the action and work it out in depth. And I beg you to let me have as much freedom as I want in this respect...'*)

He then proceeds to give an outline of his ideas. 'I am aiming at making the basic, symbolic idea more clear than it is in the Czech version. It is clearer in the novel,**) but your cuts have tended to make everything blurred. I take it that Bystrouška is supposed to mean, for everyone taking part, a kind of symbol of youth, wildness and nature. The schoolmaster, the gamekeeper and the parson have all in their lives missed their happiness. In order to simplify matters and make everything clear to the audience, I want all three of them to have been in love with the gypsy child, Terynka, although none of them have had sufficient strength to keep her for themselves. For this reason even the gamekeeper sings about Terynka and not about his sentimental memories of his wife which are, in any case, rather out of place since his wife is represented in the opera as a querulous shrew. Both the gamekeeper's reminiscences—'It's like the morning after the wedding night' (Act I, three bars after reh. No. 7) and 'How many years is it since we walked together' (Act III, five bars before reh. No. 49) — refer in my arrangement not to the gamekeeper's good wife but, after the changes, to his adventure with Terynka. He sees in the eyes of Bystrouška the memory of the wild eyes of the gypsy. In a similar way I want to derive the parson's troubles from his adventures

---

*) *Janáček — Brod*, p. 180.
**) There, on the contrary, it is not contained at all.

280

with Terynka. By doing this I hope to get some kind of unity into the book and make it comprehensible and dramatically focused.'*) Max Brod hastens, of course, to assure Janáček that 'musically, nothing will be changed.'

Janáček's reply of 16 June 1925 was on the whole positive. Thus encouraged, Brod on 22 June defined his alterations more precisely: 'Terynka... is a gypsy child—the gamekeeper took her into his cottage—then, finding her behaviour too wild, passed her on to the parson for tuition. This has given rise to gossip and the parson finds himself forced to leave the parsonage and is being trans-ferred elsewhere. In this way his case becomes an exact parallel with the pushing out of the badger ('Bystrouška expropriates'). The scene with the badger does not finish any more with the impractical dirtying of the lair but with the fox telling the animal folk that the badger (parson) made improper suggestions to her during her confirmation classes. The end is as follows: 'How can I do otherwise than give in to the seducer.' In the general hubbub of the animal folk the vixen then ostentatiously kisses the angry badger who departs with the words: 'I am morally shocked and am giving way in the face of impudent slander...' In the monologue which follows, I am letting the game-keeper (who, in the original, gives a drunken sermon to the already absent schoolmaster) ponder over the fate of the parson in order to round off the scene properly.'**)

The suggestions of Max Brod sound very tempting and are not devoid of ingenuity. However, in my opinion they show a complete lack of understanding of the work, especially for the following two reasons: Firstly, Brod completely changes not only the sense but also the basic character of most of the scenes, and secondly, his suggestions break the only possible relationship of the action to the music.

Certainly it is far from easy to find one's way among the female characters mentioned in the opera, but does not this multiplicity correspond to the erotic effervescence of the work where names are only of secondary importance? Is it not touching that while the gamekeeper is pulling the schoolmaster's leg about his old love for Veronika, he is—and after all, the gamekeeper suspects this—thinking about his new one for Terynka which then turns out to be just as ephemeral? True, the parallel between Bystrouška and Terynka is certainly not worked out to the letter, but is this altogether necessary? Is not the imaginary Terynka just another symbol like Goethe's *das ewig weibliche* rather than a real figure, and is not this made sufficiently clear by the music, since all the female characters become invested with the theme of the vixen, and especially, before any of the others, her closest double, Terynka? On the other hand, tortuous attempts made to achieve unity and logic come into con-tradiction with the music and, at times, even with the logic itself as well as with the freshness and spontaneity of the work. From the musical point of view Terynka's theme (and that of Bystrouška) has nothing gypsy about it. The most apparent contradiction between the music and Brod's version occurs in the moving epilogue of the gamekeeper in the last scene, at the moment when he stumbles on a nice large mushroom. In the original he meditates: 'How many years is it since we walked together, two young people...

---

*) Ibid, 180.
**) Ibid, p. 185.

we also went gathering mushrooms, but we trod on them because... because we could not see for love.' Instead of these touchingly simple words revealing reconciliation with life (and also, which is even more touching, with the 'querulous shrew') accompanied by the purest of music, Brod at this point gives the gamekeeper the following lines: 'The same rainy air as when I found that beautiful girl. How she scratched at first, but then she was sweet. We went deeper into the bushes.' The meaning could hardly be more different. How could 'the music remain unchanged' if its entire relationship to the words was turned upside down?

The rewriting of the parson's monologue in the forest is due to the same lack of understanding. In the original the parson declaims mechanically: 'Remember to be a righteous man,' racking his brains and trying to remember where the quotation comes from. When he reviews his life he feels bound to admit that he has failed as much in love as in his vocation. Then the words come back to him again, this time with the full force of their accusation 'Memnestho aner agathos einai!' Suddenly the good man taps his forehead with delight—he has remembered. 'It is from Xenophon's *Anabasis*,' and his mood of critical self-examination is suppressed in the trifling satisfaction of having solved an irrelevant problem. Janáček goes even further in his thorough revelation of character by disturbing the peace with a volley from the game-keeper's shotgun aimed at the vixen. The parson and the schoolmaster tremble for their lives, while the vixen, and with her the vision of all Terynkas once more—this time, probably for good—escapes beyond their reach.

In Brod's version this tragi-comic confession is deprived of its inner meaning, for the parson is seen not only as a specimen of chastity, but as its victim. In addition, Brod has made Bystrouška accuse the 'parson-badger' of 'improper suggestions' during her confirmation classes, thus turning her into a common liar. In my opinion Max Brod goes altogether too far in his efforts to keep the story within the limits of purely human concepts. Thus in the moonlit scene outside the den (Act II, Scene 4, reh. No. 51) he makes Bystrouška describe how the gamekeeper used to be 'really kind' to her, though 'with clumsy fondling', and that 'his wife was jealous'. Thus on account of these 'relation-ships' artificially constructed in his effort to 'focus' the story, Max Brod manages to make it obscure and muddled.

In the light of these glaring inconsistencies it is of comparatively small importance when, in Brod's version (Act I, reh. No. 7), the starling instead of having an affair with the cuckoo is courting a crow while the orchestra, blissfully unheeding, continues to play the cuckoo motif.

Brod's rigid 'armour of logic' fits this fantasy even less well in its details, depriving it of its refreshing naivety, as for instance during the fox's courting, and of its charming simplicity, especially at the end of the penultimate scene (Act III, reh. Nos. 45—46) where Max Brod makes the gamekeeper declare gravely: 'Now we only wait for death,' instead of his original good-natured, 'and now one is glad just to sit down and rest a bit', and again where the school-master, instead of saying 'Maybe he hasn't noticed' (namely, the tear in his eye), is made to say: 'That hurts his feelings.' Even the fox, Bystrouška's mate, is distorted. Instead of simply saying: 'I am no lying fox,' he prances about exclaiming: 'I am unlike most other foxes. When I love, it is not for the body... I am not like the average.' It is also rather out of place for the little Moravian fox cubs to start singing (in the ditty as in Ex. 312) about Szegedin in one verse and Africa in the other. One also wonders why Brod indicates that in the first scene Little Bystrouška should be acted by a child while 'her part is sung off-stage' by an adult singer. This might be adopted as a last resort if there is no small girl with a musical voice available.

And what happens to the delightful character of the poacher Harašta? Janáček makes him do little more than poke fun in a rather sly way at the somewhat slow but good-natured gamekeeper, denying the charge of poaching, while Brod makes him querulously bark back with 'irate irony' (Act III, reh. No. 11). In Janáček's version he is almost childishly looking forward to Terynka becoming his wife, while in Brod's version he awaits the opportunity of bullying her into submission. Thus an analogy, of a kind, with the sad end of Bystrouška is achieved at the price of completely distorting the character of Harašta and of upsetting the happy atmosphere of the work, but an analogy which is not more than a superficial parallel since Bystrouška does not perish as a passive victim but as a result of her overflowing elemental vitality.

My objections to Max Brod's translation of ADVENTURES OF THE VIXEN SHARP EARS are not meant to detract in any way from the tremendous debt Janáček owed to Brod for all he did by means of his enthusiastic and inspired articles, as well as his translations, to win recognition for the composer. And in the case of ADVENTURES OF THE VIXEN SHARP EARS Brod was certainly convinced that he was doing a great service to the work. Janáček, who had absolute faith in Brod and was not a little shaken by the doubtful reception of the opera after its first performances, did not object firmly enough to Brod's adaptations. (Fortunately, Janáček insisted on keeping the highly original ending with the little frog, which Brod had also declared to be 'impossible'.) At one time the composer had even been willing to alter his original in accordance with Brod's version. It is characteristic, however, that this drastic measure was never carried out and that Janáček's last letter to Brod on the subject, in which he probably took a firm stand, has been lost.

As it was, the adaptations had no more effect than the rescoring of the work which was done in Prague in 1936. Before 1953 it was produced (in Brod's version) at only one German theatre (Mainz, 1927) where it was only performed three times. But the opera's eventual success in the composer's own country lies in the delightful authenticity of the various characters both in word and in sound which, naturally, can only come into its own if the balance between these two elements is strictly maintained. And it is possible to recreate this balance only by making the most painstaking revision in accordance with the original text. This is all the more important since the German version might very easily become the only one available for use when making translations into other languages.*)

---

*) ADVENTURES OF THE VIXEN SHARP EARS was put on, however, in May 1956 by Walter Felsenstein in a truly remarkable production at the Berlin Komische Oper. Brod's adaptations were largely eradicated although, unfortunately, the gamekeeper remained in love with Terynka, thus being placed in an altogether theatrical relationship to the 'maidenly' Bystrouška as well as to Harašta; and the part of the male fox was sung by a tenor instead of a soprano, thus depriving Janáček's Octavian of much of his charm.

(35) 'The Wandering Madman'

As was Janáček's wont, ADVENTURES OF THE VIXEN SHARP EARS too had its counterpart. While in the VIXEN the almost 70-year-old composer presented the public with an optimistic or, at least, reconciled view of life and death, in the male-voice chorus THE WANDERING MADMAN he wrote a work of an utterly different nature. Once again it was linked with a personal experience.

In June 1921 Rabindranath Tagore came to Prague and recited some of his poetry in public. Janáček was present and fell under the spell of the great thinker and poet, a kind of Bengali Maeterlinck. His work appealed just as much to the down-to-earth Janáček as it had done to his compatriot, the gentle lyrical composer J. B. Foerster, who set to music Tagore's *Love Songs* as a cycle for voice and orchestra (op. 96, Universal Edition, 1914).

Tagore's silver-grey hair and beard gave him the appearance of a true philosopher and prophet. Janáček's article 'Rabindrantah Tagore', illustrated with some incredibly high *nápěvky* (speech melodies) and published in the paper *Lidové noviny* on 22 June 1921, conveys the depth of impression made by the great poet. When Tagore walked onto the stage, Janáček felt 'as though a white, holy flame had sprung up over the heads of the thousands sitting in the audience'. His looks—'An indescribable sadness.' His speech: 'He makes each of his syllables soar... I wanted to join in with a rejoicing chord.' His personality: 'I have seen and heard the prophet of his people...'

A year later, Janáček, using Tagore's words, composed THE WANDERING MADMAN, one of the most impressive choral works he had ever written.

It is a ballad about a man who spends his whole life searching for a stone which will turn ordinary objects into gold. One day a country boy asks him how he comes to have a gold chain round his neck. The man remembers that the chain was once of iron and concludes that he has therefore unwittingly come into contact with the stone. He must have held the magic stone in his hand only to throw it away. He turns to look once more for the lost treasure...

This story presented Janáček with a ready-made musical pattern, his favourite *ABA*, the words of the country boy (*B*) dividing the two wanderings of the madman (*A*). The first section rushes along in a feverish presto, slowing down several times. While some of the voices declaim the story on a single note symbolizing the fixed idea of the madman, the remaining voices alternately comment with a whispered 'Crazy man' and join in the narrative. The rhythms overlap in such a way that we almost see the madman stumbling over the stones in his path, possibly over the magic stone itself.

Following a vertiginous chord gradation framed in parallel octaves and built up from the motif of 'Just like the ocean swell' comes a sudden lull. The silence is broken by the entry of a solo soprano representing the inquisitive boy. The basses join in—first hesitantly and almost sympathetically—and then the whole choir joins in with increasing eagerness: 'Where, oh where did he come upon this wealth?' In Tagore's poem the madman first wildly beat his brow, and only then asked 'where...' and only in indirect speech. Janáček, on the other hand, has the choir come in at once with the question about the origin of the gold in direct speech. He thus creates the impression that the question is being asked not just by the madman alone, but by thousands of crazed men with him.

The recapitulation is not a simple repetition of the first section. The rests on the accented beats which were formerly the expressions of a feverish rush, now exude tiredness. The music, instead of gradation, wanes. Even the boy's lines have lost their cheekiness. The work which began in E flat comes to rest on a low B major chord as if it too could not find its way back, motionless like the uprooted tree to which the madman is compared.

The work makes special demands on the performers—the compass is three octaves from a high B in the tenors to the low B of the basses in the final chords. This is probably why, after its completion on 21 November 1922, almost two years passed before the Moravian Teachers' Choir conducted by Ferdinand Vach introduced it to the public, and then only tentatively, in the provincial town of Rosice u Brna on 21 September 1924.

(36) 'The Danube'

As soon as Janáček completed the score of ADVENTURES OF THE VIXEN SHARP EARS on 17 March 1923, he began to consider new projects. He made a journey to Bratislava, the Slovak capital on the Danube, to hear the first performance there of KATYA KABANOVA on 23 March conducted by Milan Zuna (a performance which Janáček praised very highly, especially for the idiomatic tempi) and decided to remain there for several days. He was so deeply impressed by the river that he determined to 'set it to music' in a symphony. In October 1924 he wrote:

'The light green ripples of the Danube! So many of them, one next to another, as if holding each other arm in arm.
'They wonder how they got to this place, a Czech [*sic*] shore!
'Look downstream and they seem still.
'They like it here.
'Here I am going to set my symphony.
'A long time ago, before the year 1923, the blurred image of the Bratislava riverside in my mind gave rise to:

313

'I know that the bassoon jumped in, rippling the Danube waters:

314

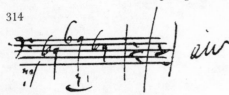

286

and then the whole thing simply vanished from my mind.

'But I know that at some moment the picture will return and this time it
will not be alone. Where did the tremolo of the four timpani come from?

315

'I believe once a work has taken root in my mind, it grows in me spontaneously.

'KATYA KABANOVA, THE WANDERING MADMAN, the suite YOUTH: none of
this will stifle the future DANUBE.

'Nor will it be stifled by the MAKROPOULOS CASE. It (the Danube) is billow-
ing and feeding on all that, unnoticed.

'Yesterday, 1 October 1924, it occurred to me that Insarov's Lola will
certainly be drowned in it.

316

'And one day, perhaps in 1925, when my mind is at ease, the work will
quickly ripen as if in the sun.'

Did it actually happen? After his death a complete sketch of the full score
of four movements of the symphony THE DANUBE was found in a cardboard
folder. But since there were other sketches also in the folder, there is a possibility
that Janáček might have wanted to add a fifth movement. Osvald Chlubna,
one of Janáček's pupils, maintains,*) however, that Janáček told him he had

---

*) In the Brno *Divadelní list*, Vol. VII. (1931—1932), p. 306.

completed a symphonic cycle in four movements called THE DANUBE. Even so, it is difficult to regard the extant four movements as the definitive version of the work, and Chlubna himself when he was preparing it for performance felt the necessity not only of adding to and altering some of the scoring, but also of structural changes. Unfortunately, even Chlubna's version, which was performed on 2 May 1948 by the Brno Radio orchestra conducted by Břetislav Bakala, did not satisfactorily solve all the riddles of the work. It would appear that Janáček, who had probably never struggled with any non-operatic work for so long, did not, in fact, arrive at a satisfactory solution of how to deal with the subject. According to an article by Adolf Veselý in the *Lidové noviny* of 2 June 1925 Janáček asked the Czechoslovak ambassador in Vienna Hugo Vavrečka to plan a trip down the Danube for him... 'I want to see the whole length of the Danube, and then I shall begin my symphony.' This seems to suggest that to Janáček the Danube was, first and foremost, an analogy to Smetana's *Vltava*.*) He managed to convince himself that the Danube was a Slav river, which was not as ludicrous as it might seem, since four Slav states were at that time situated on its banks—states in whose folk art the Danube had from time immemorial played an important part. Adolf Veselý, however, maintains that the main motto of the cycle was to be 'woman with all her passions and instincts'. This would automatically put the work among Janáček's erotically inspired compositions. One movement was to characterize the Vienna which Janáček imagined as 'a woman who had laid down the whole of her femininity on the banks of the river'. He had already hinted at a further heroine of THE DANUBE in his remark 'Insarov's Lola will be drowned in it', by which he meant the heroine of Alexander Insarov's poem *Lola* (a newspaper cutting from the *Lidové noviny* containing this poem was, in fact, found in the folder with the score)—the story of a prostitute, described in three paragraphs. In the first, Lola can command a palace and a life of pleasure. In the second she looks in vain for her desired palace, and in the third she whimpers in anguish: 'Soon the day will dawn, and no one wants me. I am cold, I am hungry, and yet I used to be a magic scarlet flame. God, if only I could warm my hands in front of a fire.'

The connection with the Danube? Janáček remained unabashed; guessing what would make a fourth paragraph of the poem, he simply jotted down: 'She throws herself into the Danube.'

As if—after MARYČKA MAGDÓNOVA and KATYA KABANOVA—there had not been enough river victims already, he took as the basis of the second movement still another similar poem, *The Drowned Girl* by Pavla Křičková (sister of the poet Petr Křička and the composer Jaroslav Křička), which had also been published in the *Lidové noviny*. In it a young girl preparing to

---

*) It is interesting to note that Richard Strauss—as Ernst Krause mentions in his biography—also began writing, for the occasion of the centenary celebrations of the Vienna Philharmonic Orchestra, a symphonic poem *The Danube* for orchestra, choir and organ. He began the composition about 1942 and it was to describe—inspired even more obviously by Smetana's *Vltava*—the river and the life along its banks. In it—a typically Straussian touch—there was to be a quotation from his *Symphonia domestica* to characterize Ingolstadt, the birthplace of his wife Pauline.

bathe suddenly sees that her nakedness is being watched by a strange boy. 'Like a wounded doe' she throws herself into the river (not necessarily the Danube, of course) and drowns.

We can only assume that the fourth movement was to be Lola's, since it contains this exuberant dance tune at the beginning:

317

and ends on a note of tragedy. There is every reason to suppose that *The Drowned Girl* was the basis for the second movement which was probably completed before the others, on 18 June 1923. Janáček wrote fragments of the poem into the score, and the viola motif:

318

is an almost exact and rudimentary setting of the words: '*Ach, je to sotva hodinu, co viděl tady dívčinu*, (Ah, it is barely an hour since he saw the girl here) which Janáček jotted down at that place. This might mislead observers into supposing that a vocal setting was intended. But Janáček was not the only composer to use vocal lines as motivic material for his symphonic works; this was also done by Dvořák.

One should not be misled by the fact that the plaintive oboe theme marked *žalostně* (woefully) in Ex. 316 (which is, according to Janáček, 'Lola drowning' and also a mere variant of the cello motif from Ex. 313) appears, in the quoted form, only in the second movement in association with Pavla Křičková's *Drowned Girl*. It reappears in the fourth movement in a clarinet variant marked 'desperately'. This duplicity of themes, possibly intentional, may be why Chlubna left the passage in the second movement out altogether. (There is less reason for some of Chlubna's other decisions suppressing Janáček's programmatic intentions as apparent from his jottings.)

The first movement—impressionistic in the beginning, later becoming more balladic in character—is built mainly on the motif:

319

The short third movement, a fragment of a kind of scherzo lacking a contrasting trio, was probably meant to represent Vienna, with its cascading

289

figurations, trills, and this colourful, buoyant theme in canonic imitation:*)

There remains the question of when this sketch was written. According to Osvald Chlubna it was finished by May 1925 at the latest. Yet this is denied by a curious answer which Janáček wrote on a postcard to Otakar Ostrčil, dated 19 August 1926.**) In answer to Ostrčil's request to conduct the first performance of THE DANUBE Janáček writes: 'This "Danube of ours" is not attractive(!) enough to make me want to finish my own Danube in a hurry!'

In my opinion this laconic answer is sufficient to prove that this special celebration of the 'Slav' Danube should be regarded, if not as unfinished, at least as not definitive, and should be judged as such.

Thus—since even Richard Strauss did not finish his *Danube*—the only hymn in praise of this mighty river still remains the famous waltz by Johann Strauss.

---

*) Owing to the amorous character which this movement should have had, Janáček included in the scoring a part for his beloved viola d'amore to which, however, he himself added the note 'better cello' and which Chlubna rescored for ordinary viola.
**) *Janáček—Ostrčil*, p. 95—96.

(37) The First Quartet

While THE DANUBE was taking shape in Janáček's mind, new operatic subjects intruded. In April 1923, shortly after Janáček finished ADVENTURES OF THE VIXEN SHARP EARS, Max Brod suggested to him the play by František Xaver Šalda *The Child* performed shortly before, on 16 March, at the National Theatre in Prague. Brod thought it 'an excellent operatic text'. At first Janáček liked the idea. 'There is plenty of new atmosphere. A certain similarity to JENŮFA does not matter. Here it is the story of a child that will live. In JENŮFA the child is murdered,' he wrote to Max Brod on 18 April 1923 and commissioned him to make the play into a libretto.*)

In July Janáček re-read *The Child* during a visit to the Štrbské Pleso lake in the Tatra mountains and at the same time studied Karel Čapek's new fantastic comedy *The Makropoulos Case* which he had seen eight months before at the Vinohrady Theatre in Prague. Čapek's play made such a powerful impression on him that he kept getting musical ideas while he was still reading it. The choice was rendered the easier for him by the fact that Šalda refused to allow his play to be used as a libretto, stating that 'it contained enough of its own inherent music'.

Čapek on the other hand had given his consent as early as February, but Janáček did not begin straight away on the new opera but quite unexpectedly wrote instead one of his most sincere and telling works, his FIRST STRING QUARTET inspired by Tolstoy's story *The Kreutzer Sonata* which in turn was written under the impact of Beethoven's famous Violin Sonata No. 9 in A, Op. 47. Janáček wrote the quartet between 30 October and 7 November 1923 after attending, at the beginning of August in Salzburg, the second festival organized by the International Society for Contemporary Music, where his VIOLIN SONATA was performed.

The FIRST QUARTET is, in fact, not Janáček's first. At the end of May and the beginning of June 1880 during his short period of study in Vienna he wrote a composition of this kind which was subsequently lost and of which only the first three movements are known to have been completed. Nor is this the only work by Janáček to be based on Tolstoy's *The Kreutzer Sonata*. As already mentioned, in the autumn of 1908 Janáček had planned to write a PIANO TRIO based on this story, which he had rewritten six months later for a performance at the Friends of Art Club in Brno on 2 April 1909 as a part

---

*) Despite this difference, Šalda's *Child* is really nothing more than a town version of JENŮFA: there are two brothers, Říša, spoiled and superficial, and Aleš, neglected but sincere. There is also the girl, the maid Františka, who is loved by Aleš but prefers his brother by whom she becomes pregnant. Aleš marries her, accepting his brother's child. But the language as well as the actions of the characters are not nearly as convincing and realistic as those in JENŮFA. ('It is not alive, it is contrived,' noted Janáček in his copy of the play.)

of the Tolstoy celebrations of that year. But since the trio is also lost it is impossible to judge how much of the material from it went into the quartet. Max Brod in his book records Janáček's words that 'several of the ideas were employed'. Pavel Dědeček who played the violin part at the Friends of Art Club performance*) has told Jarmil Burghauser that little of the material is used in the quartet. Already the first movement of the trio was quite different. It began with some agitated sextuplet figuration in the strings while the main melodic line was in the piano. Janáček was apparently heard to say that this was to evoke the idea of a train in motion to correspond exactly to the opening part of Tolstoy's story.

THE FIRST QUARTET is the last link in a spiritual chain which began in 1907 with the intended opera ANNA KARENINA and included the above-mentioned TRIO and, in particular, KATYA KABANOVA of which the FIRST QUARTET is a chamber music counterpart. The heroine of all these works is an unhappily married woman who, in her longing for happiness, throws herself into the arms of an unworthy lover and dies tragically.

Though it would be futile to seek, bar by bar, Tolstoy's story in Janáček's absorbing music, it would be equally wrong to try to analyze the FIRST QUARTET as pure absolute music, although there is the outline of a compressed sonata form in the first movement, with the second theme in the dominant introduced by no more than a dominant seventh, pizzicato. There is a residual development or, more precisely, a return leading to a memento rather than a recapitulation of the exposition. It is probably not far from the truth to assume that the opening idea of the first movement:

321
Adagio (♩)

which is strikingly similar to the 'sigh of the Volga' motif (see Ex. 277) in KATYA KABANOVA is the theme of life and death, of the heroine's tragic desire. The seducer is portrayed by its foppish viola variant which, at the opening of the second, scherzo movement,**) seems to express the short-lived satisfaction of the heroine's desire:

322

*) The cello was played by Rudolf Pavlata, the piano by Růžena Fialová.
**) Janáček may well have got his favourite idea of replacing the conventional scherzo with a Czech polka from Smetana's string quartet *From My Life*, itself prefaced, so to speak, with a motif of life-long yearning in the same key (E minor) and over a legato tremolo just as Janáček's quartet. Smetana's description of the first movement of *From My Life* in a letter dated 12 April 1879 may be applied almost word for word to the recurring motivic material in Janáček's work: '...an indescribable longing for something which I could not define clearly, but which was also a warning of my future misfortune'. (We may add that the first Czech composer to use a polka in place of a scherzo was Zdeněk Fibich, in his First Quartet from the year 1874, two years before Smetana.)

The rustling ponticello of the next section of the second movement, formed from bars two and three of Ex. 322, seems to describe the chilling pang of temptation:

It is followed first by this melody choking with overflowing emotion:

and then by a pleasantly languorous derivative in 3/2—perhaps the heroine's first confession.

The third movement opens with an affectionate violin and cello duet in canon marked 'lightly and timidly':

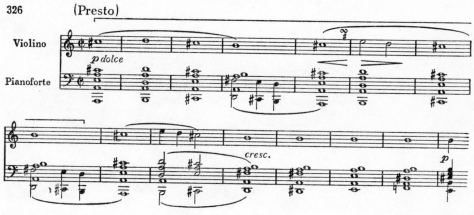

which is evidently a reminiscence of the beautiful second theme from the first movement of Beethoven's *Kreutzer Sonata*. This is particularly apparent when comparing the second appearances of both these themes:
Beethoven:

Janáček:

The frenzied diminution which cuts short the canon every time, and the agitated motif of the middle section:

328 Vivace

with its chromatic counter-melody as if pleading for compassion, portends the approaching catastrophe with which the work culminates in the last movement after an anguished introduction recalling the opening motif from Ex. 321. The climax reintroduces the motif, just as the 'sigh of the Volga' reappears at the end of KATYA KABANOVA, both as a shattering warning and as an intoxicatingly alluring reminiscence.

The FIRST QUARTET was first performed in an unforgettable way on 17 October 1924 by the Bohemian Quartet at whose instigation, in fact, the work had been written. According to the Bohemian Quartet's second violinist, the composer Josef Suk, Janáček meant the work to be a kind of moral protest against men's despotic attitude to women. Thus while Tolstoy in *The Kreutzer Sonata* ascribes to music 'the most immoral effects' (music being, according to Tolstoy, one of the main forces for encouraging adultery in our society), Janáček in his quartet uses music to the exactly opposite effect: as the voice of the conscience of humanity.

On 11 November, only four days after completing his quartet, Janáček began working on his opera in which the heroine is a strong-minded, domineering woman... 'Life, I want life!'

(38) Janáček at Seventy

Throughout the whole of the following year, 1924, the new opera held him under its spell. 'Almost two hundred pages are complete' (once more he was composing straight into the score), he announced to Brod at the end of 1923. 'This time everything flies about, completely boundless. Many motifs. How I shall get them into order I shan't be able to see until Act I is finished.' For his Christmas holidays he went once more to the Tatra mountains. 'The white calm of the covering of snow, as far as the eye can see, makes one silent and thoughtful.' In addition, the year of his seventieth birthday was the year in which a number of important events in his life took place; in particular the première of JENŮFA in Berlin.

This came about in the following way. On 22 February 1922 the Director of the Berlin State Opera, Max von Schillings, conducted the Czech Philharmonic Orchestra in a concert in Prague. The Prague musical circles made every effort to arouse von Schilings' interest in Czech opera—each camp according to its own ideas—and for Janáček, as he himself said in a letter to Kamila, 'the days were hot.' In the end (largely due to the enthusiasm of Max Brod) von Schillings decided to accept JENŮFA whose composer, according to Brod, impressed him very much.*) The Berlin première did not take place until 17 March 1924, since certain political prejudices had to be overcome. These were smoothed out thanks largely to the efforts of the Czechoslovak ambassador in Berlin, Vlastimil Tusar. (Musically, the way had been prepared by an unusually successful performance of THE DIARY OF THE YOUNG MAN WHO DISAPPEARED on 21 September 1922 at the Bechstein Hall.) Janáček arrived for the première, which took place on a Sunday, only a day before. He was too late to attend the dress rehearsal. Yet he intended to make, as he wrote in his article 'Berlin' in the *Lidové noviny* of 15 May 1924, two more journeys: 'one to the great flautist (Frederick II) who once made the whole world dance to his tune, and the other to the old settlement (Rixdorf) of our people who long ago came here in search of religious freedom'. But there he found Czech names only in the cemetery. 'In contrast to these two places where deathly silence reigns, my victory at the State Opera resounded triumphantly thanks to Mrs Zinaida Jurjewskaya (Jenůfa), Mrs Margarete Arndt-Ober (Kostelnička), Mr Soot and Mr Jöken (Laca and Števa), the charming shepherd of Miss Charlotte Värner, Mr Karl Holý's lively production and the brilliant colours of Mr Emil Pirchan's sets. On the stage, nothing but joy and enthusiasm.**) I have heard here an exemplary production of my JENŮFA.'

---

*) Von Schillings evidently heard JENŮFA at the National Theatre on 21 February 1922. His wife Barbara Kemp was originally to have sung the part of Jenůfa.
**) JENŮFA was such a success in Berlin that even the tobacconists were selling 'Jenůfa cigars'.

No wonder: the conductor was Erich Kleiber.*)

Unfortunately, the ambassador Tusar, the diplomatic pioneer of that great day, outlived it by only five days.

The day of the Berlin première became memorable for Janáček and his opera in yet another way. In a letter dated 17 March the producer of JENŮFA in Vienna, W. Wymetal, informed him from New York that the opera had been accepted for the Metropolitan. This was all the more remarkable since the director of the Metropolitan Opera House, Gatti-Casazza, was notoriously suspicious of novelties. The first performance took place on 6 December of that year and Janáček was given a full account, not only by Maria Jeritza who was once more singing Jenůfa, but also by his former pupil František Rybka**) who was choir-master and organist of Pittsburgh Cathedral. In a letter dated 28 February 1925 Rybka expresses himself in superlatives concerning the production (the costumes had been bought in Moravia), the chorus, the soloists and, in particular, Jeritza. But the Kostelnička of Margarete Matzenauer was, according to Rybka, the greatest triumph. He was not so enthusiastic about the orchestral playing nor the tempi—although his objections were the opposite of Janáček's in Berlin. ('The beginning was too fast, so was the recruits' chorus. Our intense Slav rhythm was lost.') According to Jeritza it was, nevertheless, 'a wonderful performance' and the conductor Arthur Bodanzky (who was acquainted with Czech music since he had been engaged by the German theatre in Prague from 1907 to 9) was so impressed by Janáček's music that, as will be seen later, he gave the first American performance of THE GLAGOLITIC MASS.

In June of that year the distinguished American music critic, Olin Downes, paid a visit to Janáček, and on his return published on 13 July 1924 in the

---

*) According to Dr Julius Kapp, the dramaturge of the Berlin State Opera House at the time, Janáček was so entranced by the performance (enhanced by the gift of peasant costumes from the Czechoslovak government) that during the extra dress rehearsal, which was specially arranged for Janáček's benefit, hot tears flowed down his cheeks and he kept whispering, 'I have lived to see this!' On 22 March he wrote to Kleiber: 'I am still with you in my thoughts. You gave my work so many supreme moments and filled it with brilliant sun. They used to turn the recruits' song and Jenůfa's song into an angular military march. You gave it the vitality and heat of young hearts. "Every couple of lovers has some troubles to bear" became in Prague and also in Vienna almost a funeral song. You made it smile. And that's how it should be. They used to put so many horrid "breathing pauses" into Act II. You gave such classic plasticity to your Act II. At the end of the work, in the hymn of love, one feels its burning flames in your stringendo of the motif:

329

You brought the end of each act to such an elemental climax. It is your JENŮFA that can be seen from afar—not the Prague, nor the Vienna one. If I could ask you something it would be just this: the introduction to Act I just a shade faster to make it more suggestive of unrest. And the xylophone should be on the stage near the mill-wheel. This will take the edge off its icy tone. That is all. I send you my most grateful thanks. Please give my regards to the best Kostelnička there has ever been and all the other soloists and members of the chorus.'
**) The same whom Janáček had once caught malingering and playing cards.

New York Times a long and enthusiastic article not only about his meeting with Janáček but also about Czech contemporary music in general, about Janáček's habit of jotting down speech melodies (Downes of course became a subject of this portraiture himself), about the story of THE DIARY OF THE YOUNG MAN WHO DISAPPEARED and the deep impression made on him by Janáček's choral compositions. The article was accompanied by a picture— a good likeness of Janáček drawn by Wenck. Downes also wrote of Janáček's attitude to other composers—a negative one to a greater or lesser degree, except for Chopin and Dvořák. Among other things, Janáček had told Downes that he had only heard Mussorgsky's *Boris Godunov* a year earlier and that he had been very much impressed by Charpentier's *Louise* but had liked it less on knowing it more.*)

In Janáček's own country the major part of 1924 (in particular the autumn) was dedicated to his seventieth birthday celebrations. Yet these did not consist, as might have been expected with an artist of that age, of a mere survey of his known works, for Janáček was still at the height of his creative powers. The best proof of this is given by the three premières with which he surprised the public in that year—ADVENTURES OF THE VIXEN SHARP EARS, the FIRST QUARTET and the sextet YOUTH. In addition there were a number or earlier works which had still to be performed or which had been revised or rewritten, for instance the ETERNAL GOSPEL. Thus these celebrations brought to light many unknown works. For instance, only now was the 70,000 performed at Brno on 11 October at a concert given jointly by the Moravian Teachers' and the Moravian Women Teachers' Choirs. The choral works CZECH LEGION and THE WANDERING MADMAN were also new to Brno and, for the younger members of the Brno musical public, so were THE THREAT, The SOLDIER'S LOT, and most of the works performed at a concert given by the Beseda Philharmonic Society on 19 October with Jaroslav Kvapil conducting the cantatas OUR FATHER, AMARUS, ČARTÁK and THE ETERNAL GOSPEL. On 21 October the Brno *conservatoire* organized a concert of his chamber music and on 13 December the Bohemian Quartet gave the Brno première of his FIRST QUARTET. The autumn season at the Brno Theatre included three of Janáček's operas, all conducted by František Neumann: a new production of JENŮFA, KATYA KABANOVA and the première of ADVENTURES OF THE VIXEN SHARP EARS which took place on 6 November produced by Ota Zítek with scenery by Eduard Milén.

Yet, even in Brno, Janáček was still not fully appreciated. The concert of cantatas drew only a small audience and an orchestral concert planned by the Moravian Composers' Club, at which František Neumann was to have conducted some early works including the SUITE FOR STRINGS, LACHIAN DANCES and the overture to ŠÁRKA, had to be cancelled for lack of interest. As for ADVENTURES OF THE VIXEN SHARP EARS, the warm reception by the opera public did not save it from sceptical criticism by the musical establishment. Even so erudite a critic as Vladimír Helfert, once a passionate adversary now turned determined promoter of Janáček's music and his biographer to be,

---

*) Olin Downes also published in the same paper in August 1928 an appraisal of Janáček after the composer's death.

whose Brno music magazine *Hudební rozhledy* appeared in a special double edition, thought it necessary to advise Janáček to cut out all the human characters with the possible exception of the gamekeeper in the Prologue and Epilogue.

In Prague the most important part of the celebrations was the first performance of his QUARTET by the Bohemian Quartet at a Contemporary Music Society concert at the Mozarteum on 17 September 1924. Janáček said in a letter to Kamila written on 14 September, clearly after the usual 'dress rehearsal' at home: 'I have never heard anything so magnificent as the way the Bohemian Quartet played my work. I am agitated myself and it is over a year since I wrote it.' As a point of interest it should be said that the performance in the intimate atmosphere of the Mozarteum made a much deeper impression than its next performance soon afterwards in the large Smetana Hall.

Other events included a Sunday matinée when the Prague première of YOUTH was given, and a joint concert on 8 December by the Philharmonic Choir conducted by Jaroslav Křička (with Stanislav Tauber and Marie Calma-Veselá as soloists), the Prague Teachers' Choir conducted by Method Doležil and the Czech Philharmonic Orchestra conducted by Václav Talich. This concert began—almost symbolically—with the (rewritten) ETERNAL GOSPEL and ended with TARAS BULBA—with love and defiance—two of the main characteristics of Janáček's personality, which were also apparent in the other works included in the programme, the orchestral ballad THE FIDDLER'S CHILD and the choral works MARYČKA MAGDÓNOVA and the 70,000. In the WANDERING MADMAN the 70-year-old fighter and thinker seemed to be presenting the audience with a life's memento. President Masaryk was present at this concert and invited Janáček to his box. The Prague public gave him a tremendous ovation. It was the kind of ovation not given even to Italian tenors nor the most famous virtuosi but which is reserved for a national hero when the public shows its enthusiasm by unanimously rising to its feet.

Little wonder that Janáček later admitted: 'You know, there came over me a strange wave of feeling...'*)

Similar celebrations were organized in other towns of Bohemia, Moravia and Slovakia according to the available facilities. Only the Prague National Theatre did not find it necessary to remember his jubilee, not even by a performance of JENŮFA. This opera was, however, excellently performed on his birthday at another Prague theatre by the Brno Opera company.

Janáček himself celebrated his seventieth birthday in the jolliest possible manner by composing in July 1924, in the very month of his birthday, the wind sextet YOUTH. This hymn in praise of true youth was written while he was busy working on the opera dealing with the artificial youth of Elina Makropoulos. He had apparently been inspired to write for a chamber wind ensemble after hearing the Parisian *Société moderne des instruments à vent* in Salzburg**) and the subject may very well have suggested itself to him when he was sorting out material concerning his childhood and youth for his biographer

---

*) *Československá republika* (Czechoslovak Republic), 11 December 1924, signed J. V.
**) Ludvík Kundera writing in Brno *Hudební rozhledy*, II, p. 87.

298

Max Brod and for a commemorative almanac published for the seventieth birthday by the Brno editor Adolf Veselý. He must have recalled his boyhood years at the old Brno monastery. With this period in mind he wrote, on 19 May 1924, the joyous MARCH OF THE BLUE-BOYS scored for 'piccolo, snare drums and Glockenspiel'*) and dedicated to the flautist Václav Sedláček, Janáček's truly clairvoyant copyist. This miniature composition which has so far only been published in the Brno magazine *Hudební besídka* (Vol. 4, p. 121—127)**) bears the following inscription on the manuscript: 'Whistling go the little songsters from the Queen's Monastery—blue like bluebirds.' A few weeks later the MARCH became the basis for the third movement of the sextet which is scored for flute (alternating piccolo), oboe, clarinet, horn, bassoon and bass clarinet. But even the MARCH OF THE BLUE-BOYS passed through two preliminary stages of development: the first was a sketch for a piece to be called SIEGESALLEE (also for 'piccolo, bells and tambourine') jotted down under the composer's impressions of Berlin from his visit there to hear JENŮFA. The sketch begins with the motif:

330

used subsequently (with the same accompaniment) in the MARCH OF THE BLUE-BOYS and (modified and with off-beat chords in the accompaniment) in the third movement of YOUTH (Ex. 338). The second stage consisted of the composer's article 'Berlin' published on 15 May 1924 in the *Lidové noviny*. Janáček writes in it about the *Siegesallee* ('Victory Boulevard') and reminisces about the time in Brno during the holidays of 1866 when he heard there the 'swirling roll of the little tin drums and above them the strident tunes of the high piccolos' of the Prussian military band. And he appends a manuscript illustration (starting with the second bar of the above-quoted motif, this time clearly marked 'picc., bells and drums' [*sic*]). There is also a reference to Frederick the Great, and Janáček inserts the following motif as a reminiscence of Frederick the musician:

331

Doubtless soon afterwards, on 19 May 1924, Janáček wrote the real MARCH OF THE BLUE-BOYS in which the melody of the Trio is quite similar:

---

*) The piano can only be meant as a substitute for the other two instruments, in particular the Glockenspiel.
**) As part of a series of articles dealing with the flute and flute playing.

Both melodies obviously gave rise to the trio of the third movement of YOUTH (see Ex. 340).

Thus it is evident that both the principal melodies of this playful movement belonged originally to 'blue-boys' of a different, much less benign character than the scholars of the old Brno monastery. Are we to see in this some sort of musical pun? Or is it just another proof of the multitude of meanings applicable even to the most 'realistic' music?

The light-hearted character of YOUTH is indicated by the fact that although there are the usual four movements, the first is not in sonata form but in the more diverting rondo form. The main motif:

which is said to have been developed from the speech melody of the sigh *Mládí, zlaté mládí!* (Youth, golden youth!) is at first alternated with a new melody in A flat minor:

After the main motif's fleeting reappearance in the dominant, the romping second episode bursts in:

335

Un poco più mosso

the third bar of which may be recognized as the teasing motif from the fourth bar of the main theme. In a similar way, after the return of the somewhat melancholy first episode, the main motif reasserts its cheerful mood once more, this time in unclouded B major. It pauses for a while when the horn—after the fashion of Beethoven's rondos—muses a little on its opening notes.

The concluding five bars ('presto a una battuta') are then all the more brilliant movement.

The most serious, relatively speaking, is the slow second movement in Aeolian D flat minor, with its Slav-sounding theme—a pensive andante in the true sense of the word:*)

336

In the ninth bar it is answered by a comforting variant remarkable for the extra semiquaver in the descending figure of the horn:

337

the two last notes of which are then detached to roam about under the held chords of the other instruments, thus heightening the melancholy character of the movement. Its main theme is then developed in four free variations, of which only the final one seems to put the movement's distressed mood aside and comes to rest in a reconciled D flat major.

The lively third movement is an extended scherzo (typically again in 2/4 time) of which the main section in A flat minor, with its playful trill:

338

and its imitative figures trying to outdo one another:

339

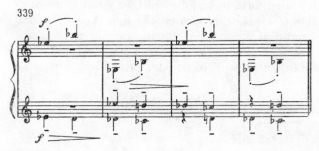

gives a graphic illustration of the musical pranks of the blue-boys. The main

*) Perhaps it should suggest Křížkovský deep in thought pacing up and down the monastery garden at night, throwing an occasional glance of reproach at the window behind which sleeps his thankless but precociously talented pupil.

section is twice alternated with a well-mannered, almost amorous souding trio in A flat major, taking its cue from the rising fifth of the preceding motif (or, in fact, the rising fourth which, at the very beginning of the movement, provides an ostinato bass):

The accompaniment of most of the themes is derived from their motivic elements, and this is true also of the main idea of the last movement in G flat (or F sharp) major:

which is related by its first bar to the main motif of the first movement (see Ex. 333). The ascending figure of its second bar, on the other hand, gives rise to the second idea, its triumphant mood still underscored by the same hammering quadruplet quavers as the main theme:

Both the themes reappear in varied form to be followed by a slowing down of the tempo and a recapitulation of ideas heard earlier: the sigh 'Youth, golden youth' as well as the second motif of the first movement, and the triumphant rising motif from Ex. 342, but in a new, serious guise. Its second and third bars give rise to a new variant full, as it were, of wisdom gained by the passage of time:

This is at first accompanied by arpeggio quadruplets derived from the original rising figure (Ex. 342). Soon a diminution of its own opening notes makes its appearance in 3/4 and in a quickening tempo. The joyful ending repeats the Beethoven-like procedure from the first movement, except that the slowed-down musing centres on the philosophical variant quoted in Ex. 343. A short fast stretta concludes the work.

This work lasts only about 18 minutes but is extremely characteristic of Janáček and brimming over with humour. The first performance was given in Brno on 21 October 1924 by professors of the Brno *conservatoire*. In spite of the excellence of the players and many rehearsals, the first performance was a disaster, though for reasons beyond the control of both the performers and the composer. The difference of temperature between the unheated artists' room and the overheated Beseda concert hall was such that the most important key on the clarinet ceased to function and the otherwise excellent player was forced to give a sketchy account of his part, almost turning the work into a quintet. The unusual quality of Janáček's writing was thus made to sound even more unusual. As soon as the performance was at an end the irate composer rushed on to the platform and declared in his acid Lachian accent: 'Ladies and gentlemen, this was not my composition! Mr K. was pretending to play but in fact did not.'

On 23 November of the same year the sextet was played at the Vinohrady Theatre by seven members of the Czech Philharmonic Orchestra (the extra player taking care of the piccolo part), and this must be regarded as the real première.

Yet another tribute was paid to Janáček during his seventieth year. It came from the Philosophical Faculty of the Masaryk University in Brno, which on 20 January 1925 conferred on him an honorary degree—a tribute which Janáček regarded with pride and gratitude since from that day he never omitted to sign himself Ph. D. Here are some characteristic remarks which he made in his speech on that occasion:

'Creating a composition requires no other line of thought than that of everyday thinking or of purely scientific work. There are no miracles in art.

'A perfect work falls from the tree like a ripe apple. And even a scientist cannot do without fantasy.

'Freedom of thought is the freedom with which the work is built.

'My little house—a composition—is fit for the countryside: in the mountains its roof is askew—inside, the room is warm from work—I can reach the walls and ceiling with my fintertips.

'And in this I join Richard Wagner, Liszt, Berlioz and the neglected...'

Here my pen stops. According to all the known printed versions of Janáček's speech, including Pazdírek's report on the whole ceremony, Janáček added 'the neglected Zoilo', leaving the world to rack its brains as to who this personage might be. Did he mean Zoilos, the ancient Greek rhetor from the fourth century B.C. who was Homer's sarcastic critic? Or perhaps Annibale Zoilo, a sixteenth century composer of church music? Or someone with a similar name, for instance Arrigo Boito who certainly fits much better into the company of the other composers mentioned by Janáček?*)

Be that as it may, no one will disagree with the closing words which Janáček

---

*) Pazdírek's report, judging by the typical layout of the speech, was based on Janáček's own manuscript and not on a shorthand record of it. Janáček was in the habit of writing Z like a B without the vertical stroke, and it is easy at the best of times to mistake t for l.

addressed to the students: 'All who want to learn a lesson from my life should note that it is necessary to create even while still learning.' (In this he agreed with Vincent d'Indy who also founded an 'organ school'—the famous Schola Cantorum in Paris.)

Janáček, in his next work, gave ample proof that this academic honour was not going to have the slightest effect on his composing, especially since it was of a type which might very easily have been academic—a piano concerto.

'The eternally young old man from Brno surprised us on Saturday with a work which was, once again, a revelation. The title: CONCERTINO—for piano, two violins, viola, clarinet, horn and bassoon. The scoring itself is pure Janáček, let alone the music, although the piano cadenza in the third movement seems reminiscent of the old type of concerto. It is not a symphony with piano, but a suite which might have been entitled "In Nature's Realm".*)

'Thus it is clear that the CONCERTINO belongs to the world of ADVENTURES OF THE VIXEN SHARP EARS while the QUARTET could be coupled with KATYA KABANOVA. Janáček's melodies are excitingly new, highly original and still folk-like, based at times on a minor scale with a raised fourth (the main themes of the first, second and to a certain extent the third movements) or at other times on the whole tone scale which has, however, quite a different colour with Janáček than with Debussy—just as melodic progressions based on chords of four or five superimposed fourths, equally dear to Debussy. Janáček's rhythms, sometimes declamatory and free, at other times dance-like and strictly controlled or given a free rein, would need a separate study of their own. The same may be said about his characteristic and yet perfectly apt instrumentation which he knows so well how to gradate by using in the first movement only the horn with the piano, in the second only the clarinet, and only from the end of the movement using the whole ensemble.**) No wonder that the success of the new work was quite exceptional. As before in Brno, it had to be repeated immediately. Everyone in the audience felt that this was the first spring day of the year.'

With these words—if I may be forgiven for quoting myself once more— I tried to express the fresh, spontaneous impression made by this work, in an article in *Československá republika* of 23 February 1926 after the first Prague performance of this CONCERTINO for piano and chamber ensemble. Janáček wrote it in the spring of 1925 in the heart of his native Hukvaldy country, finishing it on 29 April.

The inspiration to write it and the first musical ideas had come to him five

---

*) Cf. Dvořák's Overture, Op. 91. According to Štědroň's catalogue of 1959 the CONCERTINO was intended in all probability to be a suite entitled *Spring* with the individual movements called *The Beetle, The Deer, The Cricket* and *The Stream*. Janáček himself indicated something of the kind in a letter to Kamila dated 22 April 1925 from Hukvaldy: 'I have composed a piano concerto here, "Spring". There is a cricket in it, and flies, a deer, a fast stream, and — well — a man.' With the exception of the overall title, though, the names of the individual sections in either Štědroň's catalogue or Janáček's letter do not fit the music very well.

**) Dr Ludvík Kundera pointed out in an article in the Brno *Hudební rozhledy*, Vol. II (1928), p. 77, that there is increasing gradation in the piano part itself: 'In the first movement the phrases are mostly monotonal, in the second movement chordal, in the third stiffened with octaves, and in the last movement they thunder with octaves in both hands.'

months earlier in Prague after hearing the brilliant rendering of the piano part of his DIARY by Jan Heřman (1886—1946) at a rehearsal which took place in Heřman's flat one evening before the Sunday morning concert given at the Vinohrady Theatre on 23 November 1924 as part of Janáček's jubilee celebrations. Here his OVERGROWN PATH, SONGS OF HRADČANY, YOUTH, *Forebodying* and *Death* from STREET SCENE 1 OCTOBER 1905 and THE DIARY OF THE YOUNG MAN WHO DISAPPEARED were performed, with Heřman playing the first and the last two items. A letter which Janáček wrote to Heřman on 7 February 1925 contains some interesting hints relating to the content of the CONCERTINO even if they are obscured by Janáček's usual style: 'You played my DIARY as I have never yet heard it played... Under this wonderful impression... the main themes for my future concerto came to me while walking. From here to the finished composition is a long way. Much thinking!

'Why the horn in the first movement? Why the shrill derisive clarinet in the second? Why the heavy chords in the third? Why all that passion in the last? (This is exactly what it would be interesting to know from Janáček himself!) The whole thing grew from the youthful mood of the sextet YOUTH.

'I have a feeling it is like an echo of the time when I was struggling with the piano.'

If these remarks do not reveal much, there is luckily in existence yet another explanation in an article in German written by Janáček for the conductors' magazine *Pult und Taktstock*, which was printed in the double number May—June 1927, Vol. IV, p. 63—64:

'First Movement

'One spring day we prevented a hedgehog from getting to his lair lined with dry leaves in an old lime-tree.

'He was cross but he toiled in vain.

'He could not make it out. Neither could the horn in my first movement. All it could manage was this grumpy motif:

344

Should the hedgehog have stood up on his hind legs and sung a sorrowful song? The moment he stuck his nose out he had to pull it in again.

'Second Movement

'The squirrel was chatty while she was jumping high up from tree to tree. But once in the cage she screeched like my clarinet, but even so, to the great delight of the children, she twirled and danced round and round in circles.

'Third Movement

'With a bullying expression the stupid bulging eyes of the little night owl and the other censorious night-birds stare into the strings of the piano.

'Fourth Movement

'The fourth movement is like a scene from a fairy-tale: everybody is discussing the new penny.

'And the piano?

'Someone has to be the organizer.

'I think there must be three motifs in every movement. (Here Janáček quotes Examples Nos 345—351, 353, 356, 357 and 360.)

'Let this be enough for everyone's mind, even if he thinks differently from Korngold*)—it was certainly enough for the composer of this little trifle.'

Dr Ludvík Kundera**) rightly points out that 'We must not forget the purely musical impulse which gave birth to these compositions' (the FIRST QUARTET, YOUTH and CONCERTINO) and that 'Janáček's style of composition, making, as it does, frequent use of motivic diminutions, is not so far removed from the style and texture of a concerto as would at first appear.' Moreover, 'it can even give the impression of virtuosity, but—of course—since every note in Janáček's passagework has its structural validity—has its own role to play—it is a modern kind of virtuosity which is more than just a technical device.' It is certain that Janáček's choice of a chamber ensemble to accompany the piano was influenced by contemporary trends in general and the example of Hindemith in particular.

However, despite certain affinities to classical forms, especially to the ternary form *ABA*, always a favourite with Janáček, it may be said that he created in the CONCERTINO a true piano concerto of his own design which differs from the absolute forms of, for instance, Hindemith's concertos, by being admittedly programmatic and also by the strict application of the theory of linking certain themes with certain instruments.

Also the character of these themes or motifs (there are basically only three of them) is more illustrative than symphonic.

The first movement, which hints at sonata form, begins camlly with this motif in the piano followed by the horn's echoing of the last three notes but one:

The Allegro proper begins with a quickened version of the same motif after which the bracketed 'echo' motif from Ex. 345 is developed into what could be called the second subject:

---

*) Julius Korngold, music critic who wrote about the Vienna première of JENŮFA in the paper *Neue Freie Presse*.

**) In the Brno *Hudební rozhledy*, Vol. II (February 1926), p. 77.

306

and, later, into this waltz-like motif which, together with the original three-note motif, serves as the development section:

which is followed by the recapitulation in a reversed order, with the introductory bars returning at the end. The second, scherzo-like movement begins once again with the solo piano playing a teasing, fragmentary motif:

The bracketed figure in bars four and five gives rise to two ideas: the mischievous motif of the E flat clarinet in combination with the original motif from Ex. 348:

and the theme of the middle section affecting a strutting pace:

after which the first section returns followed by a coda in stretta.

The same descending three-note motif with an ascending note added provides the material for the third, march-like movement, both for its outer sections:

and for the more lyrical middle section:

354 **Vivo ad lib.**

In contrast to these three movements in ternary form, the last movement is in fact one long thematic cadenza for the piano assisted by the accompanying instruments and ending with a stretta. This movement consists of a playful struggle between the domineering descending motif:

355 **Allegro**

its admonitory afterthought:

356 *energico*

and a romping gallop derived from them both:

357

The 'admonitory' motif is then developed in combination with the 'domineering' one into a much mellower melody:

358

which, after a solo cadenza based on its diminution:

359

emerges with its rhythm boldly reshaped and its mood looking forward to the festive fanfares of the fifth movement of the GLAGOLITIC MASS, while the important opening motif (Ex. 355) is reduced to an ornamental appendage:

360

361

The work is rounded off with the gallop motif reappearing in a mischievous piano but soon working up to a vigorous forte.

The first performance of this little masterpiece took place on 16 February 1926 in Brno, and Prague followed suit four days later, yet in neither case was the piano part entrusted to Heřman as he had expected, but to Mrs Ilona Kurzová-Štěpánová. In his letter of explanation to Heřman, Janáček gave the simple though unconvincing reason that she had been the first to ask for it. 'But to you,' adds Janáček, 'I dedicate the work, because it is you I must thank for the CONCERTINO.'

As it was, the young interpreter who was the daughter of one of the best Czech piano professors Vilém Kurz (the teacher of Rudolf Firkušný), and wife of Dr Václav Štěpán, a pianist and composer mentioned earlier, gave excellent performances both in Brno and in Prague, as well as later in Germany.

In May 1926, Janáček went to Prague to attend the International Festival of Contemporary Music which included the Prague première of ADVENTURES OF THE VIXEN SHARP EARS. This took place on 18 May, conducted by Otakar Ostrčil and produced by Ferdinand Pujman. It came nearest to the smiling, realistic character of the work in its sets designed by Josef Čapek, brother of the author Karel Čapek. In spite of Emil Burian's outstanding gamekeeper, however, the work was otherwise received with puzzlement rather than enthusiasm. But the Prague visit had the merit that it wrought a reconciliation, albeit a temporary one, between the composer and his wife, soon to be sealed by a journey together to Venice.

There, the International Society for Contemporary Music continued the summer's proceedings begun earlier in Prague, with a chamber music festival from 3 until 8 September. Czech music was represented by Ladislav Vycpálek's *Awakening* and Janáček's FIRST QUARTET. The competition was stiff, since Janáček's name was quite unknown in Italy. His music had to compete with Stravinsky's Piano Sonata, Schönberg's Serenade, Opus 24, Hindemith's *Kammermusik No. 2*, Ravel's *Tzigane*, Roussel's *Joueurs de flûte*, Honegger's Cello Sonata, Fauré's *L'horizon chimérique*, Szymanowski's Quartet, Vaughan Williams' Three Rondos, Malipiero's *Le Stagioni italiche* and works by Ibert and others, also Gruenberg's *Daniel-Jazz*. Nevertheless Janáček's powerful work which was performed by the Czechoslovak Quartet (led by Richard Zika, 1897—1947) made a deep impression. Zika and his colleagues, in spite of their modern matter-of-fact approach, gave a spontaneous, musicianly account of the whole work with a particularly passionate rendering of its last movement. Afterwards, Janáček had to take several bows although he kept the audience waiting for quite some time before he appeared on the stage. All the exits in the Teatro Fenice where the concert took place lead outside and everytime Janáček tried to reach the artists he found himself in the street. Eventually, though, he was taken in his light white suit through an underground passage to his destination.

On the way to Venice, Janáček was impressed by Trieste, but his enchantment with Venice knew no bounds, and, according to Mrs Janáček, he kept repeating: 'I must come back here.' (He never did.) He was enchanted not only by the old heritage in stone, but also by the present-day life of the town, in particular by the Sunday regatta on the Grand Canal which he watched from the steps of the magnificent baroque church of Santa Maria della Salute near which he lived in a small *pension*.

There is little doubt that Janáček must have been overjoyed when on 11 November of the same year František Neumann revived his first opera ŠÁRKA in Brno, produced by Ota Zítek with scenery by Vlastislav Hofman. Zeyer's veto had kept it from the stage for 36 years. Janáček thought so highly of his first opera (especially when compared with his second one, THE BEGINNING OF A ROMANCE, which Gabriela Preissová had unsuccessfully sought to rewrite with him after JENŮFA's success), that he was not only eager to see it put on also at the National Theatre in Prague, but—as it seems from his dealings with Max Brod as late as January 1928 concerning the German translation—even considered it suitable for production abroad. Yet it seems that even Max Brod was sceptical, and in the composer's own country Fibich's *Šárka* will always stand in its way.

(39) 'The Makropoulos Case'

All inmost things, we may say, are melodious;
naturally utter themselves in Song...
See deep enough, and you see musically.

Thomas Carlyle

Everything can be set to music
if the necessary talent is there.

Richard Strauss

The revival of ŠÁRKA did not prevent Janáček from pressing onward. On 12 November—the day after the première of ŠÁRKA—he finished the opera THE MAKROPOULOS CASE. He said in an interview with Adolf Veselý:*)

'Yes, it was rather a difficult job, I rewrote the libretto three times before I got what I wanted.' But on another occasion he said: 'It gripped me. The third act, I'm rather proud of that. The flow, the suspense. That is what I felt, what I wanted. I worked on it for about a year. Before that I carried it about in my head, kept thinking about it—but then it went fast—like a machine!'**)

Thus in two years from 11 September 1923 to 12 November 1925, Janáček completed what he described as 'a modern historical opera' and what, after ADVENTURES OF THE VIXEN SHARP EARS and THE WANDERING MADMAN, was yet another survey of life.

In ADVENTURES OF THE VIXEN SHARP EARS the almost septuagenarian Janáček came to terms with human mortality by accepting the notion of the immortality of nature. Bystrouška is overtaken by the deadly bullet just as the gamekeeper is overtaken by old age. But soon enough the new little Bystrouška and, with her, a dozen others appear, and Nature continues undisturbed with its eternal song, its eternal regeneration.

In THE MAKROPOULOS CASE the problem is put in a more pressing, more defiant, even more revolutionary way: what if we could lengthen our lives at will? What if we could live for centuries not only in our posterity but in our own actual selves? It is the same question as Hamlet's 'to be or not to be', but asked less modestly or almost from the opposite point of view: to be or not to be satisfied with our ephemeral existence, with the limited span of time accorded to us by nature, which seems too short a time in which to accomplish all that we want to do, to know all that we want to know and to experience all that we long to experience. It is the question posed in the old Faustian legend and, in our time, in G. B. Shaw's *Back to Methuselah*. But while Shaw

---

*) 'Capriccio of a Creator's Autumn' by Adolf Veselý, in the paper *České slovo* of 18 November 1926.
**) In *Literární svět* (The Literary World) of 8 March 1928.

311

comes to the conclusion that the ability to live for several hundred years is the necessary pre-condition of a higher state of humanity, Karel Čapek, the author of the comedy from which Janáček made his libretto, gives the opposite answer. (It is of interest that Shaw's play was unknown to Čapek when he first began working on the subject in the form of a novel.) Presuming that there did exist an elixir of life—the Makropoulos secret—he confronts us with a 'young' woman over 300 years old with all the charms of beauty and intelligence. But instead of the desired eternal youth, we see to our horror an artificially preserved mask of youth which hides satiety, cynicism and deathly spiritual weariness, living only on monstrous memories.

The story is as follows:

Act I. Young Albert Gregor visits his lawyer Dr Kolenatý in order to find out the final verdict in the case Gregor v. Prus which has been dragging on for almost 100 years, concerning the inheritance of the two families. If the verdict turns out unfavourably for the Gregor side, there will be no other alternative for young Albert Gregor than to follow his father's example and commit suicide 'for debts contracted on account of the inheritance'. The lawyer Dr Kolenatý is not in his office and his clerk Vítek does not yet know the result of the case. Vítek's daughter Krista, a young singer, comes to the office praising enthusiastically a certain Emilia Marty who has just captured the operatic public by her magnificent singing as well as by her striking beauty. Emilia Marty herself then enters, accompanied by Dr Kolenatý. She is anxious to know more about the famous case of which she has read in the paper. Kolenatý galantly gives her the necessary information. It concerns an estate left by Baron Josef Ferdinand Prus who died in 1827 leaving no children and no will. The management of the estate was therefore taken over by his cousin, Baron Emerich Prus, to whom a certain Ferdinand Gregor, the grandfather of the present Albert Gregor, presented a claim stating that the late baron in a personal declaration to the head of the college where he was a boarder, had made him his heir. The cousin opposed this claim and produced the protocol of the last hours of the baron according to which the old man expressed a wish that the estate should go to an unknown person called Mach Gregor. At this moment Emilia Marty excitedly interrupts by declaring with surprising assurance that 'Ferdy' (i.e. Albert's grandfather Ferdinand Gregor) was Pepi's (i.e. Baron Josef Ferdinand Prus) son and that his mother was Elian MacGregor, a singer at the Imperial opera house. She goes on to explain that he chopped the prefix 'Mac' out of consideration for his mother, but it was he whom the dying man had in mind and no 'Mach' Gregor. She even knows where the written will of the old baron may be found, in which it is expressly stated that his heir is to be his illegitimate son Ferdinand. (This highly important name was left out both by Janáček and by Max Brod in the German translation!) She then challenges the lawyer to take her to the old house of the baron where he will find in a special drawer a sealed yellow envelope containing the lost will. Kolenatý, who at first thinks that the mysterious woman is pulling his leg, is at last persuaded by young Albert Gregor to comply with her wish and go to the old house. Albert Gregor is left alone with Emilia Marty and makes no effort to hide the fact that he has fallen in love with her. But she repulses his advances with an ice-cold manner and only laughs derisively when he offers to pay her for helping him to win the case. All she desires are some papers written in Greek which belonged to his grandfather and which she assumes to be in his possession. She becomes mysteriously agitated on hearing that he has no knowledge of them. Kolenatý now returns begging Emilia Marty's forgiveness. The will has been found and the case will be resumed. (Janáček altogether left out the news of the court's having decided against Gregor.) But Gregor's adversary Prus does not yet give in. He points out that there is nothing to prove that the illegitimate son Ferdinand mentioned in the will is in fact Ferdinand Gregor. Emilia Marty once again undertakes to produce the necessary proof.

Act II. Backstage at the theatre after the final curtain, in the lingering atmosphere of Emilia Marty's latest triumph, Krista tells Janek—Prus' son—that their love must from now on take second place to her training to be as great a singer one day as Marty. Everyone is eager to congratulate the *diva*. Among her admirers is a dotty, senile old man Hauk Šendorf who sees in her a certain Eugenia Montez who had been his mistress in Madrid many years ago. He does not realize that Eugenia and Emilia are one and the same woman. Strangely enough, Marty has a few kind words for him. Prus is also secretly in love with Emilia while at the same time keeping a sharp eye on his interests in the case. He has in fact discovered that the illegitimate son Ferdinand, mentioned in the will, is entered in the register of births as Ferdinand Makropoulos and that his mother is stated to be Elina Makropoulos and that therefore the inheritance is no concern of anyone called Gregor. He must therefore win the case unless someone claiming to be Ferdinand Makropoulos makes his appearance. Emilia Marty declares that this person will be found and demands of Prus that he sell her the 'envelope'. (This is a different envelope, this one containing the 'Greek' papers, with—as will be seen later—the Makropoulos secret.) However, since Prus refuses the bargain, she incites his simple-minded son Janek to steal the envelope from his father. The boy, who is enchanted by her, promises. But his father has overheard their conversation and now returns to offer to bring the envelope to Emilia. 'But when, but when?' he asks. 'This evening,' she replies suggestively.

Act III. Prus has spent a night with Marty at her hotel. He has had what he wanted and now, disappointed by the coldness of her embrace, must keep his promise and give her what she wanted. A messenger brings the news that Janek, Prus' only son, has committed suicide on finding out that his rival for Emilia's love is his own father. Prus leaves in despair and Emilia prepares to leave with Hauk for Spain. But Hauk is taken away to an asylum and Dr Kolenatý accuses Emilia publicly of fraud. In particular, the document identifying Ferdinand Gregor, with a date 100 years old is, he declares, written not long ago in modern ink and in handwriting identical with that of the signature on the photograph dedicated by Emilia Marty to Krista. Emilia proposes to explain everything as soon as she is dressed. The others in the meantime ransack her luggage and, finding many letters addressed to various names of which the initials are invariably E.M., are confirmed in their belief that she is an impostor. At last Emilia Marty returns half drunk carrying a bottle of whisky. She declares that her real name is Elina Makropoulos and that she was born in Crete in 1575—thus she is exactly 327 years old. Her father was a doctor to the Emperor Rudolf in Prague who, when he was beginning to grow old, demanded a life-giving elixir. Makropoulos gave him a prescription which would keep him young for 300 years. The Emperor ordered that it be tried out on the doctor's daughter Elina who was only 16 at the time.*) She took the potion and fell into a coma lasting several weeks. The Emperor had thrown her father into prison for fraud. But Elina pulled through and escaped abroad, taking the prescription with her. However, as no one can live normally among people for 300 years, she kept changing her name; she has been Elian Mac Gregor, Eugenia Montez, Ekaterina Mishkina and others. She had lent the miraculous prescription to her lover Josef Prus in whose house it remained until last night. The suspicious lawyer again summons her to reveal her real name but she repeats stubbornly 'Elina Makropoulos' and breaks down. Now, at last, all believe her and ask her forgiveness for their callous lack of understanding. She herself ends her confession with the desperate conclusion that 'One should not live so long. If you knew how easy it is for you to live... For you, everything has its meaning, its value. You fools! You are so happy because of that stupid accident of early death.' Thus the 'immortal one' speaks to the mortals while the voice of humanity answers in the orchestra and the chorus: 'Yes, we are all so happy... There's nothing more we can want!' Elina Makropoulos loses interest in the miraculous formula, since her long and desperate search for it has been overshadowed by a still more poignant despair of the emptiness of her own life. Surprisingly, no one else wants the formula either. In the end it is Krista who takes it, only to burn it over a candle. As the old paper turns to ash Elina Makropoulos cries out 'Pater hemon'—the first words of 'Our Father' in her mother tongue,**) and dies reconciled with life, or, as Wagner would have said, 'redeemed'.

---

*) Since in staging this opera the period 'feel' is all-important, producers should know that Janáček deliberately or more likely by accident left a number of choices open to them: When Marty first discloses her true age (vocal score p. 160, reh. No. 64), she says she is 337 years old. She puts her date of birth as 1585 (p. 163, a bar before reh. No. 71). Thus far the figures agree with those in the original play by Karel Čapek. But later on (p. 176, reh. No. 102) in reply to Dr Kolenatý's direct question how old she is, Marty screams: 'Don't confuse! Three hundred and *twenty* seven!' Bearing in mind that (a) Rudolf II reigned from 1576 to 1612 and that the 16-year-old Elina could therefore have taken the potion at either the earlier or the later date, and that (b) Dr Kolenatý's reference in Act I to Baron Josef Prus' death 'a hundred years ago' is vague, sorting out the confusion one way or another yields basically three choices:

	Jaroslav Vogel's solution	Possible intermediate solutions		Karel Čapek's solution
E. M. born	1575	1575	1585	1585
took potion in	1591	1591	1601	1601
states she is (years old)	327	337	327	337
therefore action takes place in	1902	1912	1912	1922

K. J.

**) Janáček's addition.

314

Thus even here Janáček's own answer is a manly acceptance of death, although no longer with a conciliatory smile as in ADVENTURES OF THE VIXEN SHARP EARS but resignedly with courage and fully aware of the paradox of human existence which attributes value to immortality only because of its own mortality, its ephemeral shortness alone making life's values worth living for. Because of this human content of the argument, I do not agree with the critics who at the time of the opera's première objected that the composer of JENŮFA had let himself be enticed into making an opera out of a dry legal story whose intricate plot was difficult enough to follow in a straight play, let alone in an opera where half the words were not intelligible.

True, Karel Čapek himself, although giving his consent without hesitation, did not hide his doubts. 'As I have already told you,' he wrote to Janáček on 27 February 1923 with his usual self-deprecation, 'I have too high an opinion of music—and especially your music—to be able to imagine it in combination with a play which contains so much conversation, is so unpoetic and clotted up with dialogue as my *Makropoulos Case*.*) I am afraid that you have in mind something better than my play can offer except, perhaps, the woman who is three hundred years old. There is nothing to stop you from making up a new story regardless of my play, in which a three-hundred-year-old life with all its suffering would be the centre of attention inside a better frame. After all it is not my own patent. You could base it on Ahasver, the Wandering Jew, or on the witch from František Langer's story (from the collection *Murderers and Dreamers*) or even on Miss Makropoulos, and arrange the action independently.'

'Except, perhaps, the woman who is three hundred years old' —that is where the secret of Janáček's choice lay. Admittedly, the inheritance case was not particularly poetic, neither was a lawyer's office a poetic locale even if it could be regarded as the stage on which, symbolically, human destinies are played out, just as Act II could be considered the backstage of the struggle for fame, and the hotel room in Act III a symbol of a short life's passage in this world. But once a personality like Emilia Marty walks into the office—a moment wonderfully prepared by Čapek, with Gregor's imminent tragedy on the one hand and Krista's enthusiasm on the other—it does not really matter whether all the intricacies of the case can be followed or not. It is sufficient to realize at each given moment the exceptional character of the heroine. Clearly no

---

*) Janáček did considerably reduce the dialogue, in particular at the end of the last act which he shortened from two scenes to one; but on the whole he adhered to Čapek's clean-cut diction, except for a few 'bold' expressions. He also cut out the scene in Act III in which Gregor gets dangerously near to losing the audience's sympathy by ordering Emilia's luggage to be searched in revenge for her repulsion of his advances. However, in some places Janáček went further in his cuts than was accetable for the understanding of the plot. His cut in Act II (reh. No. 95) for instance, makes Prus' sentence 'Then, the envelope will remain sealed' seem to refer to the envelope containing the testament (unless the listener is alert enough to remember at once that the will was in fact opened in Act I) whereas it actually refers to the 'Greek papers'. Max Brod pointed this out to Janáček and amended the discrepancy in his German translation. On the other hand Brod himself comes into conflict with the music in the scene in Act I (reh. No. 126) where, in an effort to restore the logic, he makes Gregor sing to the accompaniment of a triumphant G major 6/4 chord '*Plötzlich so alt!*' (Suddenly so old) instead of the original '*Jste krásná*' (You are beautiful).

Wandering Jew could replace Emilia Marty for Janáček who was attracted by her facinating and enigmatic womanhood. In other words she represented for him his Šárka, Zefka, Etherea and Terynka, all in one. He himself confirmed this when recalling a beautiful woman who had unwittingly been his model for Emilia Marty: 'You, my lady of Kounic Avenue in the black fur coat, so black that the moles themselves might have been wearing it—you were the measure for my Elina Makropoulos? You must have been surprised that I, whom you do not know, greeted you. In you and your cold beautiful face I saw Elina Makropoulos.'*)

It is true that the harsh, embittered tone of the story was reflected in music of an altogether harsher character than that inspired by the spontaneous musicality of the folk in JENŮFA or by the poetic musicality of the summer nights in KATYA or by the exciting animality of the goings on in the VIXEN. It is music which almost hurts by its insistent edginess in such scenes as that of Gregor and the 'ice-cold' heroine in Act II. It is the music of a long span of time, one end of which, the Rudolphine period, is symbolized by the trumpet, horn and timpani fanfares offstage in the opening Prelude:

362

At the other end stands the mysterious figure of the 327-year-old and yet always young Emilia Marty—symbolized by the viola d'amore with its questioning motif:

363
Act I.

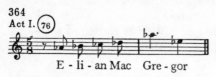

and especially by the speech melody of the heroine's name:

364
Act I. ⑦⑥

E - li - an Mac   Gre - gor

and by its numerous variants:

365
Act III.

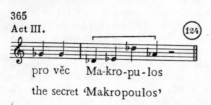

pro věc   Ma-kro-pu-los

the secret 'Makropoulos'

---

*) From an article entitled 'At Dusk' written for the paper *Venkov* and published in it on 20 January 1928. Janáček, however, had earlier (on 8 June 1927) written to Kamila: 'You are the poor Elina Makropoulos.'

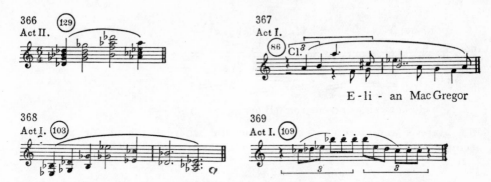

The 'Elian MacGregor' motif is at the same time the only motto theme in this work, which—exceptionally even for Janáček—is otherwise devoid of Leitmotivs. It provides the material for almost all the other ideas throughout the opera including, for instance, the soaring melody of the Prelude:

which in turn gives rise to the fanfares quoted in Ex. 362, and to the following combination (at reh. No. 10 in the Prelude):

```
371
a
b
```

and which is related to a number of motifs later on in the opera (see Exs 380, 381 and 384).

There are some remarkable touches, for instance the music of the stifling, portentous passion of Gregor for the fascinating and at the same time repulsive heroine which seems to breathe from the orchestra at the words (in Act I, five bars after reh. No. 124) 'You fired my feelings like an inferno.' Or the contrasting almost childlike romance of Krista and Janek. (How charming is her 'No, no kissing... I have other worries now'—worries which consist of being able to sing like Marty.)

Janáček, with consummate mastery, underlines every expressive point offered by the lines of the text. In Act I, for instance, Krista's admiration for Marty blossoms out in these speech-related melodies:

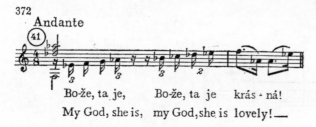

373

To ni-kdo ne-ví,   to ni-kdo ne-po-zná!

Nobody knows it,   no one can tell her age

and Marty's announcement concerning the whereabouts of the papers is accompanied by feverish suspense in the orchestra:

374

V Pruso - vě do - mě   bý-va-la ta-ko-vá   skříň,

There used to be a   cabinet   in Prus's   house

How readily Janáček takes up the desperate mood of Dr Kolenatý's decision to go and look for the papers:

375

Prestissimo

Tře-bak čer - tu!

To the devil!

and how shattering is the comment on Marty's coldness after her blunt refusal 'I won't' (seven bars after reh. No. 107), or when Krista asks (in Act II, reh. No. 23) 'D'you think that she (Marty) could have ever been in love?':

376

Moderato

How weary and yearning Janáček makes Marty's line (Act I, five bars before reh. No. 114):

377

Ev - ery-one's al - ways   dy - ing

Všech - no to jen u - mí - rá

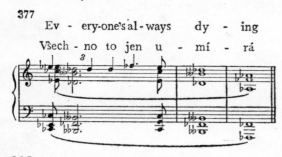

or her request (Act II, five bars before reh. No. 67):

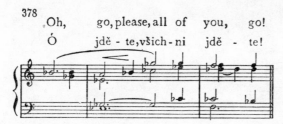

how poignant is the sorrowful sound of the orchestra when Prus reads the suicide note from his son, 'Father, be happy. As for me...' (Act III, three bars after reh. No. 22):

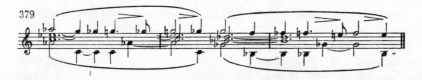

how coldly suggestive is the music in Act III when Marty recounts the mystery of the painful transfiguration of the 16-year-old Elina:

Janáček is capable of drawing music and poetic imagery or at least descriptions of characters out of such prosaic details as the sighs of old Vítek at the beginning of the work:

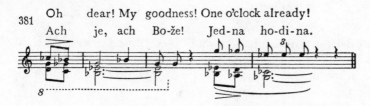

out of Vítek's reflections on the French Revolution and the old gentry (trumpet fanfare motif), or out of Krista's musing on the famous Marty (bassoon motif):

A particularly descriptive passage (still in Act I) illustrates the stage direction
'Kolenatý scribbles irritably in his papers':

384

Similarly, Vítek's earlier calling over the telephone, 'Hallo, Dr. Kolenatý?'
sounds like yodelling in the mountains—one distance evoking another (Act I,
reh. No. 30); or in Act III when the chamber-maid is about to knock on the
door in order to let in the servant bringing the news of Prus' son's suicide,
Janáček entrusts this task not to a human hand, but instead, to the xylophone—
the instrument of death.

But it is at the conclusion of the opera that Janáček gives perhaps the most
convicing justification of his approach to the material, proving at the same
time how conscious he was, despite his alleged naturalism, of the stylizing
and idealizing function of music. He transforms the conversational ending
of the play into an open-hearted, emotionally stirred epilogue for the heroine
which can only end by her death in full view of the audience. What depths
of desperate sadness—as if expressing the sadness of all humanity—Janáček
touched in the simple, folk-like motif (reminiscent, perhaps not entirely by
chance, of the earth motif in Part One of THE EXCURSIONS OF MR BROUČEK—
see Ex. 2) which acompanies Marty's words 'For me life has come to an end.
Father in heaven, it cannot go on... It's futile, Krista, singing or keeping
silent. You get tired of being good. You get tired of being bad. You get tired
of the earth, you get tired of heaven. You find that your soul has died away.'
(Act III, four bars after reh. No. 121):

385

And when, after offering Krista the miraculous prescription in vain ('You'll
be famous, you will sing like Emilia Marty'), she sinks to the ground, the curtain
falls on one of the most unreal and yet most powerful dramas of human
existence.

Luhačovice Spa in south-eastern Moravia, where Janáček spent many a summer holiday in search of company and cure for his ailments. He described the season at the spa as 'the annual congress of beautiful women'.

Page one of the full score of THE MAKROPOULOS CASE written in Janáček's own hand.

Josef Čapek's design for the opera THE MAKRO-POULOS CASE based on his brother Karel's play.

Rosa Newmarch (extreme left), Janáček, and participants of the 6 May 1926 Wigmore Hall concert: Adila Fachiri is second from the left, her accompanist Fanny Davies is on the extreme right, and second from the right is Adila's husband Alexander Fachiri. The photograph was taken by Jan Mikota in the Fachiris' garden in London after a rehearsal of Janáček's VIOLIN SONATA.

Janáček in Venice at the Chamber Music Festival organized there in September 1925 by the International Society for Contemporary Music. Second from the right is Jan Loewenbach, music critic of the Prague *Hudební revue*. Janáček's secretary, Jan Mikota, is seventh from the right. Between him and Mrs Janáčková (fifth from left) stands the Czech pianist and composer Václav Štěpán.

A page of Janáček's manuscript of THE DIARY OF THE YOUNG MAN WHO DISAPPEARED.

A programme for the 1926 London concert o Janáček's chamber works.

Janáček in London with members of the London Wind Quintette. Aubrey Brain (horn) is on the extreme left, Leon Goossens (oboe) on the extreme right, second from the right in the back row is Richard Newton (bassoon), and in the front row Haydn Draper (clarinet, left) and Robert Murchie (flute, right). Mendelssohn Draper (bass clarinet, second from left in the back row) was added for the Wigmore Hall performance of Janáček's wind sextet MLÁDÍ (Youth).

Janáček's study in the Director's house of the Organ School, now part of the Janáček Museum in Brno.

Another part of Janáček's study. The portrait is that of his friend Antonín Dvořák (1841—1904).

Kamila Stösslová, née Neumannová, who had a profound influence on the composer from their meeting in Luhačovice in 1917 until his death in 1928.

(40) Carrying the Banner

At the beginning of 1926 Janáček went to Hukvaldy where he finished his new male-voice chorus Our Flag (Naše vlajka) to words by F. S. Procházka. He dedicated it to the Moravian Teachers' Choral Society 'for the 70,000 in France' which they visited successfully the previous year. In Our Flag Janáček reveals once more his original and yet realistic powers of imagination by suggesting, in the fanfare-like main theme:

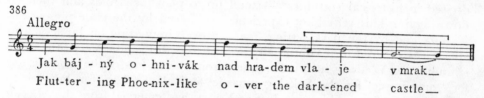

386

which rises higher and higher, the ceremonial unfurling of the flag. No less suggestive are the trills over the diminution of the last three notes of the main theme — 'Two solo sopranos fluttering over the ramparts of the male voices like a flag flying from the tower':

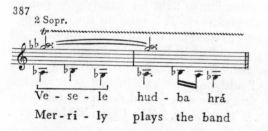

387

Similarly 'two solo tenors imitate the crowing of black ravens fleeing as the nation awakens to its freedom.*) Procházka's poem which had been published under the title *The Flag* as the last in his collection *New Songs of Hradčany* underwent Janáček's usual rough treatment. He cut its six verses to less than half but in the process managed to make it more easily understandable. He then commissioned the poet to write an additional verse which, after the Ballad of Blaník, represents a new declaration of his love of peaceful work: 'Rejoice every one of us... We shall shed blood no more... The plough will be our weapon.' The setting of its first line leans once again on the original fanfare which, in combination with the 'merry' motif (Ex. 387):

---

*) From Silvester Hippmann's critique of the first Prague performance in 1926 at the Moravian Teachers' traditional Christmas concert, published in *Listy Hudební matice*, Vol. VI, p. 122.

Re-joice, re - joice ev - ery   one   of   us
Ra - duj se,   ra - duj se,   kdo   jsi   náš

and eventually in a slowed down tempo brings the work to a festive conclusion.

On 16 February Janáček was present at the first performance in Brno of his CONCERTINO and by 1 April he was completing a further major work, the SINFONIETTA.

One sunny day in 1925 Janáček and Kamila were sitting in the local park at Písek listening to a military band concert. The well-rehearsed musicians played, among ot her things, some fanfares which took Janáček's fancy not only as such but also by the way they were performed. The players—possibly dressed in historical costumes*)—stood up to play their solos and then sat down again. This refreshing experience, enhanced by the close presence of Kamila and by the park setting, made a deep impression on Janáček who afterwards referred to it continually in his letters to Kamila. Very little extra stimulus was needed—in fact a request from the editors of the *Lidové noviny* for 'some music' for the Sokol gymnastic festival of 1926—for Janáček to write some fanfares of his own. Just as YOUTH had emerged from the MARCH OF THE BLUE - BOYS, so from these fanfares grew, movement after movement, a work about which Janáček reported to Kamila on 29 March 1926 that he was finishing a 'pretty little Symfonietta with fanfares'.**) According to his own words it expresses 'the contemporary free man, his spiritual beauty and joy, his strength, courage and determination to fight for victory'—to defend the young state and its hard-won independence. This explains the dedication ,To the Czechoslovak Armed Forces' as well as the original title *Military Symfonietta.* Janáček insisted on this title and when before the Prague première he saw it called in the programme *Sokol Symfonietta* he protested vigorously 'No *Sokol*—MILITARY SYMFONIETTA!' although he had in fact composed it for the Sokol festival. In the same programme he jotted down the following titles for the movements: 1 Fanfares. 2 The Castle. 3 The Queen's Monastery. 4 The Street. 5 The Town Hall.

At first sight these titles are bewildering. The Queen's Monastery points to Brno, while the Castle and the Town Hall, although unspecified, seem rather to point to Prague. Fortunately there is a clue to this typical Janáček mystery at the end of his article of 24 December 1927 called 'My Town'.

---

*) According to Rektorys (*The Correspondence of Leoš Janáček and Max Brod*, p. 202).

**) Owing among other things to the number of movements in a sinfonietta, its form is some-times classified under suite. However, since the first movement of Janáček's SINFONIETTA is no more than an intrada, there are in this work only the usual four movements—Allegro, Adagio, Scherzo and Finale—and they also transcend the more intimate format of the suite by their character. On the other hand the work is hardly a symphony, and Janáček could not, therefore, have chosen a more fitting title. It is interesting that he ends with a return of the festive introduction (his favourite 'da capo' form) as Tchaikovsky did in his String Serenade in C major, opus 48—a work which Janáček had once conducted in Brno and which he admired more than any other of Tchaikovsky's orchestral compositions. He was to use a similar device in his GLAGOLITIC MASS.

322

After recalling the small, inhospitable Brno of the Austro-Hungarian days, Janáček ends with the words:

'And then I saw the town undergo a miraculous change. I lost my dislike of the gloomy Town Hall, my hatred of the hill from whose depths so much pain was screaming, my distaste for the street and its throng. As if by a miracle, liberty was conjured up, glowing over the town—the rebirth of 28 October 1918. I saw myself in it. I belonged to it. And the blare of the victorious trumpets, the holy peace of the Queen's Monastery, the shadows of night, the breath of the green hill and the vision of the growing greatness of the town, of my Brno, were all giving birth to my SINFONIETTA.'

This is the key to the mystery of the titles: Here we have the Brno Town Hall—now become Czech; the castle on the hill is the notorious Špilberk with its dungeons; and the Brno streets with their new, free life.

The first movement consists entirely of fanfares scored for a special brass ensemble of nine trumpets, two tenor tubas and two bass trumpets with two pairs of timpani. The fanfares are a good example of Janáček's way of gradually hatching his motifs. From the tubas' ostinato in fifths:

there develops first another ostinato, this time in the timpani, but similarly reminiscent of the chiming of bells:

and then this fanfare for the trumpets:

which is at once combined with the two previous motifs, and then gives rise to a speeded up variant:

as well as an augmented maestoso:

Finally, this is gradated by canonic imitation.

Remembering the concert in Písek, Janáček not only asks the musicians to play standing up, but also expressly states that they should be members of a military band, even though he later dropped the word 'military' from the work's title.

The main idea of the second movement is this burlesque, dance-like tune for the oboes:

394

which is introduced by a simultaneous diminution of its own material (drawn from bar four) in the clarinets, and augmentation in the trombones:

395

The introductory demi-semiquaver figuration then accompanies a lyrical melody 'meno mosso' which is, in fact, an augmentation and development of it. Then a seemingly new tune appears which turns out to be a derivation from the repeated-note hammering of the doubled E's of the same clarinet figure (from Ex. 395):

396

This is yet another proof that Janáček did not arrive at his motivic variants by mere speculation, but did so as a full-blooded musician drawing on the living sound and its natural beat and cadence.

This 'new' theme and its fragment (bracketed in Ex. 396) provide the material for a steeply gradated development leading to trumpet fanfares in a slow, triumphal maestoso—fanfares which are nothing else than a festive-sounding variant of the main theme (Ex. 394) with the fragment from Ex. 396, suitably enlarged, fluttering once again above in a 'flag-over-the-castle-ramparts' manner:

397

After a gradated repetition in G flat and even A flat major, shimmering figures in the violins and the harp usher in and then accompany a reappearance of the main 'dance-like' idea in a new form with an enlargement attached to the

324

front of it. It seems to conjure up the blissful vision of wide open countryside. One last reminiscence of the fanfares, now subdued ('con sordini' and *pp*), and a brief and buoyant return of the burlesque dance-tune with the clarinet figuration from the opening, bring the movement sharply to an end.

If the lyrical element is present even in this movement, it is all the more pronounced in the charming third movement describing, as the title suggests, the night in and around the Old Brno Queen's Monastery of the composer's youth. The dominant pedal, low E flat in the tuba and the bass clarinet, seems to spread darkness over the earth while the muted violins and cellos play a sweetly yearning melody in parallel octaves intertwined with a soothing arpeggio figuration in the violas and the harp. After making a beautiful cadence in C flat minor, the melody passes in turn to other instruments underscoring the peaceful mood, until it subsides in open octaves in flutes and cellos. Suddenly the trombones break in with a dark and defiant syncopated motif:

398

suggestive, perhaps, of the shadows of the night. Close on its hees comes the whirling and hissing figure of the flutes and piccolo—a diminution of the earlier soothing arpeggio. The yearning melody returns in an intensified form only to be cut short by the trombones once more. The first trombone brusquely takes over the opening motif to an um-pah-pah accompaniment of the other trombones and the tuba. We can almost hear the swishing of the whip as this caricature assumes the character of a wild chase. When it passes, and after a final whirl in the flutes and piccolo, the nostalgic nocturnal melody makes a diffident reappearance.

The main and, in fact, the only theme of the fourth movement:

399

both by its character and by its 14 repetitions gives the impression of being some sort of fanfare call to a parade, but is related through its final notes D flat— E flat to the dance-like theme of the second movement. Here, too, there is no shortage of musical jokes (the movement takes the place of a scherzo)— for instance, the headlong entries of the trumpets and bells (five bars before, and at reh. No. 6) brought under control by the weight of the tutti, or the sudden prestos and the no less sudden, innocent-looking adagios, and all of it strictly and organically derived from bars one, two and four of the theme.

The fifth and last movement (Town Hall) begins with a chorus of three flutes playing a wistful, minor variant of the fanfare call from the previous movement (perhaps a joyless memory of the past?). This is interrupted in a grumpy manner by a diminution of its final notes:

400

The first three notes of the flute theme are steeply gradated over figurations in the cellos until an agitated but jubilant diminution is reached (compare the bracketed notes), soaring over sextuplet chords in the upper strings:

401

When the last tempestuous crisis is resolved, 12 trumpets in unison announce the return of the festive fanfares from the opening of the work, this time richly embroidered by fluttering trills in the rest of the orchestra, and culminating in a short coda reminiscent, by its massive power, of the conclusion of TARAS BULBA.

This may not be a coincidence since in TARAS BULBA it was a declaration wrung from pain to express faith in the indomitable strength of the Russian people, while here it is a joyful declaration of faith in the youthful power of Janáček's own resurrected nation.

It was at this time that Janáček began to be known abroad, especially through performances of his opera JENŮFA. In 1922 it was given for the first time in Yugoslavia (on 29 June, conducted by a Czech, Milan Sachs, in Zagreb and on 28 October—Czechoslovak Independence Day—in Ljubljana); in 1926 in Poland (17 March in Poznań and 30 March in Lvov, conducted by Milan Zuna) and again in 1930 in Warsaw (22 January, conducted by Stermich-Valcrociata). Apart from the opera houses already mentioned (Vienna, Berlin, New York), it was performed in German in Switzerland (Basel, 30 October 1925), in Cologne (16 November 1918 conducted by Otto Klemperer), in Frankfurt (11 December 1923 conducted by Ludwig Rottenberg and produced by W. Brügmann), in Breslau (today Wrocław in Poland, 14 November 1925 conducted by Mehlich and produced by Lothar Wallerstein), in Aachen, Altenburg, Magdeburg, Bremen, Danzig, Darmstadt, Dessau, Erfurt, Freiburg, Gera, Wiesbaden (21 January 1926), Karlsruhe, Hamburg, Düsseldorf, Coburg, Nuremberg, Augsburg, Essen, Weimar and other places, as well as the two main German theatres in Czechoslovakia—in Prague (23 October 1926 conducted by Zemlinsky) and three days later (26 October) in Brno. Altogether JENŮFA was performed that year in about 70 different opera houses.

Most important for Janáček, however, was the invitation to visit, in the spring of 1926, England where he was little known although, as has been mentioned, the tenor Mischa Léon had sung his DIARY there on 27 October 1922, and in October 1923 Sir Henry Wood had conducted THE FIDDLER'S CHILD. (In the autumn of 1928 he was to introduce TARAS BULBA to England.) Janáček was, as Jan Mikota who travelled with him as his secretary and interpreter has pointed out,*) 'after forty years, the first Czech composer since Antonín Dvořák to be invited to England.' This was due mainly to the good offices of Mrs Rosa Newmarch who did a great deal to spread the knowledge of Czech and Slovak music in England. She knew Janáček personally.**) She had gone to Czechoslovakia in the summer of 1919 at the invitation of Karel Kovařovic who wished to repay her for her tireless efforts earlier in publicizing the official tour of Britain (followed by a visit to Paris), undertaken at the time of the Peace Conference by representative Czech musical bodies including the Prague National Theatre Orchestra which was conducted by Kovařovic. In Czechoslovakia Mrs Newmarch and her daughter, accompanied by Karel Kovařovic and the director of the Vesna College, František Mareš, visited the Slovácko region and on the feast day of SS Cyril and Methodius at Velehrad saw a variety of colourful Slovácko costumes.

On returning to England Mrs Newmarch was instrumental in forming a committee of prominent English musicians to look after Janáček and introduce him to English musical circles. The members of the committee were: Director of the Royal College of Music, Sir Percy Allen, Principal of the Royal Academy of Music, Sir John McEwen, Sir Adrian Boult, at that time conductor of the City of Birmingham Symphony Orchestra who had also met Janáček earlier when, in May 1925 during the International Festival of Contemporary Music in Prague, he had conducted Vaughan Williams' Pastoral Symphony. Then there was Vaughan Williams himself, Sir Henry Wood, Miss Fanny Davies, the pianist who had on a number of occasions played with the Bohemian Quartet, and, of course, Rosa Newmarch.

The committee sent their invitation through the Czechoslovak Embassy in London and Janáček, who had just spent the Easter holidays in the Tatra mountains in Slovakia, resting after his work on the SINFONIETTA which he had completed on Maundy Thursday 1 April 1926, left on the 28th of the same month for England.

On Saturday 1 May the first rehearsal of the VIOLIN SONATA took place at the house of Adila Fachiri, granddaughter of the famous Joachim, who played the violin part and in the afternoon the FAIRY-TALE was rehearsed at the house of H. C. Colles, music critic of *The Times*. In the evening Janáček went to the Gobelin restaurant with Sir Henry and Lady Wood and Mrs and Miss Newmarch, Sir Henry inviting Janáček to spend Sunday afternoon at his country house and offering him the use of his car.

On Sunday morning the other works on the planned programme were rehearsed at the Czechoslovak Embassy. Just as at the reception at Claridges the night before, Janáček surprised everyone by his untiring freshness and

*) 'Leoš Janáček in England', *Listy Hudební matice*, Vol. V, p. 257.
**) In addition to a number of interesting articles in the British press, she was later to write a book, *The Music of Czechoslovakia* (London, 1942). Janáček dedicated his SINFONIETTA to her.

by the spirited way in which he made corrections in the parts and indicated the tempi in his QUARTET and his sextet YOUTH. His vigour seemed to communicate itself to the artists and a most significant difference could be discerned between the first run-through and the playing after Janáček's interventions.*)

In the afternoon Janáček visited Sir Henry Wood at Apple Tree Farm—his country home 20 miles from London, returning in the evening by car to London to attend a reception at the Czechoslovak Club. There he delivered this speech:

'Here I am in London. How and why? Believe me, I do not know. I feel like the Czech Johnny of the fairy-tale who leaves home and makes good. Once he even brought back a princess. But let me tell you the reason. I come with the youthful spirit of my country, with her youthful music. I am not one to look back; I prefer to look ahead. I know that we must grow, but I do not regard pain, memories of suffering and oppression, as being necessary for growth. Let us put them aside. Let us forget the past and let us once and for all realize that we must look into the future. We are a nation which should have a definite place in the world. We are the heart of Europe. And Europe needs to feel its heart.

'And now, who asked me to come? Was it a Czech? No, it was Mrs Newmarch. Someone from a quite different nation. And yet she has something in common with our people. She likes them and loves their music. She has taken a bit of a fancy to mine and knows how to publicize it. I am astonished to see how much good one person can do. Believe me, whole societies often cannot do what she has done. Appreciate her and see to it that she remains your friend. Much remains to be done here in London. May God grant her, too, a long life.

---

*) Janáček himself described his experiences in an article 'Sea, Land' (*Lidové noviny*, 13 June 1926) in which he searched for the cause of a certain reserve in the English musicians' performance and temperament, putting it down to the influence of the 'endless expanse of the sea'. (During a stormy Channel crossing, while others 'crawled like susliks into the more hospitable innards of the ship', Janáček stayed on deck exposing himself to the 'sea's rejuvenating influence', and, just as later at Flushing, made a number of sketches—not only musical ones, but also drawings depicting, for instance, a ship as if entering a wall of water.) He wrote in his article: 'The wide expanses of space evoke in the mind long stretches of time and broad, attenuated planes of emotion. This is my explanation for the English partiality for music that has been and gone—the conservatism of the English musical mind. The sea erodes and raises the banks of human nature—including the artistic nature of man: English, northern man. In league with the sea are the cold and the yellow fog. There is a correctness in the English way of drawing the bow across the string, in the blowing of the woodwind player, in the touch of the pianist. It is as if their mind was preoccupied all the time with sizing up: they discriminate the correct shades of tempo, they straighten out the tongues of the flame of power. But the warmth of emotion is not to be kindled by sticking to these marked out surfaces of pitch, timbre or idea. It is to be found in their tone. The greatest beauty of tone remains cold if the artist lacks the impulse to break without necessarily breaking, to well up without brimming over, to languish without dying, to burn without being consumed by fire, to hurry without overdoing the hurrying. The only such artist (who did not lack this impulse) was Miss Adila Fachiri, Joachim's granddaughter, playing my sonata.'

It is scarcely necessary to add that since those days English musical life has made undoubted strides forward.

'My work is no great strain. I cannot say I feel tired. I can write the things that are to be performed here in one evening, or in two or three days. But there are also works which take many years. One day you may hear them in London. They are operas. In them alone can the nation be known as it really is—firm, steadfast, unflinching—in its true likeness.'

On Monday afternoon Janáček went for a ride in the Underground and did some sightseeing. He was fortunate since on the following day the General Strike broke out and he might have missed some impressions which, according to his own words, were unique. The same day Janáček received a letter from the publishers of *Who's Who*. Their questionnaire was so thorough-going, it even asked Janáček about his likes and dislikes, his personal peculiarities, his telephone number, cable address, and even car number.

Before that, Janáček visited the Zoo which proved to be an absolute treasure trove for his collection of *nápěvky*—sketches of melodic curves. He stayed over half an hour at Monkey Hill noting down the cries of joy and sorrow of the various monkeys, and a further 20 minutes at the seals' pond watching a walrus who crawled onto a rock bellowing plaintively. Throughout the journey his notebook was always at the ready; for instance, he noted down the word 'yes' in 20 different ways. He even took down the speech melodies of the page-boy at the Langham hotel where he and his secretary Jan Mikota were staying.

In the afternoon he attended an orchestral rehearsal for students, conducted by Sir Henry Wood, which he found very interesting.

In the evening the School of Slavonic Studies and the Czech Society of Great Britain gave a small but festive reception in Dr Janáček's honour at the University building in Malet Street. The boys of the L.C.C. Mansfield Road School, Gospel Oak, under their headmaster J. B. Miles (they were among the best boys' choirs in London and had sung for George V at the opening of Ken Wood on 18 July 1925) sang English choral music from Byrd and Wilbye to Purcell and Hayes. First they sang some rounds and canons, then Hayes' 1767 composition *O come sweet Music*, then some seventeenth-century songs including *Cold's the Wind and Wet's the Rain*, then some glees and madrigals such as Thomas Morley's *Now is the Month of Maying*, Jeremy Savile's seventeenth-century *Here's a Health unto His Majesty*, William Cornyshe's fifteenth-century *Blow thy Horn, Hunter*, and Purcell's *Nymphs and Shepherds*. Herbert Hayner then sang some solo songs as well as two of Janáček's *Silesian Songs* in Rosa Newmarch's translation: No. 5 which she entitled *The Teamster* and No. 10, *Mowing in the Woods*, and the boys performed *The Lass that Loves a Sailor* which had to be repeated no less than three times. The programme ended with a speech on Anglo-Czech cultural relations by Professor Seton Watson who welcomed Janáček in the name of the Czech Society of Great Britain.

'Janáček then took the floor,' writes Jan Mikota, 'and gave an enthusiastic, in places dramatic speech, gesticulating with his hands, his eyes shining. The English had certainly never heard Czech spoken in such a way. I have already mentioned that he astonished everyone by his untiring freshness and his agility. In this speech he gave proof of both. I can still feel the youthful impression of his appearance as he stood with his legs apart in front of the guests who stared at him as if spellbound. Behind him the eight- to ten-year-old singers, on his left the modest Dr Císař from the Czechoslovak Embassy who acted as Janáček's interpreter and who did the simultaneous translation into English, and Janáček himself, greatly moved.' Janáček said:

'I do not come with a tongue but with works of music. I feel as though I were at home. When I saw these little singers singing so beautifully, I thought to myself, it is just like home. And why home? The folk song. I have lived with folk song ever since my childhood. Each folk song contains the whole man: his body, his soul, his surroundings, everything. He who grows up among folk songs, grows into a complete man. I have English folk songs. I have folk songs of all nations, and if I were to make a Czech, English, French or any other folk song without telling you where it came from, you would not be able to tell.*) The spirit of folk song is indivisible because all pure men endowed with a God-given culture belong to it—not men who have had culture grafted onto them. This is why I believe that if our music grows out of the same folk roots it will bind us all together. Folk song binds the people, nations, all of humanity together. This is why I am so glad that I have heard English folk songs here. They have brought me close to the soul of England and have made me her friend.

'There is something else I would like to say. There is not only the folk song, there is also our native tongue. They told me that the English language is ugly: now when I hear it, I find it has a beautiful melody. And when you put the two resources together—the folk song and the beautiful words with the whole culture of the language—then I am confident that real classical music is growing here, and not the kind which ignores man and his surroundings and sees only the acoustic tone. If I grow at all, then I grow only from folk song, from human speech, and I am confident that I shall grow up. I laugh at those who come to me with nothing else but acoustic tones.

'Finally—I do not want to prolong the programme—but I want to thank all those who have received me so kindly and who, as I see, feel with me and understand me. Not all men understand each other. An educated German once said to me: "What, you have grown from folk music? That shows a lack of culture." As though man on whom the sun shines, the moon pours its light, as though everything that encompasses him were not a cultural force, a part of culture. I turned away and left the man standing where he was.'

'As 4 May was thus drawing to an end,' continues Mikota, 'we began to feel the effects of the strike. There were no taxis and although, thanks to the Czechoslovak Ambassador, we were driven back to the hotel, we were worried about the outcome of Thursday's concert.

'Next day, Wednesday 5 May, Countess Lützow gave a lunch for Janáček and presented him with a book on her husband who was a great friend of the Czechs. Lord Treowen invited Janáček to his estate in Wales to enable him to study Welsh folk songs. The other guests included Lady Curry, Mrs Newmarch, Miss Dixon the novelist, Mr Young, and Dr Císař.

'In the evening the ambassador, Jan Masaryk, called for Janáček and took him to dine with Professor Seton Watson who surprised Janáček not only by

---

*) This, like so many of Janáček's remarks, should not be taken literally.

his large collection of pictures by Moravian painters but also by his thorough knowledge of conditions in Moravia and Slovakia.'

It was a miracle that the concert next day took place at all. The Wigmore Hall was not as full as had been expected for all transport was at a standstill and only those who had their own cars could attend. But the success was very real and sincere, especially since those who were present had come out of true interest. Thanks were due also to the unparalleled loyalty of the performers: Leon Goossens, the oboe player, had to walk for three hours to reach Wigmore Hall in time. Some members of the Woodhouse String Quartet had to do the same. In spite of these difficulties and the understandable tension in the air, the concert went exceedingly well.

After the STRING QUARTET had been played and again after the VIOLIN SONATA the composer was repeatedly called to the platform. Owing to the strike, no programmes had been printed, and the concert manager Fred Williams announced each work in turn and gave its details, when it had been written, who was playing it, and so on.

Then came the main work on the programme, the sextet for wind instruments—excellently played as it was by the London Wind Quintette with Mendelsssohn Draper (bass clarinet)—YOUTH, which completely captured the audience. The concert ended with the FAIRY-TALE for cello and piano played by Mr Mannucci accompanied by Fanny Davies who had earlier accompanied Adila Fachiri in the VIOLIN SONATA. The CONCERTINO which should have ended the programme had to be left out on account of insufficient rehearsals. Thus according to Janáček himself 'the strongest thing to end the programme with was missing.'*)

On the return journey Janáček stayed for two days at Flushing in Holland where he rested after his arduous visit to London which, in spite of his vitality, had made him considerably tired. Holland had an excellent effect on him. Here he found peace, there was the sea and the sound of the surf, an excursion to Domburg Spa, a visit to Middelburg, there was the Dutch countryside, the amiable country people—it all made such a strong impression that it almost made him forget London.

Although only one aspect of Janáček's output had been presented in London, his visit to England was of great importance in spreading knowledge of his work abroad. His choral music was soon to be performed in England in the autumn of the same year by the Prague Teachers' Choir conducted by Method Doležil, and, much later, by the Moravian Teachers at the International Eisteddfod in Llagollen in 1948;**) but the London performance of JENŮFA planned for the following year did not take place until 30 years later.

After his return, Janáček was feasted on 12 May at the new Umělecká Beseda (Artists' Club) where once again the almost 72-year-old composer made a speech full of vitality and charm—one of his most delightful. Just as he had done in London, he began with the modest admission that he did

---

*) As soon as the pianist's insufficient knowledge of the work became apparent, Ilona Kurzová-Štěpánová was wired in Prague, but the telegram was returned as undelivered.
**) Both these choirs sang MARYČKA MAGDÓNOVA and the 70,000. At the first official festival of Czechoslovak music in Great Britain in 1919 Janáček was not represented.

not know how, after such men as Haydn and Dvořák, he had come to be invited to England. Haydn had gone there with his symphonies, Dvořák with his oratorios, while he had taken only 'such little trifles which—as one professor has written—I write "easily and quickly" after Vymazal'.*) Here Janáček's facetious tone suddenly sharpened and with a youthful glow in his eye and an energetic thump of his fist on the table he declared amid general applause: 'Yes, gentlemen, I write easily and quickly!'

And now, on 15 May, six years after Prague, his EXCURSIONS were at last put on also in Brno—or, at least, one of them, MR BROUČEK's EXCURSION TO THE MOON. It was conducted by František Neumann and produced by Ota Zítek. Since the work is difficult, and since in those days theatres, with the exception of the National Theatre, suffered from financial insecurity, one cannot be surprised at such half-hearted treatment of the EXCURSIONS. It was long after Janáček's death, in 1937, that Milan Sachs put the matter right. What is more surprising, most critics in Brno—Janáček's Brno—found the omission of half the opera to be an asset!

But now a further success came from abroad, from Berlin, where the Charlottenburg City Opera put on KATYA KABANOVA. (This was not the first German performance, since Klemperer had conducted it on 8 December 1922 in Cologne.)

On this occasion Janáček went to Berlin in time for the dress rehearsal which took place on 29 May. The première conducted by Fritz Zweig was on Monday 31 May and Janáček said about it in Berlin: 'I did not imagine it could be so beautiful. In this production today, I think I heard my opera for the first time and, for the first time, understood it myself.' In the same sense he wrote to Max Brod from Hukvaldy: 'A wonderful performance which is beyond our dreams in Prague or Brno.' He also mentions it in the article 'Sea, Land' in *Lidové noviny*: 'Katya goes to the fatal rendezvous. The ingenious conductor put into her shuddering steps a stillness, both in the orchestra and on the stage, a stillness which then congealed into a nucleus, an unusual theme: a rest. And how the storm in Act III thundered in an orchestra of 95 players! Such performances dazzle.' The success of the work before an audience which included the composers Schrecker and Schönberg, the conductor of the Berlin JENŮFA Kleiber, the singers Jeritza and Jurjewskaya, as well as the film star Brigitte Helm, is borne out by the fact that both the City and the State opera companies wanted to produce Janáček's MAKROPOULOS CASE straight away. Otto Klemperer did, in fact, intend to put on THE MAKROPOULOS CASE with the Berlin Kroll Opera, but his plans came to nothing because—according to Dr Julius Kapp, dramaturge of the Berlin State Opera—Barbara Kemp refused to sing the principal part—a part which might have made her a second Jeritza.

---

*) 'Easily and Quickly' was the subtitle of popular language courses published by František Vymazal. The words became a term implying a slap-dash approach.

(4 I) 'Glagolitic Mass'

Let our composers grow wings large enough to carry them far,
that they may drink the waters of all the Slavs.
Perhaps only this can satisfy the composer's soul.

Janáček: Questions and Answers*)

An event equalling in importance the Berlin production of KATYA KABANOVA
was the subsequent first performance of Janáček's SINFONIETTA by the Czech
Philharmonic Orchestra conducted by Václav Talich on 26 June in Prague
on the occasion of the eighth all-Czechoslovak festival of the Sokol gymnastic
association. At the fourth festival of the International Society for Contemporary
Music in Zurich between 18 and 23 June Janáček was not represented and
did not attend.

Shortly afterwards, however, a minor event took place which pleased him
very much. On 11 July a memorial plaque was unveiled on the house of his
birth in Hukvaldy. The celebrations for this event began the day before,
Saturday, with a lunch at nearby Kopřivnice, a little town with better facilities
for putting up guests from Brno, Ostrava, and other places all over Moravia.
After speeches by the mayor of Kopřivnice, the mayor of Hukvaldy (Janáček's
schoolmate Sobotík), and the director of the Brno *conservatoire* Jan Kunc,
Janáček took the floor. Why, he said, was it so important to him that here,
in his native district, his works should be heard well played? Because they
were a part of the countryside which gave him birth. Whoever comes to know
that part of the world with its changeable weather, its frequent storms followed by the reappearance of the golden sun, whoever comes to know the people,
quick tempered but good-natured, its speech, its soul, he will understand what
it was that bound Janáček's work to his native district. The composer wanted
his music to be as close as possible to the soul of the Czech people. And Janáček
went on:

'YOUTH—the CONCERTINO—SINFONIETTA. I think I succeeded best in getting
as close as possible to the mind of the simple man in my latest work, my
SINFONIETTA. I would like to continue on that road. Although I am getting
on in years, I have a feeling that a new vein is beginning to grow in my work;
a new branch. Just as happens to the four- or five-hundred-year-old trees of
Hukvaldy. One looks and notices—there is a young twig growing from the side
of a tree. My latest creative period is also a kind of new sprouting from the
soul which has made its peace with the rest of the world and seeks only to be
nearest to the ordinary Czech man.'

In the evening two concerts took place, both crowded although they were
given almost simultaneously. At Hukvaldy musicians from Ostrava under the
aegis of Janáček's pupil František Míťa Hradil performed the FAIRY-TALE,

---

.*) 'Otázky a odpovědi', a feuilleton by Janáček in the paper *Lidové noviny*, 5 February 1922

the VIOLIN SONATA and some folk songs, while at Kopřivnice artists from Brno (the Moravian Quartet, Dr Ludvík Kundera, Stanislav Tauber and Ludmila Kudláčková) performed the FIRST QUARTET, the cycle IN THE MISTS and THE DIARY OF THE YOUNG MAN WHO DISAPPEARED, and the local choral society sang some of Janáček's choruses such as the amusing EVENING WITCH, IF YOU KNEW and others.

The Sunday celebrations at Hukvaldy were marred by heavy rain which had been pouring continuously since the evening before. For this reason the speeches had to be made in the dance-hall at Mičaník's—the local inn. Once more Janáček confessed that, in spite of his growing fame abroad, he treasured performances of his works at home even under far more modest circumstances. He said:

'People say that I have achieved something. An artist's work is seldom praised or even noticed and yet it is so important. When I now and again write something which I know is enjoyed far away from here, perhaps in South Bohemia in Písek or in the West in Plzeň or in the North in Mladá Boleslav or in the East or in Moravia or Slovakia, then it occurs to me that there is something in the power of art after all; that I have plucked at a string which resounds everywhere, which ties us all together so that we feel as one nation. This is what I value in my own art, and the most important thing is that it binds us together, that it makes us strong and defiant and proof against everything in the world. Everything else, the notes, that to me is secondary. If I can unite our nation which is so irate, so quarrelsome and disunited, if I have done this, then I feel I have not lived in vain.'

Then despite the pouring rain everyone went outside, the plaque was unveiled, the choir sang and it was all over. Janáček had been particularly impressed by the presence of the Archbishop of Olomouc Dr Leopold Prečan whose summer residence was at Hukvaldy and who had not only listened to all the speeches indoors but had stood in the rain until the end of the unveiling ceremony.

If the rain at Hukvaldy was inconvenient, at Luhačovice less than a month later (from 2 August onwards) its result was all the more positive—the composition of one of Janáček's most magnificent works, the GLAGOLITIC MASS.

'The Luhačovice rain pours and pours,' wrote Janáček in his article *Glagolskaja missa.**) 'You look out of the window at the gloomy Komonec mountain. The clouds are rolling. The wind tears them up, drives them about, just like a month ago outside the school at Hukvaldy. The darkness thickens. You peer into the dark night cut up by lightning. You light the flickering electric bulb in the high ceiling. There is nothing for it but to sketch the quiet motif of a desperate frame of mind to the words *Gospodi pomiluj* (Lord have mercy); to cry with joy *Slava, slava* (Glory, glory); there is agonizing pain in the motif *Raspet že za ny, mučen i pogreben byst* (Crucified for our sake, martyred and buried); steadfastness of faith and oath in *Věruju* (I believe); exultation and emotional exuberance are rounded off with *Amin, amin* (Amen, amen); sanctity is praised in *Svet, svet* (Holy, Holy), *Blagoslovl'en* (Blessed is he) and in *Agneče Božij* (Lamb of God).

---

*) *Lidové noviny,* 27 November 1927.

'Free from the gloom of the motifs of mediaeval monastery cells, free from the echoes of imitative parallelism, Bach's fugal 'tangles', Beethoven's pathos, Haydn's playfulness; against the paper barriers of Witt's reforms which have estranged us from Křížkovský.'

The evening storm at Luhačovice provided of course only the external stimulus and perhaps the mood for writing the GLAGOLITIC MASS, which according to Janáček's article took him only three weeks to compose.*)

In fact this work may be said to have been slumbering in Janáček's mind since the July days of 1869 when as a scholar at the Old Brno monastery he took part in the millenary celebrations at Velehrad of the death of St Cyril. Thus in the MASS Janáček reached out to Křížkovský who not only had organized that excursion to Velehrad and conducted the singing of the Blue-boys on that occasion but had also composed a cantata of his own in honour of SS. Cyril and Methodius. As Janáček's own words show,**) the cult of these two saints meant much to him: 'It has occurred to me that what is lacking in the year 1928***) is the Cyril-Methodius atmosphere. That is why I want to contribute my work in this year. I have, as a matter of fact, had it ready since 1926.'

However, the GLAGOLITIC MASS is not a religious work in the usual sense

---

*) I have been given some interesting details of how Janáček came to write the MASS by Father Josef Martínek, a retired teacher of religious knowledge:

'It was probably at the beginning of the school year 1921-2 when Janáček told me before a lesson to wait for him afterwards because he wanted to ask me something. When the students had gone he told me that he had met Archbishop Prečan and Mgre Jan Šrámek, leader of the Catholic People's Party and a government Minister, somewhere in Hukvaldy—perhaps while walking in the woods. At first they had talked about ordinary things but soon the conversation turned to music. Janáček told the archbishop that he had been to a service in a nearby church and that the music there had been poor. This was only a few years after the war, teachers had given up organ playing and the job was being taken up by amateurs or half-baked players without proper qualifications. To Janáček's talk of a decline in church music, Archbishop Prečan said: "Well, Maestro, why don't you write something worthwhile?" Janáček did not tell me what his answer had been, but he did say to me that he did not want to compose to a Latin text. "If only I could get hold of an Old Slavonic one! But I don't have one and don't even know where to look for one." He then asked me to help him to find it. I told him that this would be easy since I had the Old Slavonic text, in fact two copies of it, and I promised to bring it to my next lesson, which I did. The two copies were identical except that one of the texts, published in the church music magazine *Cyril*, had been edited by an authority on Old Church Slavonic, Dr Josef Vajs, giving the accented syllables in bold type. This was the text I recommended to Janáček, and I lent it to him so that he could copy it out for himself. And this was the text that he used in the composing of his GLAGOLITIC MASS.' He composed the MASS five years later, and it certainly took him more than three weeks. In a letter to Václav Mikota, director of the Hudební matice publishing house, dated 31 August, Janáček asked him for the Old Slavonic text admitting that he used to have his own copy—clearly, Janáček had mislaid it—and on 2 September Jaroslav Dušek sent him a copy of *Cyril* of 1921 containing Dr Vajs' article 'Masses in Honour of the Patron Saints in the Old Slavonic Language'. Then on 14 September he sent him another copy of *Cyril*, this time the 1920 edition, containing the official text of the Glagolitic Mass. Its setting to music was completed on 15 October.

**) In an interview which he gave to a correspondent of the magazine *Literární svět* (The Literary World) a day after the March 1928 Prague première of THE MAKROPOULOS CASE.

***) The tenth anniversary of Czechoslovak Independence, followed a year later by the millenary of the martyrdom of St Wenceslas, the Czech prince and patron saint.

of the word, although the Old Slavonic text is, except for a few minor cuts, the same as that of the Latin Mass, and the Roman Catholic Church exceptionally allows its liturgical use on the two Saints' day, 5 July. Janáček himself was unwilling to admit that the work was in any sense religious, and when a Brno critic wrote that 'Janáček, now an old man and a firm believer, feels with increasing urgency that the expression of his relationship to God must not be missing from his life's work,' the irate composer sent him a postcard with the laconic 'No old man, no believer'. Later on he used to add: 'Till I see for myself.'*) In the March 1928 interview he explained his real motives thus: 'I wanted to portray the nation's faith not on a religious basis but on a strong moral one which calls God to witness.'

God after all? (He had called Him to witness on the last pages of JENŮFA also.) Let me not try to catch Janáček out but rather focus the attention on what the music itself has to say. It is above all typical that Janáček did not set the usual Latin text but the Old Slavonic one translated by St Cyril himself—Janáček, one might say, set his own ancient mother tongue. This is all the more remarkable because for instance Stravinsky at that time was writing his Latin Symphony of Psalms and in his scenic oratorio *Oedipus Rex* even brought Latin back onto the stage where it had until then served the often comic purpose of giving something to say to cameo-part scholars, notaries, physicians and monks. Stravinsky declared Latin to be the language nearest to music on account of its aloofness—an approach entirely opposed to that of Janáček. In addition, a Latin Mass would have clashed with Janáček's theory of speech melodies as well as with the organic development he had undergone in his writing of church music, from his harmonizations of Czech hymns and the Old Czech HOSPODINE, POMILUJ NY (Lord Have Mercy Upon Us) to OUR FATHER and the hymnic scenes in the EXCURSION OF MR BROUČEK TO THE FIFTEENTH CENTURY, not to mention the conclusion of TARAS BULBA. His main reason for choosing the Glagolitic text may have been his instinctive feeling that here he would give full expression to the nation's spiritual and patriotic sentiments and that he could draw strength from the spiritual roots of ancient Slavdom, and inspiration from the long-lost colourful past and unspoilt Nature. He himself best expressed the part played by Nature and legend in the composition of the work:

'Always the scent of the moist Luhačovice woods—that was the incense. I felt a cathedral grow out of the giant expanse of the woods and the sky stretching far into the misty distance. A flock of little sheep were ringing the bells.

'Now I hear the voice of some arch-priest in the tenor solo, a maiden angel in the soprano, and in the choir—our people. The tall firs, their tips lit up

---

*) He was in no hurry to 'see for himself'—he was a self-confessed sufferer from an almost superstitious horror of churches. His niece Věra Janáčková has written about it in her article 'My Uncle and Death' which appeared in the *Lidové noviny* of 11 August 1940: 'At one time he went to church to feel the atmosphere; he liked the Emmaus Monastery in Prague best. In later years I could not get him to step into a church even to shelter from the rain. "A church," he told me, "is concentrated death. Tombs under the floor, bones on the altar, pictures full of torture and dying. Rituals, prayers, chants—death and nothing but death. I don't want to have anything to do with it." '

by the stars, are the candles, and during the ceremony I see the vision of St Wenceslas and I hear the language of the missionaries Cyril and Methodius.'

This, basically, is the same intimate relationship with God which finds expression in the old Czech carols and hymns. Janáček by following this folk tradition, which for him balances out his deviation from conventional church music, arrives at yet another peculiarity of his MASS: he begins and ends it with festive fanfares accompanied by drums (and, of course, orchestra). Before the final Intrada he moreover inserts the usual organ Voluntary. There are many more such novelties, all, however, springing from the Czech folk tradition. Without this novel approach and Janáček's most sincere feelings the result would doubtless have been just a conventional Mass.*)

The fanfares with which the work begins are built from this festive motif in canon:

It is taken up by violins in quaver diminution—a constant which runs through the whole of the first movement, Introduction. A melodic phrase is appended, first in the Mixolydian E flat major of the opening, then in the brighter, more majestic key of C major:

The motif which introduces the second movement (in three sections, *Gospodi pomiluj—Chrste pomiluj—Gospodi pomiluj* corresponding to *Kyrie eleison—Christe eleison—Kyrie eleison* of the Latin Mass):

is the original fanfare shifted to a low register and furnished with narrow dissonances which give it a feeling of contrition and anguish—a feeling soon to be heightened further by a steep cascade, fashioned from the motif's first three notes in diminution.

---

*) This was pointed out by Janáček himself in his criticism of Fibich's *Missa brevis* (*Hudební listy*, Vol. II, No. 8): 'We demand from a composer that he compose religious music under the influence of religious feeling; then it will certainly not result in such pale melodies and harmonies.'

When the choir enters, the motif takes on a more consonant and confident note:

The middle section accentuates the anguished feeling by quickening the tempo and by the urgent repetition of this new motif:

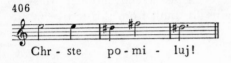

which passes from the solo soprano to the choir fortissimo. With the return of the first section, a balance is struck between the feelings of anxiety and trust.

The solo soprano then opens the all the more joyful third movement, *Slava (Gloria)*, which is built up from an idea incorporating the three main motivic elements of the whole work: the motif of the alternating upper third, the speech melody of the word *Věruju (Credo)*, and those three opening notes of the speech melody *Gospodi pomiluj (Kyrie eleison)*. They are used in the orchestra:

and, later on, in the choir:

(the motif indicated by the middle bracket in Ex. 407 looking forward to the *Credo*). The quaver figure in Ex. 408 gives rise to a busy imitative interlude leading to *Chvalim Te (Laudamus Te)*.

After a lofty postlude to this section glorifying God the Father, a new section glorifying God the Son is prefaced by a softly imploring imitative entry of flute and viola in A flat minor, and by a related staccato figuration of violins and harp, which seems to paint a picture of Christ's crown of thorns:

These instrumental ideas are followed first by this new vocal motif:

410

Vzem-ľej grě-chy mi - ra. (Qui tollis peccata mundi)

and, second, by a full-bodied variant of the opening idea from Ex. 407:

411

Condensed to its last four notes in the *Amen* section *(Amin, amin)*, it then serves to bring the movement to a splendid finish.

The words of the next movement, *Věruju (Credo)*, express in turn faith in God the Father, God the Son and the Holy Ghost, in one Apostolic Church, one christening for the forgiveness of sins, and the expectation of life eternal. The liturgical text dwells on the human figure of Christ—a cue for Janáček looking for the human aspect in every subject, to substantially extend this movement. However, his rendering of the very first word:

412

Vě - ru - ju, vě - ru - - ju (Credo)

differs very considerably from the usual demonstrative unison based on the Gregorian original and found for instance in Beethoven's *Missa Solemnis* or Bach's B minor Mass. Janáček gives the word *Věruju* an expression more of longing for faith than of an ostentatious oath. Only to the subsequent words:

413

v jedi-no-go Bo - ga, Ot - ca vse-mo-guš-ta - go

(in unum Deum, Patrem omnipotentem)

does he lend the feeling of 'steadfastness of faith and oath' by using the same austere motif with which the movement opens.

In the next section concerning Christ himself, Janáček expands melodically the *Věruju* motif in the orchestra:

414

Then, at the words *Boga ot Boga (Deum de Deo)* he develops, from the interval of a third as quoted for instance in the first bar of Ex. 411, a seemingly new melody full of loving, devotional character:

The bracketed chromaticism accompanying the mention of Christ's birth as man provides the material for the subsequent sinuous gradation suggesting the sacrifice for which the Son of God became man. Even the repetitions of the *Věruju* speech melody as well as the 'austere' opening motif now acquire a new warmth of feeling. At last the point is reached when the resolve to bring a sacrifice prevails—the section ends with three sforzato chords of A flat minor, the key signifying Christ's martyrdom throughout the work.

The long symphonic interlude which now follows was explained by Dr Ludvík Kundera in his analysis of February 1928*) as the composer's way of making up by music for the terseness of the text which nowhere describes the events in Christ's rich life before the crucifixion. Kundera's ideas were not contradicted by the composer except perhaps in the music itself— in the derivation of the interlude from the *Věruju* motif. Be that as it may, Kundera saw the three sections of the interlude as follows: one—flute recitative, then cello, accompanied by three clarinets off-stage**)—'Jesus praying in the desert'; two—fanfares built from the main motivic elements of the work (cf. Ex. 407) — 'Christ the sower of bliss':

and three—organ solo—'Christ's agony':

In contrast to this long orchestral interlude, Janáček then, in the chorus, passes almost hastily over the words of the *Crucifixus* which in both Beethoven and Bach form a major vocal section. Nevertheless, the *Crucifixus* represented for Janáček—as we have seen from his own article 'Glagolskaja missa' in the *Lidové noviny*—one of the prime ideas of the work. It seems, therefore, that he was moved by the disturbing content of the text—that, once again, he con-

---

*) *Tempo*, Vol. VII, p. 192.
**) The mysterious indication 'off-stage' (always the stage!) is to be found only in the vocal score, not in the printed full score.

ceived this passage dramatically, rather in the style of the Passions, and that he wanted—as Dr Kundera also maintained—to portray the 'culmination of Christ's human drama in all its realism and horrifying detail.'*)

The next section of the text, *I voskrse (Et resurrexit)*, which in Beethoven or Bach offers a chance of a sudden brightening after the palpably languishing *Crucifixus*, is given to the sopranos and altos piano—they are the voices of the women who have visited Christ's tomb and found it empty, and are bringing the news of the mysterious miracle. But even without such original notions Janáček would have had to set the passage unconventionally, simply to achieve contrast. Not until the solemn *Sědit o desnuju Otca (Sedet ad dexteram Patris)* does he bring in the men's voices forte, modulating from A flat minor (the 'key of Christ's martyrdom') to C flat major.

The section expressing belief in the Holy Ghost is based on the 'steadfastness of faith and oath' motif, this time in an airy piano and at a higher pitch, congealing into a more substantial forte only at the mention of the Prophets. In the final section of the movement the music broadens out, especially where it expresses belief in resurrection and eternal life, into a majestic flow still related to the *Věruju* motif:

I je - di - nu sve - tu - ju (Et unam sanctam)

Its new motivic twist is then used in the final peals of *Amin, amin (Amen, Amen)*:

Janáček joins the next two portions of the Ordinary of the Mass, *Svet (Sanctus)* and *Blagoslovl'en (Benedictus)*, to form one movement. Once again he visualizes the scene as a live one—as Dr Kundera wrote in his analysis, 'Christ the King is walking in the streets, his path strewn with flowers and the crowds chanting "Blessed is he..." (Does not the *Sanctus* of Bach's B minor Mass with its chords of women's voices undulating slowly like the palm fronds of the choirs of angels, and with its trio of bright trumpets make a similar impression?) Janáček follows the custom of giving each sentence of the text a separate section of music, each built from one instrumental and one vocal motif. The *Sanctus* is based on a Bach-like motif of the strings (compare the similar duplet upbeats in the middle section—*Et in terra pax*—of the *Gloria* in the B minor

---

*) It is nonetheless recommended that instead of preceding the *Crucifixus* with a hesitant ritardando, conductors should take the 2/4 section (one bar after reh. No. 230) at half the speed so as to allow the choir to enunciate the words properly, and to give the passage the massive weight that it needs.

Mass, or the last movement of the first part of the *St Matthew Passion*, which happens to be also in E major):

420
Moderato

The instrumental material of the next section, *Plna sut nebo* (*Pleni sunt cæli*), and later the *Benedictus*, consists of two motivic elements:

421
Con moto

Cor.

The upper element is derived from the opening figuration (Ex. 420), while the lower one is a new fanfare-like motif. The vocal material, also fanfare-like, is reminiscent of the *Amin* motif from the end of the *Credo* (bracketed in Ex. 419):

422

Pl - na sut ne - bo, ze - mlja   sla - vy tvo-jej.
(Pleni sunt cæli et terra   gloria tua)

The sixth movement, *Agneče Božij* (*Agnus Dei*), is in three sections. In the first a purely orchestral ritornello, again resembling the Passions in its devout mood, developed from a restrained, tender version of the quaver motif from the previous movement:

423
Adagio

is alternated three times with the humble prayer of the choir 'a cappella':

424
Ag - ne - če Bo - žij, ag - ne - če Bo - žij, po - mi - luj nas!

(Agnus Dei, miserere nobis)

in the melody of which we recognize the first choral entry from the *Gloria* (see Ex. 408). In the middle section the four soloists take turns in singing an

342

afflicted, syncopated setting of *Agneče Božij, vzeml'ej grěchy mira (Agnus Dei, qni tollis peccata mundi)* while the orchestra embroiders the melody of it with its own diminution (see brackets):

A return of the shortened first section closes this Mystery of pain.

With this deeply pious movement the Ordinary of the Mass— and also the participation of the soloists and the choir—comes to an end. What follows are two purely instrumental movements: the organ Voluntary, designed to release the pent-up tension in a veritable hurricane of sound in the form of a thunderous passacaglia on this ostinato motif:

and, finally, the so-called Intrada. (It stood originally at both ends of the work.) With its tumult of quaver movement in octaves suggesting, as it were, an excited throng in festive mood, and with its joyous fanfares:

it seems to cast a shaft of sunshine into the mystical gloom of the church. And in this sense the orchestral finale is an intrada after all—a marching entry into life strengthened by a new certainty and by the preceding display of the Slav spirit.

$\left(42\right)$ Defiance and Humour

Between June and October 1926, about a year after the CONCERTINO and simultaneously with the GLAGOLITIC MASS, Janáček wrote a work which presented him with a further opportunity to explore the concerto form in his own way. This was his CAPRICCIO for piano left hand and wind ensemble— flute (alternating piccolo), two trumpets, tenor tuba (usually replaced by a bass flugelhorn) and three trombones. Janáček wrote this work at the request of the pianist Otakar Hollmann who, having been wounded in the First World War, could only use his left hand. Other Czech composers had already written works for Hollmann, for instance Bohuslav Martinů his *Divertimento* for the left hand. Janáček had at first refused Hollmann's request, but eventually, on 11 November 1926, he wrote to Hollmann telling him that the CAPRICCIO was finished. He added: 'You know, to write just for the left hand would have been childishly gratuitous. More reasons were necessary; subjective and objective. When all these were encountered, the work came into existence.' Thus Janáček composed a Czech counterpart to the four compositions written at almost the same time abroad for the pianist Paul Wittgenstein (1887—1961) who had suffered a misfortune similar to Hollmann's during the war—Ravel and Prokofiev wrote concertos for him,*) and Richard Strauss his *Parergon to the Sinfonia Domestica* (1925) and *Panathenäenzug* (1926—1927).

What were these 'objective and subjective' reasons which induced Janáček to change his mind and compose the CAPRICCIO? From the objective point of view, the most important reason was certainly that having written the CONCERTINO he found he had not exhausted his new ideas for this *genre*. As for the subjective reasons, Jarmil Burghauser in his preface to the published score assumes that Janáček 'was evidently inspired by the stubborn determination and energy of a man who, although maimed in war, did not give up his intended career as a pianist and a serious artist at that. This defiance (the work was originally to have been called *Defiance*) and the clash with the drastic realities of war and its aftermath, form the spiritual content of the work which—with its hard-sounding bass notes of the brass instruments and its mood wavering between gloom and nostalgia and grotesqueness—is the reverse of the joyful SINFONIETTA whose 'military' key signature it shares. Thus the CAPRICCIO may be regarded as Janáček's protest against the senselessness and horrors of war while the soloist—the work's hero—may be said to wage an unflinching struggle with one of war's crimes.'

Burghauser's conception, while seeming to be very typical of Janáček, is probably incorrect, since the composer would hardly have chosen the title

---

*) Wittgenstein never performed Prokofiev's concerto, admitting frankly that he could not manage it.

CAPRICCIO if the work were to express the triumph of heroic endurance—
certainly the opposite of caprice. In addition, this interpretation is not borne
out by anything Janáček himself wrote or said. On the contrary, he remarked
'It is capricious, nothing but pranks and puns.'*)

Dr Bohumír Štědroň**) is probably nearer to the mark when he sees in
the CAPRICCIO 'an expression of peace and joyful contentment at the time
of Janáček's affection for Kamila in defiance of the opinion of the rest of the
world'. Except that there is rather too little peace and joyful contentment
in the work. Only the last movement manages to fight its way through to, if
not peace, then at least joyfulness. In my opinion the sometimes pugnacious,
sometimes embittered, mocking, ironical, nostalgic and again even sceptical
character of the first three movements, with the brighter mood of the finale,
could best be explained as a reflection of Janáček's own struggle as a man and
a composer. It is a struggle seen by now from the point of view of triumphant
success, with the flute (we must bear in mind Janáček's system of not only
motto themes but also motto instruments) representing the hero's beloved who,
in the last movement, lights his way and decorates his head with laurels.

The CAPRICCIO, although for a long time one of Janáček's least
performed works, is in no way inferior to his masterpieces—except perhaps
in its sound, and this may be due to the unusual technique it requires. Today,
this problem has largely been overcome. The first and second trombone
players can help by using the more agile valve instrument as was the composer's
intention in any case. It is a paradox typical oɟ Janáček that while the brass
instruments are presented with some breakneck passages, the most brilliant
instrument of the ensemble, the flute, is given no figuration at all. But there
is a reason for this, as will be seen in the analysis of the score.

The work is in four movements. The first begins with a gloomy theme in the
piano, march-like and stern in character, with soft but incisive chords in the
trombones:

428

Then all of a sudden the piano stops and the off-beat chords of the trombones
change into a sustained, eerie ostinato:

429

Above this the piano enters with an anguished, recitative-like echo of the
introductory theme, which might be called the motif of hope. This is followed
by its own inversion which might be called the motif of denial or, at the least,
doubt:

*) Adolf Veselý: 'Last interview with Leoš Janáček'. Brno *Hudební rozhledy*, 1928.
**) Prague *Hudební rozhledy*, Vol. VI, p. 613.

430

mf espress.

After a hint of a wistful waltz like a seeming reminiscence and some increasingly more curtailed and insistent entries of the motif from Ex. 430 in both its contradictory forms, the middle section is built up in an exciting gradation to a lacerating trumpet cadenza which descends steeply, ushering in a new, much weightier dialogue, maestoso, between 'hope' and 'doubt'. But soon the introductory march returns, followed by the eerie sostenuto of the trombones (this time 'con sordini') and a precipitous stretta. The introductory semiquaver motif dominates until the very end of the movement, where everything freezes once again on the mysterious trombone motif (Ex. 429) with a last sounding of 'hope' in the piano.

The second, slow, movement is again begun by the piano with a resigned melody disturbed repeatedly by the diminution of its fifth bar:

431
Adagio

dolce

Ten. tuba

This diminution, in combination with a wild, derisive motif which is nothing else than the mysterious 'eerie' motif from the first movement wearing a different mask:

432 Vivo

holds sway until a trombone pedal arrests the momentum while the flute makes its first appearance with a recitative-like entreaty addressed, it seems, to the 'wild' motif from the previous example (compare the bracketed segments):

433 Fl.

8va bassa

This, together with the opening motif and a new theme in the piano in the minor, fills up the entire middle section of the movement. Eventually, however, the 'wild' motif (Ex. 432) triumphs, capped by even greater derision than before, until the resigned melody from the opening brings the movement to a close on a note of yet greater resignation.

The third movement is a kind of scherzo in measured 2/8 time unlike the scherzo of the FIRST QUARTET of which it is also thematically reminiscent. If the main theme has humour in it, it is (and the scoring of it is) black humour:

The trombones enter with a reminder—in a modified form—of their 'eerie' croaking motif:

and the muted trumpet, mimicked ironically by the tuba, offers a mysteriously exalted version of the main theme embroidered with glissando-like scales in the piano. The main theme returns briefly in its original would-be humorous form and soon a new agitated section gets under way with the piano scales canonically interwoven. These are overriden, cavalier fashion, by the piano and brass, and gradated to a bright trumpet reprise of the main theme in G flat major (a tone higher than originally, cf. Ex. 434) accompanied by a flute counter-subject, an amiable variant of the 'denial' or 'doubt' motif from the first movement (see Ex. 430):

But the eerie, croaking trombone motif prevails once more: the scales of the piano hurry to and fro as if in fright and the amiable motif is distorted into a grimace. In the closing bars the trombones are joined by the muted trumpet with its mysteriously fanfare-like variant of the main theme. The movement ends with a sultry brass pianissimo in the relative minor of the original key.

Now the flute which, as has been said, plays no virtuoso part in the CAPRICCIO but, as an adversary of the trombones, becomes a harbinger of joy, begins the fourth and last movement straight away with a new theme:

embroidered with its own arpeggio diminution and related to the flute's earlier efforts in the scherzo. But now the mood is irrepressibly buoyant although a hint of anxiety in the second half of the theme makes this final attempt at an optimistic breakthrough all the more exciting. When the second two bars of the main theme give rise to a bracing, manly phrase in the brass:

Maestoso vivo

and when after a stormy piano cadenza dealing with the same material the original theme, splendidly augmented, returns in the bright G flat major over a dominant pedal, we feel that the struggle can no longer be lost—that we are within sight of a new shore. And although the trombones interrupt once more with their tattered motif (see Exs 429, 432 and 435), the flute theme—now in the piccolo and supported by the excited, happy tapping of the trumpets' sextuplets—and its bracing variant (as in Ex. 438) eventually triumph, bringing the work to an end in the key of so many of Janáček's apotheoses—the majestic D flat major.

If this hymnic conclusion qualifies somewhat Janáček's declaration that the CAPRICCIO was 'nothing but pranks and puns', so does the fact that the piano's cadenza in the finale—those chromatic runs of triads sharing the same note in the middle (for example C minor—C flat major, A minor—A flat major and so on)—is similar to the organ solo in the fourth movement of the GLAGOLITIC MASS, corresponding to the *Crucifixus*.

The composition which really is 'nothing but pranks and puns' and easy-going humour is the NURSERY RHYMES for vocal and instrumental ensemble, the final version of which was also completed in this prolific year of 1926.

In the wind sextet YOUTH Janáček turned to his boyhood; in his NURSERY RHYMES he entered the world of little children and—just as in the ADVENTURES OF VIXEN SHARP EARS—the world of the animal folk. The idea to write this 'living natural history', as Josef Plavec amusingly called these miniatures, came once more from the paper *Lidové noviny*. Its children's supplement used to carry charming drawings by Josef Lada, Ondřej Sekora and Rudolf Hála illustrating sayings and nursery rhymes which stirred the imagination by their amusing play on words without necessarily containing any deep meaning or story. During the summer holidays of 1925 Janáček set eight of these rhymes for three women's voices, clarinet and piano. They were performed in Brno on 26 October of the same year. Towards the end of 1926 he enlarged the collection to 18 pieces and extended the vocal and instrumental ensemble to include nine singers and ten players (two flutes—the second alternating piccolo, two clarinets—both also in E flat, two bassoons—the second alternating double-bassoon, ocarina, toy drum, double-bass and piano). Thus Janáček consciously created a Czech, and a more genial, if less demanding, counterpart to the *Pribaoutki, Cat's Cradle Songs* and other similar works of Igor Stravinsky, one of the first modern composers to amuse himself with such charming trivia culled from folk poetry. To the gallery of Leopold Mozart's Toy Symphony, Schumann's *Kinderszenen*, Debussy's *Boîte à joujoux* and Mussorgsky's song-cycle *The Nursery*, Janáček added his own present for the children. However, only the Toy Symphony can actually be played by children themselves. (A modern attempt at a similar thing are Hindemith's *Sing- und Spielmusiken* in his 'children's game' *We are building a Town*.) Janáček's NURSERY RHYMES are not exactly child's play, even for grown-up performers.

The composing of them was no easy matter for Janáček either. As we have seen, even after their first performance they gave him no peace. Perhaps he was prompted to make more of them by the mirthless impressions he formed of the 'humorous' compositions he had heard at the Venice Festival of the International Society for Contemporary Music (3—8 October 1925) where the question of humour in music presented itself in its broader sense and, paradoxically enough, its almost painful seriousness.

'The most effort was wasted on gaiety in music,' he wrote subsequently in *Lidové noviny* on 8 November 1925. 'But all that Arnold Schönberg latched onto in his Serenade, Opus 24 was Viennese strumming; Louis Gruenberg in his *Daniel Jazz*, trumpets and percussion—that was why his works reeked of taverns and their gaiety languished... This music knows how to laugh, but it is a laughter that cannot make you laugh. There is neither wit nor satire, neither humour nor joviality in it... And yet in these days there is such a demand for jolly music!'

That these works constantly reminded him of his own NURSERY RHYMES can be seen from the fact that when outlining his own idea of humour in music he quoted from them.

As has been said, writing them down, however, did not come 'easily and quickly' to Janáček. Having selected and eventually set the rhymes he wanted, he took a long time deciding how to form them into a whole. 'I had no introduction or conclusion and I had to do a lot of thinking before I hit on what to do,' he admitted in an interview with Adolf Veselý.*) How well he solved the problem in the end is shown by the short but eminently suitable introductory march of the definitive version of the work—a march during which the animal (and vegetable) folk seem to be lining up for action:

439

And in the finale the same melody is gradated to a sort of whirling dance of all the animals (one is once again reminded of the VIXEN SHARP EARS)— a caper for the animal folk to gambol off to. In between there are the 18 vocal numbers sung alternately by two sopranos, two contraltos, three tenors and two basses. The first song is still related to the introduction. We hear who it was who made up the nursery rhymes (whose 'fault' it was—the horseradish's, in fact), and then the instruments, through the mouth of the singers, express

---

*) In the article 'Capriccio of a Creator's Autumn' by Adolf Veselý in the paper *České slovo* of 18 November 1926.

their enjoyment at the prospect of the music-making ('diddlee fiddlee, diddlee dumdee')—no wonder, since they play an important part in the humour of the work. Note for instance the funny tone painting in No. 5, 'Trousers, trousers, torn in two, wind is blowing through them', or in No. 6 'Knacker's Frank scrapes on his fat bass' with a drastic double-bass solo and a jolly diminution of the vocal line in the clarinet, or in No. 8 to the couplet 'Came across a cow who seemed to be his mum, Then met a little ox—he seemed to be his dad'. The most striking touch perhaps is the use of the ocarina which warns in the introduction of the magic to come (in No. 9 'Sorcery's old witch's business') and then helps the spells along by impersonating a hooting owl.

Most important of all, the humour is neither artificial nor merely descriptive but the result of the spontaneous joy released at long last deep inside Janáček's soul by his fulfilment as a composer, and of his capacity for entering into the spirit of children's play and in the course of play bringing music to them.

If the full effect of these musical jokes is to be realized, one should not content onself with the version for two or three solo voices, viola (or violin) and piano, even though it was thus reduced by the composer himself. THE NURSERY RHYMES should be performed with their full ensemble. Janáček even went so far as to ask for slides of Josef Lada's drawings in colour to be projected during the performance and wanted to have them printed in the music. During performance, the picture was to precede each number by several seconds, and only after the audience had had time to take it in, was each nursery rhyme to be played.*)

Shortly before Christmas, when the NURSERY RHYMES were finished, this fertile year was crowned on 18 December with the first performance in Brno in the presence of many guests from home and from abroad of THE MAKROPOULOS CASE conducted by František Neumann, produced by Ota Zítek, with scenery by Josef Čapek (brother of the author Karel Čapek) and with Alexandra Čvánová singing the principal part.

During 1927—in contrast to the previous year—Janáček presented no new work to the public. From the beginning of February he was busy on a new opera—which was to be his last—THE HOUSE OF THE DEAD.

In the meantime there was news of further triumphs and honours. During the preceding year, on Sunday 24 January 1926, Janáček's bust in bronze, the last work of the sculptor Jan Štursa, was unveiled in the foyer of the Brno Theatre. A further bust by the sculptor František Hlavica was unveiled on Janáček's seventy-third birthday in the Kotouč Mountain National Park near Štramberk in north-eastern Moravia from where it looked out in the direction of Janáček's native Hukvaldy. Other countries were equally appreciative: On 10 February Janáček was elected a member of the Prussian Academy of Art together with Arnold Schönberg and Paul Hindemith (an honour which had been conferred on only one Czech before, the philologist, ethnographer and archaeologist Pavel Josef Šafařík (1795—1861).**) After the

---

*) Ludvík Kundera, Brno *Hudební rozhledy*, Vol. III, p. 110.
**) By coincidence it was Šafařík who had published a work called *Glagolitische Fragmente* (Prague, 1857).

success of JENŮFA on 8 January 1927 in Antwerp, King Albert of Belgium on 11 April made Janáček a Commander of the Order of King Leopold. In March, Otto Klemperer, Janáček's most fervent interpreter abroad, conducted the SINFONIETTA twice in New York and again, on 30 September, in Berlin*) where, after the great success of KATYA KABANOVA, a whole evening of chamber music was dedicated to Janáček's works (the FIRST QUARTET, the VIOLIN SONATA, YOUTH and the CONCERTINO with Ilona Kurzová-Štěpánová; also taking part was the Waghalter Quartet). The CONCERTINO was also very successful on 7 March 1927 in Dresden. On 30 June at the fifth festival of the International Society for Contemporary Music held from 29 June to 4 July in Frankfurt where the CONCERTINO was played by the same pianist accompanied by members of the Frankfurt Opera orchestra, it won the composer who was present the acclaim of the whole festival, although the competition— to quote Janáček**)— was 'tough'.

Janáček did not attend merely to hear his own work. Alongside the festival there was an exhibition entitled 'Music in the Life of Nations', and Janáček brought with him to Frankfurt a folk band from Myjava in Slovácko just as he had once before taken a Moravian group to Prague to the 1895 Ethnographic Exhibition. The Myjava band, together with the Moravian Teachers' choir, represented Moravia while Bohemia fielded a team of bagpipers. However, the Myjava folk musicians proved so popular that their stay had to be repeatedly extended.

Another proof of Janáček's growing fame abroad was that two German papers, the daily *Vossische Zeitung* and the critical weekly of the Berlin literary left *Die literarische Welt*, invited him to contribute to a symposium on Beethoven and his influence on modern music, organized in March 1927 on the occasion of the centenary of Beethoven's death. The somewhat problematic symposium attracted some extraordinary contributions from such diverse personalities as Ernst Křenek, Philipp Jarnach, Maurice Ravel, George Auric and others, and its results were justly criticized, for instance by Stravinsky.***) And although Janáček shared with Beethoven his love of freedom, his iconoclasm and his awareness of power, it was surely more a sign of boastfulness rather than strength on Janáček's part to write†):

'When I was 25 I knew the *Missa Solemnis* inside out. I conducted it in Brno on 2 April 1879. I cannot lie: I was never enthusiastic about Beethoven's works. They never drew me out of myself.††) They never carried me into the world of ecstasy. I got to the bottom of them too soon. [Nevertheless] Beethoven's works penetrated into my soul all the deeper. I felt in their broad flow the vault of the blue heavens while the sun of their melodies shone on a divine cloud and chased every shadow away. And pouring its yearning over all that was the moon. But it was of little avail. I want to capture the vault of the heavens

---

*) Klemperer had previously conducted the first German performance of the SINFONIETTA in Wiesbaden.
**) *Literární svět*, 8 March 1928.
***) Stravinsky: *Chroniques de ma vie*, Vol. II, pp. 67—68.
†) *Die literarische Welt*, 1927, No 12.
††) Compare quotation on p. 20.

351

at first hand. I want to bathe my own eyes in the heavenly blue. I want to grasp the sun's rays in my own fist. I want to descend into the shadows. I want to weep until I drain my yearning away. And all this *at first hand*. At the Leipzig *conservatoire* I was put in among the first basses. Karl Reinecke was conducting—this was towards the end of 1879—and the work was Beethoven's *Missa Solemnis*. But I ran away from the choir, did not go to rehearsals and evaded the performance of the work.*)

Janáček expressed himself all the more beautifully—'at first hand'—in his GLAGOLITIC MASS which was performed for the first time on 5 December 1927 in Brno at the Beseda Philharmonic Hall—Janáček's pupil Jaroslav Kvapil conducted the Brno Opera Orchestra with Alexandra Čvánová and Stanislav Tauber among the soloists. Shortly afterwards, on 8 April 1928, it was performed again by the same soloists but with the Czech Philharmonic Orchestra at the Moravian concert of the Czechoslovak Singers Society's Jubilee Festival in Prague. Very soon—but not soon enough for Janáček to live to see it—the MASS became known abroad. At Easter 1929 the Philharmonic Beseda Society of Brno performed it at the International Music Festival in Geneva, but even before that, at the beginning of 1929, it was performed in Berlin. In the autumn of 1930 it was heard in New York at a concert given by the Metropolitan Opera in a programme which included the overture to Smetana's opera *Libuše* and Dvořák's *Biblical Songs* with Edith Fleischer, Karin Branzell, Dan Gridley and Friedrich Schorr as soloists. Arthur Bodanzky, who had conducted the first performance of JENŮFA in New York six years before, was the conductor. The critics had some reservations but received the unusual 'church' composition with considerable interest demanding that it be soon performed again. The 1935 performance organised by the BBC in London was to be followed by many others. Today it is one of the most frequently performed masses of the concert repertoire.

---

*) While he blames Beethoven for Reinecke's inadequacy, Janáček after all only rephrases Debussy's 'To watch a sunrise is more useful than to hear the Pastoral Symphony'.

(43) 'The House of the Dead'

Misfortune, suffering, insanity, misery, pain, injustice, violence, privation —
this is what fills the major part of human life.
This is also a clear indication of what should fill the major part of the works
of those artists who want to be truthful and sincere.

Vladimir Vasilyevich Stasov

In his GLAGOLITIC MASS Janáček composed a work in which he rose to the
height of pure joy—more so than in any other of his compositions. Immediately
following, in his opera THE HOUSE OF THE DEAD, he descended into the darkest
depths of human existence—a descent from the most graceful upper regions
of the Slav mind down into its unfathomable pit.

Dostoyevsky in his *House of the Dead* described in the story of the fictitious
Alexander Petrovich Goryanchikov his own experiences as a political prisoner
in Siberia, on the very threshold of his career as a writer. His death sentence
(for complicity with the communist Petrashevsky) was commuted at the last
moment when the firing squad were actually taking aim, to four years *katorga*—
forced labour.*) The House of the Dead is the prison, a place where all free
will has been suppressed and all the prisoners reduced to the same level of
negative existence, distinguishable only by differences of character and the
circumstances which have brought them to gaol. Janáček's choice of this
subject was as much a surprise (especially from the theatrical point of view)
as THE MAKROPOULOS CASE had been. Janáček himself said that he was attracted by the 'play within the play'—the entertainment put on by the prisoners
in Act II, and by the originality of approach, in that the opera 'had no principal
hero.' The strongest impulse, however, was certainly the unspoken 'moral'
of the novel: 'In every creature there is a spark of God'—a moral which the
composer (who in JENŮFA showed in the character of Kostelnička that even
the most 'moral' character can be driven to crime) added as a motto to his
last score. As has been pointed out, one of his most typical characteristics was
his high-minded, proud, uncompromising ideal of human dignity, which in turn
gave rise to his compassion for the outcasts of human society, for those deprived
of happiness, and to his rude love of personal freedom—freedom as essential
to a creative man of his impulsiveness and originality as air for breathing.

He was to sing the praises of this freedom most loudly in his new opera which,
taking a cue from the symbol of the eagle, the 'Czar of the forests', culminates
in a hymn to freedom. Unlike Beethoven in *Fidelio*, Janáček in THE HOUSE
OF THE DEAD does not assume the role of a fighter for political freedom, since
he could not do so without deviating widely from the novel, just as Dostoyevsky
could not if only for reasons of censorship. Nevertheless Janáček makes Goryan-

---

*) It is perhaps surprising that Janáček did not use this shattering moment in the opera; the
execution was in fact feigned—it was part of a cruel game. But all the same, Janáček could
have used it either directly (as a prologue) or indirectly (in the form of a reminiscence).

chikov into a fighter by giving him the lines (spoken in Dostoyevsky's Chapter Eight by the Polish aristocrat Zh—sky) thrown into the face of the Commandant: 'I'm a political prisoner'—defiance for which he pays dearly. The HOUSE OF THE DEAD is no less loud and explicit a protest than KATYA KABANOVA (although most of the social motives are left out of the later opera) for being a protest which, on the surface of it, is mute.

Yet in spite of the common background of Czarist despotism (in KATYA KABANOVA the shackles were imaginary, in the HOUSE OF THE DEAD they are real) and in spite of the similarity in the characters of the Commandant and Dikoi, or Akulka and Katya (Akulka even surpasses Katya in humility), the HOUSE OF THE DEAD is, perhaps, the reverse of KATYA KABANOVA. KATYA is the tragedy of a single individual on whom is focused the whole of the composer's compassion while in the HOUSE OF THE DEAD it is an endless line of equally 'unimportant' destinies. KATYA is a work full of feminine feeling, the HOUSE OF THE DEAD is a work of masculine curtness, and its characters are almost all male (even though the feminine element is somehow or other present, largely in the prisoners' reminiscences).

The epic breadth of the novel made a number of alterations necessary. Janáček reduced the number of characters and, for instance, combined Luka with Filka (for more than reasons of economy, as we shall see) and Skuratov with Baklushin.*) He also had to cut the story and then find ways of welding it together—since he did not want the libretto, which he was writing himself, to deviate too much from the original, he decided on theatrical means rather than dramatic ones. In other words, he joined the most striking episodes together according to the laws of contrast, but did not attempt to rewrite the drama as a whole on the basis of causality even though this should, strictly speaking, be possible in a collective drama just as in any other. Fortunately, the novel contains, hidden under its grey surface, more elements of contrast than would seem at first glance. Janáček made full use of them in the most masterly way—and this in spite of the fact that when he began composing, all he apparently had was a short scenario sketched out on four sheets of paper, with cross-references to the relevant pages of the novel.**)

The fundamental antithesis around which the work revolves is that of the prisoners and their gaolers, and it is presented in Act I both indirectly in Luka's monologue and directly in the scene between the sadistic Commandant who is 'human' (in the coarse sense of the word) only when drunk, and the gentle but proud Goryanchikov.

Then there is the antithesis between the real criminals (although in gaol for crimes of passion) and the political 'trespasser' Goryanchikov; between the low-class prisoners and the aristocrat—an antithesis which (this was Janáček's

---

*) He decided upon this measure only during the course of composing, since at the beginning Baklushin exists separately as a lyric tenor. The absent-minded Janáček calls him 'Bakunin' just as in MR BROUČEK he called Etherea 'Erethea' in his letters to Rektorys, or in his article on JENŮFA published by Dr Milena Černohorská in the magazine *Divadlo* (1958, p. 512) he consistently confused Laca with Števa.

**) Leoš Firkušný: *Odkaz L. Janáčka české opeře* (Leoš Janáček's Legacy to Czech Opera), p. 58.

own addition) leads to the little Alyeya being wounded rather than Goryanchikov at the end of Act II. This provides a bridge to the first scene of Act III which takes place in the prison hospital where Goryanchikov repays his little friend Alyeya by teaching him to read—and to forgive, since that is what Isa, God's prophet, preaches.*) Alyeya, a child of unspoilt nature, feels in his feverish hallucination that Jesus is a bringer of higher humanity. Unwittingly, Alyeya becomes a link between the two prison worlds—the common folk one and the intellectual one. Between the two most gloomy sections of the work—Goryanchikov's torture in Act I and Alyeya's wounding, with the macabre night scene which follows in the primitive prison hospital—comes the bright contrast of the rest-day on the banks of the Irtysh with sunshine, bells, *pirozhki* (Russian pasties) and real 'guests', but especially the 'play within the play'. Largely a pantomime, it charms by the clumsiness of men acting women's parts, and despite the bizarre 'gaiety' of the prisoners. Moreover, its two Don Juan stories act as a preparation for the primitively erotic scene of the anonymous young prisoner with the tart, although the pantomime itself (unlike the *commedia* in *I Pagliacci*) has no connection with the action of the main drama and is only a diversion. The fact that the second of the two mimed stories (about a miller's beautiful, and charitable, young wife who has her hands full trying to hide a succession of lovers from one another—a motif inherited from the *Arabian Nights*) is a favourite with the Russians (compare Mussorgsky's *Sorochintsy Fair* and Tchaikovsky's *Cherevichki*) serves to underline the atmosphere of Eastern tradition and playful mentality.**)

The various stories of the prisoners telling of what brought them to Siberia are not mere episodes but a matter of concern to all the other prisoners. This gives Janáček still more possibilities for bringing out the typically Russian local colour: he includes Russian proverbs ('Small bird, sharp claw', or the fatalistic Slav 'What falls off the cart, is lost for ever'), folk ditties to give contrast of mood (in the prelude to Act II—the voice 'from the Kirghiz steppe', and at the end of Act II—the song, at reh. No. 39, 'Oh weep and weep, young Cossack boy') and with this mingling and criss-crossing of impressions he produces, to use his own word, real 'tangles' of expression. For instance, and this is Janáček's own inspired addition to Dostoyevsky, at the moment in Act III when Shishkov tells how he killed the innocent Akulka, Filka who had caused Akulka's and Shishkov's misfortune, and who is known in prison under the assumed name of Luka, is on the point of dying in a bed nearby, as

---

*) i.e. Jesus in Islam, since Alyeya, a Tartar boy from Daghestan, is a Muslim. Not 'Isak' as is wrongly printed in the Czech text of the vocal score. Alyeya is a still more moving relative of the little shepherd in JENŮFA, and must be also sung by a soprano or, as Janáček prescribed in the manuscript score, by a mezzo-soprano; certainly not by a tenor.

**) All these local touches, from the Tartar boy Alyeya to the Orthodox priest and the splendid Russian bells, should be reason enough for the opera not to be set in a modern barrack-like prison. The production should adhere to the typically Czarist Siberian setting. The same applies to the boat (a symbol of freedom of movement) where the prisoners' theatrical performance may take place. (Max Brod, in his German translation, sets Act I in winter and the brighter Act II in summer in order to heighten the contrast.) A sensitive producer will certainly utilize the symbolic values of the times of day and night, in particular the bright daylight at the beginning of the gentler second act and the sunrise at the end of the last act.

yet unrecognized by Shishkov. An old man's cry 'A human being has died' seems to refer to both Akulka's and Filka's death.

And where such 'tangles of expression' cannot be merged to form a symbolic whole, they follow one after another in quick succession. For instance in Act I Luka ends his description of how he was tortured with the words 'I thought I was dying…' Another composer would have added a lengthy ritornello full of compassion. Nothing of that sort in Janáček (nor in Dostoyevsky either); on the contrary, an elderly prisoner asks with a simplicity which is almost a taunt: 'And did you?'—a complete break in the atmosphere. Similarly when Skuratov in Act II tells about his unfaithful Louise, Janáček lets a drunken prisoner utter unsentimental shouts: 'Lies, it's all lies.' And when Skuratov finishes his story, instead of an epilogue, there is a raucous song sung by the prisoners, interspersed with coarse remarks whose relevance to Louise is pointed up by their motivic connection. When Shishkov in Act III eventually recognizes in the man who has just died his old rival in love Filka, instead of suppressing his hatred in the presence of death, Janáček's Shishkov implacably curses him. The orchestra alone sounds a pitying note while the elderly prisoner sings over the dead body: 'He too, had a mother.' Never has the deepest compassion for the defenceless and defeated been expressed with such merciless heartlessness—with the possible exception of Berg's *Wozzeck*, of which the night scene in the barracks (Act II, Scene 5) may possibly have influenced the 'heavy breathing of the prisoners' in the night scene (reh. No. 16) of Act III of THE HOUSE OF THE DEAD.

It is therefore not surprising that the music of THE HOUSE OF THE DEAD rarely broadens out, becomes charged with lyricism. There are exceptions, though: at the end of the opera and at the conclusion of the prelude which makes use of material originally intended for a violin concerto to be called *The Wanderings of a Little Soul.**)

The prelude opens with a balladic melody:**)

which is gradated through a lofty fanfare-like motif:

---

*) What subject Janáček had in mind and how he came to plan such a work will probably remain a mystery. Rosa Newmarch in her book *The Music of Czechoslovakia*, p. 227, says that Janáček had been thinking of it during his visit to London in 1926. Was it in some way connected with his impressions during that journey?
**) Here I cannot refrain from pointing out the crushing 4/2 augmentation of it with a simultaneous fast variant in the bass during Luka's story in Act I (reh. Nos 28–29) as Luka is nearing the point when he is to be executed.

to a combination of the two. Both these motifs give the overall impression—at least in their original—of masculine curtness.

But even this 'manly' opera is brimming over with rich musical colour. In the stories of both Luka and Shishkov it is the music of bursts and shouts keeping down unbearable memories; with primitives such as Skuratov and Shapkin it becomes almost childishly playful and helpless: it captivates in the buoyant march of Act II, yearns with the prisoners for home in Act I, is charmingly puppet-like, bizarre and eventually—in the crazy waltz that ends the pantomime in Act II—exhilarating; at the beginning of Act II where it accompanies the prisoners at work, it is refreshingly down-to-earth. Of the individual motifs, mention must be made of Skuratov's double motif first heard in Act I:

both components of which serve a wider purpose, perhaps too wide, since it is used even for the finale of Act I where Skuratov does not appear at all. The motifs in this opera do not stand in such close relation to one another as was the case with Janáček's previous operas. Nevertheless the work can be said to be monothematic in much the same way as KATYA KABANOVA was—one motif dominates the work to the point of monopoly. This is the motif of fate and, metaphorically, of the House of the Dead. Dostoyevsky, at the beginning of Chapter Eight of his novel, tries to see the psychological motive behind most crimes as the dark, elemental, instinctive drive of a man persecuted by fate to rebel at least once and break his painful spiritual shackles in a desperate outburst of free will, only to find himself in a state of yet more terrible oppression. Janáček's motif, too, at first displays a mighty, passionate, dissonant surge followed by a fall into a dark-sounding minor triad:

The motif appears straight after the prelude as a kind of warning and then it reappears again and again as a terrifying symbol, an ineluctable curse whenever in the prisoners' individual reminiscences the fateful catastrophe is imminent or whenever its consequences make themselves felt: for instance in Act I when Goryanchikov is being flogged for having declared himself to be a political prisoner (this is where Ex. 443 is taken from), or before the sad chorus of the prisoners 'Never shall I see again the land where I was born' in Act I (reh. No. 16), during Luka's story at the words 'So I lost my head as well' (Act I, reh. No. 25) and later where he describes how he knifed the tormenting officer. In Act III the motif appears when the raving Skuratov remembers the fateful moment: 'I pressed the pistol to her brow...', or when

Shishkov is telling about the unfortunate Akulka (after the words 'Get up, Akulka, you are finished') and at the glorious moment when the shackles fall from the feet of Goryanchikov (reh. No. 37) and he is to return to 'golden freedom'. (It is interesting to note the similarity between this motif and the figure:

which accompanied a similar scene ten years earlier in THE DIARY OF THE YOUNG MAN WHO DISAPPEARED (in No. 7) at the words 'Whatever will be, will be, and no man can escape it'*)—words repeated almost verbatim by the chorus in KATYA KABANOVA just before Katya's public confession of guilt.)

In contrast to this motif symbolizing oppression there is the motif of freedom. The joyful and agitated melody of the prisoners in Act I (before reh. No. 15):

O-rel car le - sů!

Forest Czar, the eagle

is a preparation for its proper appearance later. (There is a revealing psychological moment when, after the words of the elderly prisoner 'See how it (the eagle) limps', the prisoners disappointedly repeat the motif a whole seventh lower (five bars before reh. No. 15). The motif appears in its full breadth in the introduction to Act III as a solemn promise, and it then accompanies the fulfilment of this promise at the moment of Goryanchikov's release:

Svo-bo-da!   Svo-bo-dič-ka!

Freedom,   lovely freedom

From all that has been said about Janáček's posthumous opera, it is clear that it lays the least claim of all his stage works to attracting a wider public and thus gaining easy success. But although its strict unsentimentality (and its burning passion) makes it even more unusual to the popular taste than Janáček's uncommon musical language, it is this very quality which makes it unique and truthful, and which accounts for its direct appeal.

The writing of this opera was no easy task even for Janáček, as his own words in a letter to Kamila testify: 'I feel as if I was descending step by step

---

*) Brod translates these passages freely, and each turns out differently.

to the lower depths of humanity, to the most miserable of all people. And that is a difficult descent.'

Did he suspect that soon, without having seen or heard his last work, he was to descend even deeper to the place where one day we will all be submerged in the floods of time?

The thing that now remains to be discussed is the conclusion of the opera. The ending in the published edition—from Goryanchikov's release and Alyeya's last words to him, to the end—is not Janáček's, but one made at the instigation of the producer of the posthumous première Ota Zítek.*) Zítek wanted to end the work on a more optimistic note—at least on the surface of it. He wanted to avoid any possible marring of the intoxicating mirage of liberty at the end. In Janáček's version, after Goryanchikov's departure, the guard shouts 'March!' at the remaining prisoners and they limp back to their cells to the 'merry' accompaniment of the clanking of their chains (a spine-chilling counterpart to the black humour of the prisoners' play in Act II). 'Life' in the House of the Dead continues undisturbed and merciless. Only Alyeya, wearing his white hospital nightgown (perhaps forgotten by the guard and himself forgetful of everything around him since he has lost Goryanchikov) remains—according to Janáček's remark in his sketch of the scenario for the last scene—'as a symbol of God's spark in man'.

Musically, Janáček solves the problem of the conclusion by following Alyeya's last words ('God repay you') with a bridge passage of eight bars during which the guards chase the prisoners away. This leads into the final marching music in 2/4, identical with part of the second half of the interlude in Act III (Tempo I to 'con moto') where it was transferred by the arrangers anxious to gain time for the necessary scene change, at the cost of some repetitiveness in the music. Janáček's original ending (here quoted in full, starting eight bars after reh No. 39) contains just five more bars of a terse D flat major chord, which conclude the work:

*) Universal Edition now print Janáček's original ending at the end of the score. K. J.

Naturally the change in the action called for adaptations in the music. Ota Zítek asked two of Janáček's pupils—the conductor of the posthumous première Břetislav Bakala and the composer Osvald Chlubna—to make them. Starting eight bars after reh. No. 39, Bakala first repeats in the orchestra almost note for note Janáček's two preceding bars and then adds six bars, again almost identical with Janáček's music at reh. No. 38. Chlubna then added what is a combination of the motif of freedom with that of fate to form a nine-bar conclusion.

As has been said, the purpose of this arrangement was to make the end brighter and more majestic, and it must be admitted that the public does not like to be lifted from an atmosphere of oppressive gloom only to be dropped back into it again, even if the moment of brightening is only a mirage (which it is in this case). Janáček, in his definitive version, does not even keep his poetic stage direction about Alyeya and, accordingly, does not express in it

360

the music either. It is difficult to decide whether these changes were justified, just as it is difficult to judge, say, the different versions of Mussorgsky's *Boris Godunov*. Opera companies will make their own choice. Bakala's and Chlubna's conclusion is more consistent tectonically and dynamically while Janáček's is more consistent dramatically. The modified conclusion is, perhaps, more in keeping with Janáček's general principle of ending even the most tragic works on a brighter note (although KATYA KABANOVA is already an exception to this rule). However, the original conclusion is more in keeping with the specific, relentless style of THE HOUSE OF THE DEAD. The pros and cons are thus fairly equally balanced. When the present author conducted the revival of this opera at the Prague National Theatre on 10 May 1958, he decided contrary to the prevailing tradition to use Janáček's version for the following two reasons:

1. Where objective arguments are more or less of equal weight, priority should be given to the composer's wish.

2. The nine-bar finale by Chlubna deviates, due to its somewhat superficial showiness, too far from the musical style of the rest of the work.

Yet the change in the finale is not the only intrusion of the arrangers. There are some small but numerous modifications of a technical character and, in particular, an important dramatic addition, namely, Goryanchikov's frustrated attempt on the life of the Commandant at the end of Act I. Janáček's manuscript score contains nothing of that sort. After Luka's words 'Alyeya, the scissors!' the successive stage directions merely are: 'The guard brings in the punished Goryanchikov', 'Gates are closing after Goryanchikov', 'All watch the gate close after Goryanchikov', and finally, at the modulation to B Major, 'All stop working'. Nothing more.

The addition of the attempt on the Commandant's life certainly makes for an effective end to the act, but it has two weaknesses. First, there is no fitting accompaniment to it in the music, except possibly at the place where the curtain is already down; and, second, the music is based solely on Skuratov's motif. This inconsistency will remain whatever solution is adopted, but the fact is that an attempt to kill is alien to Goryanchikov's evangelical nature. Besides, it is hard to believe that having just been stripped of his own clothes and given prison ones, he would have been able to keep the 'English cobbler's knife'.*) The incident is transferred from Dostoyevsky's first chapter where the attempt is made by the prisoner Petrov—an 'old hand' who uses a brick, not a knife, and whose motivation is typical of the Russian mentality at the time: he wants to suffer.

The technical modifications, though, are on the whole justified. They deal with problems of orchestration, attribution of the vocal parts (Janáček is often inconsistent in naming the characters) and diction and tessitura which called for some minor musical changes as well. The completion of the orchestration was necessary since Janáček's manuscript is more a sketch than a score: he used to line the pages himself, according to how many staves he needed, and did not waste time on such details as doublings and fillings. Cellos and double-basses, and first and second violins, for instance, share the same staves through-

---

*) Unless, of course, he picks up Luka's. K. J.

out. Janáček composed in a feverish hurry. On 30 November 1927 he wrote to Kamila as though he was about to make his account with life: 'I am hurrying with the new opera like a baker throwing buns into the oven' (see also p. 374).

It could be claimed on the basis of a letter that Janáček wrote to Max Brod on 10 January 1928 ('I have finished THE HOUSE OF THE DEAD. The score is being copied.') that the manuscript represents Janáček's 'last will and testament' (from which it would automatically follow that the opera should be produced in its original scoring). But the score was not yet finished, as is proved by the date '24. IV. 28', which he wrote at the end of Act III. The end of Act II bears an even later date, '7. V. 1928', and to the right of it, '2. IV. 1927'—probably the date when he began composing the act. This would be in keeping with the date at the beginning of Act I, '18. II. 1927', which almost certainly indicates the day he began writing the opera. In addition, the clean copy of the score is dated '14. V. 28'—four months later than the letter in which Janáček stated 'The score is being copied out.' However, since Janáček wrote as late as 17 May 1928 to Max Brod 'THE HOUSE OF THE DEAD will still give me plenty of work', and since he took the score with him on his summer holiday that year, it is evident that he did not consider the orchestration complete even after the copyist had finished the clean copy. In fact the copyist who, unlike the composer, used normal lined paper, had left lines open for all the instruments throughout, making it easy for Janáček to add to any part as he wished.

A far more reliable guide than Janáček's vague statements is the score itself. For instance eight bars before reh. No. 28 in Act II the passage which obviously demands full orchestra is sketched out by Janáček for two clarinets and three bassoons. I have myself experienced the instrumental and harmonic bareness of parts of the original conclusion. Or take the passage in Act III (reh. No. 20) where Shishkov sings 'And I got a bull-whack ready for her': the harmony, the motivically derived rhythm, all stop and only a kind of skeleton sketch remains—a motive alternating between the violins and clarinet. Here the manuscript obviously represents no more than a basic pattern for subsequent completion. Evidently Janáček did not find time to work out some of these details, and if the opera was to be performed at all someone had to undertake the completion. Břetislav Bakala — although one might argue about the extent of intervention necessary — did it with so great a feeling for Janáček's orchestral style, that it is sometimes impossible to tell, from the sound alone,*) exactly what has been added, although in some instances he went so far as to change even details of the original skeleton orchestration. For instance at the beginning of Act III at Shapkin's words 'The pain... is no worse than when they keep pulling your ears a long time' he gives the piercing oboe motif to the E flat clarinet which does it more justice; further on (bars five and six after reh. No. 17) and at other places he even adds a motivic reminder or a rhythmic figure (as in the 4/2 time after rehearsal number 21 of Act III, where his jerky upbeat chords, scored for the horns, have a particularly Janáček-like effect).

---

*) Bakala worked in pencil in the copyist's ink copy, and his alterations are therefore clearly distinguishable.

Changes were also made in the voice parts—probably mainly by the producer Zítek—in order to sort out the diction which, in Janáček's original, is a wild medley of Czech, Russian and the Lachian dialect. The complete libretto, with a few exceptions, was put into literary Czech. (Incidentally the large quantity of Russian sentences in Janáček's original is a further indication that this opera was composed without a proper libretto, straight from Janáček's own copy of Dostoyevsky's novel in Russian.) One also cannot quarrel with the editors shifting some expressions a little or leaving others out altogether in order to smooth out the flow of the vocal exchanges on the stage.

Much was developed in the voice parts which had only been hinted at in Janáček's original. For instance, the laughter of the prisoners at the end of the first pantomime, limited in the original to bars one and two, and five to seven; or the hero of the first part of Luka's story who, in the original, is a young and childless Skuratov (though Janáček lets him refer to his children), was changed in accordance with Dostoyevsky to an 'old Khokhol'—a nickname for a Ukrainian. In spite of this, many ambiguities have remained. No one, unless he has read Dostoyevsky, will understand that Luka in his 'So I lost my head as well' is still speaking for the other convict; Shishkov's remark 'And now we'll go and tar the gate' is only understandable if 'tar her gate' is inserted as Max Brod does in his German translation; or the two sentences 'Akulka comes out of the garden. Stops at the gate' make sense only if amended to read 'He stops at the gate.' Janáček, however, changed the sense of some lines intentionally. The importance he attached to Goryanchikov's 'I am a political prisoner' has already been mentioned; similarly Skuratov's 'Then soon after, Akulka's husband turns up', quite inconsequential in Dostoyevsky, is given a deeper significance in Janáček, since it identifies Luka with Filka— the cause of Akulka's misfortune, and at the same time motivates Luka's growing irritation; or during Shapkin's story in Act III the cries of the chorus 'He's gone crazy' are made to refer in Janáček's version not to Shapkin's torturer but to Shapkin himself. Anyhow, whenever in doubt, we may find consolation in Janáček's own remarks: 'You know, this is rather odd—when someone speaks to me, I may not always understand his words, but what tone values there are in his speech! I know at once what is inside him, I know what he feels, whether he is lying, if he is agitated, and I feel, I hear, that inside, the man may even be weeping.'*) Thus in one way or another Janáček managed to reveal to us the hearts and souls of his characters.

It should be noted that Bakala also added some interpretative marks relating to dynamics, tempi, pauses and so on. These sometimes bring their own problems—for instance the 'Adagio' at the opening of Act I (after the Prelude), which seems out of place and which Janáček uses only later, at the second and third analogous place in the music; or the unnecessary break before the first sounding of the bells in Act II.

From all this it is evident that a new edition of Janáček's last opera is needed, giving not only the original ending alongside the modified one, but also indicating the various alterations that have been made, and which directions are Janáček's own and which have been added.

---

*) Interview in the magazine *Literární svět* (The Literary World), I, 1928.

(44) 'Intimate Letters'

On 4 January 1928 Janáček wrote to Kamila: 'The opera [THE HOUSE OF THE DEAD] is finished.' On 10 January he wrote the same thing to Max Brod and added: 'The score is being copied out.' He went on to admit: 'This is the first time in my life that I don't know what to do next. But I am glad. I shall go to Hukvaldy for about a fortnight. I need a rest. This past year it seemed as if my soul was being roasted.' On top of that, Janáček had just recovered from influenza which had made him cancel his visit to Leipzig to hear a performance of JENŮFA. Soon afterwards he learned that the co-author of the brightest and loveliest of his stage works, Rudolf Těsnohlídek, took his own life on 11 January.

Janáček interrupted his visit to Hukvaldy to attend the performance of KATYA KABANOVA conducted by William Steinberg at the Prague German Theatre on 21 January, and on 29 January he resumed creative work. He began his second quartet INTIMATE LETTERS (originally called LOVE LETTERS); in a letter of 20 February he explained the change of title to Kamila Stösslová, saying: 'I don't deliver my feelings to the tender mercies of fools.' This work was yet another, and direct, confession of his last love—in fact, he followed his most collectivist work with a composition of the utmost intimacy and privacy.

The catalyst was a domestic quarrel on New Year's Day (the year which was to be his last). There were no more secrets at home. But what about the world at large? With a touching frankness, Janáček—the same Janáček who had never cared a jot about what other people thought—turned to Max Brod. On 18 January he wrote to him from Hukvaldy:

'Tell me, is it possible to reveal upon which human being grew the crystals of my motifs? Has any writer ever told the public? With the painters it is no secret. But a composer? Would it be taken amiss if this spiritual relationship, this artistic relationship were to be openly admitted? (It is as if you heard Živný speaking in DESTINY!) Certainly one would have to have the consent of the attached person.*)

'She is willing because we both look to clearing ourselves of the charge of a relationship other than our purely spiritual one.'**)

Janáček then goes on, with a certain amount of *sacro egoismo,* to analyze his works from this point of view:

---

*) As is shown by the continuation of the letter, the person referred to is Kamila and not Mrs Janáčková as is assumed by the compiler of *Janáček—Brod.* (p. 232).
**) Brod was in this respect a sceptic: on 31 August 1924 he published this aphorism in the *Prager Tagblatt:* 'Friendship with a woman is not an empty phrase, it is simply an inaccurate description which forgets the essence and emphasizes the inessential.'

'I am aware of the psychological side to this tendency of the motifs to incline towards perceptions of the tangible, real.

'This is the sort of composing which has nurtured me and brought me to maturity.'

It is not known what answer Brod sent to Janáček. On Sunday 29 January Janáček wrote to Kamila, still from Hukvaldy, to announce the beginning of his confession—a new quartet. On 1 February he wrote again from Brno that he had begun writing something nice. 'Our life is going to be in it... I composed the first number at Hukvaldy. My impression when I saw you for the first time. Now I am working on the second number.' And on 6 February: 'I am writing the third of the *Love Letters*. I want to make it particularly joyful and then dissolve it into a vision like your image...' During the night of 8 February he wrote, this time probably once more about the second movement: 'Today I wrote in musical tones my sweetest desire. I struggle with it. It prevails. You are giving birth. What would be the destiny of that new-born son? What would be yours? Just as you are, laughing with tears in your eyes—that is how it sounds.' And again on 18 February, this time obviously about the third movement: 'Today I succeeded with the number "when the earth shook".*) This will be the best one... now if only the last one would turn out well, too... It will be like worrying about you.' However, on the following day he reported the last movement finished: 'The last one won't finish with fear for my pretty little weasel, but with great longing and as if its fulfilment.'**) He was burning with impatience to send the work off to his love—but not until it had been performed so that he could tell if it had any musical worth. 'You know, feelings on their own are sometimes so strong that the notes hide, run away. A great love—a weak composition. But I want it to be a great love—a great composition.'

Thus the Second Quartet is related to the first by what it expresses— fateful passion and love. The Second Quartet, however, openly concerns Janáček himself and does not end tragically but joyfully. The musical language of the quartets is closely related and both are close to Katya Kabanova. At the beginning of the first movement ('My impression when I saw you for the first time'), following a masculine opening motif:

448

---

*) This rather curious allusion is explained by a letter from Janáček to Kamila dated exactly three months later, in which he writes: 'How could I not be overjoyed that time when I felt as though the earth was trembling under my feet?'

**) Otakar Šourek in his introduction to the second edition of the score assumes that Janáček was referring on all three dates: 6, 8 and 18 February to the third movement. But if this conjecture were correct, Janáček would have been announcing the completion of the third movement twice—on 8 February ('Today I wrote...') and again on 18 February ('Today I succeeded...'). Janáček probably worked on the second and third movements, and possibly even the fourth movement, simultaneously as he had been known to do before. Or else the fourth movement (15 pages of score) would have had to be written in one day, while the third movement (only nine pages), would have taken almost a fortnight.

the viola enters (originally it was to have been viola d'amore) with a motif in the so-called gypsy scale and 'sul ponticello':

—a motif which in the second movement of the FIRST QUARTET (where it was also given to the viola sul ponticello—see Ex. 323) had the same function it has here: to express the chilling mystery of an encounter with an utterly new and potentially great experience.

Its variant, repeating the first and omitting the second note, and consisting again of three bars:

together with this lyrical motif developed by augmentation from the accompanying figure of Ex. 450:

represent—together with the constantly unfolding variations of the opening 'masculine' motif—all the material that there is in the first movement which eventually comes to rest in mostly Lydian D flat major.

The second movement (Adagio in B flat minor—KATYA's key) is for a long time dominated by a fervent melody, again introduced by the viola:

which appears in various dynamic, agogic and rhythmic guises—among others, in a combination of its own diminution and augmentation;

Then all of a sudden, after a mysterious cadenza of the second violin 'flautato'

over sustained notes in the other instruments, a playful, child-like motif appears in the first violin:

454
Presto

to be followed by a gentle variant choking with emotion:

455
rubato

A joyful, excited canonic gradation of the fervent opening melody leads to a joining together of the 'masculine' motif from the first movement (see Ex. 448) and an augmentation of the playful motif (Exs 454 and 455) which could be termed the 'feminine' one. Then just before the end of the movement, the second violin's flautato cadenza quietly returns (marked 'airily with the point of the bow') whereupon five bars of the opening motif — in a loud, festive garb and a mood of solemn thanksgiving—bring the movement to a close.

The outer sections of the third movement are developed from a new rocking motif of a distinctly Russian colouring (the accompaniment in octaves with an added third):

456
Moderato

The slow middle section ranging from the initial intimate pianissimo to an overflowing fullness of sound later, is built from a tender, loving combination of variants of the 'feminine' motifs from Exs 450 and 455, over the residual rhythm of the preceding rocking motif:

457
Adagio
dolcissimo

which quickens into agitated quintuplets:

458

('Those cries of joy, but, too, strangely enough, cries of horror after the lullaby,' Janáček wrote to Kamila on 27 June 1928.) After the recapitulation of the first section and before the loud coda, the tender theme of the middle section reappears in a brief and quiet reminiscence.

The last movement is an extended rondo with a boisterous main theme in A flat minor:

459

from the striding chordal accompaniment of which is developed, seven bars before reh. No 3, this broad motif in crotchet triplets:

460

which, together with the first episode, plays an important part later on in providing most of the material for the development.

After a short return of the main theme, the second episode opens with a pizzicato arpeggio theme in the second violin:

461

repeated at once 'legato cantabile', its mood alternately brimming over and anxiously distressed. It is reminiscent, just as the diminution of the fourth bar of the main theme is later on, of the last act of KATYA, except that here it proceeds in the direction of a definite brightening. Or does some of Janáček's anxiety about his 'pretty little weasel' remain? The episode withers away on a sweetly faint note.

The return of the main theme, this time marked feroce, is then all the more elemental. Prepared by a furious cadenza for the second violin using the triplet motive from Ex. 460, it is alternated by the hymnic pizzicato arpeggio theme two more times, before the pugnacious triplet motif brings the movement to an end on a note of triumphant defiance and in Janáček's famous key of D flat major.

Thus ends a work which, for its intensity and passion, scarcely has an equal in the chamber music repertoire, even though it was written by a seventy-four-year-old composer in the last year of his life.

368

(45) At the Height of Fame

The new creative triumph was to be followed by the winning of new laurels. The Prague première of THE MAKROPOULOS CASE took place at the National Theatre on 1 March 1928. It was conducted by Otakar Ostrčil and produced by Josef Munclinger with scenery by Josef Čapek, and with Anna Kejřová, Richard Kubla and Václav Novák in the main parts. On the following day Otakar Hollmann and members of the Czech Philharmonic Orchestra performed the CAPRICCIO, conducted by Jaroslav Řídký. Between these two performances Janáček, who naturally enough attended both of them, gave the magazine *Literární svět* (The Literary World) the interview in which apart from what has already been quoted, he spoke about contemporary opera, in particular Berg's *Wozzeck*. (A year earlier the Prague National Theatre had to withdraw *Wozzeck* after only three performances because of the demonstrations that accompanied them.) Janáček said:

'Injustice—injustice to *Wozzeck* and a grave injustice to Berg. He is a dramatist of great seriousness and deep truth. Let him speak! Today he is distraught. He suffers. Stopped in his tracks. Not another note. And each of his notes has been dipped in blood.

'The situation in the operatic world, you ask? In Berlin they asked the same thing. It will work itself out... But not just by dint of the clangour of instruments, but by the palpable existence, the essence of phenomena—that's the *raison d'être* (of opera). And it will grow as humanity will grow.'

Janáček then quoted his own work as an example:

'I penetrate because there is truth in my work; truth to its very limit. Truth does not exclude beauty, on the contrary, there should be truth as well as beauty, and more and more. Life, mainly. Always eternal youth. Life is young. It is spring. I am not afraid of living; I like it terribly.'

On 8 April Prague heard the GLAGOLITIC MASS for the first time and on 27 May Brno opened the Exhibition of Contemporary Culture with a performance of Janáček's SINFONIETTA conducted by František Neumann. At the laying of the foundation stone of the Faculty of Law building at the Brno Masaryk University, which took place on 9 June 1928, the Beseda Choral Society conducted by Jaroslav Kvapil sang a new chorus specially composed for the occasion by Janáček to words by Antonín Trýb—CHORUS FOR THE STONE-LAYING CEREMONY AT MASARYK UNIVERSITY IN BRNO.

In London in February Sir Henry Wood conducted the CONCERTINO which was to have been performed during Janáček's 1926 visit there, and then in the spring he conducted the SINFONIETTA. In March the SINFONIETTA was heard in Dresden.*) The belief that in May 1928 Klemperer introduced THE

---

*) 'In Dresden the performance of my SINFONIETTA was a riot,' wrote Janáček to Kamila

MAKROPOULOS CASE in Berlin, with Barbara Kemp in the main part,*) has already been corrected here. It is equally incorrect, as Klemperer himself has said, that in 1920 he performed THE EXCURSIONS OF MR BROUČEK in Cologne in Otto Sonnenfeld's translation.**) Both these productions were announced but came to nothing. Klemperer, however, wanted to perform THE HOUSE OF THE DEAD even before it was put on in Brno, while the Aachen opera company asked for KATYA KABANOVA. But it was mainly JENŮFA for which requests literally poured in to Universal Edition: from Bern, Graz, Dortmund, Heidelberg, Kassel, Lübeck, Hanover, Stuttgart, Munich, Mainz an other places.

In this respect it is interesting to note some occurrences which, although they mostly did not lead to any result, show the fame Janáček was acquiring abroad, especially in Germany. For instance on 26 April the Berlin daily paper *8 Uhr-Blatt* asked him whether he thought a peace anthem should be composed and whether in the form of a march, hymn or cantata, and whether the League of Nations should organize a competition for such an anthem. Janáček was asked to send them by 15 May a sketch of the rhythm and melody as he would imagine it. Two telegrams requesting his reply show the importance the paper attached to his answer. It seems that at the beginning of July the editor of the *Prager Tagblatt* Dr Franz Lederer addressed a letter to Janáček at Luhačovice asking him to contribute an article to the art magazine *Die Böttchergasse in Bremen*. However, in 1928 Janáček wrote for the Yugoslav magazine *Muzika* a small piece called VZPOMÍNKA (Souvenir), its charming progressions in thirds:

462

reminiscent of the swallows' motif from the beginning of Scene 2 of KATYA KABANOVA. He dedicated it to the Slovene composer Dr Miloje Milojevič (1884—1946) who had close links with Czech musical life. (In 1936 this piece was published by the Melpa Edition in Czechoslovakia in their collection *Moravian Composers to the Young*.)

Janáček was getting many offers of librettos from foreign librettists. As early as June 1918 the Viennese writer Franz Steffan offered him his drama *Judas*. In June 1920 the German writer K. M. von Levetzow (the son of Alexander M. von Levetzow of Diváky Castle southeast of Brno, who was a friend of the writer Alois Mrštík) offered Janáček a libretto for a ballet *Der verlorene Kopf* (The Lost Head). However, Janáček wrote to Mrštík who was acting as mediator, that he did not want to compose 'another dream' after BROUČEK. He pointed out that repetition of subjects was also the reason why he had

---

on 28 March. 'Some were applauding, others were whistling. But the former won. I am glad that they fight over the meaning of my work.'
*) Bohumír Štědroň, in the Prague *Hudební rozhledy*, Vol. VI, No. 13, p. 618. *Janáček — Ostrčil*, p. 67.
**) Commentary to *Janáček — Brod*, p. 21, where moreover a printer's error makes the date of the Berlin production of the EXCURSIONS 1900.

decided against composing the opera *The Farmer's Woman* after JENŮFA. In 1922 the Czech-German writer Schlegel-Melliwa offered him a libretto for an opera *Die Hexe* (The Witch) based on an old Czech legend. On 10 April 1924 Jaroslav Kvapil recommended to him two librettos by the French essayist William Ritter, the first of which, called *L'Ame et la Chair* (Soul and Body), set in Slovakia, revolved round a heroine in love with two men, Ondráš (Body) and Ivan (Soul). Janáček refused the story, and it fared no better with Vítězslav Novák when it was offered to him. Janáček was sympathetically inclined towards Ritter who had done much to promote Czech music and Slovak folklore, but he did not accept the second story either. That was called *Le Château en Bohême* (The Castle in Bohemia) and was probably the first libretto with aviation as its subject. (Ritter tried to arouse Janáček's interest by comparing the noise of the propeller to the clacking of the mill in JENŮFA.) In April 1926 the Berlin writer von Gellhorn offered Janáček his *Der Mantel mit den goldenen Sternen* (The Cloak with the Golden Stars)—a story from ancient Egypt. In the autumn of 1927 A. S. Pordese-Milo, another German, offered him his *Der Geisterhof* (The Haunted Manor) and Franz Feiler his *Virtschen*—a libretto with an Albanian background. And of the Czech writers, František Zavřel offered Janáček his comedy *Dědečkem proti své vůli* (A Grandfather Against his Will).*)

In the first half of May 1928 the distinguished German producer and director of the Berlin Renaissance Theatre, Gustav Hartung, asked Janáček to write incidental music to a farcical play—'a jest in six incidents'—by Gerhart Hauptmann, *Schluck und Jau,* written in 1898. Hartung was planning to put it on with the author's own assistance at the summer festival at Heidelberg Castle. The play was well suited for this purpose since the action was in a castle setting. The story was a free adaptation of the prologue to Shakespeare's *Taming of the Shrew*: At the suggestion of Carl—a man of the world who is no longer young, the Prince who wants to amuse his young wife Sidselill, allows his hunting companions to play a trick on two tramps. One of the tramps, Jau, having fallen into a drunken slumber, is dressed up as a prince and subsequently paid due honours, while the other tramp, the good-natured Schluck, is persuaded to dress up as a princess. The comedy is given full rein until Jau gets above himself. A sleeping draught is administered and the two tramps returned to their proper place, and everyone is happy—or at least seems to be.

Hartung was willing to make the journey to Brno to discuss the project, and the poet himself was very keen on the idea. But in spite of that, and in spite of Brod's intercession (Janáček worked so fast that Brod saw no obstacle in the short time limit), Janáček hesistated. 'I work fast, but I polish for a long time. They should have asked me sooner,' he wrote to Brod on 17 May. Besides, he went on, 'THE HOUSE OF THE DEAD will keep me busy for a long time yet.' In addition Janáček disliked writing to order and it took a further intercession from his faithful interpreter Otto Klemperer as well as more persuading by Max Brod before Janáček showed any interest in the subject

---

*) Dr Theodora Straková, 'Janáček's Operatic Topics and Fragments', *Musikologie III.*

at all—a subject which, in its confrontation of illusion with reality, did resemble MR BROUČEK. Between 23 and 25 May he read Hauptmann's play — a difficult job for a Czech since the two tramps speak in the broad Silesian German dialect. In the margin Janáček made his usual technical and critical notes which show that from the start he was not enthusiastic about the subject. In the second scene he rightly objected to the Prince taking a personal part in the farce. The third scene, in which Schluck is persuaded to dress up as a princess, bears the remark 'weak' and scene five, where Carl suggests playing blind man's buff, the mark 'childish'—a hasty judgment perhaps, since the suggestion is meant symbolically with an admixture of bitterness. However, it seems that Janáček liked the idea better as time went on. He is reported to have said: 'It will turn out to be funny.' His interest was probably aroused by the rebellious character of Jau. This is evident from the fact that Janáček began composing with the scene in which Jau suddenly feels like a prince. This scene he completed, and almost every sentence spoken by Jau is underlined in his copy, especially where Jau speaks like a prince. Jau's line of primitive surprise 'I am a prince?' is the only part of the text which Janáček actually quoted in the manuscript. He was also attracted by the capricious Sidselill, and underlined many of the places referring to her character.

Exactly how the music was to be used is not clear from Janáček's sketches. It was certainly to include solo and choral songs, huntsmen's horn calls, tuckets and suchlike, which are prescribed in the play. Towards the end of his copy Janáček put a number of question marks in the margin. They could mean that he was making up his mind about further musical additions. (Hartung wanted whole sections of the play to be accompanied, and he wanted the composer to turn each of the interludes between the scenes into a ballet.)*)

Janáček in fact wrote music to barely four numbers: the first piece (Andante) seems to be an introduction to Scene 1 (the hunting scene) or possibly an accompaniment to the huntsman's prologue since, after a mysterious fairy-tale beginning, there is this horn melody (strongly reminiscent of Smetana's music and, surprisingly enough, even of Tchaikovsky's First Piano Concerto):

463

(dimin.)

scored later for harp and the inevitable viola d'amore:

464

---

*) In spite of this, Janáček's remark 'They want me to write a comic opera,' (Vašek, p. 185) should not be taken literally.

372

The second piece consists entirely of simple fanfares which were obviously to be used at various points in the play. The third and largest piece (Allegretto) is the scene mentioned earlier, built from four musical ideas of which the motif:

465

is the most important. It is probably related to Jau since its maestoso variant doubtless describes his change into a prince. The fourth item (Adagio) is no more than a fragment. Judging by the progression of airy violin thirds with which it begins:

466

it was probably intended for one of Sidselill's scenes or, perhaps, for Jau's falling asleep which ends his riotous excursion into the world of illusion.

It is not clear whether these sketches remained unfinished because of Janáček's death, or whether he simply discontinued work on them. After his death they were found on his writing stand at Hukvaldy, together with the score of the DANUBE and Act III of THE HOUSE OF THE DEAD. This could mean that he was at least intending to go on working on them.

There is, perhaps, little reason to regret Janáček's not having completed SCHLUCK AND JAU since, despite the wisdom and humanity of Gerhart Hauptmann's play, he would have had to overcome not only the 'operetta' end of Act IV with Schluck cast as the 'sweet little woman', but also the two great divides of ideology and national character, even though Max Brod had thought that Janáček, on account of having been born and bred in neighbouring Czech Silesia, would be well able to find the right and natural manner for Hauptmann's two country bumpkins.*)

On 8 June Janáček finished (as far as he can be said to have finished it) his opera THE HOUSE OF THE DEAD.

On 1 July he went again to Luhačovice to take the cure and was visited by William Ritter. There he also renewed his acquaintance with his almost exact contemporary, the pianist and pupil of Smetana, Professor Josef Jiránek (1855—1940).

In an article in *Národní noviny* of 15 August 1928, F. K. Zachoval recorded a few details of Janáček's last visit to Luhačovice. Janáček was 'still full of life and went for a walk regularly every day on the esplanade. He was always carefully dressed in a white suit and greeted everybody with a warm smile.' On 20 July he sat on a bench under a large oak tree in the wood known as Na Jestřábí where he discussed THE HOUSE OF THE DEAD with Zachoval. He

*) In the end the incidental music was compiled using the works of Bedřich Smetana, by E. A. Herrmann and orchestrated by the conductor Bachenheimer.

told him that he had not yet decided to show it to the public and that he had struggled with it for a long time before finding the right way of linking the acts with a common thread. He was satisfied, however, that he had succeeded, and said that there remained only a few minor details to be worked out. He did not believe that his new opera would be produced soon and he was even doubtful about offering it to a theatre during his lifetime. He was sure that it would provoke all sorts of criticism and squabbles, but he had written it the way it had sprung up in his mind, and would change nothing.*)

At the end of July Janáček returned for a while to Brno where he attended a concert of the Lumír Choral Society. This society consisted entirely of Prussian Slavs, members of the minority group known as Lusatian Sorbs. 'Janáček listened to the entire concert which lasted two and a half hours,' wrote the leader of the Lumír group, the composer Bjarnat Krawc.**) 'He admired our active musical life, our beautiful songs and folk costumes. He was especially pleased by our national dances. He came round to the artists' room and asked to be introduced to the soloists and dancers, and said to us: "Travel, keep travelling abroad so that people may know the musical treasure of your small and worthy nation." '***)

Janáček was particularly pleased with the results of his Luhačovice cure that year—in his estimation, his rheumatism had completely gone. Unfortunately, the cure at the spa always consisted of hot mud baths which did no good to his heart. Two years earlier he suffered from giddiness and had once fallen and injured himself. Subsequently various symptoms of a weakening heart brought on gloomy premonitions from time to time, against which Janáček fought with passionate self-confidence.

On 30 November 1927 he wrote to Kamila: 'I am finishing one work after another—as if I were soon to settle my account with life.' Before this, on 12 February, he wrote to Max Brod: 'The pen seems to want to drop out of my hand. Longing and hurrying to the point of exhaustion, I am waiting, wondering whether another little star from some distant horizon will fall, ringing, into my mind...' But in the same letter he wrote: 'I feel free, I breathe like nature herself in the spring sunshine. Fresh, hopeful grass everywhere, here and there an inquisitive flower. I want only to feel the wings of the music of the spheres, waving.' Janáček's indomitable will to live and his quiet resignation are then combined in a single sentence: 'Tame as a dog, rapacious as a vulture, dry as a leaf, lapping like the surf, crackling like dry twigs in the

---

*) An utterance which need not be applied to technical details.
**) Brno *Hudební rozhledy*, Vol. IV.
***) This was not the end of his interest in folk music even at this late stage. According to the Brno literary historian Professor Pavel Váša writing in the *Lidové noviny* of 16 August 1928, he was planning for his next summer holidays a trip to Skalice in Slovakia in company with his enthusiastic collaborator Hynek Bím to hear the songs of the night-watchmen, and to the Zvolen district to hear the fuyara, a long wooden pipe, being played by shepherds. Earlier, in June, he requested Dr F. A. Cykler, who was studying in America on a Czechoslovak government scholarship, to send him a book of Negro melodies. Among Janáček's papers about 15 previously unknown harmonizations of Moravian and Slovak folk songs have been found. To within a few days of his death, Janáček worked with Váša on a collection called *Moravské písně milostné* (Moravian Love Songs), which were subsequently published during the years 1930 to 1936.

fire; I cling to every stirring in the mind; and I am dumbfounded by a holy silence.'

The one thing which remained quite unchanged was his love for Kamila. It even grew with every new creative inspiration for which he thanked her or, perhaps, his image of her. She had at last promised to spend her summer holidays with him at Hukvaldy. This brought him to the peak of elation. 'I have never known a greater love than what I feel for her. To her I dedicate my work. Flowers, bow down to her! Little birds, do not stop your song of eternal love!' This was the dedication which on 12 February he wrote for her in the vocal score of KATYA KABANOVA, alluding to the last words of the heroine of that opera; and for her he must have meant his last musical sketch entitled: 'I wait for you.' To her was also addressed his last confession—a draft for an article 'The Artist's Vision'. As though continuing where he had left off in his recent letter to Brod, Janáček ended the article with the words:

'Happiness and the power of a vision—if it can be identified with a real being. Happiness, if it thus draws the living fire. My sound is like a drizzle— you cannot get away from it. It envelops the hedges, the fields and the flowers. It even covers the little chicks with dew, even the coat of the kitten. The vision of my Louise, Alyeya and poor Akulka, my Katya and my Zefka, rings out with my sounds like pure silver. My sounds are like a mist. They would grow cold on the keyboard. They only seek life. In life they thicken into clouds, they grow hot with the storm...' And yet Janáček adds: 'It is getting darker. One has to admit it: the sign at the crossroads...'

Having reached the height of fame as well as happiness in love, he was nearer the crossroads than he himself suspected. He had, in fact, passed them.

(46) Last Holiday

On Monday 30 July—Zdeňka's birthday—Janáček, Kamila, her 11-year-old son and her husband went by slow train to Hukvaldy. Kamila's husband was to stay only a few days and then tactfully depart on a business trip. This was the first time that Janáček had made an exception to his rule of not letting himself be disturbed in his country retreat. On the contrary, in expectation of this visit he even arranged to have some hasty decorating done to his modest cottage. He had electric light put in and had the attic made into a spare bedroom, as well as having the garden tidied up. In 1924 he had become one of Hukvaldy's landowners when he purchased a piece of forest on his beloved Babí hůra. And the following year he bought a further piece. The gamekeeper Sládek looked after it for him. And Sládek's son Vinca, whom we have met already as a rich source of *nápěvky* (speech melodies), now helped with the renovations to the house and garden.

During his penultimate visit to Hukvaldy in May, Janáček corrected the final proofs of the pocket score of the LACHIAN DANCES—symbolically enough, the work in which he had first sounded his truly Lachian note and in which he declared his most sincere love—the love for his native district. In the preface which he wrote for this edition on 22 May Janáček remembers:

'Below the Hukvaldy castle, in the dale so small that you could throw a stone across it, stood the Harabiš's Inn.

'The windows glowed like embers in the darkness. Inside, dense smoke and fumes.

'Harabiš's Žofka went from one hand to another, dancing.*)

'Forty-five years have passed.

'I sit poring over the proofs of the LACHIAN DANCES. In each note, in each bar, I see the crowded room at the inn with the sweating, reddening faces. Everywhere people move and whirl around and bow...

'In memory of that warm summer night, of the starry vault overhead, of the River Ondřejnice murmuring like a tremor of love, in memory of all of you who were there that warm night and are now asleep of ever—in praise of my native countryside, my Lachia, this score filled with fleeting little notes, playful melodies—chattering or brooding, goes out into the world.

'May it spread joy and conjure up smiles.'

Kamila took possession of the new room upstairs while Janáček occupied his two rooms on the ground floor. ('He worked at his writing desk next to the large harmonium in the left-hand room which was filled with sunlight and the reflections of shining green foliage morning and afternoon.'**)

---

*) see p. 94.
**) Robert Smetana writing in the Brno *Hudební rozhledy*, IV.

On Wednesday 1 August, three days after their arrival, Janáček took his guests by carriage to Štramberk to show them the beautiful old town with its famous tower. From there they went to the National Park at Kotouč Mountain where his statue had been erected. He also took them to see the folklore collection of his friend Dr Adolf Hrstka, the local G. P. in whose house in Štramberk the Slovácko region was represented by its wine as by its peasant embroidery. 'At no other time during his last years,' wrote his host in the *Lidové noviny* of 16 August 1928, 'had I seen the maestro so cheerful, so full of good humour and joy. His eyes shone with happiness and contentment, he seemed to be overflowing with life and life's energy. "I want to work on this and on that, now that I have finished THE HOUSE OF THE DEAD," said Janáček. "I want to rewrite this and complete that, because I now feel perfectly supple in mind and healthy in body." And as he was leaving he assured us that he would be back in a week's time—with William Ritter.'

But fate changed all that...

On Monday 6 August Kamila's young son got lost while they were all out walking to Babí hůra and Janáček immediately set out to find him.*) Forgetful of his age, he crisscrossed the woods and ran up and down hills and finally sat down, overheated, on 'his' bench at 'Viewpoint' despite a strong wind. The boy eventually found his way back safely on his own. Janáček, however, caught a cold which was to prove fatal, since, out of consideration for his guest, he tried at first to conceal it. On Wednesday 8 August he even went to the hamlet of Podlesí at the foot of Babí hůra to visit his housekeeper's mother who did his laundry. On his return he felt unwell; the ear inflammation from which he had suffered in February made a painful reappearance. On Thursday morning at last he called the Hukvaldy doctor, Emil Franta, who diagnosed 'flu with laryngitis and mastoiditis, plus an irregular heart beat which, however, was attributable to the patient's long history of heart trouble and hardening of the arteries. By noon Dr Franta and Dr V. Hradečný, a consultant from Frenštát who had been called in, diagnosed the onset of pneumonia. Despite the insistence of both doctors and the Hukvaldy Mayor Sobotík, Janáček refused to be moved to hospital either in Brno or in Ostrava. Only on Friday morning, as he got noticeably worse (although he felt relatively comfortable), and especially by noon when some other disturbing symptoms appeared, he consented to be taken by car to Dr Klein's sanatorium in Ostrava. (The car had been standing by unbeknown to Janáček.) As he got into the car Janáček joked with the hospital attendants: 'Well, bring me back again soon, cured.' However, he arrived in Ostrava with a temperature of 104° and the X-ray confirmed the inflammation of the lower right-hand lobe of the lung. The general condition of the patient was found to be very serious. Nevertheless, Janáček felt easier and in good spirits at the sanatorium where in Dr Klein's absence he was attended by an experienced G. P., Dr Korbel, and Dr Klein's young assistant Dr Gross. They administered injections to increase the action of the heart and halt the drop in the patient's blood pressure. By

---

*) Janáček, in spite of his age, was a good walker. During the previous summer holidays he and his wife and the painter František Ondrůšek had climbed Radhošť (1129 m) in the Beskydy Mountains.

Saturday Janáček's condition had improved and his bed was soon strewn with music manuscript paper. 'I have a request,' he said to Dr Korbel, 'forbid these young doctors to keep pricking me with their injections. It disturbs me in my work.' During Saturday night an ominous change occurred in his condition and although constantly alert and in good spirits, he began gradually to be aware of the fact that his life was in danger. He began coughing, had difficulty in breathing, and mental tiredness set in. Dr Gross who stayed at his bedside throughout the night continued giving him stronger and stronger injections to stimulate his heart but even the strongest dose of adrenalin was of no avail. In the evening Janáček wrote a letter to a friend and, at about 2 a.m., his last will: this he wrote in pencil in Kamila's autograph book, covering four pages, with some additions on a separate scrap of paper. After that there was nothing but a painful and desperate struggle with death. When he woke up for a moment, he refused an injection, saying 'I would rather die than live like this.' According to the nurse Božena Sedláková who attended him during his last night, he even refused to be wrapped in cold sheets, saying that it was useless and that he knew he was dying. At the same time, when he fell into a feverish semi-conscious state, he called out: 'I must go back (to Hukvaldy)—I've got that child there' (Kamila's son). His old defiance did not leave him. When the nurse asked him if he wanted to make his peace with God, he said: 'Nurse, you probably don't know who I am.' And he gave Sister Siena, who took over from the nurse, the same reply.

In the early morning he had the first heart attack and after that he began weakening rapidly. Dr Korbel was summoned and in spite of Janáček's refusal of injections, was able to give him a sedative. At nine o'clock Janáček fell asleep. His blood pressure sank to a minimum and he lost consciousness. And in that state his heart stopped beating and he passed quietly away—on Sunday 12 August 1928 at exactly ten o'clock.

Only then did Kamila send a telegram to the unsuspecting Mrs Janáčková: 'Maestro seriously ill. Come immediately.'

However, Mrs Janáčková certainly guessed the truth when shortly after receiving the telegram, she was told that a car (in fact an undertaker's car) was waiting to take her to Ostrava. She travelled in the company of the family friend Stanislav Tauber, soloist of the Moravian Teachers' Choir; they drove through villages where the harvest festival was at its height.

The journey was doubly difficult for Zdeňka since she was to meet Kamila at the end of it. A vivid description of their meeting and their subsequent journey together to Hukvaldy may be found in Tauber's book *My Musical World*, page 102. A court case followed because the changes and additions made by the dying Janáček to his will benefited Kamila.*) Rivalry flared up between the private undertaker and the Brno Town Council as to who should have the

---

*) According to Zdeňka Janáčková's *Reminiscences* (p. 200), Janáček, in the autograph book, left the royalties of KATYA KABANOVA and THE HOUSE OF THE DEAD to Kamila. Although he left his wife sufficiently provided for, the principal inheritor was the Philosophical Faculty of the Masaryk University in Brno—probably in return for his honorary doctorate. But he wished that the Faculty create a department for the study of living speech and that they collect his literary works and supervise the carrying out of his will. (Robert Smetana: *Stories about Janáček*, p. 129.)

honour of burying the famous man, with the result that although the private firm finally gave way, the body of the dead composer travelled secretly to and fro (at times under cover of darkness, still wearing the garb in which he had died)—an Odyssey worthy of the pen of E. T. A. Hoffmann, Balzac or Edgar Allan Poe.

The news of Janáček's death reached Brno the same day before noon, but no one was willing to believe it at first since the health of the 'young old man' had become almost legendary. Towards the evening a black flag was hoisted on the building in which the Exhibition of Contemporary Culture was being held, and other flags were flown at half-mast. As it happened, the Myjava folk band which Janáček had a year before taken to the festival in Frankfurt, was playing at the Exhibition. The director of the Brno Theatre, František Neumann, announced the death to the packed Sunday house after the second act of Smetana's *Bartered Bride*, and the audience at once rose in memory of the dead composer, and repeated the honour after the performance when the funeral march from Beethoven's *Eroica* was played; on the stage the singers who had created so many of the parts in Janáček's operas stood with bowed heads; it was on that stage that Janáček had so often thanked them with his firm handshake or acknowledged the applause of the public with his typical short bows.

After the body had been transported to Brno (no one unfortunately thought of casting his death-mask) and after the squabbles over the funeral had been settled, the open coffin with a bunch of roses placed at the composer's feet was laid in state in the chapel of the Holy Sepulchre at the Old Brno Augustinian Monastery.

Thus Janáček ended his earthly journey at the place where he had first set out as an artist and musician. And there on Wednesday 15 August at eight o'clock in the morning the prelate Bařina sprinkled the body with holy water and the coffin was then taken to the Brno Municipal Theatre where it was placed in the foyer amidst a mass of flowers, wreaths and candles and opposite Janáček's bust which had been unveiled there two-and-a-half years previously. And there, at half past ten, the funeral began, attended by many prominent people—artists as well as public figures including, for instance, Otakar Ostrčil, Max Brod and Oskar Nedbal. The orchestra and soloists conducted by František Neumann began the beautiful finale from ADVENTURES OF THE VIXEN SHARP EARS with the gamekeeper's epilogue (sung by Arnold Flögl): 'People will bow their heads and will understand that heavenly bliss has passed by all around them...'

After speeches by the Lord Mayor of Brno, Tomeš, the composer Dr Boleslav Vomáčka who spoke for the Czech Academy of Sciences and Art, the Vice-Chancellor of the Brno Masaryk University which had bestowed its honorary degree on Janáček, Dr Jaroslav Kallab, the director of the Brno *conservatoire* Jan Kunc, and Dr Max Brod who spoke 'for the hundreds of thousands of German listeners who have enjoyed the works of Janáček's musical genius', the first part of Dvořák's *Requiem* was performed with Stanislav Tauber, Alexandra Čvánová and Marie Hloušková as soloists, and with the Brno Philharmonic Beseda Choral Society and the Orchestra of the Brno National Theatre, conducted by Janáček's pupil Jaroslav Kvapil.

The coffin was then carried out to the sound of horns and past a Sokol gymnastic association guard of honour. Three carriages filled with flowers headed the seemingly endless procession which began moving down Palacký Avenue. At that moment the sun came out, the men uncovered their heads and the street lamps were lit.

After stopping at Wilson Square, the guests went on to the cemetery where the coffin was taken to the graveside.

Here, after a religious service, the coffin was lowered into the grave, again to the sound of horns, and Janáček's closest collaborator František Neumann bade farewell 'to the father and leader' who 'had led us out of chaos'. The Opera chorus sang the national anthem and the funeral was over.*)

Another, and perhaps more significant ceremony, however, was the post-humous première of Janáček's bequest to mankind, his opera THE HOUSE OF THE DEAD, in Brno on 12 April 1930, conducted by Břetislav Bakala and produced by Ota Zítek. A number of guests from abroad attended the perform-ance, among others the composer Ernst Křenek who according to Adolf Vašek**) made no attempt to conceal his unbounded admiration. Other per-formances soon followed in Mannheim (14 December 1930), at the Prague National Theatre (21 February 1931, conducted by Vincenc Maixner and produced by Ferdinand Pujman with scenery by Vlastislav Hofman), in Oldenburg (7 May 1931, conducted by Johannes Schüller), at Berlin Kroll Opera (whose director at the time was Otto Klemperer—the première there was on 29 May 1931 with Fritz Zweig conducting***) and produced by Curjel; Caspar Neher designed the sets), then in Düsseldorf (15 May 1931), Ostrava (12 February 1932, conducted by the present author), in Coburg, Zurich and, since, in Basle (1952), Wiesbaden (12 May 1954), Amsterdam (25 June 1954), Hanover (2 March 1958) and other places.

Shortly after Janáček's death, on 11 September 1928, the Moravian Quartet (František Kudláček, Josef Jedlička, Josef Trkan and Josef Křenek) gave the first performance of the INTIMATE LETTERS at the Brno Exhibition of Con-temporary Culture. Janáček had wanted the first performance to be in Písek on account of the emotional content of the work. This was not to be, but he had studied the work with the players on 18 and 25 March so that the rendering which they subsequently gave may be considered authentic.

After Janáček's death, the ranks of those closest to him were soon to be depleted. On 25 February 1929 František Neumann died of pneumonia at the age of 55.

In 1935 Kamila Stösslová, the person who had attracted Janáček by her overwhelming vitality, died of cancer at the early age of 43. And on 17 February 1938, barely ten years after her husband's death, the 'happy unhappy' Zdeňka Janáčková also died. The retreat at the back of the *conservatoire* building was

---

*) Following the many complications over the burial, it was discovered after the funeral that Janáček had after all been buried in a private grave instead of the grave of honour. Therefore on 17 August he was quietly buried a second time.

**) *Vašek*, p. 228.

***) Dr Fritz Zweig arranged some of the music of the opera into a suite which he conducted in London on 28 February 1937. It consisted of the overture, the convicts' play from Act II and the finale, beginning at reh. No 37.

left vacant and Janáček's study—together with all his scores and papers, and (by a court order) the rights vested in them—went, thanks to the magnanimous will of Zdeňka Janáčková, to the Philosophical Faculty of the Masaryk University and the Moravian Museum, and was housed in the building of the Brno Municipal Museum in Dominican Square.*)

Now that the composer would no longer surprise the world with new works year after year, critics began to emerge who tried to maintain that the great interest in Janáček's work would eventually wear off. The concerts organized in Prague and Brno to commemorate the tenth anniversary of his death were hampered by the events following the Munich crisis.

But just as that eclipse passed, so the eclipse of Janáček's work was of short duration. The Moravian Janáček has gradually become an object of world-wide interest. And certainly the time is not far ahead when music historians will have to find him a place if not among the greatest then at least among the most original inhabitants or, better still, conquerors of the musical Parnassus.

---

*) The study has now been moved back into the Director's villa at the back of the *conservatoire* which has itself been transformed into the Musical History Department of the Moravian Museum. The first floor of the building is devoted entirely to Janáček.

APPENDIX

On the Interpretation of Janáček's Works

No, no, no, a million times no!
You musicians, you poets, prose-writers, actors, pianists, conductors,
whether of third or second or even first rank,
you do not have the right to meddle with a Shakespeare or a Beethoven,
not even to bestow on them the blessings of your knowledge and taste.
No, no, no, ten million times no!
No man, no matter who he is, has the right to compel another,
no matter who he is, to give up his own face, wear a mask,
speak in a manner that is not his, take a shape not of his choosing...

Hector Berlioz: Memoirs*)

For a composer's work to be fully appreciated it must be given an authoritative performance. But I must confess that many times, when rehearsing Janáček's music, especially his operas, I have found myself passing from the greatest admiration for its artistic essence to the most torturing doubts as to its creative design and the composer's interpretative intentions. The problems inherent in Janáček's music are more than adequately explained by the breathtaking speed with which he composed most of his masterpieces towards the end of his life—between his sixty second and seventy fourth year. During those years, apart from a number of 'lesser' works such as the DIARY OF THE YOUNG MAN WHO DISAPPEARED, TARAS BULBA, the two QUARTETS, the sextet YOUTH, the CONCERTINO, NURSERY RHYMES, the CAPRICCIO, the SINFONIETTA, the GLAGOLITIC MASS and so on, he wrote no fewer than five operas: THE EXCURSION OF MR BROUČEK TO THE FIFTEENTH CENTURY, KATYA KABANOVA, ADVENTURES OF THE VIXEN SHARP EARS, THE MAKROPOULOS CASE and THE HOUSE OF THE DEAD—a truly extraordinary achievement for an artist of his age. It would clearly be petty to blame him for having, here and there, left some problems unsolved. But the fact remains that these problems exist, and we cannot evade the question of to what extent we, Janáček's heirs, have the right or even duty to solve them.

Some particularly valuable contributions have in this respect been made by musicians who worked and studied under Janáček's supervision.**) The first

---

*) Translated by David Cairns, Victor Gollancz, London 1969.
**) Professor František Kudláček, first violinist of the Moravian Quartet, has told me, for instance, that Janáček wanted the end of his FIRST QUARTET to be played ff throughout, without the diminuendo marked in the final bars; at the beginning of the VIOLIN SONATA he wanted the prescribed staccato changed to gradually quickening long bows, and in the third movement he added—in place of the rests in the violin part in bars 12 to 14 on page 21, before the return of the allegretto—the following:

with the same expression in the piano part, and on the last page in the first four bars he changed the p to ff, in bars three and four doubled the left hand at an octave below, and the last two bars of the SONATA he wanted adagio.

problem to be considered is that of the retouching of Janáček's orchestration. Luckily no major revisions or completions of the scale of, say, Mussorgsky have been necessary, with the negligible exception of the DANUBE. Even Kovařovic's alterations and additions in JENŮFA are relatively minor. Václav Talich had the interludes before and after Scene 2 of Act II (At Pásek's Inn) of the VIXEN extended for his 1937 production at the Prague National Theatre (whereas he cut the reprise of the interlude in Act I), but these expedients were dictated by difficulties with the scenery—expedients which may well be dispensed with in other productions.

More serious than mere retouching is the surgery to which some of Janáček's scores, especially the operatic ones, have been subjected.*) Janáček, true, is not one of the world's virtuoso orchestrators even though he holds his own among them on account of his bold experimentation and his unusual combinations of instruments (for instance in the CAPRICCIO) in the best Berlioz—Stravinsky line of development. On the other hand his originality did not make his task any easier, since at the beginning of his career he lacked the necessary orchestral experience. Thus it is not surprising that his striking sound was, at least in the beginning, perhaps involuntary. After the first performance of RÁKÓS RÁKÓCZY, V. J. Novotný**) wrote that Janáček's orchestra utters 'the most peculiar sounds'. However, the same could be said today of even his most mature compositions if the orchestra is not carefully rehearsed.

Janáček was fully aware of this, and when he considered a conductor competent, he did not hesitate to give him a free hand in the matter of necessary corrections. For instance, on 17 September 1917, he wrote to Kovařovic who was rehearsing JEALOUSY with the orchestra of the Prague National Theatre for its performance in Brno: 'If you find it necessary to fill out the orchestration, do it by all means.' And on 29 January 1920 he wrote very much the same thing to Ostrčil in connection with the EXCURSIONS OF MR BROUČEK.

It will be noted, however, that these were works Janáček had not heard as yet, or not for some time, and works whose rehearsals he could not easily attend. Janáček certainly never intended to give everyone *carte blanche* for making their own alterations, especially not for changing the character and therefore the sense of his orchestration. The most that can be said to have been sanctioned by Janáček is the carrying out of his probable intentions.***) His orchestral colouring is an integral part of his originality and it may be said of him—bearing in mind the foregoing qualifications—what Weingartner said of Brahms: that 'he had what orchestration he needed.'†)

---

*) For the above-mentioned 1937 production of the VIXEN Talich—doubtless wishing to help the opera's chances of success—had the orchestration fundamentally reworked by the National Theatre's conductor František Škvor and, in part, by the composer and conductor Jaroslav Řídký who was also responsible for extending the interludes. Talich's suite from the VIXEN also uses the new orchestration. The rescoring in KATYA is less extensive and was done by Talich himself for his production, again at the Prague National Theatre, in 1938. Talich added a lot of brass during Kabanikha's invectives, also at the end of Act II (too much in view of the lyricism inherent in the scene), and especially during the storm. Prague, unlike Brno, still uses Talich's instrumentation which it has also committed to a gramophone recording.
**) In *Zlatá Praha* (Golden Prague), Vol. VIII, No. 39.
***) Since Janáček composed in full score, it sometimes happened that he put down only the

As the standard of instrumental playing goes up, it must be harnessed in the service of interpretation, for, as another conductor (Milan Sachs) said: 'If some works play themselves, Janáček's never do.' To begin with, his favourite keys, A flat minor and D flat major, and the wide, 'over-the-top' intervals which he used so often and which call for awkward fingerings—notably in the strings—are difficult. When they turn into fast diminutions, as in the second movement of the SINFONIETTA, they are especially trying. However, since they are thematic and no mere kicking up of dust, they must remain unchanged— here patience is the only answer.

One simply has to get used to the missing heavy beats without getting bogged down or irritated by the novelty of their absence. The same applies to Janáček's predilection for notation using the smallest note values. And his use of flats and sharps seems to be governed by rules of unfathomable mystery. One has to forgive him in view of the feverish haste with which he wrote, as one must also forgive his tendency to overlook the technical limits of some quite well known instruments, such as the violin. In the second scene of ADVENTURES OF THE VIXEN SHARP EARS, for instance, he asks the second violins and violas to play the following harmonics:

while the harp has the same notes without harmonics. One would assume that given this notation the notes should sound loco which, of course, is impossible. And using artificial harmonics, the nearest that the violins can get to their B flat is an octave higher, and the violas to their G flat is two octaves higher.

In the same scene of the VIXEN and elsewhere Janáček askes the double-basses for some equally impossible harmonics, so that players are often obliged to resort to the weirdest acrobatics in performing them: when the Brno State Philharmonic Orchestra was making their gramophone recording of the GLAGOLITIC MASS, for instance, the principal double-bass player helped himself out by touching the string at the fourth with his nose in order to elicit this harmonic (in the third movement):

(He should have considered tuning down and saving himself the trouble.)

Trombones, on the other hand, are often given such low notes that most players are obliged to perform them an octave higher. It is said that in Janáček's

instruments which indicated the basic tone colour he wanted. Even here, however, it should not be forgotten that a certain thinness of sound, a certain lack of stuffing in the middle parts, is the distinguishing feature of his style.
†) Talich himself admitted broadmindedly to the present author in later years: 'We wanted to help him (Janáček), and he instead crushed us all!'

time the Brno Theatre had a bass trombone player whose instrument (and lung capacity) made those depths attainable.

In Part One of TARAS BULBA, the motif:

470

is accompanied in the cymbal by a figure systematically written like this:

471

instead of the simple:

472

so that unnecessary doubts arise as to whether a simultaneous stroke on both cymbals is meant (as, for instance, Bruno Walter read it) or whether one of the two notes is intended for another percussion instrument altogether. Janáček probably envisaged a stroke (with a stick which is expressly prescribed) on one and the other cymbal in alternation. This was no momentary whim since in a similar sword-fighting scene in Act II of THE HOUSE OF THE DEAD (after reh. No. 25) he still wrote the cymbal part analogously:

473

instead of:

474

Similar riddles are sometimes the fault not so much of the composer, but of the copyist or the printer. For instance, at the beginning of the third movement of the SINFONIETTA the strings are all marked 'con sordini', except for the violas. The explanation is to be found in Janáček's manuscript score where the viola part throughout the movement, including the wild middle section, is scored for a solo viola d'amore—the instrument which Janáček from a certain point in his life kept asking for and kept having subsequently to suppress. Naturally enough, in order to hold its own against the rest of the strings it had to play 'senza sordino'.

In the same movement the manuscript score clearly indicates 'little bells', but the printed score gives only the abbreviation 'camp.' which may mean *campanelle* (little bells) just as *campane* (bells, as so many conductors wrongly understand). Unfortunately not even the manuscript score gives any pitch to the bell notes, which could mean that what Janáček had in mind was the triangle. If 'little bells' are used, they should best be given perhaps the note o f the cello and horn pedal, E flat above the middle C. In the next movement there is no problem—Janáček's manuscript clearly states 'little bells' and gives the pitch.

Janáček's way of notating tremolos is equally puzzling. He always indicates demi-semiquavers, whatever the tempo. Judging by those examples which are written or partly written out, however, one may presume that he wanted a rhythmic tapping or hammering rather than a tremolo. As a general rule, though, passages of regular symphonic flow require a regular tapping, whereas rubato passages call more for a tremolo.

A typical Janáček characteristic which makes his intentions difficult to understand is his unwillingness to disengage himself from a rhythmic pattern, even though a change of tempo demands a different rhythmic notation for the same motif. For instance, at the beginning of ADVENTURES OF THE VIXEN SHARP EARS he writes the staccato figuration of the slow 4/8 introduction in demi-semiquavers and continues to do so even after the change of tempo to the following quick waltz where it should, in fact, be written in quavers. (The relation of the tempi is, according to Janáček's own indication, ♪ = 120 : ♩. = 88, that is to say, ♪ = 240 : ♩ = 264, making the quavers of the waltz even faster than the demi-semiquavers of the previous Andante!) On the other hand I cannot agree with those who hold that a similar oversight occurred in Part Three of TARAS BULBA at the change of time signature from 3/4 to 2/4, 10 bars after reh. No. 25. The confusion was cleared up in the printed score published in 1927 when Janáček was still alive, where the editor Otakar Šourek appends ♪ = ♪. As he rightly explains in his introductory notes, any faster tempo would make nonsense of the following accelerando and obscure the motivic development in the woodwind. The solution is made easier if, starting with the preceding 2/8 presto, a tempo faster than the ♩ = 80 marked in the score is used—a procedure, in my opinion, fully justified in a re-presentation of the orgiastic dance of the Poles and of the subsequent mad gallop of Taras' Cossacks. It helps, too, if the change to the relatively calmer rhythm of the 2/4 section is pointed up by a sudden piano (the trombones excepted)—the subsequent build up (as marked in the score) is then all the more effective.

As a general rule, when Janáček changes the time signature, the unit of time that remains constant is not the bar but the small time-value. It must surely be a mistake to beat in Part Two of TARAS BULBA between reh. Nos. 18 and 21 the same one-in-a-bar beat throughout irrespective of the alternation of 3/8 time with 2/8, as for instance Bruno Walter, an otherwise distinguished promoter of Janáček's music, used to do. Equally, if the same three-in-a-bar beat is applied to the passage at reh. No. 27 in Act II of ADVENTURES OF THE VIXEN SHARP EARS where 3/4 and 3/2 bars alternate, the 3/2 bars will turn out to be twice as slow and their music ponderous—hardly appropriate to the action on stage, given as 'Harašta stumbling'.

More difficult than these rather obvious cases are those where, along with the change of time signature, Janáček presupposes a change of tempo without expressly saying so. Here, it is usually a case of analogy with previous properly marked passages. Thus it goes without saying that in Act III of the VIXEN, before and after reh. No. 6, the 6/16 bars are always to be taken twice as slow as the 3/8 ones, since similar places earlier on bear the mark : ♩. = ♪

One must not be confused also by Janáček's habit of giving a 6/16 time signature instead of a clear 3/8. He likes to switch the rhythm from three times two to two times three and back again, and the use of the signature 6/16 is a convenient way of leaving the metre open to either interpretation. For the same reason, the crotchets at the beginning of Act II of KATYA are to be played as equal irrespective of the changes of metre (3/2 instead of 6/4).

From all that has been said, it is clear that neither the studying of the score nor the rehearsals are an easy matter. And even when the technical and interpretative problems have been solved, fresh surprises are in store. The sound of the orchestra sometimes appears to be too thin—due to the absence of any sort of 'pedal'; at other times, owing to the tendency of the temperamental composer to over-emphasize the dynamics, it seems to be too compact. The former flaw, so long as it is not intentional, can easily be made good (as in the charming scene with the little shepherd in Act I of JENŮFA) by the unobtrusive addition of a held note in the bass or some such expedient. The latter flaw can be corrected by lightening the dynamics by about one degree and contenting ourselves with a sort of toned-down ardour which, nonetheless, need lose none of its tension as a consequence. The result, in the operas for instance, will be to make the words more audible and, at the same time, to bring out the motivic work where it occurs in the inner and lower parts of the orchestra. It is there that Janáček, in his striving after pure *timbres*, often scores too lightly.*) Only where lightening the dynamics would not work, or where it would weaken the effect of a climax, should one resort to retouching the orchestration by judicious doubling. For instance in Part One of TARAS BULBA, during the battle scene, one should use at least the xylophone and the first oboe to double the second oboe's fanfare in order to make it heard above the held trill of almost all the other instruments. On the other hand, since Janáček is very reserved in his use of the more fanciful instruments, in particular the percussion, it is a grave mistake and misunderstanding of his style to add to their part for the sake of effect. It is best to bear in mind that in order to make Janáček's music as clear to the listener as possible, it must never be adapted according to conventional ideas but its presentation must be as true to its extraordinary style and substance as possible.

It is music closely linked with realism, and because of that, it presents us with two specific problems of interpretation: how to integrate the illustrative touches into the overall design, and how to reconcile the earthy realism with artistic sophistication.

The rhapsodic character of some portions of Janáček's music and their supposed naturalism was long the cause of the entirely misleading idea that his musical language was a string of characteristic fragments and that the right interpretative approach was to concentrate on detail—in a word, continuous rubato. The unification of tempi was thought to be not only alien to his style,

---

*) The harp sextuplets just before the end of TARAS BULBA are a case in point: beside using two harps, the dynamics in the other parts should be toned down after the second crotchet beat of the first bar of each phrase, and only in the second bar should there be a gradual crescendo back to forte again.

but well nigh impossible.*) The temptation to reach for this conclusion was supplied mainly by Janáček's typical rubato interjections which seemed, at first sight, to break up all unity of tempo. In reality, these interjections do not break up the tempo at all, they merely suspend it. Janáček's low opinion of mere stereotyped caesuras before every sudden piano (as is often done, for instance, in JENŮFA in Act I, eight bars before reh. No. 3, or in Act II, at reh. No. 53) is clearly stated in his letter to Erich Kleiber quoted earlier in this book on page 296. Thus, unity of tempo in Janáček's music is not only possible but is in fact one of the secrets of the relative tectonic unity of his works. The performer should not let himself be misled by contradictory expression marks such as the 'più mosso' before reh. No. 5 in the second movement of the SINFONI-ETTA— the clue is in the metronome mark ♩ = 144, exactly the same as before; or at the 6/4 Andante after the 6/8 Allegro at the end of the introduction to Act III of THE MAKROPOULOS CASE where the new crotchets are doubtless meant to be identical with the previous quavers and where Janáček should have written 'doppio movimento'. One should also not be confused when deciding on the new tempo, if one finds that while one part may continue evenly, another will have its rhythm doubled or halved as for instance in the last movement of the SINFONIETTA when changing from the maestoso at reh. No. 6 to tempo primo at No. 7—augmentation and, in particular, diminution of motives are part and parcel of Janáček's technique of composition. One should also bear in mind that Janáček's 'presto' is evidently not as fast, and his 'adagio' not as slow as they often are with other composers.**)

Naturally there are moments in Janáček's music as for instance the wistful rubato introduction to the last scene but one in ADVENTURES OF THE VIXEN SHARP EARS, where it is neither desirable nor possible to maintain a unified tempo. At such moments the logic of the construction can only be sustained by the inner compulsion and cogency of the many different twists of expression, agogic accent, pause and so on.

From the aesthetic point of view, Janáček's realism makes it imperative to perform his works, where necessary, in all their roughly hewn truthfulness and elemental wildness.***) Luckily we have a number of his own pronouncements on the subject: apart from such general ones as those quoted on page 12 we know for instance that when during the rehearsals for the first performance of the SINFONIETTA the Czech Philharmonic's excellent principal flute, Nesporý,

---

*) This is why one can still hear the simple melody of No. 3 of IN THE MISTS (Ex. 185) some-times played like this:

475

Here the root of the trouble is the complete lack of another quality which, in my opinion, is essential to interpreting Janáček: mere simplicity.

**) The final presto in the chorus 70,000 bears the relatively low metronome mark ♩ = 100.

***) Even Hindemith, once thought of as the representative of the so-called 'pure' music, marks the last movement of his Solo Viola Sonata 'Wild, Tonschönheit ist Nebensache,' (Wild. Beauty of tone is beside the point.)

protested that the demi-semiquaver runs in the third movement, Prestissimo, were unplayable, Janáček said irritably: 'Playable, unplayable—it has got to be like the wind. I heard it.' (Where he could have heard it, since this was the first performance, will remain a mystery.) Stanislav Tauber notes a similar remark in his *My Musical World* (p. 70) where he describes the first rehearsal of the chorus 70,000 by the Moravian Teachers' Choral Society: 'Here they are drunk, they are making a din. It must be a din. If a note here and there falls by the wayside, it doesn't matter.' None of this should, however, be taken to mean that Janáček whose music is so full of tender poetry and subtle humour wanted to inaugurate some kind of *Schule der Beiläufigkeit* (School of Slackness). It merely means that the right way to the proper rendering of his works lies not in detours and compromises, but in directly overcoming the difficulties.

Thus it is often a case of sheer and repeated drudgery before a score begins to shine. Such unexpected discoveries are then brought to light, however, that one is obliged to admit that far less retouching is in fact needed than had appeared necessary at the outset, and that what does need revising is one's own ingrained ideas.

In the operatic works, even greater attention should be paid to the stage and its living component—the singers. Janáček makes some quite unusual demands on them: for instance the vertiginous heights required of Mr Brouček and others in the EXCURSIONS or of the singers in THE HOUSE OF THE DEAD (Skuratov with his 'Me get married, me get married?'). Janáček liked to use the high register to emphasize weak, cowardly or crooked male characters, just as Wagner did (Mime, Beckmesser) and Richard Strauss (Herod, Aegisth), in contradistinction to the lower, heroic register. It could be argued that Janáček's demands are not always fully justified. He himself apologized to Kovařovic in a letter of 26 March 1919, saying: 'The practical side, and the baking hot emotions—the two do not always coincide when I am composing.' But one simply cannot allow the great spans of his vocal lines to be spoiled for whatever reason, including the mistaken belief that his vocal style is in any case a declamatory one. Equally, it is a distortion to cast the youthful parts of the Fox, the dog Lapák, and the Cock in the VIXEN, Alyeya in THE HOUSE OF THE DEAD, and so on, as male ones in an exaggerated effort to attain realism when Janáček just as Mozart (Cherubino, for instance) or Richard Strauss (Octavian) meant them to be sung by women. Not only does this change the intended sound picture and, with it, the structure of the work, but also what is charming or touching in a female interpreter becomes all too easily ponderous or even ridiculous when performed by a man.

In Janáček's operas the singer's job does not end with the singing. Perhaps even more crucial than that is his acting.

In 1907 Janáček wrote of DESTINY, conscious perhaps of its rather muddled plot: 'I am well aware that excellent acting is necessary from the singers if the characters and the plot are to emerge clear-cut. The characters must be rooted in everyday life.' This is true of all Janáček's operas; he expected the singer to act out the text in full, as much as he expected a realistically conceived and executed rendering of the music. Although Janáček's head was often in the clouds, his feet were set firmly on his native soil. And when he once said 'I am steeped in nature but not likely to drown in it,' he might very well have said: 'I am steeped in fiction but I shall not drown in it.' Janáček can be likened to folk songs which also have the power to raise some of the most realistic and everyday happenings to a level where they become outpourings of innermost emotion. And what has just been said applies in equal measure to the interpretation of Janáček's works: it also should not be swamped by naturalism, nor by fiction and esoteric symbols; it should rather pursue the earth-bound, human characterization of the *dramatis personæ* and the story, starting with the casting—be it for the role of the Little Bystrouška or the Little Frog, or for the almost Classical Greek figure of Kostelnička or the provocatively mysterious Emilia Marty. None of the parts lack character, but the fewer the words in a part, the more suggestive must be its casting.*)

If the characterization of Janáček's figures and of their speech is always clear, the same unfortunately cannot be said of the actual words that he sometimes gives them to say. In such cases the singer must help by gesture or by modulation of expression. For instance in Act I of THE HOUSE OF THE DEAD the Tall Convict must make it clear that his otherwise incomprehensible remark 'Biryulin's cow, in calf from white bread, will calve sixteen calves for the feast' is meant to ridicule the fat Small Convict. Obviously, if the singer is quoting or mimicking someone else (as for instance when Bystrouška is telling the Fox about her 'argument' with the gamekeeper, or in the various stories told in THE HOUSE OF THE DEAD) he will differentiate by 'intonation' (to use Chaliapin's expression) and by the most effective gesture. Caricature, and the right measure of it, is more difficult to judge. For instance Shishkov in his story in Act III of THE HOUSE OF THE DEAD may possibly exaggerate when quoting his shrewish mother-in-law, but the rest of the story is too serious for him to do more than just differentiate between the other people he quotes, even though Janáček tempts him to over-act, by placing Luka's quoted words in the tenor register. (Luka is a tenor while Shishkov a baritone.)

Sometimes, however, acting and 'intonation' are not enough, and one has to resort to some textual alterations. The corrections made by the ever alert as well as tactful Max Brod in his translations of Janáček's operas may be taken as a guide. In Act II of THE MAKROPOULOS CASE for instance, Emilia scorns Gregor who has threatened to kill her if she will not love him; he insists ('I'm in love with you'), and she retorts 'Kill yourself then', accentuating (even in Čapek's original) the first word, 'Kill'. Here Brod rightly shifts the accent to the word 'yourself'. More examples will be found in the earlier discussion of his translation of KATYA. On the other hand, Brod's translations are not without their flaws or even grave mistakes. The case of the ADVENTURES OF THE VIXEN SHARP EARS has been discussed in detail; similarly, other instances have been mentioned where Brod's textual changes—though correct—contradict the general drift of the vocal line, or where his translation runs counter to the motivic signalling in the accompanying music. Moreover Brod—doubtless in an effort to enrich the libretto—replaces the word repeti-

---

*) For this reason and in spite of my admiration for Dostoyevsky, it is to my mind wrong to present Goryanchikov in THE HOUSE OF THE DEAD as Dostoyevsky himself—in any case, since Dostoyevsky is to a large extent a co-author of the work, the wider, symbolic relevance of the character is thus lost.

tions, so typical of Janáček, with new and different words even where the melody remains the same. This is not only alien to Janáček' style and the meaning of his repetitions. It is also against his express wish: 'The same *nápěvek* (speech melody) has to have the same words,' he wrote to Brod on 9 January 1927, referring to THE MAKROPOULOS CASE.

In his 1907 letter concerning DESTINY mentioned above, Janáček stresses that the *dramatis personæ* must be rooted in everyday life. This means preserving the environment in which his characters move, since it is this that determines not only their originality but also their authenticity. As we have seen, Janáček spared no pains when starting to write an opera, in travelling up and down the countryside studying the place of action. We have also seen the importance he attached to folk song and to knowing where it came from—to its 'cradle'. He took care to capture each particular *milieu* in his music, and in some cases (JENŮFA, THE VIXEN) went as far as preserving the dialect—in THE HOUSE OF THE DEAD he even inserts Russian words into the text. His letters show again and again the care with which he supervised the productions of his operas to ensure both outwardly and inwardly their faithfulness. For instance, before and even after the Prague première of JENŮFA, he urged that the stone footbridge in Act I should be replaced by a wooden one. 'A footbridge like that back at home... of stone... never!'*) And three months after the première, in August 1916, the painter Alois Kalvoda travelled at Janáček's insistence to the Javorník—Púchov district straddling the Moravian-Slovak border to see what the highland mills looked like. Gabriela Horvátová, the first Prague Kostelnička, tells how she studied the part with Janáček: 'Learning Kostelnička meant travelling all over Moravia with Janáček. He wanted me to know the customs of 'his' people down to the last detail. The journey began in his native Hukvaldy... Then we visited 'aunt' Hudečková**) of whom Bartoš had written: "A regal woman, noble, beautiful, her bearing a true model for Kostelnička..."' He also took her to some villages in the Javorníky Mountains where the women who were in mourning (there were many as it was wartime) wore white dresses to church, looking like a 'flock of humble doves'.

It is a great mistake, widely made today, to try to bring the drama nearer to the audience by neutralizing it or by transferring it to a modern setting. This not only results in a colourless levelling of the drama, but also a great deal of the charm of theatre is lost when the outward juxtaposition (and at the same time the inherent oneness) of the unique and the universal, of dreams and reality, of the distant and the near, of the past and the present, is removed. There is a Czech proverb which says 'Clothes make a man', and this is especially true of the man of the stage.

The bragging of Števa and the recruits and, later on, even of Jenůfa in Act I is psychologically impossible to imagine without their wearing the ostentatious Slovácko folk costumes. Besides, the musical and choreographic embellishments (for instance the recruits' *odzemek* dance—see p. 130) presuppose some corresponding traditional adornment in the form of folk costumes.

---

*) One wonders what he would have made of a certain West German production in which Števa turned up on stage wearing ordinary civilian town clothes and pushing a bicycle.
**) The wife of Martin Zeman who was one of Janáček's main helpers in collecting folk songs.

But even JENŮFA must never become a mere empty display of colourful peasant costumes. In particular Kostelnička—a widow—should be distinguishable from the other women by her sober workaday dress. And it is nonsense to suppose that the costumes have to be an exact copy of the original; only the fundamental character of the *milieu* and thus of the whole work must be preserved. Otherwise the contingent success (since it is difficult to stifle an opera such as JENŮFA) may be for the wrong reasons, as it very often is, for instance, with Smetana's *Bartered Bride* abroad. But that sort of success is the most bitter kind a masterpiece can have.

A true work deserves true understanding and true success.

CATALOGUE OF WORKS
BY LEOŠ JANÁČEK

Abbreviations

A	alto/contralto
APSM	Akademické pěvecké sdružení Moravan v Brně (The Academic Chorale 'Moravan' in Brno)
B	bass
Bar	baritone
BeB	Beseda brněnská (The Brno Society)
Br	Brno
c	circa
ČHF	Český hudební fond (Czech Music Fund), Prague
ded.	dedication/dedicated
ed.	editor/edited
edn.	edition
eds.	editors
HAM	Hudební archiv Moravského musea v Brně — Janáčkův archiv (Music Archives of the Moravian Museum in Brno — Janáček Archives)
HM	Hudební matice Umělecké besedy v Praze (Music Association of the Art Society in Prague)
KPU	Klub přátel umění v Brně (Friends of Art Club in Brno)
LN	*Lidové noviny* (a Brno daily newspaper)
min.	minute(s)
ND	Národní divadlo (National Theatre) in Prague
PD	Prozatímní divadlo (Provisional Theatre) in Prague
perf.	performance/performed
p(p).	page(s)

Pr	Praha (Prague)
PSMU	Pěvecké sdružení moravských učitelů (Moravian Teachers' Choral Society) in Brno
PSPU	Pěvecké sdružení pražských učitelů (Prague Teachers' Choral Society)
PSPUk	Pěvecké sdružení pražských učitelek (Prague Women Teachers' Choral Society)
rev.	revision/revised
ŘBS	Řemeslnická beseda Svatopluk (Artisan Society 'Svatopluk'), Brno
S	soprano
SATB	mixed voices (mixed choir) chorus
S, A, T, B	solo(ist) quartet
SB	Slovanská beseda v Brně (Slavonic Society in Brno)
SD	Státní divadlo (State Theatre)
SHV	Státní hudební vydavatelství v Praze (State Publishing House for Music) in Prague
SNKLHU	Státní nakladatelství krásné literatury, hudby a umění v Praze (State Publishers for Literature, Music and Arts in Prague)
T	tenor
UE	Universal Edition, Vienna
UK	Univerzitní knihovna v Brně (University Library in Brno)
ÚVU	Ústav ku vzdělání učitelů v Brně (Teachers' Training Institute in Brno)

VSMU	Vachův sbor moravských učite-	ZSH	Zpěvácký spolek Hlahol v Praze
	lek (Vach Choir of Moravian		('Hlahol' Choral Society in
	Women Teachers)		Prague)
W	Wien (Vienna)		

I. KEYBOARD

1875 PŘEDEHRA pro varhany ('Overture' for organ); Panton – Bärenreiter,
Pr – Kassel 1976, in Composizioni per
organo) (Varhanní skladby) (Compositions for organ) (rev. Miloslav Buček);
1st perf. Brno, 24 Oct. 1958 by Josef
Černocký.

1875 VARYTO pro plné varhany ('Lyre'
for full organ) (varyto = lyre instrument
used in legends by bards); Panton –
Bärenreiter, Pr – Kassel 1976, in Com-
posizioni per organo (Varhanní skladby
/Compositions for organ) (rev. Miloslav
Buček); 1st perf. Brno, 24 Oct. 1958 by
Josef Černocký.

1875 CHORÁLNÍ FANTASIE pro varhany ('Choral Fantasia' for organ);
Panton – Bärenreiter, Pr – Kassel 1976,
in Composizioni per organo (Varhanní
skladby / Compositions for organ) (rev.
Miloslav Buček); 1st perf. Praha, 23 July
1875 by L. Janáček (during the final
examination at the Organ School); 1st
of more recent performances Brno,
24 Oct. 1958 by Josef Černocký.

1880 TEMA CON VARIAZIONI (Zdeň-
činy variace) (Zdeňka's Variations) for
piano 2 hands; HM, Pr 1944, in Klavírní repertoár (Repertoire for piano),
No. 24 (ed. Vilém Kurz); critical edn.
Supraphon – Bärenreiter, Pr – Kassel
1978, in Composizioni per pianoforte/
Klavírní skladby (Compositions for piano) (eds. Ludvík Kundera and Jarmil
Burghauser); Tema – Andante, Var. 1 –
Andante, Var. 2 – Allegro, Var. 3 – Con
moto, Var. 4 – Con moto, Var. 5 – Meno
mosso, Var. 6 – Adagio, Var. 7 – Adagio;
duration c 9 min.; 1st public perf. unknown.

1884 2 SKLADBY PRO VARHANY
('2 Pieces for Organ'); Benediktinská
tiskárna (Benedictine Printing House),
Br 1884; Supraphon, Pr 1975 (rev. Jiří
Reinberger); I. – Adagio, II. – Adagio;
1st perf. unknown.

1886? NA PAMÁTKU ('In Memory'),
for piano 2 hands to three verses by Eliška
Krásnohorská, taken by the composer from
her poem 'Na rozchodu' ('Leave-Taking')

to which Janáček composed later the
male-voice chorus 'Loučení' ('Leave-
taking'), 1888 (see 'Tři mužské sbory'
in section 'Choruses'); Supraphon, Pr
1979 (ed. Jan Trojan); 1st perf. unknown.

1892 EJ, DANAJ, dance for piano 2 hands;
critical edn. Supraphon – Bärenreiter,
Pr – Kassel 1978, in Composizioni per
pianoforte/Klavírní skladby (Compositions for piano) (eds. Ludvík Kundera
and Jarmil Burghauser), section Tři moravské tance (Three Moravian Dances);
duration c 2 min.; 1st perf. Brno, 15 June
1948 by Zdeňka Průšová; later arranged
Janáček as mixed-voice chorus (SATB)
by with orchestra 'Zelené sem sela'
('Green I Sowed'), 1892, autograph in
HAM.

1893 HUDBA KE KROUŽENÍ KUŽE-
LY ('Music for Indian Club Swinging' –
music for gymnastic exercises) in 5 sections; ded. Sokol Association in Moravia-
Silesia; published by the gymnastic union
Sokol in Brno, 1895; critical edn. Supraphon – Bärenreiter, Pr – Kassel 1978, in
Composizioni per pianoforte/Klavírní
skladby (Compositions for piano) eds.
Ludvík Kundera and Jarmil Burghauser; 1st perf. probably Brno, 16 April
1893; orchestration for brass band by
Josef Kozlík and František Kmoch
(Kmoch arrangement being in the Sokol
archives in Kolín); arranged for symphonic orchestra as well, and broadcast
by Brno Radio as Čtverylka (Quadrille),
copy in HAM.

1904 MORAVSKÉ TANCE ('Moravian
Dances'), 2 dances for piano solo: 1. Če-
ladenský, 2. Pilky; A. Píša, Br 1905
(2 volumes); critical edn. Supraphon –
Bärenreiter, Pr – Kassel 1978, in Com-
posizioni per pianoforte/Klavírní skladby
(Compositions for piano) (eds. Ludvík
Kundera and Jarmil Burghauser), section
Tři moravské tance (Three Moravian
Dances); duration of No. 1 c 1.5 min., of
No. 2 c 1 min.; 1st perf. unknown.

1905 SONÁTA '1. 10. 1905', ('1 October
1905'), named 'Z ulice' ('Street Scene'), in

memory of František Pavlík; 2 movements preserved: 1. Předtucha (Foreboding), 2. Smrt (Death), 3rd lost; HM, Prague 1924; critical edn. Supraphon – Bärenreiter, Pr – Kassel 1978, in Composizioni per pianoforte (Klavírní skladby (Compositions for piano) (eds. Ludvík Kundera and Jarmil Burghauser); duration c 11 min.; 1st perf. Brno, 27 Jan. 1906 by Ludmila Tučková under the title 'Street Scene 1 October 1905'; 2nd movement orchestrated by Břetislav Bakala and performed by him with the Prague and Brno Radio Orchestras in Brno.

1908 PO ZAROSTLÉM CHODNÍČKU – Drobné skladby pro klavír ('The Overgrown Path' – Small pieces for piano), cycle of 15 pieces (originally 7 for harmonium), 1901 – 1908; in two sets: Series I (Nos. 1 – 10) – 1. Naše večery (Our Evenings), 2. Lístek odvanutý (A Leaf Gone with the Wind), 3. Pojďte s námi (Come with Us), 4. Frýdecká Panna Maria (Our Lady of Frýdek), 5. Štěbetaly jak laštovičky (They Chattered like Little Swallows), 6. Nelze domluvit (Words Fail), 7. Dobrou noc (Good Night), 8. Tak neskonale úzko (Such Infinite Anguish), 9. V pláči (In Tears), 10. Sýček neodletěl (The Little Night Owl Kept Hooting), 11. Andante, 12. Allegretto, 13. Più mosso, 14. Vivo, 15. Allegro; Nos. 1, 2 and 10 published originally in Slovanské melodie (Slav Melodies), 1901, vol. V, as well as Nos. 4 and 7, 1902, vol. VI (ed. by E. Kolář, Ivančice u Brna), No. 11 appeared originally in Večery (Evenings) (30 Sept. 1905), literary supplement to LN; entire cycle of 10 pieces published by A. Píša, Br 1911; the complete cycle of 15 pieces was not published before 1942 in 4th edn. by HM, Pr – Series I (Nos. 1 – 10) rev. by Vilém Kurz and Series II (Nos. 11 – 15) rev. by František Schäfer; critical edn. Supraphon – Bärenreiter, Pr – Kassel 1978, in Composizioni per pianoforte/Klavírní skladby (Compositions for piano) (eds. Ludvík Kundera and Jarmil Burghauser); duration – I c 26 min., II c 16 min.; 1st perf. unknown. No. 2 Lístek odvanutý (A Leaf Gone with the Wind) arranged for cello and piano by Miloš Sádlo, ed. O. Pazdírek, Br 1943, and for violin and piano by Jan Štědroň, ed. SNKLHU, Pr 1956; moreover

No. 4 Frýdecká Panna Maria (Our Lady of Frýdek) arranged for cello and piano by Miloš Sádlo (not published), the same by František Smetana (not published); Nos. 1 – 10 adapted for string quartet by Jarmil Burghauser, ed. Supraphon, Pr 1978 in Edice Hrajeme doma ('Playing at Home' series), No. 11.

1912 V MLHÁCH ('In the Mists'), piano cycle of four pieces: I. Andante, II. Molto adagio, II. Andantino, IV. Presto; KPU, Br 1913; critical edn. Supraphon – Bärenreiter, Pr – Kassel 1978, in Composizioni per pianoforte/Klavírní skladby (Compositions for piano) (eds. Ludvík Kundera and Jarmil Burghauser); duration c 13.5 min.; 1st perf. Brno, 24 Jan. 1914 by Marie Dvořáková.

1921 SLEZSKÁ NÁRODNÍ PÍSEŇ ('Silesian Folk Song'), theme with 5 variations for piano 2 hands; copy by Metoděj Janíček, dated 1921, in HAM; 1st performance unknown.

1928 VZPOMÍNKA ('Reminiscence'); ded. M. Milojevič, Beograd; published originally in the Musical Supplement of the magazine Muzika, Belgrade 1928, No. 6; 2nd edition by Melpa, Pr – Br 1936 in Moravští skladatelé mládeži (Moravian Composers to the Young) (rev. Václav Kaprál), No. 1; critical edn. Supraphon – Bärenreiter, Pr – Kassel 1978, in Composizioni per pianoforte/Klavírní skladby (Compositions for piano) (eds. Ludvík Kundera and Jarmil Burghauser); duration c 1.2 min.; 1st perf. unknown.

II. CHAMBER

1875 ZNĚLKA v A dur ('Intrada' in A major) for 4 violins; autograph dated 23 Nov. 1875 in HAM; 1st perf. Brno, 18 Oct. 1958 by Collegium musicum brunense (at the opening ceremony of the exhibition 'Leoš Janáček on World Stages').

1875 ZVUKY KU PAMÁTCE FÖRCHTGOTTA-TOVAČOVSKÉHO ('Sounds in the Memory of Förchtgott-Tovačovský) for 3 violins, viola, cello and contrabass; autograph in HAM.

1879 ROMANCE for violin and piano, originally No. 4, six others lost; HM, Pr 1938 (rev. Bohumír Štědroň); 3rd edn. Supraphon, Pr 1975 (rev. B. Štědroň); duration c 6 min.; 1st perf. Ivančice u Brna, 5 July 1904 by Rudolf Kratochvíl (violin) and Vincenc Šťastný (piano).

1880 DUMKA for violin and piano; HM, Pr 1929 (rev.Richard Zika); 4th edn. Supraphon, Pr 1975 (rev. R. Zika); 1st perf. Brno, 3 March 1885 by A. Sobotka (violin) and L. Janáček (piano).

1910 POHÁDKA ('Fairy-tale') for violoncello and piano, after the epic poem 'The story of Czar Berendey' by V. A. Zhukovsky; revised 1923; ded.J. Elgart; HM, Pr 1924 (rev.Julius Junek); 4th edn. Supraphon, Pr 1974 (rev. František Smetana); I. Con moto, II. Con moto, III. Allegro; 1st perf. of first version Brno, 13 March 1910 by Rudolf Pavlata (violoncello) and Ludmila Prokopová (piano); 1st perf. of second version Praha, 21 Feb. 1923 by Julius Junek (violoncello) and Růžena Nebušková (piano).

1910 PRESTO for violoncello and piano; Supraphon—Bärenreiter, Praha—Kassel 1970 (rev. Jan Trojan); 1st perf. Brno, 15 June 1948 by Karel Krofta (violoncello) and Zdeňka Průšová (piano).

1922 SONÁTA III ('Sonata for Violin and Piano'); composed and recomposed 1913, 1913–1921; 1st version 1. Con (moto, 2. Adagio, 3. Balada, 4. Marcia) first perf. Praha, 16 Dec. 1922 by Stanislav Novák (violin) and Václav Štěpán (piano), autograph without the 3rd movement and 2 sketches to the 4th movement in the estate of Břetislav Bakala, Brno; 2nd version (1. Con moto, 2. Adagio, 3. Balada, 4. Allegro), copy of undated score in HAM, autograph of the 4th movement in the estate of B. Bakala; 3rd version (1. Con moto, 2. Balada, 3. Allegretto, 4. Con moto), undated autograph of score without the 2nd movement in HAM; final version (1. Con moto, 2. Balada, 3. Allegretto, 4. Adagio) published by HM, Pr 1922; 5th edn. Supraphon, Pr 1974 (rev. Josef Suk); duration c 15.5 min.; 1st perf. Brno, 1922 by František Kudláček (violin) and Jaroslav Kvapil (piano); 2nd movement (Balada) published independently already 1915 in the series Česká hudba (Czech Music) in Kutná Hora.

1923 I. SMYČCOVÝ KVARTET ('String Quartet No. 1') after L. N. Tolstoy's *Kreutzer Sonata*; based on the unpreserved Pianoforte Trio, 1908–1909; HM, Pr 1925 (score and parts, arranged by Josef Suk); 4th edn. Supraphon,

Pr 1975 (score and parts, rev. Milan Škampa); 5th edn. UE, W 1979 (pocket score); duration c 17 min.; 1st perf. Praha, 17 Oct. 1924 by the Czech Quartet (Karel Hoffman, Josef Suk, Jiří Herold and Ladislav Zelenka).

1924 MLÁDÍ ('Youth'), suite for wind sextet; HM, Pr 1925 (piano score as well as full score by Břetislav Bakala), pocket score by same, 1947; 3rd edn. of parts Supraphon, Pr 1975; I. Allegro, II. Andante sostenuto, III. Vivace, IV. Allegro animato; duration c 18 min.; 1st perf. Brno, 21 Oct. 1924 by professors of the Brno Conservatoire J. Bok (flute-piccolo), M. Wagner (oboe), St. Krtička (clarinet), Fr. Jánský (horn), Fr. Bříza (basson) and J. Pavelka (bass clarinet).

1924 POCHOD MODRÁČKŮ ('March of the Blue-boys') for piccolo, carillon, tambourine or piano; ded. Václav Sedláček; employed in the 3rd movement of the Sextet Youth; complete edn. for piccolo and piano in the magazine *Hudební besídka* (Music Corner), Brno, IV-1927/29, pp. 121 et seq.; 2nd edn. Supraphon, Pr 1976; duration c 2 min.; 1st perf. unknown.

1925 CONCERTINO for piano and chamber orchestra (2 violins, viola, clarinet, horn and bassoon), originally piano concerto dedicated to the pianist Jan Heřman; HM, Pr 1926 (score and parts); 5th edn. Supraphon, Pr 1975 (rev. Otakar Šourek); I. Moderato, II. Più mosso, III. Con moto, IV. Allegro; duration c 17.5 min.; 1st perf. Brno, 16 Feb. 1926 by Ilona Štěpánová-Kurzová (piano), Fr. Kudláček (violin), J. Jedlička (violin), J. Trkan (viola), St. Krtička (clarinet), Fr. Jánský (horn) and J. Bříza (bassoon).

1924 CAPRICCIO for piano left hand and chamber orchestra (piccolo, flute, 2 trumpets, 3 trombones and tenor tuba); SNKLHU, Pr 1953 (full score and parts—ed. Jarmil Burghauser); 3rd edn. Supraphon, Pr 1974 (full score and parts—ed. J. Burghauser); duration c 17 min.; 1st perf. Praha, 2 March 1928 by Otakar Hollman (piano), V. Máček (flute), E. Šerý and Fr. Trnka (trumpets), A. Bok, J. Šimsa and G. Tyl (trombones), A. Koula (tenor tuba).

1928 II. SMYČCOVÝ KVARTET — LISTY DŮVĚRNÉ ('String Quartet No. 2—Intimate Letters'); HM, Pr 1938 pocket score and parts, rev. František

Kudláček and Ot. Nebuška); 3rd edn. SHV, Pr 1966 (pocket score and parts, rev. František Kudláček and Jaroslav Ruis); 4th edn. UE, W 1979 (pocket score); I. Andante. Con moto, II. Adagio, III. Moderato. Adagio, IV. Allegro; duration c 21 minutes; 1st perf. Brno, 18 May 1928 by the Moravian Quartet (František Kudláček, Josef Jedlička, Josef Trkan and Josef Křenek).

III. ORCHESTRAL

1877 SUITA pro smyčcový orchestr ('Suite for string orchestra'), in 6 movements; O. Pazdírek, Br 1926 (pocket score and parts); 3rd edn. Supraphon, Pr 1974; I. Moderato – II. Adagio – III. Andante con moto – IV. Presto – V. Adagio – VI. Andante; 1st perf. Brno, 2 Dec. 1877 by BeB (conductor L. Janáček).

1878 IDYLA pro smyčcový orchestr ('Idyll' for string orchestra), in 7 movements; Orbis, Pr 1951 (pocket score and parts) and 1952 (full score); 2nd edn. Supraphon, Pr 1974 (pocket score); I. Andante – II. Allegro – III. Moderato – IV. Allegro – V. Adagio – VI. Scherzo – VII. Moderato; 1st perf. Brno, 15 Dec. 1878 by BeB (conductor L. Janáček).

1890 LAŠSKÉ TANCE pro orchestr ('Lachian Dances' for full orchestra), 6 symphonic dances; originally named 'Valašské tance' ('Valachian Dances') – see VALAŠSKÉ TANCE (in section Folk Music Arrangements – 1890); HM, Pr 1928 (full score with preface by L. Janáček); Orbis, Pr 1951 (pocket score); 2nd edn. SHV, Pr 1965 (full score); I. Starodávný I – II. Požehnaný – III. Dymák – IV. Starodávný II – V. Čeladenský – VI. Pilky; duration c 20 min.; five of these 'Valachian' dances (except Starodávný II) were employed in the ballet 'Rákós Rákóczy', 1891 (q. v.); about 1893 the 'Valachian Dances' were renamed by Janáček to 'Lachian Dances'; 1st perf. Brno, 19 Feb. 1925 (as a ballet) at the Brno ND (conductor Břetislav Bakala).

1891 SUITA op. 3 pro orchestr ('Suite for orchestra, op. 3'), also known as 'Serenade'; SNKLHU, Pr 1958 (pocket and full scores); I. Con moto – II. Adagio – III. Allegretto – IV. Con moto (No. III is the Lachian dance Požehnaný, No. IV is the Lachian dance

Dymák); duration c 14 min.; 1st perf. Brno, 28 Sept. 1928 by the combined Prague and Brno Radio Orchestras (conductor Břetislav Bakala).

1891 ADAGIO pro orchestr ('Adagio for orchestra'), symphonic composition for full orchestra; SHV, Pr 1964 (full score, ed. Osvald Chlubna); UE, W 1978 (full score); duration c 5.5 min.; 1st perf. Brno, 1930 by the Symphony Orchestra of the Czechoslovak Radio (conductor Břetislav Bakala); 1st perf. in public Brno, 20 Feb. 1941 by the same orchestra (conductor Václav Kašlík).

1894 ŽÁRLIVOST ('Jealousy'), symphonic overture to the opera Her Step-Daughter (Jenůfa); SHV, Pr 1964 (full score, ed. Osvald Chlubna); UE, W 1978 (full score); duration c 5.5 min.; 1st perf. Praha, 14 Nov. 1906 by the Czech Philharmonic Orchestra (conductor František Neumann).

1899 KOZÁČEK ('Cossack Dance'), Russian folk dance for orchestra after a tune by M. N. Veveritsa; Supraphon, Pr 1977 in 'Dva tance' ('Two Dances') (full score, ed. Jarmil Burghauser); duration c 1 min.; 1st perf. Brno, 11 Jan. 1900 at SB.

1899 SRBSKÉ KOLO ('Serbian Kolo' – round dance) for full orchestra; Supraphon, Pr 1977 in 'Dva tance' ('Two Dances') (full score, ed. Jarmil Burghauser); duration c 1.5 min.; 1st perf. Brno, 11 Jan. 1900 at SB.

1912 ŠUMAŘOVO DÍTĚ ('The Fiddler's Child'), orchestral ballad after the poem by Svatopluk Čech; ded. V. Zemánek; KPU, Br 1914) (pocket score); 3rd edn. HM, Pr 1949 (pocket score, rev. Otakar Šourek); duration c 12 min.; 1st perf. Praha, 14 Nov. 1917 by the Czech Philharmonic Orchestra (conductor Otakar Ostrčil).

1918 TARAS BULBA (originally named 'Slavonic Rhapsody'), orchestral rhapsody after N. V. Gogol's novel; composed 1915 – 1918; published originally for piano 4 hands (arr. by Břetislav Bakala) – HM, Pr 1925, later full score ed. by same, 1927; 3rd edn. SHV, Pr 1967 (full score, rev. Jarmil Burghauser); Supraphon, Pr 1972 (pocket score); I. Smrt Andrijova (The Death of Andri) – II. Smrt Ostapova (The Death of Ostap) – III. Proroctví a smrt Tarase Bulby (The Prophecy and Death of Taras Bulba); duration c 24 min.;

1st perf. Brno, 9 Oct. 1921 by the orchestra of the ND (conductor František Neumann).

1920 BALADA BLANICKÁ ('The Ballad of Blaník'), symphonic poem after Jaroslav Vrchlický's poem; SNKLHU, Pr 1958 (both full and pocket scores, ed. Břetislav Bakala); duration c 8 min.; 1st perf. Brno, 21 March 1920 by the orchestra of the ND (conductor František Neumann).

1926 SINFONIETTA, originally called Vojenská symfonietta (Military Symfonietta) or Sletová symfonietta (Sokol Festival Symfonietta); in 5 movements; ded. Mrs Rosa Newmarch; Wiener Philharmonischer Verlag A. G., W 1927 (pocket score); UE, W 1927 (full score, rev. R. A. Pisk); 2nd edn. UE, W—London 1954 (pocket score); I. Allegretto — II. Andante — III. Moderato — IV. Allegretto — V. Andante con moto; duration c 25 min.; [Janáček himself placed the individual movements in the context of liberated Brno: 1. Fanfáry (Fanfares), 2. Hrad (The Castle), 3. Královė klášter (The Queen's Monastery), 4. Ulice (The Street), 5. Radnice (The Town Hall)]; 1st perf. Praha, 26 June 1926 by the Czech Philharmonic Orchestra (conductor Václav Talich).

IV. VOCAL

1897 JARNÍ PÍSEŇ ('Spring Song'), for voice and piano to a poem by Jaroslav Tichý; rev. 1905; ded. Vesna Society at Brno; O. Pazdírek, Br 1944 in Pazdírkův pěvecký repertoár (Pazdírek's Vocal Repertoire), No. 1; 1st perf. of original version Brno, 6 March 1898 by Zdeněk Lev (voice) and C. M. Hrazdira (piano), and of revised version Prostějov, 10 Dec. 1905.

1899 NÁVOD PRO VYUČOVÁNÍ ZPĚVU ('Singers' Training Manual') contains, apart from introductory text and mechanical vocal exercises, 28 authentic vocal pieces of between a few bars up to several pages for solo voice with accompaniment of a keyboard instrument and 3 pieces for two solo voices with accompaniment; published by A. Píša, Br 1899.

1918 ZÁPISNÍK ZMIZELÉHO ('The Diary of the Young Man Who Disappeared'), song cycle (in 22 sections) for tenor, contralto, three female voices (SSA) and piano to anonymous text (a mysterious set of 23 short poems published in LN with the title 'From the pen of a Self-Taught Peasant'); composed 1917—1919; O. Pazdírek, Br 1921 (pocket and full scores; latest edn. Supraphon, Pr 1972 (pocket and full scores; with German translation by Max Brod, English translation by Bernard Keefe and French translation by Hanuš Jelínek); duration c 38 min.; 1st perf. Brno, 18 April 1921 by Karel Zavřel (tenor), Ludmila Kvapilová (contralto) and Břetislav Bakala (piano); 1st stage performance Ljubljana (Yugoslavia), 28 Oct. 1926; orchestrated by Václav Sedláček and Ota Zítek for scenic production Plzeň, 26 June 1943 (producer Ota Zítek).

1927 ŘÍKADLA ('Nursery Rhymes'), 18 vocal pieces with introduction and epilogue for 9 singers (2 sopranos, 2 contraltos, 3 tenors, 2 basses) and 10 players (ocarina, 2 flutes, second alternating piccolo, 2 clarinets in B and E flat, 2 bassoons, second alternating double-bassoon, double-bass, children's drum and piano) to Bohemian, Moravian and one Ruthenian folk texts published in Dětská příloha (Children's Supplement) to LN; composed 1925—1927 under the impression of cartoons drawn by Josef Lada, Ondřej Sekora and Jan Hála to illustrate the rhymes; originally composed as 8 songs for 3 female voices, clarinet and piano, and first perf. Brno, 26 Oct. 1925 by a selected female ensemble of BeB, Stanislav Krtička (clarinet), Jaroslav Kvapil (piano); later entirely recomposed to full extent; UE, W 1928 — authorized reduction for solo voice, or 6—9 solo voices, viola or violin and piano (arranged by Erwin Stein, with German translation by R. St. Hoffmann); UE, Wien 1929 ed. full score for vocal ensemble (2S, 2A, 3T, 2B) and ten instruments; 1. Řípa se vdávala (The Turnip's Wedding), 2. Není lepší jako z jara (No Time's Better than the Spring), 3. Leze krtek (The Mole Is Crawling), 4. Karel do pekla zajel (Charles Rode to Hell), 5. Roztrhané kalhoty (Trousers Torn in Two), 6. Franta rasů hrál na basu (Knacker's Frank Played the Bass), 7. Náš pes, náš pes (Our Dog), 8. Dělám, dělám kázání (I'm Preaching a Sermon), 9. Stará bába čarovala (Sorcery's Old Witch's Business), 10. Hó,

hó, krávy dó (Ho, Ho, Cows Do Go),
11. Moje žena malučičká(My Tiny, Tiny
Wife) 12. Bába leze do bezu (Granny
Crawls in the Elder), 13. Koza bílá
hrušky sbírá (A White Goat Picking
Pears), 14. Němec brouk hrnce tlouk
(Farmer Bumpkin Smashed his Pots),
15. Koza leží na seně (The Goat is
Resting in the Hay), 16. Vašek, pašek,
bubeník (Silly Billy, Drummer-Boy),
17. Frantíku, Frantíku (Frankie, Frankie),
18. Seděť medviď (A Bear is Sitting on a
Log); duration c 16.5 min.; 1st perf.
Brno, 25 April 1927 at a concert of the
Moravian Composers' Club.

V. FOLK MUSIC ARRANGEMENTS

1889 KRÁLOVNIČKY ('Little Queens'),
10 old ritual folk dances with songs
(collected by František Xaver Bakeš)
arranged for voice and piano; undated
copy of score, authorized by Janáček,
in HAM; first published by SNKLHU,
Pr 1954 (ed. Bohumír Štědroň; with
introduction and description of the
dances by Maryna Úlehlová-Hradilová); 1st perf. unknown.
1890 VALAŠSKÉ TANCE ('Valachian
Dances'), originally a cycle of about
12 folk dances for orchestra or choir with
orchestra; composed 1889–1890; some
of them used in the ballet Rákós Rákóczy,
1891; the undated autographic score
copies of Kožich, Čeladenský and Starodávný II in HAM bear Janáček's
own handmarking 'op. 2'–the original
'Valachian Dances' were to have consisted of a set of 5 dances (Starodávný I,
Pilky, Kožich, Čeladenský, Starodávný
II), but as 'Valašské tance op. 2' there
appeared only two dances (Starodávný I
with first part of Šátečkový and Pilky
with second part of Dymák) at the
publishers Bursík & Kohout, Pr 1890,
with dedication to Mrs Marie Jungová;
these two published Valachian dances
were renamed by Janáček about 1893 to
Lachian Dances and another four were
added for the 1928 edition (see 'Lašské
tance' in the Orchestral section–1890);
1st perf. probably Brno, 23 May 1898 at
ND (conductor Ferdinand Vach).
1890 HANÁCKÉ TANCE ('Dances from
Haná'), 10 folk dances for piano, both
2 hands and 4 hands, as well as for

orchestra or choir with orchestra; composed 1889–1890; Tetka (Auntie), Holubička (Little Dove), Sekerečka (Little
Axe), Kalamajka (Round Dance), Ko-
nopě (Hemp) alias Coufavá (Step-back
Dance), Troják tovačovský, (Threesome
from Tovačov), Rožek (Kerchief), Silnice
(Road), Kukačka (Cuckoo), Trojky
(Triplets); published in Národní tance
na Moravě (National Dances in Moravia), vol. I, II, III (1891–1893) (see
below); 8 of them (Troják, Silnice, Kukačka, Tetka, and Trojky, Sekerečka,
Kalamajka, Rožek) are used–arranged
for orchestra or choir and orchestra–in
the ballet Rákós Rákóczy (see in section
Stage–1891); 1st perf. Tovačov, May
1889 (rehearsed by Xaverie Běhálková)
and Brno, 1 Jan. 1891 by A. Nikodé-
mová and A. Kumpoštová (pianos).
1890 MORAVSKÉ TANCE I ('Moravian
Dances I'), 5 folk dances for orchestra:
1. Kožich (Fur), 2. Kalamajka (Round
Dance), 3. Trojky (Triplets), 4. Silnice
(Road), 5. Rožek (Kerchief); composed
1889 to 1890; score and parts copied
by ČHF, Pr 1958; this set of dances was
compiled and entitled by editor or edn.
of full score at Supraphon-UE, Pr–
Mainz 1971 (ed. Jarmil Burghauser);
1st perf. unknown.
1893 NÁRODNÍ TANCE NA MORAVĚ
('National Dances in Moravia'), 21 folk-
dances in 3 volumes; compiled and edited
by Lucie Bakešová, Xaverie Běhálková
and Leoš Janáček, with cooperation of
Martin Zeman, too; volume 1 contains
6 dances, volume 2 also 6 dances for
piano both 2 hands and 4 hands, volume 3
lastly 9 dances for piano solo and voice
with piano; published at composer's own
expenses by A. Píša, Br 1891 (2 volumes)
and 1893 (volume 3); 3rd edn. Supraphon, Pr 1977 (rev. Bohumír Štědroň,
with description of dances by Maryna
Úlehlová-Hradilová).
1898 UKVALSKÁ LIDOVÁ POESIE
V PÍSNÍCH ('Hukvaldy Folk Poetry
in Songs'), 13 folk songs for voice and
piano; ded. Circle 'Pod akátem' ('Under
the Acacia Tree') in Hukvaldy; A. Píša, Br
1899; 3rd edn. HM, Pr 1949 (rev. Bohumír Štědroň); 1st perf. Brno, 18 Dec.
1898 by J. Harfner and Fr. Vojtěchovský
(voices) and L. Janáček (piano).
1899 UKVALSKÉ PÍSNĚ ('Hukvaldy
Songs'), 6 folk songs for mixed voices
(SATB); ded. Choral and Reading

Society 'Pod Hukvaldy' ('At Hukvaldy'); HM, Pr 1949 (ed. Bohumír Štědroň); 1st perf. Ostrava, 13 Dec. 1947 by Pěvecký kroužek Sokola na Hukvaldech (Sokol Gymnastic Association Choral Circle at Hukvaldy) (conductor Miloň Dohnal) over the Ostrava Radio (only the first two: Ondráš and Hukvaldy Little Church (Ten ukvalský kostelíček), the complete six songs Frýdek-Místek, 25 May 1948 by the mixed choir of the Frýdek-Místek Grammar School (conductor Gabriel Štefánek).

1908 MORAVSKÁ LIDOVÁ POESIE V PÍSNÍCH ('Moravian Folk Poetry in Songs'), 53 folk songs for voice and piano, compiled by František Bartoš and Leoš Janáček (piano accompaniment) about 1892 and 1901 as Kytice z národních písní moravských ('A Bouquet of Moravian Folk Songs'); Vol. I, Nos. 1–15 published by E. Šolc, Telč (without year of edition); Vol. II, Nos. 16–53 (38 folk songs) published by same, 1901; Vol. I ded. A. Ondříčková, vol. II R. Maturová, preface by L. Janáček; 2nd edn. published under the title 'Moravská lidová poesie v písních – 53 nejkrásnějších písní z Kytice od Fr. Bartoše a L. Janáčka' ('Moravian Folk Poetry in Songs – 53 of the Most Beautiful Songs from the Bouquet by Fr. Bartoš and L. Janáček'), published by same (undated) about 1908; newest edn. in 1 vol. as Moravská lidová poesie v písních (Moravian Folk Poetry in Songs) by Supraphon – Bärenreiter, Pr – Kassel 1975 (with German translation by Kurt Honolka).

1909 NARODIL SE KRISTUS PÁN ('Christ the Lord Is Born'), Czech folk carol arranged for piano with underlying text after a carol melody in the Lehner Hymnbook; appeared in Janáček's short story Světla jitřní (Lights of Morn) in LN of 24 Dec. 1909; published in L. Janáček: Fejetony z Lidových novin) (Articles from LN), Brno 1958; 1st perf. unknown.

1911 PODME, MILÁ, PODME ('Come, Dear, Come'), folk song for voice and piano; facsimile of Janáček's autograph in L. Janáček and Pavel Váša: Z nové sbírky národních písní moravských ('From the New Collection of Moravian Folksongs') published in Večery (Evenings), 23 Dec. 1911 (literary supplement of LN, No. 19); reproduced in L. Janáček: Fejetony z Lidových novin (Brno, 1958); 1st perf. Brno, 24 Feb. 1949 by M. Juře-

nová (voice) and B. Štědroň (piano) over the Brno Radio.

1912 KRAJCPOLKA ('Crossover Polka'), folk song for voice and piano; facsimile of Janáček's autograph in Večery (17 Feb. 1912), literary supplement No. 20 of LN; published in the magazine Hudební výchova (Musical Education) III-1955, p. 90 (supplement); reproduced also in L. Janáček: Fejetony z Lidových novin (Brno, 1958); 1st perf. Brno, 24 Feb. 1949 by M. Juřenová (voice) and B. Štědroň (piano).

1917 DVACET ŠEST BALAD LIDOVÝCH ('Twenty-six Folk Ballads') in 4 sections; published as a collection first in 1922 by HM, Pr; Vol. I – ŠEST NÁRODNÍCH PÍSNÍ, jež zpívala Gabel Eva ('Six folk songs which Eva Gabel sang'), 6 Slovak folk songs for solo voice and piano, composed about 1909, German translation by Max Brod; 1st perf. Brno, 5 March 1911 by M. Vytopilová (voice) and M. Dvořáková (piano); Vol. II – LIDOVÁ NOKTURNA: Večerní zpěvy slovenského lidu z Rovného ('Folk Nocturnes: Evening songs of the Slovak people from Rovné'), 7 Slovak folk songs for 2 female voices and piano; composed 1906; 1st perf. Brno, 5 Dec. 1907 at KPU; arrangement for string orchestra, 2 clarinets and cymbal by Břetislav Bakala in the archives of the Brno Radio; Vol. III – PÍSNĚ DETVANSKÉ (zbojnické, balady) ['Songs of Detva' (brigand songs and ballads)], 8 Slovak folk songs for solo voice and piano; composed 1916; 1st perf. unknown; Vol. IV – PĚT NÁRODNÍCH PÍSNÍ ('Five Folk Songs') for male voice and chorus (T, TTBB) with piano or harmonium; composed 1916–1917; 1st perf. Brno, 1934 by Moravské vokální kvarteto (Moravian Vocal Quartet) over the Brno Radio; 2nd edn. of the whole collection HM, Pr 1950.

1918 SLEZSKÉ PÍSNĚ ('Silesian Songs'), 10 folk songs (from the collection of Helena Salichová) for voice and piano; ed. B. Svoboda, Br 1920; 2nd edn. SNKLHU, Pr 1954 (rev. Bohumír Štědroň); 1st perf. Brno, 25 May 1919; Nos. 1, 4, 7, 8 arranged by Břetislav Bakala to accompaniment of flute, violin, viola and violoncello (1951).

1921 MORAVSKÉ LIDOVÉ PÍSNĚ ('Moravian Folk Songs'), 15 folk songs for piano with text added; HM, Pr 1950 (rev. B. Štědroň); Panton, Pr 1978 — facsimile of Janáček's autograph under the title 'Patnáct moravských lidových písní' ('Fifteen Moravian Folk Songs'); 1st perf. Brno, 24 Feb. 1949 by Libuše Domanínská and Eduard Hrubeš (voices) and Bohumír Štědroň (piano) over the Brno Radio.

1923 RADUJTE SE VŠICHNI ('Rejoice All of You'), folk song for solo voice accompanied by string instrument (violin); Janáček used a melody recorded in his notebook 1898 – 1899; facsimile in 'Starosta Smolík' ('Mayor Smolík'), article by Janáček in LN (18 March 1923); reproduced in L. Janáček: *Fejetony z Lidových novin* (Articles from LN), Brno 1958; 1st perf. 1958 by the Czechoslovak Radio Brno.

1923 SKLENOVSKÉ POMEZÍ ('Sklenov Borderland'), folk song with single-voiced instrumental accompaniment marked 'whistling of air-draught'; Janáček used a melody recorded in his notebook 1898 – 1899; facsimile in Janáček's article 'Starosta Smolík' ('Mayor Smolík') in LN, 18 March 1923, reproduced in L. Janáček: *Fejetony z Lidových novin*, Brno 1958; 1st perf. 1958 by the Czechoslovak Radio Brno.

1923 POĎTE, POĎTE, DĚVČATKA ('Come Along, Lassies'), folk song with triad accompaniment marked 'Svit měsíce' ('Moonlight'); Janáček used a tune recorded in his notebook 1898 – 1899; facsimile in Janáček's article 'Starosta Smolík' ('Mayor Smolík') in LN, 18 March 1923, reproduced in L. Janáček: *Fejetony z Lidových novin*, Brno 1958; 1st perf. 1958 by the Czechoslovak Radio Brno.

1978 LIDOVÉ PÍSNĚ A BALADY ('Folk Songs and Ballads'), 7 songs for voice and piano: 1. Ej duby, duby (Oh Oaks, Oaks), 2. Ten ukvalský kostelíček (The Little Church of Hukvaldy), 3. Tovačov (village), 4. Pilařská (Sawmaker's Song), 5. Aj ženy (Oh Women!), 6. Vandrovali hudci (Wandering Fiddlers), 7. Ballada (opening words: Rychtarova Kačenka — The Mayor's Kate); undated autographs in HAM; 1st ed. Panton-Bärenreiter, Pr — Kassel 1978 (rev. Josef Ceremuga, with German translation by Adolf Langer); 1st perf. unknown.

? 2 folk songs for voice and piano: RODINU MÁM ('I Have a Family'), SEDĚL VĚZEŇ ('A Prisoner Doing Time'); undated autographs in HAM; 1st perf. unknown.

VI. FOLK SONG EDITIONS

1890 KYTICE Z NÁRODNÍCH PÍSNÍ MORAVSKÝCH ('A Bouquet of Moravian Folk Songs'), compiled by František Bartoš and Leoš Janáček about 1890; 174 folks ongs for single voice without accompaniment; published in the form of a pocket song-book by Emil Šolc, Telč 1890; 2nd (1892) and 3rd (1901) edns. by same (195 songs — Czech and Slovak songs added; 4th edn. SNKLHU, Pr 1953 (rev. Al. Gregor and B. Štědroň); with detailed introductions by L. Janáček to all editions (as well as to Fr. Bartoš's earlier collection 'Národní písně moravské nově nasbírané' ('Folk Songs of Moravia Newly Collected'), Brno 1889).

1901 NÁRODNÍ PÍSNĚ MORAVSKÉ V NOVĚ NASBÍRANÉ ('Folk Songs of Moravia Newly Collected'), in 2 volumes with L. Janáček's fundamental treatise 'O hudební stránce národních písní moravských' ('About the Musical Aspects of Moravian Folk Songs'); 2057 folk songs compiled by František Bartoš and Leoš Janáček (with other collaborators, esp. Martin Zeman); ed. Česká akademie (Czech Academy), Pr 1899 (Volume I) and 1901 (Volume II).

1930 MORAVSKÉ PÍSNĚ MILOSTNÉ ('Moravian Love Songs') contain 150 groups of folk song variants with annotations to melodies and texts, compiled and classified by Leoš Janáček (1927 to 1928) and Pavel Váša; introduction by L. J. and P. V., index of melodies by Vladimír Helfert; ed. Státní ústav pro lidovou píseň v ČSR (State Institute for Folk Songs in ČSR), Pr 1930 (524 pp.).

VII. OTHER ARRANGEMENTS

1877 A. DVOŘÁK: ŠEST MORAVSKÝCH DVOJZPĚVŮ ('Six Moravian Duets') for mixed voices (SATB) and piano; 4 numbers (Dyby byla kosa nabróšená, Slavíkovské polečko, Holub na javoře, V dobrým jsme se sešli) arranged 1877, 1st perf. Brno, 2 Dec. 1877 under the title 'Čtvero písní s průvodem klavíru' ('Four Songs with Piano Accompaniment') by BeB (conductor L. Janáček); 2 other songs (Šípek, Zelenaj se) arranged 1884, 1st perf. Brno, 8 Nov. 1884 by BeB (conductor Jan Havlíček); published as private edn. by Josef Plavec, Pr 1939; newest edn. Panton-Bärenreiter, Pr — Kassel 1978 (full score and choral score, with German translation by Kurt Honolka).

1901 MŠE B dur podle Messe pour orgue Ference Liszta ('Mass in B flat major after the Messe pour orgue by Franz Liszt') for mixed choir and organ; Supraphon — UE, Pr — W 1978 (ed. Jarmil Burghauser); duration c 12.5 min.; 1st perf. of Credo in Brno, 24 Nov. 1901 and of the complete Mass at the beginning of 1902.

1902 E. GRIEG: OLAV TRYGVASON — Zabrání země ('Taking Land'), choral section from the cantata for solo voices, mixed choir and orchestra, arr. by Janáček for male-voice choir with accompaniment of piano and harmonium; autograph of piano and harmonium parts in HAM; 1st perf. unknown.

1920? J. A. KOMENSKÝ: UKOLÉBAVKA ('Lullaby'), piano accompaniment to a lullaby from J. A. Komenský's *Informatorium školy mateřské* (The Nursery School Informatorium); ed. Ústřední spolek učitelský a na Moravě ve Slezsku (Teachers' Central Society in Moravia and Silesia), Br 1920 in *Kniha Komenského* (The Comenius Book) (ed. František Pražák); 1st perf. unknown.

? ZACHOVEJ NÁM, HOSPODINE ('God Save the Emperor'), Janáček's arrangement of the Imperial Austrian Anthem by J. Haydn for voice an d organ, with fragmentary Czech text without title; undated autograph in HAM.

VIII. CHORUSES

1873 ORÁNÍ ('Ploughing') for male voices (TTBB) to folk text (from František Sušil, 'Moravské písně národní' ('Moravian Folk songs'), 1859, p. 517); HM, Pr 1923 in 'Čtyři lidové mužské sbory' ('Four Male-Voice Folk Choruses'), No. 1; latest edn. SNKLHU, Pr 1954 in 'Rok české hudby' ('Year of Czech Music'); 1st perf. Brno, 27 April 1873 by ŘBS (conductor L. Janáček).

1873 VÁLEČNÁ ('War Song'), festive chorus for male voices (TTBB), piano, trumpet and 3 trombones to anonymous text; autograph of score and parts in HAM; 1st perf. Brno, 5 July 1873 by ŘBS (conductor L. Janáček).

1873 NESTÁLOST LÁSKY ('The Fickleness of Love') for male voices to folk text; Supraphon — UE, Pr — W 1978 in 'Tři mužské sbory' ('Three Male-Voice Choruses'), No. 1 (rev. Jan Trojan; with German translation by Friedrich Saathen); 1st perf. Brno, 9 Nov. 1873 by ŘBS (conductor L. Janáček).

1874 OSAMĚLÁ BEZ ÚTĚCHY ('Alone without Comfort') for male voices to folk text; revised 1898 and 1925; Supraphon — UE, Pr — W 1978 in 'Tři mužské sbory' ('Three Male-Voice Choruses'), No. 2 (rev. Jan Trojan; with German translation by Friedrich Saathen); 1st perf. Brno, 14 March 1874 by ŘBS (conductor L. Janáček).

1876 LÁSKA OPRAVDIVÁ ('True Love') for male voices to folk text; Melpa, Pr — Br 1937 in 'Ohlas národních písní' ('Echoes of Folk Songs'), No. 1 (ed. Vilém Steinman); latest edn. Supraphon, Pr 1976 in 'Ohlas národních písní', No. 1 (ed. Jan Trojan); 1st perf. Brno, 23 Jan. 1876 by ŘBS (conductor L. Janáček).

1876 DIVÍM SE MILÉMU ('I Wonder at my Beloved') for male voices to folk text; composed 1875 — 1876; Melpa, Pr — Br 1937 in 'Ohlas národních písní' ('Echoes of Folk Songs'), No. 2 (ed. Vilém Steinman); latest edn. Supraphon, Pr 1976 in 'Ohlas národních písní', No. 2 (ed. Jan Trojan); 1st perf. unknown.

1876 VÍNEK STONULÝ ('A Drowned Wreath') for male voices to folk text (from František Sušil, 1860, No. 214); composed 1875 — 1876; Melpa, Pr — Br 1937, No. 3 in 'Ohlas národních písní' ('Echoes of Folk Songs') (ed. Vilém Steinman); latest edn. Supraphon, Pr 1976, No. 3 in 'Ohlas národních písní' (ed. Jan Trojan); 1st perf. unknown.

1876 KDYŽ MNE NECHCEŠ, COŽ JE VÍC? ('If You Don't Want Me, What Is Left?') for male voices to text by František Ladislav Čelakovský; only tenor voice and arrangement as song with piano have been preserved, autographs in HAM; 1st perf. Brno, 23 Jan. 1876 by ŘBS (conductor L. Janáček).

1876 ZPĚVNÁ DUMA ('Choral Elegy') for male voices to text by Fr. L.

Čelakovský; Supraphon—UE, Pr—W 1979 (ed. Jan Trojan; with German translation by Friedrich Saathen); 1st perf. Brno, 3 April 1876 by BeB (conductor L. Janáček).

1877 SLAVNOSTNÍ SBOR ('Festive Chorus') for mixed voices (T, T, B, B SA TTBB) and piano to text by Karel Kučera; Supraphon-Bärenreiter, Pr—Kassel 1972 (ed. Jan Trojan; with German translation by Kurt Honolka); 1st perf. Brno 15 July 1877 by the choir of ÚVU (conductor L. Janáček).

1878 OSUDU NEUJDEŠ ('No Escape from Fate') for male voices (TTBB) to Serbian folk text (from 'Zpěvy lidu srbského' ('Serbian Folk Songs')—Czech translation by Siegfried Kapper); Supraphon—UE, Pr—W 1978, No. 3 in 'Tři mužské sbory' ('Three Male-Voice Choruses') (rev. Jan Trojan; with German translation by Friedrich Saathen); probably similar to the lost chorus 'Ženich vnucený' (see Section XIII Lost—1873).

1880 NA KOŠATEJ JEDLI DVA HOLUBI SEĎÁ ('In the Spreading Fir Tree Two Pigeons Are Perched') for male voices to folk text; composed probably between 1878—1880; copied from the property of Josef Kozlík at the University Library in Brno; 1st perf. Praha, 1 Dec. 1957 by APSM (conductor Josef Veselka).

1880 PÍSEŇ V JESENI ('Autumn Song') for mixed voices (SATB) to poem by Jaroslav Vrchlický; ded. Beseda brněnská; Orbis, Pr 1951, No. 1 in Smíšené sbory (Mixed Choruses) (ed. Bohumír Štědroň); 1st perf. Brno, 12 Dec. 1880 by BeB (conductor L. Janáček).

1883 AVE MARIA for male voices to text by G. G. Byron ('Don Juan', Canto III, paragraph 102, translation into Czech by Josef Durdík); first published in the magazine *Varyto* XIII/1890, No. 1, Brtnice u Jihlavy; new edn. Supraphon, Pr. 1979 (rev. Jan Trojan); 1st perf. unknown.

1885 NA PRIEVOZE ('At the Ferry') for male voices (TTBB) to Slovak folk ballad: composed probably 1883—1885; undated copy from the bequest of Vojtěch Blatný in HAM and from the bequest of Josef Kozlík in UK; 1st perf. Praha, 1 Dec. 1957 by APSM (conductor Josef Veselka).

1885 ČTVEŘICE MUŽSKÝCH SBORŮ ('Four Male-Voice Choruses'), originally 'Mužské sbory' ('Male-Voice Choru-

ses'): 1. Výhrůžka (The Threat), 2. Ó lásko (Ah Love), 3. Ach vojna, vojna (The Soldier's Lot), 4. Krásné oči tvé (Your Beautiful Eyes); texts of Nos.1—3 formed by settings of folk poetry, text of No.4 by Jaroslav Tichý; dedicated to Antonín Dvořák 'in token of deepest respect'; K. Winkler, Br 1886; latest edn. SHV, Pr 1962 (with German translation by Max Brod); 1st perf. of Nos. 2, 3 Brno, 14 Nov. 1886 by BeB (conductor L. Janáček), of No. 1 Brno, 23 May 1889 by BeB (conductor Jaroslav Kvapil), of No. 4 unknown.

1885 Ó LÁSKO ('Ah Love'), male-voice chorus to folk text; separate edn. SHV, Pr 1963 in 'Sborový repertoár — Mužské sbory bez doprovodu' ('Choral Repertoire—Male-voice choruses without accompaniment'), p. 30.

1885 KAČENA DIVOKÁ ('The Wild Duck') for mixed voices (SATB) to folk text; J. Barvič, Br 1885 in 'Zpěvník pro školy střední a měšťanské II' ('Songbook II for secondary schools'), compiled by B. Žalud, pp. 141—149; 2nd edn. Orbis, Pr 1951 in 'Smíšené sbory' ('Mixed-voice choruses'), No. 2 (rev. Bohumír Štědroň); 1st perf. Brno, 17 March 1901 by mixed choir of the 2nd Czech Gymnasium in Old Brno (conductor L. Janáček).

1888 TŘI MUŽSKÉ SBORY ('Three Male-Voice Choruses'): 1. Holubička (The Little Dove) to text by Eliška Krásnohorská, 2. Loučení (Leave-Taking) to text by Eliška Krásnohorská, 3. Žárlivec (The Jealous Man) with baritone solo, to Slovak folk text; SNKLHU, Pr 1959 (ed. Miroslav Venhoda; with German translation by Kurt Honolka and English translation by John Clapham); 1st perf. of Nos. 1 and 2 Přerov, 1 Sept. 1956 by PSMU (conductor Jan Šoupal); 1st perf. of No. 3 Vizovice, 9 April 1941 by PSMU (conductor Jan Šoupal).

1890 NAŠE PÍSEŇ ('Our Song') for mixed voices (SATB) to text by unquoted author; Orbis, Pr 1951 in 'Smíšené sbory' ('Mixed-voice choruses'), No.3 (ed. Bohumír Štědroň; 1st known perf. Brno, 11 Dec. 1930 by mixed choir of the Czechoslovak Radio at Brno (conductor Břetislav Bakala); melody used for the final septet, No. 16, in the one-act opera 'Počátek románu' ('The Beginning of a Romance'), 1891, as well as in the mixed-voice chorus with orchestra 'Sivy sokol zaletěl' ('The Ash-grey Falcon Flew

Away') to text of Silesian folk song, 1890.

1890 SIVY SOKOL ZALETĚL ('The Ash-grey Falcon Flew Away') for mixed voices with orchestra to folk text; authorized copy dated 12 June 1890 in HAM; origin see 'Naše píseň'; 1st perf. unknown.

1892 ZELENÉ SEM SELA ('Green I Sowed') for mixed voices and orchestra to folk text (originally 'Ej, danaj' for piano 2 hands, 1892); undated authorized copy of score and choral parts in HAM; 1st perf. Brno, 20 Nov. 1892 by orchestra of PD and mixed choir (conductor L. Janáček).

1893 COŽ TA NAŠE BŘÍZA ('Our Birch Tree') for male voices to text by Eliška Krásnohorská; ded. Řemeslnická beseda Svatopluk (ŘBS); first published in 'Památník Svatopluka' ('Svatopluk Album'), Br 1893; reprinted by HM, Pr 1923 in 'Čtyři lidové mužské sbory' ('Four Male-Voice Folk Choruses'), No. 2; latest edn. by same, 1948, No. 2; 1st perf. Brno, 21 May 1893 by ŘBS (conductor M. Koblížek).

1893 VÍNEK ('The Garland') for male voices to folk text; HM, Pr 1923 in 'Čtyři lidové mužské sbory' ('Four Male-Voice Folk Choruses'), No. 3; latest edn. by same, 1948, No. 3; 1st perf. unknown.

1894 UŽ JE SLÚNKO Z TEJ HORY VEN ('The Sun Has Risen above that Hill') for baritone and mixed voices (Bar SATB) with piano to folk text; copy from the property of Josef Kozlík in UK; 1st perf. Brno, 13 May 1894.

1897 SLAVNOSTNÍ SBOR ('Festive Chorus') for male voices to text by Vladimír Šťastný; intended probably for and performed at the consecration of the banner of St Joseph Union for Youths and Men in Old Brno (1898), therefore also being denoted as St Joseph festive chorus; authorized copy of voices in HAM; ed. Supraphon – UE, Pr – W 1978 (ed. Jan Trojan; with German translation by Friedrich Saathen); 1st perf. Brno, 24 April 1898 by boarders of ÚVU (conductor L. Janáček).

1904 ČTVERO MUŽSKÝCH SBORŮ MORAVSKÝCH ('Four Moravian Male-Voice Choruses'): 1. Dež viš (If You Knew) to text by Ondřej Přikryl, 2. Komáři (Mosquitoes) to folk text, 3. Klekánica (The Evening Witch) to text by Ondřej Přikryl, 4. Rozloučení (Parting) to folk text; ded. PSMU; Moj-

mír Urbánek, Pr 1906; 2nd edn. HM, Pr 1950 (rev. Bohumír Štědroň); Nos. 3, 4 with German text by W. Henzen published by R. Forberg, Leipzig 1908 in 'Männerchöre aus dem Repertoire des Sängerbundes mährischer Lehrer', Nos. 9, 10 (Die Abendhexe, Wanderschaft); 1st perf. of Nos. 1, 3 Přerov, 26 Nov. 1905 by PSMU (conductor Ferdinand Vach), of No. 2 Vyškov, 3 Feb. 1907 by PSMU (conductor Ferdinand Vach), of No. 4 Brno, 23 Feb. 1908 by BeB (conductor Rudolf Reissig).

1904 DEŽ VIŠ ('If You Knew'), male-voice chorus to text by Ondřej Přikryl; separately ed. by Supraphon, Pr 1968 in 'Sborový repertoár – Z repertoáru PSMU' ('Choral repertoire – From the repertoire of PSMU').

1906 KANTOR HALFAR ('Schoolmaster Halfar') for male voices to poem by Petr Bezruč; ded. Ferdinand Vach; HM, Pr 1923; latest edn. SHV – Alkor, Pr – Kassel 1958 (with German translation by Kurt Honolka); 1st perf. Luhačovice, 3 Aug. 1918 by PSMU (conductor F. Vach).

1907 MARYČKA MAGDÓNOVA for male voices to poem by Petr Bezruč; first version completed in autumn 1906, second version in spring 1907; ded. Ferdinand Vach; F. A. Urbánek, Pr 1909; latest edn. SHV – Alkor, Pr – Kassel 1959 (with German translation by Kurt Honolka); 1st perf. (2nd version!) Prostějov, 12 April 1908 by PSMU (conductor F. Vach).

1909 70,000 or SEDMDESÁT TISÍC ('The Seventy Thousand') for male voices to poem by Petr Bezruč; ded. František Spilka; HM, Pr 1923; latest edn. Supraphon, Pr 1976; 1st perf. Praha, 4 April 1914 by PSPU (conductor Fr. Spilka).

1914 PERINA ('The Eiderdown') for male voices to folk text; published by HM, Pr 1923 as No. 4 in 'Čtyři lidové mužské sbory' ('Four Male-Voice Folk Choruses'); latest edn. by same, 1948, No. 4; 1st perf. unknown.

1916 VLČÍ STOPA ('The Wolf's Tracks') for female voices and piano to poem by Jaroslav Vrchlický; autograph of score in HAM; ed. Supraphon, Pr 1968 (ed. Jan Ledeč; with German translation by Peter Korff); 1st perf. Nová Paka, 18 Aug. 1916 by VSMU (conductor Ferdinand Vach).

1916 HRADČANSKÉ PÍSNIČKY ('Songs

of Hradčany'), cycle of 3 choruses for female voices with accompaniment to poems by František Serafín Procházka: 1. Zlatá ulička (Golden Lane), SSAA, 2. Plačící fontána (The Weeping Fountain), S SSAA and flute, 3. Belveder (Belvedere), S A SSAA and harp; HM, Pr 1922 (harp part arranged by Helena Nebeská-Kličková); latest edn. Supraphon, Pr 1977 (ed. Zbyněk Mrkos; with German translation by Peter Korff, English translation by Malcolm Rayment); 1st perf. of only the 'Golden Lane' Praha, 26 Dec. 1916; 1st perf. of the whole cycle Brno, 27 Nov. 1918 by VSMU (conductor F. Vach).

1916 KAŠPAR RUCKÝ. Ballad for female voices with soprano solo. Anno Domini 1612, (S S, S, A, A SSAA) to poem by František Serafín Procházka, German translation by Max Brod; HM, Pr 1925; latest edn. Supraphon, Pr 1976 (with German translation by Max Brod); 1st perf. Praha, 6 April 1921 by PSPUk (conductor Metod Doležil).

1918 ČESKÁ LEGIE ('The Czech Legion'), epopee for male voices to poem by Antonín Horák; in memory of 28 October 1918; autograph of score dated 15 Nov. 1918 in HAM, a hectographed copy dated 23 Jan. 1920 there contains an inserted sheet with autographic score amendment by Janáček; 1st perf. Kroměříž, 26 Feb. 1920 by PSMU (conductor Ferdinand Vach).

922 POTULNÝ ŠÍLENEC ('The Wandering Madman'), male-voice chorus with soprano solo (S T, Bar TTBB) to poem by Rabindranath Tagore (Czech translation by F. Balej, German translation by F. Adler); HM, Pr 1925; latest edn. Supraphon, Pr 1976; 1st perf. Rosice u Brna, 21 Sept. 1924 by PSMU (soprano solo Eliška Janečková, conductor Ferdinand Vach).

1923 ČTYŘI LIDOVÉ MUŽSKÉ SBORY ('Four Male-Voice Folk Choruses'), 1st edn. HM, Pr 1923 (latest edn. HM, Pr 1948): 1. Orání – 1873, 2. Což ta naše bříza – 1893, 3. Vínek – 1893, 4. Perina – 1914 (see the respective choruses).

1926 NAŠE VLAJKA ('Our Flag') for male voices with 2 solo sopranos (S, S TTBB) to poem by F. S. Procházka; composed 1925–1926; ded. PSMU; undated autograph in HAM; 1st perf. Přerov, 16 Oct. 1926 by PSMU (conductor F.Vach).

1928 SBOR PŘI KLADENÍ ZÁKLADNÍHO KAMENE MASARYKOVY UNIVERSITY V BRNĚ ('Chorus for the Stone-Laying Ceremony at Masaryk University in Brno') for male voices (TTBBBB) to text by Antonín Trýb; autograph of score dated 2 April 1928 as well as sketches and text dated 24 March 1928 in HAM; 1st perf. Brno, 9 June 1928 by BeB (conductor Jaroslav Kvapil).

1928 PENZISTŮM UČITELŮM PO 50 LETECH MATURIT ('To Retired Teachers after 50 Years of Matriculation Examinations'), male-voice chorus (TTBB) to anonymous text; copy of score by Metoděj Janíček, dated 6 July 1928, in HAM.

1937 OHLAS NÁRODNÍCH PÍSNÍ ('Echoes of Folk Songs'), 3 male-voice choruses to folk texts, 1st edn. Melpa, Pr – Br 1937 (latest edn. Pr 1976, Supraphon, ed. Jan Trojan): 1. Láska opravdivá – 1876, 2. Divím se milému – 1876; 3. Vínek stonulý – 1876; (see the respective choruses).

1978 TŘI MUŽSKÉ SBORY ('Three Male-Voice Choruses') to folk texts, 1st edn. Supraphon-UE, Pr – W 1978 (ed. Jan Trojan): 1. Nestálost lásky – 1873, 2. Osamělá bez útěchy – 1874, 3. Osudu neujdeš – 1878; (see the respective choruses).

IX. CANTATAS

1897 AMARUS, lyrical cantata for solo voices (S, T, Bar), mixed voices (SATB) and orchestra, set to poem by Jaroslav Vrchlický; rev. 1901 and 1906; HM, Pr 1938 (vocal score by Otakar Nebuška); SNKLHU, Pr 1957 (vocal score by O. Nebuška, rev. Karel Šolc; with Preface by Vladimír Helfert and summaries of cantata text in Russian and French; German translation of text by Kurt Honolka, English translation by Bernard Keefe); ČHF, Pr 1957 (copied full score); SNKLHU, Pr 1958 (choral score, only with German and English texts); I. Moderato, II. Andante, III. Moderato, IV. Adagio, V. Epilog – Tempo di marcia funebre; duration c 30 min.; 1st perf. (without Epilogue) Kroměříž, 2 Dec. 1900 by local choral society Moravan (rehearsed by Ferdinand Vach, conductor L. Janáček); 1st perf. of final section—Epilogue (Funeral march) Brno, 20 March 1898 by Orchestr české kapely (Orchestra of the Czech Band), (conductor L. Janáček).

1903 ELEGIE NA SMRT DCERY OLGY ('Elegy on the Death of Daughter Olga'), chamber cantata for tenor solo, mixed voices and piano to Russian text by Maria Nikolayevna Veveritsa (translation into Czech by B. Zavadil); ded. 'In memory to my Olga'; completed on 28 April 1903 under the impression of the death of the composer's daughter Olga (26 Feb. 1903), revised 28 March 1904; SNKLHU, Pr 1958 (rev. Theodora Straková, preface by Vladimír Helfert; full score; German translation by Kurt Honolka, English translation by Malcolm Rayment; 1st perf. Brno, 20 Dec. 1930 by the Brno Radio (conductor Břetislav Bakala).

1911 NA SOLÁNI ČARTÁK ('Čarták on the Soláň'), cantata for tenor solo, male voices and orchestra, set to poem by Martin Kurt (pseudonym of Max Kunert); ded. Pěvecký spolek (Choral Society) Orlice in Prostějov; ČHF, Pr 1958 (copied full score); SNKLHU, Pr 1958 (piano score by Břetislav Bakala; with German translation by Kurt Honolka and English translation by Bernard Keefe); duration c 6.5 min.; 1st perf. Prostějov, 23 March 1912 by 'Orlice' (conductor Vilém Steinman).

1914 VĚČNÉ EVANGELIUM ('The Eternal Gospel'), legend for solo voices (S, T), mixed voices (SATB) and orchestra, set to poem by Jaroslav Vrchlický; ČHF, Pr 1958 (copied full score); SNKLHU, Pr 1958 (vocal score by Břetislav Bakala, with German translation by Kurt Honolka and English translation by Malcolm Rayment) (rev. Karel Šolc); I. Con moto, II. Adagio, III. Con moto, IV. Andante; duration c 22 min.; 1st perf. Praha, 5 Feb. 1917 by ZSH (conductor Jaroslav Křička).

1926 MŠA GLAGOLSKAJA ('Glagolitic Mass') for solo quartet (S, A, T, B), mixed choir (SATB), organ and orchestra, in 8 sections; Old Slav text arranged by Miloš Weingart; ded. Leopold Prečan; UE, W 1928 (vocal score by Břetislav Bakala, with German translation by R. St. Hoffmann; 2nd edn. by same, 1930 (with English text by Rosa Newmarch added); latest edn. SHV-UE, Pr—W 1966 (vocal score by Ludvík

Kundera; preface by Miloš Weingart with revised Latin and Old Slav texts; with German translation by R. St. Hoffmann); I — Úvod (Introitus), II — Gospodi pomiluj (Kyrie eleison), III — Slava (Gloria), IV — Věruju (Credo), V — Svet (Sanctus), VI — Agneče božij (Agnus Dei), VII — Postludium (Organ solo), VIII — Intrada (Exodus); duration c 40 min.; 1st perf. Brno, 5 Dec. 1927 by BeB (conductor Jaroslav Kvapil).

X. SACRED

1870 FIDELIS SERVUS, Communion for mixed voices (SATB); autograph in HAM.

1870 GRADUALE IN FESTO PURIFICATIONIS B. V. M. (Suscepimus) for mixed voices; revised 1887; autograph in the archives of the Augustinian Monastery in Brno; Supraphon-UE, Pr—Mainz 1971 (ed. Jan Trojan).

1874 GRADUALE (Speciosus forma) for mixed voices with organ accompaniment; autograph in HAM.

1874 INTROITUS (In festo Ss Nominis Jesu) for mixed voices with organ accompaniment; autograph in HAM.

1875 BENEDICTUS for soprano solo and mixed voices (S SATB) with organ accompaniment; autograph in HAM.

1875 COMMUNIO for mixed voices; autograph in HAM.

1875 EXAUDI DEUS for mixed voices with organ accompaniment; autograph dated 3 Feb. 1875 in HAM.

1875 EXAUDI DEUS for mixed voices, unaccompanied; autograph dated 10 Feb. 1875 in HAM; ed. in the magazine *Cecilia* IV-1877, Supplement No. 3 (Janáček's first published composition); 1st perf. unknown.

1875 ODPOČIŇ SI ('Rest in peace'), funeral chorus for male voices (TTBB) to text by František Sušil; HM, Pr 1926; arrangement for wind instruments by Vilém Tauský; 1st perf. unknown.

1878 REGNUM MUNDI for mixed voices; score copy dated 1900 and part copies dated 1878—1879, 1888 and 1891 (two of the parts in Janáček's hand) in the archives of the Old Brno Church; 1st perf. unknown.

1881 DESET ČESKÝCH CÍRKEVNÍCH ZPĚVŮ Z LEHNEROVA MEŠNÍHO

KANCIONÁLU ('Ten Czech Hymns from the Lehner Hymnbook') for organ with text incipits only; K. Winkler, Br 1881–1882; 2nd edn. by same, 1889 as České církevní zpěvy (Czech Church Hymns); 1st perf. unknown.

1896 HOSPODINE POMILUJ NY ('Lord Have Mercy Upon Us') for solo quartet (S, A, T, B) and mixed double choir (SATB, SATB) with accompaniment of organ, harp, 3 trumpets, 4 trombones and tuba; Supraphon–Bärenreiter, Praha–Kassel 1977 (rev. Jan Trojan); 1st perf. Brno, 19 April 1896 by mixed choir of ÚVU (conductor L. Janáček).

1900 VENI SANCTE SPIRITUS for male voices; Supraphon, Pr 1978 (rev. Jan Trojan); UE, W 1979; 1st perf. Brno 13 April 1947 by the male-voice choir of the Czechoslovak Radio in Brno (conductor Bohumír Štědroň).

1901 OTČENÁŠ ('Lord's Prayer') (originally 'Moravský Otčenáš' – 'Moravian Lord's Prayer'), tableaux vivants to a cycle of paintings by the Polish painter J. Krzesz-Męcina for tenor solo, mixed voices and piano or harmonium, in 5 sections; ded. Ženské útulně v Brně (to the Women's Home in Brno); SHV, Pr 1963 (full score and parts, with German text of prayer added) (ed. Bohumír Štědroň); 2nd edn. Supraphon, Pr 1974 (full score and parts, with German text of prayer added) (ed. B. Štědroň); 1. Andante – Otče náš (Our Father), 2. Moderato – Buď vůle Tvá (Thy will be done), 3. Con moto – Chléb náš vezdejší (Give us this day our daily bread), 4. Adagio – A odpusť nám naše viny (And forgive us our trespasses), 5. Energico moderato – Neuvoď nás v pokušení (Lead us not into temptation); duration c 14 min.; 1st perf. Brno, 15 June 1901 at PD (tenor solo Miloslav Lazar, piano Ludmila Tučková, conductor L. Janáček, producer Josef Villart) with 5 tableaux; rearranged 1906 for T, SATB, harp and organ; 1st perf. as chamber cantata (without tableaux, but with two harps and organ) Praha, 18 Nov. 1906 by ZSH (conductor Adolf Piskáček) with the cooperation of L. Janáček.

1902 SVATÝ VÁCLAVE ('St Wenceslas'), organ accompaniment to the St Wenceslas Hymn; undated autograph in HAM.

1903 CONSTITUES for male voices with organ accompaniment; composed before 1903, revised 1903; Supraphon-UE, Praha – Mainz 1971 (ed. Jan Trojan); 1st perf. unknown.

1904 ZDRÁVAS MARIA ('Ave Maria') for tenor solo, mixed voices and organ; arranged by Janáček also for soprano or tenor solo to the accompaniment of violin or piano (organ); ded. Countess Leopoldyna Serenyi; Supraphon-UE, Pr – W 1979 (rev. Břetislav Bakala; with prayer text in Czech and German); 1st perf. unknown.

1904 CÍRKEVNÍ ZPĚVY ČESKÉ VÍCEHLASNÉ Z PŘÍBORSKÉHO KANCIONÁLU ('Czech Hymns for Several Voices from the Příbor Hymnbook'); a) Christmas hymns: 1. Slavně budem zpívati ('Rejoice and Sing' – for 3 voices), 2. Narodil se syn boží ('The Son of God is Born' – for 3 voices), 3. Kristus, syn boží ('Christ, the Son of God' – for mixed voices), 4. Prorokovali proroci ('The prophets have prophesied' – for mixed voices); b) Easter hymns: 1. Na den božího vzkříšení ('On the day of God's Resurrection' for – ? voices), 2. Vstalť jest této chvíle ('Risen hath He at that moment' – for ? voices), 3. Třetího dne vstal Stvořitel ('On the third day the Creator rose' – for ? voices); undated score manuscript of the Christmas hymns (Nos. 1–4) in HAM; score manuscript of the Easter hymns in the estate of Karel Hradil, Brno; 1st perf. Brno, 7 Oct. 1954 by the Hradil Mixed Choir (conductor Karel Hradil) under the title 'Staročeské vícehlasé církevní zpěvy z Příborského kancionálu' ('Old Czech Hymns for Several Voices from the Příbor Hymnbook').

XI. STAGE

1887 ŠÁRKA, opera in 3 acts; libretto by Julius Zeyer; original version 1887, revised 1888, second revision 1918–1919, final version 1924–1925, act III orchestrated by Osvald Chlubna; authorized copy (3 volumes of vocal score) dated 18 June 1888, authorized copy of vocal score dated 1919 and autograph of libretto in HAM, authorized copy of full score (probably 1925) at UE; later (not corrected) copy of full score in HAM; 1st perf. Brno, ND, 11 Nov. 1925 (conductor František Neumann, producer

Ota Zítek, designer Vlastislav Hofman).

1891 RÁKÓS RÁKÓCZY, 'Scene from Slovácko', folk ballet in 1 act, a collection of Lachian-Valachian and Haná dances and folk songs (q.v. — Orchestral, 1890) for solo voice as well as for choir with orchestra (altogether 41 items — 18 songs and 23 dances); libretto by Jan Herben, ballet arrangement by Augustin Berger; undated copy of score at ND, Praha, item No.263, libretto text in HAM; Dilia, Pr 1957 (copied full score); Dilia-UE, Pr — W 1978 (copied vocal score by Ladislav Matějka); 1st perf. Praha, ND, 24 July 1891 (conductor Mořic Anger, producer František Kolár, choreographer Augustin Berger).

1891 POČÁTEK ROMÁNU ('The Beginning of a Romance'), opera in 1 act; libretto versified by Jaroslav Tichý after a short story by Gabriela Preissová; incomplete autograph of vocal score dated 15 May — 2 July 1891, copy of score (Introduction No. 1) and undated copy of libretto with Janáček's annotations in HAM; sections later destroyed were reconstructed by Břetislav Bakala (1931, 1954); Dilia — Alkor, Praha — Kassel 1978 (copied vocal score by Evžen Holiš); 1st perf. Brno, PD, 10 Feb. 1894 (conductor L. Janáček); reconstructed opera performed in Brno, 22 June 1954 by the Operatic Studio of the Janáček Academy of Music and Dramatic Art (conductor Břetislav Bakala, producer Lubomír Selinger, designer Josef Adamíček).

1903 JEJÍ PASTORKYŇA ('Her Step-Daughter') ('Jenůfa'), opera in 3 acts; libretto adapted by composer from Gabriela Preissová's drama; composed 1894 to 1903; in memory of Olga Janáčková; revised 1906; full score revised and orchestration adapted by Karel Kovařovic 1916; KPU, Brno 1908 (1st vocal score); UE, W 1917 (vocal score by J. V. von Wöss, German text by Max Brod; full score); SNKLHU, Pr 1955 (6th vocal score, rev. by Vladimír Helfert); libretto first in German (Hugo Reichenberger) by UE, W 1917 and 1918, libretto in Czech (latest edition) by SNKLHU, Pr 1959; UE, W 1969 (full score, ed. J. M. Dürr; with German translation by Max Brod and English translation by O. Kraus and E. Downes); 1st perf. Brno, ND, 21 Jan. 1904 (conductor C. M. Hrazdira, producer J. Malý).

1904 OSUD ('Destiny'), opera in 3 acts, called also 'Fatum', 'Slepý osud' ('Blind Fate') or 'Plamenné růže' ('Fiery Roses'); libretto versified by Fedora Bartošová from a story by the composer; composed 1903 — 1904, rev. 1906 — 1907; undated autographs of score and libretto in HAM; Dilia — Alkor, Praha — Kassel 1978 (vocal score copied by Václav Nosek; with the original as well as the revised text by Rudolf Vonásek); 1st perf. (radio only) Brno Radio (conductor Břetislav Bakala) on 1 Sept. 1934; 1st staging Brno, SD, 25 Oct. 1958 (dramaturgical rearrangement by Václav Nosek, conductor František Jílek, producer Václav Věžník, designer Josef A. Šálek).

1917 VÝLETY PÁNĚ BROUČKOVY ('The Excursions of Mr Brouček'), opera in 2 parts:
Part I — VÝLET PANA BROUČKA DO MĚSÍCE ('Mr Brouček's Excursion to the Moon') in 2 acts; original libretto by the composer after the novel 'Pravý výlet pana Broučka do Měsíce' ('Mr Brouček's True Excursion to the Moon') by Svatopluk Čech, with additional text by Viktor Dyk, František Gellner, Karel Mašek, František Serafín Procházka and others; composed 1908 to 1917; original epilogue discarded when 2nd Excursion added;
Part II — VÝLET PANA BROUČKA DO XV. STOLETÍ ('Mr Brouček's Excursion to the Fifteenth Century') in 2 acts and 2 scene changes; libretto by František Serafín Procházka after Svatopluk Čech's novel 'Nový epochální výlet pana Broučka tentokráte do XV. století' ('Mr Brouček's New Epoch-making Excursion, this time to the Fifteenth Century'); composed 1917. UE, W 1919 (complete vocal score by Roman Veselý) and 1920 (complete libretto); UE, W 1959 (vocal score only with 'updated' German text by Karl Heinz Gutheim); Supraphon-UE, Pr — W 1967 (vocal score by Roman Veselý, only with Czech text); 1st perf. (of the complete operatic 'bilogy' 'The Excursions of Mr Brouček') Praha, ND, 23 April 1920 (conductor Otakar Ostrčil, producer Gustav Schmoranz, designer Karel Štapfer).

1921 KÁŤA KABANOVÁ, opera in 3 acts; libretto adapted by composer from Vincenc Červinka's Czech translation of the play 'The Storm' by A. N. Ostrovsky;

composed 1919–1921; German text by Max Brod; UE, W 1922 (full score as well as vocal score by Břetislav Bakala and libretto in Czech); UE, London 1951 (English libretto by Norman Tucker); Supraphon–UE, Pr–W 1969 (latest vocal score); UE, W (unpublished full score, ed. Sir Charles Mackerras); 1st perf. Brno, ND, 23 Nov. 1921 (conductor František Neumann, producer Vladimír Marek, designer A. V. Hrska).

1923 PŘÍHODY LIŠKY BYSTROUŠKY ('Adventures of the Vixen Sharp Ears'), opera in 3 acts; libretto by the composer after Rudolf Těsnohlídek's novel 'Liška Bystrouška' ('Bystrouška the Vixen'), based on a series of 193 drawings by Stanislav Lolek; composed 1921–1923, revised 1924; UE, W 1924 (vocal score by Břetislav Bakala; 2nd edn. undated by same (with German text by Max Brod added); libretto in Czech by same, 1924, libretto in German by same, 1925; new edn. of Czech libretto SNKLHU, Pr 1961; new German version of libretto by Walter Felsenstein Reclam Verlag, Leipzig 1962; new score edition Supraphon–UE, Pr–W 1969 (vocal score with German translation by Max Brod); 1st perf. Brno, ND, 6 Nov. 1924 (conductor František Neumann, producer Ota Zítek, designer Eduard Milén); orchestral suite from Příhody lišky Bystroušky arranged and scored by Václav Talich (1937).

1925 VĚC MAKROPULOS ('The Makropoulos Case'), opera in 3 acts; libretto by the composer after Karel Čapek's play; composed 1923–1925; UE, W 1926 (vocal score by Ludvík Kundera, German text by Max Brod), libretto by same, 1926; new edn. SNKLHU–UE, Pr–W 1958 (vocal score); SHV, Pr 1961 (Czech libretto); UE, W 1978 (full score, ed. Sir Charles Mackerras); 1st perf. Brno, ND, 18 Dec. 1926 (conductor Fr. Neumann, producer O. Zítek, designer Fr. Foltýn).

1928 Z MRTVÉHO DOMU ('The House of the Dead'), opera in 3 acts; libretto by the composer after F. M. Dostoyevsky's original novel ('From the House of the Dead') composed 1927–1928; Czech text by the composer, German text by Max Brod; UE, W 1930 (full score revised and reorchestrated by Osvald Chlubna and Břetislav Bakala, vocal score by B. Bakala, German translation by Max Brod); libretto (rev. Ota Zítek) by same, 1930; vocal score with original ending as appendix by same, 1958; latest edn. of vocal score with original ending as appendix Supraphon–UE, Pr–W 1967; 1st perf. Brno, ND, 12 April 1930 (with music arrangements by Břetislav Bakala and Osvald Chlubna as well as textual corrections by Ota Zítek) (conductor Břetislav Bakala, producer Ota Zítek, designer František Hlavica).

XII. FRAGMENTS

1875 ZNĚLKA v g moll ('Intrada' in G minor) for 4 violins; autograph dated 25 November 1875 in HAM.

1877 RONDO for piano 2 hands; page 1 of autograph dated 8 July 1877 in HAM.

1878 SKLADBA PRO VARHANY ('A Piece for Organ'); composed 4 August 1878 in Oettingen, incomplete; autographic inscription on first page of 'Idyll for Orchestra';'published in Vladimír Helfert: Leoš Janáček, Vol. I, Brno 1939 (p. 9, No. 41).

1885 POSLEDNÍ ABENCERAGE ('The Last Abencerage'), projected opera in 3 acts after François René de Chateaubriand's story, Les aventures du dernier des Abencerages'; sketch of action in Janáček's notebook 1885 (HAM).

1889 POD RADHOŠTĚM ('At the Foot of Mt Radhošť'), projected ballet in 1 act; Janáček's notebook 1888–1889 with respective ballet scenario in HAM.

1889 VALAŠSKÉ TANCE ('Valachian Dances', idyllic scene), projected ballet in 1 act to an idea of Václav Kosmák; incomplete undated autograph of the scenario by Janáček with 11 items, with dramatic and dance scenes in HAM.

1901 ANDĚLSKÁ SONÁTA ('Angelic Sonata'), projected opera in 4 acts after the novel by Josef Merhaut; Janáček's notebook 1903 with his unfinished sketch of the scenario and Merhaut's text in HAM.

1904 GAZDINA ROBA ('The Farmer's Woman'), projected opera in 3 acts to the drama by Gabriela Preissová; April 1904 and August 1907; autographic sketches and Preissová's text with annotations by Janáček in HAM.

1905 HONZA HRDINA ('Johnny the Hero'), fairy-tale operatic idea (in 3 acts) suggested to Janáček by K. Dostál-Lutinov whose libretto dated Blatnice 29

Jnue 1905 with several Janáček's melody sketches on back cover is in HAM.

1906 PANÍ MINCMISTROVÁ ('The Mintmaster's Wife'), projected comic opera in 1 act to the comedy by Ladislav Stroupežnický; end of 1906, beginning of 1907; autographic sketches to Scene I and Stroupežnický's text with annotations by Janáček in HAM.

1907 ANNA KARENINA, projected opera directly to the Russian text of L. N. Tolstoy's novel; 20 pp. of autographic sketches written 5—29 Jan. 1907 lost, but some of them published in Gracian Černušák's article 'Janáčkova Anna Karenina' (Janáček's A. K.) (LN, 9 Aug. 1936).

1908 MŠE Es dur—Nedokončená mše ('Mass in E flat major—Unfinished Mass') for soloists (S, A, T, B), mixed choir (SATB) and organ; composed during the school-year 1907—1908 together with pupils of the Brno Organ School, unfinished; the Kyrie and parts of the Credo and Agnus were discovered by Janáček's pupil Vilém Petrželka who completed the Credo; HM, Pr 1946 (choral parts); Supraphon, Pr 1972 (vocal score with organ); duration c 8 min.; 1st perf. Brno, 7 March 1943 by choir of the St Cyril and Method Church (conductor Karel Hradil); the Kyrie, Credo and Agnus were orchestrated 1944 by Vilém Petrželka; 1st perf. of this version Praha, 1 March 1946 by the Czech Philharmonic Orchestra (conductor Rafael Kubelík).

1916 ŽIVÁ MRTVOLA ('The Living Corpse'), projected opera to Russian text of L. N. Tolstoy's drama; September 1916; Janáček's score sketches of Scene I (22 pp.) and 7 pp. of libretto autograph as well as Tolstoy's text with annotations by Janáček in HAM.

1920 DIVOŠKA ('The Girl Scamp'), projected comic opera in 3 acts to Viktor Krylov's comedy ('The Third One' in Czech translation by Jiří Ščerbinský with the subheading (Divoška.—Šotek.) (Girl scamp.—Imp.); probably used by Janáček for his opera composition class; text dated 26 October 1920 with Janáček's annotations in HAM.

1923 DÍTĚ ('The Child'), projected opera after F. X. Šalda's drama; the libretto was to be written by Max Brod; Šalda's text dated 10 July 1923 with Janáček's annotations in HAM.

1928 DUNAJ ('The Danube'), symphonic poem in 4 movements; 1923—1928; not finished by Janáček; incomplete autograph of score (second movement being dated 18 June 1923) in HAM; I. Andante, II.—, III. Allegro, IV.—; completed and partly even reorchestrated and recomposed by Janáček's pupil Osvald Chlubna, 1948; Chlubna's version of full score in the Brno Radio Archive; 1st perf. Brno, 2 May 1948 by the Orchestra of the Czechoslovak Radio (conductor Břetislav Bakala).

1928 HOUSLOVÝ KONCERT 'PUTOVÁNÍ DUŠIČKY' (Violin Concerto 'The Wandering of a Little Soul'); sketches 1927—1928; used in the Introduction to the opera 'The House of the Dead'; the respective sketches are on the autograph back sides of Introduction to the 'House of the Dead' in HAM (from fragments of the score in the estate of Břetislav Bakala, Brno).

1928 SCHLUCK UND JAU, stage music to Gerhardt Hauptmann's play; incomplete undated score autograph (88 pp.). I. Introduction—Andante, II. Allegretto, III. Adagio, IV.—(sketches) and Hauptmann's text dated 25 May 1928 in HAM.

VIII. LOST WORKS

1870 MŠE ('Mass'), composed at some time in the seventies for the Old Brno Church.

1873 SRBSKÁ LIDOVÁ PÍSEŇ ('Serbian Folk Song'), chorus for mixed voices (SATB) to folk text; 1st perf. Brno, 27 April 1873 by ŘBS (conductor L. Janáček).

1873 ŽENICH VNUCENÝ ('The Imposed Bridegroom'), chorus for male voices (TTBB) to Serbian folk text; 1st perf. Brno, 27 April 1873 by ŘBS (conductor L. Janáček); possibly similar to 'Osudu neujdeš', 1878 q. v.

1876 SMRT ('Death'), melodrama for narrator and orchestra to M. J. Lermontov's poem 'On the Poet's Death'; 1st perf. Brno, 13 Nov. 1876 by BeB (narrator Antonín Peka, conductor L. Janáček).

1878 SARABANDA for string quintet; 1st perf. Brno, 8 Dec. 1878 by boarders of ÚVU (probably conducted by L. Janáček).

1879 DUMKA for piano 2 hands; 1st

perf. Rožnov pod Radhoštěm, 8 Sept. 1879 by L. Janáček.

1879 SONÁTA Es dur ('Sonata in E flat major') for piano 2 hands; completed 6 Oct. 1879 in Leipzig.

1879 NOKTURNO PRO KLAVÍR ('Nocturne for Piano'), finished 16 Oct. in Leipzig.

1879 DIE ABENDSCHOPPEN, song with piano to text by Karl Mayer; begun 25 Oct. 1879 in Leipzig.

1879 ROMANCE ('Romances') for violin and piano; 7 pieces composed 26 Oct. — 16 Nov. 1879 in Leipzig; in the final arrangement there were only 4 pieces to be performed under the title 'České romance' ('Czech Romances'); of those only No. 4 has been preserved (see 'Romance' for violin and piano in section Chamber — 1879.

1879 PÍSEŇ PRO GRILLA ('A Song for Grill') with piano accompaniment; finished 10 Nov. 1879 in Leipzig (during Janáček's studies with Leo Grill).

1879 SANCTUS for mixed-voice choir; composed 18—23 Nov. in Leipzig

1879 SMUTEČNÍ POCHOD ('Funeral March') for piano 2 hands; finished 10 Dec. in Leipzig.

1880 ZDEŇČIN MENUET ('Zdeňka's Minuet') for piano 2 hands; completed 8 Jan. 1880 in Leipzig.

1880 FUGY ('Fugues') for piano 2 hands; altogether 17 pieces; composed between 9 Oct, 1879 and 12 Jan. 1880 in Leipzig; three of them played by Janáček on 14 Feb. 1880 at a soirée of the Leipzig Conservatoire.

1880 SONÁTA I pro housle a klavír ('Sonata I' for violin and piano), probably only the first 2 movements, 14—18 Jan. in Leipzig.

1880 SCHERZO for symphony orchestra; completed 25 Jan. in Leipzig (as part of planned symphony).

1880 RONDA ('Rondos') for piano 2 hands composed during February 1880 in Leipzig.

1880 FRÜHLIHGSLIEDER, song cycle with piano accompaniment to text by Vinzenz Zusner; composed 23 April — 7 May 1880 in Vienna.

1880 SONÁTA II pro housle a klavír ('Sonata II' for violin and piano'), completed between 20 April and 12 May 1880 in Vienna.

1880 SMYČCOVÝ KVARTET ('String Quartet'), composed from 25 May to the beginning of June 1880 in Vienna.

1880 MENUETTO a SCHERZO ('Minuetto' and 'Scherzo') for clarinet and piano; composed probably towards the end of 1880; lst perf. Brno, 6 Jan. 1881 by V. Ženíšek (clarinet) and L. Janáček (piano).

1899 OŘÍŠEK LÉSKOVÝ ('The Hazelnut'), song transcription for piano; performed in Brno, 5 March 1899 by Bohumír Fialka.

1899 PÍSNĚ ('Songs') with piano accompaniment; without further description; lst perf. Brno, 5 March 1899.

1904 MODERATO pro orchestr (for orchestra), fragment of a composition from about 1904.

1909 KLAVÍRNÍ TRIO ('Piano Trio') after L. N. Tolstoy's *Kreutzer Sonata;* composed in autumn 1908, recast March to April 1909; lst perf. Brno, 2 April 1909 at KPU; used in String Quartet No. 1 (see section Chamber — 1923).

? KOMÁR ('The Mosquito'), fragment of intended piece for violin 'sul ponticello' and piano.

1912 JARNÍ PÍSEŇ (íSpring Song'), piano cycle.

WORKS REFERRED TO
IN THE TEXT

As the works listed below are known by different titles in different languages the following is a guide to finding them in the bibliography. The reference number given after each author refers to the number given before the author's name in the bibliography below. For further details see Bibliography.

Brod Czech version *see* (24), German original *see* (10), second edition *see* (11)
Helfert see (27)
Janáček—Bartoš see Catalogue of Works, VI, Janáček, L. and Bartoš, F. *Národní písně morav-ské v nově nasbírané* (Folk Songs of Moravia Newly Collected) Prague, vol. 1, 1899, vol. 2, 1901.
Janáček—Brod see (87)
Janáček—Calma-Veselá see (86)
Janáček—Horvátová see (84)
Janáček—Kovařovic see (85)
Janáček—Librettists see (83)
Janáček—Ostrčil see (80)
Janáček—Procházka see (81)
Janáček—Rektorys see (82)
Musikologie III see (30)
Vašek see (44)
Veselý—Janáček see (45)
Zdeňka Janáčková see (29)

BIBLIOGRAPHY

BIBLIOGRAPHIES AND GUIDES TO INFORMATION ABOUT JANÁČEK

(1) Racek, J. ed. *Leoš Janáček. Obraz života a díla. Prameny, literatura, ikonografie a katalog výstavy.* (Leoš Janáček. A Portrait of His Life and Work. Sources, Bibliography, Iconography, and Exhibition Catalogue.) Brno: Výbor pro pořádání oslav Leoše Janáčka, 1948.

(2) Racek, J. *Leoš Janáček.* In Černušák, G. *et al. Československý hudební slovník osob a institucí.* (Czechoslovak Music Dictionary of People and Institutions.) Praha: Státní hudební vydavatelství, 1963. vol. 1, pp. 557–566, vol. 2, p. 1050. Includes a bibliography of main sources.

(3) Racek, J. *K historii janáčkovského bádání v Brně: Problémy heuristické a ediční.* (A propos the History of Janáček Research in Brno: The Heuristic and Editorial Problems.) Sborník prací filosofické fakulty brněnské university. Řada hudebněvědná H 7, 1972: 21 (7), 100.

(4) Straková, T. *ed. Iconographia Janáčkiana – k 120. výročí narození Leoše Janáčka.* (On the 120th Anniversary of the Birth of Leoš Janáček.) Brno: Moravské muzeum, 1975.

(5) Straková, T., *et al. Průvodce po archivních fondech Ústavu dějin hudby Moravského musea v Brně,* (A Guide to the Archive Stock of the Institute of the History of Music of the Moravian Museum in Brno.) Brno: Ústav dějin hudby Moravského muzea, 1971, pp. 165–168. Describes the Janáček archive.

(6) Štědroň, B. *Dílo Leoše Janáčka. Abecední seznam Janáčkových skladeb a úprav. Bibliografie a diskografie.* (Leoš Janáček's Work. An Alphabetical List of Janáček's Compositions and Arrangements. Bibliography and Discography.) Knižnice Hudebních rozhledů 1959: 5 (9).

(7) Telec, V. *comp. Leoš Janáček, 1854–1928: výběrová bibliografie.* (Leoš Janáček, 1854–1928: A Selected Bibliography.) Brno: Universitní knihovna, 1958.

BOOKS IN ENGLISH, FRENCH AND GERMAN

(8) *Acta Janáčkiana I* (International Colloquia on Janáček's Operatic Work. Brno: 1965). Ed, by T. Straková et al. Brno: Moravské muzeum, 1968.

(9) Brod, M. *Sternenhimmel: Musik- und Theatererlebnisse.* Munich: Kurt Wolff Verlag, 1923. Various essays about Janáček.

(10) Brod, M. *Leoš Janáček: Leben und Werk.* Vienna: Wiener Philharmonischer Verlag, 1925.

(11) Brod, M. *Leoš Janáček.* Rev. ed. Vienna: Universal, 1956.

(12) Černohorská, M. *Leoš Janáček.* Trans. by J. Layton-Eislerová. Prague: Státní hudební vydavatelství, 1966.

(13) Chisholm, E. *The Operas of Leoš Janáček.* Ed. by K. Wright. Oxford: Pergamon Press, 1971.

(14) *Colloquium Leoš Janáček et musica Europaea, Brno 1968.* Ed. by R. Pečman. Brno: International Musical Festival, 1970. (Colloquia on the History and Theory of Music, 3.)

(15) Ewans, M. *Janáček's Tragic Operas.* London: Faber, 1977.

(16) Geck, A. *Das Volksliedmaterial Leoš Janáčeks: Analysen der Strukturen unter Einbeziehung von Janáčeks Randbemerkungen und Volksliedstudien.* Thesis, Berlin University, 1970.

(17) Hollander, H. *Leoš Janáček: his life and work.* Trans. by P. Hamburger. London: Calder, 1963.

(18) Hollander, H. *Leoš Janáček — Leben und Werk.* Zürich: Atlantis Verlag, 1964.

(19) Kneif, T. *Bühnenwerke von Leoš Janáček.* Vienna: Universal, 1974.

(20) Muller, D. *Leoš Janáček.* Paris: Les Éditions Rieder, 1930.

(21) Richter, H. *Leoš Janáček.* Leipzig: Breitkopf u. Härtel, 1958.

(22) Šeda, J. *Leoš Janáček.* Trans. by M. Milner and V. Fried. Prague: Orbis, 1956.

(23) Štědroň, B. *Zur Genesis von Leoš Janáčeks Oper Jenůfa.* (Opera Universitatis Purkynianae Brunensis Facultas Philosophiae 139) Brno: Universita J. E. Purkyně, 1968.

SELECTED BOOKS IN CZECH

(24) Brod, M. *Leoš Janáček.* Trans. from German by Dr. A. Fuchs. Prague: Hudební matice Umělecké besedy, 1924.

(25) Cigler, R. *Soupis zahraničních inscenací Janáčkových oper.* (A List of Janáček's Operatic Productions Abroad.) Brno: Moravské museum, 1958.

(26) Firkušný, L. and Kunc, J. *Odkaz Leoše Janáčka české opeře.* (Janáček's Legacy to Czech Opera.) Brno: Dědictví Havlíčkovo, 1939.

(27) Helfert, V. *Leoš Janáček — obraz životního a uměleckého boje. I. V poutech tradice.* (Leoš Janáček — A portrait of His Struggle as a Man and an Artist. I. Shackled by Tradition.) Brno: Pazdírek, 1939.

(28) Helfert, V. *O Janáčkovi: Soubor statí a článků.* (About Janáček. A Collection of Essays and Articles.) Prague: Hudební matice Umělecké besedy, 1949.

(29) Janáčková, Z. *Můj život.* Sestavila Marie Trkanová (My life. Compiled by Marie Trkanová.) Typescript, 1939. Parts of it were published in Racek, J. *Z duševní dílny Leoše Janáčka.* (From the Workshop of Leoš Janáček's Mind.) Brno: Hudební archiv Zemského musea, 1936.
Also in *Divadelní listy* 1935 — 1936: 11 (10), 215 — 224; 11 (11), 243 — 252; 11 (12), 270 — 279; 11 (13), 294 — 304; 11 (14), 334 — 341; 11 (15) 350 — 357; 11 (17), 397 — 411.

(30) *K stému výročí narození Leoše Janáčka.* (On the 100th Anniversary of the Birth of Janáček.) Prague: Státní nakladatelství krásné literatury, hudby a umění, 1955. (*Musikologie,* vol. 3.)

(31) Kožík, F. *Po zarostlém chodníčku: sblížení s Leošem Janáčkem.* (On the Overgrown Path: Getting Acquainted with Leoš Janáček.) Prague: Československý spisovatel, 1967.

(32) *Leoš Janáček a soudobá hudba: mezinárodní hudebněvědecký kongres, Brno 1958.* (Leoš Janáček and Contemporary Music: The International Musicological Congress, Brno 1958.) Prague: Knižnice Hudebních rozhledů, 1963.
Also contains text in German.

(33) Nosek, V. ed. *Opery Leoše Janáčka na brněnské scéně.* (The Operas of Leoš Janáček on the Brno Stage.) Brno: Státní divadlo, 1958.

(34) Procházka, J. *Lašské kořeny života i díla Leoše Janáčka.* (The Lachian Roots of the Life and Works of Leoš Janáček.) Prague: Hudební matice Umělecké besedy, 1948. Published for the festival *Janáčkovo hudební Lašsko* 1948 at Frýdek-Místek.

(35) Racek, J. *Leoš Janáček: člověk a umělec.* (Leoš Janáček: Man and Artist.) Brno: Krajské nakladatelství, 1963.

(36) Racek, J. *Leoš Janáček a současní moravští skladatelé — nástin k slohovému vývoji soudobé moravské hudby* (Leoš Janáček and Contemporary Moravian Composers: An Outline *à propos* the Stylistic Development of Contemporary Moravian Music.) Brno: Unie českých hudebníků z povolání, 1940.

(37) Racek, J. *Leoš Janáček v mých vzpomínkách.* (Leoš Janáček as I Remember Him.) Prague: Vyšehrad, 1975.

(38) Šeda, J. *Leoš Janáček.* Prague: Státní hudební vydavatelství, 1961.

(39) Slavický, J. *Listy důvěrné: Z milostné korespobennce Leoše Janáčka.* (Intimate Letters: From the Love Letters of Leoš Janáček.) Prague: Panton, 1966.

(40) Smetana, R. *Vyprávění o L. Janáčkovi.* (Stories about L. Janáček.) Olomouc: Velehrad, 1948.

(41) Štědroň, B. *Leoš Janáček: k jeho lidskému a uměleckému profilu.* (Leoš Janáček: On His Profile as a Man and an Artist.) Prague: Panton 1976.
Stejskalová, M. *see* Trkanová, M.

(42) Trkanová, M. *U Janáčků, podle vyprávění Marie Stejskalové.* (At the Janáčeks, As Told by Marie Stejskalová.) Prague: Panton, 1964.

Trkanová, M. *see also* Janáčková, Z.

(43) Tučapský, A. *Mužské sbory Leoše Janáčka a jejich interpretační tradice.* (Janáček's Male-Voice Choruses and the Tradition of Their Interpretation.) Prague: Státní pedagogické nakladatelství, 1971. (Spisy pedagogické fakulty v Ostravě, svazek 16.)

(44) Vašek, A. E. *Po stopách dra L. Janáčka.* (In the Steps of Dr. L. Janáček.) Brno: Brněnské knižní nakladatelství, 1930.

(45) Veselý, A. *Leoš Janáček: Pohled do života a díla.* (Leoš Janáček: A Survey of His Life and Work.) Prague: F. Borový, 1924.

SELECTED ARTICLES IN ENGLISH

(46) Andrews, H. 'Neglected Modernist of Moravia'. *Music Teacher.* September 1930: vol. 8, no. 9, 513—514.

(47) Davis, P. G. 'Janáček Case'. *Opera News.* 21 December 1974: vol. 39, no. 8, 10—13.

(48) Ewans, M. 'Janáček'. *The Listener,* 17 January 1974: vol. 91, no. 2338, 90—91.

(49) Gorer, R. *and* Černušák, G. 'Janáček, Leoš'. *In* Blom, E., *ed. Grove's Dictionary of Music and Musicians.* London: Macmillan, 1954: vol. 4, 578—584.

(50) Hollander, H. 'Leoš Janáček and His Operas'. *Musical Quarterly.* January 1929: vol. 15, no. 1, 29—36.

(51) Hollander, H. 'Leoš Janáček—Slav Genius'. *Music and Letters.* July 1941: vol. 22, no 3, 248—251.

(52) Hollander, H. 'Leoš Janáček—A Centenary Appreciation'. *Musical Times.* June 1954: vol. 95, no. 1336, 305—306.

(53) Hollander, H. 'The Music of Leoš Janáček—Its Origin in Folklore'. *Musical Quarterly.* April 1955: vol. 41, no. 2, 171—176.

(54) Hollander, H. 'Janáček's Development'. *Musical Times.* August 1958: vol. 99, no. 1386, 427.

(55) Kubelík, R. 'Katya Kabanova'. *Foyer.* 1952: no. 1, 18—20.

(56) Mackerras, C. 'Janáček's "Makropoulos"'. *Opera.* February 1964: vol. 15, no. 2, 79—86.

(57) Mason, C. 'Janáček, a Victim of History'. *The Listener.* May 1953: vol. 50, 561.

(58) Mellers, W. 'Janáček'. *New Statesman.* 21 February 1964: vol. 67, 307.

(59) Mellers, W. 'The World of Janáček'. *New Statesman.* 11 September 1964: vol. 68, 367.

(60) Mellers, W. 'Leoš Janáček (1854—1928)'. *In* Bacharach, A. L., *ed., The Music Masters.* London: Cassell, 1952: vol. 3, 191—197.

(61) Mellers, W. 'A Great Czech Composer'. *The Listener.* 20 April 1939: vol. 21, 861.

(62) Newmarch, R. 'Janáček, Leoš'. *In* Colles, H. C., *ed., Grove's Dictionary of Music and Musicians.* London: Macmillan, 1927: vol. 2, 756—762.

(63) Newmarch, R. 'Leoš Janáček'. (Obituary) *Slavonic Review*. January 1929: vol. 7, no. 20, 416–418.

(64) Newmarch, R. 'Leoš Janáček'. (Obituary). *Musical Times*, September 1928: vol. 69, no. 1027, 846.

(65) Newmarch, R. 'Leoš Janáček and Moravian Music Drama'. *Slavonic Review*. December 1922: vol. 1, no. 2, 362–379.

(66) Poole, G. 'The Lone Czech'. *Music and Musicians*. April 1972: vol. 20, no. 8, 40–49.

(67) 'Rebirth of an Eccentric'. *Time*. December 5, 1969: vol. 94, no. 23, 58.

(68) Shawe-Taylor, D. 'The Operas of Leoš Janáček'. *Proceedings of the Royal Musical Association*. 85th Session 1958–1959, 49–64.

(69) Shawe-Taylor, D. 'Janáček's Celebrations at Brno'. *Opera*. January 1959: vol. 10, no. 1, 18–24.

(70) Shawe-Taylor, D. 'Leoš Janáček'. *New Statesman*. 15 January, 1949: vol. 37, 53–54.

(71) Tyrrell, J. 'The Musical Prehistory of Janáček's *Počátek románu* (The Beginning of a Romance) and its Importance in Shaping the Composer's Dramatic Style'. *Časopis Moravského muzea*. 1967, vol. 52, 245–268.

(72) Tyrrell, J. 'Mr Brouček's Excursion to the Moon'. *Časopis Moravského muzea*. 1968/1969: vol. 53–54 no. 2, 89–122.

(73) Tyrrell, J. 'How Domšík Became a Bass'. *Musical Times*. January 1973: vol. 114, no. 1559, 29–30.

(74) Tyrrell, J. 'Janáček and the Speech-Melody Myth'. *Musical Times*. August 1970: vol. 111, no. 1530, 793–796.

(75) Tyrrell, J. 'Mr. Brouček at Home: An Epilogue to Janáček's Opera'. *Musical Times*, January 1979: vol. 120, No. 1631, 30–33.

(76) Tyrrell, J. Record notes in *Káťa Kabanová*, Vienna Philharmonic Orch., *cond.* Sir Charles Mackerras, Decca D51D 2, 1977.

(77) Tyrrell, J. Record notes in *Věc Makropulos* ('The Makropulos Case'), Vienna Philharmonic Orch., *cond.* Sir Charles Mackerras, Decca D144D 2, 1979.

(78) Tyrrell, J. Record notes in *Z mrtvého domu* ('From the House of the Dead'), Vienna Philharmonic Orchestra, *cond.* Sir Charles Mackerras, Decca D224D 2, 1980.

(79) Tyrrell, J. 'Janáček, Leoš'. *In* Sadie, S., ed., *The New Grove Dictionary of Music and Musicians*. London: Macmillan, 1980: vol. 9, 474–490.

JANÁČEK'S CORRESPONDENCE

(80) *Korespondence Leoše Janáčka s Otakarem Ostrčilem*. (Correspondence of Janáček with Otakar Ostrčil.) *Ed.* by A. Rektorys. Prague: Hudební matice Umělecké besedy, 1948. (*Janáčkův archiv*, vol. 2.)

(81) *Korespondence Leoše Janáčka s F. S. Procházkou*. (Correspondence of L. Janáček with F. S. Procházka.) *Ed.* by A. Rektorys. Prague: Hudební matice Umělecké besedy, 1949. (*Janáčkův archiv*, vol. 3.)

(82) *Korespondence Leoše Janáčka s Artušem Rektorysem*. (Correspondence of L. Janáček with Artuš Rektorys.) *Ed.* by A. Rektorys with notes by V. Helfert, 2nd enl. ed. Prague: Hudební matice Umělecké besedy, 1949. (*Janáčkův archiv*, vol. 4.)

(83) *Korespondence Leoše Janáčka s libretisty 'Výletů Broučkových'*. (Correspondence of L. Janáček with the Librettists of the 'Excursions of Mr Brouček'.) *Ed.* by A. Rektorys. Prague: Hudební matice Umělecké besedy, 1950. (*Janáčkův archiv*, vol. 5.)

(84) *Korespondence Leoše Janáčka s Gabrielou Horvátovou*. (Correspondence of L. Janáček with)

Gabriela Horvátová.) *Ed.* by A. Rektorys. Prague: Hudební matice Umělecké besedy, 1950. (*Janáčkův archiv*, vol. 6.)

(85) *Korespondence Leoše Janáčka s Karlem Kovařovicem a ředitelstvím Národního divadla.* (Correspondence of L. Janáček with Karel Kovařovic and with the Management of the Prague National Theatre.) *Ed.* by A. Rektorys. Prague: Hudební matice Umělecké besedy, 1950. (*Janáčkův archiv*, vol. 7.)

(86) *Korespondence Leoše Janáčka s Marií Calmou a MUDr Františkem Veselým.* (Correspondence of L. Janáček with Marie Calma and Dr František Veselý.) *Ed.* by J. Racek and A. Rektorys. Prague: Státní nakladatelství krásné literatury, hudby a umění, 1953. (*Janáčkův archiv*, vol. 8.)

(87) *Korespondence Leoše Janáčka s Maxem Brodem.* (Correspondence of Leoš Janáček with Max Brod.) *Ed.* by J. Racek and A. Rektorys. Prague: Státní nakladatelství krásné literatury, hudby a umění, 1953. (*Janáčkův archiv*, vol. 9.)

(88) Štědroň, B. *Janáček ve vzpomínkách a dopisech.* (Janáček in Reminiscences and Letters.) Prague: Topičova edice, 1946.

(89) *Leoš Janáček: Dopisy Zdeňce.* (Letters to Zdeňka.) Ed. by F. Hrabal. Trans. from the German by O. Fiala. Prague: Supraphon, 1968.

(90) *Leoš Janáček: Letters and Reminiscences.* (Edited, with a list of compositions, arrangements and literary works, and a bibliography by B. Štědroň.) Tr. by G. Thomsen. Prague: Artia, 1955.

(91) *Leoš Janáček in Briefen und Erinnerungen;* (*Ed.* B. Štědroň.) Prague: Artia, 1955.

JANÁČEK'S VISIT TO BRITAIN

(92) Mikota, J. 'Leoš Janáček v Anglii'. (Leoš Janáček in England.) *Listy Hudební matice,* April – May 1926: vol. 5, No. 7 – 8, 257 – 268.

(93) Mikota, J. 'Janáček in London'. *About the House,* March 1968: vol. 2, no. 9, 20 – 23.

A GENERAL MAP CZECHOSLOVAKIA

A MAP OF MORAVIA AND SILESIA

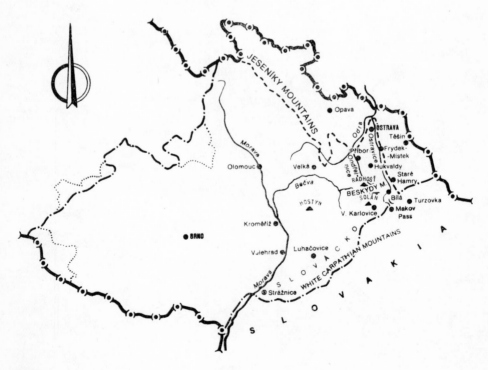

INDEX

424

431

INDEX OF JANÁČEK'S WORKS

JANÁČEK'S WRITINGS MENTIONED IN THE TEXT